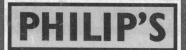

STREET ATLAS

C000201073

Merseyside

First published in 1997 by

Philip's, a division of
Octopus Publishing Group Ltd
2-4 Heron Quays, London E14 4JP

Third edition 2004
First impression 2004

ISBN 0-540-08520-0 (spiral)

Printed and bound in Spain
by Cayfosa-Quebecor

Contents

II **Merseyside rail network map**

III **Key to map symbols**

IV **Key to map pages**

VI **Route planning**

VIII **Administrative and Postcode boundaries**

1 **Street maps** at 3½ inches to 1 mile

90 **Street map of Liverpool city centre** at 7 inches to 1 mile

91 **Index** of towns and villages

92 **Index** of streets, hospitals, industrial estates, railway stations, schools, shopping centres and universities and places of interest

Digital Data

The exceptionally high-quality mapping found in this atlas is available as digital data in TIFF format, which is easily convertible to other bitmapped (raster) image formats.

The index is also available in digital form as a standard database table. It contains all the details found in the printed index together with the National Grid reference for the map square in which each entry is named.

For further information and to discuss your requirements, please contact Philip's on 020 7644 6932 or james.mann@philips-maps.co.uk

Merseyrail NETWORK MAP

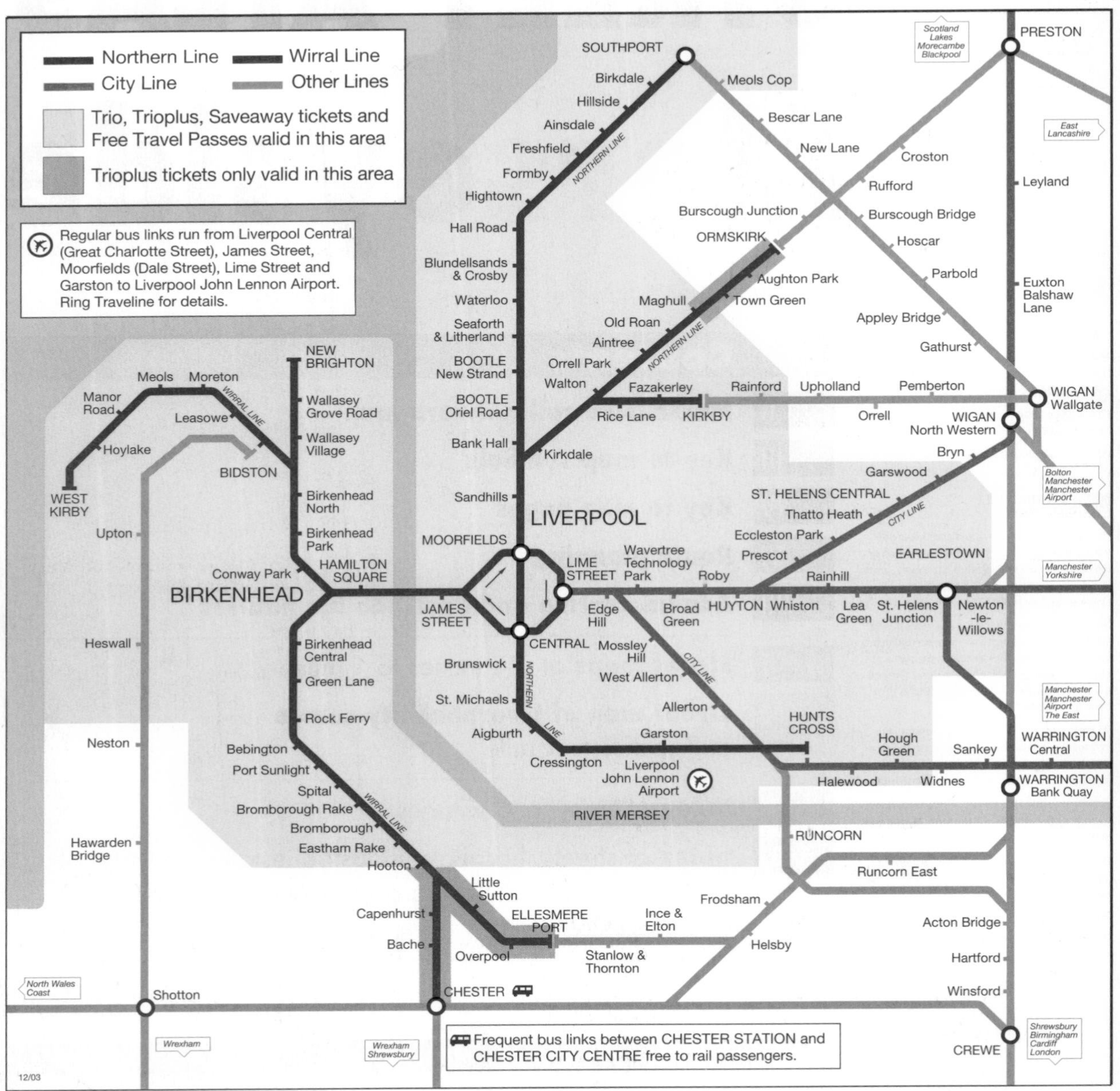

Map reproduced by permission of Merseyside Passenger Transport Authority and Executive

(22a)	**Motorway** with junction number
	Primary route – dual/single carriageway
	A road – dual/single carriageway
	B road – dual/single carriageway
	Minor road – dual/single carriageway
	Other minor road – dual/single carriageway
	Road under construction
	Tunnel, covered road
	Rural track, private road or narrow road in urban area
	Gate or obstruction to traffic (restrictions may not apply at all times or to all vehicles)
	Path, bridleway, byway open to all traffic, road used as a public path
	Pedestrianised area
DY7	**Postcode boundaries**
	County and unitary authority boundaries
	Railway, tunnel, railway under construction
	Tramway, tramway under construction
	Miniature railway
Walsall	**Railway station**
	Private railway station
South Shields	**Metro station**
	Tram stop, tram stop under construction
	Bus, coach station

◆	**Ambulance station**
◆	**Coastguard station**
◆	**Fire station**
◆	**Police station**
✚	**Accident and Emergency entrance to hospital**
H	**Hospital**
+	**Place of worship**
i	**Information Centre** (open all year)
P	**Parking**
P&R	**Park and Ride**
PO	**Post Office**
X	**Camping site**
	Caravan site
▶	**Golf course**
✕	**Picnic site**
Prim Sch	**Important buildings, schools, colleges, universities and hospitals**
River Medway	**Water name**
	River, weir, stream
	Canal, lock, tunnel
	Water
	Tidal water
	Woods
	Built up area
Church	**Non-Roman antiquity**
ROMAN FORT	**Roman antiquity**
87 / 228	**Adjoining page indicators and overlap bands** The colour of the arrow and the band indicates the scale of the adjoining or overlapping page (see scales below)

Acad	**Academy**	Inst	**Institute**	Recn Gd	**Recreation Ground**
Allot Gdns	**Allotments**	Ct	**Law Court**		
Cemy	**Cemetery**	L Ctr	**Leisure Centre**	Resr	**Reservoir**
C Ctr	**Civic Centre**	LC	**Level Crossing**	Ret Pk	**Retail Park**
CH	**Club House**	Liby	**Library**	Sch	**School**
Coll	**College**	Mkt	**Market**	Sh Ctr	**Shopping Centre**
Crem	**Crematorium**	Meml	**Memorial**	TH	**Town Hall/House**
Ent	**Enterprise**	Mon	**Monument**	Trad Est	**Trading Estate**
Ex H	**Exhibition Hall**	Mus	**Museum**	Univ	**University**
Ind Est	**Industrial Estate**	Obsy	**Observatory**	W Twr	**Water Tower**
IRB Sta	**Inshore Rescue Boat Station**	Pal	**Royal Palace**	Wks	**Works**
		PH	**Public House**	YH	**Youth Hostel**

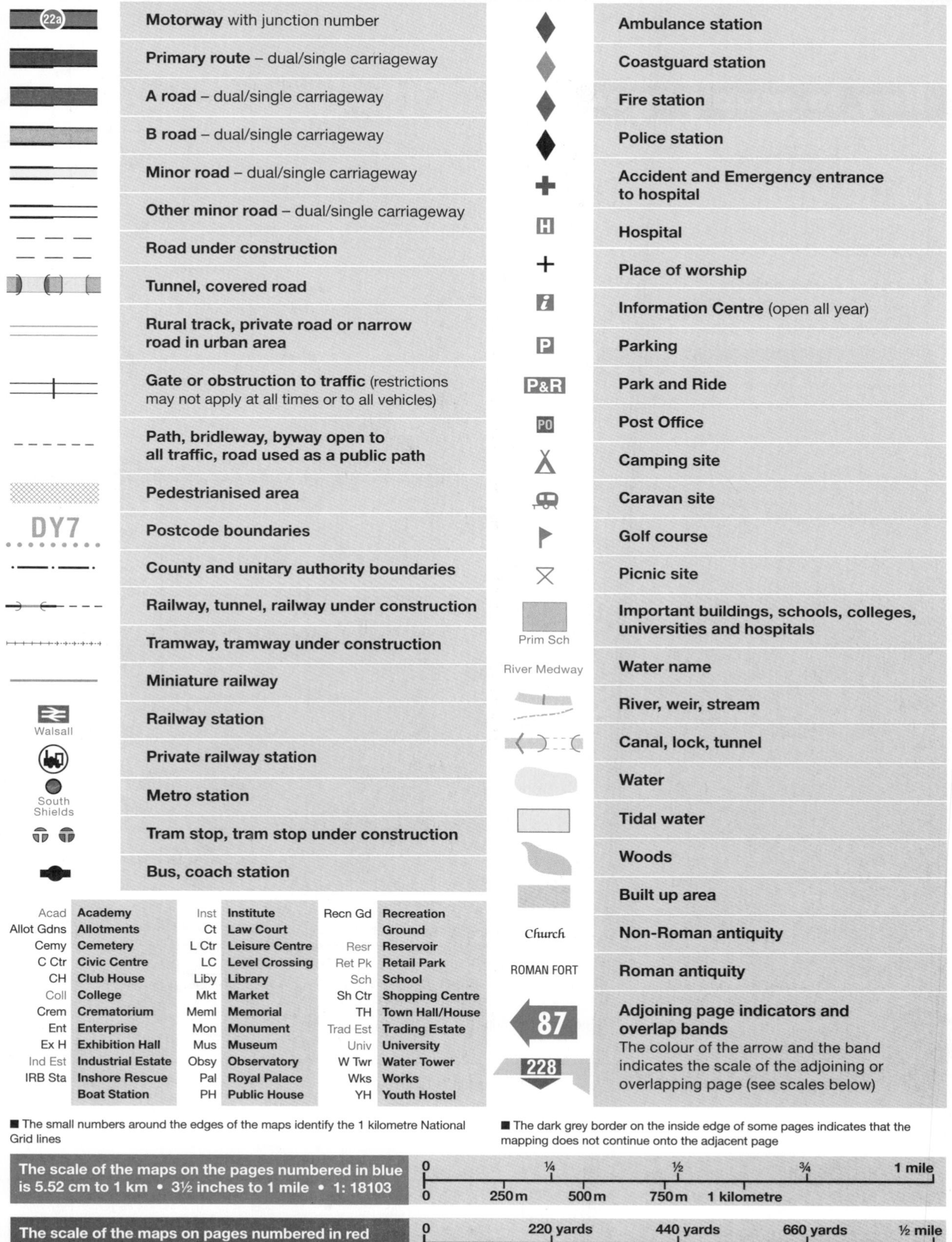

■ The small numbers around the edges of the maps identify the 1 kilometre National Grid lines

■ The dark grey border on the inside edge of some pages indicates that the mapping does not continue onto the adjacent page

The scale of the maps on the pages numbered in blue is 5.52 cm to 1 km • 3½ inches to 1 mile • 1: 18103

0	¼	½	¾	1 mile
0	250 m	500 m	750 m	1 kilometre

The scale of the maps on pages numbered in red is 11.04 cm to 1 km • 7 inches to 1 mile • 1: 9051

0	220 yards	440 yards	660 yards	½ mile
0	125 m	250 m	375 m	½ kilometre

Key to map pages

Map pages at
3½ inches to 1 mile

45

Map pages at
7 inches to 1 mile

90

Scale

0 1 2 3 4 5 6 7 8 8 10 km

0   1   2   3   4   5 miles

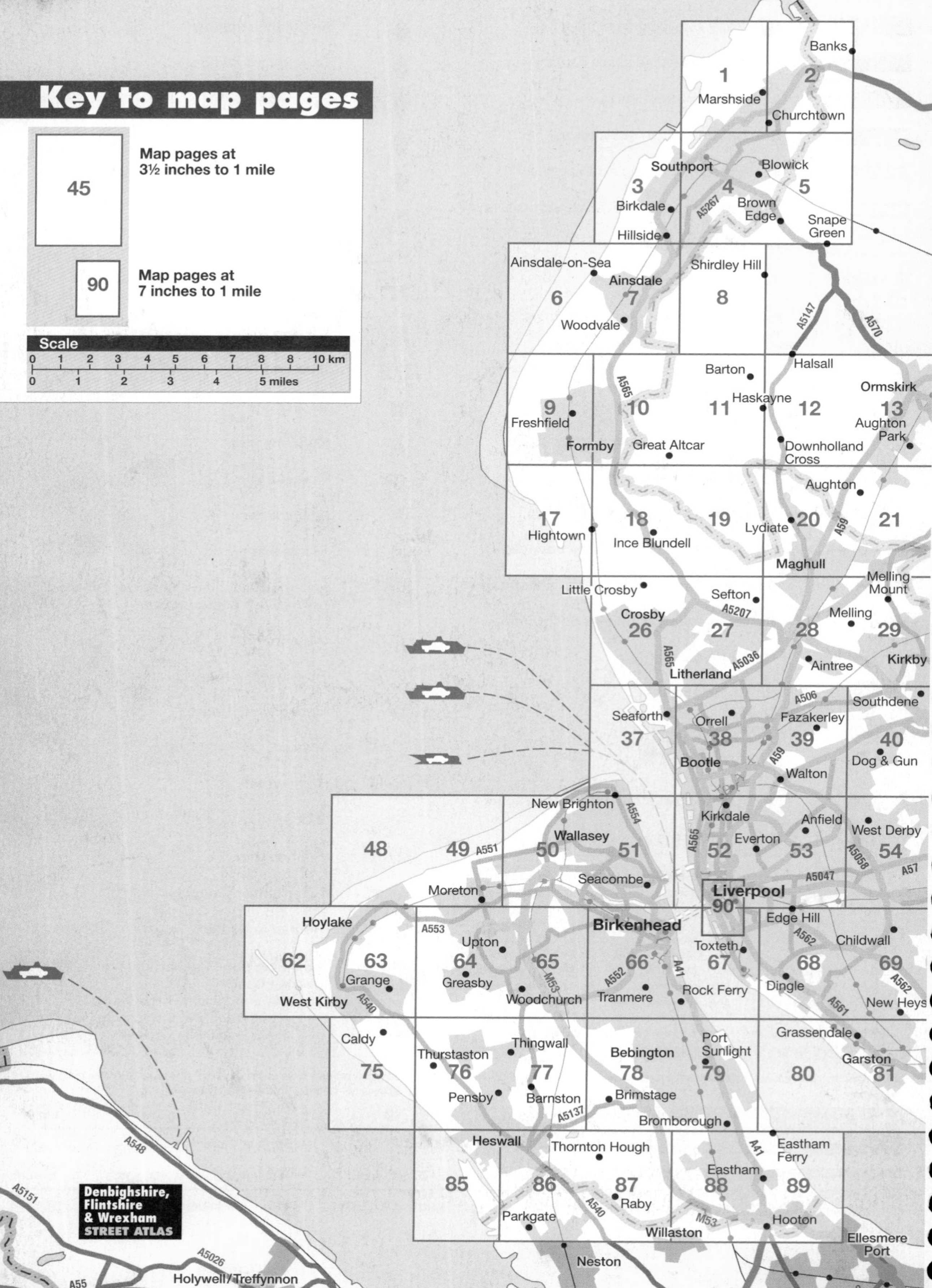

Banks

1   **2**

Marshside

Churchtown

Southport   Blowick

3   **4**   **5**

Birkdale   Brown   A5267   Edge   Snape
Green

Hillside

Ainsdale-on-Sea   Shirley Hill

6   Ainsdale   **8**

7

Woodvale   A5147   A570

Barton   Halsall

A565   Haskayne   Ormskirk

9   **10**   **11**   **12**   **13**

Freshfield   Aughton
Park

Formby   Great Altcar   Downholland
Cross

Aughton

17   **18**   **19**   Lydiate   **20**   A59   **21**

Hightown   Ince Blundell   Maghull

Melling
Mount

Little Crosby   Sefton   Melling
A5207

Crosby   **27**   **28**   **29**
26

A565   A5036   Kirkby

Litherland   Aintree

A506   Southdene

Seaforth   Orrell   Fazakerley

37   **38**   **39**   **40**

Bootle   A59   Dog & Gun

Walton

New Brighton   A554   Kirkdale   Anfield

Wallasey   Everton   West Derby
48   **49** A551   **50**   **51**   A565   **52**   **53**   **54**   A57
A5058
Seacombe   A5047

Moreton   **Liverpool**   Edge Hill
90

Hoylake   A553   Upton   **Birkenhead**   Toxteth   Childwall

62   **63**   **64**   **65**   **66**   **67**   **68**   **69**
A552   A41   A562   A561   A562
Grange   Greasby   Rock Ferry   Dingle   New Heys
West Kirby   A540   Woodchurch   Tranmere

Caldy   Thingwall   Grassendale

Thurstaston   Port   Garston
Bebington   Sunlight

75   **76**   **77**   **78**   **79**   **80**   **81**

Pensby   Barnston   Brimstage
A5137   Bromborough

Heswall   Thornton Hough   Eastham
Ferry
A41

85   **86**   **87**   **88**   Eastham   **89**
A540   Raby   M53   Hooton
Parkgate   Ellesmere
Willaston   Port

Neston

A548

A5151

**Denbighshire,
Flintshire
& Wrexham**
STREET ATLAS

A5026

A55   Holywell/Treffynnon

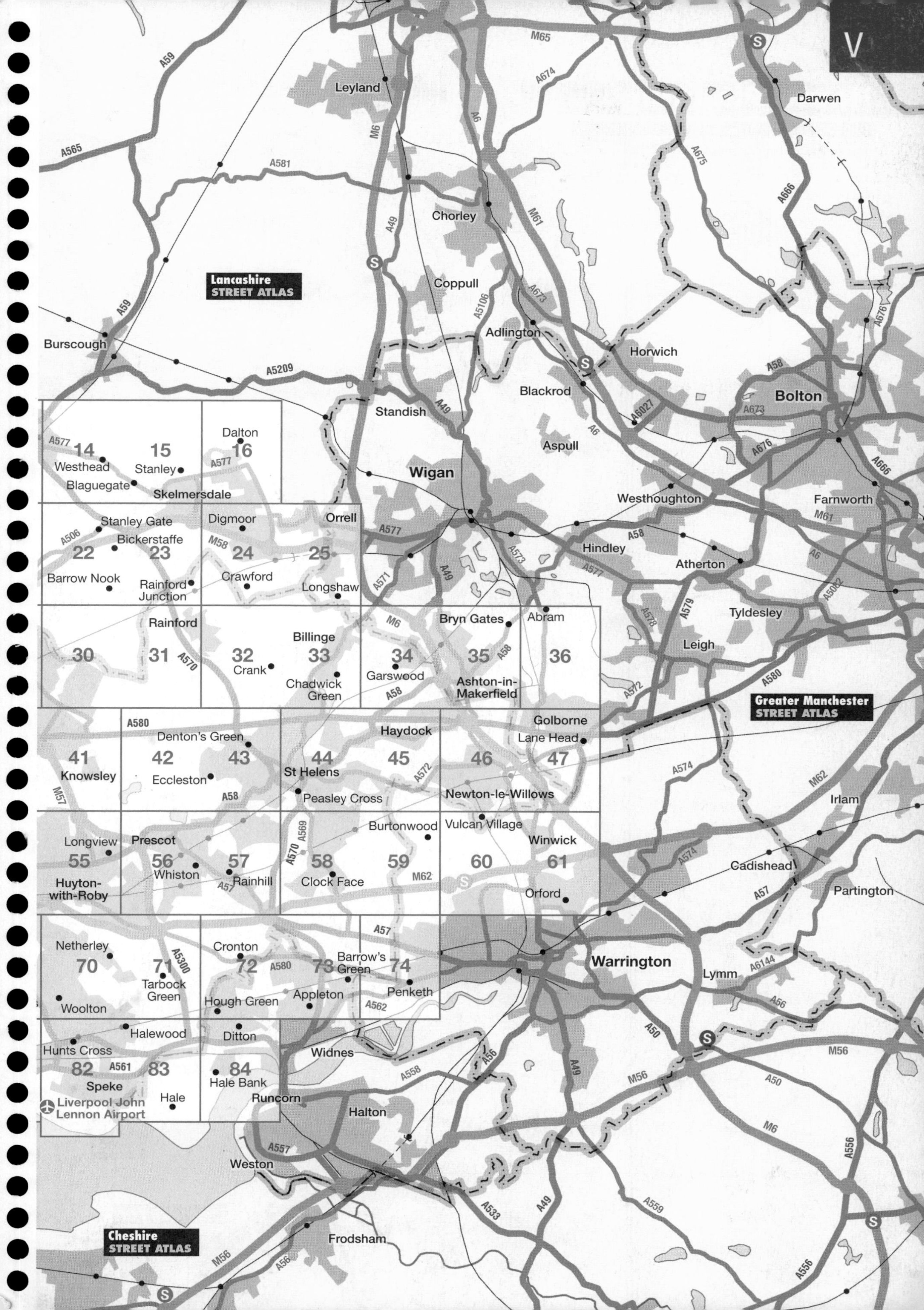

Lancashire STREET ATLAS
Greater Manchester STREET ATLAS
Cheshire STREET ATLAS
Leyland
Darwen
Chorley
Coppull
Adlington
Horwich
Burscough
Standish
Blackrod
Bolton
Aspull
Wigan
Westhoughton
Farnworth
Hindley
Atherton
Tyldesley
Leigh
Abram
Dalton 16
14 Westhead
15 Stanley
Blaguegate
Skelmersdale
Stanley Gate
Bickerstaffe
22
23
Barrow Nook
Rainford Junction
Digmoor
24
Crawford
Orrell
25
Longshaw
30
Rainford
31
32 Crank
Billinge
33
Chadwick Green
34 Garswood
Bryn Gates
35
Ashton-in-Makerfield
36
41 Knowsley
Denton's Green
42
43
Eccleston
44 St Helens
Haydock
45
Peasley Cross
46
Newton-le-Willows
Golborne
Lane Head
47
Longview
55
Huyton-with-Roby
Prescot
56
Whiston
57
Rainhill
58
Clock Face
Burtonwood
59
Vulcan Village
60
Winwick
61
Orford
Irlam
Cadishead
Partington
Netherley
70
Woolton
71
Tarbock Green
Cronton
72
Hough Green
73
Barrow's Green
Appleton
74
Penketh
Warrington
Lymm
Halewood
Hunts Cross
82
Speke
83
Hale
Ditton
84
Hale Bank
Widnes
Runcorn
Halton
Liverpool John Lennon Airport
Weston
Frodsham
M65
M6
M61
M58
M62
M56
M57
A59
A565
A581
A674
A6
A675
A666
A49
A5106
A673
A676
A5209
A58
A6027
A577
A573
A571
A579
A578
A5082
A570
A580
A572
A574
A57
A569
A562
A5300
A561
A580
A6144
A56
A50
A558
A557
A533
A559
A556

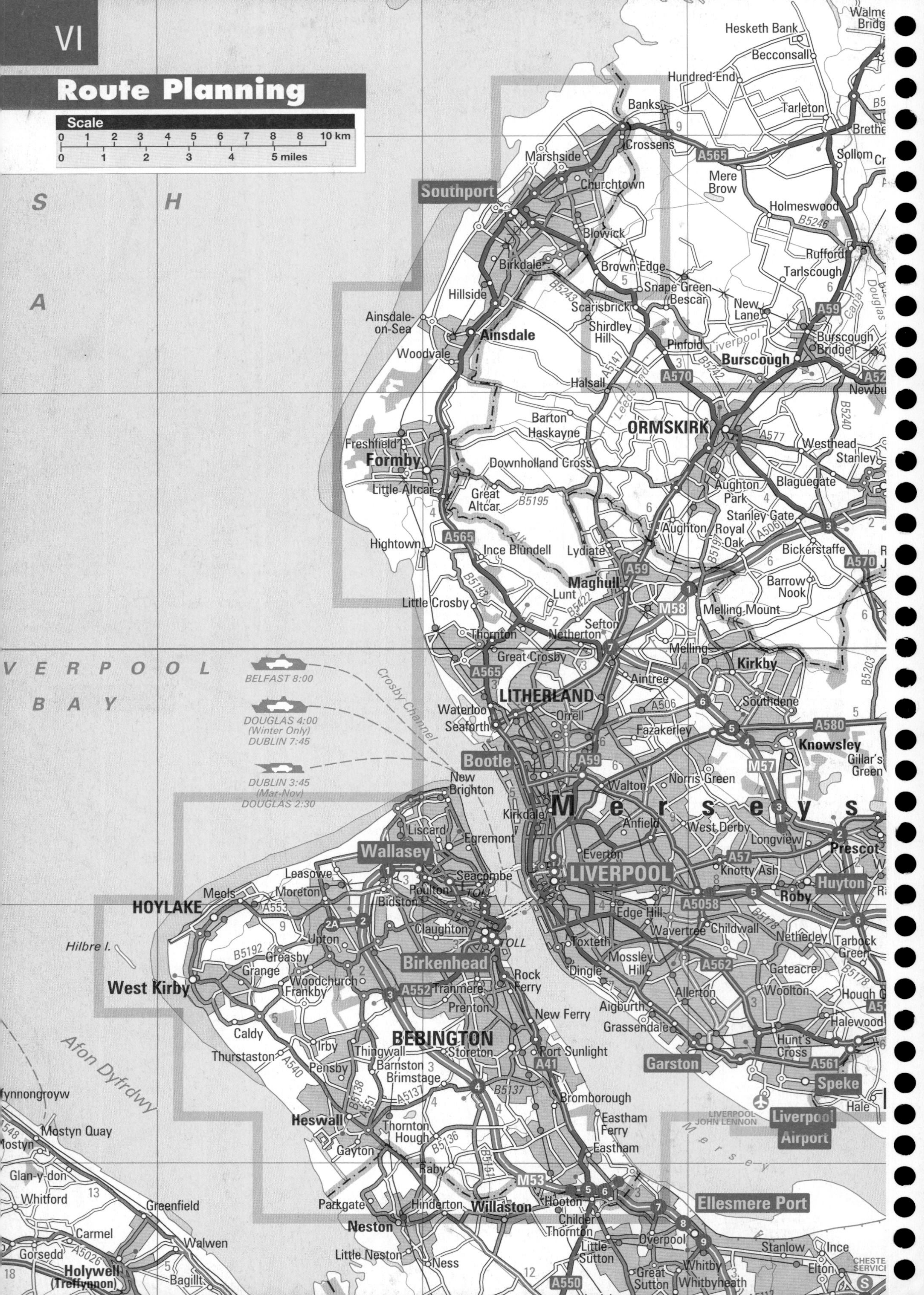

Route Planning

Scale

0 1 2 3 4 5 6 7 8 8 10 km

0 1 2 3 4 5 miles

S H

A

S

V E R P O O L
BAY

BELFAST 8:00

DOUGLAS 4:00
(Winter Only)
DUBLIN 7:45

DUBLIN 3:45
(Mar-Nov)
DOUGLAS 2:30

Crosby Channel

Hesketh Bank
Becconsall
Hundred End
Banks
Tarleton
Crossens
Marshside
Churchtown
Mere Brow
Holmeswood
Southport
Blowick
Rufford
Birkdale
Brown Edge
Tarlscough
Hillside
Snape Green
New Lane
Burscough Bridge
Scarisbrick
Bescar
Shirdley Hill
Pinfold
Burscough
Ainsdale-on-Sea
Ainsdale
Woodvale
Halsall
Newbu
Barton
Haskayne
ORMSKIRK
Westhead
Stanley
Freshfield
Downholland Cross
Aughton Park
Blaguegate
Formby
Stanley Gate
Little Altcar
Great Altcar
Aughton
Royal Oak
Bickerstaffe
Hightown
Ince Blundell
Lydiate
Barrow Nook
Maghull
Lunt
Melling Mount
Little Crosby
Sefton
Netherton
Thornton
Melling
Kirkby
Great Crosby
Aintree
Southdene
LITHERLAND
Waterloo
Orrell
Knowsley
Seaforth
Fazakerley
Gillar's Green
Bootle
Norris Green
Knowsley
New Brighton
Walton
Kirkdale
Liscard
M e r s e y s
Wallasey
Egremont
Anfield
West Derby
Longview
Prescot
Seacombe
Everton
Knotty Ash
Huyton
Leasowe
Poulton
LIVERPOOL
Roby
Meols
Moreton
Bidston
Edge Hill
HOYLAKE
Upton
Claughton
Wavertree
Childwall
Netherley
Tarbock Green
Hilbre I.
Greasby
Birkenhead
Toxteth
Mossley Hill
Woolton
Grange
Woodchurch
Tranmere
Rock Ferry
Aigburth
Allerton
Hough
West Kirby
Frankby
Prenton
New Ferry
Grassendale
Caldy
BEBINGTON
Gateacre
Irby
Thingwall
Storeton
Port Sunlight
Garston
Thurstaston
Pensby
Barnston
Brimstage
Bromborough
Hunt's Cross
Heswall
Thornton Hough
Eastham Ferry
Speke
Gayton
Eastham
Hale
Raby
Liverpool Airport
Mostyn Quay
LIVERPOOL JOHN LENNON
Glan-y-don
Parkgate
Hinderton
Hooton
Whitford
Greenfield
Willaston
Ellesmere Port
Carmel
Neston
Childer Thornton
Holywell (Treffynnon)
Walwen
Little Neston
Ness
Little Sutton
Overpool
Stanlow
Ince
Bagillt
Great Sutton
Whitby
Whitbyheath
Elton

18

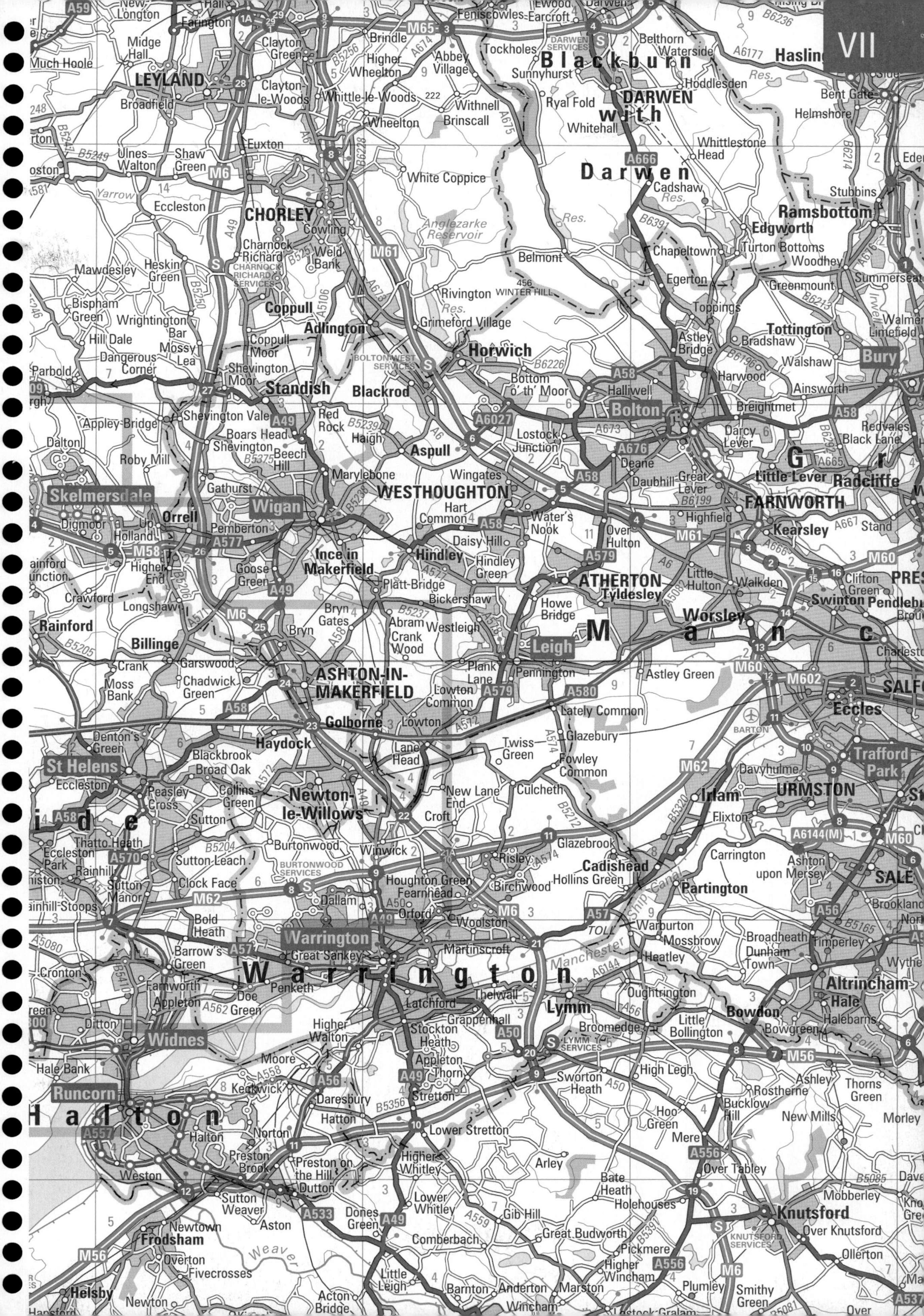
Much Hoole
Midge Hall
Farington
Clayton Green
Brindle
Higher Wheelton
Abbey Village
Feniscowles
Earcroft
Tockholes
Blackburn
Sunnyhurst
Belthorn
Waterside
Haslingden
LEYLAND
Broadfield
Clayton-le-Woods
Whittle-le-Woods
Withnell
Brinscall
Wheelton
DARWEN
Ryal Fold
Whitehall
Hoddlesden
Bent Gate
Helmshore
Darwen with Darwen
Whittlestone Head
Euxton
Ulnes Walton
Shaw Green
White Coppice
Cadshaw
Stubbins
Yarrow
Eccleston
CHORLEY
Cowling
Anglezarke Reservoir
Ramsbottom
Edgworth
Turton Bottoms
Woodhey
Charnock Richard
Weld Bank
CHARNOCK RICHARD SERVICES
Mawdesley
Heskin Green
Belmont
Chapeltown
Egerton
Greenmount
Summerseat
Bispham Green
Wrightington Bar
Coppull
Rivington
WINTER HILL
Toppings
Walmersley
Hill Dale
Mossy Lea
Adlington
Grimeford Village
Tottington
Dangerous Corner
Coppull Moor
Horwich
Astley Bridge
Bradshaw
Bury
Parbold
Shevington Moor
BOLTON WEST SERVICES
Walshaw
Standish
Blackrod
Bottom o' th' Moor
Halliwell
Harwood
Ainsworth
Appley Bridge
Shevington Vale
Red Rock
Bolton
Breightmet
Dalton
Boars Head
Shevington
Haigh
Aspull
Lostock Junction
Darcy Lever
Redvales
Black Lane
Roby Mill
Beech Hill
Deane
Marylebone
Wingates
Daubhill
Great Lever
Little Lever
Radcliffe
Skelmersdale
Gathurst
Wigan
WESTHOUGHTON
FARNWORTH
Digmoor
Up Holland
Orrell
Pemberton
Hart Common
Water's Nook
Highfield
Kearsley
Stand
Over Hulton
Ince in Makerfield
Hindley
Daisy Hill
Hindley Green
Rainford Junction
Higher End
Goose Green
ATHERTON
Tyldesley
Little Hulton
Walkden
Clifton Green
Swinton
Pendlebury
Crawford
Longshaw
Platt Bridge
Bickershaw
Howe Bridge
Worsley
Rainford
Bryn Gates
Abram
Westleigh
Billinge
Bryn
Crank Wood
Leigh
Manchester
Crank
Garswood
Chadwick Green
Moss Bank
ASHTON-IN-MAKERFIELD
Plank Lane
Pennington
Astley Green
Charlestown
Lowton Common
SALFORD
Golborne
Lowton
Lately Common
Eccles
Denton's Green
Haydock
Glazebury
BARTON
Blackbrook
Twiss Green
Trafford Park
St Helens
Broad Oak
Lane Head
Fowley Common
Davyhulme
Eccleston
Peasley Cross
Collins Green
Newton-le-Willows
New Lane End
Culcheth
URMSTON
Sutton
Croft
Irlam
Flixton
Thatto Heath
Eccleston Park
Rainhill
Burtonwood
Winwick
Glazebrook
Carrington
Ashton upon Mersey
SALE
Sutton Leach
BURTONWOOD SERVICES
Risley
Cadishead
Rainhill Stoops
Sutton Manor
Clock Face
Houghton Green
Fearnhead
Birchwood
Hollins Green
Partington
Brooklands
Dallam
Orford
Woolston
Bold Heath
Warburton
Mossbrow
Broadheath
Dunham Town
Timperley
Warrington
Martinscroft
Manchester Ship Canal
Barrow's Green
Great Sankey
Heatley
Cronton
Farnworth
Doe Green
Penketh
Thelwall
Lymm
Oughtrington
Altrincham
Hale
Halebarns
Wythenshawe
Appleton
Latchford
Grappenhall
Broomedge
Little Bollington
Bowdon
Bowgreen
Ditton
Higher Walton
Stockton Heath
Widnes
LYMM SERVICES
Moore
Appleton Thorn
Hale Bank
Sworton Heath
High Legh
Ashley
Thorns Green
Runcorn
Keckwick
Daresbury
Stretton
Rostherne
Halton
Hatton
Hoo Green
Bucklow Hill
New Mills
Morley
Norton
Lower Stretton
Mere
Preston Brook
Preston on the Hill
Higher Whitley
Arley
Over Tabley
Weston
Dutton
Bate Heath
Mobberley
Sutton Weaver
Aston
Lower Whitley
Holehouses
Dones Green
Knutsford
Newtown
Gib Hill
Great Budworth
KNUTSFORD SERVICES
Over Knutsford
Frodsham
Comberbach
Pickmere
Ollerton
Weaver
Overton
Fivecrosses
Higher Wincham
Little Leigh
Barnton
Anderton
Marston
Helsby
Newton
Plumley
Smithy Green
Wincham
Acton Bridge
Over
Lostock Gralam
M6
M61
M65
M56
M58
M60
M62
M602
A6144(M)
A666
A49
A58
A6027
A676
A579
A580
A57
A56
A50
A556
A533
A557
A570
A577
A6
A673
A5082
A572
A574
A6144
A5080
A562
A558
A559
B5256
B6228
B6391
B6226
B5239
B5375
B5238
B5237
B5206
B5205
B5204
B5250
B5251
B5246
B5249
B5247
B5356
B5397
B5085
B5081
B5165
B5320
B5212
B6199
B6213
B6214
B6236
B6196
B6292
A6177
A675
A674
A5106
A665
A667
A676
A56
A537

Major administrative and Postcode boundaries

Scale

| 0 | 5 | 10 | 15 km |
| 0 | 5 | 10 miles |

County and unitary authority boundaries

Postcode boundaries

Area covered by this atlas

Blackburn with Darwen

Bolton

Salford

Trafford

SD
SJ

Lancashire

Wigan

WN2
WN4
WN5
WN8

Orrell

Bryn
Billinge

Ashton-in-Makerfield

WA3
WA2
WA12
WA5

Winwick

Burtonwood

Haydock

Newton-le-Willows

Skelmersdale

Rainford

St Helens
WA11
WA9
WA10

Sutton

St Helens

Warrington

Halton
Runcorn
WA8

Widnes

Cheshire

L40

L39

L37

Bickerstaffe

Ormskirk

Haskayne

L33
L32
L31
L30
L29
L23
L22
L21
L20

Kirkby
Knowsley
L34

Knowsley
Huyton-with-Roby
L36
L14
L35
L27
L26

Halewood

Speke
L24
Hale

PR9
PR8

Marshside

Southport

Ainsdale

L38
L28

Maghull

Lunt

Litherland

Fazakerley

L9
L10
L11
L12
L13
L7
L4
L5
L6
L3
L2
L1
L8
L17
L18
L19
L25
L16
L15

Liverpool
Woolton
Netherley

Garston

Bebington

CH62
CH65
CH66

Crosby

Waterloo

Seaforth

Bootle

Toxteth

CH45
CH44
CH41
CH43
CH49
CH42
CH63
CH64
CH60
CH61

Eastham

Sefton

Formby

Hightown

Wallasey

Birkenhead

Upton

Irby

Heswall

Wirral

CH46
CH47
CH48

Hoylake

West Kirby

Flintshire

Denbighshire

SD
SJ

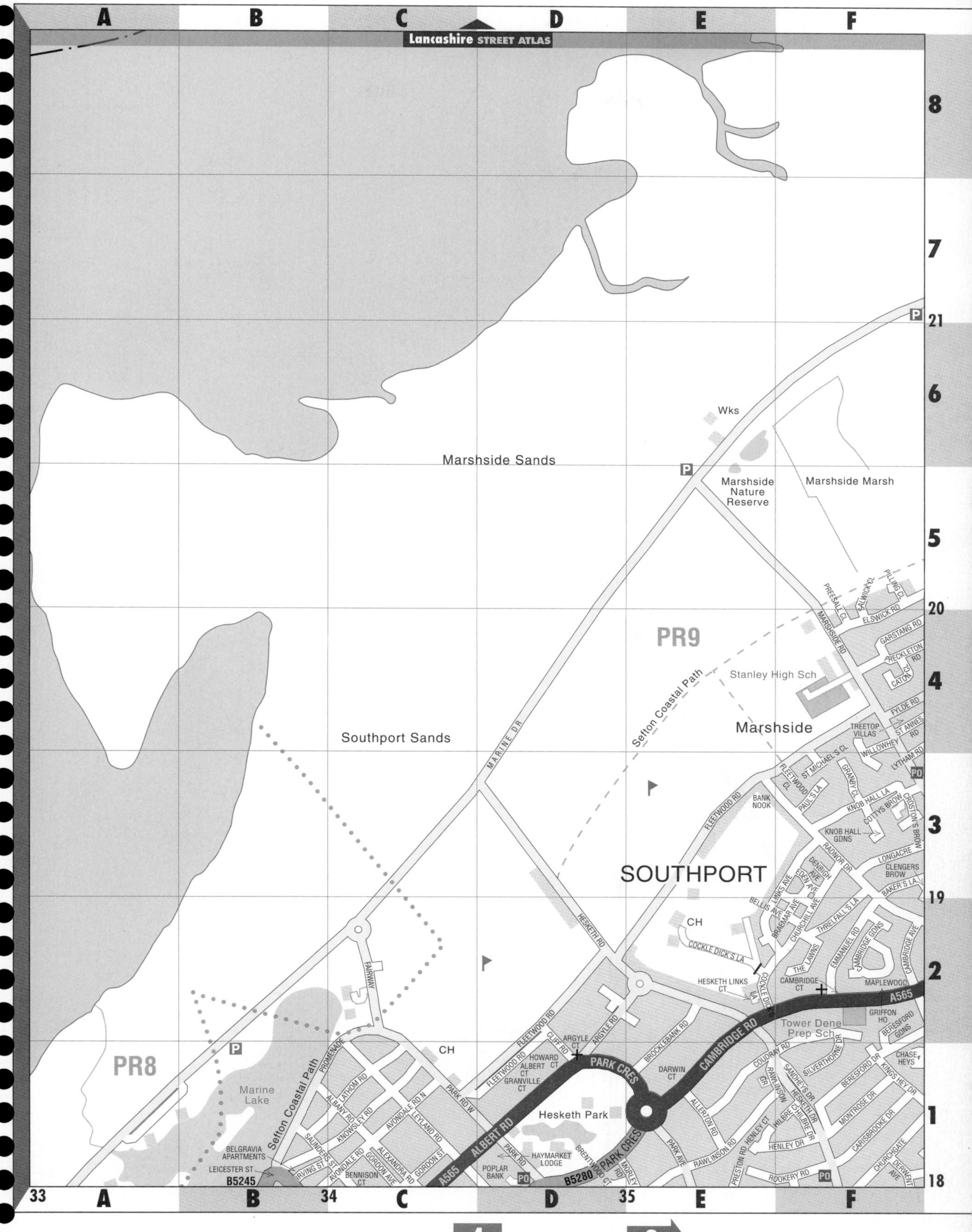

Marshside Sands

Wks

P

Marshside Nature Reserve

Marshside Marsh

PR9

Stanley High Sch

PRESSALL CT

FALMIKCKL

PILLING CL

ELSWICK RD

GARSTANG RD

MARSHSIDE RD

PRECKLETON

CATON

FYLDE RD

Marshside

Southport Sands

Sefton Coastal Path

TREETOP VILLAS

ST ANNES

WILLOWHEY

LYTHAM RD

PO

MARINE DR.

FLEETWOOD RD

ST MICHAEL'S CL

GRANEY

PAUL'S LA

CL

KNOB HALL LA

COTTYS BROW

CROSTON'S BROW

BANK NOOK

KNOB HALL GDNS

RADNOR DR

LONGACRE

CLENGERS BROW

SOUTHPORT

BELLIS AVE

LIVING AVE

BRABAR AVE

CHURCHILL AVE

THREEFALLS LA

BAKER'S LA

19

HESKETH RD

CH

COCKLE DICK'S LA

EMMANUEL RD

CAMBRIDGE GDNS

CAMBRIDGE AVE

THE LAWNS

HESKETH LINKS CT

CAMBRIDGE CT

MAPLEWOOD

2

FAIRWAY

FLEETWOOD RD

CLIFF RD

ARGYLE CT

ARGYLE RD

BROCKLEBANK RD

CAMBRIDGE RD

A565

GRIFFON HO

BERESFORD GDNS

TOWER DENE PREP SCH

CHASE HEYS

CH

HOWARD ALBERT CT

GRANVILLE CT

PARK CRES

DARWIN CT

ALLERTON RD

COURDAT

SILVERTHORNE DR

BERESFORD DR

KINGS HEY DR

PR8

PROMENADE

LATHOM RD

ALBANY RD

KNOWSLEY RD

AVONDALE RD N

LEYLAND RD

PARK RD W

GORDON ST

CH

ALBERT RD

PARK RD

HESKETH PARK

HAYMARKET LODGE

PARK AVE

RAWLINSON RD

PRESTON RD

HENLEY DR

PO

Marine Lake

BELGRAVIA APARTMENTS

LEICESTER ST

B5245

IRVING ST

SAUNDERS

AVONDALE

BENNISON CT

ALEXANDRA RD

GORDON ST

POPLAR BANK

PO

B5280

BRENTWOOD

PARK CRES

MORLEY

HONLEY CT

ROOKERY RD

CARISBROOKE DR

MONTROSE DR

CHURCHGATE

DERWENT AVE

21

20

8

7

6

5

4

3

2

1

18

33   34   35

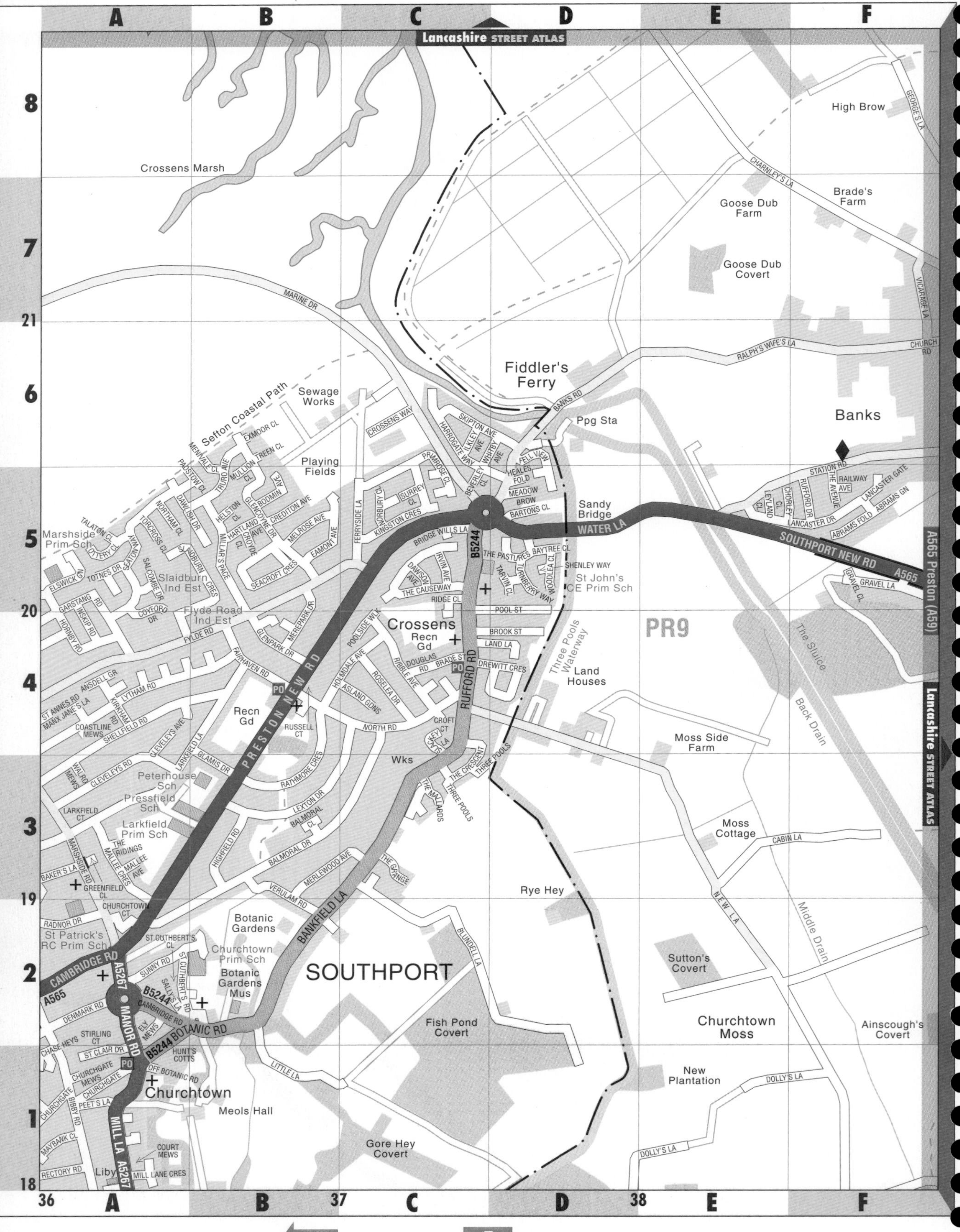

Lancashire STREET ATLAS

A B C D E F

8

Crossens Marsh

High Brow

7

Goose Dub Farm

Brade's Farm

21

Goose Dub Covert

MARINE DR

CHARNLEY'S LA

6

Sewage Works

Fiddler's Ferry

Banks

BANKS RD

Ppg Sta

RALPH'S WIFE'S LA

CHURCH RD

VICARAGE LA

GEORGE'S LA

Sefton Coastal Path

Playing Fields

CROSSENS WAY

SKIPTON AVE

HARROGATE WAY

ILKLEY AVE

BEVERLEY CL

WHARFE AVE

FELL VIEW

HEALES FOLD

MEADOW BROW

BARTONS CL

Sandy Bridge

STATION RD

THE AVENUE

LANCASTER GATE

RAILWAY

CHORLEY

RUFFORD DR

ABRAMS FOLD

ABRAMS GN

LANCASTER DR

LEYLAND

GRAVEL LA

Marshside Prim Sch

MEMORIAL CL

EXMOOR CL

MULLION

TREEN CL

PADSTOW CL

TRURO CL

HELSTON

MARAZION CL

CREDITON AVE

MELROSE AVE

SEACROFT CRES

EAMONT AVE

KINGSTON CRES

SURREY CL

PRIMROSE CL

FERRYSIDE LA

KINGSBURY CL

POOLSIDE WALK

BRIDGE WILLS LA

IRVIN AVE

B5244

THE PASTURES

BAYTREE CL

TURNBERRY WAY

WOODLEA CL

SHENLEY WAY

St John's CE Prim Sch

WATER LA

SOUTHPORT NEW RD

A565

A565 Preston (A59)

5

20

Slaidburn Ind Est

Flyde Road Ind Est

ELSWICK CL

GARSTANG

HORNBY RD

TOTTERY CL

TOTNES DR

COVFORD DR

NORTHALL CL

MERE PARK DR

GLENPARK DR

FAIRHAVEN RD

DAISY AV

THE CAUSEWAY

RIDGE CL

POOL ST

BROOK ST

LAND LA

Crossens

Recn Gd

BRADE ST

DREWITT CRES

Three Pools Waterway

Land Houses

PR9

The Sluice

Moss Side Farm

Back Drain

4

St ANNES RD

MARK JANE LA

ANSDELL GR

LYTHAM RD

Coastline Mews

SHELLFIELD RD

KIRKHAM RD

CLEVELEYS AVE

LARKFIELD LA

GLAMIS DR

Recn Gd

PO

RUSSELL CT

HOLMDALE AVE

ASLAND GDNS

ROSELEA DR

RIBBLE AVE

NORTH RD

Wks

CROFT

KEY CT

ELY LA

THE CRESCENT

THE MALLARDS

Three Pools

RUFFORD RD

PO

Moss Cottage

CABIN LA

3

WILBY RD

CLEVELEYS RD

Peterhouse Sch

Pressfield Sch

LARKFIELD CT

THE RIDINGS

MALLEE AVE

Larkfield Prim Sch

RATHMORE CRES

LEXTON DR

BALMORAL CL

HIGHFIELD RD

BALMORAL DR

THE GANGE

NEW LA

Middle Drain

19

BAKER'S LA

Greenfield CL

CHURCHTOWN CL

MERLEWOOD AVE

VERULAM RD

BANKFIELD LA

Rye Hey

Sutton's Covert

2

RADNOR DR

St Patrick's RC Prim Sch

CAMBRIDGE RD

A5267

A565

DENMARK RD

MANOR RD

B5244

CAMBRIDGE RD

St CUTHBERT'S CL

SUNNY RD

St CUTHBERT'S RD

ELY MEWS

Botanic Gardens

Churchtown Prim Sch

Botanic Gardens Mus

SOUTHPORT

BLUNDELL LA

LITTLE LA

Fish Pond Covert

Churchtown Moss

Ainscough's Covert

STIRLING CT

CHASE HEYS

St CLAIR DR

PO

BOTANIC RD

B5244

HUNT'S COTTS

OFF BOTANIC RD

New Plantation

DOLLY'S LA

1

CHURCHGATE MEWS

CHURCHGATE

BIBBY RD

St PEET'S LA

CHURCHGATE

MILL LA

A5267

Churchtown

Meols Hall

Gore Hey Covert

DOLLY'S LA

18

MAYBANK RD

RECTORY RD

Liby

COURT MEWS

MILL LANE CRES

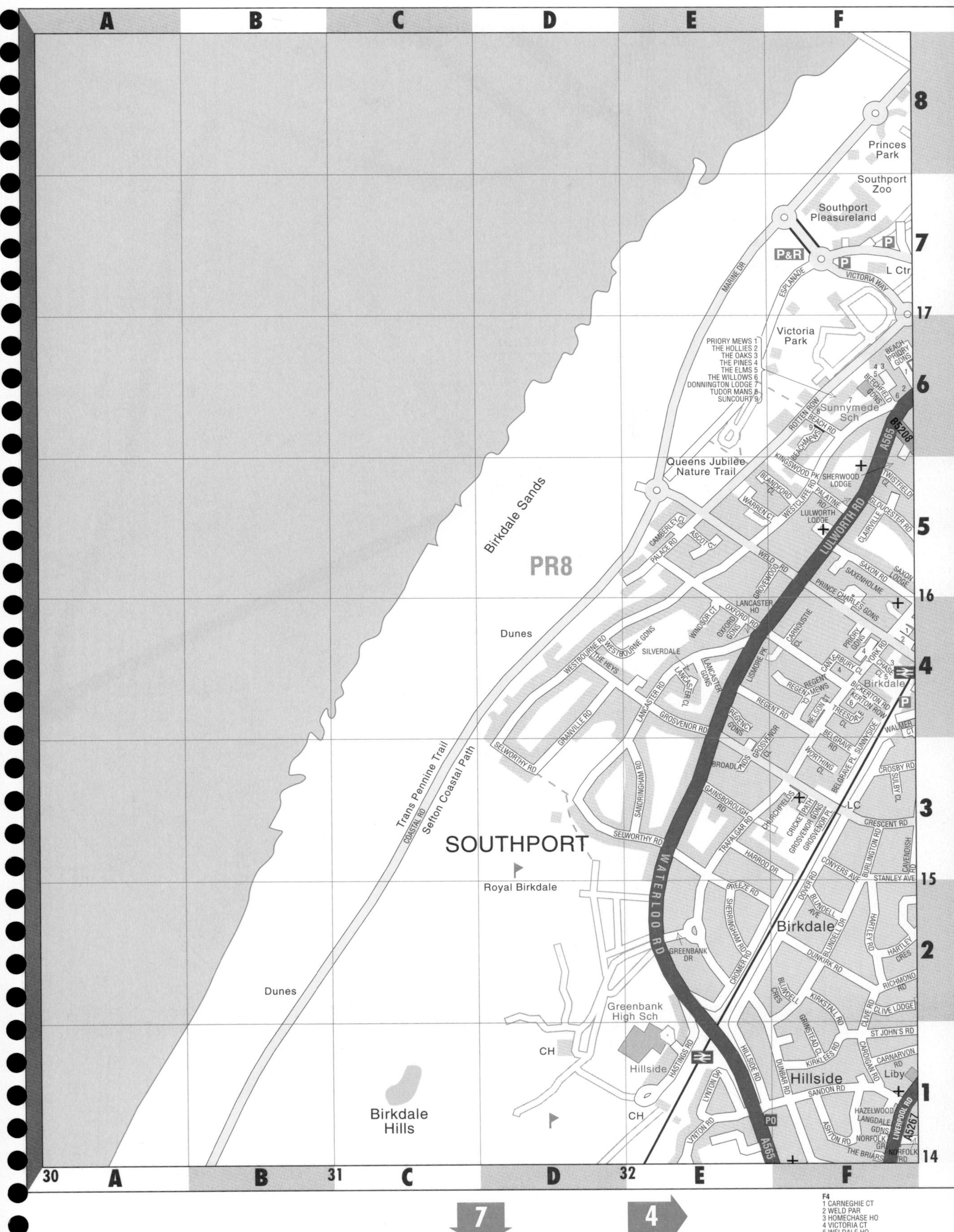

A   B   C   D   E   F

8

Princes
Park

Southport
Zoo

Southport
Pleasureland

7

P&R   P   P

L Ctr

ESPLANADE   VICTORIA WAY

17

MARINE DR

Victoria
Park

PRIORY MEWS 1
THE HOLLIES 2
THE OAKS 3
THE PINES 4
THE ELMS 5
THE WILLOWS 6
DONNINGTON LODGE 7
TUDOR MANS 8
SUNCOURT 9

BEACH PRIORY GDNS

6

BEECHFIELD

A565

B5208

Sunnymede
Sch

ROTTEN ROW

BEACH RD

KINGSWOOD PK

BLEACHMERS

SHERWOOD
LODGE

TWISTFIELD

Queens Jubilee
Nature Trail

BLANDFORD

WESTCLIFFE RD

PALATINE

LULWORTH
LODGE

CLAIRVILLE

GLOUCESTER RD

LULWORTH RD

WARREN CT

CAMBERLEY

PALACE RD

ASCOT CL

WELD RD

GREENWOOD

PRINCE CHARLES GDNS

SAXON RD

SAXON
LODGE

5

Birkdale Sands

PR8

SAXONHOLME

16

LANCASTER
HO

WINDSOR CT

OXFORD RD

OXFORD
GDNS

CARNOUSTIE
CL

PRIORY
GDNS

YORK
CLOSE

YORK
CHASE

Dunes

WESTBOURNE RD

THE HEYS

WESTBOURNE GDNS

SILVERDALE

LANCASTER RD

LANCASTER
GDNS

LISMORE PK

CANTERBURY CL

BICKERTON RD

KERTON ROW

TREESDALE
CL

Birkdale

P

4

WALMER

WESTBOURNE RD

GRANVILLE RD

LANCS LR CL

GROSVENOR RD

REGENT
MEWS

MELTON
CL

REGENT RD

REGENCY
GDNS

BELGRAVE
CL

BELGRAVE PL

DUNKIRK CL

CROSBY RD

SELBY CL

SELWORTHY RD

WORTHING
CL

3

BROADLANDS

GROSVENOR

LC

Trans Pennine Trail
Sefton Coastal Path

COASTAL RD

SANDRINGHAM RD

GAINSBOROUGH RD

CHURCHFIELDS

CRICKET PATH

GROSVENOR GDNS

GROSVENOR RD

CONYERS AVE

CRESCENT RD

BURLINGTON RD

STANLEY AVE

CAVENDISH

15

SELWORTHY RD

TRAFALGAR RD

HARROD DR

DOVER RD

BLINDELL
AVE

CLIVE RD

CLIVE LODGE

SOUTHPORT

BREEZE RD

SHERRINGHAM RD

CROMER RD

HARTLEY RD

HARTLEY
CRES

Royal Birkdale

Birkdale

RICHMOND
RD

2

WATERLOO RD

GREENBANK
DR

BLINDELL
CRES

KIRKSTALL RD

KIRKI EES RD

GRIMSTEAD

HILLSIDE RD

CLIVE RD

ST JOHN'S RD

Dunes

Greenbank
High Sch

CH

LANGDALE
GDNS

HAZELWOOD

CARDIGAN RD

LIVERPOOL RD

Liby

1

CARNARVON
RD

Hillside

HASTINGS RD

Hillside

SANDON RD

ASHTON RD

NORFOLK
GR

A5267

NORFOLK
RD

Birkdale
Hills

CH

LYNTON DR

LYNTON RD

THE BRIARS

PO

A565

14

30   A   B   31   C   D   32   E   F

F4
1 CARNEGHIE CT
2 WELD PAR
3 HOMECHASE HO
4 VICTORIA CT
5 WELDALE HO
6 OXFORD CT

A6
1 WELLINGTON ST
2 PERCIVAL CT
3 VICEROY CT
4 ST PAULS MANS

C8
1 SANDOWN CT
2 REGENT CT
3 THISTLETON MEWS
4 YORK TERR
5 MARLBOROUGH GDNS
6 HALSALL BLDGS

C8
7 QUEENS CTYD
8 ALEXANDRA MEWS
9 BOWLAND CT
10 TOWER BLDGS

D6
1 Rosehill Bsns Pk
2 ST LUKE'S BLDG
3 LARKSPUR CL

3
1

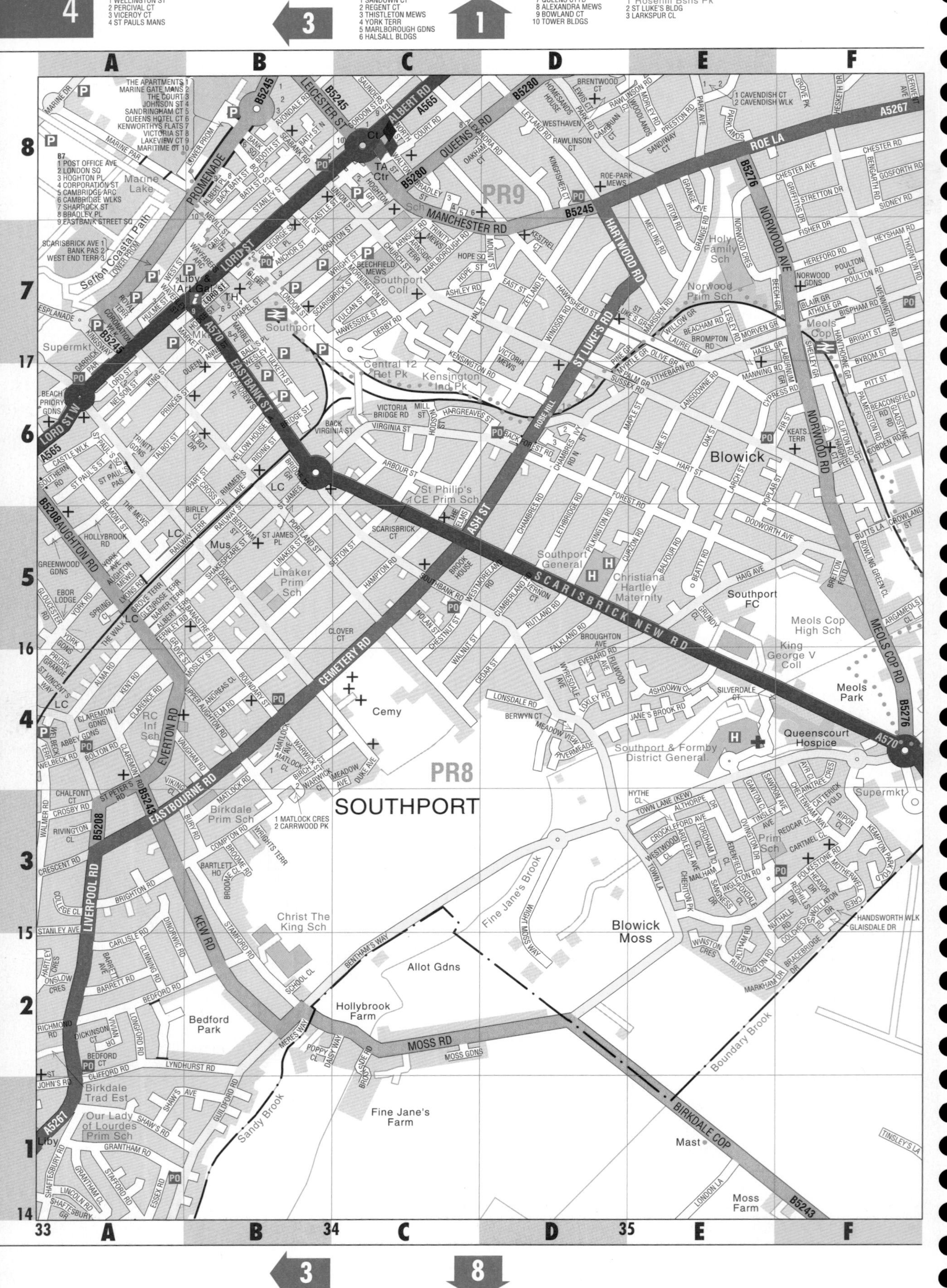

3
8

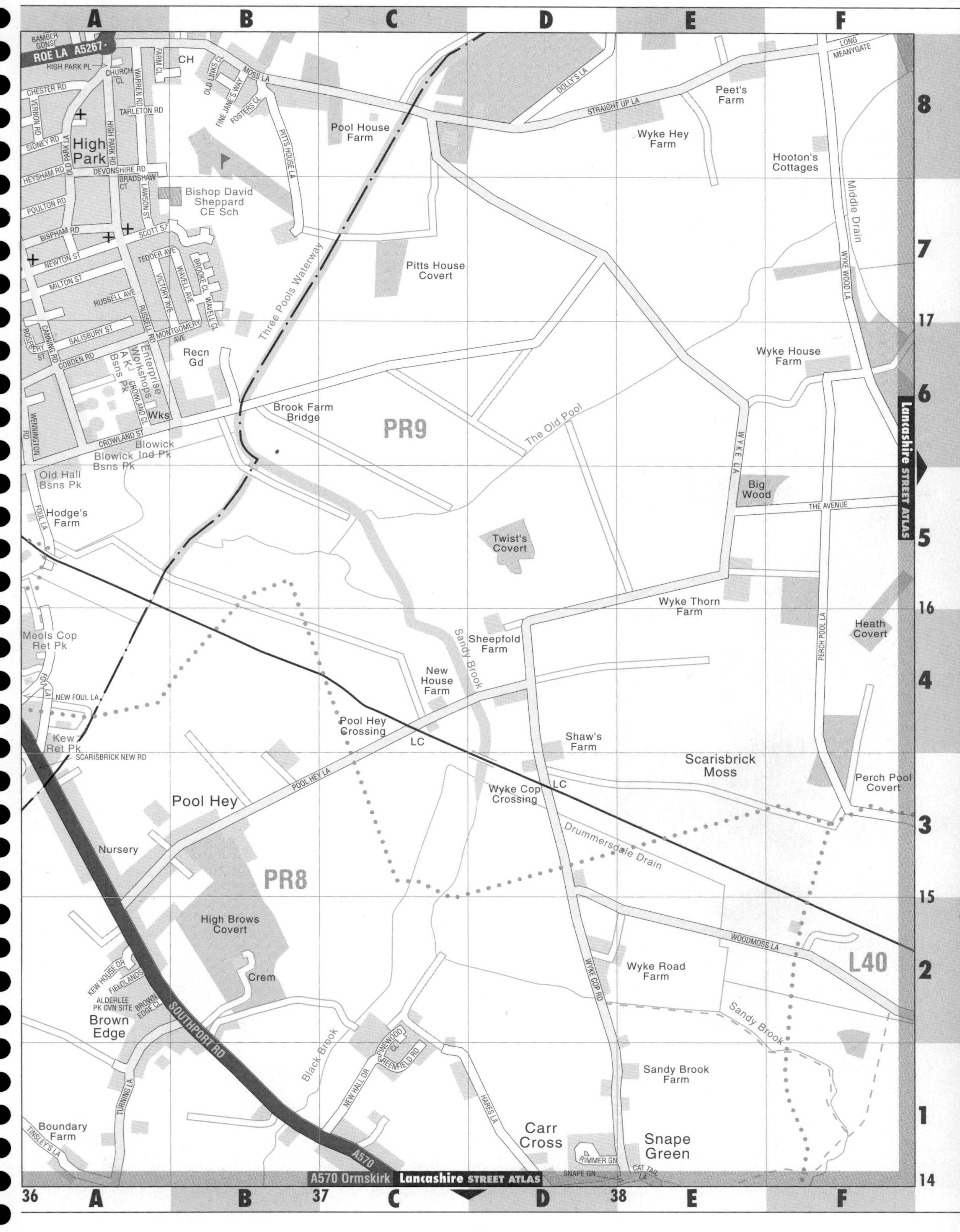

A **B** **C** **D** **E** **F**

8

BAMBER GDNS
ROE LA A5267-
HIGH PARK PL
CH
Old Links Cl
Moss La
CHESTER RD
WARREN CL
FARM CL
CHURCH CL
TARLETON RD
FINE JAMES WAY
FOSTERS CL
PITTS HOUSE LA
Pool House Farm
DOLLY'S LA
STRAIGHT UP LA
Peet's Farm
LONG MEANYGATE

VERNON RD
SIDNEY RD
HEYSHAM RD
POULTON RD
BISPHAM RD
High Park
HIGH PARK RD
DEVONSHIRE RD
BRADSHAW CT
LAWSON ST
SCOTT ST
Bishop David Sheppard CE Sch
TEDDER AVE
BROOKE CL
WAFELL CL
WAFELL CT
VICTORY AVE
Pitts House Covert
Wyke Hey Farm
Hooton's Cottages
Middle Drain

8

NEWTON ST
MILTON ST
RUSSELL AVE
SALISBURY ST
RUSSELL RD
MONTGOMERY AVE
Three Pools Waterway
WYKE WOOD LA

7

ROSSERY ST
CANNING ST
COBDEN RD
Enterprise Workshops
A K Bsns Pk
CROWLAND CT
Recn Gd
17

WERNINGTON RD
FOUL LA
CROWLAND ST
Blowick
Blowick Ind Pk
Bsns Pk
Brook Farm Bridge
PR9
The Old Pool
Wyke House Farm
6

Old Hall Bsns Pk
Hodge's Farm
Big Wood
WYKE LA
THE AVENUE
Lancashire STREET ATLAS

5

FOUL LA
Twist's Covert
Wyke Thorn Farm
PERCH POOL LA
Heath Covert
16

Meols Cop Ret Pk
FOUL LA
NEW FOUL LA
Sheepfold Farm
Sandy Brook
New House Farm
4

Kew Ret Pk
SCARISBRICK NEW RD
Pool Hey Crossing
LC
Shaw's Farm
Scarisbrick Moss
Perch Pool Covert

POOL HEY LA
Wyke Cop Crossing
LC
3

Pool Hey
Drummersdale Drain
WOODMOSS LA
L40
2

Nursery
PR8
High Brows Covert
Wyke Road Farm
15

KEW HOUSE DR
FIELDLANDS
Crem
SOUTHPORT RD
Sandy Brook

ALDERLEE PK CVN SITE
BROWN EDGE CL
Black Brook
PINEWOOD
GREENFIELD RD
WYKE COP LA
Sandy Brook Farm

Brown Edge
TURNING LA
NEW HALL DR
HARES LA
2

Boundary Farm
TINSLEY'S LA
A570
Carr Cross
MIMMER GN
SNAPE GN
Snape Green
CAT TAIL LA
1

14

A **B** **C** **D** **E** **F**

36   37   38

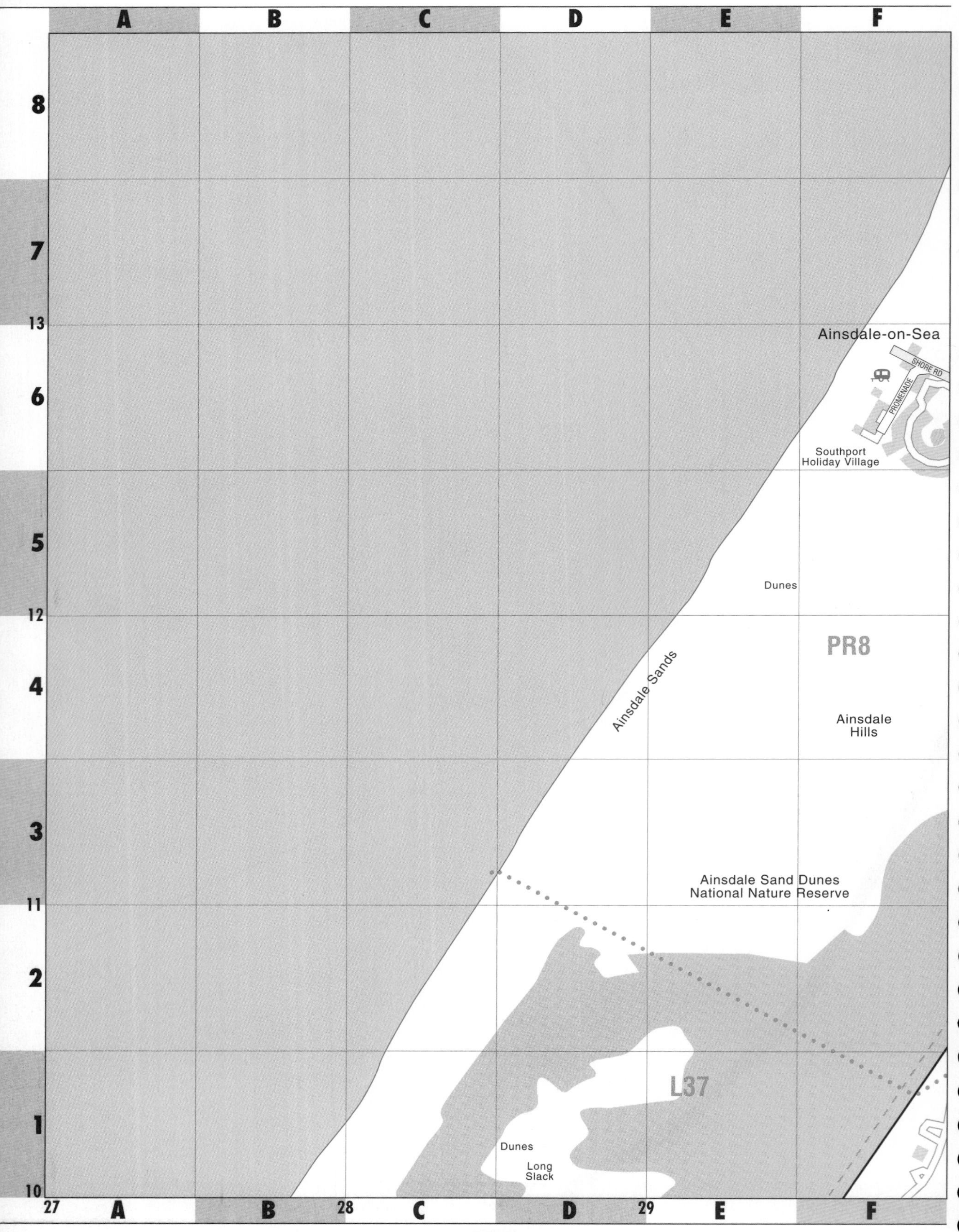

Ainsdale-on-Sea

SHORE RD

PROMENADE

Southport
Holiday Village

Dunes

PR8

Ainsdale Sands

Ainsdale
Hills

Ainsdale Sand Dunes
National Nature Reserve

L37

Dunes

Long
Slack

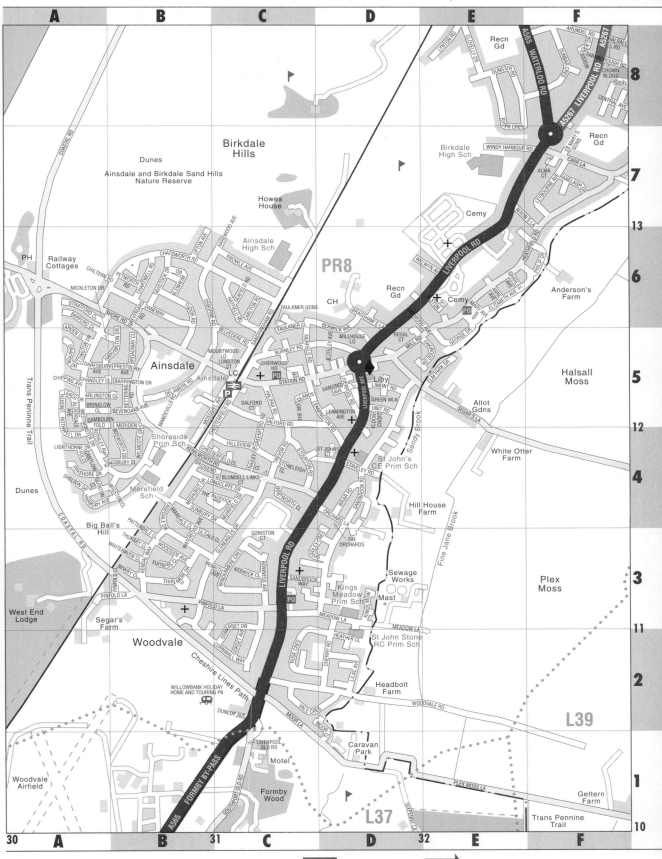

3
8

A B C D E F

8
7
13
6
5
12
4
3
11
2
1
10

Birkdale Hills

Dunes

Ainsdale and Birkdale Sand Hills Nature Reserve

Howes House

Ainsdale High Sch

PR8

Birkdale High Sch

Recn Gd

Cemy

A565 WATERLOO RD

A5267 LIVERPOOL RD

LIVERPOOL RD

WINDY HARBOUR RD

CARR LA

Sch

PH

Railway Cottages

COASTAL RD

Ainsdale

LC

Trans Pennine Trail

CH

Liby

Allot Gdns

SEGAR'S LA

Halsall Moss

Anderson's Farm

White Otter Farm

Sandy Brook

Shoreside Prim Sch

Merefield Sch

St John's CE Prim Sch

Hill House Farm

Fine Jane Brook

Dunes

Big Ball's Hill

Sewage Works

Mast

Kings Meadow Prim Sch

Plex Moss

West End Lodge

Segar's Farm

Woodvale

St John Stone RC Prim Sch

Cheshire Lines Path

Headbolt Farm

WILLOWBANK HOLIDAY HOME AND TOURING PK

WOODVALE RD

L39

Caravan Park

Motel

Woodvale Airfield

Formby Wood

A565 FORMBY BY-PASS

L37

PLEX MOSS LA

Gettern Farm

Trans Pennine Trail

30 A B 31 C D 32 E F

10
8

A   B   C   D   E   F

Lancashire STREET ATLAS

8

SHAFTESBURY AVE
SUFFOLK RD
ESSEX RD
HALSALL RD
BLYTHE RD
BLYTHE MEWS
GUILDFORD RD
CENTRAL AVE
NEW CUT LA

Farnborough Road Inf & Jun Schs

Gorsehill Farm

Fine Jane's Brook

Boundary Brook

PR8

White Moss Farm

BIRKDALE COP
HEATHEY LA
B5243

Hodge's Farm

7

East Crantum Farm

London Farm

LONDON LA

Renacres Moss

13

King's Covert

The Willows

Shirdley Hill
SHAW CL

6

New Moss

NEW CUT LA

Short Ranks Farm

RENACRES LA

SHAWS GARTH

Old Canal

Halsall Moss

Manor House Farm

Olverston House

5

CABIN LA

BARLOW'S LA

12

HEADBOLT LA

L39

4

SEGAR'S LA

New Cut Brook

Rain Bag

SPENCER'S LA

Barn House Farm
Front Covert

3

MICHAEL'S LA

11

Heather Farm

Green Kettle House

2

Plex Moss

Gettern Mere Farm

CARR MOSS LA

PLUMPTON LA

Colonel's Holt

1

Holt Farm

Carr Moss

10

PLEX MOSS LA

33   A   B   34   C   D   35   E   F

6
10

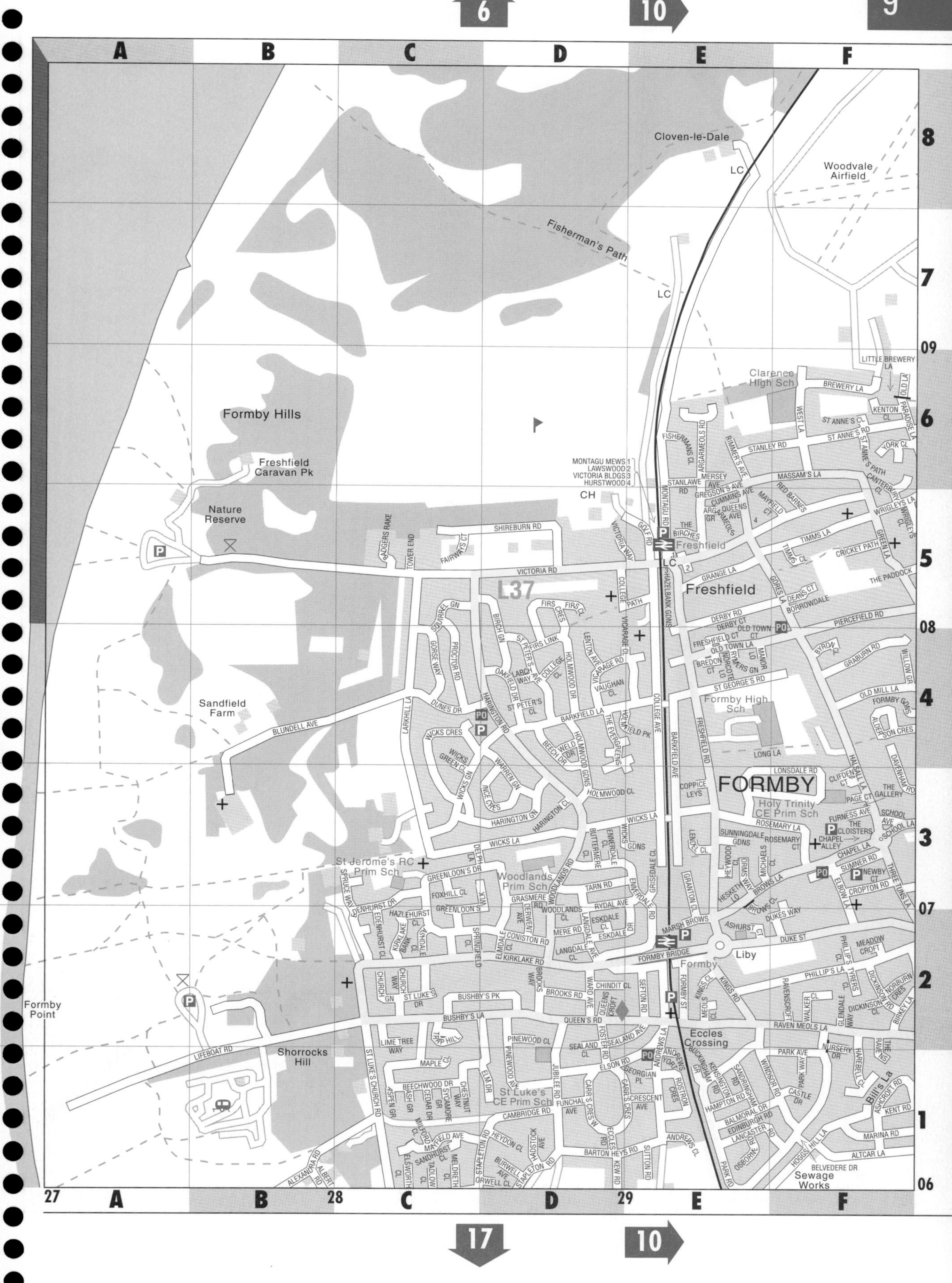
A
B
C
D
E
F
Cloven-le-Dale
Woodvale Airfield
Fisherman's Path
Formby Hills
Freshfield Caravan Pk
Nature Reserve
Clarence High Sch
Freshfield
L37
Sandfield Farm
Formby High Sch
FORMBY
Holy Trinity CE Prim Sch
St Jerome's RC Prim Sch
Woodlands Prim Sch
Formby Point
Shorrocks Hill
Eccles Crossing
St Luke's CE Prim Sch
Liby
Sewage Works
VICTORIA RD
BLUNDELL AVE
LIFEBOAT RD
COLLEGE AVE
FRESHFIELD RD
BARKFIELD AVE
WICKS LA
KIRKLAKE RD
BUSHBY'S LA
QUEEN'S RD
DUKE ST
CHAPEL LA
GRANGE LA
DERBY RD
ST GEORGE'S RD
FORMBY BRIDGE
PHILLIP'S LA
RAVEN MEOLS LA
CAMBRIDGE RD
BARTON HEYS RD
ALTCAR LA
27
28
29
8
7
09
6
5
08
4
3
07
2
1
06

17
10

9 7

	A	B	C	D	E	F

8

Woodvale Airfield

Formby Hall

Formby Hall Farm

Golf Driving Range

CH

Camp Site

White Grass

Formby Moss

Fine Jane Brook

7

Sandy Brook

GORSEY LA

Trans Pennine Trail

09

North Moss La

North Moss Farm

Fine Jane Pumping Sta

Shalom

Sixteen Acre La

Rose Farm

6

South Moss Farm

CHESHIRE LINES PATH

L39

Warren Farm

HEATHER CL

B5424 SOUTHPORT RD

St Peter's CE Prim Sch

Pasture La

Downholland Brook

MOSS LA

5

FORMBY BY-PASS

CLIFTON RD

NEW RD

RYEGROUND LA

LITTLE HEY LA

Freshfield Prim Sch

MOSS SIDE

L37

DOWNHOLLAND MOSS LA

08

Southern Heys Farm

Thirty Acre La

4

CHURCH RD

Altcar La

Downholland Moss

HIGHER MOSS LA

FORMBY

Formby Moss

3

Our Lady Of Compassion RC Prim Sch

Formby Bsns Pk

STEPHENSON WAY

MITTEN'S LA

Formby's Farm

BROAD LA

SUTTON'S LA

MIDDLE MOSS LA

07

B5195 ALTCAR RD

BUCKFAST

Rose Nursery

Sutton's Farm

Tyrer's Farm

DOCTOR'S LA

LIVESLEY'S LA

2

Superstore
1 BATTLE WAY
2 CLEVE WAY
3 CROWLAND WAY
4 KIRKSTALL DR
5 FORMBY LA
6 CLOISTER GN

Redgate Prim Sch

LORD SEFTON WAY

ASHINHALL CRES

BROAD LA B5195

1

LIVERPOOL RD

Mayflower Ind Est

River Cl

B5424

NEW CSWY

Altcar Hall

Great Altcar

Tatlock's Farm

ENGINE LA

06

B5424 Little Altcar

A565

9 18

8
12

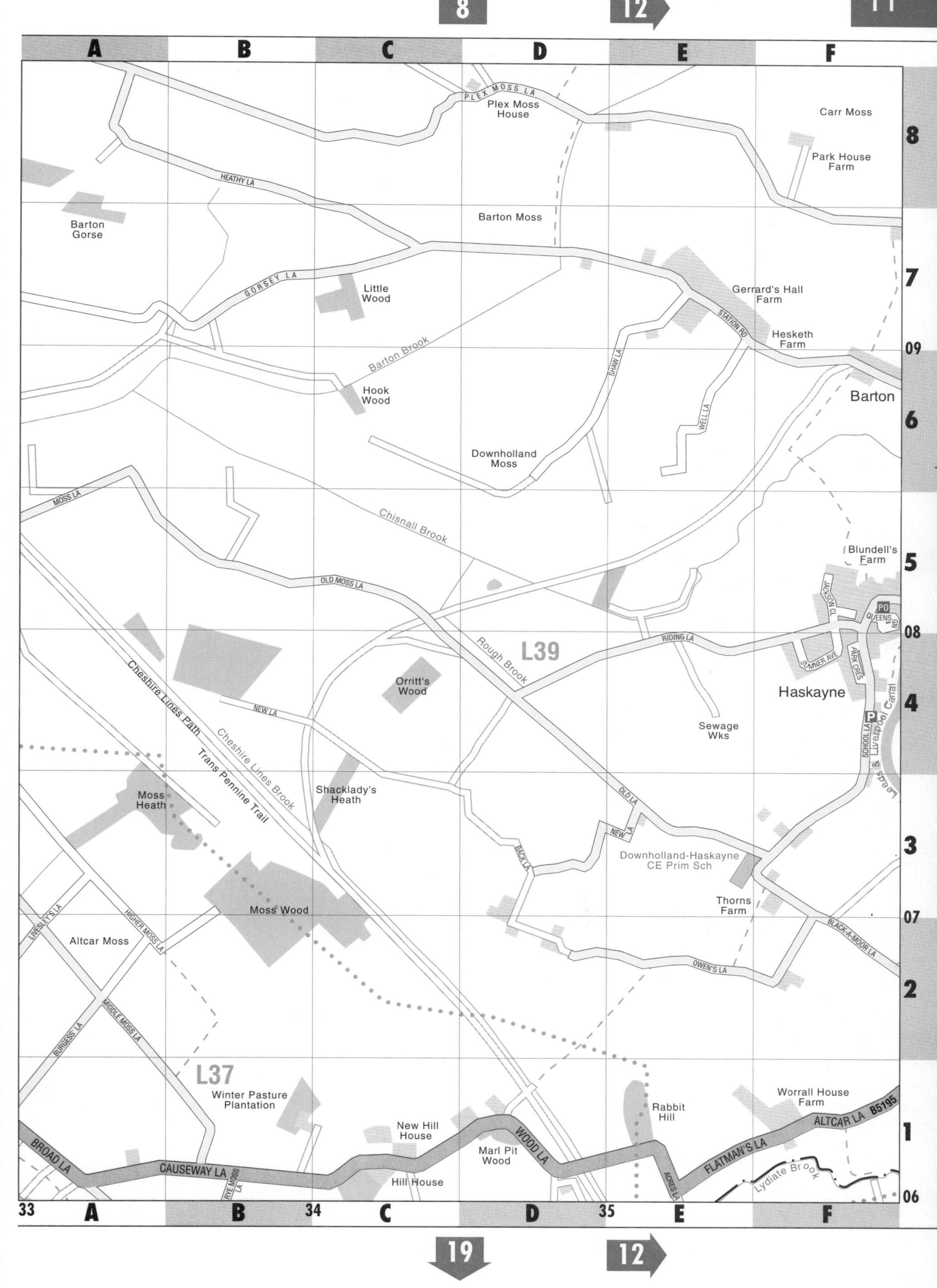
A
B
C
D
E
F
PLEX MOSS LA
Plex Moss House
Carr Moss
Park House Farm
HEATHY LA
Barton Gorse
Barton Moss
GORSEY LA
Little Wood
Gerrard's Hall Farm
STATION RD
Hesketh Farm
Barton Brook
Hook Wood
SHAW LA
WELL LA
Barton
Downholland Moss
MOSS LA
Chisnall Brook
Blundell's Farm
OLD MOSS LA
JACKSON CL
PO
QUEENS
Rough Brook
L39
RIDING LA
SUMNER AVE
PARK CRES
Orritt's Wood
Haskayne
Cheshire Lines Path
NEW LA
P
SCHOOL LA
Leeds & Liverpool Canal
Sewage Wks
Cheshire Lines Brook
Trans Pennine Trail
Moss Heath
Shacklady's Heath
OLD LA
NEW LA
BACK LA
Downholland-Haskayne CE Prim Sch
Thorns Farm
Moss Wood
LIVESLEY'S LA
HIGHER MOSS LA
Altcar Moss
BLACK-A-MOOR LA
OWEN'S LA
MIDDLE MOSS LA
BURGESS' LA
L37
Winter Pasture Plantation
Rabbit Hill
Worrall House Farm
New Hill House
WOOD LA
ALTCAR LA
B5195
BROAD LA
CAUSEWAY LA
RYE MOSS LA
Marl Pit Wood
Hill House
ACRES LA
FLATMAN'S LA
Lydiate Brook
8
7
09
6
5
08
4
3
07
2
1
06
33
34
35

19
12

11

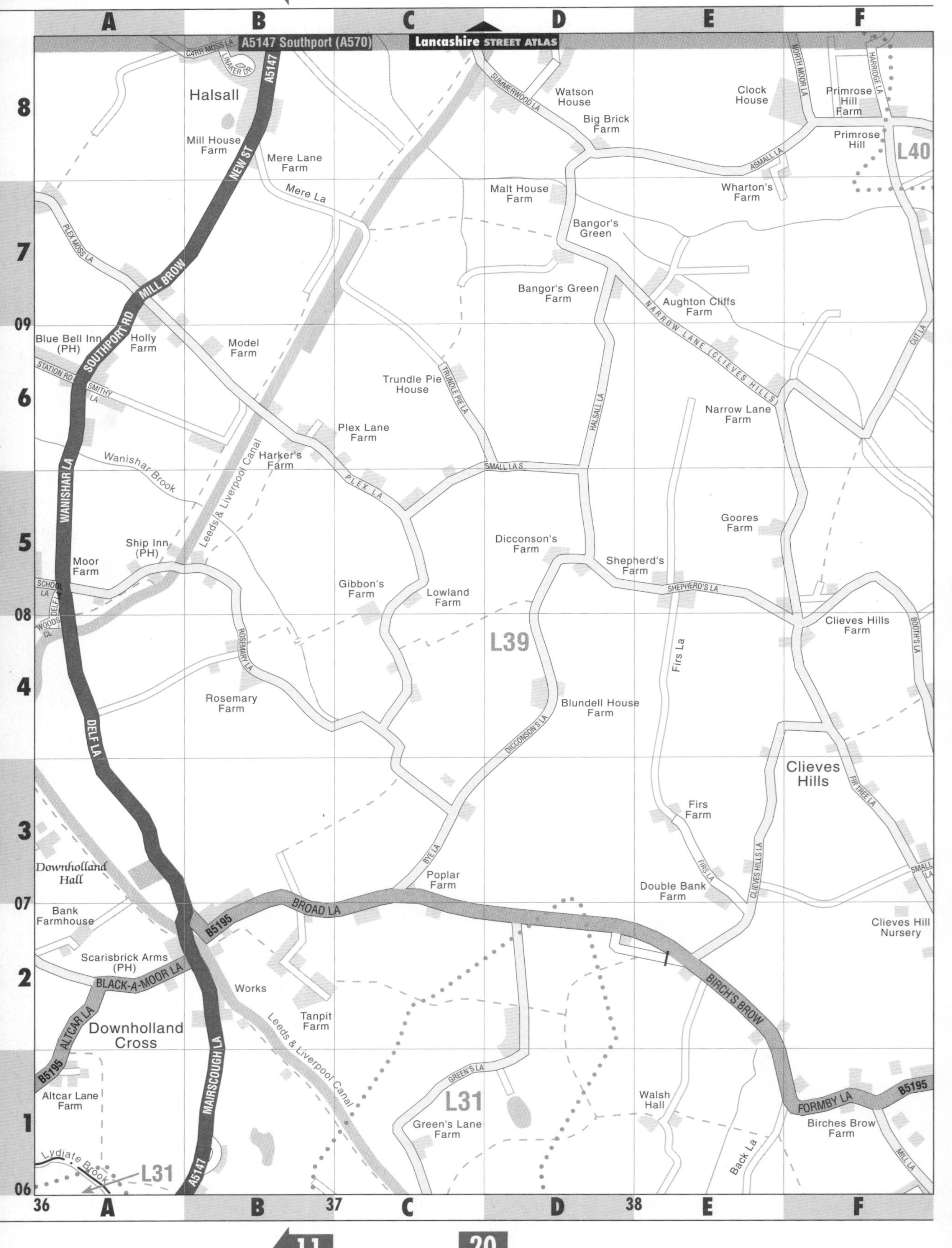
A5147 Southport (A570)
Lancashire STREET ATLAS
Halsall
Mill House Farm
Mere Lane Farm
Mere La
NEW ST
MILL BROW
SOUTHPORT RD
PLEX MOSS LA
Watson House
Big Brick Farm
Malt House Farm
Bangor's Green
Bangor's Green Farm
Clock House
Primrose Hill Farm
Primrose Hill
Wharton's Farm
ASMALL LA
L40
Aughton Cliffs Farm
NARROW LANE (CLIEVES HILLS)
Narrow Lane Farm
Blue Bell Inn (PH)
Holly Farm
Model Farm
Trundle Pie House
TRUNDLE PIE LA
Plex Lane Farm
Harker's Farm
Leeds & Liverpool Canal
Wanishar Brook
WANISHAR LA
PLEX LA
SMALL LA S
HALSALL LA
Goores Farm
Ship Inn (PH)
Moor Farm
Gibbon's Farm
Lowland Farm
Dicconson's Farm
Shepherd's Farm
SHEPHERD'S LA
Clieves Hills Farm
L39
ROSEMARY LA
Rosemary Farm
Blundell House Farm
DICCONSON'S LA
Firs La
DELF LA
Clieves Hills
FIR TREE LA
Firs Farm
Downholland Hall
Poplar Farm
BYE LA
Double Bank Farm
CLIEVES HILLS LA
Bank Farmhouse
BROAD LA
B5195
Clieves Hill Nursery
Scarisbrick Arms (PH)
BLACK-A-MOOR LA
Works
BIRCH'S BROW
Tanpit Farm
ALTCAR LA
Downholland Cross
MAIRSCOUGH LA
Leeds & Liverpool Canal
GREEN'S LA
L31
Green's Lane Farm
Walsh Hall
FORMBY LA
Birches Brow Farm
Back La
MILL LA
Altcar Lane Farm
Lydiate Brook
L31
A5147

11
20

14

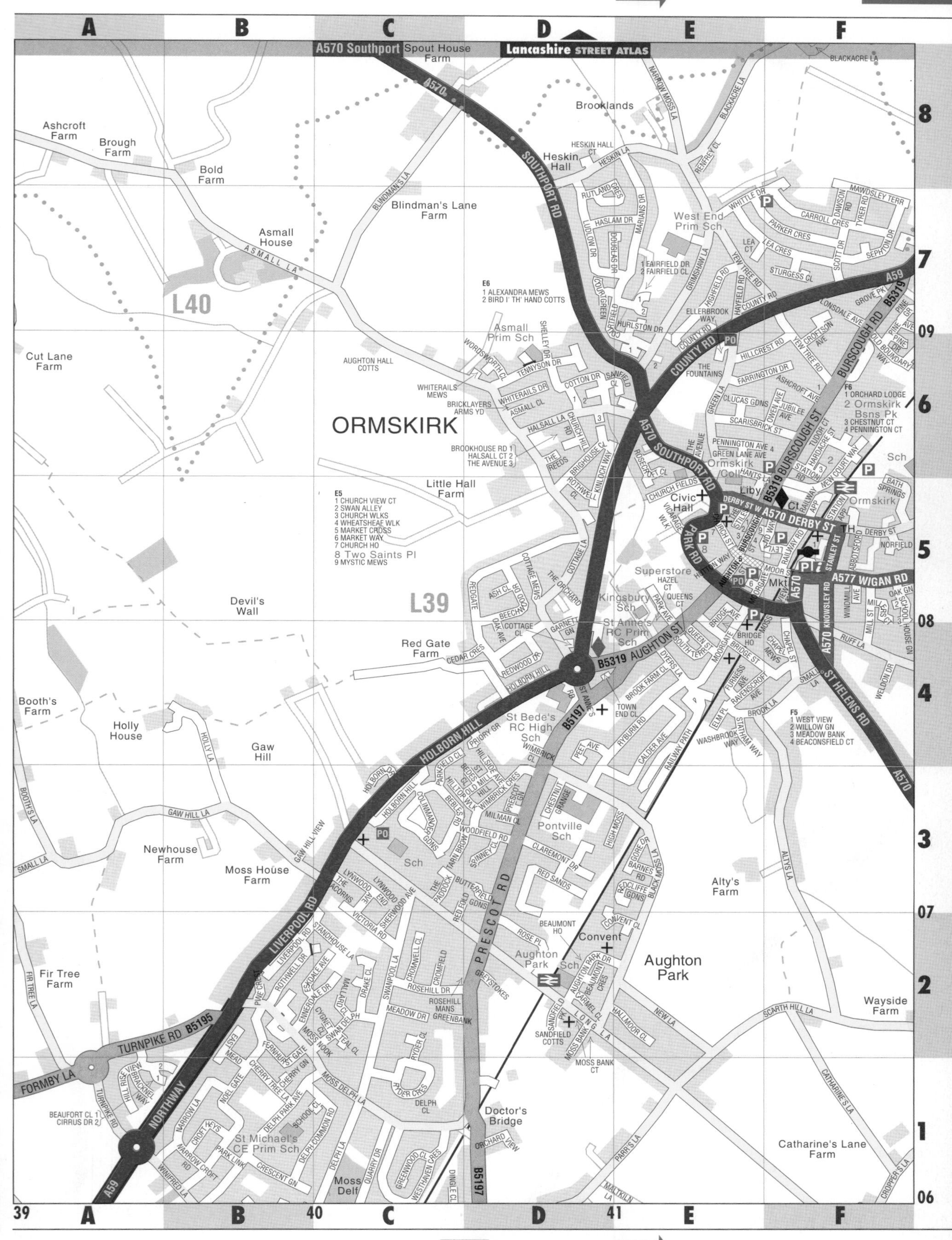

A
B
C
D
E
F
A570 Southport
Spout House Farm
Lancashire STREET ATLAS
BLACKACRE LA
8
7
09
6
5
08
4
3
07
2
1
06
Ashcroft Farm
Brough Farm
Bold Farm
Brooklands
Heskin Hall
HESKIN HALL CT
HESKIN LA
SOUTHPORT RD
NARROW MOSS LA
BLACKACRE LA
RENFREY CL
Blindman's Lane Farm
BLINDMAN'S LA
Asmall House
ASMALL LA
L40
West End Prim Sch
RUTLAND CRES
HASLAM DR
LUDLOW DR
DOUGLAS DR
MARIANS DR
1 FAIRFIELD DR
2 FAIRFIELD CL
WHITTLE DR
MAWDSLEY TERR
CARROLL CRES
DAWSON RD
TYRER RD
PARKER CRES
LEA CT
LEA CRES
SCOTT DR
SEPHTON DR
STURGESS CL
GRIMSHAW LA
YEW TREE RD
HIGHFIELD RD
HAYFIELD RD
COUNTY RD
ELLERBROOK WAY
HURLSTON DR
A59
B5319
GROVE PK
LONSDALE AVE
BURSCOUGH RD
E6
1 ALEXANDRA MEWS
2 BIRD I' TH' HAND COTTS
Cut Lane Farm
Asmall Prim Sch
AUGHTON HALL COTTS
WORDSWORTH CL
SHELLEY DR
TENNYSON DR
COTTON DR
SANFIELD CL
THE FOUNTAINS
HILLCREST RD
CROFTSON AVE
FARRINGTON DR
ASHCROFT AVE
WHITERAILS MEWS
WHITERAILS DR
BRICKLAYERS ARMS YD
ASMALL CL
HALSALL LA
CHURCH HILL RD
ORMSKIRK
CLUCAS GDNS
OWEN AVE
JUBILEE AVE
SCARISBRICK ST
F6
1 ORCHARD LODGE
2 Ormskirk Bsns Pk
3 CHESTNUT CT
4 PENNINGTON CT
BROOKHOUSE RD 1
HALSALL CT 2
THE AVENUE 3
THE REEDS
BRIGHOUSE CL
KINLOCH WAY
ROTHWELL CL
A570
GREEN LA
PENNINGTON AVE
GREEN LANE AVE
Ormskirk Coll
BURSCOUGH ST
TUDOR CT
HARDACRE ST
STATION RD
NEW COURT WAY
Sch
BATH SPRINGS
Little Hall Farm
E5
1 CHURCH VIEW CT
2 SWAN ALLEY
3 CHURCH WLKS
4 WHEATSHEAF WLK
5 MARKET CROSS
6 MARKET WAY
7 CHURCH HO
8 Two Saints Pl
9 MYSTIC MEWS
CHURCH FIELDS
Civic Hall
Liby
DERBY ST W
A570 DERBY ST
Ormskirk
DERBY ST
NORFIELD
PARK RD
VICARAGE WLK
MOOR ST
Mkt
A577 WIGAN RD
KNOWSLEY RD
STANLEY ST
WINDMILL AVE
MILL ST
SCHOOL HOUSE GR
OAK GN
Superstore
HAZEL CT
QUEENS CT
Kingsbury Sch
COTTAGE LA
THE ORCHARD
COTTAGE MEWS
REDGATE
ASH CL
BEECH DR
OAK AVE
COTTAGE CL
L39
Devil's Wall
GARNETT GN
St Anne's RC Prim Sch
PARK AVE
QUEEN ST
BRIDGE AVE
MOORGATE
BRIDGE HO
CHAPEL ST
RUFF LA
Red Gate Farm
CEDAR CRES
REDWOOD DR
HOLBORN HILL
B5319 AUGHTON ST
DYERS LA
SOUTH TERR
BRIDGE ST
FURNESS AVE
RAVENSCROFT AVE
ST HELENS RD
WELDON DR
Booth's Farm
Holly House
HOLLY LA
Gaw Hill
St Bede's RC High Sch
ST ANNE'S RD
B5197
TOWN END CL
BROOK FARM CL
RYBURN RD
CALDER AVE
RAILWAY PATH
ELMA PL
STATHAM WAY
WASHBROOK WAY
BROOK LA
F5
1 WEST VIEW
2 WILLOW GN
3 MEADOW BANK
4 BEACONSFIELD CT
PRIORY GR
WIMBRICK CL
PEET AVE
BOOTH'S LA
GAW HILL LA
HOLBORN DR
PARKFIELD CL
HILLSIDE AVE
WIMBRICK CRES
CHESTNUT GRANGE
HIGH MOSS
Pontville Sch
MILMAN CL
WOODFIELD RD
Newhouse Farm
SMALL LA
GAW HILL VIEW
Moss House Farm
Sch
TARN BROW
SPINNEY CL
CLAREMONT DR
RED SANDS
BARNES RD
REDCLIFFE GDNS
BLACK MOSS LA
Alty's Farm
ALTYS LA
LIVERPOOL RD
LYNWOOD AVE
LYNWOOD END
SHERWOOD AVE
VICTORIA RD
THE ACORNS
THE PADDOCK
BUTTERFIELD GDNS
RED FOLD
PRESCOT RD
BEAUMONT HO
CONVENT CL
Convent
Aughton Park
Aughton Park Sch
AUGHTON PARK DR
BEAUMONT CRES
Fir Tree Farm
FIR TREE LA
STANDHOUSE LA
ROTHWELL DR
ESKDALE AVE
DRAKE CL
SWANPOOL LA
CROMWELL CL
CROMFIELD
ROSEHILL DR
ROSE PL
GREYSTOKES
ROSEHILL MANS
GREENBANK
MEADOW DR
MALLARD CL
TEAL CL
SWAN DELPH
MOSS NOOK
CYGNET CL
CARMEL CL
SANDFIELD PK
SANDFIELD COTTS
LONG LA
HALLMOOR CL
NEW LA
SCARTH HILL LA
Wayside Farm
TURNPIKE RD
B5195
FORMBY LA
HILL RISE VIEW
BRACKNELL WAY
PINE CREST
FERNHURST GATE
CHERRY TREE LA
CHERRY GN
MEAD
NOEL GATE
MOSS DELPH LA
RYDER CL
RYDER CRES
DELPH CL
MOSS BANK
MOSS BANK CT
CATHARINE'S LA
NORTHWAY
TURNPIKE RD
BEAUFORT CL 1
CIRRUS DR 2
NARROW LA
CROFT KEYS
DELPH PARK AVE
SCHOOL CL
DELPH COMMON RD
St Michael's CE Prim Sch
Doctor's Bridge
ORCHARD VIEW
PARK LINK
NARROW CROFT RD
CRESCENT GN
DELPH LA
QUARRY DR
GREENWOOD CL
WESTHAVEN CRES
DINGLE CL
Moss Delf
PARR'S LA
MALTKILN LA
Catharine's Lane Farm
CROPPER'S LA
WINIFRED LA
A59
39
40
41

21

14

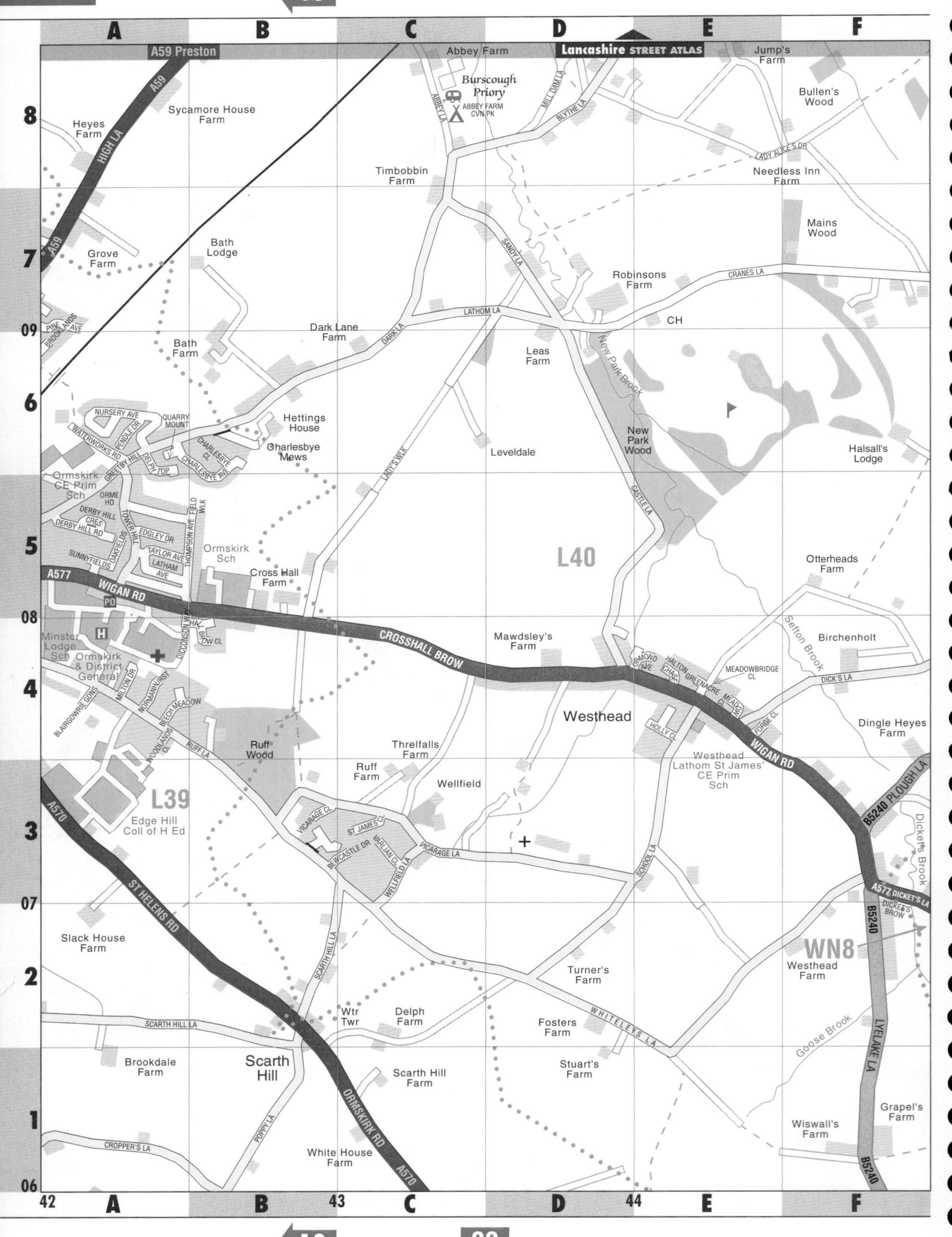

A59 Preston

Abbey Farm

Jump's Farm

Heyes Farm

Sycamore House Farm

Burscough Priory
ABBEY FARM CVN.PK

Bullen's Wood

HIGH LA

A59

Timbobbin Farm

MILL DAM LA

BLYTHE LA

LADY ALICE'S DR

Needless Inn Farm

Bath Lodge

Mains Wood

Grove Farm

A59

Robinsons Farm

CRANES LA

DARK LA

Dark Lane Farm

SANDY LA

LATHOM LA

CH

Bath Farm

BROOKLANDS AVE

Leas Farm

New Park Wood

Halsall's Lodge

NURSERY AVE

QUARRY MOUNT

Hettings House

Charlesbye Mews

LADY'S WLK

Leveldale

New Park Wood

WATERWORKS RD
PENDLE DR
DELPH TOP
GREETBY HILL
CHARLESBYE CL
CHARLESBYE AVE

Ormskirk CE Prim Sch

ORME HO
ORME

DERBY HILL CRES
DERBY HILL RD

TOWER HILL
DANTHELOR
EDGLEY DR
TAYLOR AVE
LATHAM AVE

THOMPSON AVE
FIELD WLK

CASTLE LA

NEW PARK BROOK

L40

Otterheads Farm

SUNNYFIELDS

Ormskirk Sch

Cross Hall Farm

A577

WIGAN RD

PO

DISCONSON WY
RAC BROW CL

CROSSHALL BROW

Mawdsley's Farm

ORMOND AVE

SEFTON BROOK

Birchenholt

Minster Lodge Sch
H
Ormskirk & District General

Westhead

HALTON GREENACRE CL
MEADOWBRIDGE CL

DICK'S LA

BLAIRGOWRIE GDNS
MILTON DR
NORMANHURST
BEECH MEADOW
WOODLANDS

RUFF LA

Ruff Wood

Threlfalls Farm

HOLLY CL

FORGE CL

Dingle Heyes Farm

A570

L39

Edge Hill Coll of H Ed

Ruff Farm

Wellfield

Westhead Lathom St James' CE Prim Sch

B5240 PLOUGH LA

WIGAN RD

VICARAGE CL
ST JAMES' CL
BEWCASTLE DR
VARLIAN CL
WELLFIELD LA

VICARAGE LA

SCHOOL LA

Dickers Brook

ST HELENS RD

A577 DICKET'S LA

DICKET'S BROW

B5240

SCARTH HILL LA

Slack House Farm

WN8

Westhead Farm

Turner's Farm

WHITELEYS LA

GOOSE BROOK

LYELAKE LA

SCARTH HILL LA

Wtr Twr

Delph Farm

Fosters Farm

Brookdale Farm

Scarth Hill

POPPY LA

Scarth Hill Farm

Stuart's Farm

Grapel's Farm

CROPPER'S LA

ORMSKIRK RD

White House Farm

A570

Wiswall's Farm

B5240

16

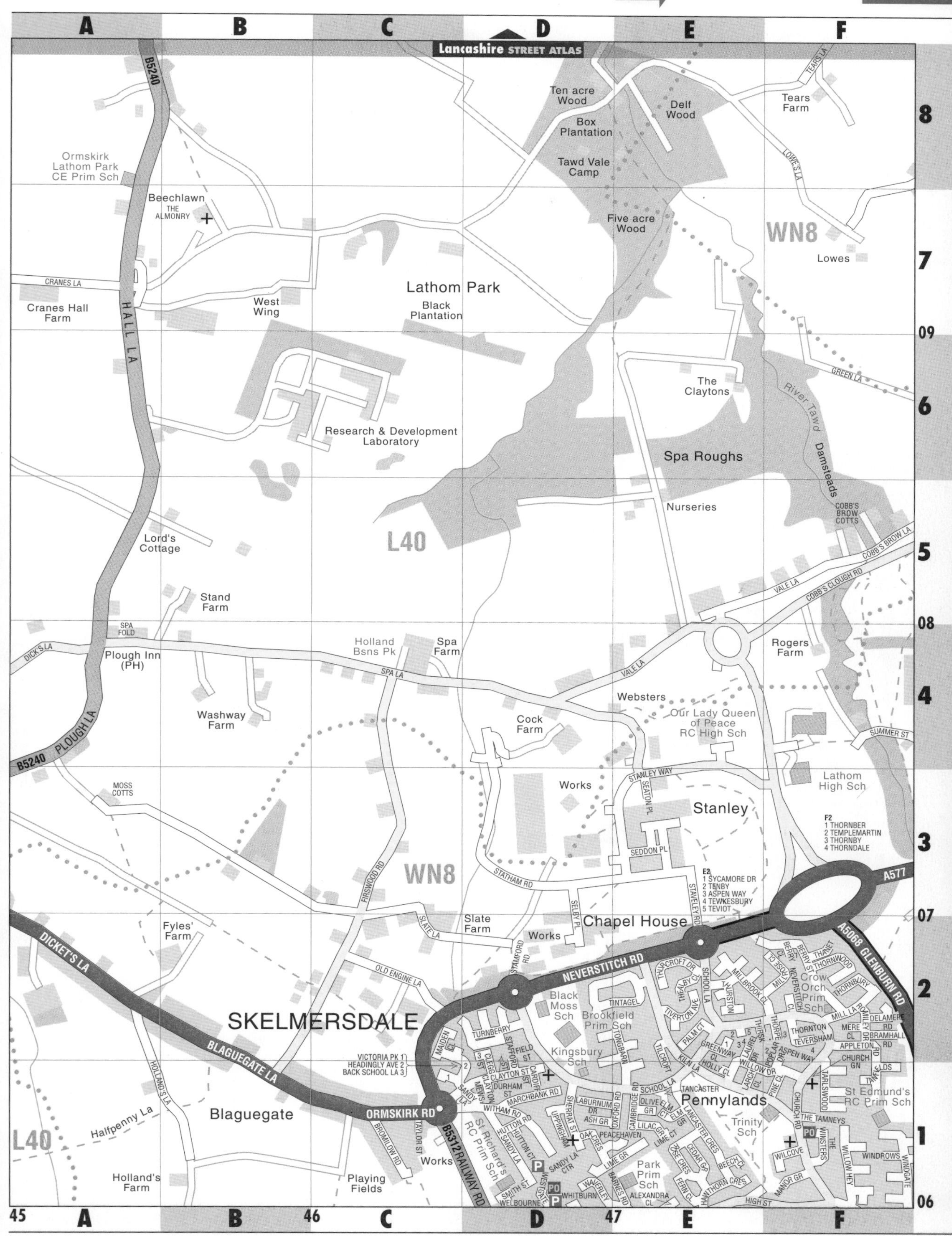
Lancashire STREET ATLAS
A
B
C
D
E
F
8
7
09
6
5
08
4
3
07
2
1
06
45
46
47
Ten acre Wood
Delf Wood
Box Plantation
Tawd Vale Camp
Five acre Wood
Tears Farm
Lowes
WN8
Ormskirk Lathom Park CE Prim Sch
Beechlawn
THE ALMONRY
CRANES LA
Cranes Hall Farm
HALL LA
B5240
West Wing
Lathom Park
Black Plantation
The Claytons
River Tawd
Research & Development Laboratory
Spa Roughs
Damsteads
Nurseries
COBB'S BROW COTTS
L40
Lord's Cottage
COBB'S BROW LA
COBB'S CLOUGH RD
VALE LA
Stand Farm
SPA FOLD
DICK'S LA
Plough Inn (PH)
Holland Bsns Pk
Spa Farm
SPA LA
Rogers Farm
Websters
Washway Farm
Cock Farm
Our Lady Queen of Peace RC High Sch
SUMMER ST
PLOUGH LA
MOSS COTTS
Works
STANLEY WAY
SEATON PL
Stanley
Lathom High Sch
F2
1 THORNBER
2 TEMPLEMARTIN
3 THORNBY
4 THORNDALE
SEDDON PL
FIRSWOOD RD
WN8
STATHAM RD
E2
1 SYCAMORE DR
2 TENBY
3 ASPEN WAY
4 TEWKESBURY
5 TEVIOT
A577
Fyles' Farm
DICKET'S LA
Slate Farm
SLATE LA
SELBY PL
Chapel House
STAVELEY RD
A5068 GLENBURN RD
Works
STAMFORD RD
NEVERSTITCH RD
OLD ENGINE LA
Black Moss Sch
TINTAGEL
Brookfield Prim Sch
Crow Orch Prim Sch
SKELMERSDALE
Kingsbury Sch
Pennylands
St Edmund's RC Prim Sch
BLAGUEGATE LA
VICTORIA PK
HEADINGLY AVE
BACK SCHOOL LA
Blaguegate
ORMSKIRK RD
Halfpenny La
HOLLAND'S LA
Trinity Sch
L40
St Richard's RC Prim Sch
B5312 RAILWAY RD
Works
Holland's Farm
Playing Fields
Park Prim Sch
BROMILOW RD
TAYLOR ST
ALEXANDRA CL
HIGH ST
WINDROWS
WINDGATE

23
16

15

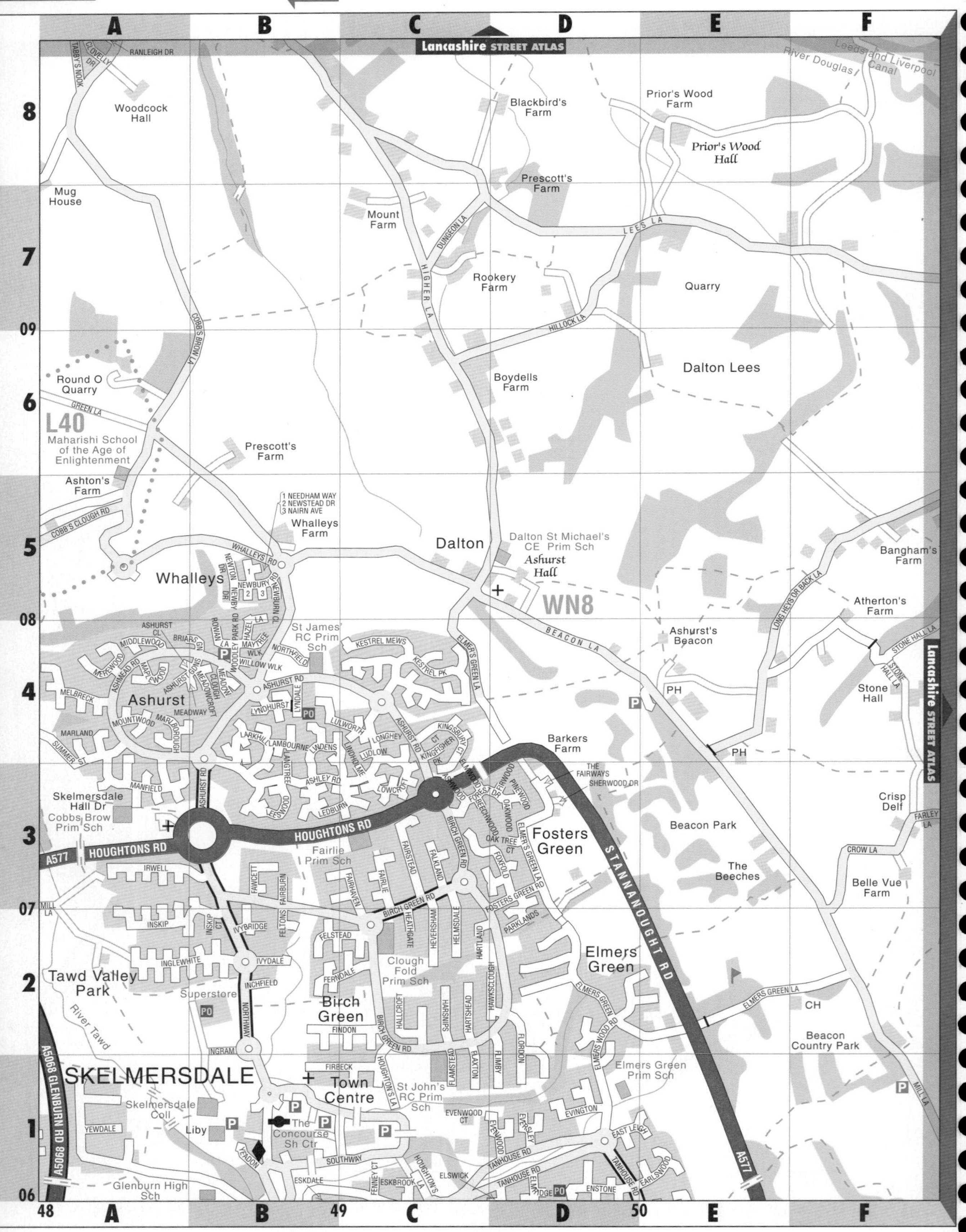
Lancashire STREET ATLAS
A
B
C
D
E
F
8
7
09
6
5
08
4
3
07
2
1
06
48
49
50
Woodcock Hall
Mug House
Round O Quarry
L40
Maharishi School of the Age of Enlightenment
Ashton's Farm
Prescott's Farm
Whalleys Farm
Whalleys
Blackbird's Farm
Prescott's Farm
Mount Farm
Rookery Farm
Boydells Farm
Dalton
Dalton St Michael's CE Prim Sch
Ashurst Hall
WN8
Prior's Wood Farm
Prior's Wood Hall
Quarry
Dalton Lees
Bangham's Farm
Atherton's Farm
Ashurst's Beacon
Stone Hall
Crisp Delf
Beacon Park
The Beeches
Belle Vue Farm
Barkers Farm
Fosters Green
Elmers Green
Beacon Country Park
Elmers Green Prim Sch
St James' RC Prim Sch
Ashurst
Skelmersdale Hall Dr
Cobbs Brow Prim Sch
Fairlie Prim Sch
Clough Fold Prim Sch
Birch Green
Tawd Valley Park
Superstore
SKELMERSDALE
Town Centre
St John's RC Prim Sch
Skelmersdale Coll
Liby
The Concourse Sh Ctr
Glenburn High Sch
River Douglas
Leeds and Liverpool Canal
River Tawd
LEES LA
HILLOCK LA
DUNGEON LA
HIGHER LA
COBB'S BROW LA
GREEN LA
COBB'S CLOUGH RD
WHALLEYS RD
BEACON LA
ELMERS GREEN LA
LONG HEYS OR BACK LA
STONE HALL LA
FARLEY LA
CROW LA
MILL LA
HOUGHTONS RD
A577
STANNANOUGHT RD
A5068 GLENBURN RD B5068
1 NEEDHAM WAY
2 NEWSTEAD DR
3 NAIRN AVE
RANLEIGH DR
TABBY'S NOOK
CLOVELLY DR
ASHURST CL
MIDDLEWOOD
MELBRECK
MARLAND
SUMMER ST
MANFIELD
MOUNTWOOD
MEADWAY
KESTREL MEWS
KESTREL PK
LULWORTH
LONGHEY
LUDLOW
LAMBOURNE
LINDENS
ASHLEY RD
LEDBURN
LEESWOOD
IRWELL
INSKIP
INGLEWHITE
IVYDALE
IVYBRIDGE
INCHFIELD
NORTHWAY
INGRAM
FAWCETT
FAIRBURN
FELTONS
FELSTEAD
FERNDALE
FAIRHAVEN
FAIRLIE
FAIRSTEAD
FALKLAND
BIRCH GREEN RD
HEATHGATE
HEVERSHAM
HELMSDALE
HARTLAND
HAWKSCLOUGH
HALLCROFT
HARSNIPS
HARTSHEAD
FINDON
FIRBECK
FLAMSTEAD
FLAXTON
FLIMBY
FLORDON
FOXFOLD
PARKLANDS
FOSTERS GREEN RD
OAK TREE CT
THE FAIRWAYS
SHERWOOD DR
PINEWOOD
FIRWOOD
ELMERS WOOD RD
EVINGTON
EVENWOOD CT
EVERSLEY
TANHOUSE RD
EAST LEIGH
EARLSWOOD
ENSTONE
ELSWICK
ESKBROOK
ESKDALE
SOUTHWAY
YEADON
YEWDALE
FENNEY CT
HOUGHTON'S LA
PH
CH
P
PO

15
24

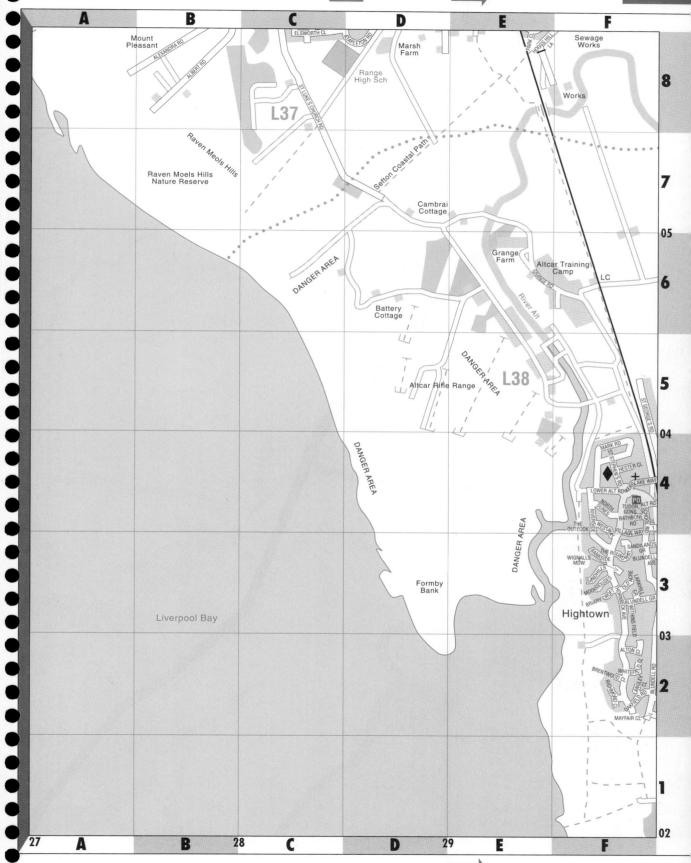

A B C D E F

Mount Pleasant

ALEXANDRA RD

ALBERT RD

ELSWORTH CL

STAPLETON RD

PARK CL

HOGGS HILL LA

Marsh Farm

Sewage Works

Works

Range High Sch

ST LUKE'S CHURCH RD

L37

Raven Meols Hills

Raven Meols Hills Nature Reserve

Sefton Coastal Path

7

05

Cambrai Cottage

DANGER AREA

Grange Farm

GRANGE RD

Altcar Training Camp

LC

6

Battery Cottage

River Alt

DANGER AREA

L38

5

04

DANGER AREA

Altcar Rifle Range

ST GEORGE'S RD

MARK RD

ST STEPHEN'S RD

HESTER CL

LAKE WAY

4

LOWER ALT RD

ALT RD

PO

TUDOR GDNS

RATHBONE RD

THE OUTLOOK

NORTH DUNES

RIVERSIDE

WEST VW

VILLAGE WAY

DANGER AREA

WIGNALLS MDW

SANDILANDS

BARNSIDE

THE ROUND

SANDILANDS GR

BLUNDELL AVE

LARKHILL

LADY GR

BLUNDELL GR

WITHINS FIELD

Formby Bank

MOORHOUSES

BRIARY CROFT

THORNBECK AVE

BLUNDELL RD

3

03

Liverpool Bay

Hightown

ALTON CL

WHITE PK CL

BRENTWOOD CL

LANGLEY CL

RICHMOND CL

OAKFIELD RD

BLUNDELL RD

2

MAYFAIR CL

1

02

17
10

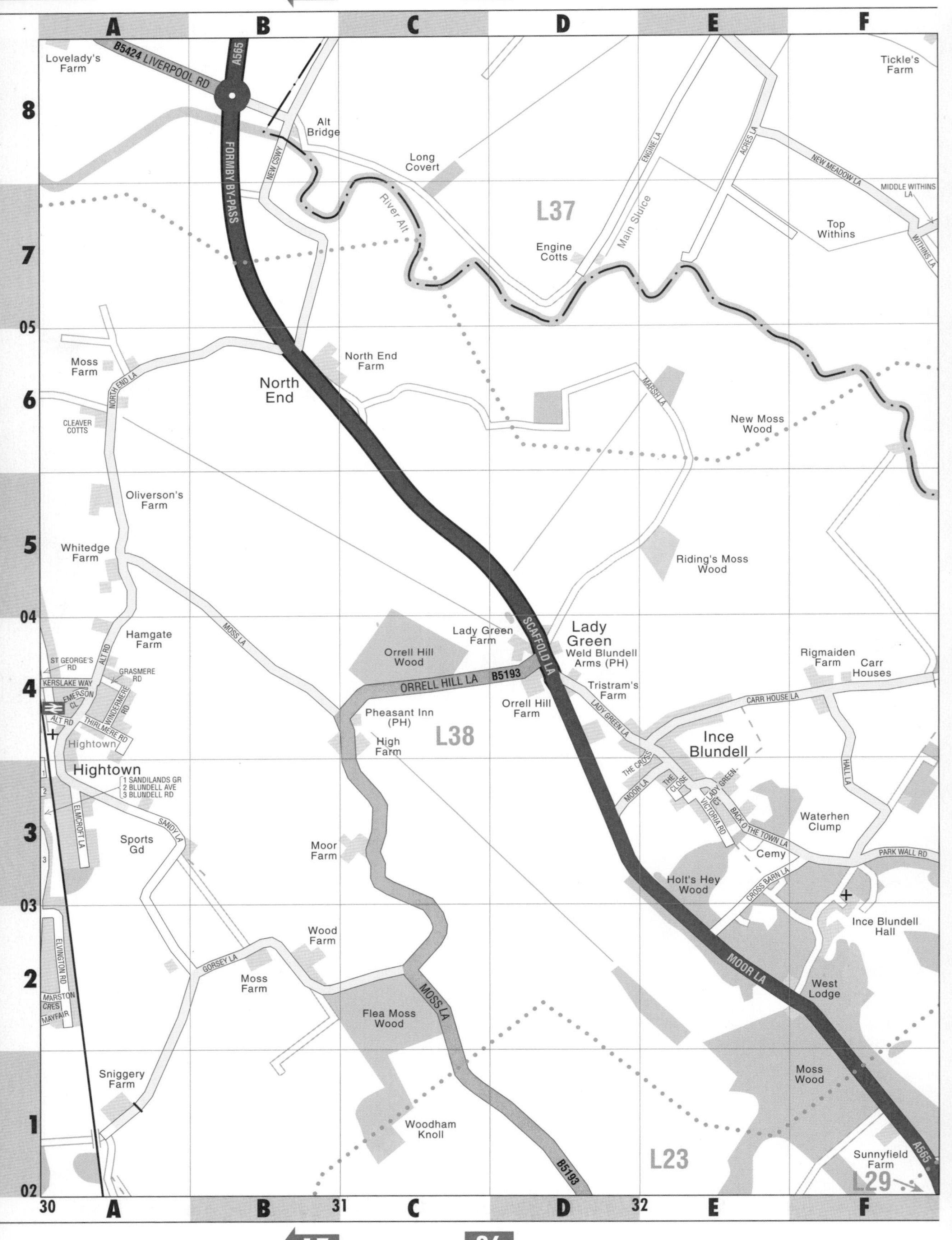
Lovelady's Farm
B5424 LIVERPOOL RD
A565
FORMBY BY-PASS
Alt Bridge
NEW CSWY
Long Covert
River Alt
L37
ENGINE LA
Main Sluice
ACRES LA
NEW MEADOW LA
MIDDLE WITHINS LA
Tickle's Farm
Top Withins
WITHINS LA
Engine Cotts
Moss Farm
NORTH END LA
North End
North End Farm
CLEAVER COTTS
MARSH LA
New Moss Wood
Oliverson's Farm
Whitedge Farm
Riding's Moss Wood
MOSS LA
Hamgate Farm
ALT RD
ST GEORGE'S RD
GRASMERE RD
KERSLAKE WAY
EMERSON CL
WINDERMERE RD
ALT RD
THIRLMERE RD
Hightown
Orrell Hill Wood
Lady Green Farm
SCAFFOLD LA
Lady Green
Weld Blundell Arms (PH)
ORRELL HILL LA
B5193
Tristram's Farm
Rigmaiden Farm
Carr Houses
Orrell Hill Farm
Pheasant Inn (PH)
LADY GREEN LA
CARR HOUSE LA
High Farm
L38
Ince Blundell
THE CROSS
MOOR LA
THE CLOSE
LADY GREEN CT
VICTORIA RD
HALL LA
Hightown
1 SANDILANDS GR
2 BLUNDELL AVE
3 BLUNDELL RD
SANDY LA
ELMCROFT LA
Sports Gd
Moor Farm
BACK O' THE TOWN LA
Waterhen Clump
Cemy
PARK WALL RD
Holt's Hey Wood
CROSS BARN LA
Ince Blundell Hall
ELVINGTON RD
Wood Farm
GORSEY LA
MOOR LA
Moss Farm
MARSTON CRES
MAYFAIR
MOSS LA
West Lodge
Flea Moss Wood
Sniggery Farm
Moss Wood
Woodham Knoll
B5193
L23
Sunnyfield Farm
A565
L29
A
B
C
D
E
F
8
7
05
6
5
04
4
3
03
2
1
02
30
31
32

17
26

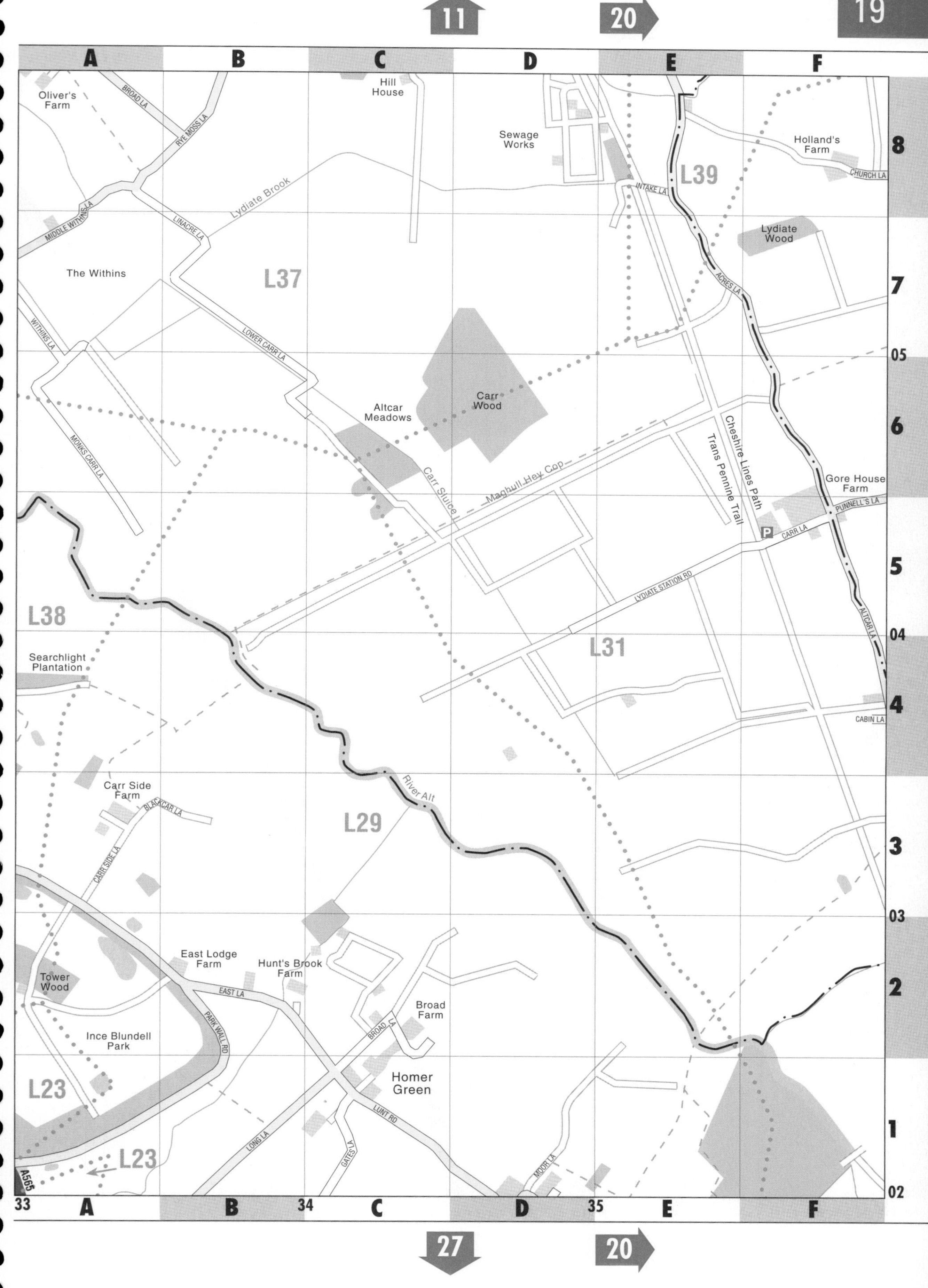
11
20
A
B
C
D
E
F
Oliver's Farm
BROAD LA
RYE MOSS LA
Hill House
Sewage Works
Holland's Farm
CHURCH LA
L39
INTAKE LA
Lydiate Brook
MIDDLE WITHINS LA
LINACRE LA
Lydiate Wood
The Withins
L37
ACRES LA
WITHINS LA
LOWER CARR LA
Carr Wood
Altcar Meadows
MONKS CARR LA
Carr Sluice
Maghull Hey Cop
Cheshire Lines Path
Trans Pennine Trail
Gore House Farm
PUNNELL'S LA
CARR LA
LYDIATE STATION RD
L38
ALTCAR LA
Searchlight Plantation
L31
CABIN LA
Carr Side Farm
BLACKCAR LA
River Alt
L29
CARR SIDE LA
East Lodge Farm
Hunt's Brook Farm
Tower Wood
EAST LA
Broad Farm
BROAD LA
PARK WALL RD
Ince Blundell Park
Homer Green
L23
LUNT RD
LONG LA
GATES LA
L23
A565
MOOR LA
8
7
05
6
5
04
4
3
03
2
1
02
33
34
35
27
20

19
12

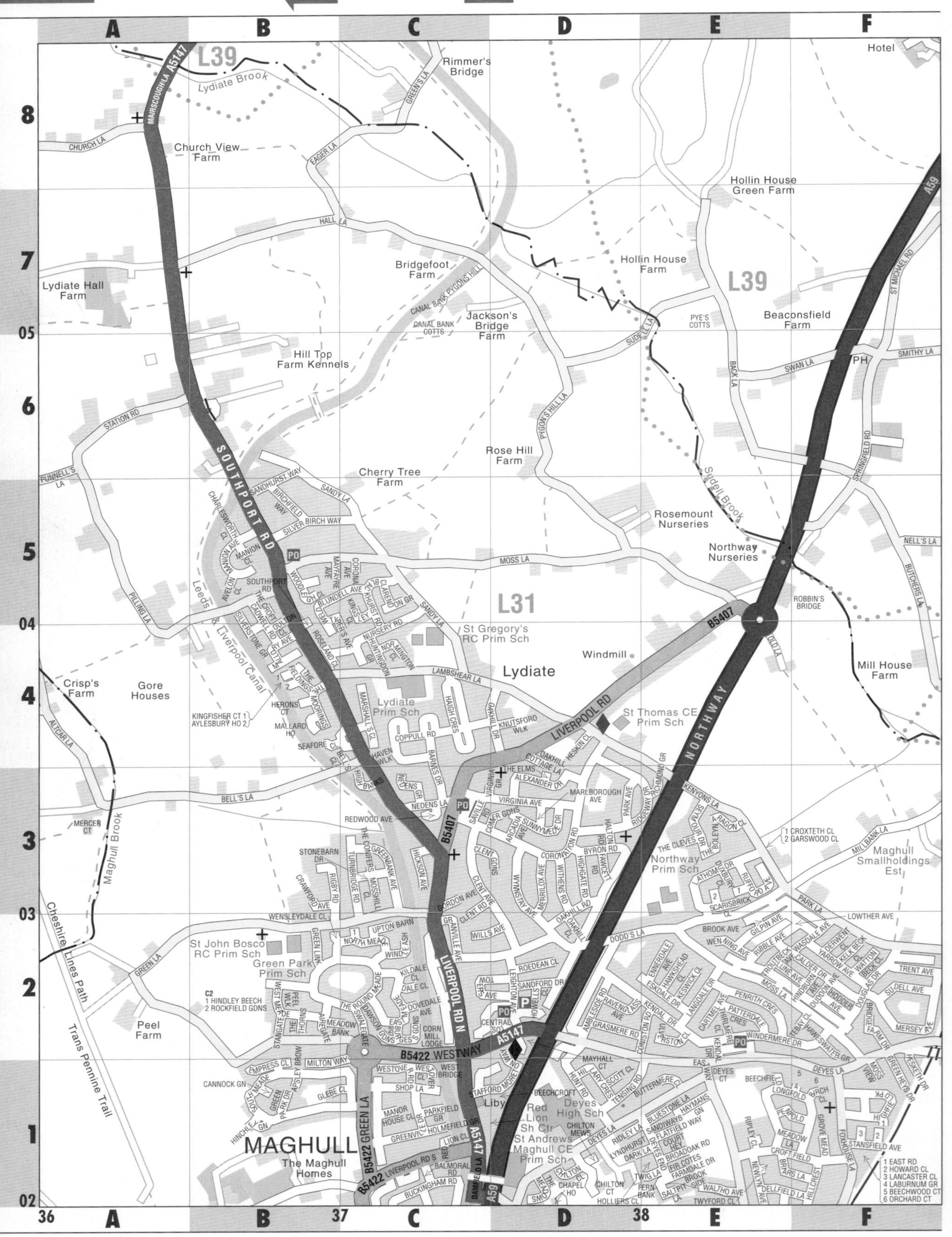
L39
Lydiate Brook
Rimmer's Bridge
Church View Farm
Hollin House Green Farm
Hotel
Bridgefoot Farm
Hollin House Farm
Lydiate Hall Farm
Jackson's Bridge Farm
Beaconsfield Farm
Hill Top Farm Kennels
Rose Hill Farm
Cherry Tree Farm
Rosemount Nurseries
Northway Nurseries
SOUTHPORT RD
Leeds & Liverpool Canal
L31
St Gregory's RC Prim Sch
Windmill
Lydiate
Lydiate Prim Sch
St Thomas CE Prim Sch
Crisp's Farm
Gore Houses
Mill House Farm
NORTHWAY
LIVERPOOL RD
Maghull Brook
Northway Prim Sch
Maghull Smallholdings Est
Cheshire Lines Path
St John Bosco RC Prim Sch
Green Park Prim Sch
Trans Pennine Trail
Peel Farm
B5422 WESTWAY
LIVERPOOL RD N
Deyes High Sch
Red Lion Sh Ctr
St Andrews Maghull CE Prim Sch
MAGHULL
The Maghull Homes
A B C D E F
8 7 05 6 5 04 4 3 03 2 1 02
36 37 38

19
28

13
22

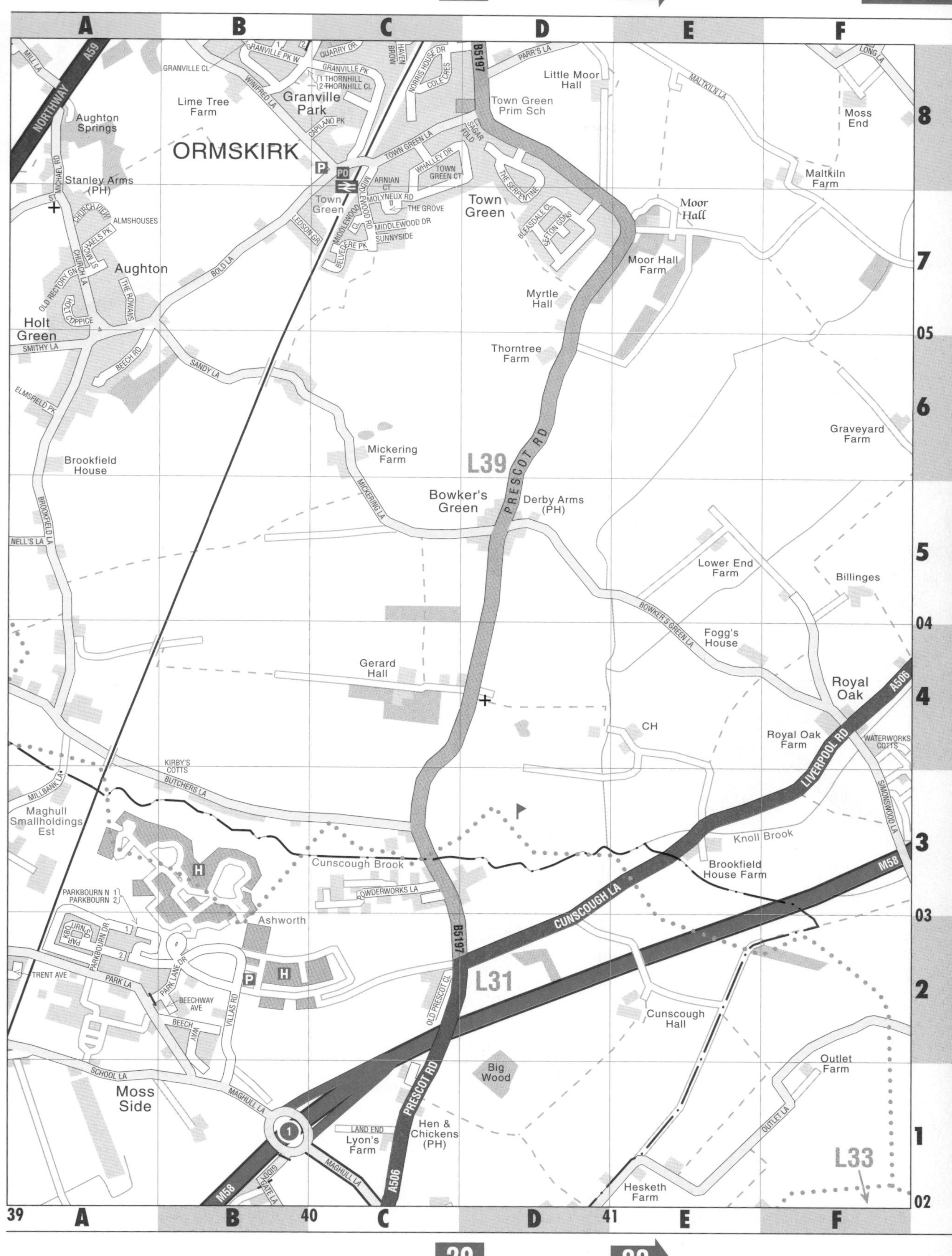
ORMSKIRK
Granville Park
Lime Tree Farm
Aughton Springs
Stanley Arms (PH)
Town Green
Aughton
Holt Green
Little Moor Hall
Town Green Prim Sch
Moss End
Maltkiln Farm
Moor Hall
Moor Hall Farm
Myrtle Hall
Thorntree Farm
Graveyard Farm
Mickering Farm
Brookfield House
L39
PRESCOT RD
Bowker's Green
Derby Arms (PH)
Lower End Farm
Billinges
Fogg's House
Gerard Hall
Royal Oak
Royal Oak Farm
CH
Maghull Smallholdings Est
Cunscough Brook
Knoll Brook
Brookfield House Farm
Ashworth
L31
Cunscough Hall
Big Wood
Outlet Farm
Moss Side
Hen & Chickens (PH)
Lyon's Farm
Hesketh Farm
L33
B5197
A59
A506
M58
NORTHWAY
LIVERPOOL RD
CUNSCOUGH LA
BOWKER'S GREEN LA
MICKERING LA
SANDY LA
BOLD LA
SCHOOL LA
MAGHULL LA
PARK LA
BUTCHERS LA
KIRBY'S COTTS
MILLBANK LA
BROOKFIELD LA
NELL'S LA
SMITHY LA
ELMSFIELD PK
CHURCH LA
TOWN GREEN LA
PARR'S LA
MALTKILN LA
LONG LA
OUTLET LA
SIMONSWOOD LA
WATERWORKS COTTS
POWDERWORKS LA
OLD PRESCOT CL
VILLAS RD
PARK LANE DR
TRENT AVE
BEECHWAY AVE
LAND END
A B C D E F
8 7 6 5 4 3 2 1
05 04 03 02
39 40 41

29
22

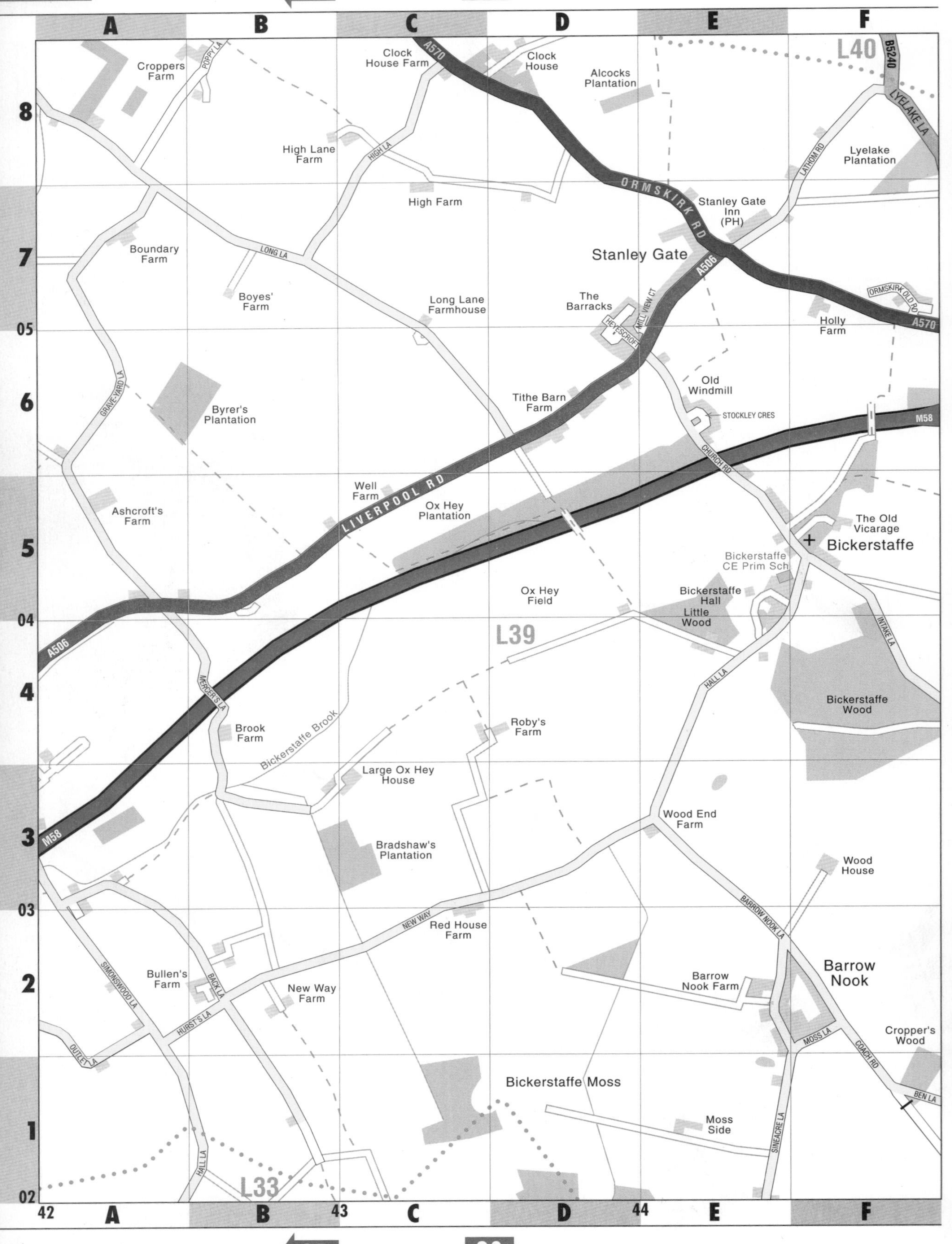

21
14

L40

B5240

Croppers Farm

POPPY LA

Clock House Farm

Clock House

Alcocks Plantation

LYELAKE LA

High Lane Farm

HIGH LA

Lyelake Plantation

LATHOM RD

8

High Farm

ORMSKIRK RD

Stanley Gate Inn (PH)

Boundary Farm

LONG LA

Stanley Gate

A506

ORMSKIRK OLD RD

7

Boyes' Farm

Long Lane Farmhouse

The Barracks

HEY'S CROFT

MILL VIEW CT

Holly Farm

A570

05

GRAVEYARD LA

Byrer's Plantation

Old Windmill

Stockley Cres

M58

6

Tithe Barn Farm

CHURCH RD

The Old Vicarage

Well Farm

Ashcroft's Farm

LIVERPOOL RD

Ox Hey Plantation

Bickerstaffe CE Prim Sch

Bickerstaffe

5

Ox Hey Field

Bickerstaffe Hall

Little Wood

04

A506

L39

HALL LA

Bickerstaffe Wood

INTAKE LA

4

MERCER'S LA

Brook Farm

Bickerstaffe Brook

Roby's Farm

Large Ox Hey House

Wood End Farm

Wood House

3

M58

Bradshaw's Plantation

BARROW NOOK LA

03

NEW WAY

Red House Farm

Barrow Nook

Bullen's Farm

SIMONSWOOD LA

BACK LA

New Way Farm

Barrow Nook Farm

Cropper's Wood

2

HURST'S LA

MOSS LA

COACH RD

OUTLET LA

BEN LA

Bickerstaffe Moss

Moss Side

SINEACRE LA

1

HALL LA

L33

02

42
43
44

15
24

L40

A   B   C   D   E   F

Blaguegate Moss

Primrose
Farm

8

Lyelake
Farm

WELBOURNE   WAVERLEY
B5312   Liverpool Rd
WESTGATE   WALLCROFT
LIVERPOOL RD   WALDRON
ASHWALL ST
WHEATACRE
Railway Rd

West
Gillibrands
Ind Est

Woodcroft
WOLVERTON
B5312   WIGAN RD   WINDGATE

GLENBURN RD
A5068

SKELMERSDALE RD

Four Lane
Ends

Lyelake La
B5240

B5312

Stanley
Farm

Colliery Plantation

White Moss Rd
White Moss Rd S

Peel
Farm

SKELMERSDALE

WN8

White Moss

West Gillibrands

GILLIBRANDS RD
GERRARD PL

8

05
7

M58
4

Moss La View

Nursery

Moss La

6

3

Rainford Rd

Wash
Farm

Rose
Farm

Ivy House

Rainford Rd

Bickerstaffe
Moss

Higherend
Farm

Hey's
Crossing

Moss Lane
Farm

Moss Lane
Farm

5

04

Long
Plantation

L39

Coal Pit La

Barker's Brook

Rainford Rd

Brookdale

Holly Lane
Farm

Holly La

Big Ferny
Knoll Farm

Holly Fold La

Ferny Knoll Rd

Ferny
Knoll

4

Intake
Farm

Intake La

Ben Lane Ct

Ben Lane
Farm

Ben La

Lodge
Farm

Holly Fold
Farm

WA11

03

Park Hill

Ormskirk Rd

Lodge La

PH

Red
Delph
Farm

Bushey La

Spring Field

Keswick Way 1
Coniston Way 2
Windermere Dr
Buttermere Cres
Kendal Dr
Kendal Ct

News La

Rainford
Junction

PO
Rail Cl
PH

Rainford

3

03

2

Moss House
Farm

Coach Rd

Kenyon's
Wood

Rigby's
Wood

Siding La

Siding La

Ormskirk Rd
A570   B5203

Red Delph La

Junction Rd

Bridge
Farm

1

02

45   A   B   46   C   D   47   E   F

31
24

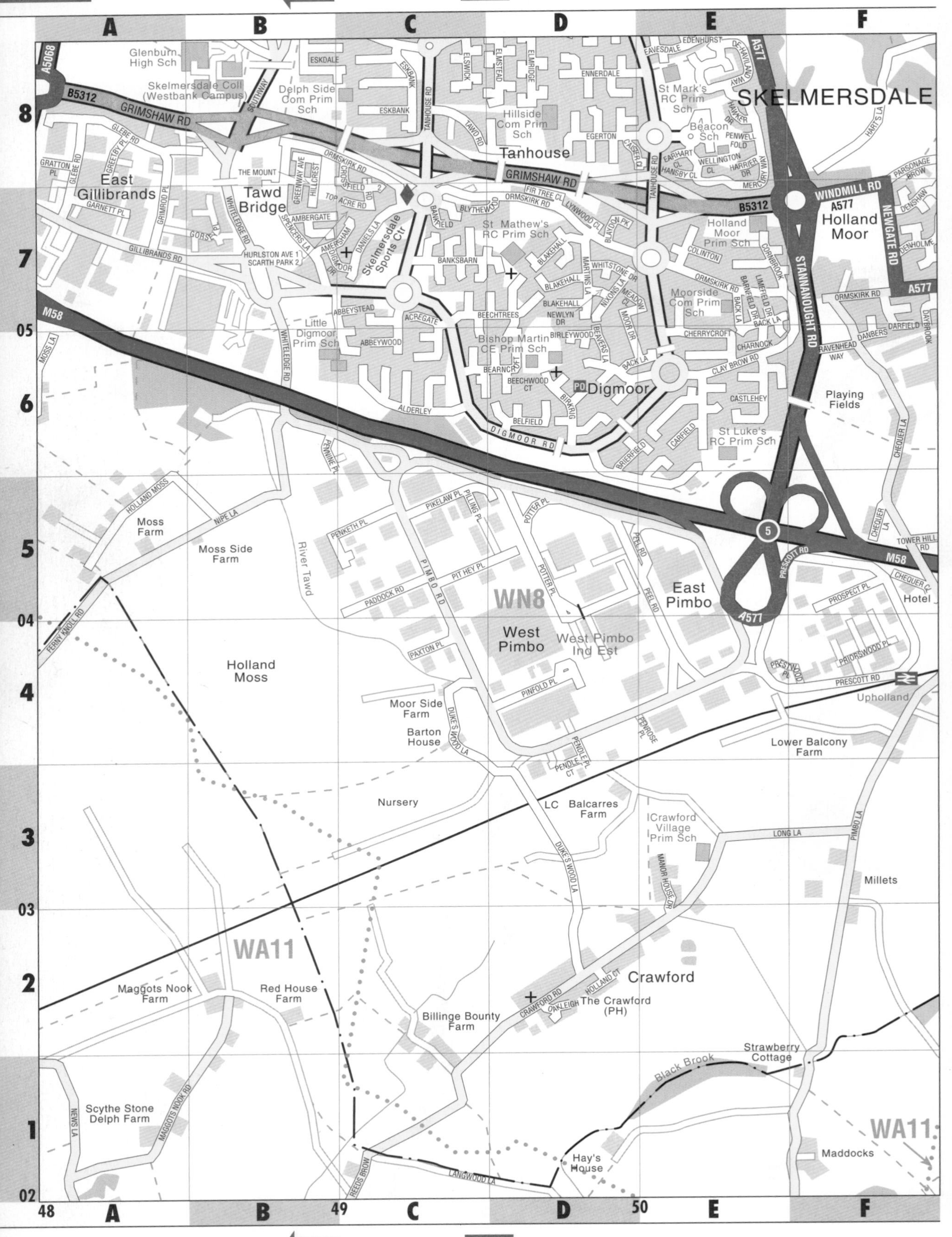

SKELMERSDALE

Glenburn High Sch

EDENHURST

Skelmersdale Coll (Westbank Campus)

B5312 GRIMSHAW RD

East Gillibrands

Delph Side Com Prim Sch

Eskdale

Eskbank

Eskbank

Elswick

Elmstead

Elmridge

Ennerdale

St Mark's RC Prim Sch

Beacon Sch

Penwell Fold

Tawd Bridge

THE MOUNT

ORMSKIRK RD

GREENWAY AVE

HILLCRES

Top Acre Rd

GRIMSHAW RD

Hillside Com Prim Sch

Egerton

Wellington CL

Harrier DR

Windmill Rd

A577

Holland Moor

Hurlston Ave 1 Scarth Park 2

Skelmersdale Sports Ctr

Ambergate

Bankfield

Blythewood

St Mathew's RC Prim Sch

Fir Tree Cl

Lynwood Cl

Blayton

B5312

A577

Holland Moor Prim Sch

Newgate Rd

Gillibrands Rd

Banksbarn

Beechtrees

Blakehall

Blakehall

Whitstone Dr

Martins La

Colinton

Moorside Com Prim Sch

Ormskirk Rd

Darfield

Daybrook

M58

Little Digmoor Prim Sch

Abbeystead

Acregate

Abbeywood

Bishop Martin CE Prim Sch

Newlyn Dr

Birleywood

Cherrycroft

Charnock

Ravenhead Way

Chequer La

Alderley

Bearncr

Beechwood Ct

Birkrig

Digmoor

Back La

Clay Brow Rd

Castlehey

Playing Fields

Belfield

DIGMOOR RD

Carfield

St Luke's RC Prim Sch

Stannanought Rd

M58

5

A577

Tower Hill Rd

Chequer La

Hotel

Holland Moss

Moss Farm

Moss Side Farm

Nipe La

River Tawd

Penketh Pl

Paddock Rd

Pikelaw Pl

Pilling Pl

Potter Pl

Pit Hey Pl

Pimbo Rd

WN8

West Pimbo

West Pimbo Ind Est

East Pimbo

Prescott Rd

Prospect Pl

Chequer C.

Holland Moss

Moor Side Farm

Paxton Pl

Duke's Wood La

Pinfold Pl

Peel Rd

Penrose Pl

Prestwood

Friorswood Pl

Prescott Rd

Upholland

Barton House

Pendle Pl

Lower Balcony Farm

Nursery

LC Balcarres Farm

Pendle Ct

Crawford Village Prim Sch

Long La

Pimbo La

Millets

WA11

Maggots Nook Farm

Red House Farm

Billinge Bounty Farm

Crawford Rd

Oakleigh

Holland Ct

The Crawford (PH)

Crawford

Manor House Dr

Black Brook

Strawberry Cottage

Scythe Stone Delph Farm

News La

Maggots Nook Rd

Reeds Brow

Hay's House

Langwood La

WA11

Maddocks

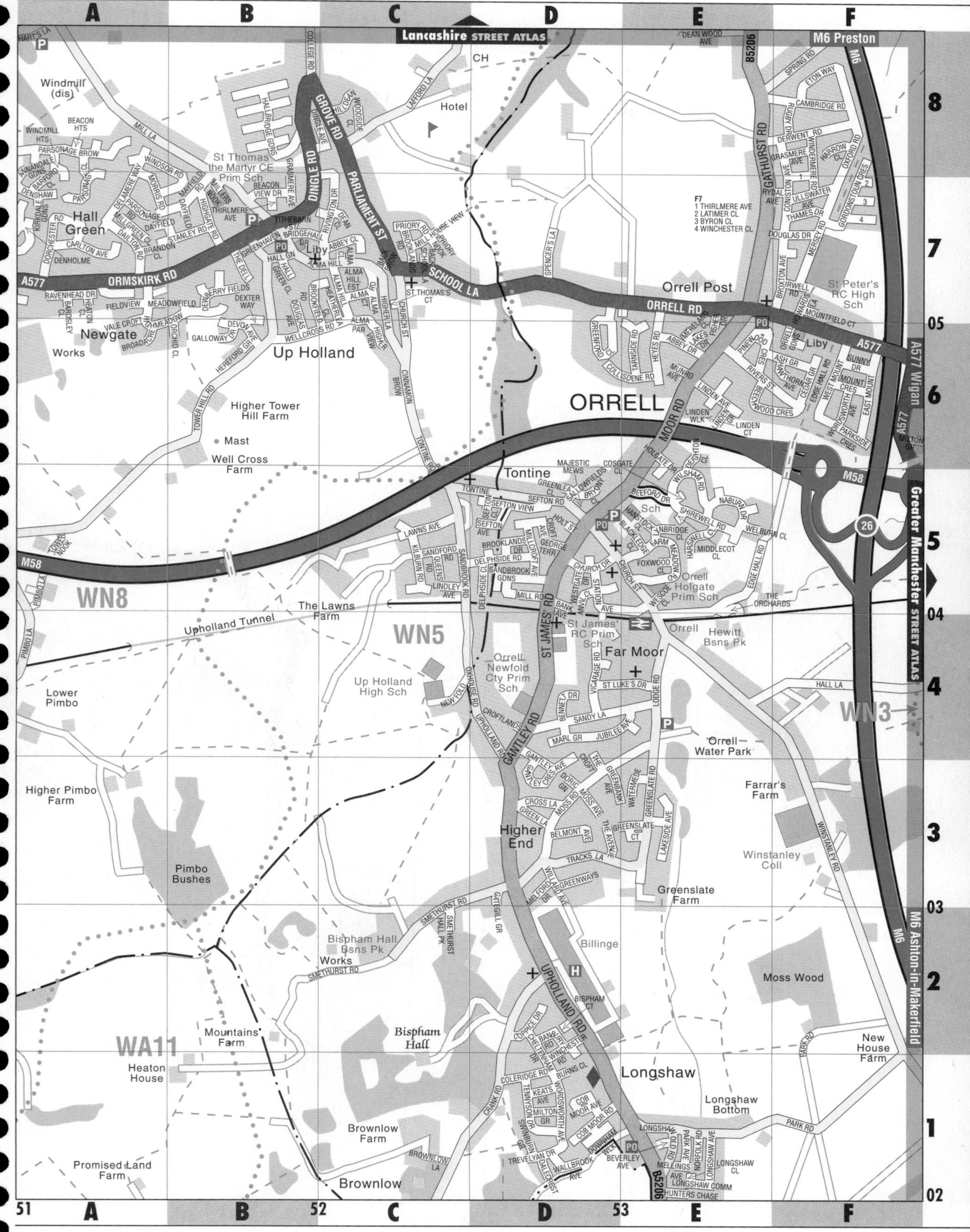

A
B
C
D
E
F
Lancashire STREET ATLAS
M6 Preston
Greater Manchester STREET ATLAS
A577 Wigan
M6 Ashton-in-Makerfield
Windmill (dis)
Hall Green
Newgate
Works
Up Holland
St Thomas the Martyr CE Prim Sch
Higher Tower Hill Farm
Mast
Well Cross Farm
Hotel
CH
ORRELL
Orrell Post
St Peter's RC High Sch
Tontine
ORMSKIRK RD
SCHOOL LA
ORRELL RD
PARLIAMENT ST
DINGLE RD
GROVE RD
MOOR RD
GATHURST RD
M58
WN8
WN5
WN3
WA11
The Lawns Farm
Upholland Tunnel
Up Holland High Sch
Orrell Newfold Cty Prim Sch
St James' RC Prim Sch
Far Moor
Orrell Holgate Prim Sch
Hewitt Bsns Pk
Lower Pimbo
Higher Pimbo Farm
Pimbo Bushes
Orrell Water Park
Farrar's Farm
Winstanley Coll
Higher End
Greenslate Farm
Billinge
Bispham Hall Bsns Pk
Works
Moss Wood
Mountains Farm
Heaton House
Bispham Hall
Longshaw
Longshaw Bottom
New House Farm
Brownlow Farm
Brownlow
Promised Land Farm
F7
1 THIRLMERE AVE
2 LATIMER CL
3 BYRON CL
4 WINCHESTER CL
51
52
53
8
7
6
5
4
3
2
1
05
04
03
02

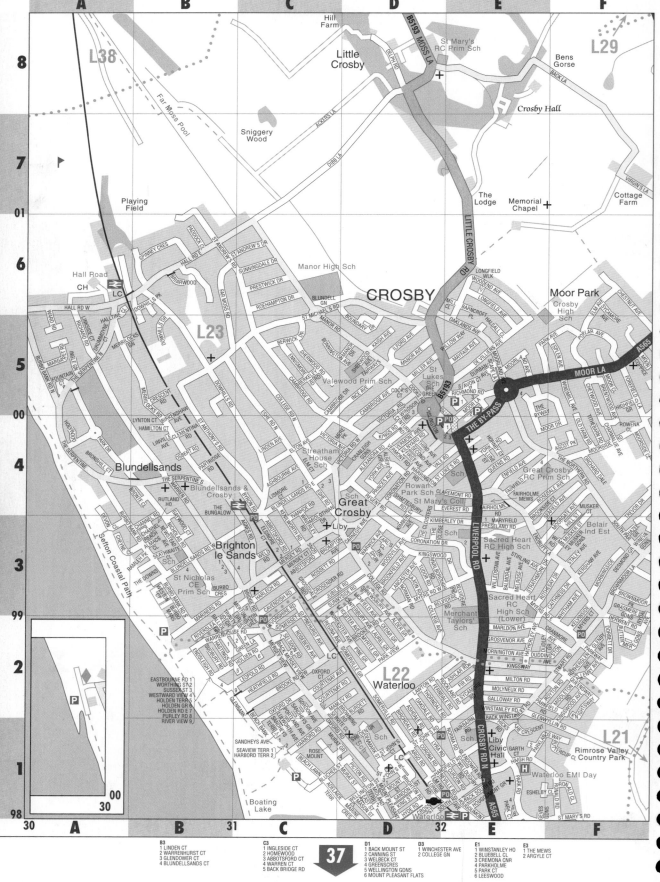

C4
1 HOMEDOVE HO
2 SANDHURST
3 FORTON LO

D5
1 CLAREMONT TERR
2 SPRINGFIELD COTTS
3 PINFOLD CT

E4
1 CHURCH RD
2 CENTRAL BLDGS
3 CROWN BLDGS
4 THE PRECINCTS

E5
1 ALLENGATE
2 GLENN BLDGS
3 TELEGRAPH HO
4 MOOR HO
5 RICHMOND CT

B3
1 LINDEN CT
2 WARRENHURST CT
3 GLENDOWER CT
4 BLUNDELLSANDS CT

C3
1 INGLESIDE CT
2 HOMEWOOD
3 ABBOTSFORD CT
4 WARREN CT
5 BACK BRIDGE RD

37

D1
1 BACK MOUNT ST
2 CANNING ST
3 WELBECK CT
4 GREENSCRES
5 WELLINGTON GDNS
6 MOUNT PLEASANT FLATS

D3
1 WINCHESTER AVE
2 COLLEGE GN

E1
1 WINSTANLEY HO
2 BLUEBELL CL
3 CREMONA CNR
4 PARKHOLME
5 PARK CT
6 LEESWOOD

E3
1 THE MEWS
2 ARGYLE CT

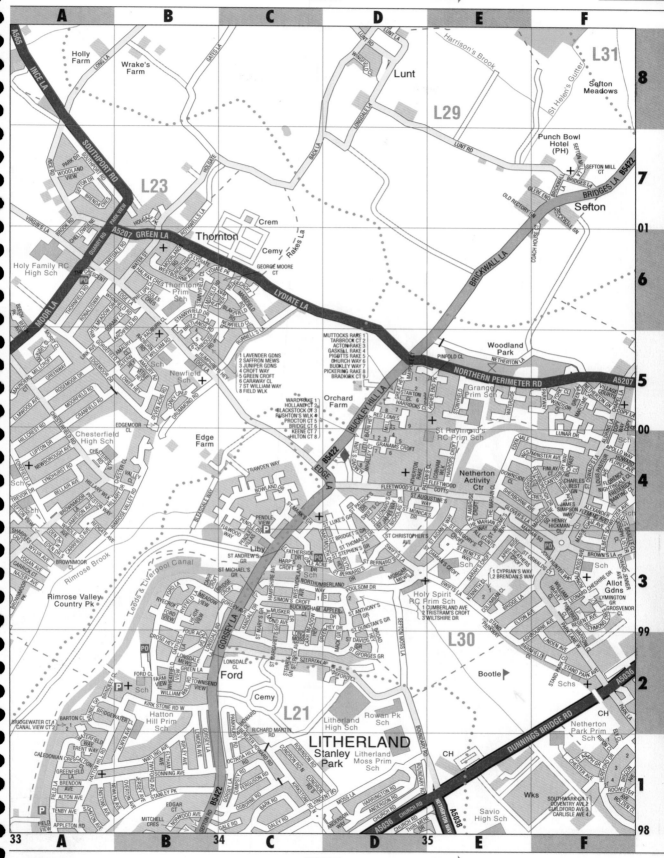

19
28

A B C D E F

8 7 01 6 5 00 4 3 99 2 1 98

Holly Farm
Wrake's Farm
Lunt
L31
Sefton Meadows
L29
Punch Bowl Hotel (PH)
L23
Sefton
Crem
Thornton
Cemy
Holy Family RC High Sch
Thornton Prim Sch
Newfield Sch
Woodland Park
Orchard Farm
Grange Prim Sch
St Raymond's RC Prim Sch
Edge Farm
Chesterfield High Sch
Netherton Activity Ctr
Liby
Rimrose Valley Country Pk
Leeds & Liverpool Canal
Rimrose Brook
Holy Spirit RC Prim Sch
Allot Gdns
L30
Ford
Cemy
L21
Bootle
Schs
Hatton Hill Prim Sch
Litherland High Sch
Rowan Pk Sch
LITHERLAND
Stanley Park
Litherland Moss Prim Sch
Netherton Park Prim Sch
Wks
Savio High Sch

1 LAVENDER GDNS
2 SAFFRON MEWS
3 JUNIPER GDNS
4 CROFT WAY
5 GREEN CROFT
6 CARAWAY CL
7 ST WILLIAM WAY
8 FIELD WLK

MUTTOCKS RAKE 1
TARBROCK CT 2
ACTON RAKE 3
GASKELL RAKE 4
PIGOTTS RAKE 5
CHURCH WAY 6
BUCKLEY WAY 7
PICKERING RAKE 8
BRADKIRK CT 9

WARD RAKE 1
HOLLAND CT 2
BLACKSTOCK CT 3
RUSHTON'S WLK 4
PROCTOR CT 5
BRIDGE CT 6
KEENE CT 7
HILTON CT 8

1 CYPRIAN'S WAY
2 BRENDAN'S WAY

1 CUMBERLAND AVE
2 TRISTRAM'S CROFT
3 WILTSHIRE DR

BRIDGEWATER CT 1
CANAL VIEW CT 2

SOUTHWARK GR 1
COVENTRY AVE 2
GUILDFORD AVE 3
CARLISLE AVE 4

33 34 35

38
28

27
20

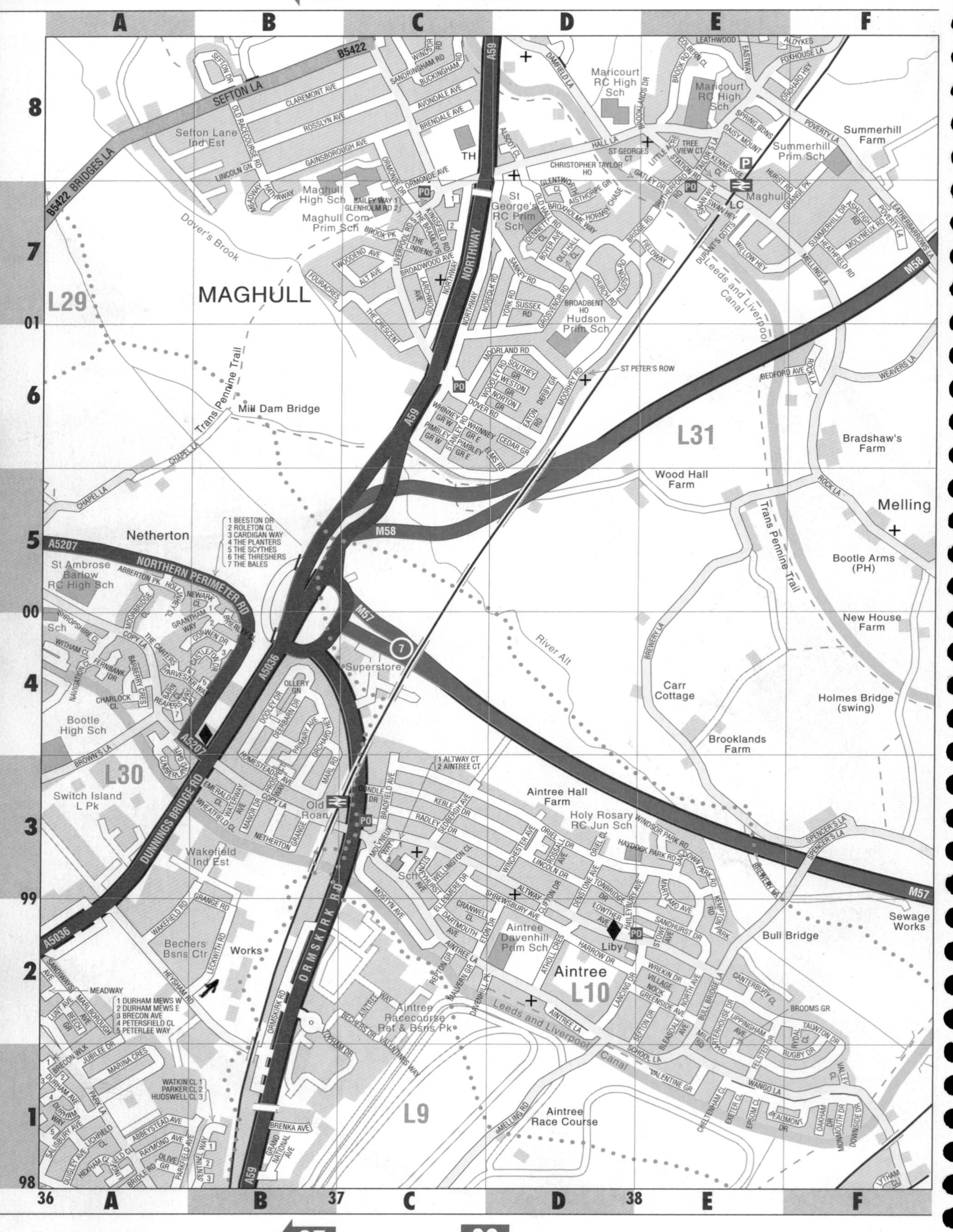
MAGHULL
Sefton Lane Ind Est
Maghull High Sch
Maghull Com Prim Sch
Dover's Brook
Maricourt RC High Sch
Summerhill Farm
Summerhill Prim Sch
St George's RC Prim Sch
Hudson Prim Sch
Leeds and Liverpool Canal
L29
Trans Pennine Trail
Mill Dam Bridge
L31
Bradshaw's Farm
Wood Hall Farm
Melling
Netherton
St Ambrose Barlow RC High Sch
Bootle Arms (PH)
New House Farm
River Alt
Superstore
Carr Cottage
Holmes Bridge (swing)
Bootle High Sch
Brooklands Farm
L30
Switch Island L Pk
Aintree Hall Farm
Holy Rosary RC Jun Sch
Old Roan
Wakefield Ind Est
Sewage Works
Bull Bridge
Aintree Davenhill Prim Sch
Becher's Bsns Ctr
Works
Aintree
L10
Aintree Racecourse Ret & Bsns Pk
L9
Aintree Race Course
A59
M58
M57
A5036
A5207
B5422
NORTHWAY
NORTHERN PERIMETER RD
DUNNINGS BRIDGE RD
ORMSKIRK RD
1 BEESTON DR
2 ROLETON CL
3 CARDIGAN WAY
4 THE PLANTERS
5 THE SCYTHES
6 THE THRESHERS
7 THE BALES
1 ALTWAY CT
2 AINTREE CT
1 DURHAM MEWS W
2 DURHAM MEWS E
3 BRECON AVE
4 PETERSFIELD CL
5 PETERLEE WAY
WATKIN CL 1
PARKER CL 2
HUDSWELL CL 3
ST PETER'S ROW
A B C D E F
8 7 6 5 4 3 2 1
01 00 99 98
36 37 38

27
39

C1
1 TRENTHAM WLK
2 PATELEY CL
3 AMPLEFORTH CL
4 STRATTON WLK
5 HALSTEAD WLK
6 MARNWOOD WLK

C2
1 EMSTREY WLK
2 FRANTON WLK
3 BOLTON WLK
4 CORBET WLK

F2
1 KRAMAR WLK
2 BURNARD WLK
3 HARGATE WLK
4 TARVES WLK
5 RETFORD WLK

29
22
Brookfield Farm
Voces Farm
Hesketh's Shroggs
Walkden Cotts
Walkden House Farm
Sewage Works
Grayson's Farm
Simonswood Brook
New Bridge Farm
Barrow Nook Hall
Caravan Site
L39
High Barn Farm
Abram's Farm
Wood House Farm
Stopgate La
Siding La
Hall's Folly
Wild Goose Slack
Shevington's La
Gate House Bridge
Timber Yard
Simonswood Ind Pk
1 Gardeners View
2 Windfield Cl
3 Greenside Cl
4 Whitely Gr
5 Blackley Gr
6 Epsom Gr
1 Winmoss Dr
2 Spring Cl
3 Brompton Ave
4 Loughlin Dr
5 Sunset Cl
6 Kale Gr
7 Dorchester Dr
8 Crofters La
9 Glendale Gr
10 Birchwood Way
11 Cherry View
Woodwards Plantation
Woods Farm
Southead
Bridge Farm
1 Lapford Wlk
2 Byton Wlk
3 Northfield Cl
4 Woodcote Cl
5 Whitburn Rd
6 Kenbury Cl
L33
North Perimeter Rd
Spencer's House Farm
Eccleston House
Simonswood Moss
Dale La
Acorn Venture Urban Farm
Works
Ashcroft's Plantation
WA11
North Mersey Bsns Ctr
Depot Rd
Woodward Rd
Moss End Way
1 Jade Cl
2 Wingate Wlk
3 Brook Hey Wlk
4 Quernmore Wlk
5 Changford Gn
6 Birbeck Wlk
7 Fairthorn Wlk
8 Burwell Cl
9 Harleston Wlk
10 Kenmay Way
Marl Rd
Hammond Rd
Bradman Rd
Sch
Northwood
Moss La
Ashcroft Rd
Courtyard Works
Newstet Rd
Quarryside Dr
Retford Rd
1 Colwall Wlk
2 Simonswood Wlk
3 Lifton Rd
Knowsley Ind Pk
Birchill Rd
Stockpit Rd
Draw Well Rd
Acornfield Rd
Perimeter Rd
Top House Farm
Boundary La
KIRKBY
Football Academy
Kirkby Bank Rd
Orchard Works
Capitol Trad Est
Cranston Rd
Arbour La
Lees Rd
Webber Rd
Acorn Bsns Ctr
Yardley Ctr
Yardley Rd
Gladeswood Rd
Kirkby Moss
Charley Wood
Venture Works
Charley Wood Rd
4 Westhead Wlk
5 Westhead Cl
Sports Ctr
L32
A5208
County Rd
Cusson Rd
Enterprise Workshops
Deltic Way
Gores Rd
Mosslawn Rd
A B C D E F
8 7 01 6 5 00 4 3 99 2 1 98
42 43 44
29
41

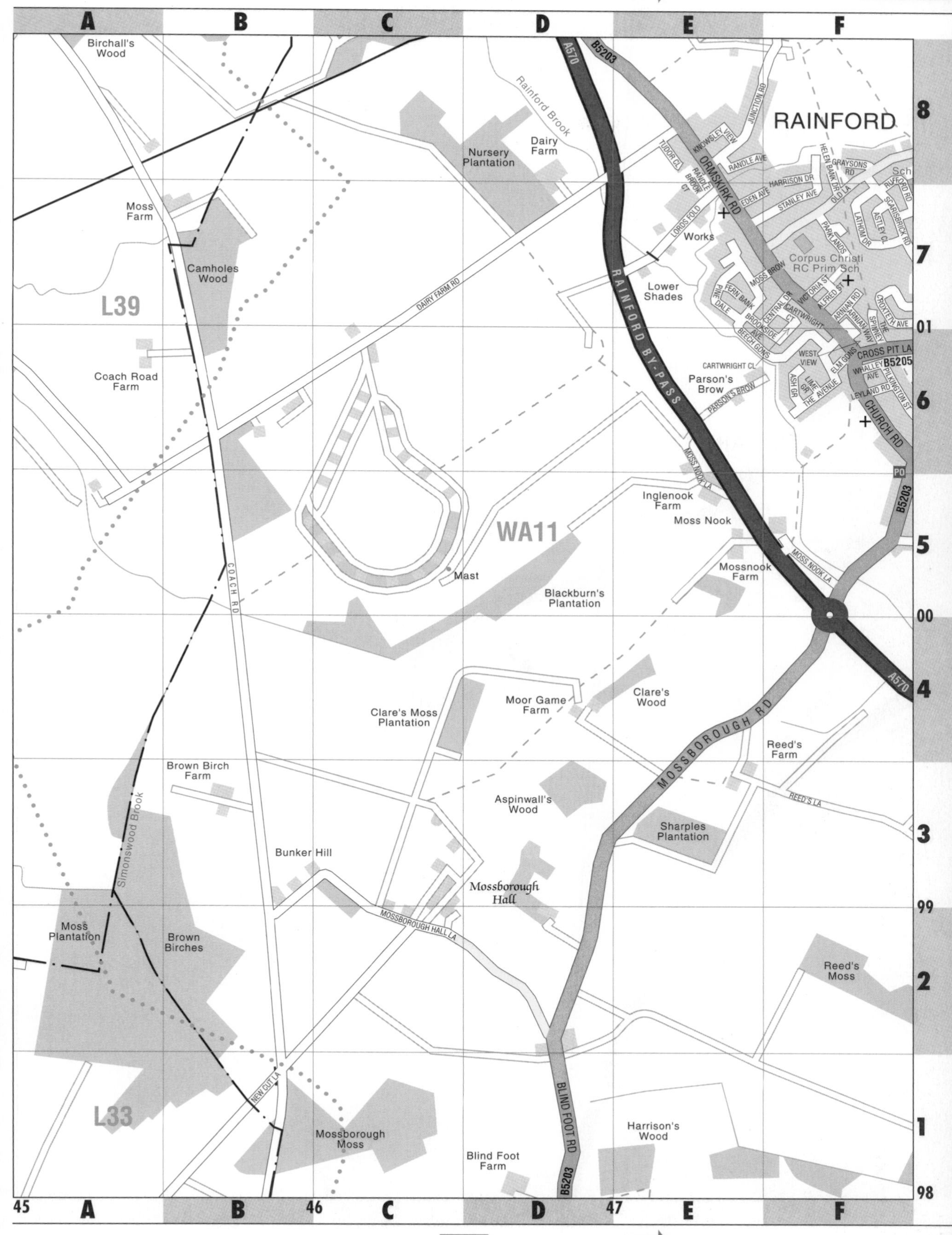

A · B · C · D · E · F

8
7
01
6
5
00
4
3
99
2
1
98

RAINFORD

Birchall's Wood

Nursery Plantation

Dairy Farm

Rainford Brook

A570 · B5203

Moss Farm

Camholes Wood

L39

Dairy Farm Rd

Coach Road Farm

COACH RD

Rainford By-Pass

Knowsley View
Tudor Cl · Randle Grove Cl
Randle Ave
Lords Fold · Eden Ave
Works
Lower Shades
Fern Bank · Moss Brow · Central Ave · Cartwright
Pine Dale · Brookside Ave · Beech Gdns
West View
Cartwright Cl
Parson's Brow
Ash Gr · Lime Gr · The Avenue
Flat Gdns
Junction Rd
Helen Bank Dr · Old La
Harrison Dr
Stanley Ave
Parklands
Victoria St · Fred St · Kernan Rd · Kernan Ave
Graysons Rd
Rivington Rd
Scarisbrick Rd
Astley Cl
Cathon Rd
Croften Ave
Whalley Ave
Pilkington St
Leyland Rd
Cross Pit La · B5205
Church Rd
B5203
PO

Corpus Christi RC Prim Sch
Sch

WA11

Mast

Blackburn's Plantation

Moss Nook La

Inglenook Farm

Moss Nook

Mossnook Farm

Moss Nook La

Mossborough Rd

Clare's Moss Plantation

Moor Game Farm

Clare's Wood

Reed's Farm

Reed's La

Brown Birch Farm

Simonswood Brook

Aspinwall's Wood

Sharples Plantation

Bunker Hill

Mossborough Hall

Moss Plantation

Brown Birches

Mossborough Hall La

Reed's Moss

New Cut La

L33

Mossborough Moss

Blind Foot Rd

Blind Foot Farm

Harrison's Wood

B5203

45 · 46 · 47

31
24

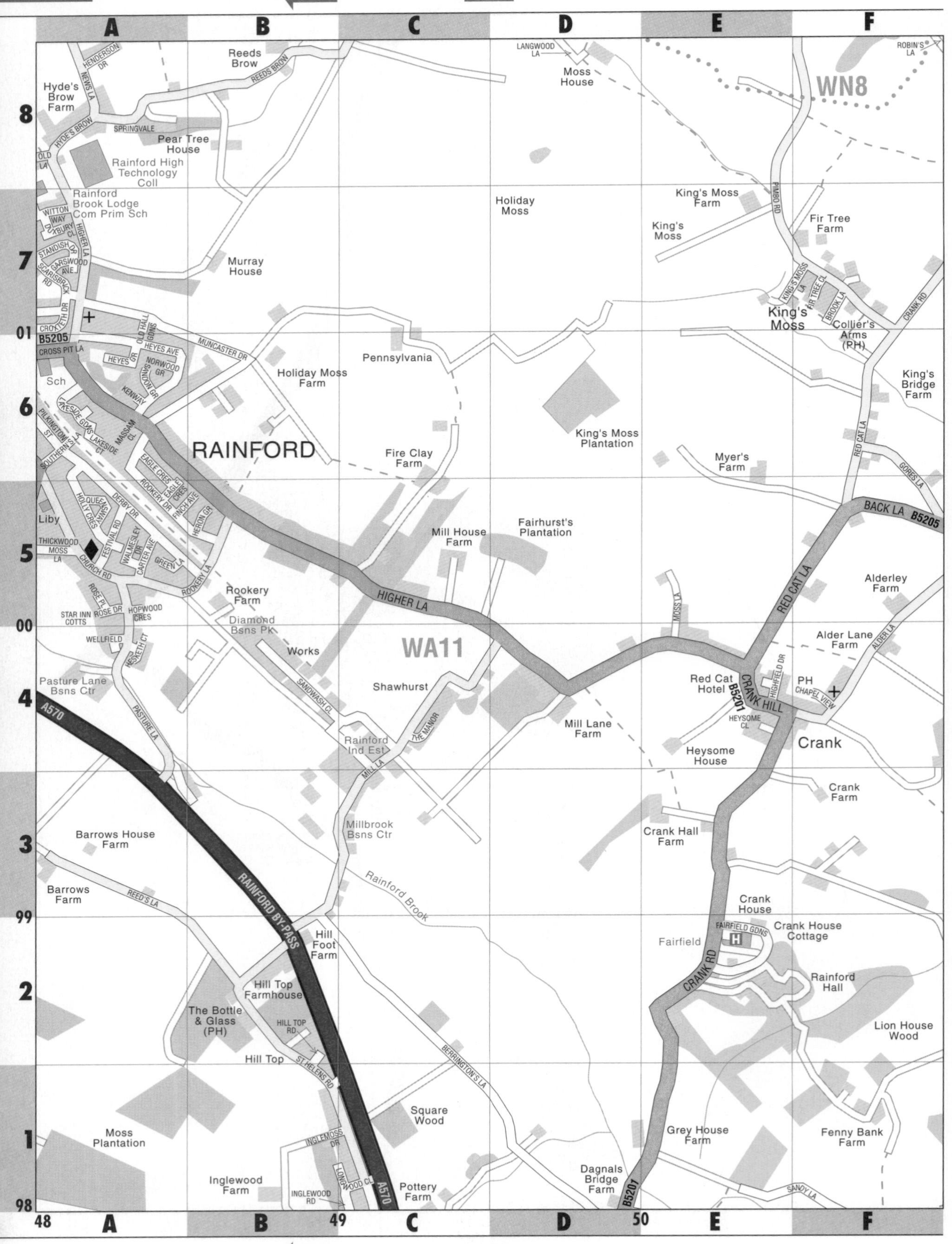
A
B
C
D
E
F
8
7
01
6
5
00
4
3
99
2
1
98
48
49
50
Reeds Brow
REEDS BROW
HENDERSON DR
NEWS LA
Hyde's Brow Farm
HYDE'S BROW
SPRINGVALE
Pear Tree House
Rainford High Technology Coll
Rainford Brook Lodge Com Prim Sch
WITTON WAY
DUXBURY CL
HIGHER LA
STANDISH DR
GARSWOOD AVE
SCARISBRICK RD
CROXTETH DR
OLD HALL GDNS
B5205
CROSS PIT LA
HEYES AVE
HEYES GR
NORWOOD GR
SANDON GR
MUNCASTER DR
KENWAY
MASSAM CL
Sch
LAKESIDE GDNS
LAKESIDE CT
PILKINGTON ST
SOUTHERN ST
RAINFORD
EAGLE CRES
ROOKERY DR
FINCH AVE
HERON GR
DERBY DR
HOLLY CRES
QUEENS AVE
FESTIVAL RD
WALMESLEY DR
CARTER AVE
GREEN LA
ROOKERY LA
Liby
THICKWOOD MOSS LA
CHURCH RD
ROSE PL
ROSE DR
HOPWOOD CRES
STAR INN COTTS
WELLFIELD
HESKETH CT
Pasture Lane Bsns Ctr
PASTURE LA
A570
Murray House
Holiday Moss Farm
Rookery Farm
Diamond Bsns Pk
Works
SANDWASH CL
Rainford Ind Est
MILL LA
THE MANOR
Shawhurst
Pennsylvania
Fire Clay Farm
Mill House Farm
Fairhurst's Plantation
HIGHER LA
WA11
LANGWOOD LA
Moss House
Holiday Moss
King's Moss Plantation
Mill Lane Farm
ROBIN'S LA
WN8
King's Moss Farm
King's Moss
PIMBO RD
Fir Tree Farm
KING'S MOSS LA
FIR TREE CL
BROOK LA
King's Moss
Collier's Arms (PH)
CRANK RD
King's Bridge Farm
Myer's Farm
RED CAT LA
GORES LA
BACK LA
B5205
RED CAT LA
Alderley Farm
MOSS LA
Alder Lane Farm
ALDER LA
Red Cat Hotel
B5201
HIGHFIELD DR
CRANK HILL
PH
CHAPEL VIEW
HEYSOME CL
Crank
Heysome House
Crank Farm
Crank Hall Farm
Barrows House Farm
Barrows Farm
REED'S LA
Millbrook Bsns Ctr
Rainford Brook
RAINFORD BY-PASS
Hill Foot Farm
Hill Top Farmhouse
The Bottle & Glass (PH)
HILL TOP RD
Hill Top
ST HELENS RD
BERRINGTON'S LA
Crank House
FAIRFIELD GDNS
Crank House Cottage
Fairfield
CRANK RD
Rainford Hall
Lion House Wood
Square Wood
Moss Plantation
INGLEMOSS DR
LONGWOOD CL
Inglewood Farm
INGLEWOOD RD
Pottery Farm
Dagnals Bridge Farm
B5201
Grey House Farm
Fenny Bank Farm
SANDY LA

31
43

25 34

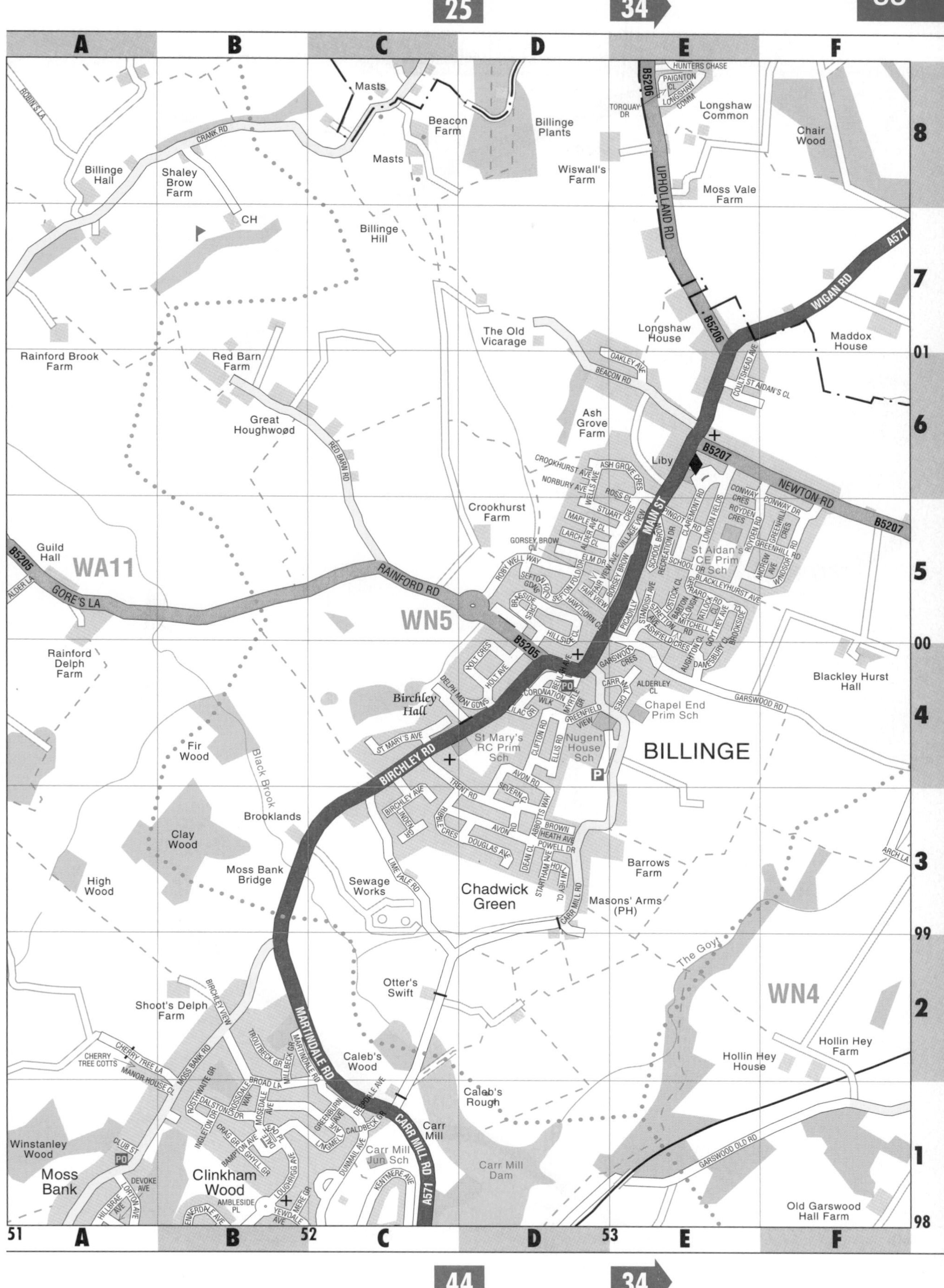
A
B
C
D
E
F
8
7
01
6
5
00
4
3
99
2
1
98
51
52
53
Masts
Beacon Farm
Billinge Plants
HUNTERS CHASE
PAIGNTON CL
LONGSHAW COMM
TORQUAY DR
B5206
Longshaw Common
Chair Wood
ROBIN'S LA
CRANK RD
Billinge Hall
Shaley Brow Farm
Masts
Wiswall's Farm
UPHOLLAND RD
Moss Vale Farm
CH
Billinge Hill
A571
WIGAN RD
Longshaw House
The Old Vicarage
Maddox House
Rainford Brook Farm
Red Barn Farm
OAKLEY AVE
BEACON RD
COULTSHEAD AVE
ST AIDAN'S CL
Great Houghwood
RED BARN RD
Ash Grove Farm
B5207
Liby
CROOKHURST AVE
ASH GROVE CRES
NORBURY AVE
WELLS AVE
ROSS CL
STUART CL
MAIN ST
NEWTON RD
CONWAY CRES
CONWAY DR
ROYDEN CRES
Crookhurst Farm
MAPLE AVE
LARCH CL
ALDER AVE
ELM DR
GORSEY BROW CL
ROBY WELL WAY
VILLAGE VIEW
SCHOOL BROW
RECREATION DR
CLAREMONT RD
PINGOT RD
LONDON FIELDS
St Aidan's CE Prim Sch
ROYDEN RD
GREENHILL CRES
GREENHILL RD
ANDREW AVE
WINDSOR
Guild Hall
WA11
B5205
ALDER LA
GORE'S LA
RAINFORD RD
WN5
SEFTON GDNS
SEFTON FOLD DR
HAWTHORN CL
FAIR VIEW
BRAESIDE CRES
HILLSIDE CL
PICADILLY
STANDISH AVE
STRETTON AVE
ASHFIELD CRES
LOSTOCK CL
BLACKLEYHURST AVE
MITCHELL RD
TATLOCK CL
GOYT HEY AVE
BROOKSIDE
AUGHTON CL
DANESBURY CL
Rainford Delph Farm
HOLT CRES
HOLT AVE
BEULAH AVE
GARSWOOD CRES
CARR MILL CRES
ALDERLEY CL
Blackley Hurst Hall
GARSWOOD RD
Birchley Hall
DELPH MDW GDNS
CORONATION WLK
LILAC GR
MYRTLE GR
GREENFIELD VIEW
Chapel End Prim Sch
ST MARY'S AVE
St Mary's RC Prim Sch
CLIFTON RD
ELLIS RD
Nugent House Sch
BILLINGE
Fir Wood
Black Brook
BIRCHLEY RD
AVON RD
TRENT RD
SEVERN CL
ABBOTTS WAY
BIRCHLEY AVE
LINDEN GR
RIBBLE CRES
AVON RD
BROWN HEATH AVE
DOUGLAS AVE
POWELL DR
Brooklands
Clay Wood
Barrows Farm
ARCH LA
High Wood
Moss Bank Bridge
Sewage Works
LIME VALE RD
Chadwick Green
DEAN CL
STARTHAM AVE
HOLLY HEY CL
CARR MILL RD
Masons' Arms (PH)
The Goyt
WN4
Otter's Swift
Shoot's Delph Farm
BIRCHLEY VIEW
MARTINDALE RD
Hollin Hey Farm
Hollin Hey House
CHERRY TREE COTTS
CHERRY TREE LA
MANOR HOUSE CL
MOSS BANK RD
TROUTBECK GR
MILLBECK GR
Caleb's Wood
BROAD LA
ROSTHWAITE GR
DALSTON DR
CROSSDALE WAY
MOSEDALE AVE
DEEPDALE AVE
Caleb's Rough
INGLETON DR
CRAG GR
BAMPTON AVE
GHYLL GR
GREENBURN AVE
CALDBECK GR
CARR MILL RD
Carr Mill
Winstanley Wood
CLUB ST
Carr Mill Jun Sch
DUNMAIL AVE
Carr Mill Dam
GARSWOOD OLD RD
Moss Bank
DEVOKE AVE
LORTON AVE
HILLBRAE AVE
Clinkham Wood
LOUGHRIGG AVE
AMBLESIDE PL
ENNERDALE AVE
YEWDALE AVE
MERE GR
KENTMERE AVE
A571
Old Garswood Hall Farm
PO
P

44 34

33

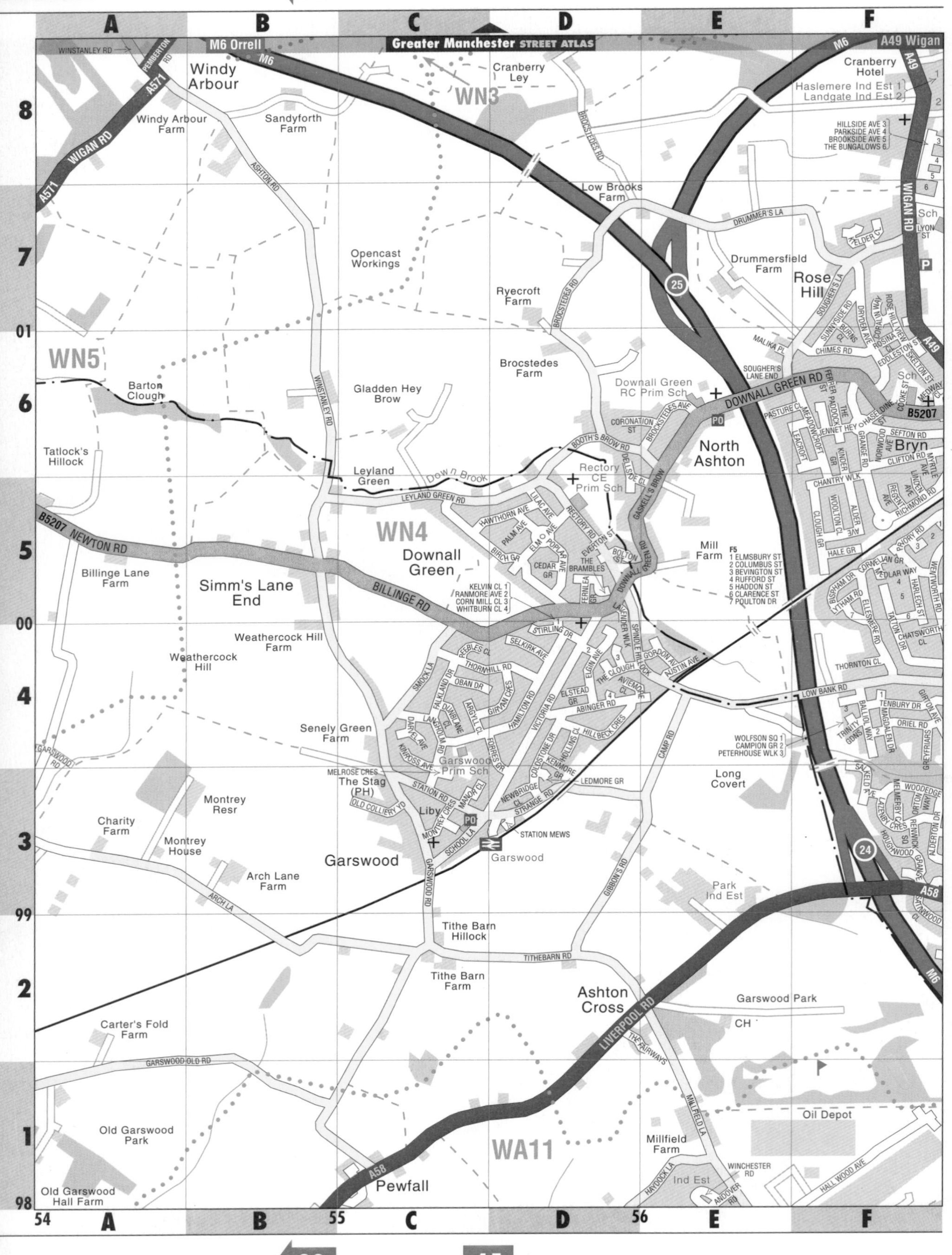
A
B
C
D
E
F
8
7
01
6
5
00
4
3
99
2
1
98
54
55
56
M6 Orrell
Greater Manchester STREET ATLAS
A49 Wigan
M6
WINSTANLEY RD
PEMBERTON RD
A571
WIGAN RD
Windy Arbour
Windy Arbour Farm
Sandyforth Farm
Cranberry Ley
WN3
Cranberry Hotel
Haslemere Ind Est 1
Landgate Ind Est 2
HILLSIDE AVE 3
PARKSIDE AVE 4
BROOKSIDE AVE 5
THE BUNGALOWS 6
ASHTON RD
BROCSTEDES RD
Low Brooks Farm
DRUMMER'S LA
WIGAN RD
Sch
LYON ST
KELDER CL
Opencast Workings
Drummersfield Farm
Rose Hill
25
Ryecroft Farm
SOUGHER'S LA
SUNNYSIDE RD
BURNS CL
DRYDEN AVE
CORALIN WAY
ROSE HILL VIEW
ROSINA CL
EDDLESTON ST
SKELTON ST
A49
MALIKA PL
CHIMES RD
WN5
Brocstedes Farm
SOUGHER'S LANE END
Barton Clough
Gladden Hey Brow
WINSTANLEY RD
Downall Green RC Prim Sch
DOWNALL GREEN RD
FERRER ST
PADDOCK
HASELDINE
COOKE ST
MEDWAY CL
B5207
PASTURE CL
MEADOWCROFT
THE ST
JENNET HEY
GRANGE RD
NORWOOD AVE
SEFTON RD
CORONATION ST
BROCKSTEDES AVE
PO
North Ashton
Bryn
Tatlock's Hillock
BOOTH'S BROW RD
LEACROFT
KINDER GR
CLIFTON RD
MYRTLE AVE
Leyland Green
Down Brook
Rectory CE Prim Sch
DELLSIDE CL
GASKELL'S BROW
CHANTRY WLK
REGENT AVE
LINDEN AVE
RICHMOND RD
LEYLAND GREEN RD
WOOLTON CL
ALDER AVE
HAWTHORN AVE
LILAC AVE
RECTORY RD
CLOUGH GR
PRIORY RD
B5207 NEWTON RD
WN4
PALM AVE
ELM AVE
POPLAR AVE
EVERTON ST
Mill Farm
HALE GR
Downall Green
BIRCH GR
CEDAR GR
THE BRAMBLES
BOLTON ST
DOWNALL GREEN RD
F5
1 ELMSBURY ST
2 COLUMBUS ST
3 BEVINGTON ST
4 RUFFORD ST
5 HADDON ST
6 CLARENCE ST
7 POULTON RD
CORNELIAN GR
MEDLAR WAY
WENTWORTH RD
Billinge Lane Farm
Simm's Lane End
KELVIN CL 1
RANMORE AVE 2
CORN MILL CL 3
WHITBURN CL 4
FERNLEA GR
BISPHAM DR
LYTHAM RD
ELLESMERE RD
HARLECH ST
TATTON DR
CHATSWORTH CL
BILLINGE RD
LAVENDER WLK
SPINDLE HILLOCK
GORDON AV
AUSTIN AVE
STIRLING DR
SELKIRK AVE
PEEBLES CL
THORNHILL RD
ELGIN AVE
THE CLOUGH
AVIEMORE CL
Weathercock Hill Farm
Weathercock Hill
THORNTON CL
SMOCK LA
FALKLAND DR
OBAN DR
GIRVAN CRES
HAMILTON RD
VICTORIA RD
ELSTEAD GR
ABINGER RD
LOW BANK RD
TENBURY DR
GIRTON AVE
ORIEL RD
DUNBLANE AVE
ARGYLL CL
LANGHOLM RD
BALLIOL WAY
MAGDALEN DR
GREYFRIARS
Senely Green Farm
DARWELL AVE
HILLBECK CRES
TRINITY GDNS
WOLFSON SQ 1
CAMPION GR 2
PETERHOUSE WLK 3
GARSWOOD RD
KINROSS AVE
FORRES GR
COLDSTONE DR
HOLLINS CL
KENMORE GR
CAMP RD
Garswood Prim Sch
MELROSE CRES
The Stag (PH)
Long Covert
Montrey Resr
STATION RD
LEDMORE GR
SALKELD AVE
WOODEDGE
OLD COLLIERY YD
NEWBRIDGE CL
STRANGE RD
MELMERBY CRES
ALDERTON DR
Charity Farm
Liby
MANOR CL
PO
MONTREY CRES
SCHOOL LA
STATION MEWS
RENWICK SQ
Montrey House
24
Garswood
Garswood
Arch Lane Farm
GIBBON'S RD
Park Ind Est
A58
ARCH LA
GARSWOOD RD
Tithe Barn Hillock
TITHEBARN RD
Tithe Barn Farm
Ashton Cross
Garswood Park
CH
LIVERPOOL RD
Carter's Fold Farm
THE FAIRWAYS
GARSWOOD OLD RD
MILLFIELD LA
Oil Depot
Old Garswood Park
WA11
Millfield Farm
WINCHESTER RD
HAYDOCK LA
HALL WOOD AVE
A58
Ind Est
ANDOVER RD
Pewfall
Old Garswood Hall Farm

33
45

36

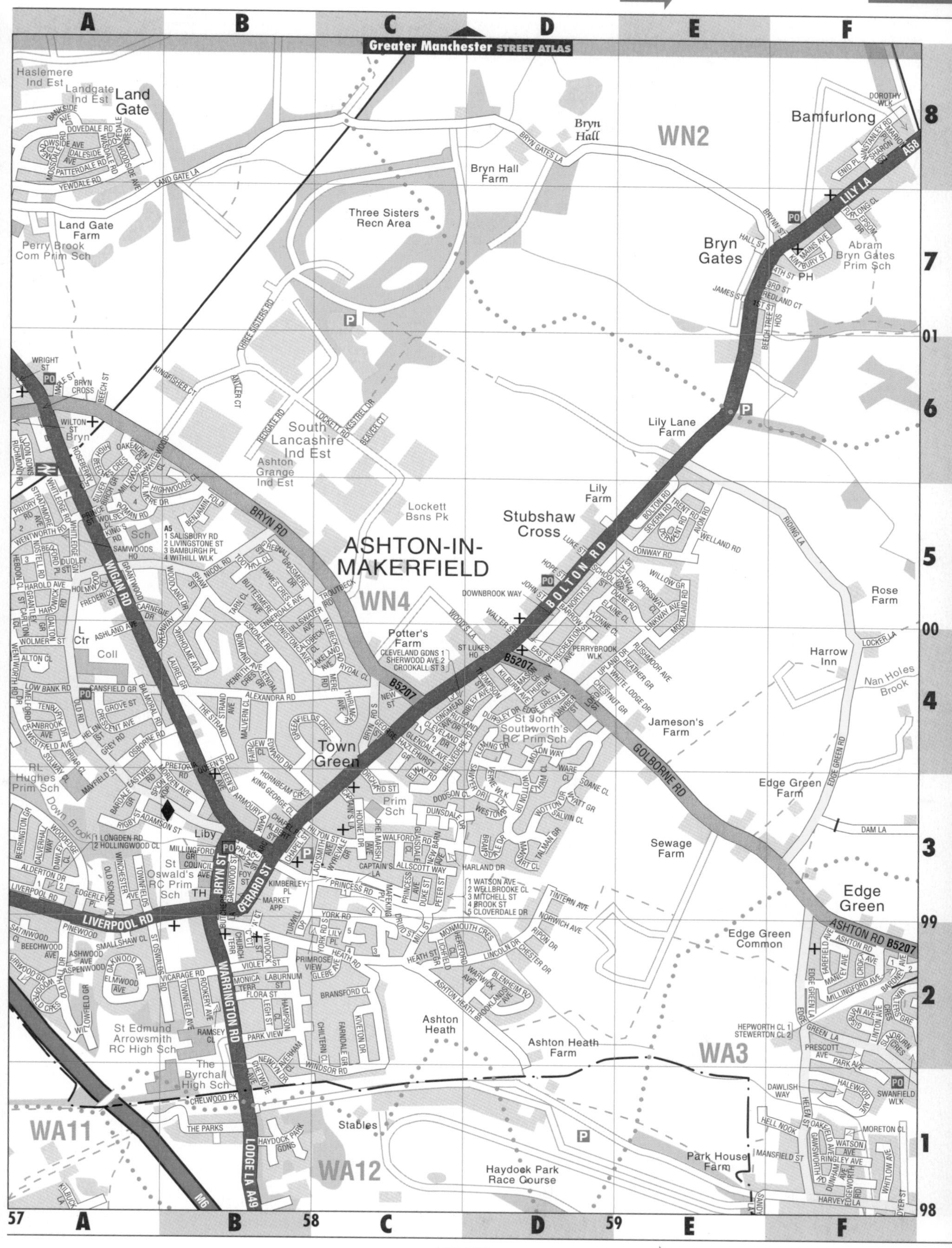
Greater Manchester STREET ATLAS
A
B
C
D
E
F
8
7
01
6
5
00
4
3
99
2
1
98
57
58
59
Haslemere Ind Est
Landgate Ind Est
Land Gate
Land Gate Farm
Perry Brook Com Prim Sch
Bryn Hall
Bryn Hall Farm
WN2
Bamfurlong
Three Sisters Recn Area
Bryn Gates
Abram Bryn Gates Prim Sch
South Lancashire Ind Est
Ashton Grange Ind Est
Lily Lane Farm
Lockett Bsns Pk
Lily Farm
Stubshaw Cross
ASHTON-IN-MAKERFIELD
WN4
Rose Farm
Potter's Farm
Harrow Inn
Nan Holes Brook
Jameson's Farm
St John Southworth's RC PrimSch
Town Green
Edge Green Farm
RL Hughes Prim Sch
Prim Sch
Sewage Farm
Liby
St Oswald's RC Prim Sch
Edge Green
Edge Green Common
St Edmund Arrowsmith RC High Sch
Ashton Heath
Ashton Heath Farm
WA3
The Byrchall High Sch
WA11
Stables
WA12
Haydock Park Race Course
Park House Farm
BRYN GATES LA
LAND GATE LA
LILY LA
A58
BOLTON RD
BRYN RD
WIGAN RD
B5207
GOLBORNE RD
GERARD ST
BRYN ST
LIVERPOOL RD
WARRINGTON RD
LODGE LA A49
ASHTON RD B5207
M6
DAM LA
RIDING LA

46

36

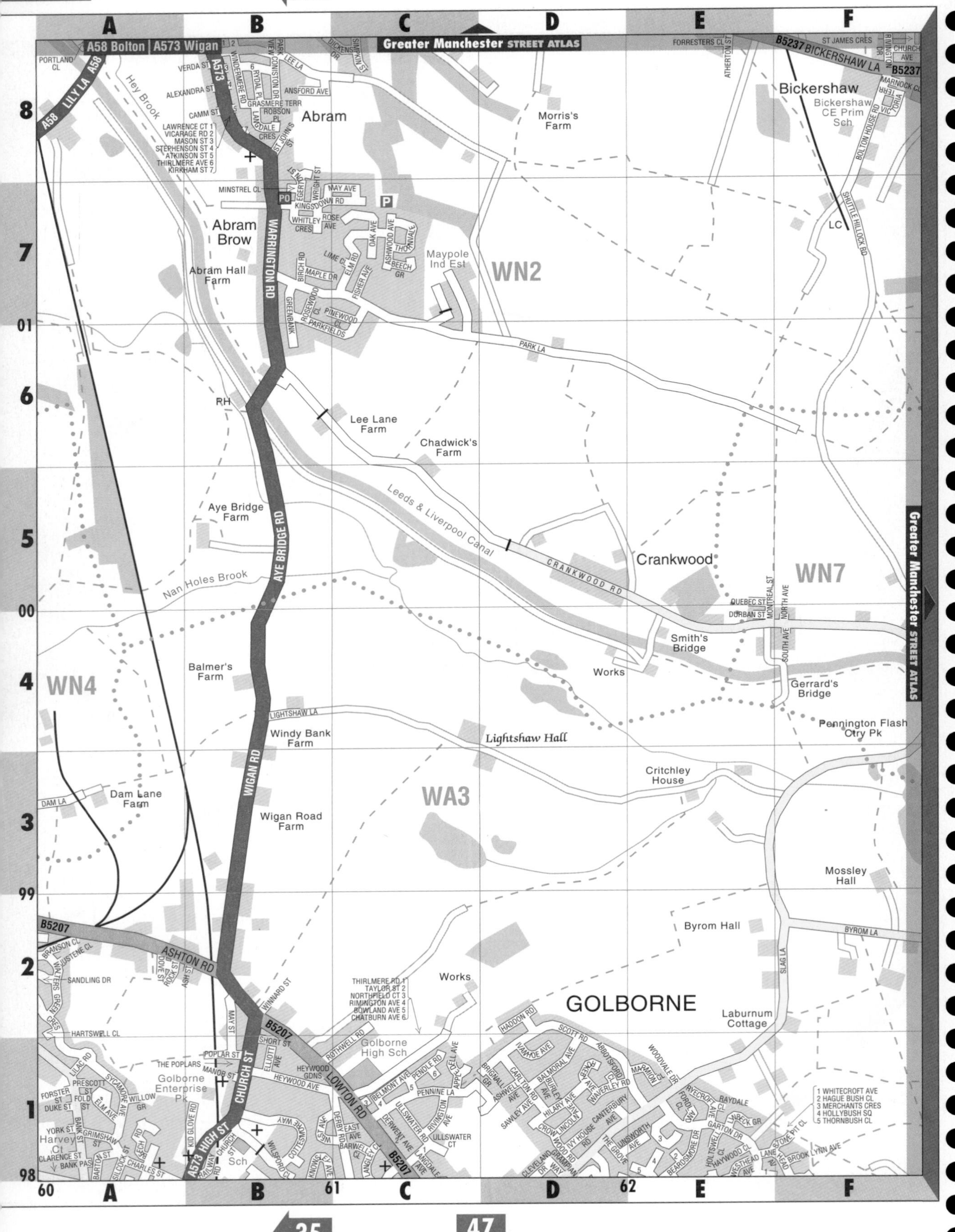

Greater Manchester STREET ATLAS

A | B | C | D | E | F

8

A58 Bolton | A573 Wigan

PORTLAND CL

LILY LA A58

Hey Brook

VERDA ST

ALEXANDRA ST

CAMM ST

LAWRENCE CT 1
VICARAGE RD 2
MASON ST 3
STEPHENSON ST 4
ATKINSON ST 5
THIRLMERE AVE 6
KIRKHAM ST 7

Abram

PARK VIEW
CONISTON ST
LEE LA
DICKENSON DR
SIMPKIN ST

FORRESTERS CL

ATHERTON ST

B5237 BICKERSHAW LA

St JAMES CRES

CHURCH AVE

B5237

Morris's
Farm

Bickershaw

MARNOCK CL

Bickershaw
CE Prim
Sch

BOLTON HOUSE RD

SHUTTLE HILLOCK RD

LC

7

MINSTREL CL

Abram
Brow

WARRINGTON RD

Abram Hall
Farm

PO

MAY AVE

KINGSDOWN RD

P

WHITLEY
CRES

ROSE
AVE

GRASMERE TERR
RYDAL AVE
ROBSON
PL
LANSDALE
CRES
St JOHN'S
EGERTON ST
WRIGHT ST

ASHWOOD
AVE

THORVALE

MAYPOLE
IND EST

BIRCH RD
MAPLE DR
ELM RD
FISHER AVE
LIME GR
ELM AVE
BEECH
GR
OAK AVE
THORVALE

GREENBANK

ROSEWOOD

PINEWOOD
PARKFIELDS

WN2

PARK LA

01

6

RH

Lee Lane
Farm

Chadwick's
Farm

Aye Bridge
Farm

AYE BRIDGE RD

Leeds & Liverpool Canal

Nan Holes Brook

CRANKWOOD RD

Crankwood

WN7

5

QUEBEC ST
DURBAN ST

MONTREAL ST
NORTH AVE

SOUTH AVE

00

Balmer's
Farm

Smith's
Bridge

Works

Gerrard's
Bridge

4

WN4

WIGAN RD

LIGHTSHAW LA

Windy Bank
Farm

Lightshaw Hall

Pennington Flash
Cntry Pk

WA3

Critchley
House

DAM LA

Dam Lane
Farm

Wigan Road
Farm

Mossley
Hall

3

99

Byrom Hall

BYROM LA

SLAG LA

2

B5207

BRANSON CL
JUSTENE CL
CARTERS CL
GREEN CRES
SANDLING DR

ASHTON RD

DOVE ST

HARTSWELL CL

MAY ST

WINNARD ST

CHURCH RD

WHINNEY
DERBY EAST

B5207

SHORT ST

ROTHWELL ST

THIRLMERE RD 1
TAYLOR ST 2
NORTHFIELD CT 3
RIMINGTON AVE 4
BOWLAND AVE 5
CHATBURN AVE 6

Works

GOLBORNE

Laburnum
Cottage

1

FORSTER ST
DUKE ST
YORK ST
CLARENCE ST
BANK PAS

PRESCOTT
FOLD
SYCAMORE AVE
ELM LANE
WILLOW ST

Golborne
Enterprise
Pk

THE POPLARS

POPLAR ST

MANOR RD

ELLIOTT ST

HEYWOOD
GDNS

HEYWOOD AVE

BELMONT AVE

ULLSWATER RD

LOWTON RD

PENDLE RD

PENNINE LA

APPLE CL
CRABTREE
PENDLE AVE

HADDON RD

SCOTT RD

HILARY AVE
BRIDHALL
CARLTON RD
ASHWELL
SAWLEY AVE
CROW NICOLYN

BALMORAL
BILSLEY
AVE
MAGNOLIA AVE

WOODVALE DR

HAGUE AVE
WAVERLEY RD

1 WHITECROFT AVE
2 HAGUE BUSH CL
3 MERCHANTS CRES
4 HOLLYBUSH SQ
5 THORNBUSH CL

98

Harvey
Ct

GRIMSHAW
CLOCK FACE
CHARLES ST
BARTHOLOMEW

A573 HIGH ST

CHURCH ST

MID GLOVE RD

WILSON CL

DERWENT
DERBY
LANGLEY
BARWELL

ROSEWOOD
CANTERBURY
IVY HOUSE
RIVINGTON
ANGLE

CLEVELAND
HAYWOOD LANE
WESTHEAD
AVE

RYECROFT
GARTON DR
POND CL
HOLCROFT

BRIARFIELD DR

LYNN AVE

60 | A | B | 61 | C | D | 62 | E | F

Greater Manchester STREET ATLAS

26
38

A
B
C
D
E
F
8
7
97
6
5
96
4
3
95
2
1
94
30
31
32
Sefton Coastal Path
Marine Lake
L22
Radar Sta
Seaforth Nature Reserve
Seaforth
Port of Liverpool Euro Rail Terminal
Royal Seaforth Container Terminal
L21
Wind Turbines
Royal Seaforth Dock
Mast
Gladstone Dock
L20
Alexandra Dock
River Mersey
Rock Lighthouse
Perch Rock
CH45
Marine Lake
A554 KING'S PAR
KING'S PAR
MARINE PROM
UNION TERR
ROWSON ST
A554
WELLINGTON RD
PORTLAND ST
ATHERTON ST
BURLINGTON RD
WATERLOO RD
WINDSOR ST
RICHMOND ST
BELMONT RD
VIRGINIA RD
BALMORAL RD
VICTORIA PAR
ALBERT ST
TOLLEMACHE ST
TOWER PROM
LB Sta
1 MARINE PARK MANS
2 BECKENHAM RD
1 TIVOLI VILLA'S
2 WATERS EDGE APARTMENTS
ALBERT RD 1
DEACON CL 2
CHAPEL HO 3
DEAN HO 4
E8
1 WATER ST
2 SANDRINGHAM AVE
3 MELROSE PK
F7
1 BEDFORD PL
2 GLADSTONE AVE
3 RIVERSDALE RD
4 BELGRAVE RD
5 SANDY HO
6 CHURCHILL HO
7 ALEXANDER HO
8 MONTGOMERY HO
F6
1 LATHOM CL
2 LATHOM AVE
3 CLARENDON RD
4 ELM GDNS
CROSBY RD N A565
CROSBY RD S
A565
A5036 PRINCESS WAY
B5421
SANDY RD
LAKESIDE VIEW
BOSSOM CT
MARINE TERR
THE ESPLANADE
ALEXANDRA RD
CHATHAM CT
VICTORIA RD
CAMBRIDGE RD
MARLBOROUGH RD
KINROSS RD
MELROSE RD
SANDRINGHAM RD
GREENBANK
BROOKLANDS AVE
BROOK VALE
BRAMHALL RD
PARK TERR
HEREFORD RD
DURHAM RD
WOODLAND RD
PARKER AVE
PRITCHARD AVE
RAWSON CL
RAWSON RD
CLAREMONT RD
BEACONSFIELD RD
HARROWBY RD
GORDON RD
CECIL RD
ELM DR
ELM RD
HOLLY GR
POPLAR GR
BARKELEY DR
CHURCH RD
CHURCH GR
VERDI ST
SHORE RD
REGENT RD
GRECIAN ST
DORIC ST
IONIC ST
CORINTHIAN ST
ADELAIDE RD
CHESNUT RD
SANDOWN RD
KINGS PK
GLADSTONE RD
DEWLANDS RD
LC
Sch
TH

51
38

A6
1 ELM GDNS
2 WOOLFALL TERR
3 HOGARTH ST
4 VALE CT
5 MARY STOCKTON CT
6 CRESCENT CT
7 WILLOW HO
8 SANDON LODGE

37 27

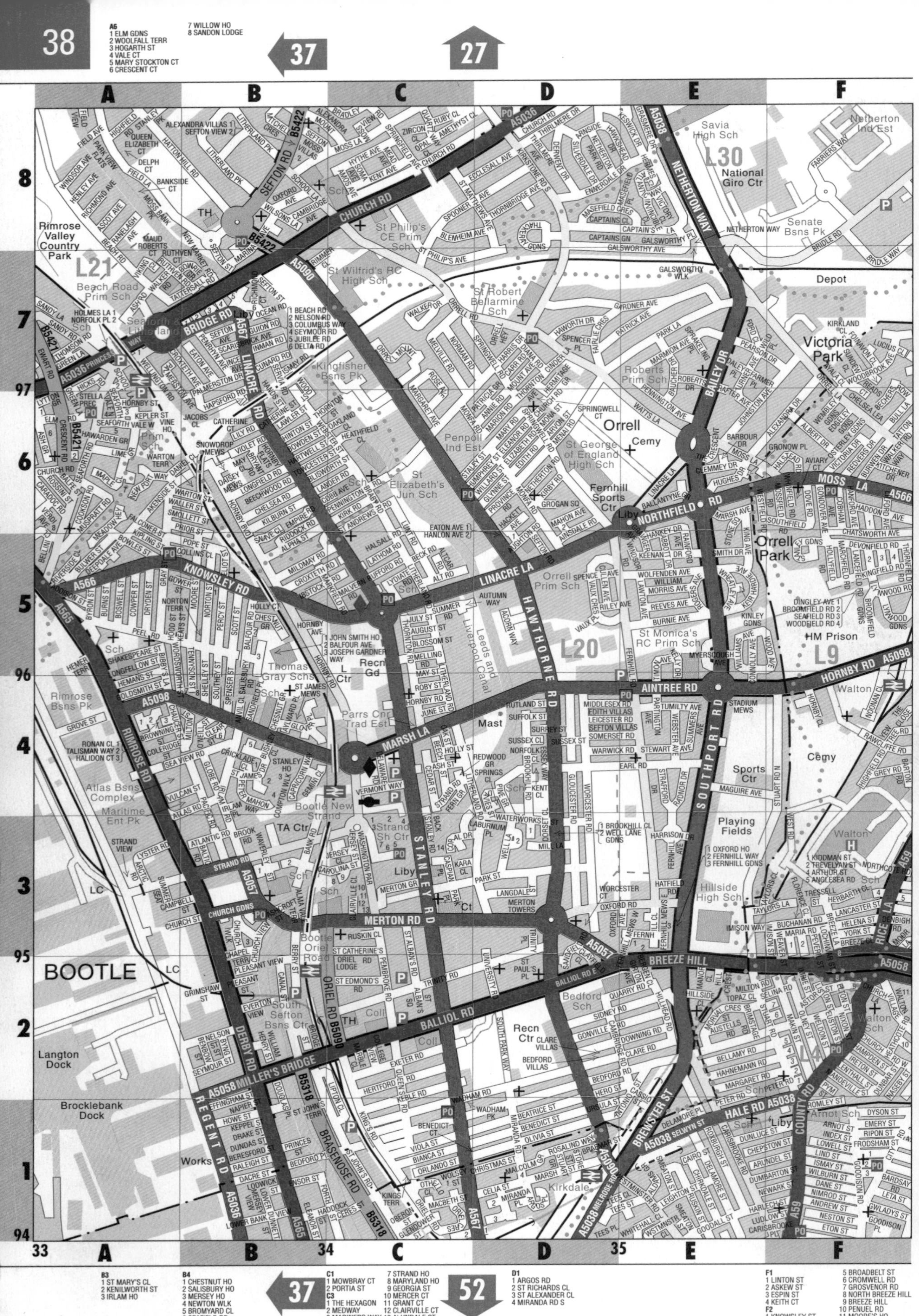

B3
1 ST MARY'S CL
2 KENILWORTH ST
3 IRLAM HO

B4
1 CHESTNUT HO
2 SALISBURY HO
3 MERSEY HO
4 NEWTON WLK
5 BROMYARD CL
6 SEAFIELD RD
7 AVALON TERR
8 CAMELOT TERR

37

C1
1 MOWBRAY CT
2 PORTIA ST

C3
1 THE HEXAGON
2 MEDWAY
3 MARINERS WAY
4 THE ESPLANADE
5 MONS SQ
6 THE PALATINE
7 STRAND HO
8 MARYLAND HO
9 GEORGIA ST
10 MERCER CT
11 GRANT CT
12 CLAIRVILLE CT
13 ALUNDALE CT
14 GARDEN VIEW

52

D1
1 ARGOS RD
2 ST RICHARDS CL
3 ST ALEXANDER CL
4 MIRANDA RD S

F1
1 LINTON ST
2 ASKEW ST
3 ESPIN ST
4 KEITH CT

F2
1 KNOWSLEY ST
2 PENNINGTON ST
3 WYNDHAM ST
4 BRIDE ST
5 BROADBELT ST
6 CROMWELL RD
7 GROSVENOR RD
8 NORTH BREEZE HILL
9 BREEZE HILL
10 PENUEL RD
11 MOORE'S HO

28
40

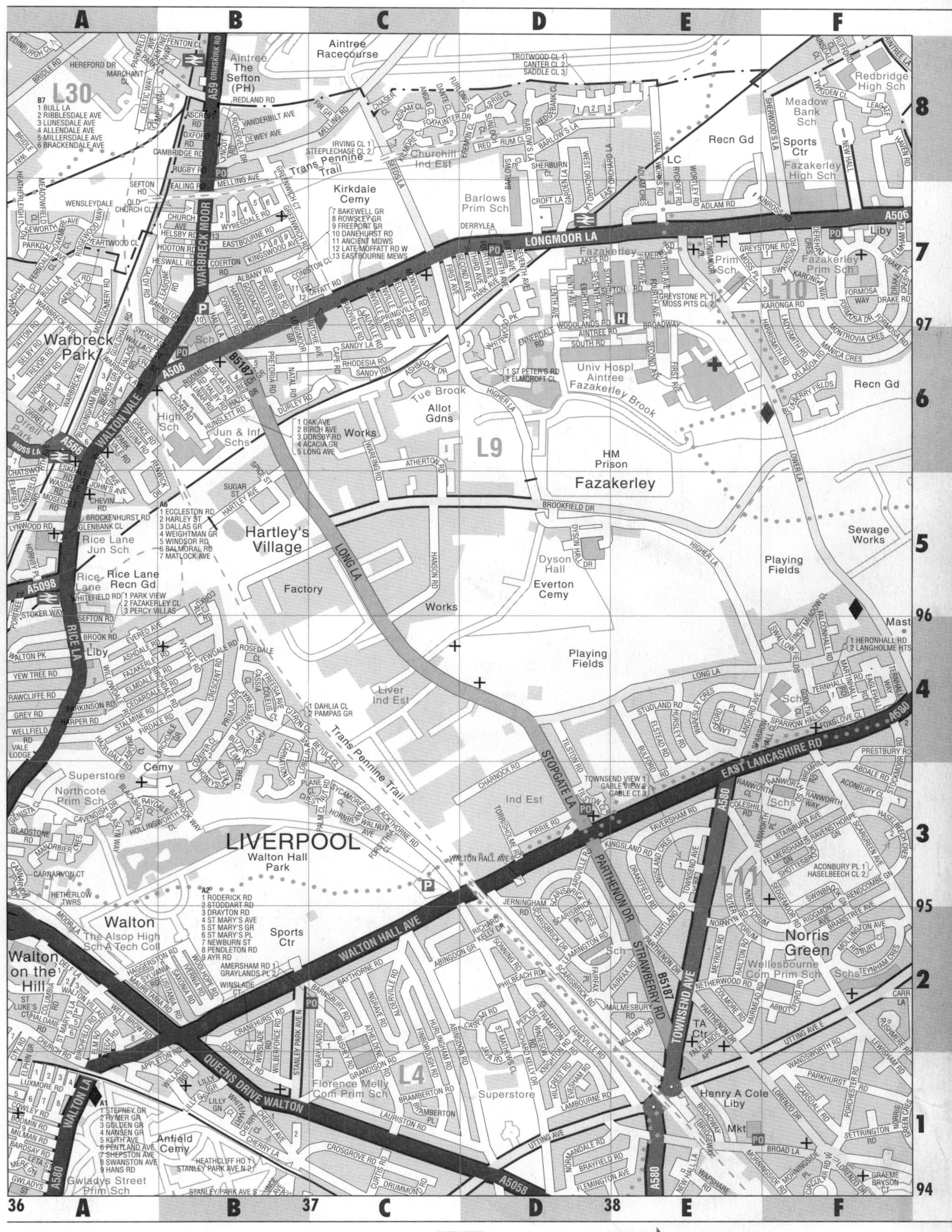
A
B
C
D
E
F
8
7
97
6
5
96
4
3
95
2
1
94
36
37
38
L30
L10
L9
L11
L4
Aintree Racecourse
Aintree
The Sefton (PH)
Redbridge High Sch
Meadow Bank Sch
Sports Ctr
Fazakerley High Sch
Recn Gd
Kirkdale Cemy
Churchill Ind Est
Trans Pennine Trail
Barlows Prim Sch
LONGMOOR LA
A506
Fazakerley
Prim Sch
Fazakerley Prim Sch
Liby
Warbreck Park
WARBRECK MOOR
A59 ORMSKIRK RD
WALTON VALE
Univ Hospl Aintree
Fazakerley Brook
Tue Brook
Allot Gdns
Works
HM Prison
Fazakerley
Orrell Park
MOSS LA
A566
High Sch
Jun & Inf Schs
B5187
LONG LA
Hartley's Village
Rice Lane Jun Sch
Rice Lane
Rice Lane Recn Gd
A5098
Factory
Dyson Hall
Everton Cemy
Playing Fields
Sewage Works
Mast
RICE LA
Liver Ind Est
Superstore
Cemy
Northcote Prim Sch
LIVERPOOL
Walton Hall Park
Ind Est
STOPGATE LA
EAST LANCASHIRE RD
A580
PARTHENON DR
STRAWBERRY RD
Schs
Walton
The Alsop High Sch A Tech Coll
Walton on the Hill
Sports Ctr
WALTON HALL AVE
Norris Green
Wellesbourne Com Prim Sch
TOWNSEND AVE
TA Ctr
Henry A Cole Liby
Mkt
QUEENS DRIVE WALTON
Florence Melly Com Prim Sch
Superstore
Anfield Cemy
Gwladys Street Prim Sch
WALTON LA
A5058

53
40

39
29

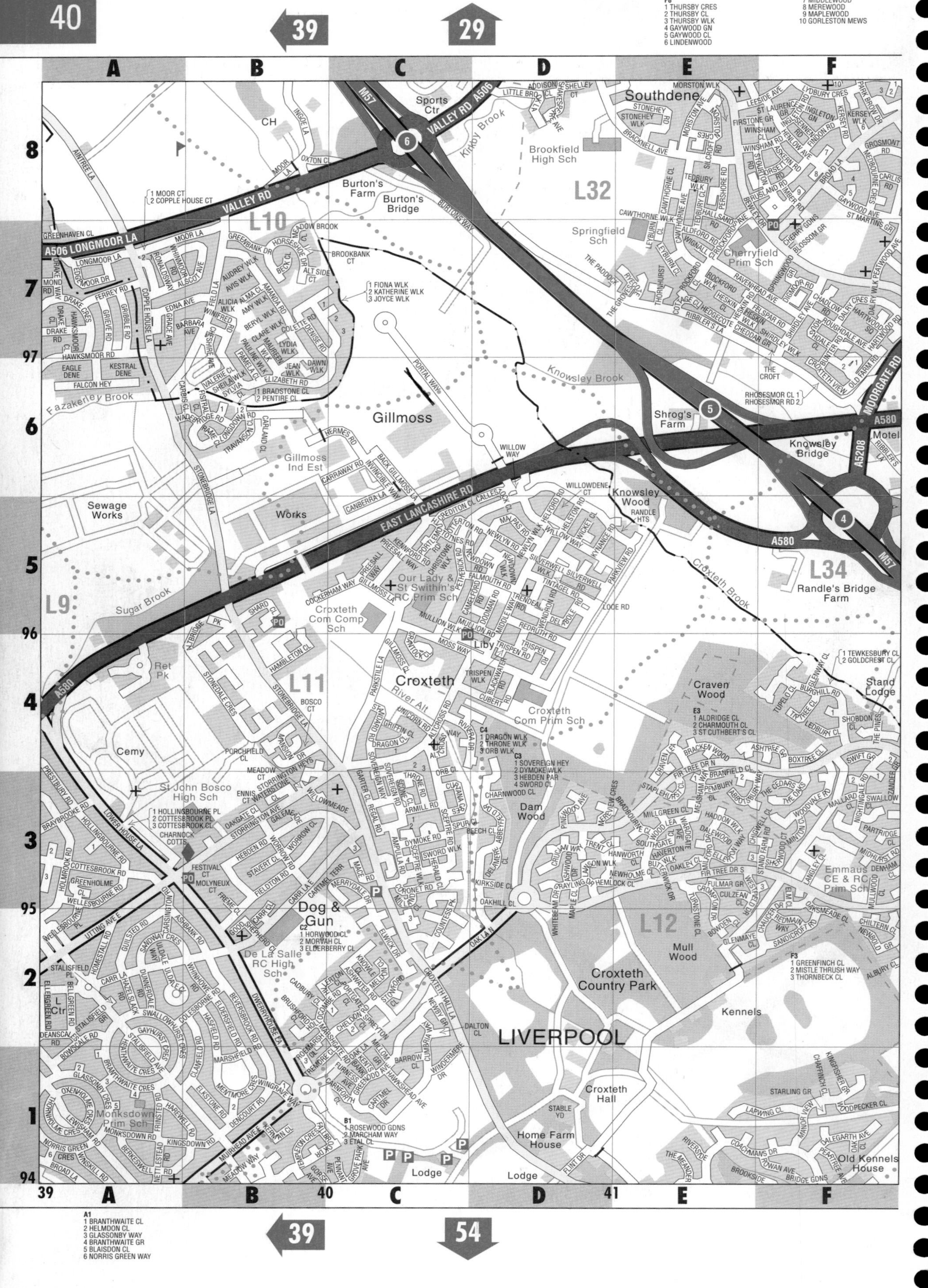
F8
1 THURSBY CRES
2 THURSBY CL
3 THURSBY WLK
4 GAYWOOD GN
5 GAYWOOD CL
6 LINDENWOOD
7 MIDDLEWOOD
8 MEREWOOD
9 MAPLEWOOD
10 GORLESTON MEWS
A
B
C
D
E
F
8
7
97
6
5
96
4
3
95
2
1
94
39
40
41
Southdene
Sports Ctr
VALLEY RD
A506
M57
CH
Brookfield High Sch
L32
L10
Burton's Farm
Burton's Bridge
Springfield Sch
Cherryfield Prim Sch
A506 LONGMOOR LA
1 MOOR CT
2 COPPLE HOUSE CT
1 FIONA WLK
2 KATHERINE WLK
3 JOYCE WLK
Gillmoss
Gillmoss Ind Est
Knowsley Brook
Shrog's Farm
Motel
Knowsley Bridge
A580
A5208
MOORGATE RD
Knowsley Wood
Sewage Works
Works
EAST LANCASHIRE RD
L34
Randle's Bridge Farm
Croxteth Brook
L9
Sugar Brook
Fazakerley Brook
Our Lady & St Swithin's RC Prim Sch
Croxteth Com Comp Sch
Liby
Croxteth
River Alt
L11
Ret Pk
Cemy
St John Bosco High Sch
Croxteth Com Prim Sch
Craven Wood
Stand Lodge
E3
1 ALDRIDGE CL
2 CHARMOUTH CL
3 ST CUTHBERT'S CL
1 TEWKESBURY CL
2 GOLDCREST CL
C4
1 DRAGON WLK
2 THRONE WLK
3 ORB WLK
C3
1 SOVEREIGN HEY
2 DYMOKE WLK
3 HEBDEN PAR
4 SWORD CL
Dam Wood
1 HOLLINGBOURNE PL
2 COTTESBROOK PL
3 COTTESBROOK CL
CHARNOCK COTTS
Emmaus CE & RC Prim Sch
Dog & Gun
C2
1 HORWOOD CL
2 MORVAH CL
3 ELDERBERRY CL
De La Salle RC High Sch
L12
Mull Wood
F3
1 GREENFINCH CL
2 MISTLE THRUSH WAY
3 THORNBECK CL
Croxteth Country Park
Kennels
L Ctr
LIVERPOOL
Croxteth Hall
Monksdown Prim Sch
B1
1 ROSEWOOD GDNS
2 MARCHAM WAY
3 ETAL CL
STABLE YD
Home Farm House
Lodge
Old Kennels House
A1
1 BRANTHWAITE CL
2 HELMDON CL
3 GLASSONBY WAY
4 BRANTHWAITE GR
5 BLAISDON CL
6 NORRIS GREEN WAY

39
54

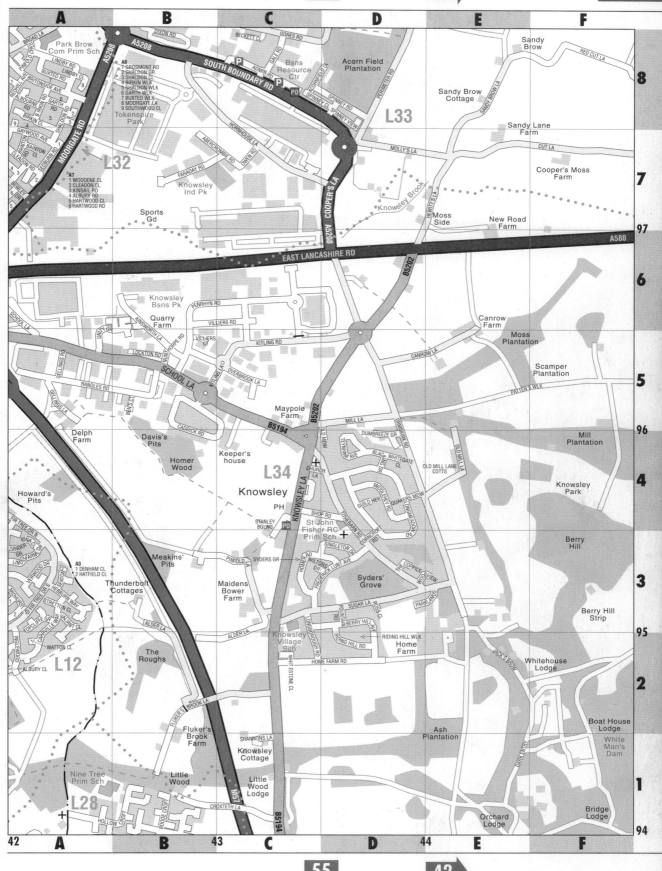

41
31

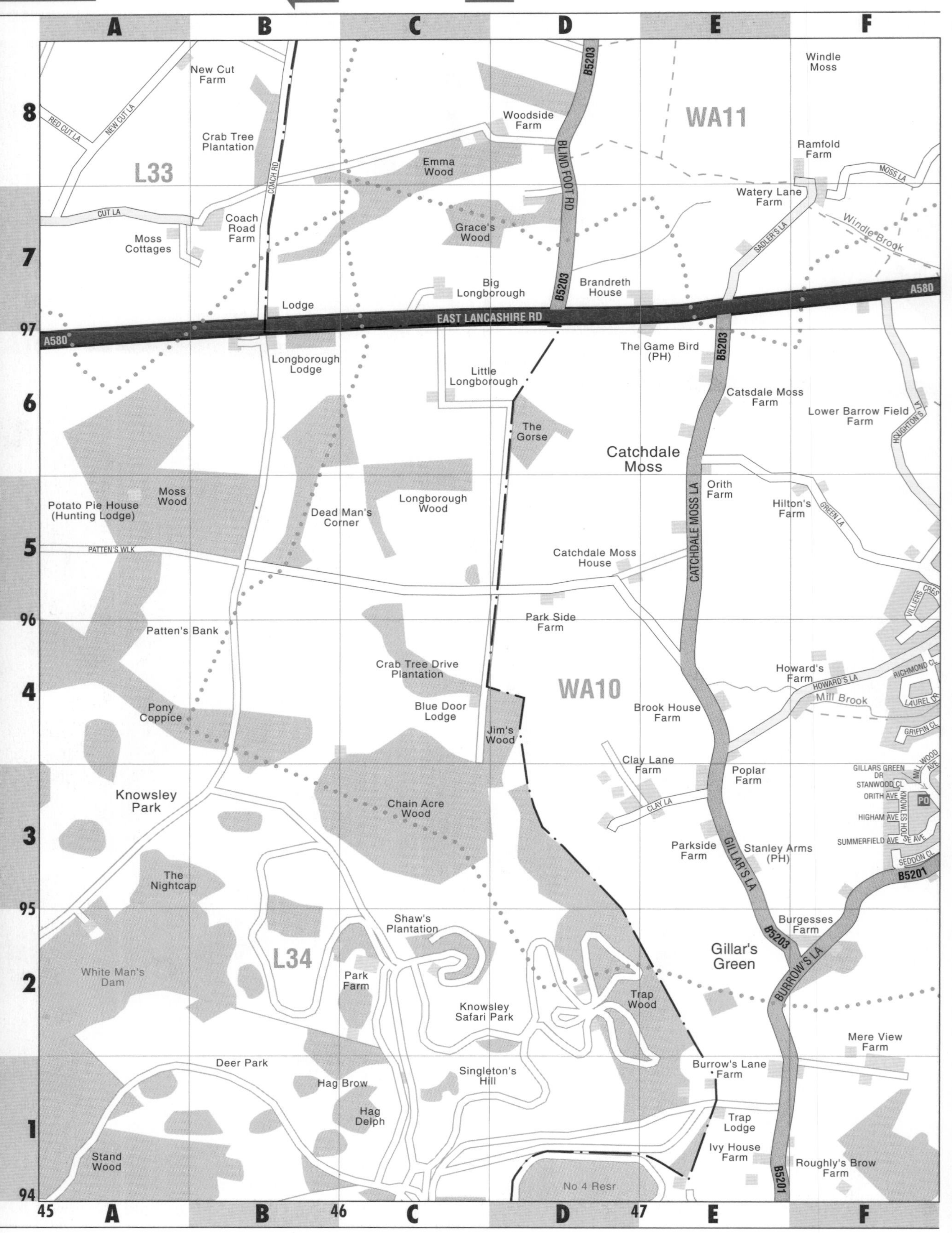
A
B
C
D
E
F
New Cut Farm
Windle Moss
WA11
L33
Crab Tree Plantation
Woodside Farm
Emma Wood
Ramfold Farm
Watery Lane Farm
Coach Road Farm
Moss Cottages
Grace's Wood
Windle Brook
Big Longborough
Brandreth House
Lodge
EAST LANCASHIRE RD
A580
B5203
BLIND FOOT RD
COACH RD
CUT LA
RED CUT LA
NEW CUT LA
MOSS LA
SADLER'S LA
The Game Bird (PH)
Longborough Lodge
Little Longborough
Catsdale Moss Farm
Lower Barrow Field Farm
The Gorse
Catchdale Moss
Orith Farm
Hilton's Farm
Moss Wood
Potato Pie House (Hunting Lodge)
Dead Man's Corner
Longborough Wood
PATTEN'S WLK
Catchdale Moss House
CATCHDALE MOSS LA
GREEN LA
Park Side Farm
Patten's Bank
Crab Tree Drive Plantation
WA10
Howard's Farm
HOWARD'S LA
Mill Brook
Blue Door Lodge
Brook House Farm
Pony Coppice
Jim's Wood
Clay Lane Farm
CLAY LA
Poplar Farm
Knowsley Park
Chain Acre Wood
Parkside Farm
Stanley Arms (PH)
GILLAR'S LA
The Nightcap
Shaw's Plantation
Burgesses Farm
L34
Gillar's Green
BURROW'S LA
White Man's Dam
Park Farm
Trap Wood
Knowsley Safari Park
Mere View Farm
Deer Park
Singleton's Hill
Burrow's Lane Farm
Hag Brow
Hag Delph
Trap Lodge
Ivy House Farm
Roughly's Brow Farm
Stand Wood
No 4 Resr
B5201
VILLIERS CRES
RICHMOND CL
LAUREL DR
GRIFFIN CL
GILLARS GREEN DR
STANWOOD CL
ORITH AVE
HIGHAM AVE
SUMMERFIELD AVE
SEDDON CL
MILL WOOD AVE
KNOWLES HO
PO
HOUGHTON'S LA
8
7
97
6
5
96
4
3
95
2
1
94
45
46
47

41
56

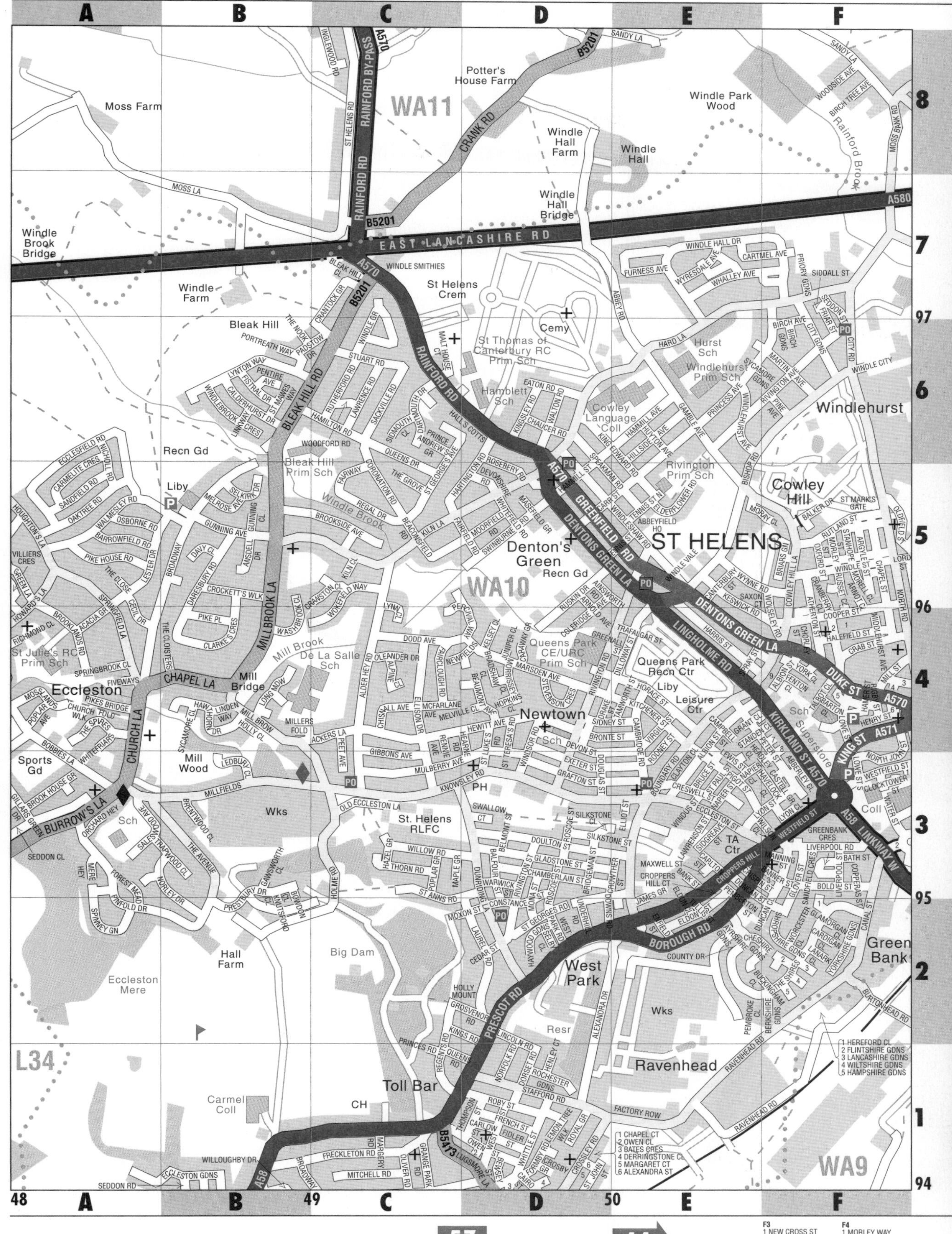

F3
1 NEW CROSS ST
2 CHALON WAY W
3 BANNER WLK

F4
1 MORLEY WAY
2 OXFORD ST
3 VOLUNTEER ST
4 LEACH ST
5 RANDON GR
6 NEW CROSS ST
7 PALMER CL
8 BURNELL CL
9 PATRICIA CT

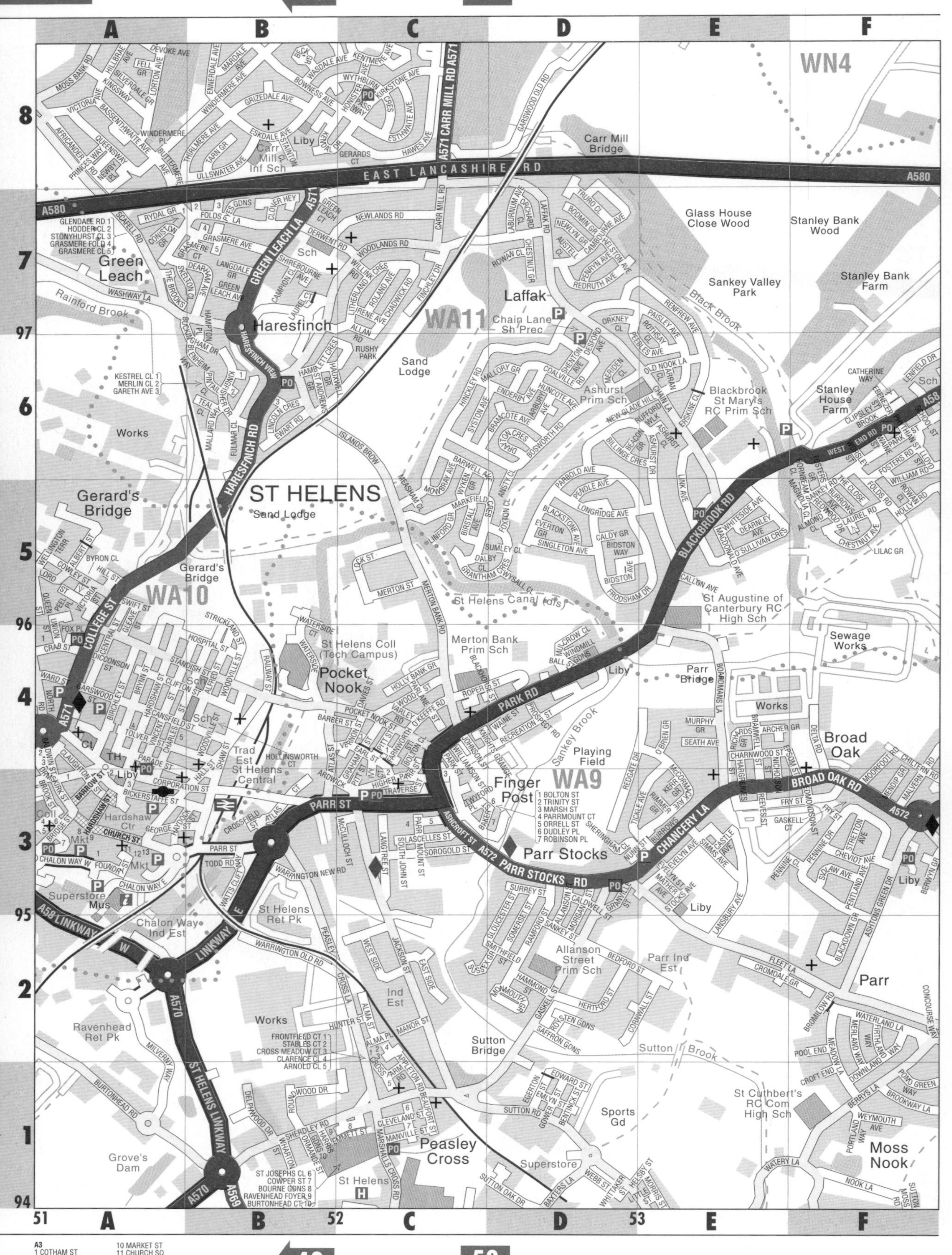

A3
1 COTHAM ST
2 VICTORIA SQ
3 LIBRARY ST
4 WATERLOO ST
5 CROSS ST
6 MILK ST
7 EXCHANGE ST
8 LAGRANGE ARC
9 PALATINE ARC

10 MARKET ST
11 CHURCH SQ
12 ST MARY'S ARC
13 BROWNLOW ARC

A4
1 NORMAN SALISBURY CT
2 WILLIAM ST
3 JOHN ST
4 TOLVER HO
5 PROVIDENCE CT

34
46

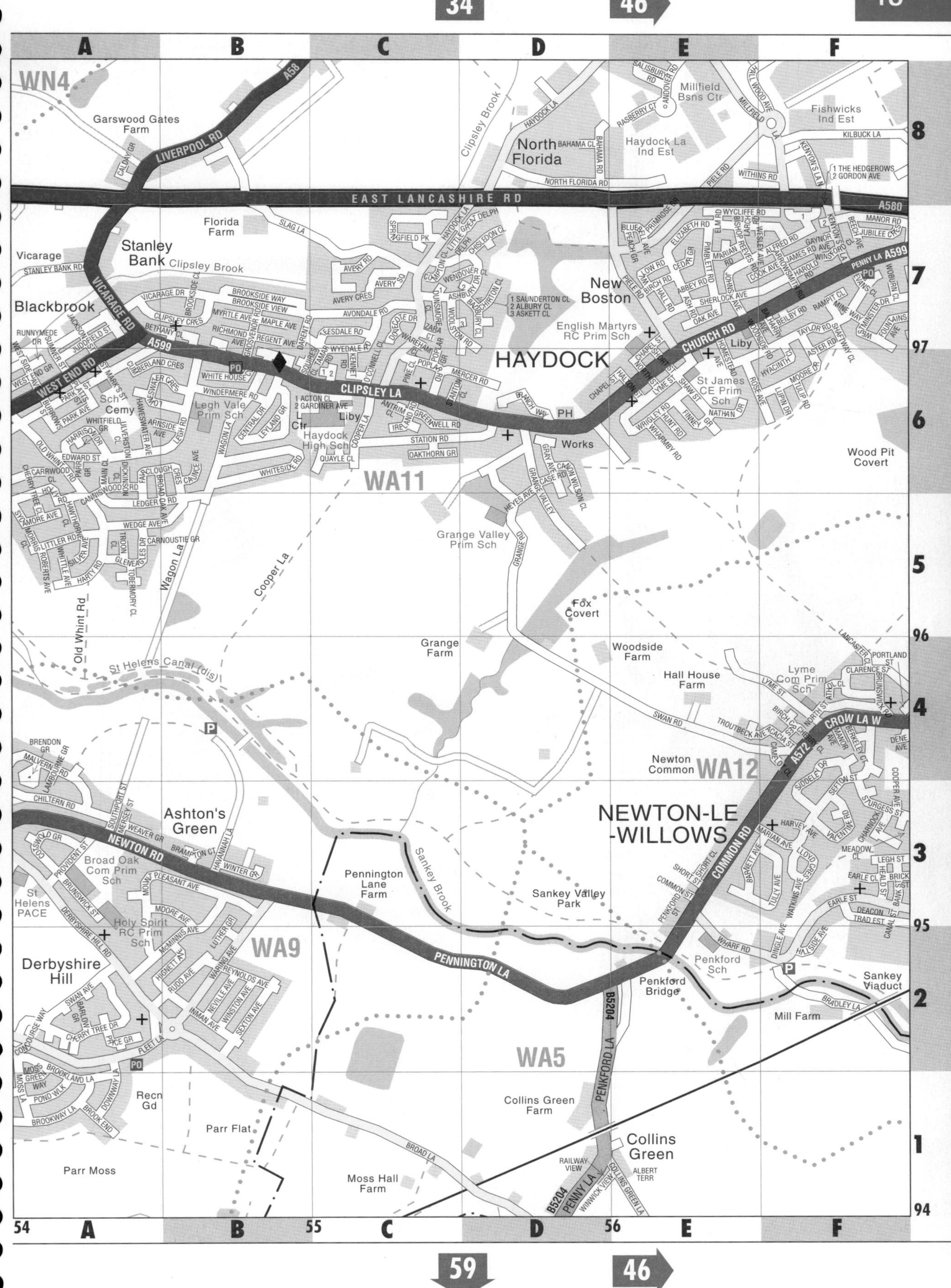
A
B
C
D
E
F
8
7
97
6
5
96
4
3
95
2
1
94
54
55
56
WN4
A58
Garswood Gates Farm
LIVERPOOL RD
EAST LANCASHIRE RD
A580
Florida Farm
SLAG LA
Stanley Bank
Clipsley Brook
Vicarage
STANLEY BANK RD
VICARAGE RD
Blackbrook
WEST END RD
A599
CLIPSLEY LA
North Florida
NORTH FLORIDA RD
HAYDOCK LA
Millfield Bsns Ctr
Haydock La Ind Est
Fishwicks Ind Est
KILBUCK LA
WITHINS RD
PIELE RD
1 THE HEDGEROWS
2 GORDON AVE
New Boston
HAYDOCK
CHURCH RD
PENNY LA
English Martyrs RC Prim Sch
St James CE Prim Sch
Liby
PH
Works
1 SAUNDERTON CL
2 ALBURY CL
3 ASKETT CL
1 ACTON CL
2 GARDINER AVE
Haydock High Sch
Legh Vale Prim Sch
Cemy
Sch
STATION RD
OAKTHORN GR
WA11
Grange Valley Prim Sch
GRANGE VALLEY
Wood Pit Covert
Wagon La
Cooper La
Old Whint Rd
Fox Covert
Grange Farm
Woodside Farm
Hall House Farm
St Helens Canal (dis)
Lyme Com Prim Sch
SWAN RD
CROW LA W
A572
Newton Common
WA12
NEWTON-LE-WILLOWS
COMMON RD
Ashton's Green
NEWTON RD
Broad Oak Com Prim Sch
St Helens PACE
Holy Spirit RC Prim Sch
Pennington Lane Farm
Sankey Brook
Sankey Valley Park
PENNINGTON LA
WA9
Derbyshire Hill
Penkford Sch
Penkford Bridge
B5204
Sankey Viaduct
Mill Farm
BRADLEY LA
WA5
PENKFORD LA
Collins Green Farm
Collins Green
Recn Gd
Parr Flat
Parr Moss
BROAD LA
Moss Hall Farm
PO
P

59
46

45
35

A
B
C
D
E
F
8
7
97
6
5
96
4
3
95
2
1
94
57
58
59
HAYDOCK
Yew Tree Farm Trad Est
Old Boston Trad Est
Old Boston
Hotel
Haydock Park
Haydock Park Racecourse
White Door Covert
Lady Hill Plantation
White Door Dam
GOLBORNE
WA3
SPRINGFIELD AVE 1
HIGHFIELD AVE 2
CLIFTONMILL MEADOWS 3
A580
A599
EAST LANCASHIRE RD
M6
A49
LODGE LA
23
Haydock Park Farm
Fox Covert
Dean Dam
Dean Dam Farm
WA11
Ellam's Brook
Ellam's Rough
Newton-Haydock Bridge
Woodlands Ind Est
Lawson's Farm
Hollows Bridge
CH
VISTA RD
B5209
ASHTON RD
Newton-le-Willows Com High Sch
WA12
LANGTON CL 1
GLADSTONE WAY 2
BROTHERTON WAY 3
Newton Bank Sch
St Mary's RC Inf Sch
Liby
A572
CROW LA W
CROW LA E
HIGH ST
CHURCH ST
THE COURTYARD
Newton Lake
WATERWORKS DR
1 NORTHWOOD AVE
2 WOODLAND AVE
SOUTHWORTH RD
The District CE Prim Sch
St Helens Coll Newton Campus
St Mary's RC Jun Sch
St Aelred's RC Tech Coll
St Peter's CE Prim Sch
Newton-le-Willows Prim Sch
Newton-le-Willows
Stones Crossing
Mill Green Sch
MILL LA
Earlestown
Wargrave
Newton Park Farm
NEWTON PARK DR
1 PARK VIEW
2 CRABTREE CL
3 OWLSFIELD
Deacon Trad Est
Mast
NEWTON-LE-WILLOWS
WELLINGTON GDNS 1
WELLINGTON CL 2
WOODS CT 3
GRAFTON ST 4
BACK BRIDGE ST 5
Sankey Valley Ind Est
Earlestown
Newton Community
Cemy
Newton Brook
WINWICK RD
Wargrave House Sch
Sch
Sankey Canal (dis)
Sankey Brook
HAVERTY PREC 1
NOON CT 2
CAUNCE AVE 3
LANGLEY AVE 4
SCOTT WLK 5
THOMPSON CL 6
INGHAM AVE 7
FEARNLEY WAY 8
KENT WAY 9
OLD HEY WLK 10
WA5
Vulcan Ind Est
Works
Red Bank
New Hey Farm
WA2

45
60

36

61

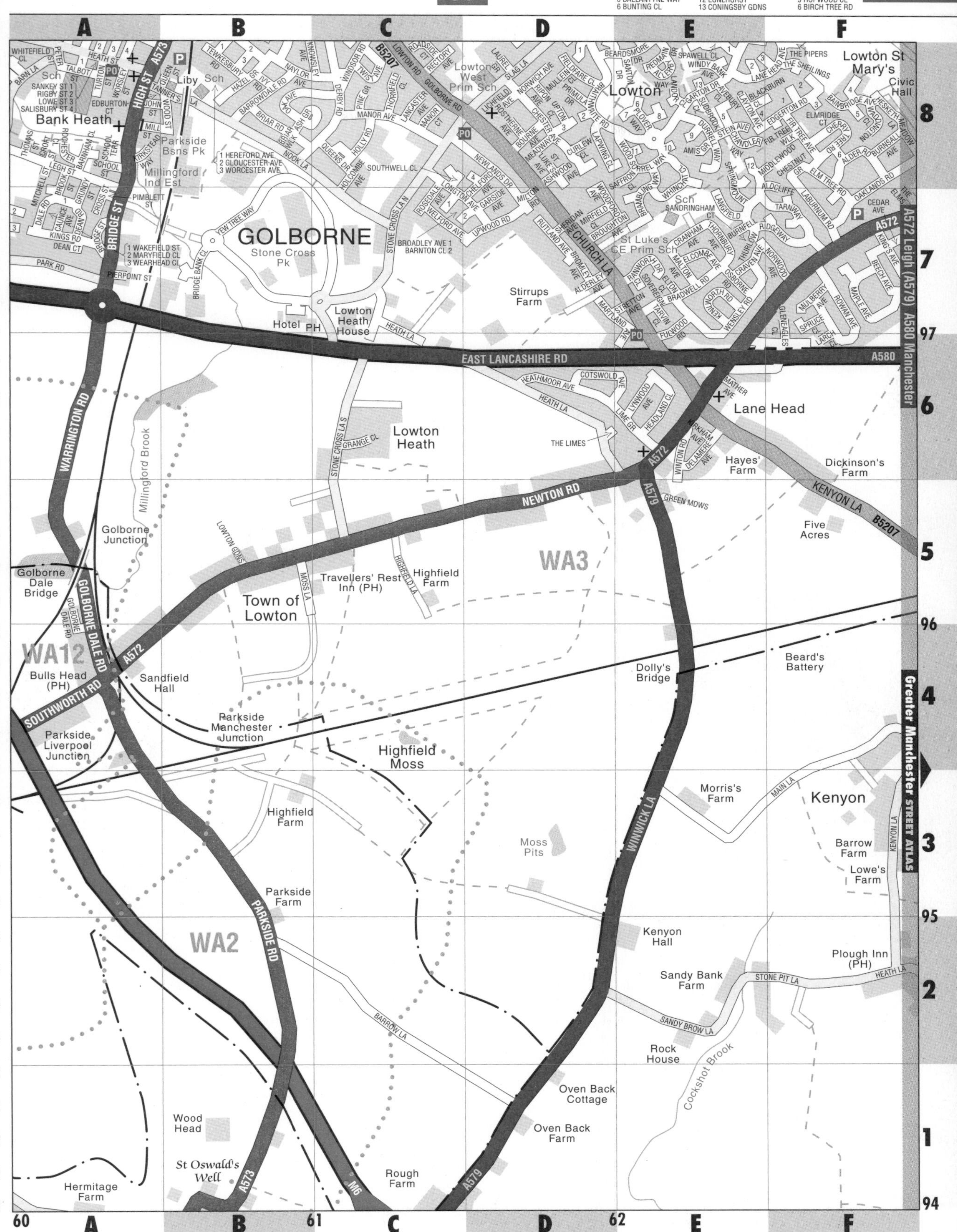

D8
1 SARSFIELD AVE
2 FOXGLOVE CL
3 GROSVENOR AVE
4 RIDGEWELL AVE

E8
1 TURRET HALL DR
2 ROYSTON CL
3 SANDFIELD CL
4 ARIEL WLK
5 BALLANTYNE WAY
6 BUNTING CL

7 REDSTART CL
8 WILD ARUM CL
9 HUDSON GR
10 STONECHAT CL
11 SPEEDWELL CL
12 LUNEHURST
13 CONINGSBY GDNS

F8
1 SCOTIA WLK
2 TYLER WLK
3 ROBSON WAY
4 HORNCASTLE CL
5 HOPWOOD CL
6 BIRCH TREE RD

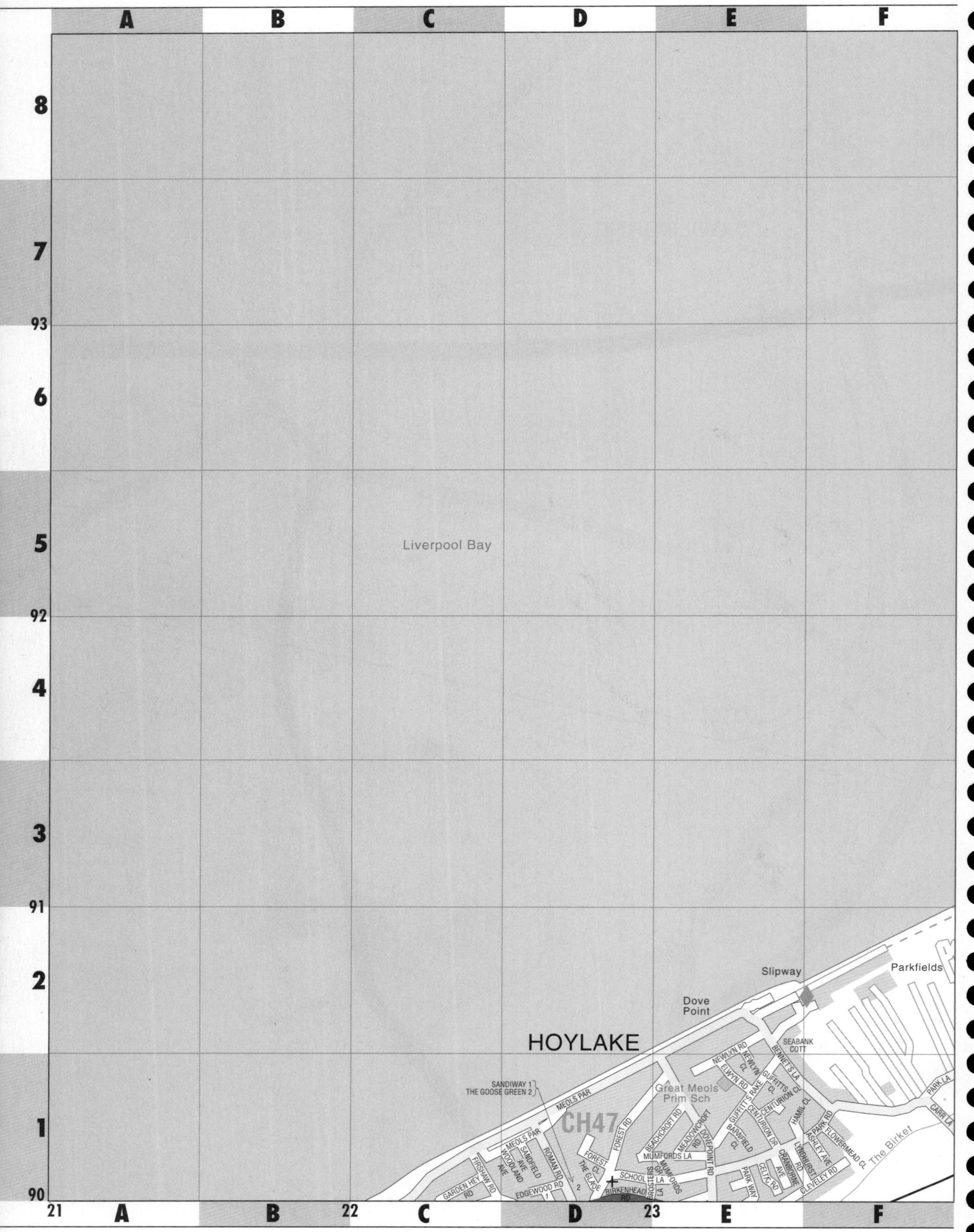

A B C D E F

8

7

93

6

5

92

Liverpool Bay

4

3

91

2

Slipway   Parkfields

Dove
Point

1

HOYLAKE   SEABANK
COTT

SANDIWAY 1
THE GOOSE GREEN 2

Great Meols
Prim Sch

MEOLS PAR

NEWLYN RD
THE WIEM
BERNET'S LA

ELWYN RD
GUFFIT'S CL

CH47   FOREST RD

GUFFIT'S BAKE

CENTURION DR

PARK RD

PARK LA

CABR LA

MEOLS PAR

FOREST CL

BEACHCROFT RD

NEWTON CROFT

MUMFORDS LA

TIDEPOINT RD

CRANSTONE

HAMIL CL

FLOWERMEAD RD

FRESHAW RD

SANDFIELD
AVE

WOODLAND
AVE

ROMAN RD

THE GLADE

FOREST
CL

SCHOOL

HUMFORDS

BARNFIELD
CL

PARK WAY

PAISLEY AVE
CELTS CL

LYNDHURST RD

CLEVELEY RD

The Birket

GARDEN HEY RD

EDGEWOOD RD

2

BIRKENHEAD
RD

HROSSERS LA

HUMFORDS
LA

CELTS CL

90

21 A   B   22 C   D   23 E   F

Liverpool Bay

North Wirral Coastal Park

CH

Leasowe Castle Hotel

A551

1 SHANNON HO
2 LAGAN HO
3 CAUSEWAY HO

LEASOWE RD

CASTLEFIELDS

MURRAYFIELD DR

Wallasey Embankment

Leasowe Common

P

MEREHEATH GDNS

THE SANDY

CRONTON AVE

FARNWORTH AVE

BLACKHEATH DR

TWICKENHAM DR

REEDS AVE E

Lighthouse (dis)

P

The Birket

CHELTENHAM CRES

EPSOM RD

NEWBURY WAY

REEDS LA

BIRKET AVE

P

Parkfield House

Lingham Farm

Ditton Lane Nature Area

DUNSTALL CL

GOODWOOD DR

BIRKET SQ

WALLASEY

91

Works

Leasowe Hotel (PH)

REEDVILLE GR

TARRAN WAY N

TARRAN WAY W

TARRAN WAY S

TARRAN DR

Sunnyside

Moreton

PASTURE RD

Station App

2

CH46

CH47

PASTURE AVE

PASTURE CRES

SUNFIELD RD

KINGSMEAD RD

Arrowe Brook

WASTDALE CT 1
WASTDALE MEWS 2

CURLEW CT

BERRYLANDS RD

BRAMBLE WAY

WEST WAY

YEW TREE RD

SAXON RD

DANESWELL DR

PARK LA

TERN WAY

WASTDALE DR

BRADMAN RD

GLASIER RD

MEADFOOT RD

BERRYLANDS CL

WESTWAY

WITLEY AVE

Eastway Prim Sch

RUSSELL RD

DUNKIRK LA

LC

ASHBY

MILLHOUSE LA

BALLARD WAY

BLEAMCR RD

HEATH VIEW

HARVEST LA

FLAXHILL

WITLEY CL

BLUNDELLS LA

Sacred Heart RC Prim Sch

AVONDALE AVE

CH47

ESKDALE AVE

TOWN MEADOW LA

KESTREL RD

Lingham Prim Sch

EDGEHILL RD

EVERGREEN CL

FELICITY GR

MAURICE JONES CT

KNUTSFORD RD

A553

HOYLAKE RD

P

LC

GLENFIELD CL

CATMOUTSIE CL

TURNBERRY CL

BERNULLA RD

E1
1 GARDEN LA
2 OAKENHOLT RD

MARYLAND LA

OLD MARYLAND LA

WILLASTON RD

LITHERLAND AVE

DIGG LA

Liby

FAIRMEAD RD

BURNLEY GR

STUART AVE

TANWORTH GR

CARR LA

24

25

26

49

A
B
C
D
E
F
8
7
93
6
5
92
4
3
91
2
1
90
27
28
29
Liverpool Bay
Slipway
Dunes
PH
CH
Harrison Park
Wallasey Grove Road
CH45
Greenleas Prim Sch
Wallasey Village
St Mary's RC Coll
St George's Prim Sch (Annexe)
St George's Prim Sch
Liby
LEASOWE RD
KING'S PAR
A554
A551
B5477 HARRISON DR
BAYSWATER RD
WALLASEY VILLAGE
Our Lady of Lourdes RC Sch
Leasowe
Castleway Prim Sch
Leasowe Prim Sch
CH46
L Ctr
Wallasey Sch
The Birket
WALLASEY
The Mosslands Sch
Recn Gd
CH44
Junction One Ret Pk
Superstore
Bidston Ind Est
Bidston Moss
A5139
M53
Sch & Coll
B5145
BRECK RD
Factory
Bidston
LC
CH43
Leasowe
P&R
Clare Mount Sch
Fender Bridge
FENDER LA
A553
Fender Farm
St Oswald's Bidston CE Prim Sch
Vyner Prim Sch
Bidston
Bidston Hall
HOYLAKE RD
BOUNDARY RD
B5151
Sports Ctr
CH41
Works
Birkenhead North
Holy Cross RC Prim Sch
WALLASEY BRIDGE RD
A5088
A5030
E6
1 MARSHLANDS RD
2 TOWN FIELDS
3 GRANVILLE CT
F4
1 BLETCHLEY AVE
2 BRYNMOSS AVE
3 CROMARTY RD
4 MILLTHWAITE CT
PENINSULA CL 1
CORMORANT CT 2
REDCAP CL 3
DUNLINS CT 4
ROSEATE CT 5
COMPASS CT 1
ENNERDALE CT 2

49
65

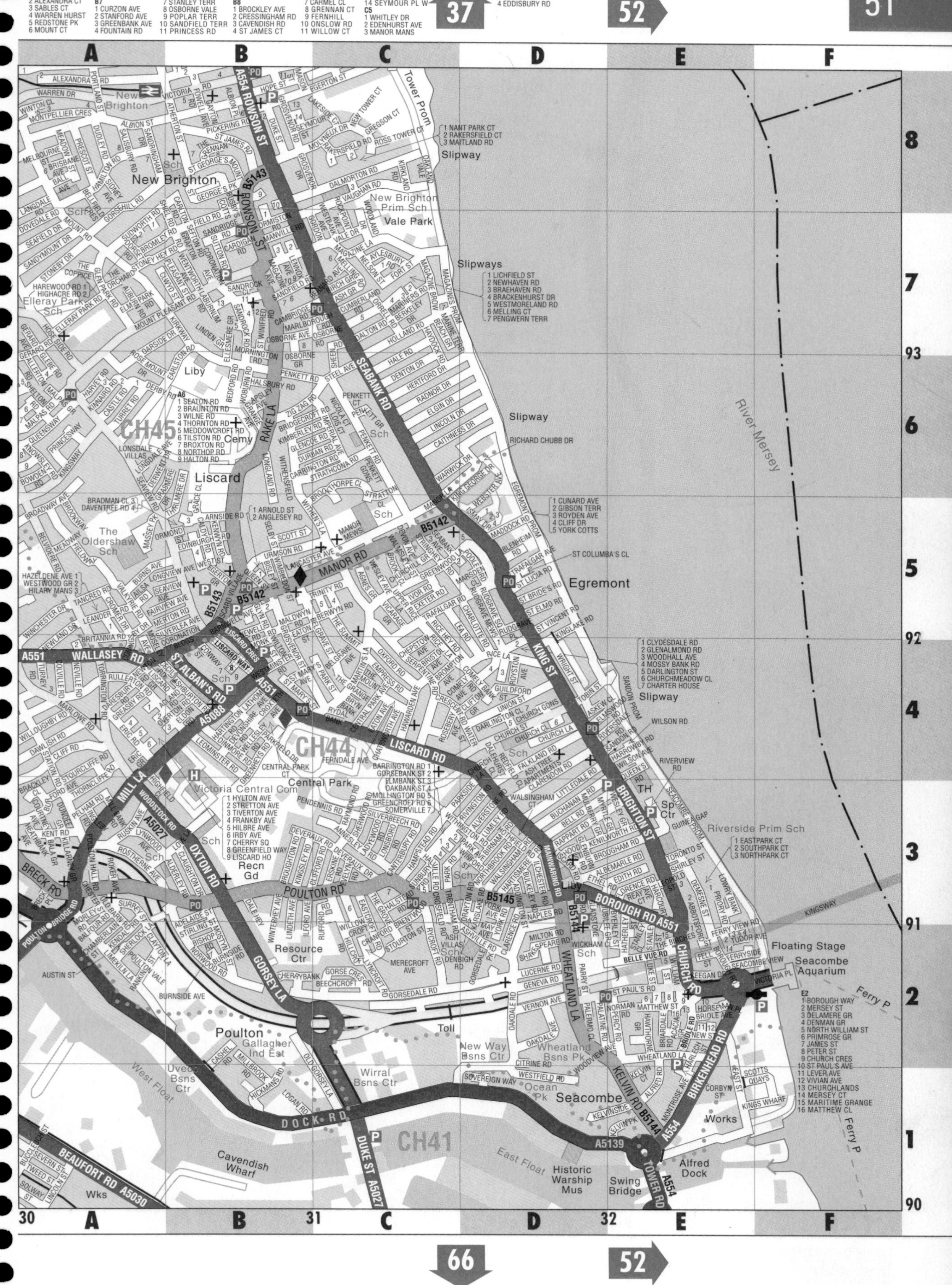
A8
1 WELLINGTON RD
2 ALEXANDRA CT
3 SABLES CT
4 WARREN HURST
5 REDSTONE PK
6 MOUNT CT
7 OCEAN VIEW
8 KENHAM CT
B7
1 CURZON AVE
2 STANFORD AVE
3 GREENBANK AVE
4 FOUNTAIN RD
5 SOUTH VILLAS
6 CYPRUS TERR
7 STANLEY TERR
8 OSBORNE VALE
9 POPLAR TERR
10 SANDFIELD TERR
11 PRINCESS RD
12 MARSDEN CT
13 SANDHEYS RD
B8
1 BROCKLEY AVE
2 CRESSINGHAM RD
3 CAVENDISH RD
4 ST JAMES CT
5 CAVENDISH CT
6 ROWSON CT
7 CARMEL CL
8 GRENNAN CT
9 FERNHILL
10 ONSLOW RD
11 WILLOW CT
12 EGERTON CT
13 PRIMROSE CT
14 SEYMOUR PL W
C5
1 WHITLEY DR
2 EDENHURST AVE
3 MANOR MANS
37
C5
3 KINGSWOOD RD
4 EDDISBURY RD
52
A
B
C
D
E
F
8
7
93
6
5
92
4
3
91
2
1
90
30
31
32
New Brighton
Liscard
Egremont
Seacombe
Poulton
River Mersey
CH45
CH44
CH41
Vale Park
Central Park
Slipway
Slipways
Tower Prom
Elleray Park Sch
The Oldershaw Sch
Victoria Central Com
Riverside Prim Sch
Floating Stage
Seacombe Aquarium
Alfred Dock
Swing Bridge
Historic Warship Mus
Cavendish Wharf
West Float
East Float
DOCK RD
SEABANK RD
KING ST
BRIGHTON ST
WALLASEY RD
LISCARD RD
MANOR RD
POULTON RD
BOROUGH RD
WHEATLAND LA
KELVIN RD
BIRKENHEAD RD
CHURCH RD
BRECK RD
GORSEY LA
DUKE ST
BEAUFORT RD
TOWER RD
OXTON RD
MILL LA
ST ALBAN'S RD
RAKE LA
ROWSON ST
A554
A551
A5027
A5088
A5139
A5030
B5142
B5143
B5144
B5145
E2
1 BOROUGH WAY
2 MERSEY ST
3 DELAMERE GR
4 DENMAN GR
5 NORTH WILLIAM ST
6 PRIMROSE GR
7 JAMES ST
8 PETER ST
9 CHURCH CRES
10 ST PAUL'S AVE
11 LEVER AVE
12 VIVIAN AVE
13 CHURCHLANDS
14 MERSEY CT
15 MARITIME GRANGE
16 MATTHEW CL
66
52

D5
1 ST AUGUSTINE ST
2 McKEOWN CL
3 WESTMORELAND PL
4 WILBRAHAM PL
5 St Anthony's Sh Ctr

D7
1 JAMES HOPKINS WAY
2 WULSTAN ST
3 PINCROFT WAY
4 FOUNTAINS CT
5 EASBY RD
6 ELSTOW ST

51

D7
7 SWINDON CL
8 CHELMSFORD CL
9 SHARPEVILLE CL
10 BACK BLACKFIELD TERR

38

E8
1 DELAMORE ST
2 CHIRKDALE ST
3 BACK WESTMINSTER RD
4 BRUNSWICK CL
5 DRYBURGH WAY
6 WARDEN ST
7 BRADEWELL CL
8 ROCKLEY ST
9 ST HILDA ST
10 LONGRIDGE WLK
11 MILNTHORPE CL

F7
1 TEULON CL
2 LUTYENS CL
3 COCKERELL CL
4 HARTLEY CL
5 WYRE RD
6 GOSCHEN ST
7 ELM BANK
8 YORK VILLAS
9 PULFORD ST
10 BALFOUR ST
11 GORST ST
12 RANDOLPH ST
13 GURNALL ST
14 HAYFIELD ST
15 ATTWOOD ST
16 NORGATE ST
17 SAKER ST
18 LAMBRIGG ROW

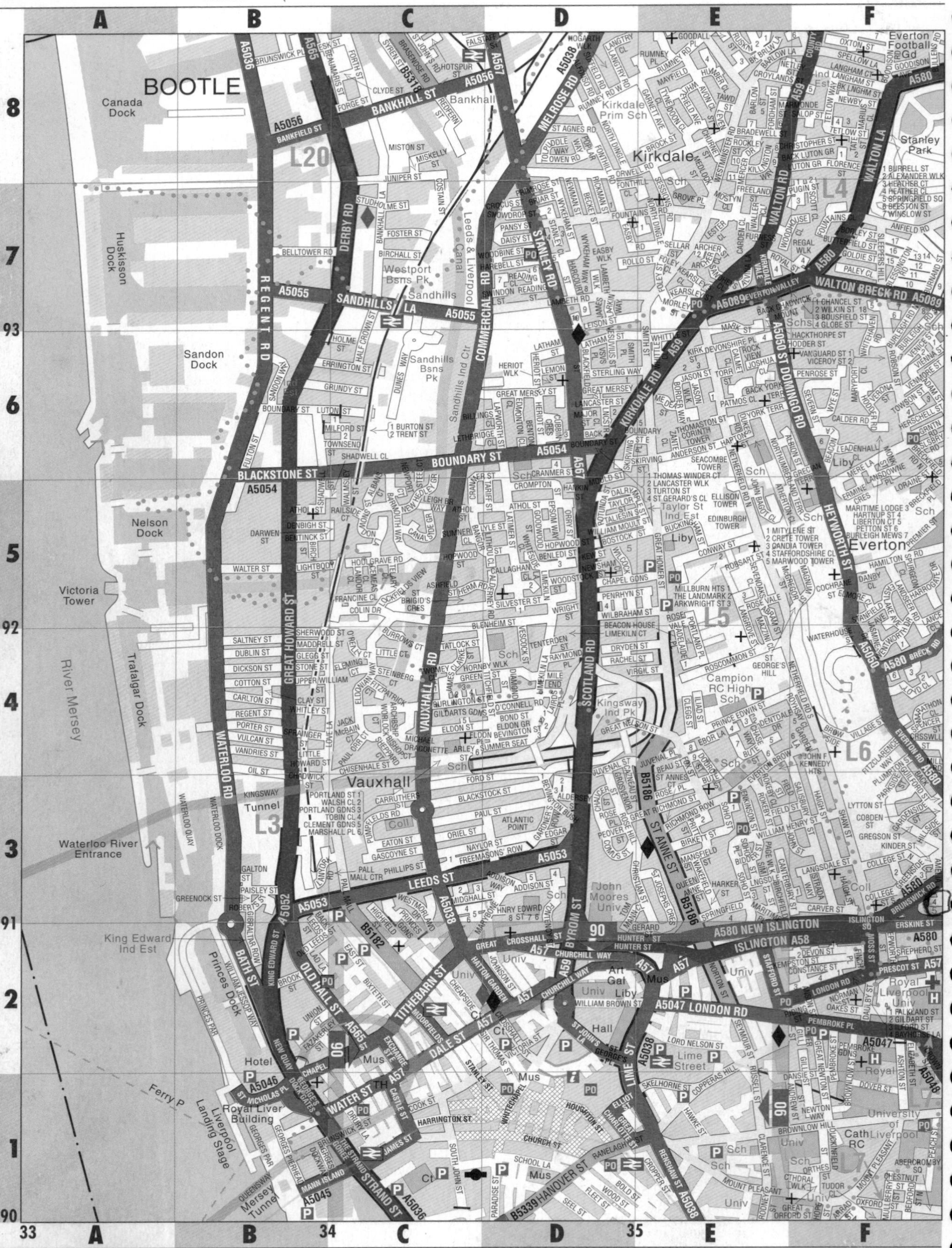

A
B
C
D
E
F
8
7
93
6
5
92
4
3
91
2
1
90
33
34
35
BOOTLE
Canada Dock
Huskisson Dock
Sandon Dock
Nelson Dock
Victoria Tower
Trafalgar Dock
River Mersey
Waterloo River Entrance
King Edward Ind Est
Princes Dock
Royal Liver Building
Liverpool Landing Stage
Mersey Tunnel
Kirkdale
Everton
Everton Football Gd
Stanley Park
Vauxhall
Sandhills
Westport Bsns Pk
Sandhills Bsns Pk
Leeds & Liverpool Canal
Kingsway Ind Pk
Campion RC High Sch
John Moores Univ
Lime Street
University of Liverpool
Royal Liverpool Univ
L20
L4
L5
L6
L3
L7
REGENT RD
GREAT HOWARD ST
WATERLOO RD
DERBY RD
COMMERCIAL RD
VAUXHALL RD
SCOTLAND RD
STANLEY RD
KIRKDALE RD
MELROSE RD
WALTON RD
WALTON LA
HEYWORTH ST
ST DOMINGO RD
EVERTON VALLEY
WALTON BRECK RD
BANKHALL ST
SANDHILLS LA
BOUNDARY ST
BLACKSTONE ST
LEEDS ST
BYROM ST
NEW ISLINGTON
ISLINGTON
LONDON RD
OLD HALL ST
TITHEBARN ST
DALE ST
WATER ST
STRAND ST
HANOVER ST
CHURCHILL WAY
ST ANNE ST
LIME ST
RENSHAW ST
MOUNT PLEASANT
BATH ST
90

For full street detail of the highlighted area see page 90.

51

C3
1 GLADSTONE ST
2 STOCKDALE CL
3 WALDRON CL
4 MARLBOROUGH ST
5 MARLBOROUGH PL
6 PICKOP ST

D3
1 LIMEKILN LA
2 WELLINGTON ST

67

D3
3 NICHOLAS ST
4 ST STEPHENS PL
5 HOLY CROSS CL
6 BISPHAM HO
7 ADLINGTON ST
8 ADLINGTON HO

D4
1 BURROUGHS GDNS
2 BEVINGTON HILL
3 ENNERDALE ST
4 KINGSWAY CT

E3
1 BICKERSTAFFE ST
2 DRINKWATER GDNS
3 RODERICK ST
4 TRINITY WLK

E4
1 ST MARTIN'S MEWS
2 CLIFTON GR
3 SHERIFF CL
4 HIGHAM SQ
5 UPPER BUTE ST
6 WATMOUGH ST
7 BERESFORD ST
8 BACK BEAU ST
9 UPPER BEAU ST

F3
1 CANTERBURY WAY
2 TICHBOURNE WAY
3 MELDA CL
4 TRAFALGAR WAY
5 Erskin Ind Est

F4
1 NORTHCOTE CL
2 FISHGUARD CL
3 SPINDLE CL
4 EMBER CRES
5 RICHARD ALLEN WAY
6 ST AMBROSE WAY

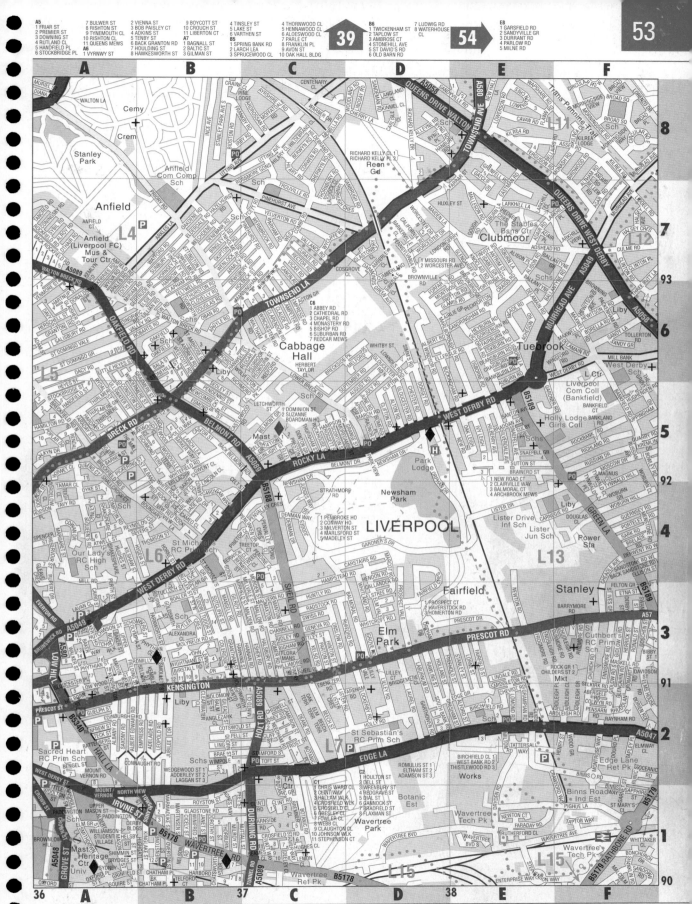

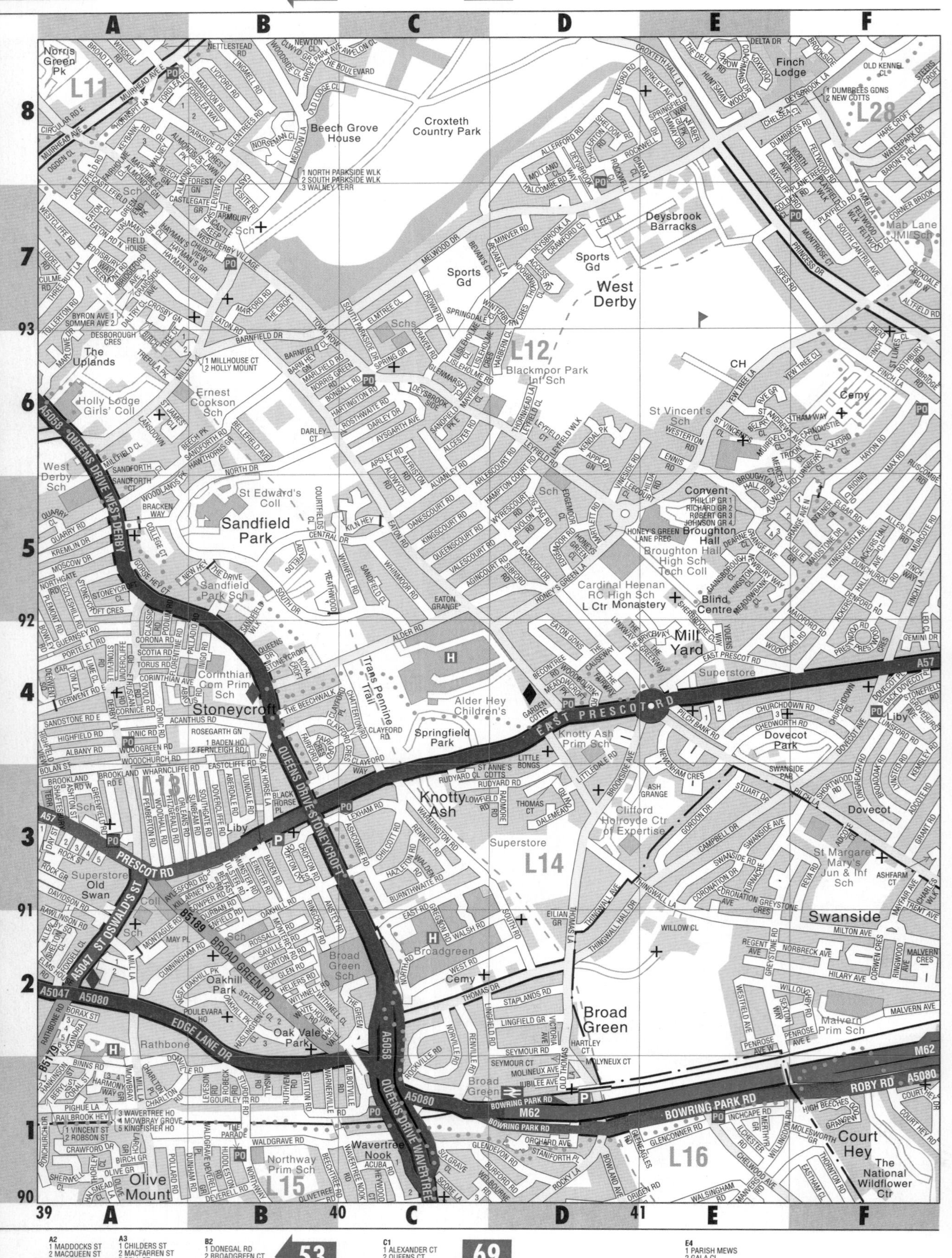

A2
1 MADDOCKS ST
2 MACQUEEN ST
3 AUGUSTA CL
4 STEPHENSON RD
5 ARMOUR GR
6 WILTON GR

A3
1 CHILDERS ST
2 MACFARREN ST
3 BELL ST
4 BATLEY ST
5 BOOTH ST
6 RAVENSWOOD RD
7 BEATTY RD

B2
1 DONEGAL RD
2 BROADGREEN CT
3 DALLINGTON CT

C1
1 ALEXANDER CT
2 QUEENS CT
3 GLENAVON RD

E4
1 PARISH MEWS
2 GALA CL
3 CHURCHDOWN GR

41
56

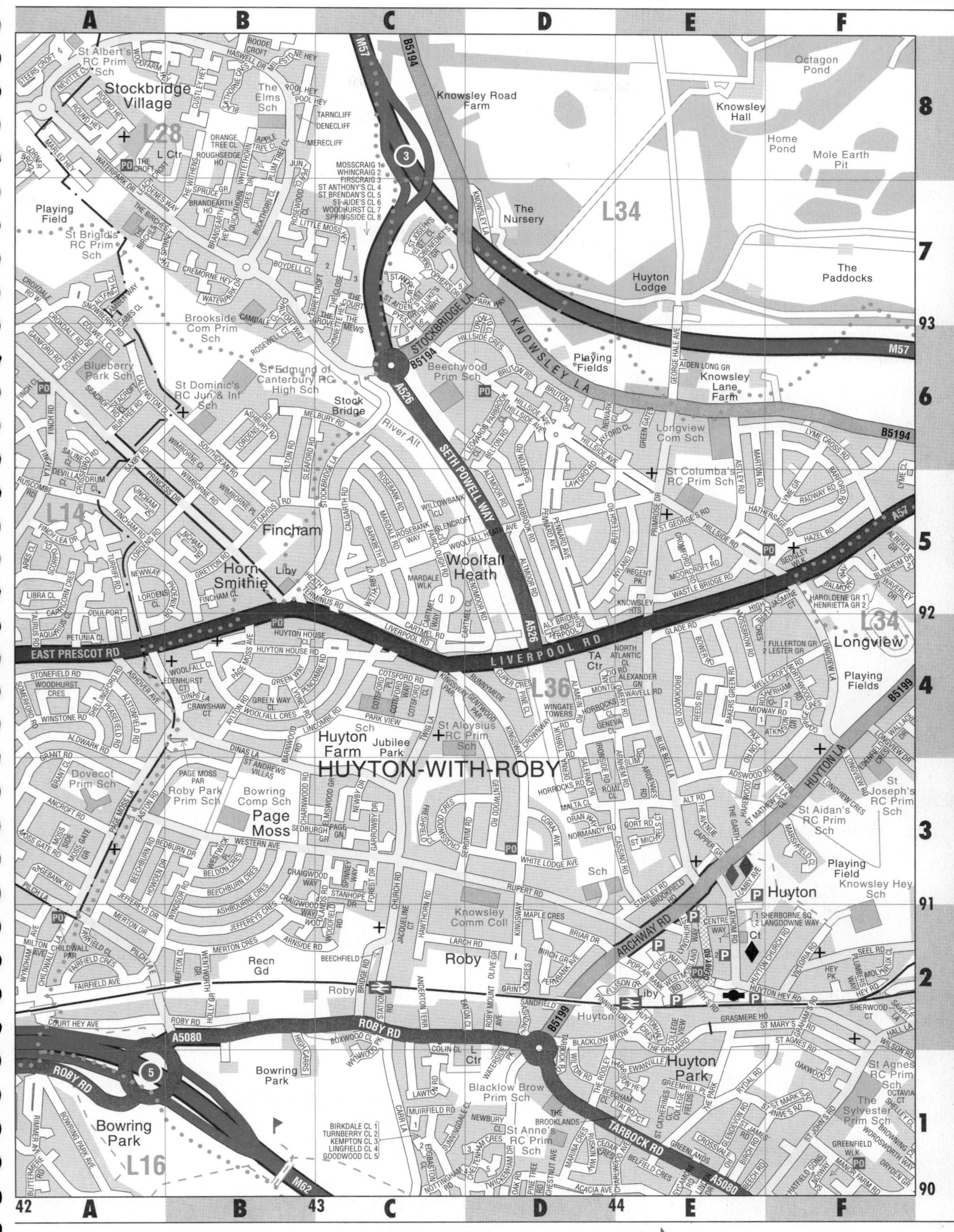
A
B
C
D
E
F
8
7
93
6
5
92
4
3
91
2
1
90
42
43
44
Stockbridge Village
L28
St Albert's RC Prim Sch
The Elms Sch
L Ctr
Playing Field
St Brigid's RC Prim Sch
Brookside Com Prim Sch
Blueberry Park Sch
St Dominic's RC Jun & Inf Sch
St Edmund of Canterbury RC High Sch
Stock Bridge
River Alt
Knowsley Road Farm
The Nursery
L34
Octagon Pond
Knowsley Hall
Home Pond
Mole Earth Pit
Huyton Lodge
The Paddocks
Playing Fields
Knowsley Lane Farm
Longview Com Sch
St Columba's RC Prim Sch
Beechwood Prim Sch
M57
B5194
A526
SETH POWELL WAY
KNOWSLEY LA
STOCKBRIDGE LA
L14
Fincham
Horn Smithie
Liby
Woolfall Heath
EAST PRESCOT RD
LIVERPOOL RD
A57
Longview
Playing Fields
TA Ctr
L36
Wingate Towers
Huyton Farm
Jubilee Park
St Aloysius RC Prim Sch
HUYTON-WITH-ROBY
Dovecot Prim Sch
Roby Park Prim Sch
Bowring Comp Sch
Page Moss
Knowsley Comm Coll
Sch
Recn Gd
Roby
B5199
HUYTON LA
St Joseph's RC Prim Sch
St Aidan's RC Prim Sch
Playing Field
Knowsley Hey Sch
Huyton
Ct
ARCHWAY RD
Liby
Huyton
ROBY RD
A5080
Bowring Park
L16
M62
Blacklow Brow Prim Sch
St Anne's RC Prim Sch
L Ctr
Huyton Park
TARBOCK RD
St Agnes RC Prim Sch
The Sylvester Prim Sch
BIRKDALE CL 1
TURNBERRY CL 2
KEMPTON CL 3
LINGFIELD CL 4
GOODWOOD CL 5
MOSSCRAIG 1
WHINCRAIG 2
FIRSCRAIG 3
ST ANTHONY'S CL 4
ST BRENDAN'S CL 5
ST JUDE'S CL 6
WOODHURST CL 7
SPRINGSIDE CL 8
HAROLDENE GR 1
HENRIETTA GR 2
FULLERTON GR 1
LESTER GR 2
SHERBORNE SQ 1
LANGDOWNE WAY 2

70
56

← 55

↑ 42

D6				
1 SEDDONS CT	7 HILL ST	14 PRESCOT CTR	E6	7 LAVENDER CRES
2 WYCHERLEY ST	8 LEYLAND ST	15 GREENALL CT	1 POTTERY FIELDS	8 DERBY SQ
3 SALISBURY ST	9 ATHERTON ST		2 SMITH ST	9 PEMBERTONS CT
4 DUKE ST	10 CHAPEL ST		3 TINLING CL	10 FAIRHURST TERR
5 CARLTON ST	11 ACKERS ST		4 HUNTER CT	
6 STONE ST	12 VICTORIA HO		5 MENAI MEWS	
	13 BEACONSFIELD		6 OLIVER LYMM HO	

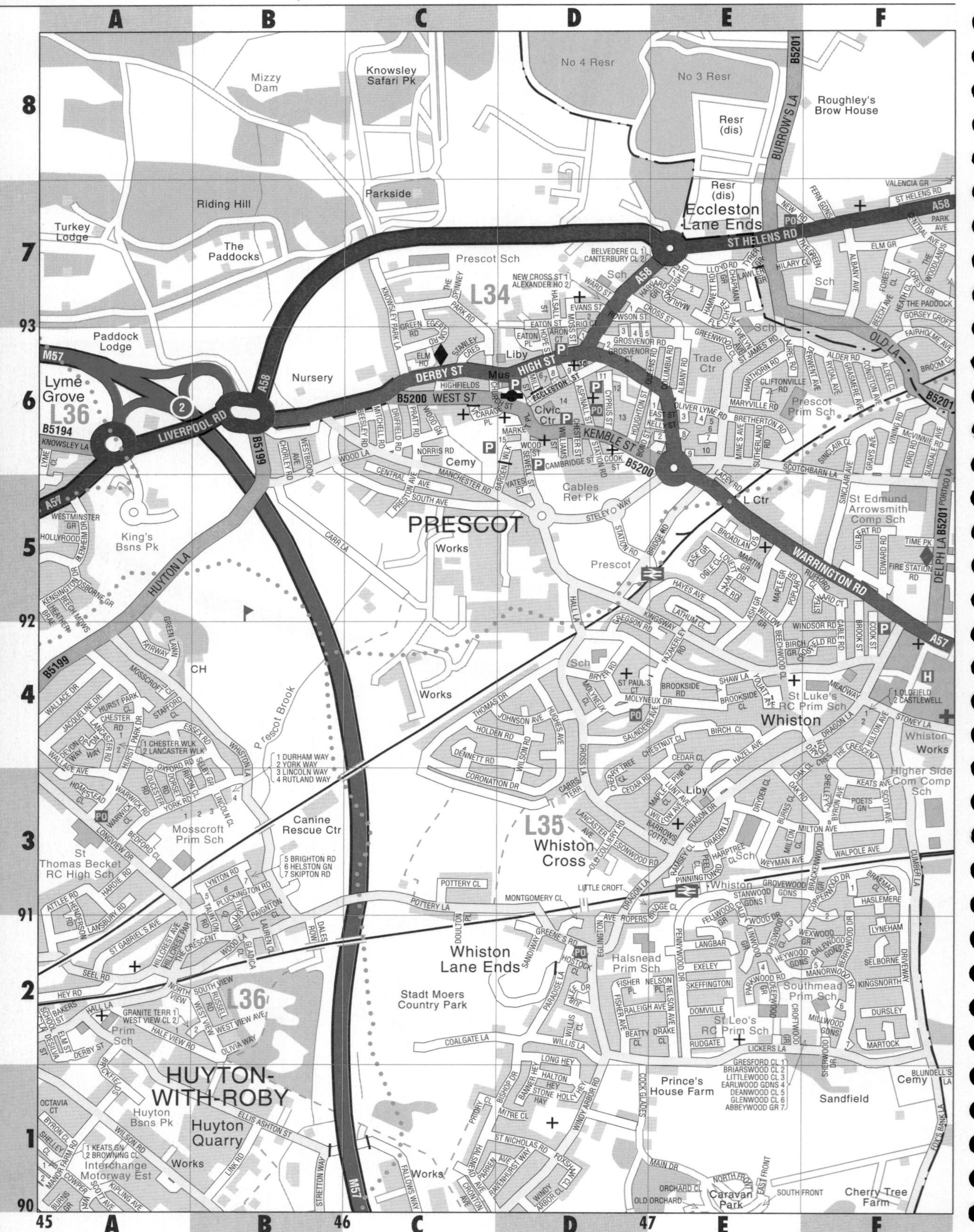

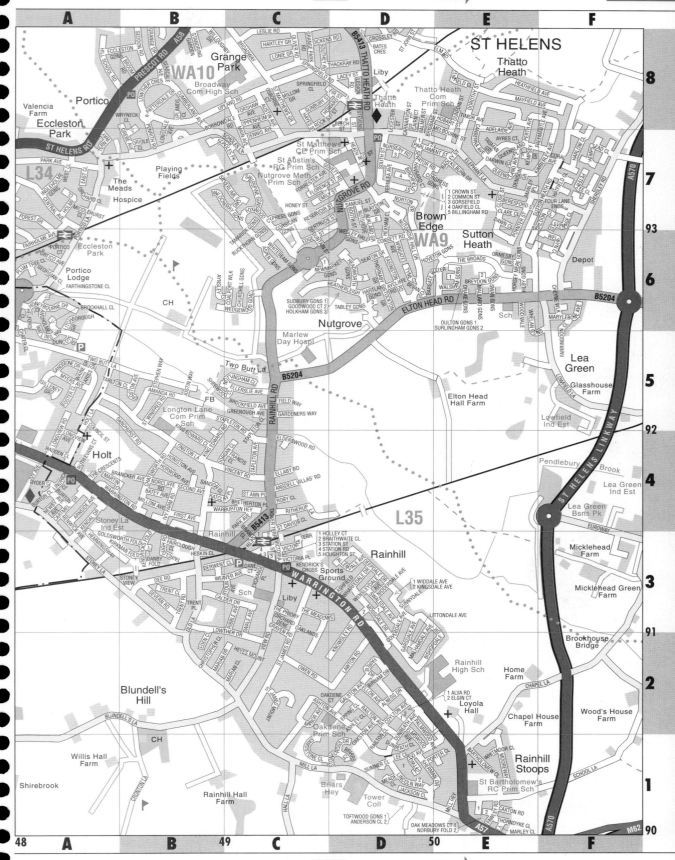

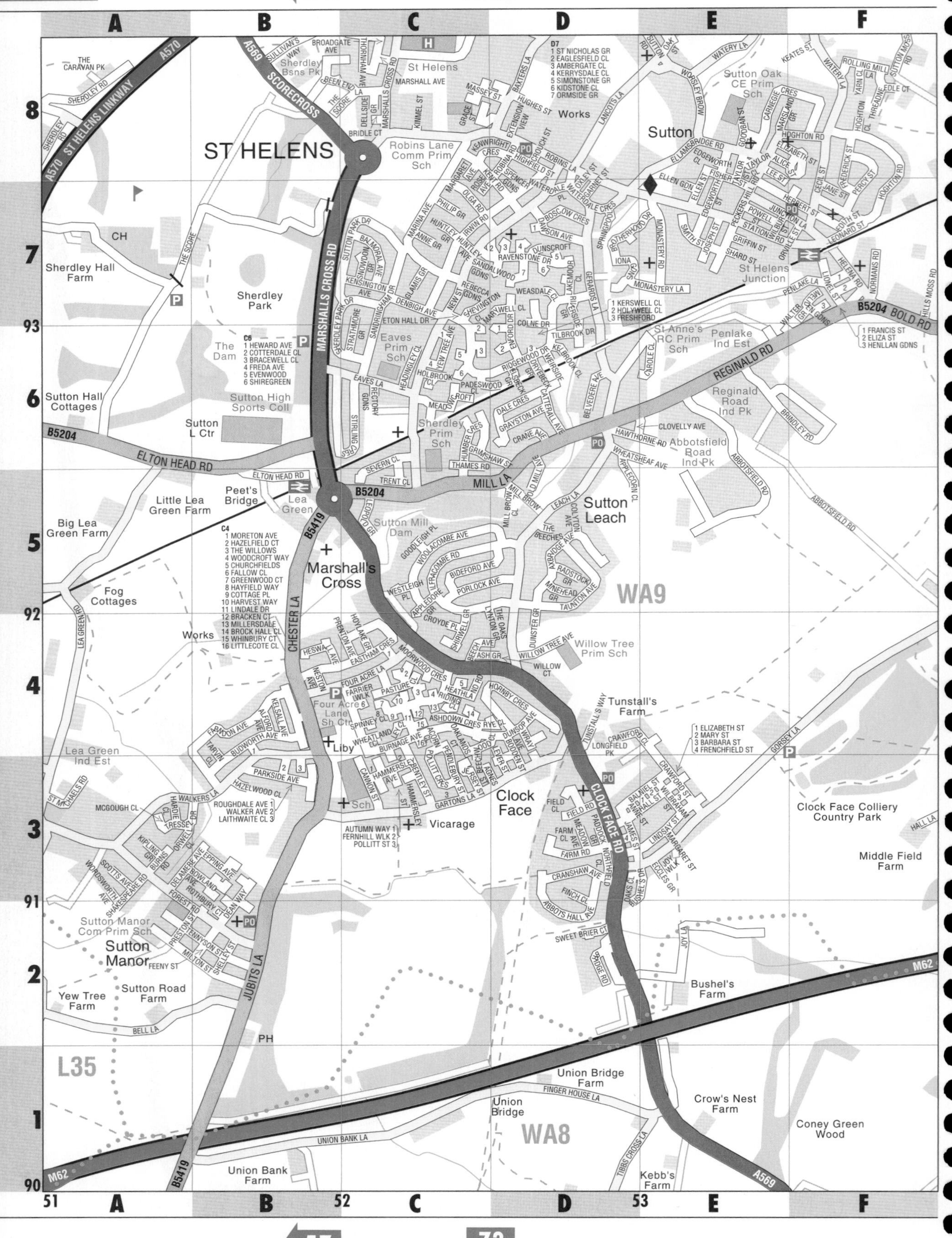

57
44

A B C D E F

8

7

93

6

5

92

4

3

91

2

1

90

51 A B 52 C D 53 E F

57
73

THE CARAVAN PK
ST HELENS LINKWAY
A570
A569
SCORECROSS
A570
SULLIVAN'S WAY
BROADGATE AVE
Sherdley Bsns Pk
MARSHALL AVE
St Helens
Works
D7
1 ST NICHOLAS GR
2 EAGLESFIELD CL
3 AMBERGATE CL
4 KERRYSDALE CL
5 SIMONSTONE GR
6 KIDSTONE CL
7 ORMSIDE GR
Sutton Oak
CE Prim Sch
WATERY LN
Sutton

CH
ST HELENS
Sherdley Hall
Farm
Sherdley
Park
Robins Lane
Comm Prim Sch
St Helens
Junction

Sutton Hall
Cottages
The
Dam
Sutton High
Sports Coll
C6
1 HEWARD AVE
2 COTTERDALE CL
3 BRACEWELL CL
4 FREDA AVE
5 EVENWOOD
6 SHIREGREEN
Eaves
Prim
Sch
St Anne's
RC Prim
Sch
Penlake
Ind Est
B5204 BOLD RD
1 FRANCIS ST
2 ELIZA ST
3 HENLLAN GDNS

B5204
ELTON HEAD RD
Sutton
L Ctr
ELTON HEAD RD
Peet's
Bridge
Lea
Green
B5204
Sherdley
Prim
Sch
MILL LA
REGINALD RD
Reginald
Road
Ind Pk
Abbotsfield
Road Ind Pk

Little Lea
Green Farm
Big Lea
Green Farm
C4
1 MORETON AVE
2 HAZELFIELD CT
3 THE WILLOWS
4 WOODCROFT WAY
5 CHURCHFIELDS
6 FALLOW CL
7 GREENWOOD CT
8 HAYFIELD WAY
9 COTTAGE PL
10 HARVEST WAY
11 LINDALE DR
12 BRACKEN CT
13 MILLERSDALE
14 BROCK HALL CL
15 WHINBURY CT
16 LITTLECOTE CL
Marshall's
Cross
Sutton Mill
Dam
Sutton Leach
WA9
Willow Tree
Prim Sch

Fog
Cottages
Works
Lea Green
Ind Est
Liby
Sch
Vicarage
Clock
Face
Tunstall's
Farm
1 ELIZABETH ST
2 MARY ST
3 BARBARA ST
4 FRENCHFIELD ST
Clock Face Colliery
Country Park
Middle Field
Farm

McGOUGH CL
AUTUMN WAY 1
FERNHILL WLK 2
POLLITT ST 3
CLOCK FACE RD

Sutton Manor
Com Prim Sch
Sutton
Manor
Yew Tree
Farm
Sutton Road
Farm
BELL LA
PH
JUBITS LA
B5419
L35
M62
Bushel's
Farm
M62

Union Bank LA
UNION BANK LA
Union Bridge
Farm
FINGER HOUSE LA
Union
Bridge
WA8
Crow's Nest
Farm
Coney Green
Wood

M62
B5419
Union Bank
Farm
Kebb's
Farm
A569
TIBBS CROSS LA

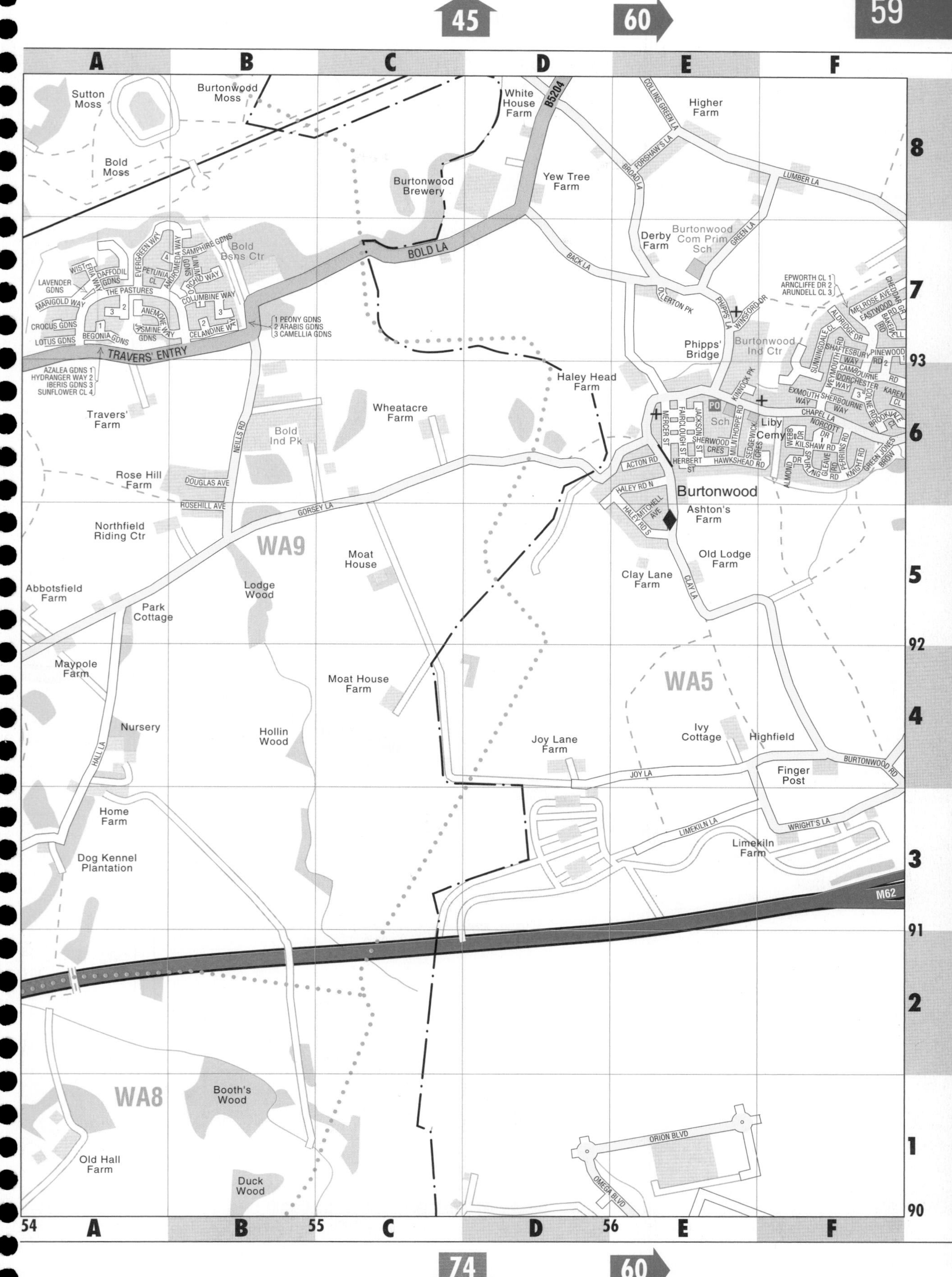
45
60
A
B
C
D
E
F
Sutton Moss
Burtonwood Moss
White House Farm
B5204
Higher Farm
Bold Moss
Burtonwood Brewery
Yew Tree Farm
LUMBER LA
Bold Bsns Ctr
BOLD LA
BACK LA
Derby Farm
Burtonwood Com Prim Sch
TRAVERS' ENTRY
Phipps' Bridge
Burtonwood Ind Ctr
Haley Head Farm
Travers' Farm
Wheatacre Farm
Bold Ind Pk
Liby
Cemy
Rose Hill Farm
Burtonwood
Ashton's Farm
Northfield Riding Ctr
GORSEY LA
WA9
Moat House
Old Lodge Farm
Clay Lane Farm
Abbotsfield Farm
Lodge Wood
Park Cottage
Maypole Farm
Moat House Farm
WA5
Nursery
Hollin Wood
Joy Lane Farm
Ivy Cottage
Highfield
JOY LA
Finger Post
BURTONWOOD RD
Home Farm
LIMEKILN LA
WRIGHT'S LA
Limekiln Farm
Dog Kennel Plantation
M62
WA8
Booth's Wood
ORION BLVD
Old Hall Farm
Duck Wood
OMEGA BLVD
8
7
93
6
5
92
4
3
91
2
1
90
54
55
56
74
60

59
46

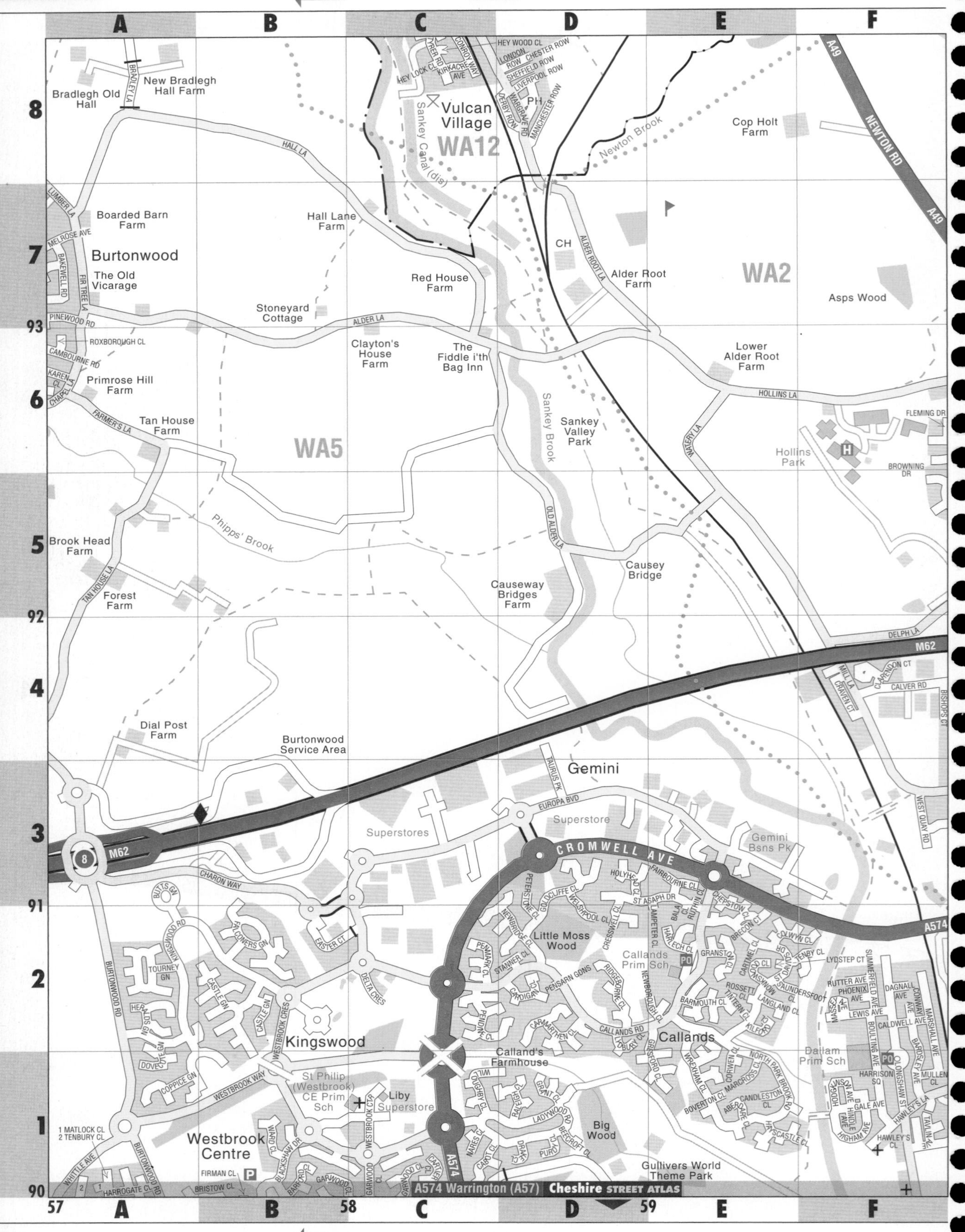
A
B
C
D
E
F
Bradlegh Old Hall
New Bradlegh Hall Farm
Vulcan Village
WA12
Sankey Canal (dis)
Newton Brook
Cop Holt Farm
NEWTON RD
A49
Boarded Barn Farm
Hall Lane Farm
CH
Burtonwood
The Old Vicarage
Red House Farm
Alder Root Farm
WA2
Asps Wood
Stoneyard Cottage
ALDER LA
Clayton's House Farm
The Fiddle i'th Bag Inn
Lower Alder Root Farm
HOLLINS LA
Primrose Hill Farm
Tan House Farm
Sankey Brook
Sankey Valley Park
WA5
Hollins Park
Phipps' Brook
Brook Head Farm
Causey Bridge
Causeway Bridges Farm
Forest Farm
DELPH LA
M62
Dial Post Farm
Burtonwood Service Area
Gemini
EUROPA BVD
Superstore
Superstores
Gemini Bsns Pk
CROMWELL AVE
CHARON WAY
Little Moss Wood
Callands Prim Sch
A574
Kingswood
Callands
Dallam Prim Sch
Calland's Farmhouse
St Philip (Westbrook) CE Prim Sch
Liby
Superstore
Big Wood
Westbrook Centre
Gullivers World Theme Park
1 MATLOCK CL
2 TENBURY CL
57
58
59
8
7
93
6
5
92
4
3
91
2
1
90

59

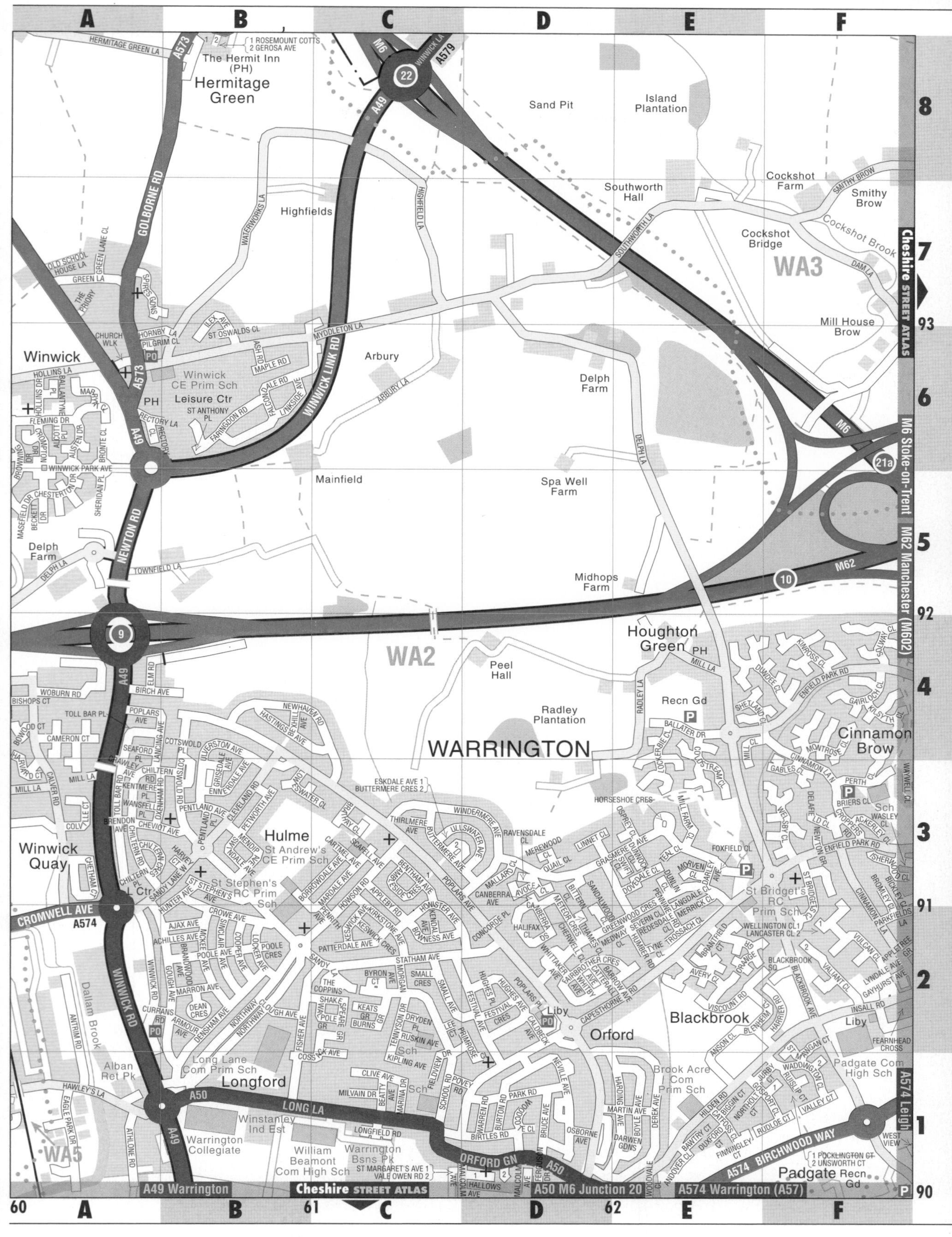

A B C D E F

8

7

Cheshire STREET ATLAS

93

6

5

92

4

91

3

2

1

90

60 A B 61 C D 62 E F

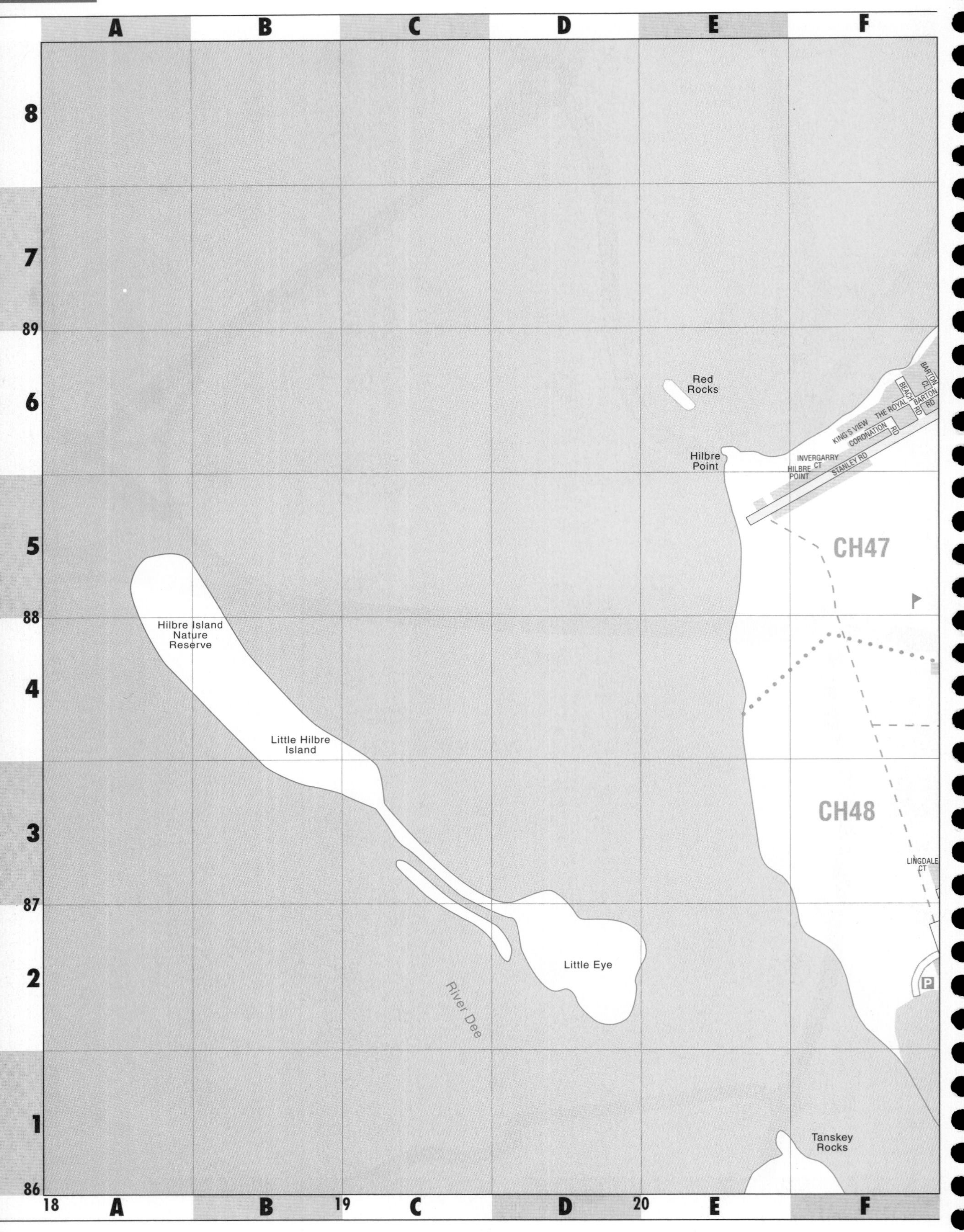

A   B   C   D   E   F

8

7

89

6

Red Rocks

Hilbre Point

CH47

5

88

4

Hilbre Island Nature Reserve

Little Hilbre Island

87

3

CH48

LINGDALE CT

Little Eye

2

River Dee

P

1

Tanskey Rocks

86

18 A   B 19 C   D 20 E   F

KING'S VIEW
CORONATION
INVERGARRY
HILBRE CT
POINT
STANLEY RD
THE ROYAL
BEACH
BARTON RD
BARTON RD

48
64

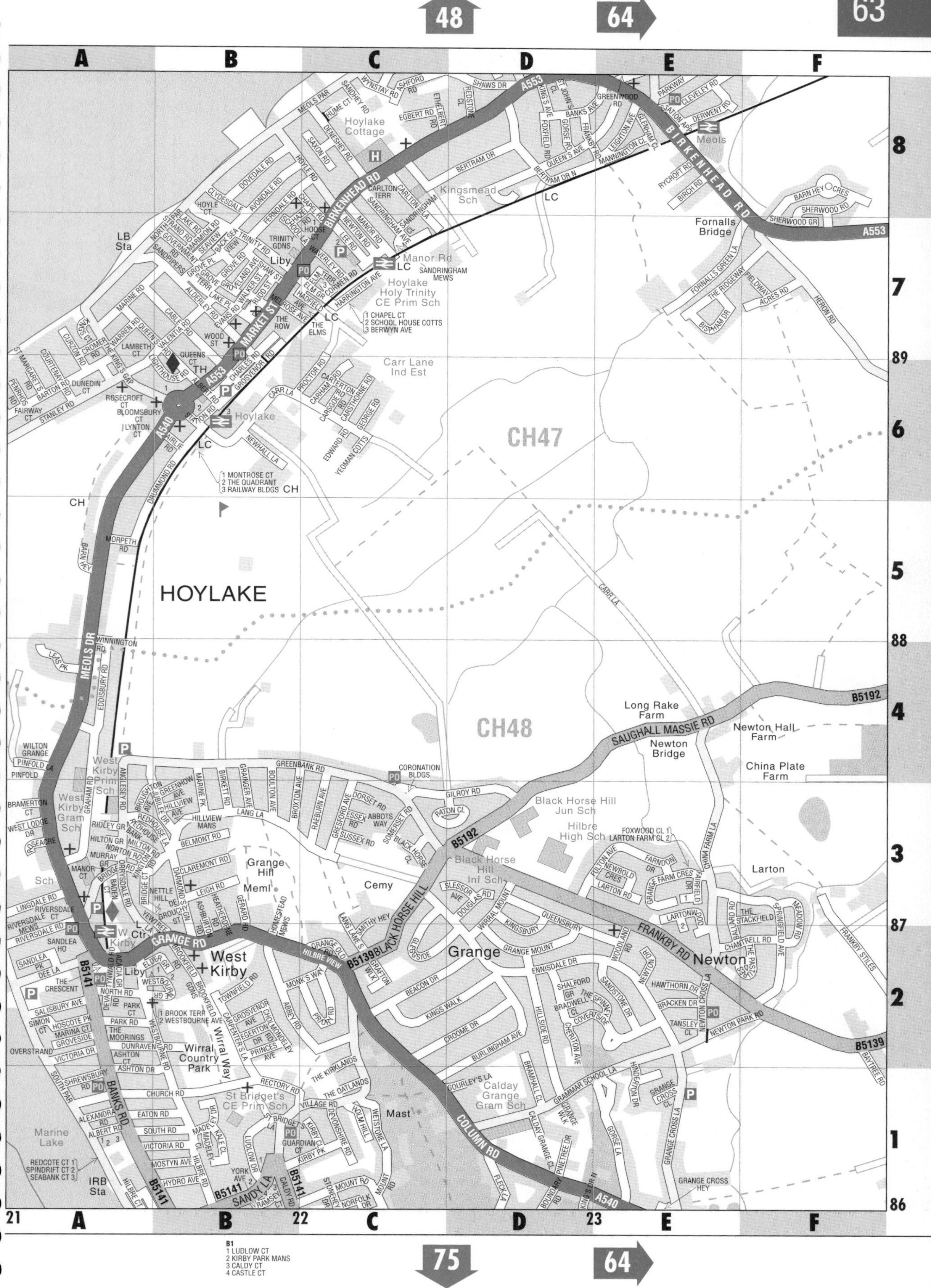

B1
1 LUDLOW CT
2 KIRBY PARK MANS
3 CALDY CT
4 CASTLE CT

75
64

63
49

A   B   C   D   E   F

8

7

CH47   CH46

Carr Farm

Works

B8
1 TAMWORTH GR
2 EARLSWOOD CL
3 LAPWORTH CL
4 WESTRY CL
5 HUNTINGDON CL
6 HUXLEY CL
7 HORNBEAM CL
8 MILLERS CL

Carr Hall Farm

A553 BIRKENHEAD RD

HOYLAKE RD

Foxfield Sch

Christ Church CE Prim Sch

UPTON RD

E7
1 ROSSLYN PK
2 BRISCOE AVE

89

Saughall Massie

Mast

M53   (2a)

A5027

MORETON RD

Overchurch Jun Sch
Overchurch Inf Sch

Upton

6

Saughall Hotel (PH)

D6
1 BLAKENHALL WAY
2 HAWKSMORE CL

The Heyes

SAUGHALL MASSIE RD   B5192

PO

Upton Hall Sch

5

Oldfield Manor Farm

Three Lanes End Farm

SAUGHALL MASSIE RD

THREE LANES END

CH49

Arrowe Brook

COWLEY CL 1
IFFLEY CL 2
BOTLEY CL 3
GLEN RONALD DR 4

UPTON BY PASS

GREASBY RD

B5139

A5027

88

B5192

C4
1 STOURPORT CL
2 MALMESBURY CL
3 FINCHDEAN CL
4 THRESHER AVE

The Planters

Brightwell CL

4

CH48

C3
1 DAYS MEADOW
2 REDCROFT

Greasby Brook

FRANKBY RD

Brookdale Prim Sch

The Wirral Bsns Pk   Factory

3

Manor House Farm

Royden Hall

Libry

Greasby

Playing Fields

Arrowe Brook Farm

Arrowe Bridge

87

Frankby

PO   The Nook

Our Lady of Pity RC Prim Sch

Greasby Copse

Gorse Covert

2

B5139

B5140   HILLBARK RD

Cemy

The Farmers Arms (PH)

Greasby Jun Sch

Arrowebrook Farm

Nicholson's Plantation

FB

1

BIRCH HEYS

B5140 MONTGOMERY HILL

Royden Park

HILLBARK RD

FB

86

24   A   B   25   C   D   26   E   F

63
76

50
66

F8
1 BERTHA GDNS
2 MIRIAM PL
3 VULCAN ST
4 GILLBROOK SQ
5 LANSDOWNE PL
6 LANSDOWNE CT

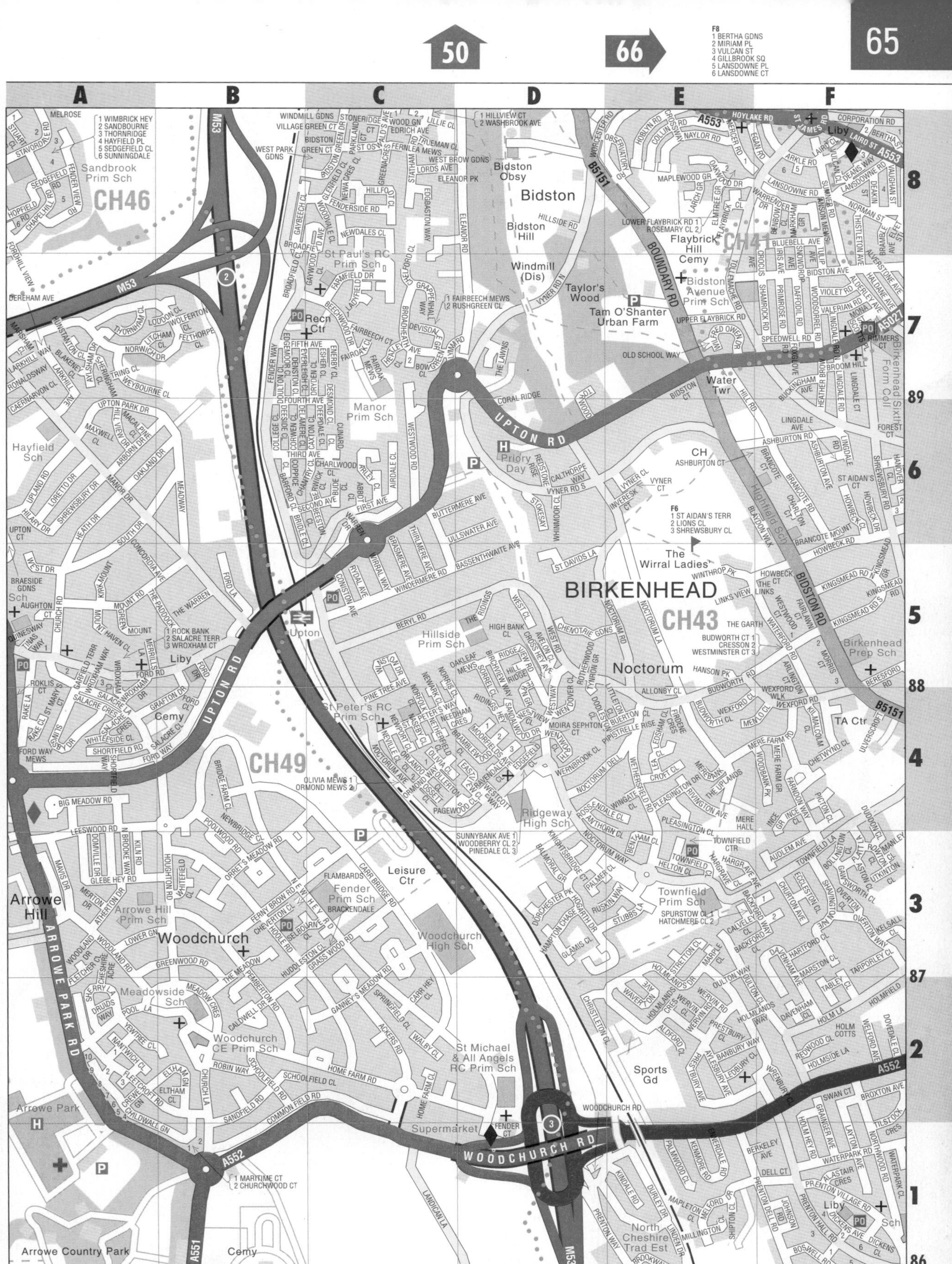

A2
1 ARCHERS WAY
2 GOODAKER'S MDW
3 TROUTBECK CL
4 CHESWOOD CT
5 BERKELEY CT
6 PARKLAND CT
7 ARROWE CT
8 BRENTWOOD CT
9 ARCHERS CT
10 GOODAKERS CT

77
66

F1
1 GOLDSMITH RD
2 GOLDSMITH WAY
3 ROTHESAY GDNS
4 CAITHNESS GDNS
5 MELROSE GDNS
6 BALMORAL GDNS

66
C5
1 RAVENSCROFT RD
2 KINGSTON LO
3 THE LINDENS
4 BRIMSTAGE ST
5 MOUNT GROVE PL
6 TURNER ST
7 CARNFORTH CL
8 WINDERMERE CT
9 GRASMERE CT
10 BUTTERMERE CT
11 CARTMEL CL
12 BELMONT GR
13 TOWN VIEW
65
C5
14 TOWN VIEW MEWS
15 GRANGE VIEW
16 CARLISLE MEWS
17 MIDLAND ST
18 WILKINSON ST
19 MARITIME PK
51
C5
20 QUARRYBANK ST
21 BARTON ST
22 CLAYTON PL
23 WEST ALFRED CT
D5
1 THE WOODLANDS
2 WHALLEY RD
3 RAWCLIFFE RD
4 WHETSTONE CT
5 HOLLYBANK CT
6 THE MOORINGS
D6
1 EXMOUTH WAY
2 CLWYD ST
3 EXMOUTH GDNS
4 VINCENT ST
5 HORATIO ST
6 ST JOHN'S PAVEMENT
7 MILTON PAVEMENT
8 COVENTRY ST
E6
1 CAMDEN PL
2 CLWYD ST
3 BURLINGTON ST
4 BANK ST
5 ALMA ST
6 HINSON ST
7 THOMAS ST
8 GRANGE RD E
9 BACK OLIVER ST
10 BOROUGH PL
11 CLIFTON CRES
12 GRANGE RD
13 ST WERBURGH'S SQ
14 PRINCESS PAVEMENT
15 KENDAL ST
16 WALTON ST
17 LORN CT
18 DOUGLAS ARC
A B C D E F
8 7 89 6 5 88 4 3 87 2 1 86
30 31 32
BIRKENHEAD
Birkenhead Park
Claughton
Oxton
Prenton
Devonshire Park
Tranmere
Mersey Park
Victoria Park
Egerton Park
Rock Ferry
Wallasey Dock
Vittoria Dock
Morpeth Dock
River Mersey
CH41
CH42
CH43
CH63
CORPORATION RD
CLEVELAND ST
LAIRD ST
PARK RD N
CONWAY ST
BOROUGH RD
NEW CHESTER RD
OLD CHESTER RD
CHURCH RD
BEBINGTON RD
STORETON RD
SINGLETON AVE
TALBOT RD
ARGYLE ST
CHESTER ST
TOWER RD
WATSON ST
EXMOUTH ST
WHETSTONE LA
BEDFORD AVE
BEDFORD RD
A5030 A553 A5027 A554 A5029 A552 A41 B5146 B5148 B5147 B514 B5151 B5172 B5136 B5149
Prenton Park (Tranmere Rovers FC)
Allot Gdns
Playing Field
Art Gal & Mus
Mkt Hall
Conway Park
Birkenhead Central
Hamilton Square
Heritage Ctr
Tower Quays
Queensway Tunnel
St Anselm's Coll
Ashton House
Prenton Prep Sch
Park High Sch
Oxton St Saviour's CE Prim Sch
Well Lane Prim Sch
Bedford Drive Prim Sch
Prenton High Sch
Cole Street Prim Sch
Marcus Street Workshops
Odyssey Ctr
D7
1 LAURENCE DEACON CT
2 CHARLES ST
3 BROOKLANDS
4 ROBERT ST
5 ST ANNE ST
6 ST ANNE'S CL
7 VICTORIA CT
8 KEIGHTLEY ST
9 McGILL CT
10 ST LAURENCE CL
11 ST LAURENCE DR
65
78
B5
1 GROSVENOR CT
2 ST MARKS CT
3 MATHER CT
4 CHARLESVILLE CT
5 BEAUMARIS CT
6 FOXES CT
D4
1 WHITFIELD CT
2 BEECH CT
3 DEWBERRY CL
4 SPRUCE CL
F1
1 WORDSWORTH AVE
2 KIPLING AVE
3 TENNYSON AVE
4 THE BEECHES
5 CASTLEBRIDGE CT
F2
1 ST PAUL'S VILLAS
2 MEADOW PK
3 MEADOWFIELD CL
4 DORIC ST
5 CORINTHIAN ST
6 CLYDE ST
F3
1 BEACONSFIELD CL
2 COBDEN AVE
3 COBDEN PL
4 GRENVILLE RD
5 GLADSTONE RD
6 LYDBROOK CL
7 STRATHLORNE CL
8 ROYAL STANDARD WAY

52

68
F8
7 BEDFORD WLK
8 HOPE WAY
9 BACK CATHARINE ST
10 ST BRIDE ST
11 BACK ST BRIDE ST
12 LITTLE ST BRIDE ST

F8
1 SOUTH HUNTER ST
2 BACK BEDFORD ST
3 SUGNALL ST
4 UPPER HOPE PL
5 PHILHARMONIC CT
6 BEDFORD CL

13 SIR HOWARD ST
14 SIR HOWARD WAY
15 SANDON ST
16 CAMBRIDGE CT
17 AGNES JONES HO
18 BLACKBURNE TERR
19 MOSSLAKE

79

68
F6
1 UPPER HILL ST
2 MAKEPEACE WLK
3 RADLEY'S CT
4 COMBERMERE ST
5 WINDSOR CT
6 THACKERAY CT
7 THACKERAY ST

F7
1 LITTLE CANNING ST
2 BACK LITTLE CANNING ST
3 BACK HUSKISSON ST
4 BACK EGERTON ST N
5 BACK EGERTON ST S
6 BIRLEY CT
7 MAHON CT
8 SELBORNE ST
9 ALEXANDRA TERR

10 PRINCES AVE
11 RIALTO CL
12 BEDFORD CT

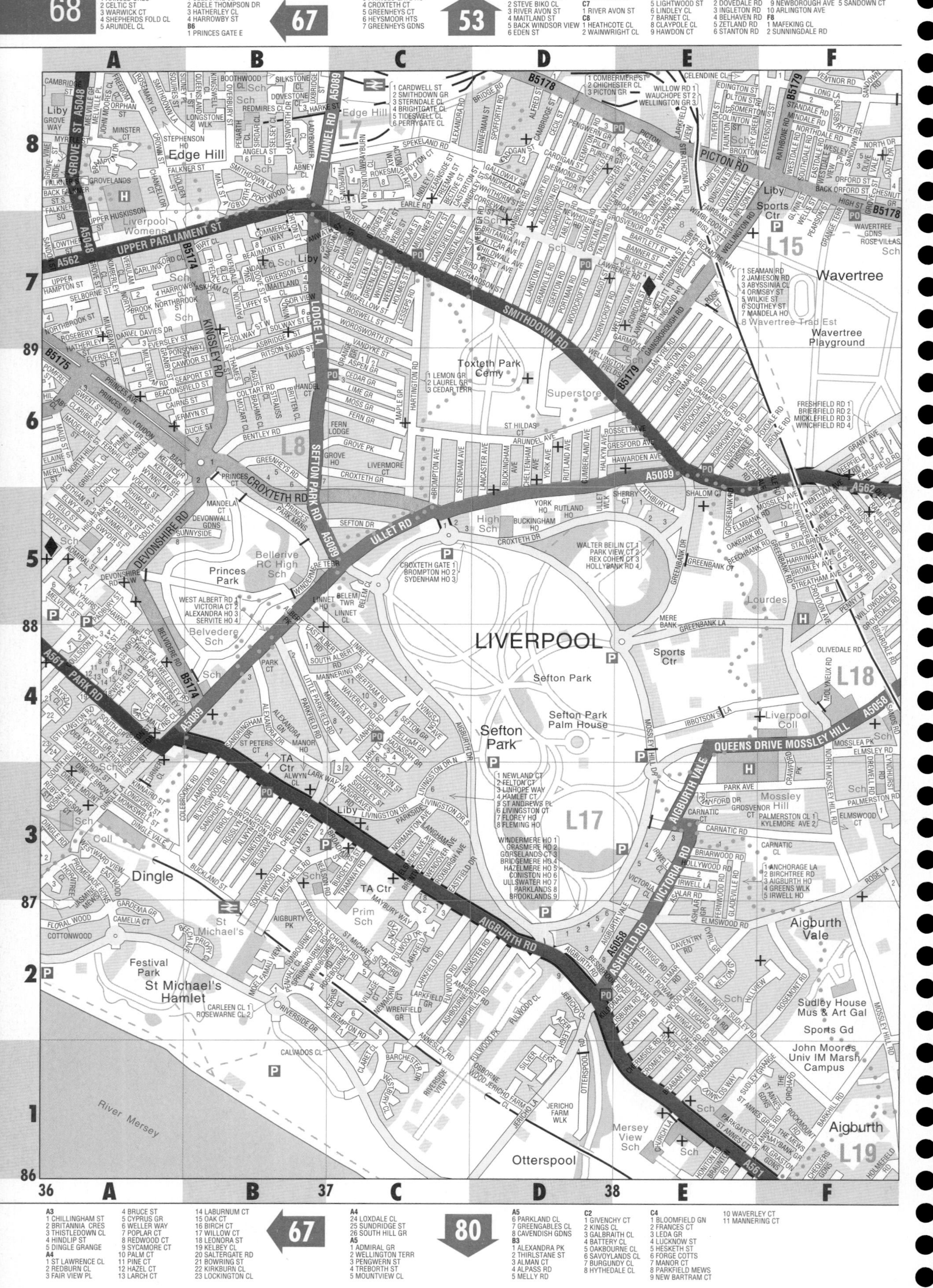
68
A6
1 ARNOLD CRES
2 CELTIC ST
3 WARWICK CT
4 SHEPHERDS FOLD CL
5 ARUNDEL CL
A7
1 SELBORNE CL
2 ADELE THOMPSON DR
3 HATHERLEY CL
4 HARROWBY ST
B6
1 PRINCES GATE E
67
2 PRINCES GATE W
3 PRINCES GATE HO
4 CROXTETH CT
5 GREENHEYS CT
6 HEYSMOOR HTS
7 GREENHEYS GDNS
53
B7
1 BUTTERMERE ST
2 STEVE BIKO CL
3 RIVER AVON ST
4 MAITLAND ST
5 BACK WINDSOR VIEW
6 EDEN ST
7 ST BERNARD'S CL
8 EMBLEDON ST
C7
1 RIVER AVON ST
C8
1 HEATHCOTE CL
2 WAINWRIGHT CL
3 LIGHTWOOD DR
4 WILFER CL
5 LIGHTWOOD ST
6 LINDLEY CL
7 BARNET CL
8 CLAYPOLE CL
9 HAWDON CT
F5
1 BLENHEIM RD
2 DOVEDALE RD
3 INGLETON RD
4 BELHAVEN RD
5 ZETLAND RD
6 STANTON RD
7 BECKENHAM AVE
8 NORBURY AVE
9 NEWBOROUGH AVE
10 ARLINGTON AVE
F8
1 MAFEKING CL
2 SUNNINGDALE RD
3 BACK SANDOWN LA
4 VICTORIA AVE
5 SANDOWN CT
A B C D E F
8 7 89 6 5 88 4 3 87 2 1 86
36 37 38
Edge Hill
Edge Hill
L7
L8
L15
L17
L18
L19
LIVERPOOL
Wavertree
Wavertree Playground
Toxteth Park Cemy
Superstore
Princes Park
Bellerive RC High Sch
Belvedere Sch
Sefton Park
Sefton Park Palm House
Sports Ctr
Lourdes
Liverpool Coll
Mossley Hill
Dingle
St Michael's
Festival Park
St Michael's Hamlet
River Mersey
Otterspool
Mersey View Sch
Jericho Farm Wlk
Aigburth Vale
Aigburth
Sudley House Mus & Art Gal
Sports Gd
John Moores Univ IM Marsh Campus
Liverpool Womens
UPPER PARLIAMENT ST
SMITHDOWN RD
LODGE LA
SEFTON PARK RD
ULLET RD
CROXTETH RD
DEVONSHIRE RD
KINGSLEY RD
PARK RD
AIGBURTH RD
QUEENS DRIVE MOSSLEY HILL
AIGBURTH VALE
ASHFIELD RD
VICTORIA RD
PICTON RD
TUNNEL RD
A
B
37
C
67
A3
1 CHILLINGHAM ST
2 BRITANNIA CRES
3 THISTLEDOWN CL
4 HINDLIP ST
5 DINGLE GRANGE
A4
1 ST LAWRENCE CL
2 REDBURN CL
3 FAIR VIEW PL
4 BRUCE ST
5 CYPRUS GR
6 WELLER WAY
7 POPLAR CT
8 REDWOOD CT
9 SYCAMORE CT
10 PALM CT
11 PINE CT
12 HAZEL CT
13 LARCH CT
14 LABURNUM CT
15 OAK CT
16 BIRCH CT
17 WILLOW CT
18 LEONORA ST
19 KELBEY CL
20 SALTERGATE RD
21 BOWRING ST
22 KIRKBURN CL
23 LOCKINGTON CL
A4
24 LOXDALE CL
25 SUNDRIDGE ST
26 SOUTH HILL GR
A5
1 ADMIRAL GR
2 WELLINGTON TERR
3 PENGWERN ST
4 TREBORTH ST
5 MOUNTVIEW CL
80
A5
6 PARKLAND CL
7 GREENGABLES CL
8 CAVENDISH GDNS
B3
1 ALEXANDRA PK
2 THIRLSTANE ST
3 ALMAN CT
4 ALPASS RD
5 MELLY RD
C2
1 GIVENCHY CT
2 KINGS CL
3 GALBRAITH CL
4 BATTERY CL
5 OAKBOURNE CL
6 SAVOYLANDS CL
7 BURGUNDY CL
8 HYTHEDALE CL
C4
1 BLOOMFIELD GN
2 FRANCES CT
3 LEDA GR
4 LUCKNOW ST
5 HESKETH ST
6 FORGE COTTS
7 MANOR CT
8 PARKFIELD MEWS
9 NEW BARTRAM CT
10 WAVERLEY CT
11 MANNERING CT

A5
1 CRAMOND AVE
2 DUDDINGSTON AVE
3 WESTGATE RD
4 CRONTON RD
5 SMITHDOWN PL
6 SUNSDALE RD

54
70

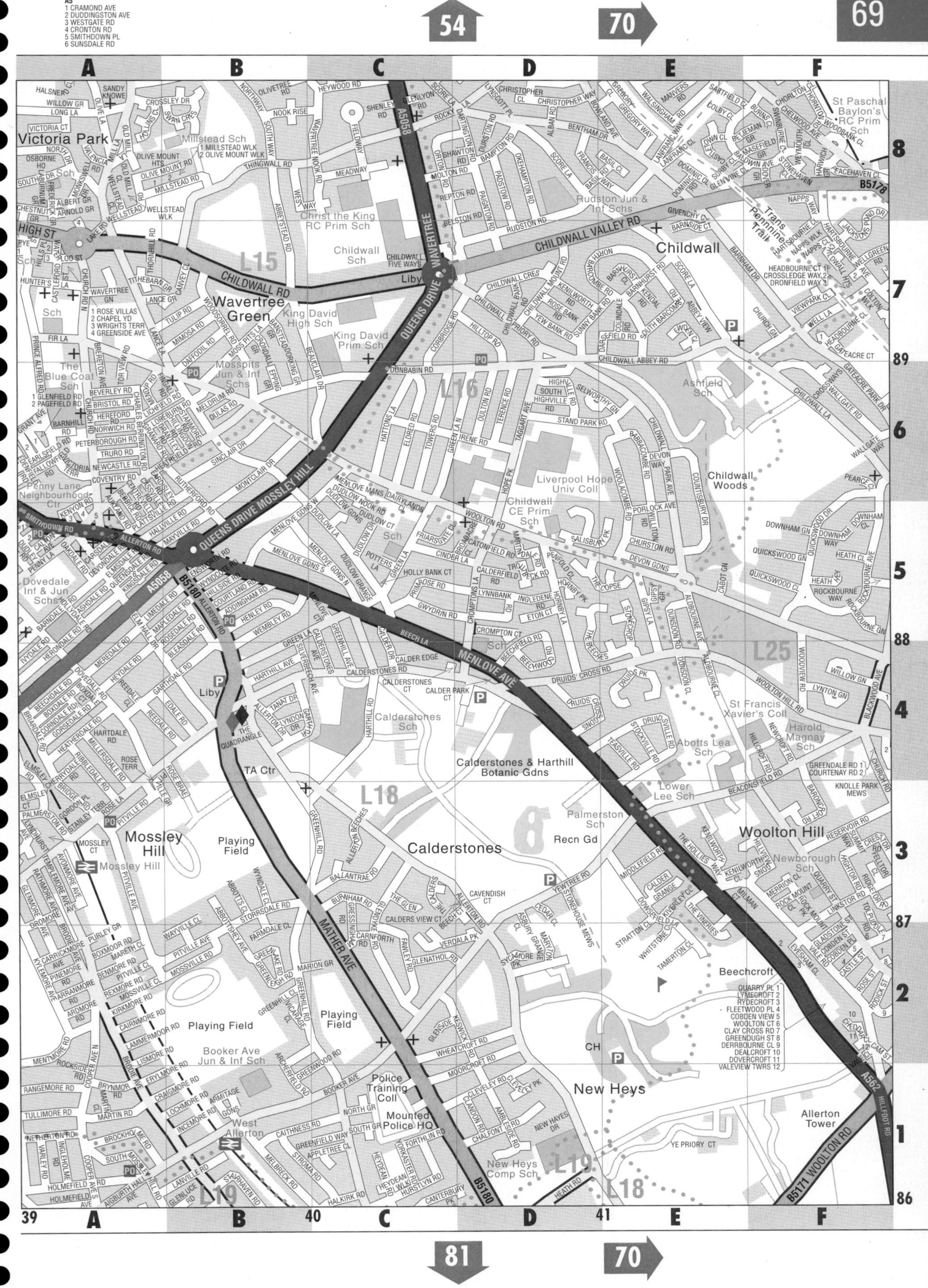

81
70

69
55

A B C D E F

8

L16

Sports Gd

St Paschal

1 MARCHWOOD WAY
2 LOWER FARM RD
3 WELLGREEN WLK
4 DRONFIELD WAY
5 HARTSBOURNE WLK

HUYTON-WITH-ROBY

L36

WHEAT HILL

7

1 CORNWOOD CL
2 KENTON CL
3 LOXWOOD CL
4 ROADWATER CL
5 MILDENHALL WAY
6 MURRAYFIELD WLK
7 MERIDEN RD
8 MARLBROOK RD
9 TRELAWNEY
10 MAYFORD CL

Wheathill Farm

Hope Sch

CH

L35

89

1 CRANWELL WLK
HARTOPP WLK

1 BARNSTREAM CL
2 MULLREA CL
3 CALLARD CL

CRANBERRY CL 1
CLOUDBERRY CL 2
BRAMBLEWOOD CL 3
MAPLEWOOD CL 4

Sewage Works

6

Our Lady of the Assumption RC Prim Sch

CHILDWALL VALLEY RD

L27

Wheathills Ind Est

PH

Belle Vale Sh Ctr

CHURCH COTTS 1
VICARAGE LAWN 2
GORSEWOOD CL 3

Superstore

B5171

NETHERLEY RD B5178

5

Dunlin Ct

Gateacre Com Comp Sch

Gateacre

BELLE VALE RD

Netherley

The Norman Pannell Sch

Sch

Kenwood Cl

Blue Jay Cl

Swallow Cl

88

Woolton Hill Rd

Grange Mews
York Cotts

CH

Stonechat Cl

Langshaw Lea

Lingfor

4

Trans Pennine Trail

ST STEPHENS CT

LIVERPOOL

1 RIBBLE HO
2 DEE HO
3 WEAVER HO
4 DEE CT
5 WEAVER CT

Cross Farm Prim Sch

SHERFORD CL 1
BEESANDS CL 2
WOODLANDS SQ 3
ULVERSTON LAWN 4
SELSIDE WLK 5
DOWNLANDS RD 6
CANOVA CL 7
ROOKLEY CL 8

TOTLAND

Woodlands

3

Woolton Park

L25

Woolton Jun & Inf Sch

Sewage Works

North End

Gerrard's Farm

87

Bishop Martin CE Prim Sch

Superstore

1 KINGHAM CL
2 KINGHAM MEWS

Foxhill House

2

Superstore

Liby

Woolton

Watergate Sch

1 GOLDFINCH CL
2 GOLDCREST MEWS
3 GREENFINCH CL
4 SPARROWHAWK CL
5 GERMANDER CL
6 SANDPIPER GR

Halewood Farm House

L26

1 BLACKBERRY GR 1
MAGNOLIA GR 2
HONEYSUCKLE CL 3
REDWING WAY 4
WILLOWHERB CL 5

1

Woolton Manor

St Julie's RC High Sch

1 FROME WAY
2 LANCING WAY
3 LANCING RD
4 HUNTSMAN CL

Mackets Prim Sch

Holy Family RC Prim Sch

86

B5171

A562

42 A B 43 C D 44 E F

56
72

A
B
C
D
E
F
Interchange Motorway Est
Warehouse
Windy Arbor
Hotel
Round Clump
Big Water
Cvn Pk
Halsnead Park
M62
SHAW ENTRY
Old Halsnead
1 CONEY LA
2 BOUNDARY WLK
3 CARNABY CL
4 WARKWORTH CL
L36
Works
Huyton Bsns Pk
TARBOCK RD
CRONTON RD
A5080
A5300
M57
PH
COPPICE LA
6
FOX'S BANK LA
PENNY LA
DACRE'S BRIDGE LA
CRONTON RD
Higher Park Farm
A5080
Ochre Brook
OX LA
WHITEFIELD LA
Yew Tree Farm
Yew Tree Farm
White House Farm
PRESCOT RD
Mill Bridge
Tarbock Hall
L35
Water Lane Farm
Four Oaks
Wayside Farm
WATER LA
Mill Bridge Farm
Water Lane Bridge
KNOWSLEY EXPRESSWAY
Dog Clog Brook
ALDER LA
Dog Clog Bridge
1 EGREMONT LAWN
2 EGREMONT CL
3 KIRKBRIDE WLK
4 KIRKBRIDE LAWN
5 HEALY CL
6 WOODLANDS SQ
7 SELSIDE LAWN
8 APPLEBY WLK
9 APPLEBY LAWN
Dale Farm
Brewery Farm
Marklands Farm
STOCKSWELL RD
Stockswell Farm
Tarbock Green
10 HEYSHAM LAWN
11 MARDALE LAWN
12 MARDALE WLK
13 MARDALE CL
14 LAKESIDE LAWN
15 RIDSDALE LAWN
16 HONISTER WLK
17 SCAFELL LAWN
Brick Wall Inn (PH)
NETHERLEY RD
WA8
Georgeson's Farm
L27
Netherley Brook
Dye House Farm
Green's Bridge Farm
Barn Hey Farm
Foxhill Farm
L26
GREENSBRIDGE LA
Cross Hillocks Farm
B5178
Plumptons Farm
Bridgefield Forum (L Ctr)
Green's Bridge Plantation
1 AMBASSADOR DR
2 ABINGDON GR
Ditton Brook
GARNETTS LA
Spring Farm
Springfield Farm
A5300
PH
Halewood CE Prim Sch
8
7
89
6
5
88
4
3
87
2
1
86
45
46
47

83
72

71
57

A B C D E F
8
7
89
6
5
88
4
3
87
2
1
86
48 49 50
Mill Wood
L35
M62
A57
M62
WARRINGTON RD A57
WATKINSON WAY A557
Sandhill Farm
Higher Shaw Farm
Rough Head
Fox's Bank Brook
Cronton Wood
Visitor Ctr
Pex Hill
Norland's House
Nicolford Hall
Hotel
Town End
Penny Lane Farm
Holy Family RC Prim Sch
Cronton CE Prim Sch
A5080
Nursery
Mast
Cronton Farm
CRONTON RD
CRONTON LA
The Globe (PH)
Smaller Gorse Farm
Caxton Lodge
Cronton
Widnes & Runcorn Coll
Upton Rocks
WA8
Rose Farm
Holly Farm
Upton
Stock's Well House
All Saints Upton CE Prim Sch
St Basil's RC Prim Sch
Cemy
WIDNES
Rugby Football Ground
Ball o' Ditton
Saints Peter & Paul RC High Sch
Hough Green
B5178
The Bankfield Sch
Ditton CE Prim Sch
LIVERPOOL RD
Ditton Prim Sch
Ashley Sch
Chestnut Lodge Spl Sch
CH
PH

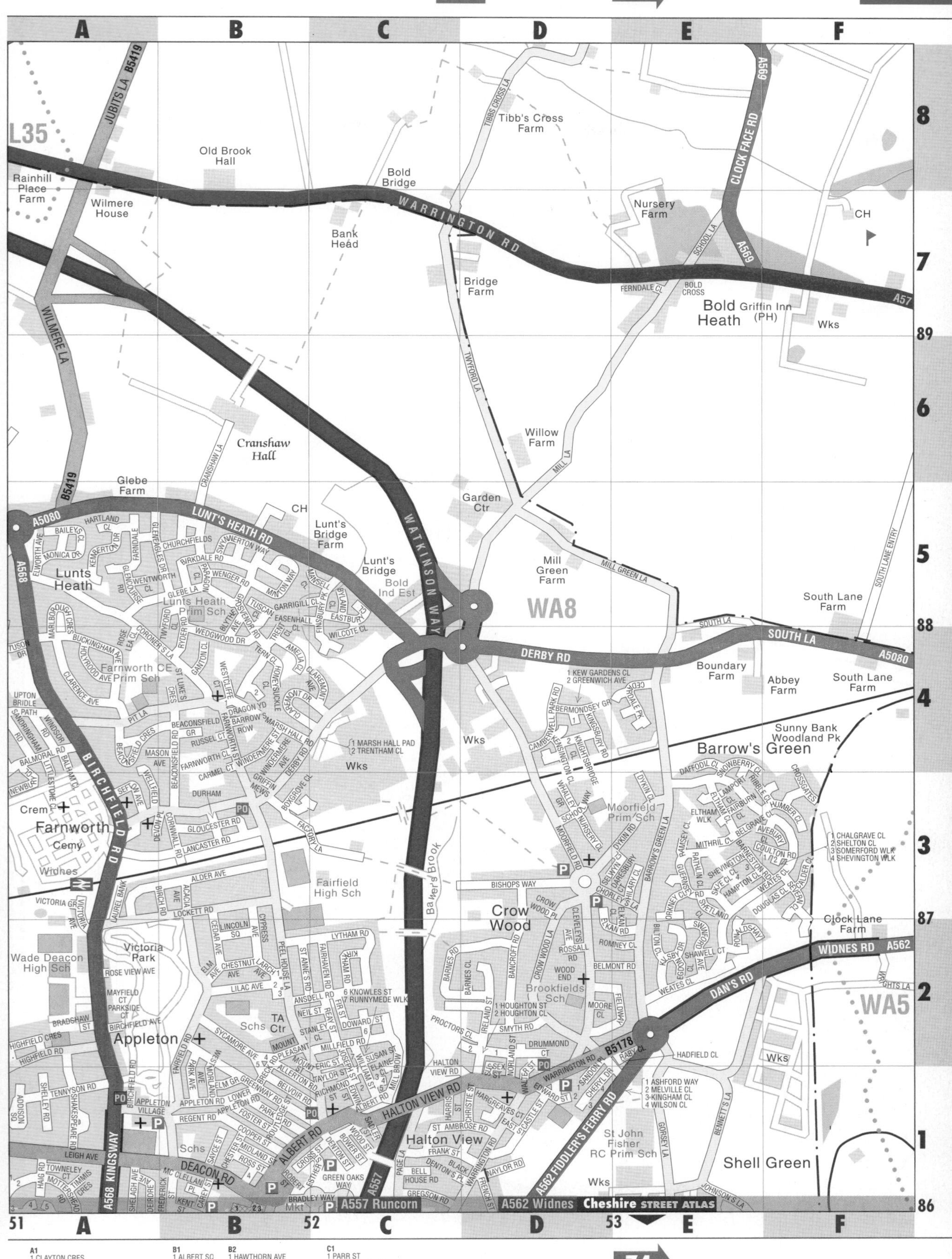

A1
1 CLAYTON CRES
2 HENDERSON RD
3 SQUIRES AVE
4 BRUNNER RD
5 MOND RD

B1
1 ALBERT SQ
2 ALBERT RD
3 BROOK ST
4 SAXON TERR

B2
1 HAWTHORN AVE
2 WILLOW AVE
3 LIME AVE
4 PINE AVE
5 MAPLE AVE

C1
1 PARR ST
2 RUNNYMEDE CT
3 CLIFFE ST
4 HENRY ST
5 RUNNYMEDE GDNS

A B C D E F

8 Eccles Plantation Finch's Plantation Lingley Mere
South Park Plantation LINGLEY GREEN AVE L Ctr
Park Farm Whittle Brook Great Sankey High Sch
Barrow Hall Lane Com Prim Sch Brow Farm

7 Bargyloo Lingley Green
WARRINGTON RD Dawson House
89 A57

6 Hayfield Farm SANDY LA The Trigger Pond (PH) Liverpool Rd
Greenside Farm Laburnum Farm LIVERPOOL RD
Sandy Lane Farm Park Road Com Prim Sch
Sankey For Penketh

5 WA8 WARRINGTON Sch Penketh High Sch

88 Camp (dis) A5080 WA5 Penketh Com Prim Sch Recn Gd

4 SOUTH LA Four Top'd Oak Brook Farm Penketh
FARNWORTH RD A5080 WARRINGTON RD A562

3 Fowl Farm Doe Green St Vincent's RC Prim Sch
MOWCROFT LA WIDNES RD Penketh South Com Prim Sch

87 Cuerdley Cross A562 Cross Lane Farm Cottages CH
Trans Penine Trail

2 Marsh End Farm River Mersey
Swing Bridge Ferry Inn (PH) Fiddler's Ferry Riverside Trad Est WA5

1 Power Station Fiddler's Ferry St Helens Canal (disused) WA4

86
54 55 56

73

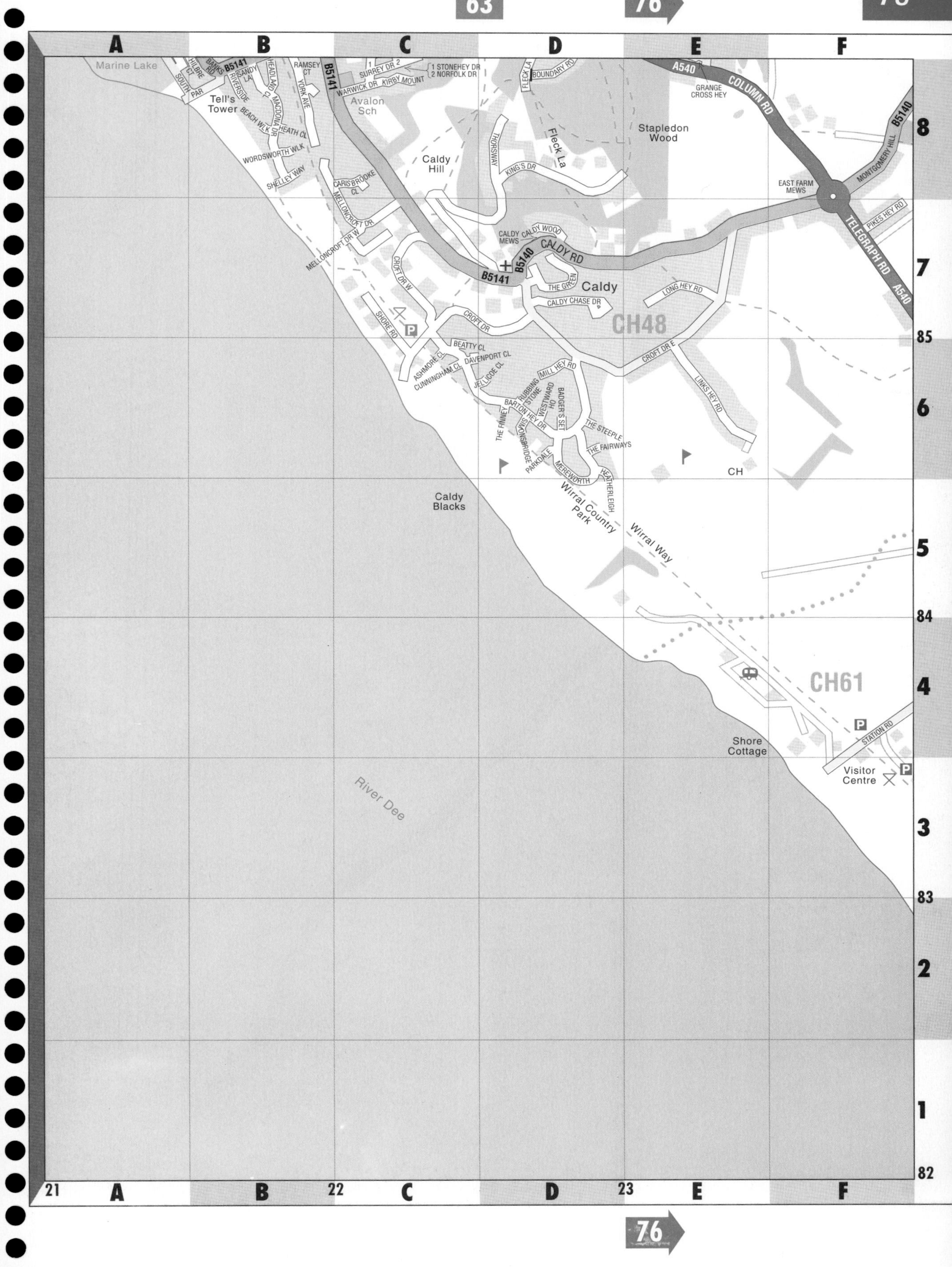
Marine Lake
Tell's Tower
Avalon Sch
Caldy Hill
Fleck La
Stapledon Wood
Caldy
CH48
CH
Caldy Blacks
Wirral Country Park
Wirral Way
River Dee
CH61
Shore Cottage
Visitor Centre
A540
COLUMN RD
TELEGRAPH RD
B5140
B5141
CALDY RD
CROFT DR
CROFT DR E
CROFT DR W
MELLONCROFT DR
MELLONCROFT DR W
LONG HEY RD
LINKS HEY RD
CALDY CHASE DR
THE GREEN
STATION RD
PIKES HEY RD
MONTGOMERY HILL
EAST FARM MEWS
GRANGE CROSS HEY
KING'S DR
THORSWAY
BOUNDARY RD
FLECK LA
WARWICK DR
KIRBY MOUNT
SURREY DR
1 STONEHEY DR
2 NORFOLK DR
RAMSEY CT
YORK AVE
HEATH CL
MACDONA DR
HEADLAND CL
SANDY LA
RIVERSIDE
BANKS RD
HILBRE CT
SOUTH PAR
BEACH WLK
WORDSWORTH WLK
SHELLEY WAY
CARISBROOKE CL
SHORE RD
BEATTY CL
DAVENPORT CL
ASHMORE CL
CUNNINGHAM CL
JELLICOE CL
MILL HEY RD
RUBBING STONE
WESTWARD HO
BADGER'S SET
BARTON HEY DR
THE FINNEY
STONEBRIDGE
PARKDALE
MEREWORTH
HEATHERLEIGH
THE STEEPLE
THE FAIRWAYS
CALDY MEWS
CALDY WOOD
A B C D E F
8 7 6 5 4 3 2 1
85 84 83 82
21 22 23

A B C D E F

8

Royden Park
Hill Bark
Visitor Ctr
Irby Hill
Redstones Farm
ARROWE BROOK LA
UMBROLA LA
CH49
Arrowe Country Park

CH48
Thurstaston Common
Irby Hill Farm
Arrowe Brook
Neilson's Plantations

7
Thurstaston Hill
SANDY LA
MILL HILL RD
THORSTONE DR
NORTON DR
LESTER DR
HILLVIEW RD
LEACH WAY
SANDY LA
FROST DR
HOWBECK DR
PURBECK RD
EASTLEIGH
CALNE CL
HEATHBANK AVE
FROME CL
WIMBORNE WAY
ISLIP CL
SUMMERWOOD
COPSE CR
BROOK MEADOW
DENNING DR
DEVIZES DR
LEISTON CL
COMBRE RD
Limbo Lane Plantation

85
A540
FAR MEADOW LA
COOMBE AVE
COTSWOLDS
SEAVIEW AVE
VERNON DR
HAZEL GR
LABURNUM GR
GLENWOOD DR
Irby Prim Sch
WOODSIDE RD
LYNNWOOD DR
THINGWALL RD
ELM RD
MENLO AVE
MAYEW RD
BRIAN AVE
WALSTON CL
DALEY CL
BARKER RD
WALLEY LA
DALE CL

6
DAWPOOL COTTS
SCHOOL LA
THURSTASTON RD
Thurstaston Dawpool CE Prim Sch
MARTIN CL
LOOMSWAY
Irby
SEAVIEW LA
THE ROSERY
ROSS HEY DR
Village Ct
MANOR RD
Harrock Wood
HARROCK WOODS CL
LEAFIELD CL
DALESIDE CL
KING'S DR
EXMOOR DR
CORNELIUS DR
THE CRESCENT
BENTLEY RD
NORWSHERA AVE
SANDRIDGE RD
RIDGEMERE RD
RIDGEFIELD RD

Dawpool
PH
LYNDHURST RD
GREENHEYS RD
SOUTH DR
DAMESH RD
Liby
MANOR CT

5
Thurstaston
DAWPOOL FARM
CHURCH LA
Rectory
CH61
Irby Hall
PENRHYD RD
BACKFORD CL
DRAYTON CL
WOODLANDS RD
PORTO HEY RD
SOUTH HEY RD
TOWNSHEND AVE
GRANTHAM CL
SMALLRIDGE CL
KENILWORTH DR
ARUNDEL DR
CHATSWORTH RD
RIDGEWOOD DR
WOODEND
Pensby

84
STATION RD
Thurstaston Hall
SUSSEX CL
SOMERSET RD
CHEDDON
DASSEX DEVON DR
BEESTON DR
HADDON DR

4
GREENWAY
DEVONSHIRE RD
WOODFIELD RD
BARLEYFIELD RD
BRIDGENORTH RD
FISHERS LA
HOLMES WAY
NICHOLLS DR
DERWENT DR
RUSLAND RD
KENTMERE DR
LANGDALE AVE
RYDAL CL
ASHLEA RD
ROSEMEAD AVE
Pensby High Sch for Boys
Pensby Park Prim Sch
COLUMBUS DR
PO
NELSON DR
GRENVILLE CL
PORTAL MEWS
PORTAL RD
GIBSON
GREENBANK DR
Pensby Schs

3
▲
The Dungeon
Pensby High Sch for Girls
Cemy
KYLEMORE CL
HANNAH CL
ALEXANDER DR
Ladymount RC Prim Sch
KYLEMORE WAY
1 BENNETT WLK
2 CHESHIRE WAY
LARDHWOOD CL
FAIRVIEW WAY
STEWART AVE
HAWTHORN DR
WOODCROFT RD
ASHCROFT
HILLFIELD RD
BERWYN DR

83
Oldfield Farm
MERE LA
FairHall CL
PENDALL CL
QUARRY RD
WOODCROFT RD
HAMMOND WAY
HILL LANGTON DR
CH60
PINE WAY
BIRCHMERE
BRILLERNE GR
QUARRY CL
ELMWOOD CL
HILLINGDON AVE

2
Wirral Country Park
OLDFIELD COTTS
HALYARD HO
OLDFIELD DR
OLDFIELD LA
Cleaver Heath
THE RIDGE
STRATHALLAN CL
OLDFIELD CL
QUARRY CT
Heswall Prep Sch
TOWER RD
QUARRY RD E
ERICA CL
SMALLWOODS MEWS
BRACKENDALE
GRANGE HIGHFIELD CL
GRANGE CR
FLORENCE AVE

OLDFIELD GDNS
DALE
OLDFIELD RD
OLDFIELD WAY
LAUREL BANKS
CIRCULAR DR
QUAKER LA
Poll Hill

1
PIPER'S LA
FERNS CL
BROOMFIELD CL
HEATHSIDE
Dale Farm
WARREN CL
HATTON CL
The Dales
THURSTASTON RD
WOODCOT
HEATH DR
ROCK DALE
POLL HILL RD
RYE DALE
GRANGE MOUNT
1 HIGHFIELDS
2 DALE CT

82
River Dee
BROAD LA
A540

78

A B C D E F

Arrowe Park
CH
P
Crem
Cemy
A551
ARROWE PARK RD
Home Farm
CH49
LANDICAN LA
Landican
North Cheshire Trad Est
BROOK WAY
BADGER WAY
PARKVALE AVE
PRENTON WAY
M53
BYRON CL
GARRICK RD
PRENTON DELL RD
Old Hall Farm
LANDICAN RD
LANDICAN LA
CH43
RICHMOND WAY
B5138
THINGWALL RD E
HAZELDENE WAY
TORRINGTON DR
TORRINGTON GDNS
The Farm
Cow Hey Covert
LANDICAN LA
Thingwall Prim Sch
HEYWOOD CL
HEYWOOD BVD
Stanley Sch
HAZELDENE AVE
BEAUMARIS DR
BEVERLEY GDNS
MILL RD
MILL YARD
HOWARDS RD
CLEMERE DR
MILTON GN
Cvn Pk
THINGWALL DR
AMBLESIDE CL
BERWYN AVE
PENRHYN AVE
THE FOXES
QUARRY LA
NURSE RD
SPARKS LA
TURMAR AVE
THE LEAS
PH
Stanley Wood
ANDERSON CL
WHALEY LA
HEATHFIELD HOUSE
PO
Liby
LOWER THINGWALL LA
BENTY FARM GR
AINSDALE CL
WIMBOURNE AVE
SEVEN ACRES LA
REGENTS CL
AXHOLME RD
BARNSDALE AVE
Murrayfield
H
Prenton Brook
CORNELIUS DR
LYNDHURST CL
AXHOLME CL
Thingwall
ANTONS RD
PENSBY CL
CESTRIAN DR
GWENDOLINE CL
CH61
NORTHRIDGE RD
HESWALL MOUNT
RYLAND PK
Cross Hill
HOLMWOOD AVE
Mast
RIDGEMERE RD
RIDGEWOOD DR
SOUTHRIDGE RD
HOLMWOOD DR
STATION RD
PRIVATE DR
OVERDALE AVE
SUNNINGDALE DR
DEVEN CL
THORNCROFT DR
MARLFIELD LA
FISHERS LA
BEECH AVE
LOW WOOD GR
WOODLANDS DR
DALE END RD
New Hay Covert
GILLS LA
LAURELHURST AVE
1 SHEARMAN CL
2 SHEARMAN RD
3 CHRISTOPHERS CL
PENSBY RD
FENDER WAY
Tree Tops
ELM CL
MARKSWAY
BARNSTON RD
STORETON LA
Liby
OAKS LA
ROSEMEAD AVE
BELMONT DR
Ley Farm
ASHLEA RD
PH
Beech Farm
Bank Farm
Barnston
GREENBANK DR
HILLFIELD DR
KINGSLEY CL
LYNDHURST AVE
Manor Farm
KYLEMORE DR
PINE VIEW DR
Carnsdale Farm
BERWYN DR
NAPPS WAY
Greenhayes Cottages
IRBY RD
RAVENSWOOD RD
DOWNHAM RD N
OAKLANDS TERR
OAKLANDS DR
CH63
RABY CT
MARANATHA BGLWS
Heswall Prim Sch
Whitehouse Farm
Fairfield
ROSEBRAE CT
HEATHER RD
BENT WAY
WHITFIELD LA
HESWALL
CH60
The Brooklet
A5137
SANDY LA
SHREWSBURY RD
BRUNSTATH CL
WHITEHOUSE LA
HESKETH DR
DOWNHAM RD S
BROOKLET RD
BARCOMBE RD
B5138
CONSTANTINE AVE
GORSEHILL RD
FIELDWAY
MEADOWCROFT
BRIMSTAGE RD
MANOR RD
MILTON CRES
Whitfield Common
MILNER RD
A551
PEAR TREE CL
NORTHWAY
Dunster House
BRIARY CL
BUFFS LA
PARK RD
PINE RD
MAPLE TREE GR
ACRE LA
A5137
EPPING CT
FOREST RD

8 7 85 6 5 84 4 3 83 2 1 82

27 A B 28 C D 29 E F

86
78

A B C D E F

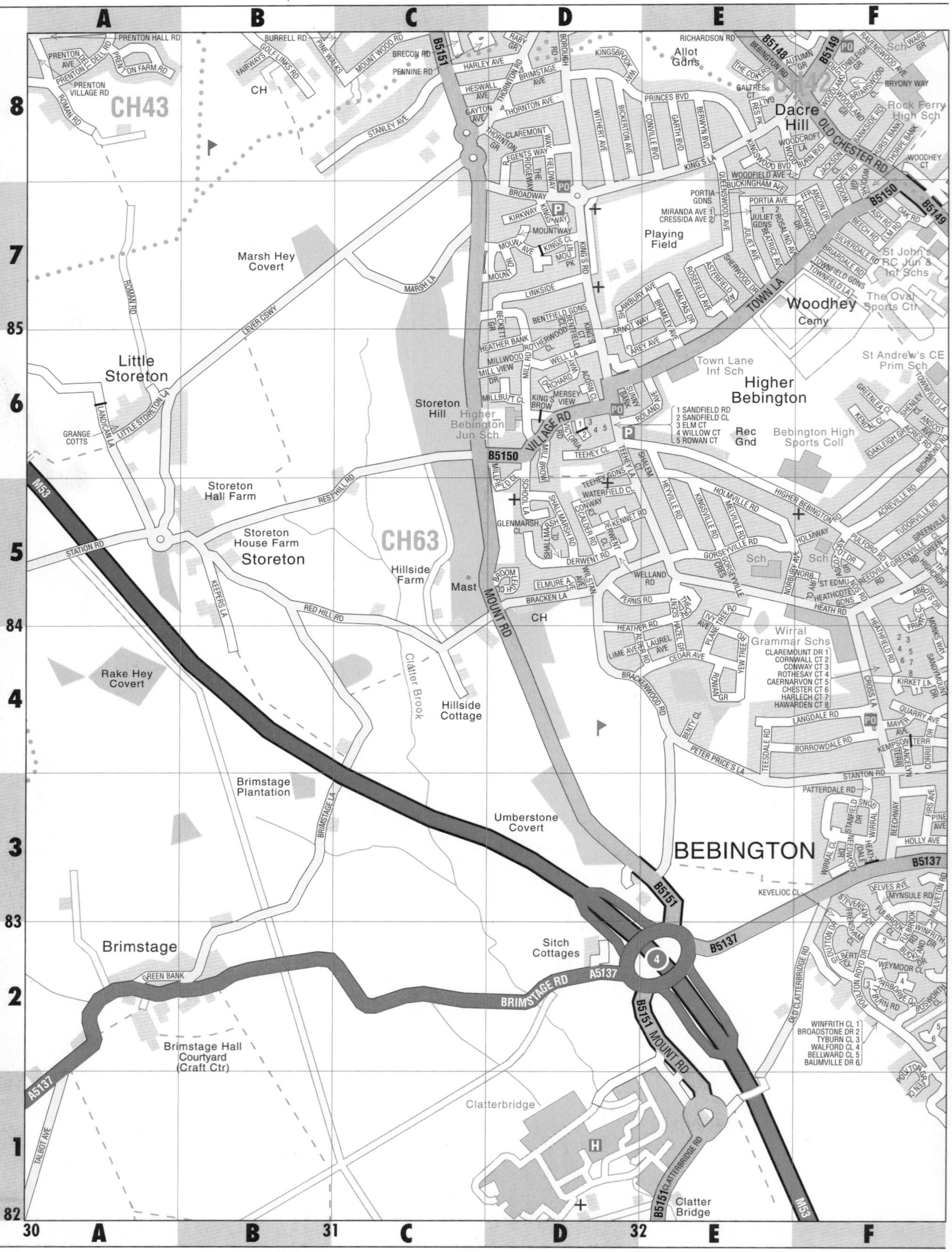

8

7

85

6

5

84

4

3

83

2

83

1

82

30 31 32

CH43

CH63

CH42

Prenton Hall Rd
Prenton Ave
Prenton Dell Rd
On Farm Rd
Prenton Village Rd
Roman Rd
Prenton Village Rd

Burrell Rd
Golf Links Rd
Fairways
Pine Walks
Mount Wood Rd
Brecon Rd
Pennine Rd
CH

Marsh Hey Covert

Stanley Ave
Lever Cswy
Marsh La

Little Storeton
Little Storeton La
Landican La
Grange Cotts
Storeton Hall Farm
Keepers La
Rest Hill Rd
Red Hill Rd

Storeton
Storeton House Farm
Station Rd

Hillside Farm
Mast
CH
Clatter Brook
Hillside Cottage

Rake Hey Covert

Brimstage Plantation
Brimstage La

Umberstone Covert

Brimstage
Green Bank
Talbot Ave
A5137
Brimstage Hall Courtyard (Craft Ctr)

Brimstage Rd
A5137

Sitch Cottages

Clatterbridge
H
Old Clatterbridge Rd
Clatterbridge Rd
Clatter Bridge
B5151

Raby Gr
Borough Rd
Kingsbrook
Richardson Rd
Allot Gdns
The Cokes
Galtres
Autumn
Beaconswood Gr
Seaward Gr
Bryony Way
Rock Ferry High Sch
Woodhey Ct
Old Chester Rd
B5148
B5149
B5149
B5150
B5150

Heswall Ave
Gayton Ave
Thornton Ave
Harley Ave
Brimstage Ave
Harley Ave
Withens La
Princes Bvd
Berwyn Ave
Bickerton Ave
Conville Bvd
Garth Bvd
King's La
Buckingham Ave
Portia Gdns
Miranda Ave
Cressida Ave
Juliet Gdns
Portia Ave
Juliet Ave
Beatrice Ave
Rosalind Ave

Playing Field

Claremont Way
The Ridgeway
Broadway
Kirkwall
Mountway
Kings Rd
Kings Pk
Mount La
Linkside
Bentfield Gdns
Beckett Gr
Heather Bank
Millwood
Mill View Dr
Millwood
Millbut Cl
Storeton Hill
Higher Bebington Jun Sch
Kings Brow
Mersey View
Richard
King's Brow
Village Rd
B5150
School La
Small Marsh Rd
Glenmarsh
Derwent Rd
Broom Ho
Elmure Ave
Bracken La
Teehey Cl
Teehey Gdns
Conway
Calder Dr
Kennet Rd
Waterfield Cl
Shelbourne Rd
Bishopton Cl
Rowson
Welland Rd
Ferns Rd

Teehey La
Sunny Rd
Roland
Heyville Rd
Holmville Rd
Melville Rd
Kingsville Rd
Gorseyville Cres
Higher Bebington Rd
Holmaway
Norbreck
Norbury Ave
St Edmu
Sch
Sch
Acreville Rd
Greenville Rd
Redville Rd
Greenville
Tudorville Rd
Richmond
Oakdale
Greenlea Cl
Kenwyn
Townfield La
Arrowcroft
Oakleigh Gr
Graceley Rd

Shrewsbury Rd
Sherwood Dr
Town La
Townfield Gdns
Townfield La
Silverdale Rd
Briardale Rd
Beech Rd
Oak Rd

Woodhey
Cemy
Higher Bebington
1 Sandfield Rd
2 Sandfield Cl
3 Elm Ct
4 Willow Ct
5 Rowan Ct
Rec Gnd
Bebington High Sports Coll
St Andrew's CE Prim Sch

St John's RC Jun & Inf Schs
The Oval Sports Ctr

Dacre Hill
Woodcroft La
Kingswood Bvd
Jackson
Hope Farm Rd
Thorpe Bank

Heather Rd
Lime Ave
Laurel Ave
Cedar Ave
Plane Tree Rd
Hazel Ave
Yew Tree Ave
Brackenwood Rd
Beaty Cl
Peter Price's La
Langdale Rd
Teesdale Rd
Borrowdale Rd
Patterdale Rd
Stanton Rd
Mount Rd

Claremount Dr 1
Cornwall Ct 2
Conway Ct 3
Rothesay Ct 4
Caernarvon Ct 5
Chester Ct 6
Harlech Ct 7
Hawarden Ct 8
Wirral Grammar Schs

Abbey
Kirket La
Quarry Ave
Mayer Ct
Kempson Corrie Terr

BEBINGTON
B5137
B5151
Kevelioc Cl
B5137
Delves Ave
Mynsule Rd
Stevenson Dr
Broad Winfrith
Dutton La
Gilbert
Weymoor Cl
Harborne Dr
Barn Rd
Roft

4

Winfrith Cl 1
Broadstone Dr 2
Tyburn Cl 3
Walford Cl 4
Bellward Cl 5
Baumville Dr 6

M53
Mount Rd
B5151

Woodhey
Higher Bebington

67
80

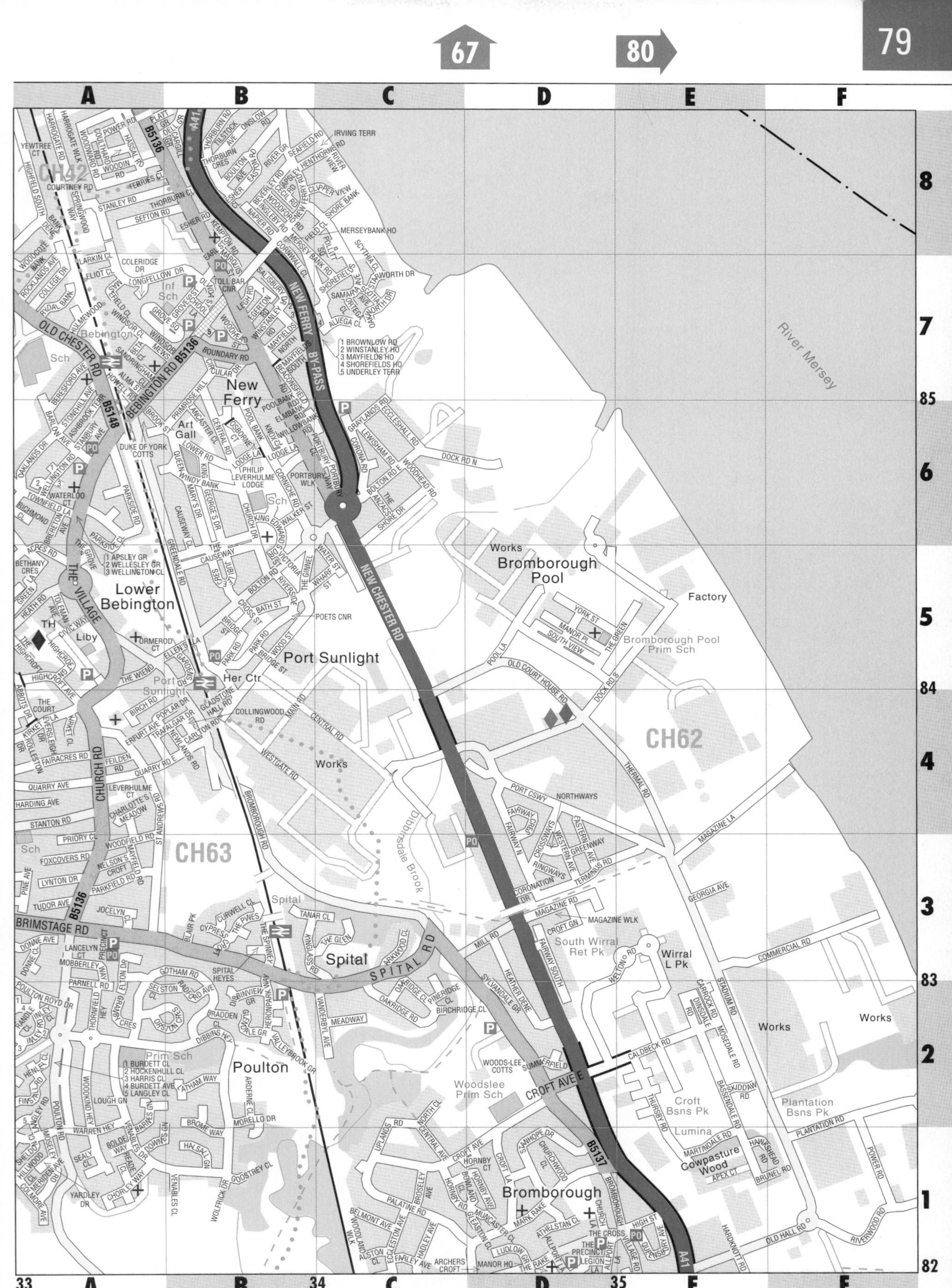
A
B
C
D
E
F
8
7
85
6
5
84
4
3
83
2
1
82
33
34
35
CH42
CH62
CH63
River Mersey
New Ferry
Lower Bebington
Port Sunlight
Bromborough Pool
Spital
Poulton
Bromborough
NEW FERRY BY-PASS
NEW CHESTER RD
OLD CHESTER RD
BEBINGTON RD
THE VILLAGE
CHURCH RD
BRIMSTAGE RD
SPITAL RD
CROFT AVE E
B5136
B5148
B5137
A41
Works
Factory
Bromborough Pool Prim Sch
South Wirral Ret Pk
Wirral L Pk
Croft Bsns Pk
Lumina
Cowpasture Wood
Plantation Bsns Pk
Woodslee Prim Sch
Art Gall
Inf Sch
Sch
Prim Sch
Liby
TH
Her Ctr
Bebington
Port Sunlight
DOCK RD N
DOCK RD S
OLD COURT HOUSE RD
THERMAL RD
MAGAZINE LA
GEORGIA AVE
COMMERCIAL RD
STADIUM RD
PLANTATION RD
OLD HALL RD
RIVERWOOD RD
POWER RD
PORT CSWY
NORTHWAYS
MAGAZINE RD
MAGAZINE WLK
BROMBOROUGH RD
POETS CNR
CENTRAL RD
WESTGATE RD
COLLINGWOOD RD
Dibbinsdale Brook
1 BROWNLOW RD
2 WINSTANLEY HO
3 MAYFIELDS HO
4 SHOREFIELDS HO
5 UNDERLEY TERR
1 APSLEY GR
2 WELLESLEY GR
3 WELLINGTON CL
1 BURDETT CL
2 HOCKENHULL CL
3 HARRIS CL
4 BURDETT AVE
5 LANGLEY CL
IRVING TERR
MERSEYBANK HO

88
80

79
68

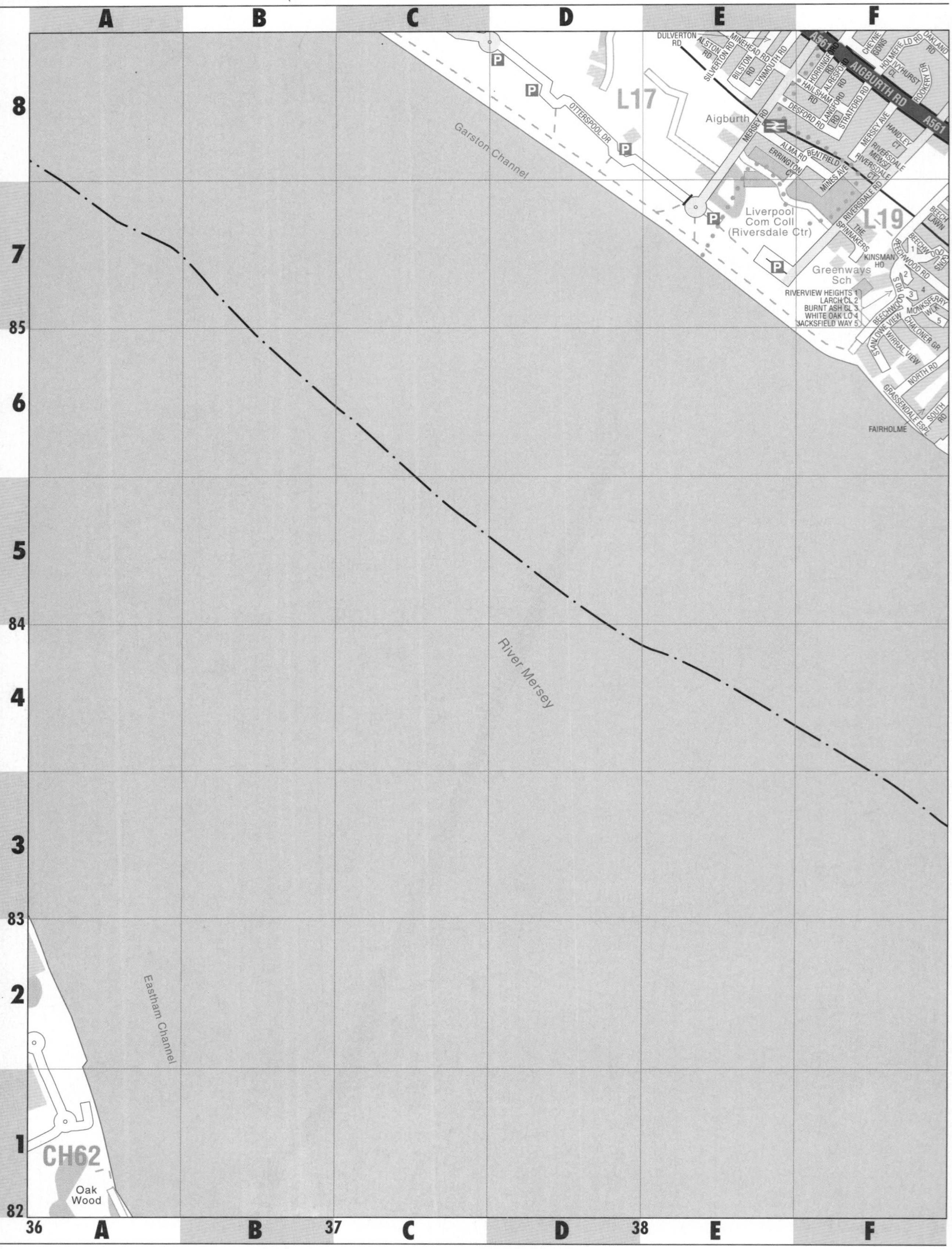

A B C D E F

8
7
85
6
5
84
4
3
83
2
1
82

Garston Channel

L17

DULVERTON RD
ALSTON RD
SILVERTON RD
MINEHEAD RD
LYNMOUTH RD
BILSTON RD
ALRESCO RD
HORRINGFORD RD
HAILSHAM RD
LANGFORD RD
STRATFORD RD
ASH
AIGBURTH RD
CHEYNE
HOLMEFIELD RD
IVYHURST
OAKLAND
A561

Aigburth

OTTERSPOOL DR

MERSEY RD
DESFORD RD
ALMA RD
ERRINGTON
BEATFIELD
MINST AV
THE SPINNAKERS
MERSEY
RIVERSDALE RD
MANOR
RIVERSDALE CT

Liverpool
Com Coll
(Riversdale Ctr)

L19

BEECH LAWN

BEECHWOOD RD
BEECH RD
BEECHEN CT

KINSMAN
HO

Greenways
Sch

RIVERVIEW HEIGHTS 1
LARCH CL 2
BURNT ASH CL 3
WHITE OAK LO 4
JACKSFIELD WAY 5

SANDOWN VIEW
WIRRAL VIEW
BEECHEN VIEW
CHALONER GR
MONKS FERRY
NORTH RD

WITHY RD
GRASSENDALE ESP
SOUTH RD

FAIRHOLME

River Mersey

Eastham Channel

CH62

Oak
Wood

36 A B 37 C D 38 E F

79
89

69
82

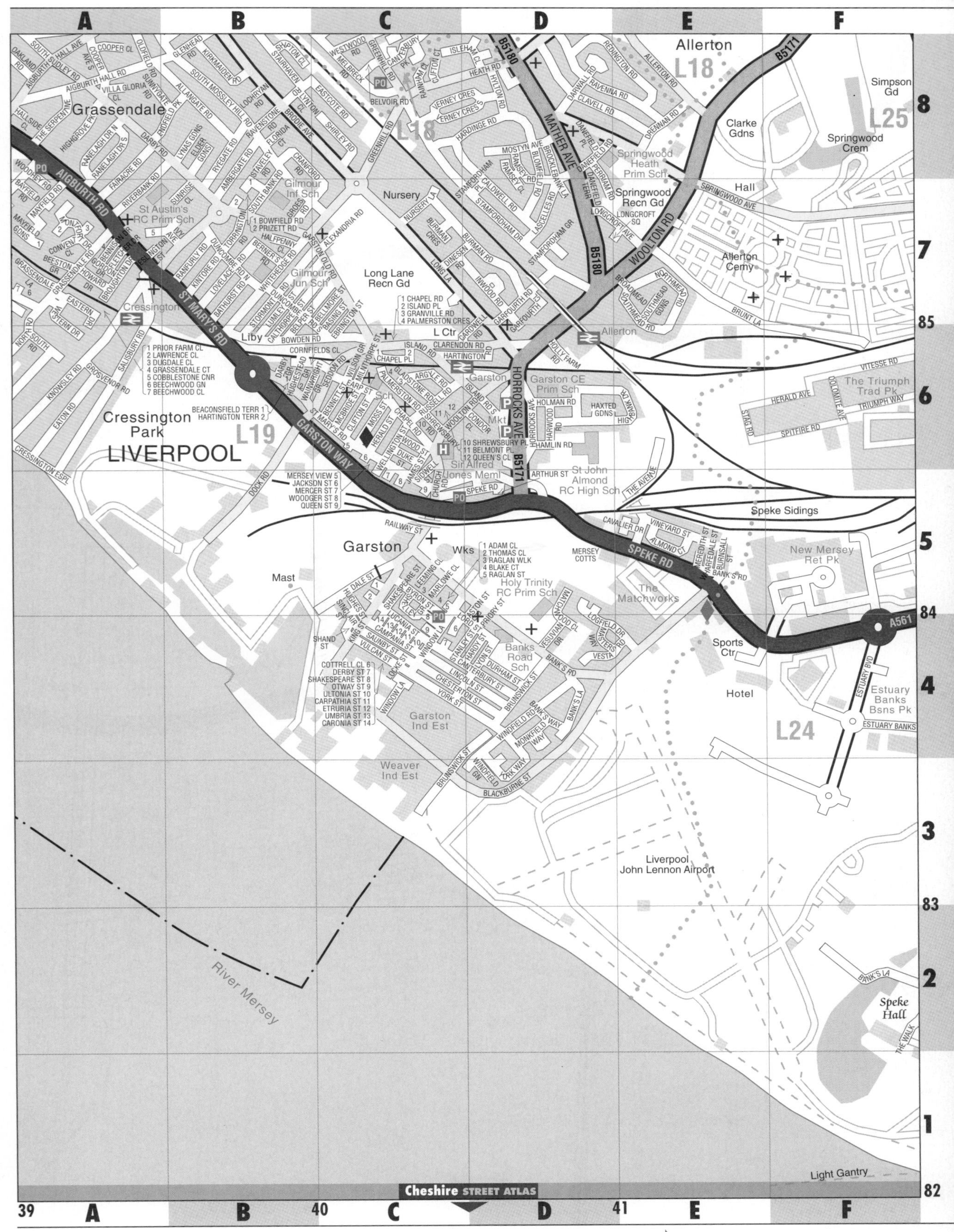
Allerton
Grassendale
Cressington
Cressington Park
LIVERPOOL
Garston
Long Lane Recn Gd
Nursery
Springwood Crem
Allerton Cemy
Speke Sidings
New Mersey Ret Pk
The Triumph Trad Pk
The Matchworks
Garston Ind Est
Weaver Ind Est
Estuary Banks Bsns Pk
Liverpool John Lennon Airport
River Mersey
Speke Hall
Light Gantry
AIGBURTH RD
ST MARY'S RD
GARSTON WAY
SPEKE RD
WOOLTON RD
MATHER AVE
HORROCKS AVE
A561
B5180
B5171
L18
L19
L24
L25

82

81
70

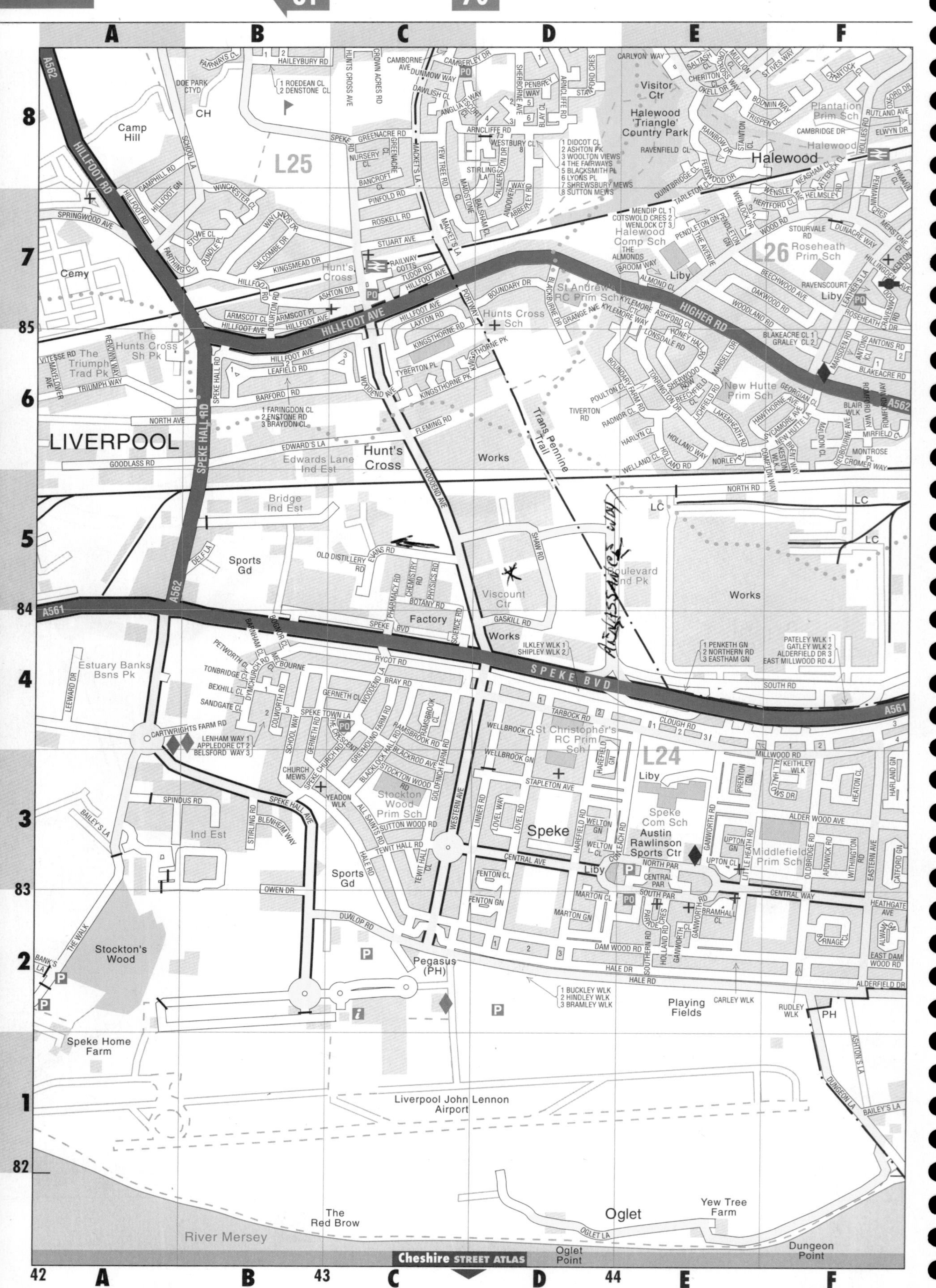
A
B
C
D
E
F
8
7
85
6
5
84
4
3
83
2
1
82
42
43
44
A562
A561
LIVERPOOL
Camp Hill
CH
Cemy
L25
L26
L24
HILLFOOT RD
HILLFOOT AVE
HIGHER RD
SPEKE HALL RD
SPEKE BVD
WOODEND AVE
WESTERN AVE
CENTRAL AVE
CENTRAL WAY
Hunt's Cross
Hunts Cross Sch
The Hunts Cross Sh Pk
The Triumph Trad Pk
Visitor Ctr
Halewood 'Triangle' Country Park
Halewood
Halewood Comp Sch
Plantation Prim Sch
Roseheath Prim Sch
St Andrew's RC Prim Sch
New Hutte Prim Sch
Trans Pennine Trail
Edwards Lane Ind Est
Bridge Ind Est
Works
Sports Gd
Viscount Ctr
Boulevard Ind Pk
Factory
Estuary Banks Bsns Pk
St Christopher's RC Prim Sch
Stockton Wood Prim Sch
Speke
Speke Com Sch
Austin Rawlinson Sports Ctr
Middlefield Prim Sch
Ind Est
Stockton's Wood
Pegasus (PH)
Playing Fields
PH
Speke Home Farm
Liverpool John Lennon Airport
The Red Brow
Oglet
Yew Tree Farm
River Mersey
Oglet Point
Dungeon Point
NORTH RD
SOUTH RD
HALE RD
DAM WOOD RD
DUNGEON LA
BAILEY'S LA
OGLET LA
THE WALK
NORTH AVE
EDWARD'S LA
GOODLASS RD
OLD DISTILLERY RD
EVANS RD
SHAW RD
GASKILL RD
BOTANY RD
RYCOT RD
BRAY RD
SPEKE TOWN LA
SPEKE HALL AVE
CARTWRIGHTS FARM RD
SPINDUS RD
OWEN DR
DUNLOP RD
HALE DR
ALDERFIELD DR
MILLWOOD RD
CLOUGH RD
TARBOCK RD
STAPLETON AVE
ALDER WOOD AVE
HEATHGATE AVE
EASTERN AVE
KINGSMEAD DR
STUART AVE
ROSKELL RD
PINFOLD RD
SPEKE RD
BOUNDARY RD
PORTWAY
MACKETS LA
YEW TREE RD
WOOD RD
OAKWOOD RD
WOODLAND RD
BEECHWOOD AVE
ROSEHEATH DR
BLAKEACRE RD
NORLEY

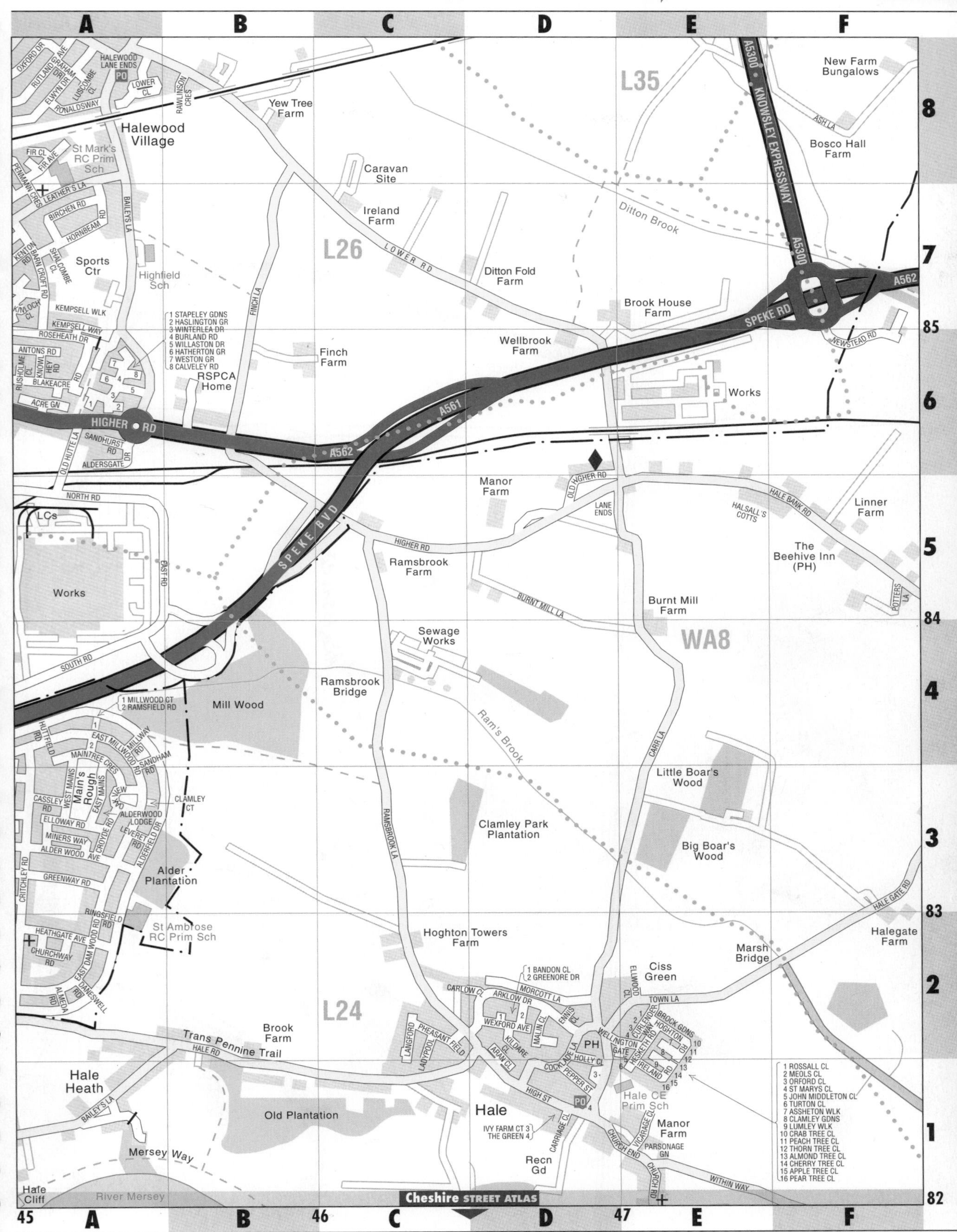
71
84
A
B
C
D
E
F
8
7
85
6
5
84
4
3
83
2
1
82
45
46
47
Halewood Village
St Mark's RC Prim Sch
Yew Tree Farm
L35
New Farm Bungalows
Bosco Hall Farm
KNOWSLEY EXPRESSWAY
A5300
Caravan Site
Ireland Farm
Ditton Brook
L26
LOWER RD
Sports Ctr
Highfield Sch
Ditton Fold Farm
Brook House Farm
A562
SPEKE RD
NEWSTEAD RD
Finch Farm
Wellbrook Farm
1 STAPELEY GDNS
2 HASLINGTON GR
3 WINTERLEA DR
4 BURLAND RD
5 WILLASTON DR
6 HATHERTON GR
7 WESTON GR
8 CALVELEY RD
RSPCA Home
Works
A561
HIGHER RD
A562
FINCH LA
Manor Farm
OLD HIGHER RD
LANE ENDS
HALE BANK RD
HALSALL'S COTTS
Linner Farm
NORTH RD
LCs
SPEKE BVD
HIGHER RD
Ramsbrook Farm
The Beehive Inn (PH)
Works
EAST RD
BURNT MILL LA
Burnt Mill Farm
POTTERS LA
SOUTH RD
Sewage Works
WA8
Ramsbrook Bridge
1 MILLWOOD CT
2 RAMSFIELD RD
Mill Wood
Ram's Brook
CARR LA
Little Boar's Wood
Main's Rough
CLAMLEY CT
Clamley Park Plantation
RAMSBROOK LA
Big Boar's Wood
Alder Plantation
HALE GATE RD
Halegate Farm
St Ambrose RC Prim Sch
Hoghton Towers Farm
Marsh Bridge
Ciss Green
1 BANDON CL
2 GREENORE DR
CARLOW CL
ARKLOW DR
MORCOTT LA
TOWN LA
L24
Brook Farm
Trans Pennine Trail
HALE RD
PH
Hale Heath
BAILEY'S LA
Old Plantation
Hale
HIGH ST
PO
Hale CE Prim Sch
Manor Farm
IVY FARM CT 3
THE GREEN 4
CARRIAGE CL
CHURCH END
PARSONAGE GN
Recn Gd
Mersey Way
WITHIN WAY
CHURCH RD
1 ROSSALL CL
2 MEOLS CL
3 ORFORD CL
4 ST MARYS CL
5 JOHN MIDDLETON CL
6 TURTON CL
7 ASSHETON WLK
8 CLAMLEY GDNS
9 LUMLEY WLK
10 CRAB TREE CL
11 PEACH TREE CL
12 THORN TREE CL
13 ALMOND TREE CL
14 CHERRY TREE CL
15 APPLE TREE CL
16 PEAR TREE CL
Hale Cliff
River Mersey
Cheshire STREET ATLAS

84

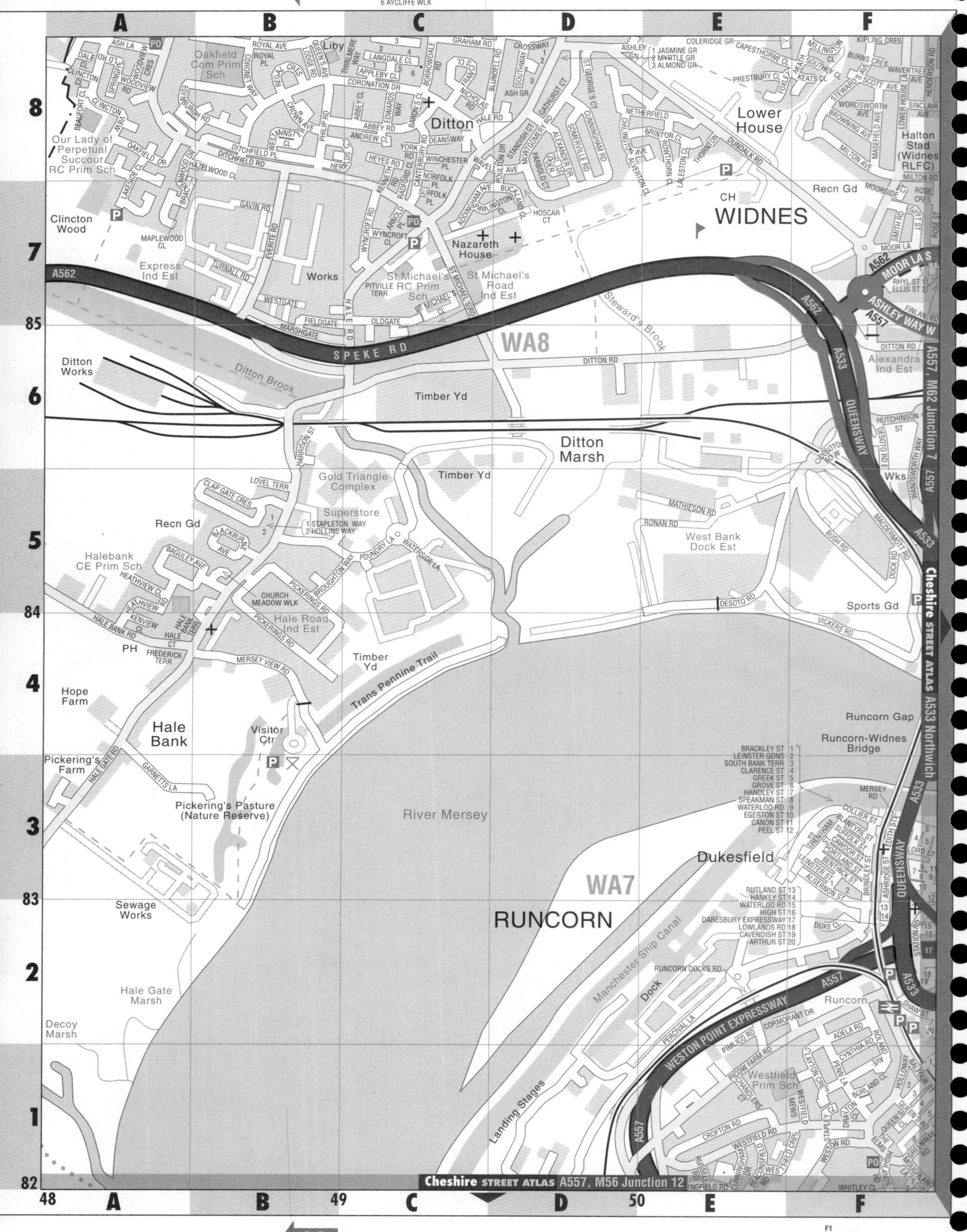

C8
1 LEVENS WAY
2 RIDSDALE
3 LONSDALE CL
4 LEIGH GREEN CL
5 APPLEBY WLK
6 AYCLIFFE WLK

Royal Ave
Liby
Langdale Cl
Graham Rd
Crossway
Coleridge Gr
Capesthorne Cl
Kipling Cres

Oakfield Com Prim Sch
Royal Pl
Thirlmere Way
Appleby Cl
Ashley Gn
1 Jasmine Gr
2 Myrtle Gr
3 Almond Gr
Burns Cres
Wavertree Ave

Our Lady of Perpetual Succour RC Prim Sch
Prestbury Cl
Keats Cl
Scott Ave
Sinclair Ave

Ditton
Deansway
Nicholas
Ash Gr
St George's
Netherfield
Wordsworth Ave
Rose Cres

Lower House

Clincton Wood

8

Clincton Wood

Express Ind Est
Turnall Rd
Works

Nazareth House

WIDNES

Recn Gd
Moorside

Halton Stad (Widnes RLFC)

7

St Michael's RC Prim Sch
St Michael's Road Ind Est

CH

Moor La S

85

Ditton Works

WA8

Steward's Brook

Ditton Rd

Alexandra Ind Est

6

Ditton Brook

Timber Yd

Ditton Marsh

Queensway

Hutchinson St

Wks

Gold Triangle Complex

Timber Yd

Bush Rd

Cheshire STREET ATLAS A533 Northwich

5

Recn Gd

Superstore
1 STAPLETON WAY
2 HOLLINS WAY

Ronan Rd

Mathieson Rd

West Bank Dock Est

Halebank CE Prim Sch

Church Meadow Wlk

Desoto Rd

84

Hale Road Ind Est

Sports Gd

Vickers Rd

Mersey View Rd

Timber Yd

4

Hope Farm

Trans Pennine Trail

Runcorn Gap

Runcorn-Widnes Bridge

Hale Bank

Visitor Ctr

Pickering's Farm

BRACKLEY ST 1
LEINSTER GDNS 2
SOUTH BANK TERR 3
CLARENCE ST 4
GREEK ST 5
GROVE ST 6
HANDLEY ST 7
SPEAKMAN ST 8
WATERLOO RD 9
EGERTON ST 10
CANON ST 11
PEEL ST 12

Mersey Rd

3

Pickering's Pasture (Nature Reserve)

River Mersey

WA7

Dukesfield

Sewage Works

RUNCORN

RUTLAND ST 13
HANKEY ST 14
HIGH ST 16
DARESBURY EXPRESSWAY 17
LOWLANDS RD 18
CAVENDISH ST 19
ARTHUR ST 20

83

Hale Gate Marsh

Manchester Ship Canal

Dock

Runcorn Docks Rd

Runcorn

2

Decoy Marsh

WESTON POINT EXPRESSWAY

Percival La

Westfield Prim Sch

Landing Stages

Westfield

1

Crofton Rd

PO

82

| 48 | A | | B | 49 | C | | D | 50 | E | | F |

F1
1 PICOW ST
2 ELAINE PRICE CT
3 HAVERGAL ST
4 CURZON ST
5 LIGHTBURN ST
6 STANLEY VILLAS
7 SOUTHLANDS MEWS
8 SOUTHLANDS CT

HESWALL

CH60

CH64

River Dee

Sewage Works

Wirral Country Park

Gayton Cott

Wirral Way

85
77

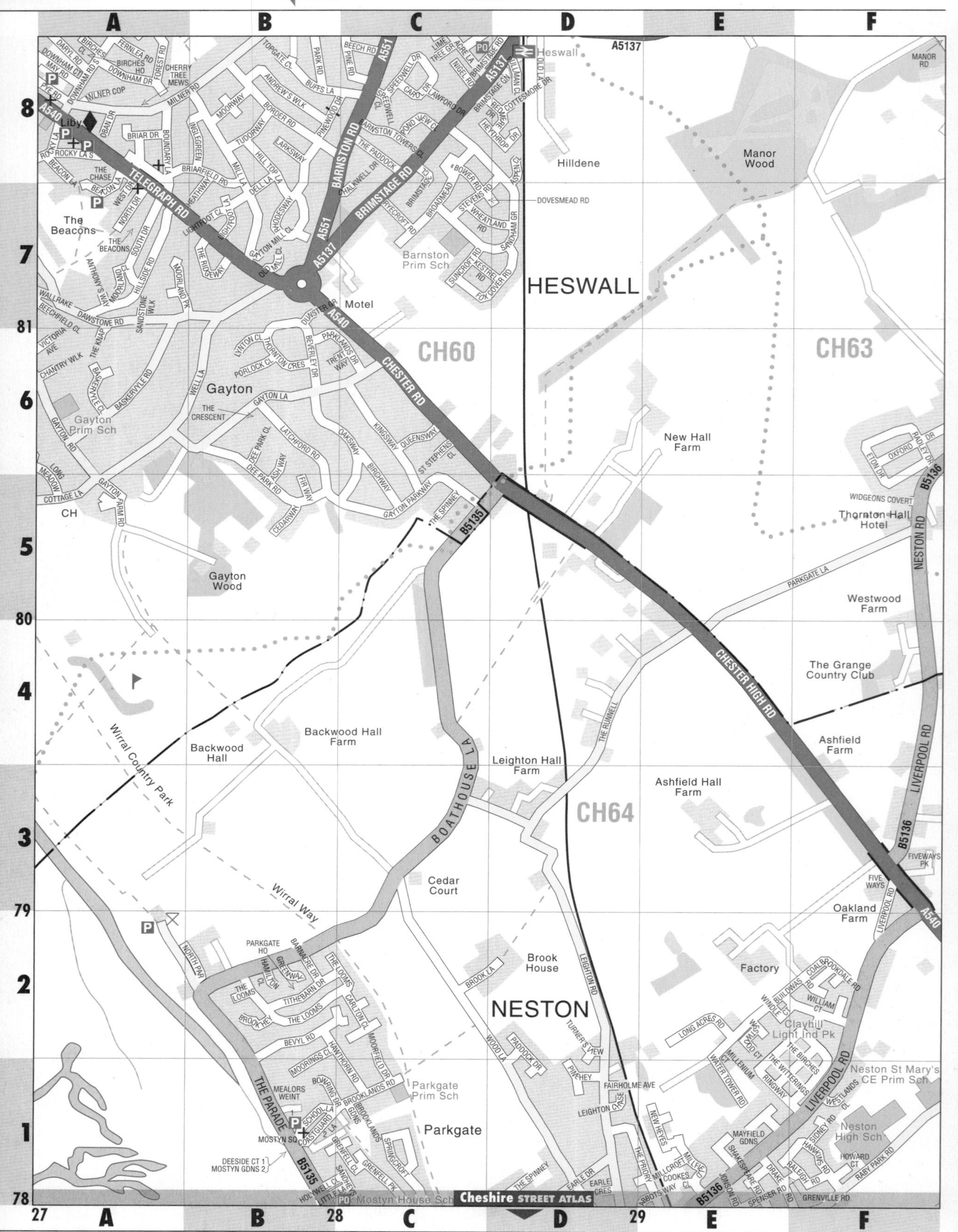
A
B
C
D
E
F
HESWALL
Heswall
A5137
Manor Wood
Hilldene
DOVESMEAD RD
TELEGRAPH RD
BARNSTON RD
BRIMSTAGE RD
A551
A540
The Beacons
Barnston Prim Sch
Motel
CH60
CHESTER RD
CH63
Gayton
Gayton Prim Sch
New Hall Farm
Thornton Hall Hotel
Gayton Wood
B5135
Westwood Farm
The Grange Country Club
CHESTER HIGH RD
Wirral Country Park
Backwood Hall
Backwood Hall Farm
Leighton Hall Farm
Ashfield Farm
Ashfield Hall Farm
CH64
BOATHOUSE LA
Cedar Court
Wirral Way
Oakland Farm
Brook House
Factory
NESTON
LIVERPOOL RD
NESTON RD
B5136
Clayhill Light Ind Pk
Neston St Mary's CE Prim Sch
Parkgate Prim Sch
Parkgate
Neston High Sch
THE PARADE
Mostyn House Sch
LEIGHTON RD
PARKGATE LA
8
7
81
6
5
80
4
3
79
2
1
78
27
28
29

85

78
88

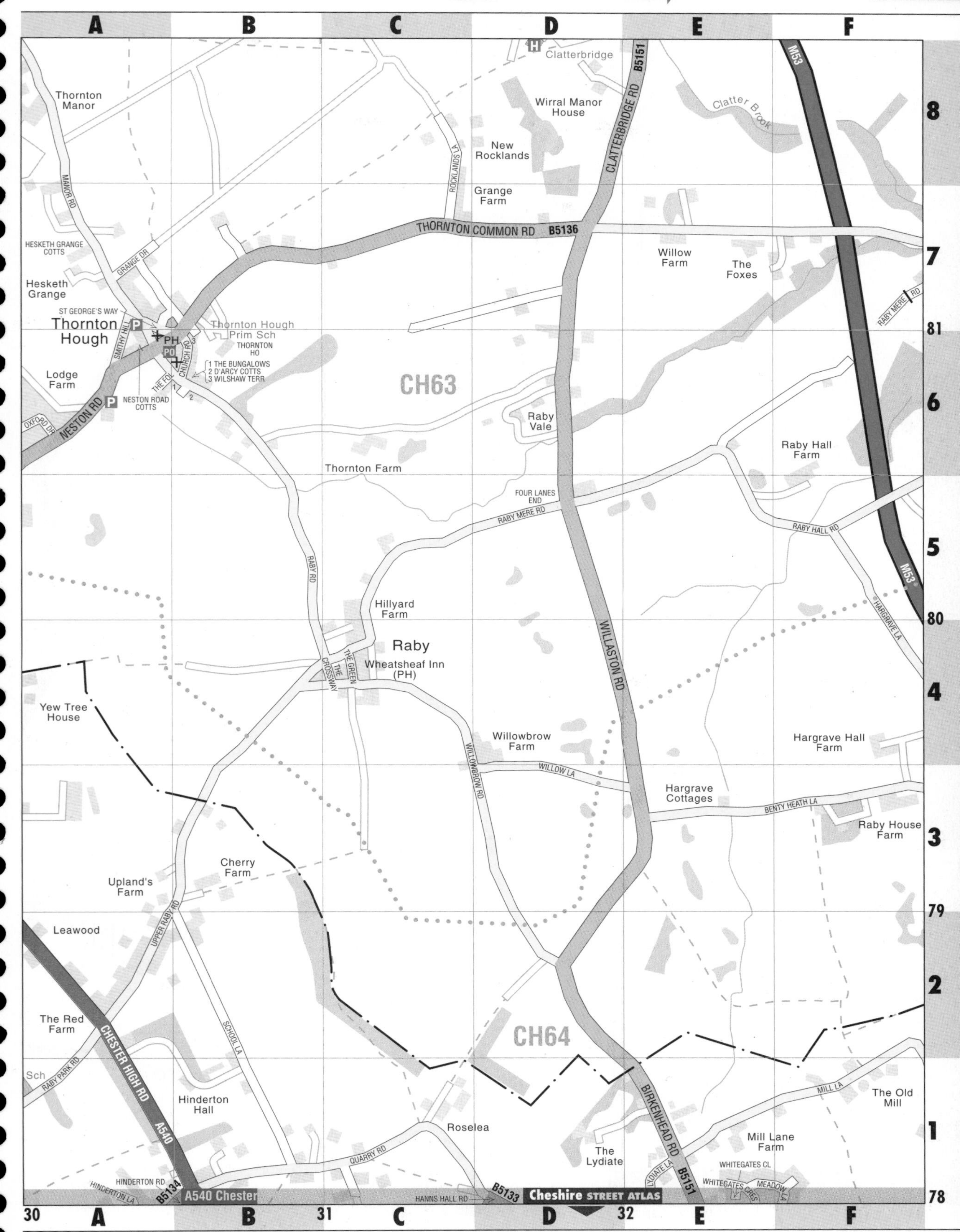
A
B
C
D
E
F
Clatterbridge
Thornton Manor
Wirral Manor House
Clatter Brook
M53
B5151
CLATTERBRIDGE RD
New Rocklands
ROCKLANDS LA
Grange Farm
MANOR RD
HESKETH GRANGE COTTS
THORNTON COMMON RD
B5136
Willow Farm
The Foxes
GRANGE DR
Hesketh Grange
ST GEORGE'S WAY
Thornton Hough
Thornton Hough Prim Sch
THORNTON HO
SMITHY HILL
CHURCH RD
1 THE BUNGALOWS
2 D'ARCY COTTS
3 WILSHAW TERR
RABY MERE RD
Lodge Farm
THE FOL
CH63
NESTON ROAD COTTS
NESTON RD
OXFORD DR
Raby Vale
Raby Hall Farm
Thornton Farm
FOUR LANES END
RABY MERE RD
RABY HALL RD
RABY RD
Hillyard Farm
HARGRAVE LA
Raby
THE CROSSWAY
THE GREEN
Wheatsheaf Inn (PH)
WILLASTON RD
Yew Tree House
Willowbrow Farm
Hargrave Hall Farm
WILLOWBROW RD
WILLOW LA
Hargrave Cottages
BENTY HEATH LA
Raby House Farm
Cherry Farm
Upland's Farm
UPPER RABY RD
Leawood
SCHOOL LA
The Red Farm
CH64
CHESTER HIGH RD
A540
Sch
RABY PARK RD
Hinderton Hall
BIRKENHEAD RD
MILL LA
The Old Mill
Roselea
Mill Lane Farm
The Lydiate
QUARRY RD
WHITEGATES CL
LYDIATE LA
B5151
WHITEGATES CRES
MEADOW LA
HINDERTON RD
HINDERTON LA
B5134
A540 Chester
HANNS HALL RD
B5133
Cheshire STREET ATLAS
8
7
81
6
5
80
4
3
79
2
1
78
30
31
32

88

87
79

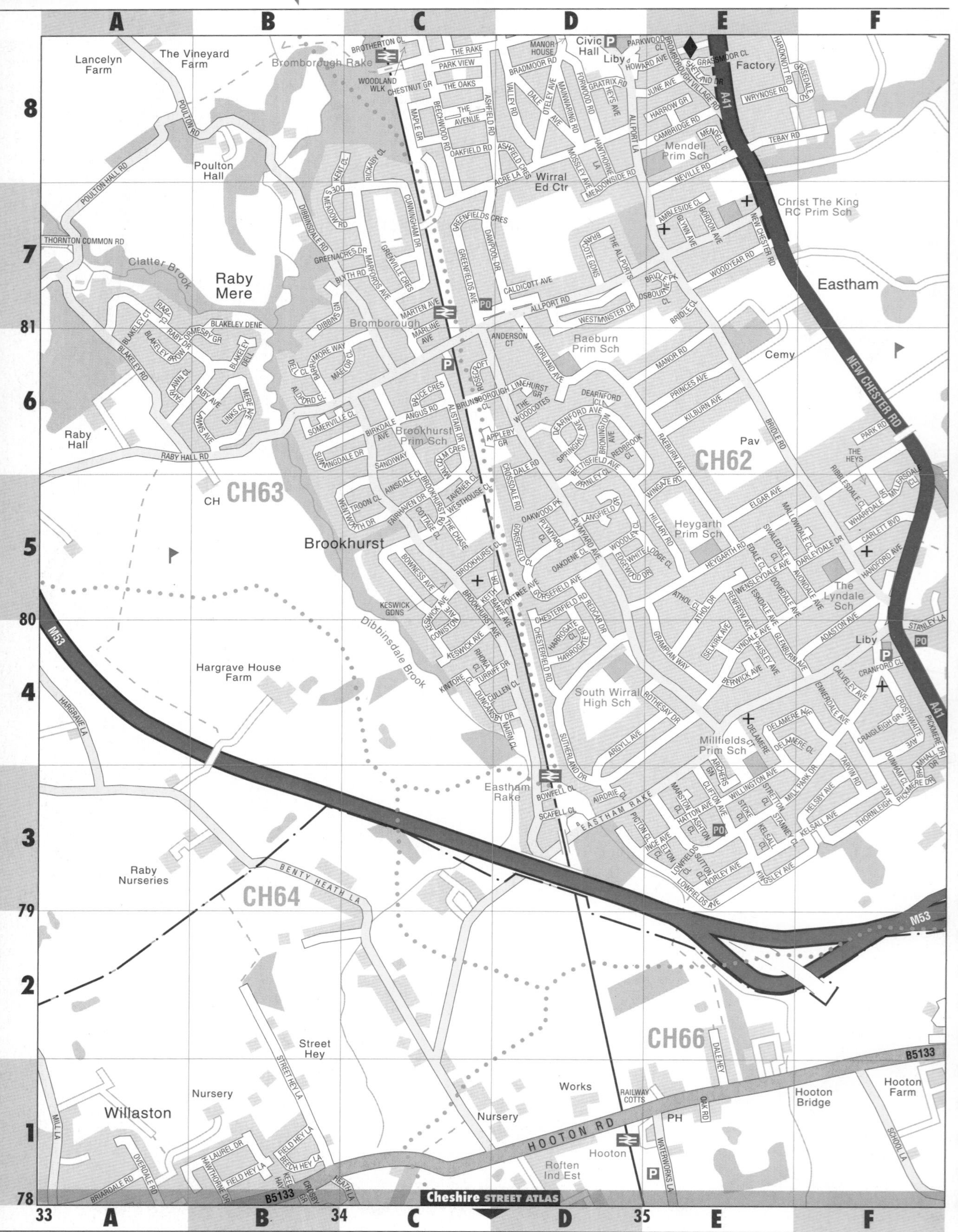
A
B
C
D
E
F
8
7
81
6
5
80
4
3
79
2
1
78
33
34
35
Lancelyn Farm
The Vineyard Farm
Bromborough Rake
BROTHERTON CL
WOODLAND WLK
CHESTNUT GR
THE RAKE
PARK VIEW
THE OAKS
MANOR HOUSE
BRADMOOR RD
Civic Hall
Liby
PARKWOOD CL
HOWARD AVE
BROMBOROUGH VILLAGE RD
GRASSMOOR CL
SHETLAND DR
Factory
HARDKNOTT RD
GRISEDALE RD
WRYNOSE RD
TEBAY RD
A41
POULTON RD
Poulton Hall
POULTON HALL RD
THORNTON COMMON RD
Clatter Brook
Raby Mere
DIBBINSDALE RD
KENT CL
RICKABY CL
MAPLE GR
BEECHWOOD RD
THE AVENUE
ASHFIELD RD
VALLEY RD
DALE AVE
OTELEY AVE
MAINWARING RD
FORWOOD RD
GRATRIX RD
HEYS AVE
ALLPORT LA
JUNE AVE
HARROW GR
CAMBRIDGE RD
MENDELL CL
Mendell Prim Sch
OAKFIELD RD
ASHFIELD CRES
ACRE LA
MOSSLEY AVE
HAWTHORNE LA
MEADOWSIDE RD
Wirral Ed Ctr
NEVILLE RD
Christ The King RC Prim Sch
AMBLESIDE CL
GLYNN AVE
GORDON AVE
NEW CHESTER RD
CUNNINGHAM DR
GREENFIELDS CRES
DAWPOOL DR
GREENFIELDS AVE
THE ALLPORTS
GREENACRES DR
GRENVILLE CRES
MARFORDS AVE
BLYTH RD
DIBBINS GN
MARTEN AVE
MARLINE AVE
Bromborough
PO
CALDICOTT AVE
ALLPORT RD
WESTMINSTER DR
BRIDLE PK
OSBOURNE CL
WOODYEAR RD
BRIDLE CL
Eastham
RABY DR
BLAKELEY DENE
MESBY GR
BLAKELEY CT
BLAKELEY BROW
BLAKELEY DELL
BLAKELEY RD
FAIRLAWN CL
RABY AVE
LINKS CL
MERE AVE
LAWNS AVE
BARRYMORE WAY
MAELOR CL
DELL CL
ALDFORD CL
ANDERSON CT
MORLAND AVE
Raeburn Prim Sch
MANOR RD
Cemy
PRINCES AVE
KILBURN AVE
SOMERVILLE CL
BIRKDALE AVE
SPRUCE CRES
ANGUS RD
ALISTAIR DR
BRUNSBOROUGH CL
LINEHURST GR
THE WOODCOTES
DEARNFORD CL
DEARNFORD AVE
Brookhurst Prim Sch
APPLEBY GR
SPRINGHILL AVE
BRONINGTON AVE
REDBROOK CL
RAEBURN AVE
Pav
BRIDLE RD
CH62
PARK RD
THE HEYS
Raby Hall
RABY HALL RD
SUNNINGDALE DR
SANDIWAY
MALCOLM CRES
TAVENER CL
WESTHOUSE CL
CROSSDALE RD
DALE RD
BETTISFIELD AVE
BRINLEY CL
WINGATE RD
ELGAR AVE
MALLOWDALE CL
RIBBLESDALE CL
WHARFDALE CL
MILLERSDALE CL
CH
CH63
TROON CL
WENTWORTH DR
AINSDALE CL
FAIRHAVEN DR
BROOKHURST RD
COTTAGE CL
THE CHASE
OAKWOOD PK
PLYMYARD CL
LANGFIELD GR
PLYMYARD AVE
HILLARY RD
Heygarth Prim Sch
SWALEDALE CL
DARLEYDALE DR
CARLETT BVD
Brookhurst
GORSEFIELD CL
OAKDENE CL
WOODLEY CL
EDGEWOOD DR
WHITE LODGE CL
HEYGARTH RD
EDALE CL
WENSLEYDALE AVE
HANDFORD AVE
BOWNESS AVE
BROOKHURST CL
KEITH DR
BANFF AVE
PORTREE AVE
GORSEFIELD AVE
ATHOL CL
ATHOL DR
RENFREW AVE
ESKDALE AVE
DOVEDALE AVE
AVONDALE AVE
The Lyndale Sch
KESWICK GDNS
KESWICK AVE
KESWICK CL
CONISTON AVE
BROOKHURST AVE
CHESTERFIELD RD
HARROGATE CL
REDCAR DR
GRAMPIAN WAY
SELKIRK AVE
LYNDALE AVE
PAISLEY AVE
GLENBURN AVE
ADASTON AVE
STANLEY LA
Liby
PO
M53
Dibbinsdale Brook
TESWICK AVE
RHONA CL
TURRIFF DR
KINTORE CL
CULLEN CL
DUNCANSBY DR
NAIRN CL
HARROGATE RD
CHESTERFIELD RD
South Wirral High Sch
ROTHESAY DR
BERWICK AVE
ENNERDALE AVE
CALVELEY AVE
CRANFORD CL
Hargrave House Farm
HARGRAVE LA
SUTHERLAND DR
ARGYLL AVE
DELAMERE AVE
DELAMERE CL
Millfields Prim Sch
CROSTHWAITE AVE
CRAIGLEIGH GR
TARVIN RD
PICKMERE DR
BRAMHALL DR
DUNHAM CL
Eastham Rake
BOWFELL CL
SCAFELL CL
AIRDRIE CL
EASTHAM RAKE
ARCHERS GN
MANSTON CL
CLIFTON AVE
WILLINGTON AVE
STRETTON CL
MILL PARK DR
HELSBY AVE
THORNLEIGH AVE
KELSALL AVE
HATTON AVE
ASHTON CL
STOKE CL
STANNEY CL
PICTON CL
INCE AVE
ELTON CL
KELSALL CL
LOWFIELDS CL
SUTTON CL
NORLEY AVE
KINGSLEY AVE
LOWFIELDS AVE
Raby Nurseries
BENTY HEATH LA
CH64
M53
Street Hey
STREET HEY LA
CH66
DALE HEY
B5133
Hooton Farm
Hooton Bridge
Works
RAILWAY COTTS
OAK RD
PH
Nursery
Willaston
MILL LA
Nursery
HOOTON RD
Hooton
WATERWORKS LA
SCHOOL LA
Roften Ind Est
LAUREL DR
HAWTHORNE DR
FIELD HEY LA
BEECH HEY LA
KEEL HAY
CROSBY GR
HEATH LA
OVERDALE RD
BRIARDALE RD
B5133
Cheshire STREET ATLAS

87

A   B   C   D   E   F

8
7
81
6
5
80
4
3
79
2
1
78

Eastham Ctry Pk
Visitor Ctr
Eastham Ferry
Eastham Ferry Hotel
The Warrens Farm
Wirral Metropolitan Coll
Custom House
Eastham Locks
Queen Elizabeth II Dock
River Mersey

ST DAVID RD
ST JOHN S RD
CH62
Tanks
Tanks
Oil Storage Depot
Tanks
Tanks
Manchester Ship Canal

FERRY RD
MAYFIELD DR
SEAVIEW AVE
CH
LOCK RD
CHRISTOPHER DR

B5132
EASTHAM VILLAGE RD
VICARAGE ROW
Sch
HALL FARM
Eastham House
Eastham Mews
BANKFIELDS DR

Tanks
LC
Hooton Park
LC
Tanks
ERIC FOUNTAIN RD
CH65
NORTH RD
Booston Wood

David's Rough
HERTON RD
DUDLEY CRES
RIVACRE RD
5
6
Kennel Wood
NEW CHESTER RD

REDVERS AVE
VERNON AVE
HOOTON WAY
HOOTON RD
B5133
Hooton
CHRISTIE CL
GRANGE CRES
CONISTON CL
DERWENT DR
HOOTON GN
Park Farm
HOOTON LA
WOOD CL
CH66
NEW SCHOOL LA
Motor Vehicle Works

A550
WELSH RD
CHESTER RD
A41
SCHOOL LA
Rivacre Wood
B5132
7
M53
M53 Chester (A56)
B5132

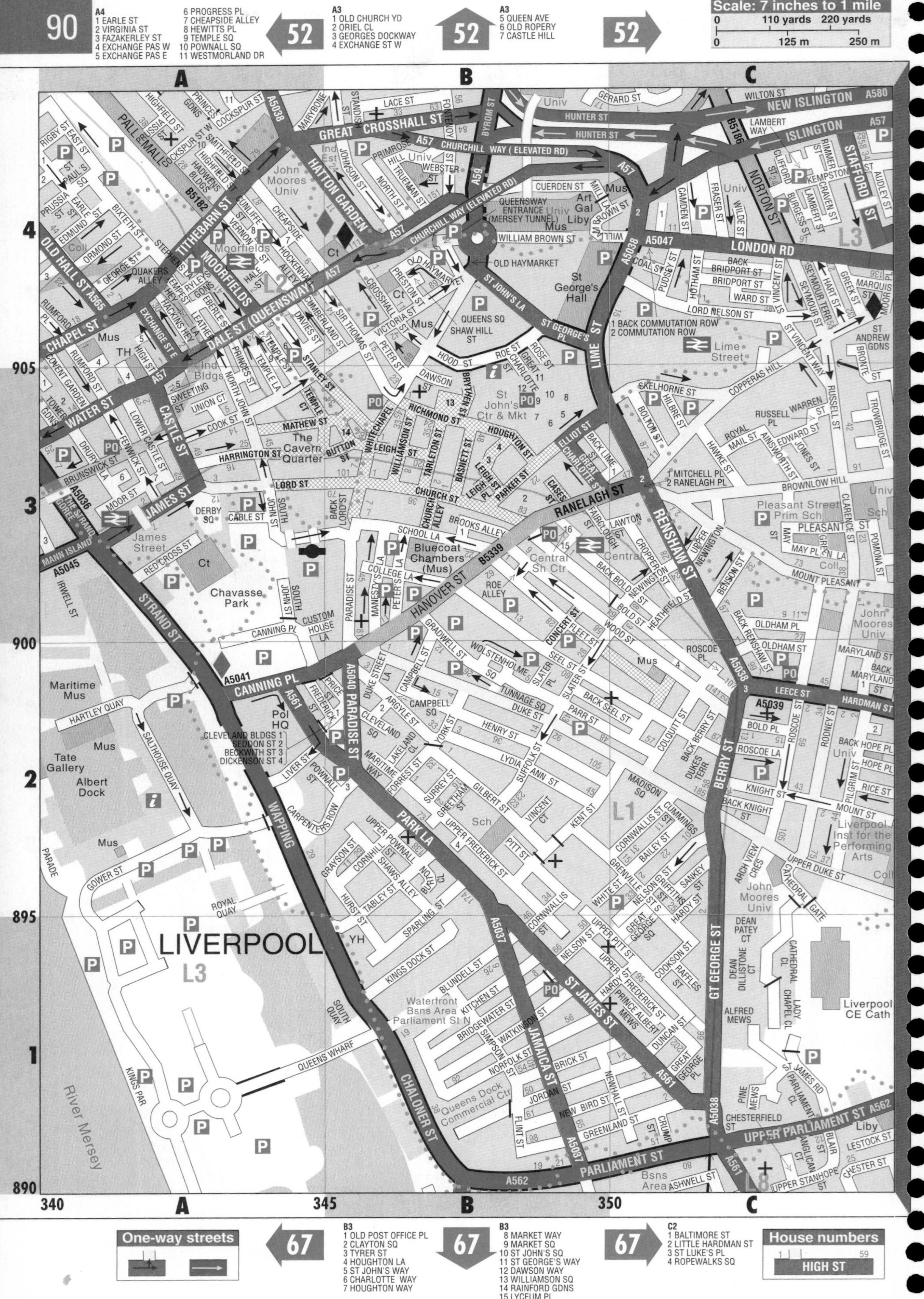
90
A4
1 EARLE ST
2 VIRGINIA ST
3 FAZAKERLEY ST
4 EXCHANGE PAS W
5 EXCHANGE PAS E
6 PROGRESS PL
7 CHEAPSIDE ALLEY
8 HEWITTS PL
9 TEMPLE SQ
10 POWNALL SQ
11 WESTMORLAND DR
52
A3
1 OLD CHURCH YD
2 ORIEL CL
3 GEORGES DOCKWAY
4 EXCHANGE ST W
52
A3
5 QUEEN AVE
6 OLD ROPERY
7 CASTLE HILL
52
Scale: 7 inches to 1 mile
0 110 yards 220 yards
0 125 m 250 m
A B C
4 905 3 900 2 895 1 890
340 345 350
LIVERPOOL
L1 L2 L3 L8
River Mersey
Albert Dock
Tate Gallery
Maritime Mus
Chavasse Park
St George's Hall
Lime Street
Liverpool CE Cath
John Moores Univ
Moorfields
James Street
Central
Pleasant Street Prim Sch
Bluecoat Chambers (Mus)
Central Sh Ctr
St John's Ctr & Mkt
The Cavern Quarter
Queens Dock Commercial Ctr
Waterfront Bsns Area Parliament St N
Liverpool Inst for the Performing Arts
Art Gal Liby
QUEENSWAY ENTRANCE (MERSEY TUNNEL)
OLD HAYMARKET
GREAT CROSSHALL ST
CHURCHILL WAY (ELEVATED RD)
HATTON GARDEN
TITHEBARN ST
MOORFIELDS
DALE ST (QUEENSWAY)
WATER ST
CASTLE ST
JAMES ST
STRAND ST
WAPPING
CANNING PL
HANOVER ST
PARADISE ST
PARK LA
ST JAMES ST
JAMAICA ST
CHALONER ST
PARLIAMENT ST
UPPER PARLIAMENT ST
GT GEORGE ST
BERRY ST
RENSHAW ST
RANELAGH ST
LIME ST
LONDON RD
ISLINGTON
NEW ISLINGTON
HUNTER ST
LEECE ST
HARDMAN ST
MOUNT PLEASANT
BROWNLOW HILL
BOLD ST
SEEL ST
DUKE ST
QUEENS WHARF
CLEVELAND BLDGS 1
SEDDON ST 2
BECKWITH ST 3
DICKENSON ST 4
1 BACK COMMUTATION ROW
2 COMMUTATION ROW
1 MITCHELL PL
2 RANELAGH PL
67
One-way streets
B3
1 OLD POST OFFICE PL
2 CLAYTON SQ
3 TYRER ST
4 HOUGHTON LA
5 ST JOHN'S WAY
6 CHARLOTTE WAY
7 HOUGHTON WAY
67
B3
8 MARKET WAY
9 MARKET SQ
10 ST JOHN'S SQ
11 ST GEORGE'S WAY
12 DAWSON WAY
13 WILLIAMSON SQ
14 RAINFORD GDNS
15 LYCEUM PL
16 LYCEUM ST
67
C2
1 BALTIMORE ST
2 LITTLE HARDMAN ST
3 ST LUKE'S PL
4 ROPEWALKS SQ
House numbers
1 59
HIGH ST

Church Rd 6 Beckenham BR2..........53 C6

Place name
May be abbreviated on the map

Location number
Present when a number indicates the place's position in a crowded area of mapping

Locality, town or village
Shown when more than one place has the same name

Postcode district
District for the indexed place

Page and grid square
Page number and grid reference for the standard mapping

Public and commercial buildings are highlighted in magenta   **Places of interest** are highlighted in blue with a star★

Abbreviations used in the index

Acad	**Academy**	Comm	**Common**	Gd	**Ground**	L	**Leisure**	Prom	**Prom**
App	**Approach**	Cott	**Cottage**	Gdn	**Garden**	La	**Lane**	Rd	**Road**
Arc	**Arcade**	Cres	**Crescent**	Gn	**Green**	Liby	**Library**	Recn	**Recreation**
Ave	**Avenue**	Cswy	**Causeway**	Gr	**Grove**	Mdw	**Meadow**	Ret	**Retail**
Bglw	**Bungalow**	Ct	**Court**	H	**Hall**	Meml	**Memorial**	Sh	**Shopping**
Bldg	**Building**	Ctr	**Centre**	Ho	**House**	Mkt	**Market**	Sq	**Square**
Bsns, Bus	**Business**	Ctry	**Country**	Hospl	**Hospital**	Mus	**Museum**	St	**Street**
Bvd	**Boulevard**	Cty	**County**	HQ	**Headquarters**	Orch	**Orchard**	Sta	**Station**
Cath	**Cathedral**	Dr	**Drive**	Hts	**Heights**	Pal	**Palace**	Terr	**Terrace**
Cir	**Circus**	Dro	**Drove**	Ind	**Industrial**	Par	**Parade**	TH	**Town Hall**
Cl	**Close**	Ed	**Education**	Inst	**Institute**	Pas	**Passage**	Univ	**University**
Cnr	**Corner**	Emb	**Embankment**	Int	**International**	Pk	**Park**	Wk, Wlk	**Walk**
Coll	**College**	Est	**Estate**	Intc	**Interchange**	Pl	**Place**	Wr	**Water**
Com	**Community**	Ex	**Exhibition**	Junc	**Junction**	Prec	**Precinct**	Yd	**Yard**

Index of localities, towns and villages

1

1st St WN2 35 E7

3

3rd St WN2 35 E7

4

4th St WN2 35 F7

A

A K Bsns Pk PR9 5 A6
'A' Ct WN4 35 B2
Abacus Rd L13 54 B4
Abberley Cl WA10 43 F3
Abberley Rd L25 82 D7
Abberton Pk L30 28 A5
Abbey Cl Birkenhead CH41 66 F5
Formby L37 10 B2
Kirkby L33 29 F2
Up Holland WN8 25 C7
Widnes WA8 84 C8
Abbey Ct L25 70 B2
Abbey Dr WN5 25 E6
Abbey Farm Cvn Pk L40 14 C8
Abbey Gdns PR8 4 A4
Abbey La L40 14 C8
Abbey Rd Haydock WA11 45 E7
1 Liverpool L6 53 C6
St Helens WA10 43 E7
West Kirby CH48 63 B2
Widnes WA8 84 C8
Abbey St CH41 66 F5
Abbey View L16 69 F7
Abbeyfield Dr L12 40 D3
Abbeyfield Ho WA10 43 E5
Abbeystead WN8 24 C7
Abbeystead Ave L30 28 A1
Abbeystead Rd L15 69 B7
Abbeyvale Dr L25 70 C6
Abbeyway N WA11 46 A7
Abbeyway S WA11 46 A7
Abbeywood WN8 24 C6
Abbeywood Gr L35 56 F2
Abbot Cl CH43 65 C6
Abbots Cl L37 10 A1
Abbots Dr CH63 78 F5
Abbots Hall Ave WA9 58 D2
Abbots Quay CH41 67 A6
Abbots Way Formby L37 10 B1
Neston CH64 86 E1
West Kirby CH48 63 C3
Abbotsbury Way L12 40 E3
Abbotsfield Rd
St Helens WA9 58 E5
St Helens WA9 58 F5
Abbotsfield Rd Ind Pk WA9 58 E6
Abbotsford L39 13 F5
Abbotsford Cl WA3 36 D1
Abbotsford Ct 3 L23 26 C3
Abbotsford Gdns L23 26 C3
Abbotsford Rd Crosby L23 26 C3
Liverpool L11 39 F2
Abbotsford St CH44 51 E2
Abbott Dr L20 38 E5
Abbotts Cl L18 69 B3
Abbotts Way WN5 33 D3
Abbottshey Ave L18 69 B2
Abdale Rd L11 39 F3
Aber St 4 L6 53 A3
Abercrombie Rd L33 41 C7
Abercromby Sq L7 52 F1
Aberdale Rd L13 54 B3
Aberdare Cl WA5 60 E1
Aberdeen St CH41 66 C7
Aberford Ave CH45 50 E5
Abergele Rd L13 53 F2
Abingdon Gr
Liverpool,Halewood L26 71 A1
Liverpool,Walton L4 39 C2
Abingdon Rd
Birkenhead CH49 64 B3
Liverpool L4 39 C2
Abinger Rd WN4 34 D4
Abney Cl L7 68 B8
Abotts Lea Sch L25 69 E4
Aboyne Cl L9 39 A4
Abram Bryn Gates Prim Sch WN2 35 F7
Abram St L5 52 E5
Abrams Fold PR9 2 F5
Abrams Gn PR9 2 F5
Abratio St CH41 66 D6
Abyssinia Cl L15 68 E7
Acacia Ave
Huyton-w-R L36 55 D1
Widnes WA8 73 B3
Acacia Cl CH49 64 C2
Acacia Gr
Liverpool L9 39 B6
St Helens WA10 43 A4
Wallasey CH44 51 E2
West Kirby CH48 63 A2
Acacia St WA12 45 F4
Acanthus Rd L13 54 B4
Access Rd L12 54 D7
Acer Leigh L17 68 D2
Acheson Rd L13 53 E6
Achilles Ave WA2 61 B2
Ackerley Cl WA2 61 F3
Ackers Hall Ave L14 54 F5
Ackers Hall Cl L14 54 F5
Ackers La Crosby L23 26 C7
St Helens WA10 43 C4
Ackers Rd CH49 65 C2
Ackers St 11 L34 56 D6
Acland Rd CH44 51 B4
Aconbury Cl L11 39 F3
Aconbury Pl L11 39 F3
Acorn Bsns Ctr L33 30 B1
Acorn Cl Bebington CH63 78 D6
St Helens WA9 58 C4
Acorn Ct L8 67 F6
Acorn St WA12 46 D3
Acorn Venture Urban Farm★ L33 30 D4
Acorn Way L20 38 D5
Acornfield Cl L33 41 C8
Acornfield Rd L33 30 D2
Acorns The L39 13 C3
Acre Gn L26 83 A6
Acre La Bebington CH62 88 D8
Heswall CH60 77 C1
Acrefield Ct CH42 66 B1
Acrefield Pk L25 70 A3
Acrefield Rd
Birkenhead CH42 66 C1
Liverpool L25 70 A3
Widnes WA8 72 B1
Acregate WN8 24 C7
Acres Cl L25 70 A7
Acres La Great Altcar L37 18 E8
Maghull L31,L39 19 E7
Acres Rd Bebington CH63 78 F6
Hoylake CH47 63 F7
Acresgate Ct L25 70 A6
Acreville Rd CH63 78 F5
Acton Cl WA11 45 C6
Acton Gr L6 53 C6
Acton La CH46 64 C7
Acton Rake L30 27 D5
Acton Rd
Birkenhead CH42 67 A1
Burtonwood WA5 59 E6
Kirkby L32 29 C2
Acton Way L7 68 C8
Acuba Gr CH42 66 E4
Acuba Rd L15 54 C1
Adair Pl L13 53 E7
Adair Rd L13 53 E7
Adam Cl L19 81 C5
Adam St L5 52 F6
Adams Cl WA12 46 D2
Adamson St
Ashton-in-M WN4 35 A3
Liverpool L7 53 D2
Adaston Ave CH62 88 F4
Adcote Cl L14 54 F3
Adcote Rd L14 54 F3
Adderley St L7 53 B2
Addingham Ave WA8 84 C7
Addingham Rd L18 69 B5
Addington St CH44 51 D3
Addison Cl L32 40 D8
Addison Sq WA8 73 A1
Addison St Bootle L20 38 A5
Liverpool L3 52 D3
Addison Way L3 52 D3
Adela Rd WA7 84 F2
Adelaide Ave WA9 57 E7
Adelaide Pl L5 52 E4
Adelaide Rd
Birkenhead CH42 66 C4
Liverpool L7 53 B2
Seaforth L21 37 F7
Adelaide St CH44 51 B3
Adelaide Terr L22 26 C1
Adele Thompson Dr 2 L8 68 A7
Adelphi St CH41 66 E6
Adkins St 4 L5 53 A6
Adlam Cres L9 39 E7
Adlam Rd L10,L9 39 E7
Adlington Ho 8 L3 52 D3
Adlington St 7 L3 52 D3
Admin Rd L33 41 C8
Admiral Gr 1 L8 68 A5
Admiral St L8 68 A5
Adrian's Way L32 29 E2
Adshead Rd L13 53 E7
Adstone Rd L25 70 C5
Adswood Rd L36 55 E3
Africander Rd WA11 44 A8
Afton WA8 72 A2
Agar Rd L11 53 F7
Agate St L5 53 A5
Agincourt Rd L12 54 C5
Agnes Gr CH44,CH45 51 C5
Agnes Jones Ho 17 L7,L8 67 F8
Agnes Rd
Birkenhead CH42 66 E3
Crosby L23 26 C3
Agnes St WA9 58 C3
Agnes Way L7 53 B1
Aiden Long Gr L34 55 E6
Aigburth Dr L17 68 C4
Aigburth Gr CH46 64 D8
Aigburth Hall Ave L19, L18 81 A8
Aigburth Hall Rd L19 81 A8
Aigburth Ho L17 68 E3
Aigburth Rd L17,L8 68 D2
Aigburth St L7 68 B8
Aigburth Sta L17 80 E8
Aigburth Vale
Liverpool L17 68 D2
Liverpool L17,L18 68 E3
Aigburty Pk L17 68 B2
Ailsa Rd CH45 51 A5
Ainsdale & Birkdale Sand Hills Nature Reserve★ PR8 7 B7
Ainsdale Cl
Bebington CH63 88 C5
Heswall CH61 77 A5
Liverpool L10 39 F8
Warrington WA5 74 F4
Ainsdale High Sch PR8 7 C6
Ainsdale Rd L20 38 D6
Ainsdale Sand Dunes Nature Reserve★ PR8 6 E3
Ainsdale Sta PR8 7 C5
Ainsworth Ave CH46 64 C6
Ainsworth La L34 41 B6
Ainsworth Rd WA10 43 D5
Ainsworth St L3 90 C3
Aintree Cl CH46 49 F3
Aintree Cres PR8 4 F4
Aintree Ct L10 28 C3
Aintree Davenhill Prim Sch L10 28 D2
Aintree La Aintree L10,L9 28 C3
Liverpool L10 40 A8
Aintree Race Course L9 28 D1
Aintree Racecourse Ret & Bsns Pk L9 28 C2
Aintree Rd Bootle L20 38 E4
Liverpool L9 39 D6
Aintree Sta L30 39 B8
Aintree Way L9 28 C2
Airdale Cl CH43 65 C6
Airdale Rd L15 68 F6
Airdrie Cl CH62 88 D3
Aire WA8 72 B2
Airedale Cl WA5 74 F7
Airegate L31 20 B2
Airlie Gr L13 53 D6
Airlie Rd CH47 63 C8
Aisthorpe Gr L31 28 D7
Ajax Ave WA2 61 B2
Akbar The CH60 76 C2
Akenside St L20 38 A6
Alabama Way CH41 66 F6
Alamein Rd L36 55 D4
Alans Way L33 29 E4
Alastair Cres CH43 65 F1
Alban Rd L16 69 D8
Alban Ret Pk WA2 61 A1
Albany Ave L34 56 F7
Albany Rd
Birkenhead CH42 66 E2
Liverpool,Elm Pk L7 53 A2
Liverpool,Stonycroft L13 54 A4
Liverpool,Warbreck Pk L9 39 B7
Prescot L34 56 E6
Southport PR9 1 C1
Albemarle Rd CH44 51 E3
Albert Ct PR9 1 D1
Albert Dock★ L3 90 A2
Albert Dr Liverpool L20,L9 38 F6
Warrington WA5 74 D6
Albert Edward Rd L7 53 A2
Albert Gr Crosby L23 26 D4
Liverpool L15 69 A8
Albert Pk L17 68 B5
Albert Pl PR9 4 B8
Albert Rd Birkenhead CH42 66 C4
Formby L37 17 B8
Hoylake CH47 63 B6
Liverpool L13 53 D6
Seaforth L22 37 D8
Southport PR9 1 D1
West Kirby CH48 63 A1
2 Widnes WA8 73 B1
Albert Schweitzer Ave L30 27 F4
Albert Sq 1 WA8 73 B1
Albert St Ashton-in-M WN4 35 B3
Liverpool L7 53 A1
St Helens WA10 44 A5
Wallasey CH45 37 C1
Albert Terr
Collins Green WA5 45 E1
Southport PR8 4 A5
Alberta Gr L34 55 F5
Albion Pl CH45 51 B8
Albion St Birkenhead CH41 66 F6
Birkenhead CH41 66 F7
Liverpool L5 52 F6
St Helens WA10 43 E4
Wallasey CH45 51 A8
Albourne Rd L32 41 A8
Albury Cl Haydock WA11 45 D7
Liverpool L12 41 A2
Albury Rd 4 L32 41 A7
Alcester Rd L12 54 C6
Alcott Pl WA2 61 A6
Aldams Gr L4 38 E1
Aldbourne Ave L25 69 E5
Aldbourne Cl L25 69 E4
Aldcliffe WA3 47 F8
Alder Ave
Ashton-in-M WN4 34 F5
Billinge WN5 33 D5
Huyton-w-R L36 71 A8
Widnes WA8 73 B3
Alder Cl L34 56 F6
Alder Cres L32 29 D3
Alder Gr L22 26 D2
Alder Hey Children's Hosp L14 54 C4
Alder Hey Rd WA10 43 C4
Alder La
Burtonwood WA2,WA5 60 C7
Crank WA11 32 F4
Cronton WA8,L35 72 A5
Formby L37,L39 10 E7
Knowsley L34 41 C2
Alder Rd Bebington CH63 78 E4
Golborne WA3 47 F8
Liverpool L12 54 C4
Prescot L34 56 F6
Alder Root La WA5 60 D7
Alder St WA12 46 C3
Alder Wood Ave L24 82 F3
Alderbank Rd WA5 74 F6
Alderdale Ave PR8 7 A5
Alderfield Dr L24 83 A3
Alderlee Pk Cvn Site PR8 5 A2
Alderley WN8 24 C6
Alderley Ave
Birkenhead CH41 65 F7
Golborne WA3 47 D7
Alderley Cl WN5 33 E5
Alderley Rd Hoylake CH47 63 B7
Wallasey CH44 51 B3
Alderney Rd L5 52 D5
Aldersey St L3 52 D3
Aldersgate CH42 66 F2
Aldersgate Dr L26 83 A6
Alderson Cres L37 9 F4
Alderson Rd L15 68 D8
Alderville Rd L4 39 C2
Alderwood Ct WA8 72 E4
Alderwood Lo L24 83 A3
Aldford Cl Bebington CH63 88 B6
Birkenhead CH43 65 E2
Aldford Rd L32 40 E7
Aldridge Cl 1 L12 40 E3
Aldridge Dr WA5 59 F7
Aldrins La L30 27 F5
Aldwark Rd L14 55 A4
Aldwych Rd L12 54 C5
Aldykes L31 28 F8
Alex Cl L8 67 F6
Alexander Ct 1 L13 54 C1
Alexander Dr
Heswall CH61 76 E3
Maghull L31 20 D3
Widnes WA8 84 D8
Alexander Fleming Ave L30 27 F4
Alexander Gn L36 55 E4
Alexander Ho Prescot L34 56 D7
7 Seaforth L21 37 F7
Alexander Way 10 L8 67 F4
Alexander Wlk L4 52 F8
Alexandra Cl Liverpool L6 53 B3
Skelmersdale WN8 15 E1
Alexandra Ct 2 CH45 51 A8
Alexandra Dr
Birkenhead CH42 66 E1
Bootle L20 38 F6
Liverpool L17 68 B4
St Helens WA10 43 D2
Alexandra Gn L17 68 B4
Alexandra Ho L17 68 B4
Alexandra Ind Est WA8 84 F7
Alexandra Mews
1 Ormskirk L39 13 E6
8 Southport PR9 4 C8
Alexandra Mount L21 38 B8
Alexandra Pk 1 L17 68 B3
Alexandra Rd
Ashton-in-M WN4 35 B4
Birkenhead CH43 66 C5
Crosby L23 26 D4
Formby L37 9 B1
Liverpool L7 68 C8
Liverpool,Stanley L13 54 A2
Seaforth L22 37 E8
Southport PR9 4 D8
Wallasey CH45 51 A8
West Kirby CH48 63 A1
Alexandra St Abram WN2 36 B8
St Helens WA10 43 D1
Alexandra Terr 9 L8 67 F7
Alexandra Villas L21 38 B8
Alexandria Rd L19 81 C7
Alfonso Rd L4 52 D8
Alford Ave WA9 58 B4
Alford St L7 53 E2
Alfred Mews L1 90 C1
Alfred Rd Birkenhead CH43 66 C5
Haydock WA11 45 F7
Wallasey CH44 51 E1
Alfred St Liverpool L15 68 D8
Newton-le-W WA12 46 E3
Rainford WA11 31 F7
St Helens WA10 44 B4
Alfriston Rd L12 54 C6
Algernon St WA7 84 F3
Alice St WA9 58 E8
Alicia Wlk L10 40 B7
Alison Ave CH42 66 F3
Alison Pl L13 53 E7
Alison Rd L13 53 E7
Alistair Dr CH63 88 C6
All Saints Cl L30 27 E3
All Saints RC High Sch L32 29 E1
All Saints RC Prim Sch
Golborne WA3 47 B8
Liverpool L4 53 B6
All Saints Rd L24 82 C3
All Saints Upton CE Prim Sch WA8 72 B3
Allan Rd WA11 44 C7
Allangate Cl CH49 64 C2
Allangate Rd L19 81 B8
Allanson St WA9 44 D3
Allanson Street Prim Sch WA9 44 D2
Allcot Ave CH42 66 D2
Allenby Ave L22,L23 26 F2
Allenby Sq L13 54 A2
Allendale Ave
4 Liverpool L9 39 B7
Rainhill L35 57 D3
Allengate 1 L23 26 E5
Allerby Way WA3 47 E8
Allerford Rd L12 54 D8
Allerton Beeches L18 69 C3
Allerton Dr L18 69 B4
Allerton Gr CH42 66 E3
Allerton Rd
Birkenhead CH42 66 E3
Liverpool L18 69 B5
Liverpool,Calderstones L18, L25 69 D3
Liverpool,Wavertree L18 69 A5
Liverpool,Woolton L25 70 A2
Southport PR9 1 E1
Wallasey CH45 51 A6
Widnes WA8 73 B1
Allerton Sta L19 81 D6
Allesley Rd L14 54 F5
Alleyne Rd L4 53 D8
Allington St L17 68 B3
Allonby Cl CH43 65 E4
Allport La CH62 88 D8
Allport Rd CH62,CH63 88 D7
Allports The CH62 88 D7
Allscott Way WN4 35 C3
Alma Cl
Liverpool L10 40 B7
Up Holland WN8 25 C7
Alma Ct
Southport PR8 7 F7
Up Holland WN8 25 C7
Alma Hill WN8 25 C7
Alma Hill Est WN8 25 C7
Alma Par WN8 25 C7
Alma Pl WA9 44 C2
Alma Rd
Liverpool L17 80 E8
Southport PR8 4 A4
Up Holland WN8 25 C7
Alma St
Bebington CH62 79 A7
5 Birkenhead CH41 66 E6
Newton-le-W WA12 46 B3
St Helens WA9 44 C2
Alma Vale Terr L20 38 B3
Almacs Cl L23 26 B3
Alman Ct 3 L17 68 B3
Almeda Rd L24 83 A2
Almond Ave L30 27 C3
Almond Cl Liverpool L26 82 E7
St Helens WA11 44 F5
Almond Ct L19 81 E5
Almond Dr WA5 59 F6
Almond Gr WA8 84 D8
Almond Pl CH46 64 F8
Almond Tree Cl L24 83 E1
Almond Way CH49 64 C2
Almond's Gn L12 54 A8
Almond's Gr L12 54 A8
Almond's Turn L30 27 D4
Almonds Pk L12 54 A8
Almonds The L26 82 E7
Almonry The L40 15 B7
Almshouses L39 21 A7
Alness Dr L35 57 D2
Alnwick Dr CH46 64 C8
Aloeswood Cl 6 L6 53 B5
Alpass Rd 4 L17 68 B3
Alpha Dr CH42 67 A1
Alpha St L20,L21 38 B5
Alpine Cl WA10 43 C4
Alpine St WA12 46 A3
Alresford Rd L19 80 F8
Alroy Rd L4 53 A7
Alscot Ave L10 40 B7
Alscot Cl L31 28 D8
Alsop High Sch A Tech Coll The L4 39 A2
Alston Cl CH62 79 C1
Alston Ct PR8 7 E6
Alston Rd L17 80 E8
Alstonfield Rd L14 55 A4
Alt WA8 72 B2
Alt Ave L31 28 C7
Alt Bridge Rd L36 55 D4
Alt Rd Bootle L20 38 C5
Formby L37 10 B2
Hightown L38 18 A4
Huyton-w-R L36 55 E3
Alt Side Ct L10 40 B7
Alt St L8 68 B7
Altbridge Pk L11 40 B4
Altcar Ave L15 68 D7
Altcar Dr CH46 64 D7
Altcar La Formby L37 9 F1
Haskayne L39 12 A2
Maghull L31 19 F5
Altcar Rd Bootle L20 38 C5
Formby L37 10 B2
Altcross Rd L11 40 C4
Altcross Way L11 40 C4
Altfield Rd L14 54 F7
Altfinch Cl L14 55 A7
Altham Rd
Liverpool L11 53 F8
Southport PR8 4 E2
Althorp St L8 67 F3
Althorpe Dr PR8 4 E3
Altmoor Rd L36 55 D5

Alton Ave L21 27 A1
Alton Cl Ashton-in-M WN4 35 A4
Hightown L38 17 F2
Alton Ct CH43 66 A4
Alton Rd Birkenhead CH43 66 A5
Liverpool L6 53 D5
Altway L10 28 D3
Altway Ct L10 28 C3
Altys La L39 13 F3
Alundale Ct 13 L20 38 C3
Alundale Rd L12 54 E5
Alva Rd L35 57 D2
Alvanley Gn L32 29 C2
Alvanley Pl CH43 66 C6
Alvanley Rd Kirkby L32 29 C2
Liverpool L12 54 C6
Alvega Cl CH62 79 C7
Alverstone Ave CH41 65 F7
Alverstone Cl WA5 74 C7
Alverstone Rd
Liverpool L18 68 F5
Wallasey CH44 51 D3
Alverton Cl WA8 84 D8
Alvina La Kirkby L33 30 A5
Liverpool L4 52 E7
Alwain Gn L24 82 F2
Alwen St CH41 50 F1
Alwyn Ave L21 27 B1
Alwyn Cl L17 68 B3
Alwyn Gdns CH46 64 F8
Alwyn St L17 68 B3
Amanda Rd Liverpool L10 40 B7
Rainhill L35 57 B5
Amanda Way L31 29 B4
Amaury Cl L23 27 B5
Amaury Rd L23 27 B5
Ambassador Dr L26 71 A1
Amber Way L14 55 A7
Ambergate WN8 24 B7
Ambergate Cl 3 WA9 58 D7
Ambergate Rd L19 81 B8
Amberley Ave CH46 64 C7
Amberley Cl
Birkenhead CH46 64 C7
Liverpool L6 53 D7
Ambleside Ave CH46 64 D8
Ambleside Cl
Bebington CH62 88 E7
Heswall CH61 77 A6
Ambleside Cres WA2 61 C3
Ambleside Pl WA11 33 B1
Ambleside Rd
Liverpool L18 69 D1
Maghull L31 20 D2
Ambrose Ct 3 L4 53 B6
Amelia Cl Liverpool L6 52 F3
Widnes WA8 73 B4
Amersham WN8 24 C7
Amersham Rd L4 39 C2
Amery Gr CH42 66 C2
Amethyst Cl Litherland L21 38 C8
5 Liverpool L6 53 B4
Amherst Rd L17 68 C2
Amis Gr WA3 47 E8
Amity St L8 67 F5
Amos Ave L21 38 C8
Ampleforth Cl 3 L32 29 C1
Ampthill Rd L17 68 D2
Ampulla Rd L11 40 C3
Amy Wlk L10 40 B7
Ancaster Rd L17 68 D2
Ancholme Cl L35 57 A6
Anchor St PR9 4 B7
Anchorage La L18 68 E3
Anchorage The L3 67 D6
Ancient Mdws L9 39 B7
Ancroft Rd L14 55 A3
Ancrum Rd L33 29 D6
Anders Dr L33 30 A5
Anderson Cl Heswall CH61 77 A6
Rainhill L35 57 D1
Anderson Ct CH62 88 D6
Anderson Rd L21 27 D1
Anderson St L5 52 E6
Anderson Way L21 27 D1
Anderton Terr L36 55 C2
Andover Cl WA2 61 E1
Andover Rd
Ashton-in-M WA11 34 E1
Haydock WA11 45 E8
Andover Way L25 82 D8
Andreas Cl PR8 4 B4
Andrew Ave Billinge WN5 33 F5
Kirkby L31 29 B3
Andrew Cl WA8 84 C8
Andrew St L4 38 F1
Andrew's Wlk CH60 86 B8
Andrews Cl L37 9 E1
Andrews La L37 9 E1
Andrews Yort L37 9 E1
Andromeda Way WA9 59 B7
Anemone Way WA9 59 A7
Anfield (Liverpool FC) Mus & Tour Ctr★ L4 53 A7
Anfield Com Comp Sch L4 53 B7
Anfield Ct L4 53 A7
Anfield Inf Sch L4 53 B6
Anfield Jun Sch L4 53 B6
Anfield Rd L4 53 A7
Angela St L7 68 B8
Angers La L31 29 B6
Anglesea Rd L9 38 F3
Anglesea Way L8 67 F4
Anglesey Rd
Wallasey CH44 51 B5
West Kirby CH48 63 A3
Anglezark Cl L7 53 B2
Anglia Way L25 82 C8
Anglican Ct L8 90 C1
Anglo Cl L9 39 C8
Angus Rd Bebington CH63 88 C6
Liverpool L11 53 F8
Ann St WN8 23 E8
Annan Gr WN4 35 E5
Annandale Cl L33 29 D6
Annandale Gdns WN8 25 A7
Anne Ave PR8 7 E6
Anne Gr WA9 58 C7
Anne St WA9 58 D3
Annerley St L7 68 C8
Annesley Rd Liverpool L17 68 C1
Wallasey CH44 51 C3
Annette Ave WA12 46 A5
Annie Rd L20 38 D6
Anscot Ave CH63 78 F6
Ansdell Dr WA10 43 B5
Ansdell Gr PR9 2 A4
Ansdell Rd WA8 73 C2
Ansdell Villas' Rd L35 57 C4
Ansford Ave WN2 36 B8
Anson Cl WA2 61 E2
Anson Mews CH43 65 F8
Anson St L3 52 F2
Anstey Cl CH46 49 B1
Anstey Rd L13 54 B2
Ansty Cl WA11 44 D6
Anthony's Way CH60 86 A7
Anthorn Cl CH43 65 D4
Antler Ct WN4 35 B6
Antonio St L20 38 E1
Antons Cl L26 82 F6
Antons Rd Heswall CH61 77 A5
Liverpool L26 82 F6
Antrim Cl WA11 45 C6
Antrim Rd WA2 61 A2
Antrim St L13 53 E7
Anvil Cl Bootle L20 38 B4
Orrell WN5 25 D5
Anzacs The CH62 79 C6
Anzio Rd L36 55 D4
Apartments The PR9 4 B8
Apex Ct CH62 79 E1
Apollo Cres L33 29 E4
Apollo Way Litherland L30 27 F4
Liverpool L6 53 B5
Apostles Way L33 29 D5
Appin Rd CH41 66 E5
Apple Ct 3 L6 53 B3
Apple Dell Ave WA3 36 C1
Apple Tree Cl Hale L24 83 E1
Huyton-w-R L28 55 B8
Appleby Cl WA8 84 C8
Appleby Dr L30 27 D3
Appleby Gn L12 54 D6
Appleby Gr CH62 88 D6
Appleby Lawn L27 71 A4
Appleby Rd Kirkby L33 29 E5
Warrington WA2 61 C3
Appleby Wlk Liverpool L27 71 A4
5 Widnes WA8 84 C8
Applecorn Cl WA9 58 D5
Appledore Ct L24 82 B4
Appledore Gr WA9 58 C5
Applegarth CH46 64 C6
Appleton Dr CH49 64 E3
Appleton Rd
Litherland L21 27 A1
Liverpool L4 39 A1
Skelmersdale WN8 15 F2
St Helens WA9 44 C1
Widnes WA8 73 B1
Appleton Village WA8 73 B1
Appletree Cl L18 69 C1
Appletree Gr WA2 61 F2
April Gr L6 53 D5
April Rise L30 27 E3
Apsley Ave CH45 51 B6
Apsley Brow L31 20 B1
Apsley Gr CH63 79 A6
Apsley Rd Bebington CH62 79 B8
Liverpool L12 54 C6
Aquarius Cl L14 55 A4
Arabis Gdns WA9 59 B7
Aragon Cl L31 20 E3
Aran Cl L24 83 D1
Arborn Dr CH49 65 A6
Arbour La L33 30 B2
Arbour St PR8 4 C6
Arbury Ave WA11 44 D6
Arbury La WA2 61 C6
Arcadia Ave L31 20 D3
Arch La WN4 34 B3
Arch View Cres L1 90 C2
Archbishop Beck RC High Sch & Sports Coll L9 39 B6
Archbishop Blanch CE High Sch L7 53 A1
Archbishop Warlock Ct L3 52 C4
Archbrook Mews L13 53 E5
Archer Cl L4 52 E7
Archer Gr WA9 44 E4
Archer St L4 52 E7
Archerfield Rd L18 69 B1
Archers Croft CH62 79 D1
Archers Ct 9 CH49 65 A2
Archers Fold L31 29 B4
Archers Gn CH62 88 E3
Archers Way 1 CH49 65 A2
Archway Rd L36 55 E2
Archway Wlk WA12 46 E3
Arctic Rd L20 38 A3
Arden WA8 72 A2
Arden Cl PR8 7 A5
Ardennes Rd L36 55 E3
Arderne Cl CH63 79 B2
Ardleigh Ave PR8 4 E3
Ardleigh Cl L13 53 F2
Ardleigh Gr L13 53 F2
Ardleigh Pl L13 53 F2
Ardleigh Rd L13 53 F2
Ardmore Rd L18 69 A2
Ardrossan Rd L4 53 C8
Ardville Rd L11 39 D3
Ardwick Rd L24 82 F3
Ardwick St WA9 44 C3
Argameols Cl PR8 4 F5
Argarmeols Gr L37 9 E5
Argarmeols Rd L37 9 E6
Argo Rd L22 26 D1
Argos Pl L20 38 D1
Argos Rd 1 L20 38 D1
Argyle Ct 2 Crosby L23 26 E3
Southport PR9 1 D1
Argyle Rd
Liverpool,Cabbage Hall L4 53 B6
Liverpool,Garston L19 81 C6
Southport PR9 1 D2
Argyle St Birkenhead CH41 66 E6
Liverpool L1 90 B2
St Helens WA10 43 F5
Argyle St S CH41 66 E5
Argyle Street Hamilton Sq CH41 66 E7
Argyll Ave CH62 88 D4
Argyll Cl WN4 34 C4
Ariel Wlk 4 WA3 47 E8
Aries Cl L14 55 A5
Ariss Gr L35 57 A5
Ark Royal Way CH41 66 F4
Arkenstone Cl WA8 72 C2
Arkle Rd CH43 65 F8
Arkles La L4 53 B7
Arkles Rd L4 53 A6
Arklow Dr L24 83 D2
Arkwood Cl CH62 79 C3
Arkwright St L5 52 E5
Arlescourt Rd L12 54 D6
Arley Cl CH43 65 C6
Arley Dr WA8 72 B2
Arley St L3 52 C4
Arlington Ave 10 L18 68 F5
Arlington Cl PR8 7 A5
Arlington Ct CH43 65 F5
Arlington Dr WA5 74 E4
Arlington Rd CH45 50 E6
Armill Rd L11 40 C3
Armitage Gdns L18 69 B1
Armley Rd L4 53 B7
Armour Ave WA2 61 B2
Armour Gr 5 L13 54 A2
Armoury Bank WN4 35 B3
Armoury The L12 54 B7
Armscot Cl L25 82 B7
Armscot Pl L25 82 B7
Armstrong Quay L3 67 F3
Arncliffe Dr WA5 59 F6
Arncliffe Rd L25 82 D8
Arnhem Rd L36 55 E3
Arnian Ct L39 21 C7
Arnian Rd WA11 31 F7
Arnian Way WA11 31 F7
Arno Ct CH43 66 B3
Arno Rd CH42,CH43 66 B3
Arnold Ave WA10 43 D5
Arnold Cl WA9 44 C1
Arnold Cres 1 L8 68 A6
Arnold Gr L15 69 A8
Arnold Pl WA8 84 C7
Arnold St Liverpool L8 67 F6
Wallasey CH45 51 B5
Arnot Cl WA10 43 F5
Arnot Com Prim Sch L4 38 F1
Arnot St L4 38 F1
Arnot Way CH63 78 D7
Arnside L21 38 D8
Arnside Ave
Haydock WA11 45 B6
Rainhill L35 57 A4
Arnside Rd
Birkenhead CH43 66 A4
Huyton-w-R L36 55 B2
Liverpool L7 53 C1
Southport PR9 4 C7
Wallasey CH45 51 B5
Arnside Terr PR9 4 C7
Aron Ct L34 56 D6
Arrad St L1,L7 67 F8
Arran Cl WA11 44 E6
Arranmore Rd L18 69 A2
Arrowe Ave CH46 64 D7
Arrowe Brook Ct CH49 64 E4
Arrowe Brook La CH49 64 E1
Arrowe Brook Rd CH49 64 E3
Arrowe Ct 7 CH49 65 A2
Arrowe Ctry Pk★
Birkenhead CH49 65 A1
★ Birkenhead CH49 76 F8
Arrowe Hill Prim Sch CH49 65 A3
Arrowe Park Hospl CH49 65 A2
Arrowe Park Rd CH49 65 A2
Arrowe Rd CH49 64 E3
Arrowe Side CH49 64 E4
Arrowsmith Rd WA11 45 F7
Arthur St Birkenhead CH41 66 C7
Birkenhead CH41 66 C8
Liverpool,Garston L19 81 D5
Liverpool,Walton L9 38 F3
Runcorn WA7 84 F2
Arundel Ave Liverpool L17 68 D6
Wallasey CH45 50 F6
Arundel Cl Heswall CH61 76 E5
Arundel Cl *continued*
5 Liverpool L8 68 A6
Arundel Rd PR8 7 F8
Arundel St L4 38 F1
Arundell Cl WA5 59 F6
Arvon St L20 38 D6
Asbridge St L8 68 B7
Asbury Cl L18 69 D3
Asbury Rd CH45 50 D6
Ascot Ave L21 38 A8
Ascot Cl PR8 3 E5
Ascot Dr Bebington CH63 78 F5
Kirkby L33 29 E5
Ascot Gr CH63 78 F5
Ascot Pk L23 26 F4
Ascroft Rd L9 39 B8
Ash Ave WA12 46 C2
Ash Cl Liverpool L15 68 E8
Ormskirk L39 13 D5
Ash Cres L36 70 E8
Ash Gr Formby L37 9 C1
Golborne WA3 47 B8
Liverpool L15 68 D8
Orrell WN5 25 F6
Prescot L35 56 E5
Rainford WA11 31 F6
Seaforth L21 38 A6
Skelmersdale WN8 15 D1
St Helens WA9 58 C4
Wallasey CH45 51 C7
Widnes WA8 84 D8
Ash Grange L14 54 E3
Ash Grove Cres WN5 33 E6
Ash La WA8 84 A8
Ash Priors WA8 72 D3
Ash Rd Bebington CH63 78 F7
Birkenhead CH42 66 D4
Haydock WA11 45 E7
Litherland L21 38 A7
Warrington WA5 74 F4
Winwick WA2 61 B6
Ash St Bootle L20 38 C4
Golborne WA3 36 B2
Southport PR8 4 C5
Ash Tree Apartments CH44 51 D3
Ash Vale L15 68 E8
Ash Villas CH44 51 C2
Ash Way CH60 86 B6
Ashbank Rd L11 40 B2
Ashbourne Ave
Crosby L23 26 C4
Litherland L30 27 E2
Ashbourne Cres L36 55 B3
Ashbourne Rd L17 68 C2
Ashbrook Dr L9 39 C6
Ashbrook Terr CH63 79 A6
Ashburn Ave L33 29 E4
Ashburton Ave CH43 65 F6
Ashburton Cl CH43 65 E6
Ashburton Rd
Birkenhead CH43 65 F6
Wallasey CH44 51 B4
West Kirby CH48 63 B2
Ashbury Dr WA11 45 D7
Ashbury Rd L14 55 B6
Ashby Cl CH46 49 B1
Ashcombe Rd L14 54 C3
Ashcroft Ave L39 13 F6
Ashcroft Dr CH61 76 F3
Ashcroft Rd Formby L37 9 F1
Kirkby L33 30 C3
Ashcroft St Bootle L20 38 B3
St Helens WA9 44 C3
Ashdale L36 55 D2
Ashdale Cl L37 9 C2
Ashdale Pk CH49 64 B4
Ashdale Rd Crosby L22 26 D2
Liverpool,Hartley's Village L9 39 A4
Liverpool,Mossley Hill L18 69 A5
Ashdown Cl PR8 4 E4
Ashdown Cres WA9 58 C4
Ashdown Dr CH49 64 C2
Ashdown Gr L26 71 A1
Ashfarm Ct L14 54 F3
Ashfield Liverpool L15 68 D8
Rainhill L35 57 D3
Ashfield Cres
Bebington CH62 88 D8
Billinge WN5 33 E4
Ashfield Rd
Bebington CH62 88 C8
Liverpool L17 68 E2
Ashfield Sch L16 69 E6
Ashfield St L5 52 C5
Ashford Cl L26 82 E7
Ashford Rd
Birkenhead CH41,CH42 66 C4
Hoylake CH47 63 C8
Ashford Way WA8 73 D1
Ashland Ave WN4 35 A4
Ashlar Gr L17 68 E2
Ashlar Rd Crosby L22 26 E2
Liverpool L17 68 E3
Ashlea Rd CH61 77 A3
Ashleigh Rd L31 28 F7
Ashley Ave CH47 48 F1
Ashley Cl Kirkby L33 29 E5
Rainhill L35 57 D2
Ashley Gn WA8 84 D8
Ashley Rd
Skelmersdale WN8 16 B3
Southport PR9 4 C7
Ashley Sch WA8 72 D1
Ashley St CH42 66 F2
Ashley Way W WA8 84 F7
Ashmead Rd WN8 16 A4
Ashmore Cl CH48 75 C6
Ashmuir Hey L32 29 F1
Ashover Ave L14 55 A4
Ashridge St WA7 84 F3
Ashton Ave L35 57 C2
Ashton Cl CH62 88 E3
Ashton Ct CH48 63 A2
Ashton Dr Liverpool L25 82 C7
West Kirby CH48 63 A1
Ashton Grange Ind Est WN4 35 B6
Ashton Heath WN4 35 C2
Ashton House Hospl CH43 66 B4
Ashton Pk L25 82 D8
Ashton Rd Golborne WA3 36 A2
Newton-le-W WA12 46 C5
Southport PR8 3 F1
Windy Arbour WN4,WN5 34 B8
Ashton Sq L25 70 B1
Ashton St Liverpool L3 52 F1
Liverpool,Stanley L13 54 A3
Ashton's La L24 82 F1
Ashtons Green Dr WA9 44 F3
Ashtree Gr L12 40 F4
Ashurst Cl Liverpool L25 70 B4
Skelmersdale WN8 16 A4
St Helens WA11 44 E6
Ashurst Ct L37 9 E2
Ashurst Dr WA11 44 E6
Ashurst Gdns WN8 16 B4
Ashurst Prim Sch WA11 44 D6
Ashurst Rd WN8 16 B4
Ashville Rd
Birkenhead CH41,CH43 66 B7
Wallasey CH44 51 D2
Ashwall St WN8 23 E8
Ashwater Rd L12 40 C2
Ashwell Ave WA3 36 D1
Ashwell St L8 90 C1
Ashwood WN8 16 C3
Ashwood Ave
Abram Brow WN2 36 C7
Ashton-in-M WN4 35 A2
Golborne WA3 47 D8
Ashwood Cl Kirkby L33 29 E5
Liverpool L27 70 E5
Ashwood Ct CH43 50 C1
Ashwood Dr L12 40 D3
Ashworth Hospl L31 21 B2
Askern Rd L32 40 F8
Askett Cl WA11 45 C7
Askew Cl CH44 51 D4
Askew St 2 L4 38 F1
Askham Cl L8 68 B7
Asland Gdns PR9 2 C4
Asmall Cl L39 13 D6
Asmall La
Haskayne L39,L40 12 E8
Ormskirk L39,L40 13 B7
Asmall Prim Sch L39 13 D6
Aspen Cl Heswall CH60 86 D8
Kirkby L33 29 F6
Aspen Gdns WA9 57 C6
Aspen Gr Formby L37 9 C1
Liverpool L8 68 C6
Aspen Way 3 WN8 15 E2
Aspendale Rd CH42 66 D4
Aspenwood WN4 35 A2
Aspes Rd L12 54 E7
Aspinall Cres L37 10 F1
Aspinall St
Birkenhead CH41 66 C7
Prescot L34 56 D6
Asquith Ave CH41 66 B7
Asser Rd L11 53 F8
Assheton Cl WA12 46 B4
Assheton Wlk L24 83 E2
Assissian Cres L30 27 E4
Aster Dr L33 29 D5
Aster Rd WA11 45 F7
Asterfield Ave CH63 78 E7
Astley Cl Rainford WA11 31 F7
Widnes WA8 72 C3
Astley Rd L36 55 E5
Aston Cl CH43 65 F3
Aston St L19 81 D5
Astonwood Rd CH42 66 D3
Astor St L4 38 F2
Atheldene Rd L4 39 C2
Athelstan Cl CH62 79 D1
Atherton Cl L5 52 E5
Atherton Dr CH49 65 A3
Atherton House Sch L23 26 D4
Atherton Rake L30 27 D4
Atherton Rd L9 39 C6
Atherton St
Bickershaw WN2 36 E8
9 Prescot L34 56 D6
St Helens WA10 43 F4
Wallasey CH45 51 B8
Athlone Rd WA2 61 A1
Athol Cl Bebington CH62 88 E5
Newton-le-W WA12 45 F4
Athol Dr CH62 88 E5
Athol St Birkenhead CH41 66 E7
Liverpool L5 52 B5
Liverpool L5 52 C5
Liverpool L5 52 D5
Athole Gr PR9 4 F7
Atholl Cres L10 28 D2
Atkinson Gr L36 55 F4
Atkinson St WN2 36 B8
Atlanta Ct L33 29 D6
Atlantic Point L3 52 D3

Bradshaw St WA8 73 A2
Bradshaw's La PR8 7 D6
Bradstone Cl L10 40 B6
Bradville Rd L9 39 C7
Bradwell Cl CH48 63 D2
Bradwell Rd WA3 47 E7
Brae St L7 53 B2
Braehaven Rd CH45 51 C7
Braemar Ave PR9 1 E2
Braemar Cl L35 56 F3
Braemar St L20 38 D1
Braemore Rd CH44 50 F4
Braeside Cres WN5 33 D5
Braeside Gdns CH49 64 F5
Brahms Cl L8 68 B6
Braid St CH41 66 D8
Brainerd St L13 53 E5
Braithwaite Cl L35 57 C3
Braithwaite Rd WA3 47 D8
Bramberton Pl L4 39 C1
Bramberton Rd L4 39 C1
Bramble Ave CH41 65 F8
Bramble Cl WA5 74 E3
Bramble Way CH46 49 D2
Brambles The WN4 34 D5
Bramblewood Cl L27 70 E5
Brambling Pk L26 70 E1
Brambling Way WA3 47 E7
Bramcote Ave WA11 44 D6
Bramcote Cl L33 30 A4
Bramcote Rd L33 30 A4
Bramcote Wlk L33 29 F4
Bramerton Ct CH48 63 A3
Bramford Cl CH49 64 E5
Bramhall Cl Liverpool L24 82 E2
West Kirby CH48 63 D1
Bramhall Dr CH62 88 F4
Bramhall Rd Seaforth L22 37 E8
Skelmersdale WN8 15 F2
Bramley Ave CH63 78 E7
Bramley Cl L27 70 E5
Bramley Way L32 29 C3
Bramley Wlk L24 82 D2
Bramleys The L31 28 C7
Brampton Ct WA9 45 B3
Brampton Dr L8 68 A8
Bramwell Ave CH43 66 A1
Bramwell St WA9 44 E4
Branch Way WA11 45 D6
Brancker Ave L35 57 B4
Brancote Ct CH43 65 F6
Brancote Gdns CH62 88 D7
Brancote Mount CH43 65 F6
Brancote Rd CH43 65 F6
Brandearth Hey L28 55 B7
Brandearth Ho L28 55 B7
Brandon WA8 72 B2
Brandon Cl WN8 25 A7
Brandon St CH41 66 F6
Brandreth Cl L35 57 C3
Brandwood Ave WA2 61 B2
Branfield Cl L12 40 E3
Bransdale Cl WA5 74 F7
Bransdale Dr WN4 35 D3
Bransford Cl WN4 35 C2
Branson Cl WA3 36 A2
Branstree Ave L11 39 F2
Brantfield Ct WA2 61 E2
Branthwaite Cl [1] L11 40 A1
Branthwaite Cres L11 40 A1
Branthwaite Gr [4] L11 40 A1
Brasenose Rd L20 38 C1
Brassey St
Birkenhead CH41 66 B8
Liverpool L8 67 E6
Brathay Cl WA2 61 C3
Brattan Rd CH41 66 C4
Braunton Rd Liverpool L17 68 E1
[2] Wallasey CH45 51 A6
Bray Rd L24 82 C4
Bray St CH41 66 B8
Braybrooke Rd L11 40 A3
Braydon Cl L25 82 C6
Brayfield Rd L4 39 D1
Brechin Rd L33 29 F2
Breck Pl CH44 51 A3
Breck Rd Liverpool L6 53 A5
Wallasey CH44 50 F4
Widnes WA8 73 B1
Breckfield Comm Comp Sch
L5 52 F5
Breckfield Pl L5 52 F5
Breckfield Prim Sch L5 52 F6
Breckfield Rd N L5 53 A5
Breckfield Rd S L6 53 A5
Breckside Ave CH44 50 E4
Breckside Pk L6 53 C6
Brecon Ave L30 27 F1
Brecon Ct WA5 60 E2
Brecon Rd Bebington CH42 78 C8
Birkenhead CH42 66 C1
Brecon Wlk L30 28 A1
Bredon Ct L37 9 E4
Breeze Cl L9 38 F3
Breeze Hill Bootle L20,L4 38 E2
[9] Liverpool L4 38 F2
Breeze La L9 38 F3
Breeze Rd PR8 3 E2
Brelade Rd L13 53 F4
Bremhill Rd L11 39 F3
Bremner Cl L7 53 C1
Brenda Cres L23 27 A7
Brendale Ave L31 28 C8
Brendan's Way L30 27 E3
Brendon Ave
Litherland L21 27 A1
Warrington WA2 61 A3
Brendon Gr WA9 45 A4
Brendor Rd L25 70 B1
Brenig St CH41 50 F1
Brenka Ave L9 28 B1
Brent Way L26 82 F6
Brentfield WA8 72 D2
Brentwood Ave
Crosby L23 26 F5
Liverpool L17 68 C3
Brentwood Cl
Hightown L38 17 F2
St Helens WA10 43 B3
Brentwood Ct
[8] Birkenhead CH49 65 A2
Southport PR9 1 D1
Brentwood Gr L33 29 E6
Brentwood St CH44 51 C3
Brereton Ave
Bebington CH63 79 A6
Liverpool L15 69 A7
Bretherton Pl L35 57 C4
Bretherton Rd L34 56 E6
Bretlands Rd L23 27 B6
Brett St CH41 66 B8
Bretton Fold PR8 4 F5
Brewery La Aintree L31 28 E4
Formby L37 9 F6
Brewster St L20,L4 38 E1
Breydon Gdns WA9 57 E6
Brian Ave CH61 76 F6
Briar Cl WN4 35 A4
Briar Dr Heswall CH60 86 A8
Huyton-w-R L36 55 D2
Briar Rd Golborne WA3 47 B8
Southport PR8 7 D4
Briar St L4,L5 52 D7
Briar Wlk WA3 47 B8
Briardale Rd
Bebington CH63 78 F7
Birkenhead CH42 66 C4
Liverpool L18 69 A4
Wallasey CH44 51 E2
Willaston CH64 88 A1
Briarfield Ave WA8 72 A1
Briarfield Rd CH60 86 B8
Briars Cl L35 57 D1
Briars Gn
Skelmersdale WN8 16 B4
St Helens WA10 43 F5
Briars Hey L35 57 D1
Briars La L31 20 E1
Briars The PR8 3 F1
Briarswood Cl
Bebington CH42 78 F8
Prescot L35 56 F3
Briarwood L23 26 B6
Briarwood Rd L17 68 E3
Briary Cl CH60 77 B1
Briary Croft L38 17 F3
Brick St Liverpool L1 90 B1
Newton-le-W WA12 45 F3
Brickfields L36 56 A1
Bricklayers Arms Yd L39 13 D6
Brickwall Gn L29 27 F7
Brickwall La L29,L30 27 E6
Bride St [4] L4 38 F2
Bridge Ave L39 13 E5
Bridge Bank Cl WA3 47 B7
Bridge Croft L21,L30 27 C3
Bridge Ct Litherland L30 27 D4
West Kirby CH48 63 A3
Bridge Farm Cl CH49 65 B4
Bridge Farm Dr L31 20 F2
Bridge Gdns L12 40 F1
Bridge Gr PR8 4 B6
Bridge Ho L39 13 E4
Bridge Ind Est L24 82 B5
Bridge La L30 27 E3
Bridge Rd Bootle L21 38 B7
Crosby L23 26 C3
Huyton-w-R L36 55 C2
Liverpool L7 68 D8
Liverpool,Mossley Hill L18 69 A3
Maghull L31 28 D7
Prescot L34,L35 56 E5
St Helens WA9 58 D2
West Kirby CH48 63 A3
Bridge St Bebington CH62 79 B5
Birkenhead CH41 66 E7
Bootle L20 38 B2
Golborne WA3 47 A7
Newton-le-W WA12 46 B3
Ormskirk L39 13 E4
Southport PR8 4 B6
St Helens WA10 44 A3
Bridge Wills La PR9 2 C5
Bridgecroft Rd CH45 51 B6
Bridgefield Cl L25 70 B7
Bridgefield Forum (L Ctr)
L26 71 A2
Bridgeford Ave L12 54 A7
Bridgehall Dr WN8 25 B7
Bridgeman St WA10 43 D3
Bridgemere Cl L7 53 D3
Bridgemere Ho L17 68 D2
Bridgend Cl WA8 72 D3
Bridgend Dr PR8 7 B4
Bridgenorth Rd CH61 76 E4
Bridges La
Maghull L29,L31 28 A8
Sefton L29 27 F7
Bridgeview Dr L33 29 F4
Bridgewater Cl L21 27 A2
Bridgewater Ct L21 27 A2
Bridgewater St L1 90 B1
Bridgewater Way L36 71 A8
Bridgeway L11 39 E1
Bridle Ave CH44 51 E2
Bridle Cl Bebington CH62 88 E7
Bridle Cl *continued*
Birkenhead CH43 65 B6
Bridle Ct WA9 58 C8
Bridle Pk CH62 88 E7
Bridle Rd Bebington CH62 88 E6
Bootle L30 38 F8
Litherland L30 28 A1
Wallasey CH44 51 E2
Bridle Way Bootle L30 38 F7
Kirkby L33 29 D6
Bridport St L3 90 C4
Brierfield WN8 24 D6
Brierfield Rd L15 68 F6
Brierley Cl L30 28 B4
Briers Cl WA2 61 F3
Briery Hey Ave L33 29 F2
Brighouse Cl L39 13 D6
Bright St Birkenhead CH41 66 C6
[6] Liverpool L6 53 A3
Southport PR9 4 F7
Brightgate Cl L7 68 B8
Brighton Rd Crosby L22 26 D1
Huyton-w-R L36 56 B3
Southport PR8 4 A3
Brighton St CH44 51 E3
Brighton Vale L22 26 C2
Brightwell Cl
Birkenhead CH49 64 F4
Warrington WA5 74 E5
Brignall Gr WA3 36 D1
Brill St CH41 66 B8
Brimelow Cres WA5 74 E3
Brimstage Ave CH63 78 D8
Brimstage Cl CH60 86 C8
Brimstage Gn CH60 86 D8
Brimstage Hall Courtyard
(Craft Ctr)★ CH63 78 A2
Brimstage La CH63 78 B3
Brimstage Rd
Bebington CH63 78 D2
Heswall CH60 86 C7
Liverpool L4 38 E2
Brimstage St [4] CH41 66 C5
Brindley Cl L21 27 A2
Brindley Rd Kirkby L32 29 C2
St Helens WA9 58 F6
Brindley St Liverpool L8 67 D6
Runcorn WA7 84 F3
Brinklow Cl PR8 7 A5
Brinley Cl CH62 88 D5
Brinton Cl Liverpool L27 70 D6
Widnes WA8 84 E8
Brisbane Ave CH45 51 A8
Brisbane St WA9 57 D8
Briscoe Ave [2] CH46 64 E7
Briscoe Dr CH46 64 E7
Bristol Ave CH44 51 C4
Bristol Rd L15 69 A6
Bristow Cl WA5 60 B1
Britannia Ave L15 68 D7
Britannia Cres [2] L8 68 A3
Britannia Ho CH41 66 F6
Britannia Rd CH45 51 A4
British Lawnmower Mus★
PR8 4 B5
Britonside Ave L32 41 A8
Brittarge Brow L27 70 E4
Britten Cl L8 68 B6
Broad Green Rd L13 54 B2
Broad Green Sta L14 54 D1
Broad Hey L30 27 D3
Broad Hey Cl L25 70 B3
Broad La Billinge WA11 33 B1
Burtonwood WA5 59 E8
Formby L37 10 E2
Haskayne L39 12 B2
Haydock WA5,WA9 45 C1
Heswall CH60 85 C8
Kirkby L32 40 F8
Liverpool L11,L4 39 F1
Maghull,Great Altcar L37,
L38 19 A8
Maghull,Homer Green L29 19 C2
Broad Oak Ave
Haydock WA11 45 A6
Warrington WA5 74 E4
Broad Oak Com Prim Sch
WA9 45 A3
Broad Oak Rd WA9 44 F3
Broad Pl L11 53 F8
Broad Sq L11 53 F8
Broad Square Com Prim Sch
L11 53 F8
Broad View L11 53 F8
Broadacre WN8 25 A6
Broadacre Cl L18 69 D5
Broadbelt St [5] L4 38 F2
Broadbent Ho L31 28 D7
Broadfield Ave CH43 65 C8
Broadfield Cl CH43 65 B8
Broadgate Ave WA9 58 C8
Broadgreen Ct [2] L13 54 B2
Broadgreen High Sch Tech
Coll L13 54 C2
Broadgreen Hospl L13 54 C2
Broadgreen Prim Sch
L13 54 B2
Broadheath Ave CH43 65 C7
Broadheath Terr WA8 72 D1
Broadhurst St L17 68 C3
Broadlands Prescot L35 56 E5
Southport PR8 3 E3
Broadley Ave WA3 47 C7
Broadmead Heswall CH60 86 C7
Liverpool L19 81 E7
Broadoak Rd Liverpool L14 54 F3
Maghull L31 20 E1
Broadoaks CH49 64 E6
Broads The WA9 57 E6
Broadstone Dr CH63 78 F2
Broadway Bebington CH63 78 D7
Birkenhead CH49 64 E4
Liverpool L11 39 E1
Liverpool,Fazakerley L9 39 E7
St Helens,Grange Pk WA10 57 C8
St Helens,Windlehurst
WA10 43 B5
Wallasey CH45 50 F5
Widnes WA8 72 A1
Broadway Ave CH45 50 F5
Broadway Cl PR8 7 B5
Broadway Com High Sch
WA10 57 C8
Broadwood Ave L31 28 C7
Broadwood St L15 68 E7
Brock Gdns L24 83 E2
Brock Hall Cl [14] WA9 58 C4
Brock St L4 52 E8
Brockenhurst Rd L9 39 A5
Brockhall Cl L35 57 A6
Brockholme Rd L18,L19 69 A1
Brocklebank La L19 81 D8
Brocklebank Rd PR9 1 E2
Brockley Ave [1] CH45 51 B8
Brocksteds Ave WN4 34 E6
Brocstedes Rd WN4 34 D7
Brodie Ave L18,L19 69 A1
Bromborough Pool Prim Sch
CH62 79 D5
Bromborough Rake Sta
CH62 88 C8
Bromborough Rd CH62,
CH63 79 B4
Bromborough Sta CH63 88 C7
Bromborough Village Rd
CH62 79 E1
Brome Way CH63 79 B2
Bromilow Rd
Skelmersdale WN8 15 C1
St Helens WA9 44 F2
Bromley Ave
Golborne WA3 47 D7
Liverpool L18 68 F5
Bromley Cl Heswall CH60 85 E7
Liverpool L26 71 A1
Warrington WA2 61 F3
Bromley Rd CH45 51 A7
Brompton Ave Crosby L23 26 C3
Kirkby L33 30 A5
Liverpool L17 68 C6
Wallasey CH44 51 C4
Brompton Ho L17 68 C5
Brompton Rd PR8 4 E7
Bromsgrove Rd CH49 64 C4
Bromyard Cl [5] L20 38 B4
Bronington Ave CH62 88 D6
Bronte Cl Crosby L23 26 B4
Winwick WA2 61 A6
Bronte St Liverpool L3 90 C4
St Helens WA10 43 D4
Brook Acre Com Prim Sch
WA2 61 E1
Brook Ave L31 20 E2
Brook Cl Cronton WA8 72 C6
Wallasey CH44,CH45 51 C5
Brook End WA9 45 A1
Brook Farm Cl L39 13 E4
Brook Hey CH64 86 B2
Brook Hey Dr L33 30 A3
Brook Hey Wlk L33 30 A3
Brook Ho PR8 4 C5
Brook House Gr WA10 43 A3
Brook La Crank WA11 32 F7
Neston CH64 86 C2
Ormskirk L39 13 E4
Brook Lynn Ave WA3 36 F1
Brook Mdw CH61 76 E7
Brook Pk L31 28 C7
Brook Rd Bootle L20 38 B3
Crosby L23 27 A7
Liverpool L9 39 A4
Maghull L31 28 E8
Brook Side L31 20 E1
Brook St Ashton-in-M WN4 35 C2
Bebington CH62 79 A6
Birkenhead CH41 66 D8
Golborne WA3 47 A8
Liverpool L3 52 B2
Prescot L35 56 F4
Southport PR9 2 D4
St Helens WA10 44 A3
[3] Widnes WA8 73 B1
Brook St E CH41 66 E7
Brook Terr CH48 63 B2
Brook Vale L22 37 F8
Brook Way CH43 77 E8
Brook Wlk CH61 76 D7
Brookbank Ct L10 40 B7
Brookbridge Rd L13 53 E6
Brookdale WA8 72 A3
Brookdale Ave N CH49 64 E4
Brookdale Ave S CH49 64 E3
Brookdale Cl CH49 64 E4
Brookdale Prim Sch
CH49 64 E3
Brookdale Rd L15 68 E6
Brooke Cl PR9 5 B7
Brooke Rd E L22,L23 26 D2
Brooke Rd W L22 26 C2
Brookfield Ave
Crosby L23 26 D3
Rainhill L35 57 C5
Seaforth L22 37 F8
Brookfield Dr L9 39 D5
Brookfield Gdns CH48 63 B2
Brookfield High Sch L32 40 D8
Brookfield Ho L36 55 E3
Brookfield La L39 21 A5
Brookfield Prim Sch
WN8 15 D2
Brookfield Rd
Up Holland WN8 25 B7
West Kirby CH48 63 B2
Brookfield St WA12 46 B3
Brookfields Sch WA8 73 D2
Brookhill Cl L20 38 D3
Brookhill Rd L20 38 D4
Brookhouse Rd L39 13 D6
Brookhurst Ave CH63 88 C5
Brookhurst Cl CH63 88 C5
Brookhurst Prim Sch
CH63 88 C6
Brookhurst Rd CH63 88 C5
Brookland La WA9 45 A1
Brookland Rd CH41 66 D5
Brookland Rd E L13 54 A3
Brookland Rd W L13 54 A3
Brooklands
[3] Birkenhead CH41 66 D7
Liverpool L17 68 D2
Ormskirk L39 14 A6
Brooklands Ave
Ashton-in-M WN4 35 D2
Seaforth L22 37 E8
Brooklands Dr
Maghull L31 28 D8
Orrell WN5 25 D5
Brooklands Gdns CH64 86 C1
Brooklands Rd
Neston CH64 86 C1
St Helens WA10 43 A4
Up Holland WN8 25 C7
Brooklands The L36 55 E1
Brooklet Rd CH60 77 C1
Brooks Alley L1 90 B3
Brooks Rd L37 9 D2
Brooks The WA11 44 A7
Brooks Way L37 9 D2
Brookside L12 54 F8
Brookside Ave
Ashton-in-M WN4 34 F8
Liverpool L14 54 D3
Rainford WA11 31 E7
Seaforth L22 37 F8
St Helens WA10 43 C5
Brookside Cl Billinge WN5 33 E5
Haydock WA11 45 B7
Prescot L35 56 E4
Brookside Com Prim Sch
L28 55 B7
Brookside Cres CH49 64 E5
Brookside Ct L23 26 E4
Brookside Dr CH49 64 E5
Brookside Rd Prescot L35 56 E4
Southport PR8 4 C2
Brookside View WA11 45 B7
Brookside Way WA11 45 B7
Brookthorpe Cl CH45 51 C6
Brookvale Cl WA5 59 F6
Brookway
Birkenhead,Upton CH49 64 E5
Wallasey CH45 51 A5
Brookway La WA9 45 A1
Brookwood Rd L36 55 E4
Broom Cl L34 56 F6
Broom Hill CH43 65 F7
Broom Rd WA10 57 B8
Broom Way L26 82 E7
Broome Cl PR8 4 B3
Broome Rd PR8 4 B3
Broomfield Cl CH60 76 C1
Broomfield Gdns L9 38 F5
Broomfield Rd L9 38 F5
Broomhill Cl L27 70 D6
Broomlands CH60 85 E8
Broomleigh Cl CH63 78 D5
Brooms Gr L10 28 E2
Broseley Ave CH62 79 C1
Broster Ave CH46 64 C8
Broster Cl CH46 64 C8
Brosters La CH47 48 D1
Brotherhood Dr WA9 58 D7
Brotherton Cl CH62 88 C8
Brotherton Way WA12 46 B4
Brougham Ave CH41 66 F3
Brougham Rd CH44 51 E3
Brougham Terr [11] L6 53 A3
Broughton Ave
Golborne WA3 47 D7
Southport PR8 4 D4
West Kirby CH48 63 A3
Broughton Dr L19 81 A7
Broughton Hall High Sch
Tech Coll L14 54 E5
Broughton Hall Rd L12 54 E5
Broughton Rd CH44 51 B3
Broughton Way WA8 84 B5
Brow La CH60 85 F7
Brow Rd CH43 50 D1
Brow Side L5,L6 52 F4
Brown Edge Cl PR8 5 A2
Brown Heath Ave WN5 33 D3
Brown's La L30 28 A3
Brownbill Bank L27 70 E5
Browning Ave
Birkenhead CH42 66 F1
Widnes WA8 84 F8
Browning Cl L36 56 A1
Browning Dr WA2 61 A6
Browning Rd Crosby L22 26 D2
Liverpool L13 53 F6

Browning Rd *continued*
Wallasey CH45 .... 50 D5
Browning St L20 .... 38 A4
Brownlow Arc 13 WA10 .. 44 A3
Brownlow Hill L1,L3,L7 ... 52 F1
Brownlow La WN5 ...... 25 C1
Brownlow Rd CH62 .... 79 B7
Brownlow St L3 .... 52 F1
Brownmoor Cl L23 ...... 27 A3
Brownmoor La L23 .... 26 F3
Brownmoor Pk L23 ...... 26 F3
Brownville Rd L13 ...... 53 E6
Brows Cl L37 .... 9 E3
Brows La L37 .... 9 E3
Broxholme Way L31 ..... 28 D7
Broxton Ave
Birkenhead CH43 .... 65 F2
Orrell WN5 .... 25 F7
West Kirby CH48 .... 63 B3
Broxton Cl WA8 .... 72 C3
Broxton Rd 7 CH45 ..... 51 A6
Broxton St L15 .... 68 E8
Bruce Ave WA2 .... 61 D1
Bruce Cres CH63 .... 88 C6
Bruce St 4 Liverpool L8 .. 68 A4
St Helens WA10 .... 43 E3
Brunel Dr L21 .... 27 A2
Brunel Rd CH62 .... 79 E1
Brunner Rd 4 WA8 ...... 73 A1
Brunsborough Cl CH62 .. 88 C6
Brunsfield Cl CH46 ...... 64 C7
Brunstath Cl CH60 ...... 77 C1
Brunswick Bsns Pk L3 .. 67 D4
Brunswick Cl 4 L4 ...... 52 E8
Brunswick Ct CH41 ...... 66 E7
Brunswick Ent Ctr L3 ... 67 D5
Brunswick Mews
Birkenhead CH41 .... 66 E7
Seaforth L22 .... 37 E7
Brunswick Par L22 ...... 37 E8
Brunswick Pl L20 .... 52 B8
Brunswick Rd Liverpool L6 52 F3
Newton-le-W WA12 .... 45 F4
Brunswick St
Liverpool L2,L3 .... 90 A3
Liverpool,Garston L19 ..... 81 C3
St Helens WA9 .... 45 A3
Brunswick Sta L8 .... 67 E4
Brunswick Way L3 ...... 67 D5
Brunt La L19,L24 .... 81 E7
Brushford Cl L12 .... 40 B2
Bruton Rd L36 .... 55 D6
Bryanston Rd
Birkenhead CH42 .... 66 A2
Liverpool L17 .... 68 B3
Bryant Rd L21 .... 38 B6
Bryceway The L12 .... 54 E4
Brydges St L7 .... 53 A1
Bryer Rd L35 .... 56 D4
Bryn Bank CH44 .... 51 C4
Bryn Cross WN4 .... 35 A6
Bryn Gates La WN2 ..... 35 D8
Bryn Rd WN4 .... 35 B5
Bryn Rd S WN4 .... 35 C4
Bryn St WN4 .... 35 B3
Bryn St Peter's CE Prim Sch
WN4 .... 34 F6
Bryn Sta WN4 .... 35 A6
Brynmor Rd L18 .... 69 A1
Brynmoss Ave 2 CH44 ... 50 F4
Brynn St Ashton-in-M WN2 . 35 F7
St Helens WA10 .... 44 A4
Bryony Cl WN5 .... 25 D5
Bryony Way CH42 .... 78 F8
Brythen St L1 .... 90 B3
Bsns Resource Ctr L33 .. 41 C8
Buccleuch St CH41 ...... 50 F1
Buchanan Rd Liverpool L9 . 38 F3
Wallasey CH44 .... 51 D3
Buckfast Ave WA11 ...... 46 A7
Buckfast Cl Litherland L30 . 27 F4
Warrington WA5 .... 74 E3
Buckfast Dr L37 .... 10 B2
Buckingham Ave
Bebington CH63 .... 78 E7
Birkenhead CH43 .... 65 F7
Liverpool L17 .... 68 D6
Widnes WA8 .... 73 A4
Buckingham Cl
Litherland L30 .... 27 C3
St Helens WA10 .... 43 F2
Buckingham Ct L33 ...... 29 F4
Buckingham Dr WA11 ... 44 B6
Buckingham Gr L37 ...... 9 E1
Buckingham Ho L17 .... 68 D5
Buckingham Rd
Liverpool,Tuebrook L13 .... 53 E5
Liverpool,Warbreck Pk L9 .. 39 A6
Maghull L31 .... 28 C8
Wallasey CH44 .... 50 F4
Buckingham St L5 ...... 52 E5
Buckland Cl WA8 .... 84 D7
Buckland Dr CH63 .... 78 F2
Buckland St L17 .... 68 B3
Buckley Hill La L23,L29,
L30 .... 27 D5
Buckley Way L30 .... 27 D5
Buckley Wlk L24 .... 82 D2
Buckthorn Cl L28 .... 55 B7
Buckthorn Gdns WA9 .... 57 C6
Bude Cl CH43 .... 65 C6
Bude Rd WA8 .... 72 E2
Budworth Ave
St Helens WA9 .... 58 B4
Widnes WA8 .... 72 D2
Budworth Cl CH43 .... 65 E4
Budworth Ct CH43 .... 65 F5
Budworth Dr L25 .... 70 D2
Budworth Rd CH43 ...... 65 E5
Buerton Cl CH43 .... 65 E4
Buffs La CH60 .... 86 B8
Buildwas Rd CH64 .... 86 F2
Bulford Rd L9 .... 39 E3
Bulkeley Rd CH44 .... 51 D3
Bull Bridge La L10 ...... 28 E2
Bull Cop L37 .... 10 B3
Bull La 1 L9 .... 39 B7
Bullens Rd Kirkby L32 .... 29 F1
Liverpool L4 .... 52 F8
Bullfinch Ct L26 .... 70 E1
Bullrush Dr CH46 .... 50 A2
Bulrushes The L17 ...... 67 F3
Bulwer St
Birkenhead CH42 .... 66 F2
Bootle L20 .... 38 A5
7 Liverpool L5 .... 53 A5
Bundoran Rd L17 .... 68 E2
Bungalow Rd WA12 ...... 46 E1
Bungalow The L23 .... 26 B4
Bungalows The
Ashton-in-M WN4 .... 34 F7
Thornton Hough CH63 .... 87 B6
Bunter Rd L32 .... 40 F7
Bunting Cl 6 WA3 ...... 47 E8
Bunting Ct L26 .... 70 D2
Burbo Bank Rd L23 ...... 26 B3
Burbo Bank Rd N L23 .... 26 A5
Burbo Bank Rd S L23 .... 26 B3
Burbo Cres L23 .... 26 B3
Burbo Mans L23 .... 26 B3
Burbo Way CH45 .... 50 E8
Burden Rd
Birkenhead CH46 .... 64 C8
Wallasey CH46 .... 49 C1
Burdett Ave CH63 .... 79 A2
Burdett Cl CH63 .... 79 A2
Burdett Rd Crosby L22 ... 26 D2
Wallasey CH45 .... 50 D5
Burdett St L17 .... 68 C3
Burford Ave CH44 .... 51 A3
Burford Rd L16 .... 54 D1
Burgess Gdns L31 .... 20 C2
Burgess St L3 .... 90 C4
Burgess' La L37 .... 11 A2
Burghill Rd L12 .... 40 F4
Burgundy Cl 7 L17 ...... 68 C2
Burkhardt Dr WA12 ...... 46 E3
Burland Cl WA7 .... 84 F1
Burland Rd L26 .... 83 A6
Burleigh Mews L5 .... 52 F6
Burleigh Rd N L4,L5 ..... 52 F7
Burleigh Rd S L4,L5 ..... 52 F6
Burley Ave WA3 .... 36 D1
Burley Cl L32 .... 29 F1
Burlingham Ave CH48 ... 63 D2
Burlington Ave L37 ...... 10 B3
Burlington Rd
Southport PR8 .... 3 F3
Wallasey CH45 .... 37 B1
Burlington St
3 Birkenhead CH41 ...... 66 E6
Liverpool L3,L5 .... 52 C4
Burman Cres L19 .... 81 C7
Burman Rd L19 .... 81 D7
Burnage Ave WA9 .... 58 C4
Burnage Cl L24 .... 82 F2
Burnand St L4 .... 52 F7
Burnard Cl L33 .... 29 F2
Burnard Cres L33 .... 29 F2
Burnard Wlk 2 L33 ...... 29 F2
Burnell Cl 8 WA10 ...... 43 F4
Burnfell WA3 .... 47 E7
Burnham Cl
Warrington WA5 .... 74 F5
Widnes WA8 .... 72 C3
Burnham Rd L18 .... 69 C3
Burnie Ave L20 .... 38 E5
Burnley Ave
Birkenhead CH46 .... 64 F8
Southport PR8 .... 7 D5
Burnley Cl L6 .... 53 A4
Burnley Gr CH46 .... 49 F1
Burnley Rd
Birkenhead CH46 .... 64 F8
Southport PR8 .... 7 C5
Burns Ave CH45 .... 51 A5
Burns Cl Ashton-in-M WN4 . 34 F6
Liverpool L16 .... 69 F8
Longshaw WN5 .... 25 D1
Prescot L35 .... 56 E3
Burns Cres WA8 .... 84 F8
Burns Gr Huyton-w-R L36 .. 56 A1
Warrington WA2 .... 61 C2
Burns Rd WA9 .... 58 A3
Burns St L20 .... 38 A5
Burnsall Ave WA3 .... 47 F8
Burnsall Dr WA8 .... 72 C3
Burnsall St L19 .... 81 E5
Burnside Ave CH44 ...... 51 B2
Burnside Rd CH44 .... 51 B2
Burnt Ash Cl L19 .... 80 F7
Burnt Mill La WA8 ...... 83 D5
Burnthwaite Rd L14 ..... 54 C3
Burrell Cl CH42 .... 66 C1
Burrell Ct CH42 .... 66 C1
Burrell Dr CH46 .... 64 E7
Burrell Rd Bebington CH42 78 B8
Birkenhead CH42 .... 66 C1
Burrell St L4 .... 52 F8
Burroughs Gdns 1 L3 .... 52 D4
Burrow's La L34,WA10 ... 42 E2
Burrows Ave WA11 .... 44 F5
Burrows Ct Liverpool L3,L5 52 C4
Burrows Ct *continued*
St Helens WA9 .... 44 E3
Burrows St WA11 .... 45 A6
Bursar Cl WA12 .... 46 D4
Burscough Rd L39 .... 13 F7
Burscough St L39 .... 13 F6
Burton Ave Rainhill L35 ... 57 A4
Wallasey CH45 .... 50 E5
Burton Cl Liverpool L1 .... 90 B2
Rainhill L35 .... 57 A4
Widnes WA8 .... 72 F3
Burton Rd WA2 .... 61 D1
Burton St L5 .... 52 C6
Burtonhead Ct WA9 ..... 44 B1
Burtonhead Rd WA9,
WA10 .... 44 A1
Burtons Way L10,L32 .... 40 C8
Burtonwood Com Prim Sch
WA5 .... 59 E7
Burtonwood Ind Ctr WA5 59 E7
Burtonwood Rd WA5 .... 60 A2
Burtree Rd L14 .... 55 A6
Burwell Ave L37 .... 9 D1
Burwell Cl L33 .... 30 A3
Burwen Dr L9 .... 38 F6
Bury Rd PR8 .... 4 B3
Busby's Cotts CH45 ..... 51 B8
Bush Rd WA8 .... 84 F5
Bush Way CH60 .... 85 D8
Bushby's La L37 .... 9 C2
Bushby's Pk L37 .... 9 D2
Bushel's Dr WA9 .... 58 E3
Bushey La WA11 .... 23 E2
Bushey Rd L4 .... 39 C1
Bushley Cl L20 .... 38 B4
Butchers La
Ashton-in-M WN4 .... 35 B3
Maghull L39 .... 21 B3
Bute St Liverpool L3 ..... 52 E3
Liverpool L5 .... 52 E4
Butleigh Rd L36 .... 55 E5
Butler Cres L6 .... 53 B3
Butler St L6 .... 53 B3
Buttercup Cl Crosby L22 .. 26 F1
Wallasey CH46 .... 50 A2
Buttercup Way L9 .... 39 B4
Butterfield Gdns L39 .... 13 D3
Butterfield St L4 .... 52 F7
Buttermere Ave
Ashton-in-M WN4 .... 35 B5
Birkenhead CH43 .... 65 C6
St Helens WA11 .... 44 A8
Warrington WA2 .... 61 C3
Buttermere Cl Formby L37 . 9 D3
Kirkby L33 .... 29 D4
Maghull L31 .... 20 E1
Buttermere Cres
Rainford WA11 .... 23 F2
Warrington WA2 .... 61 C3
Buttermere Ct 10 CH41 .. 66 C5
Buttermere Gdns L23 .... 26 F2
Buttermere Rd L16 ...... 70 A8
Buttermere St 1 L8 ...... 68 B7
Butterton Ave CH49 ..... 64 D6
Butterwick Dr L12 .... 40 E3
Button St L2 .... 90 B3
Butts Gn WA5 .... 60 A3
Butts La PR8 .... 4 F5
Buxted Rd L32 .... 41 A8
Buxted Wlk 7 L32 .... 41 A8
Buxton La CH44 .... 50 E5
Buxton Rd CH42 .... 67 A2
By-Pass The L23 .... 26 E5
Bye La L39 .... 12 C3
Byerley St CH44 .... 51 E3
Byland Cl Formby L37 .... 10 B2
Widnes WA8 .... 73 C5
Byles St L8 .... 68 A4
Byng Pl L4 .... 53 D8
Byng Rd L4 .... 53 D8
Byng St L20 .... 38 B2
Byrchall High Sch The
WN4 .... 35 B1
Byrne Ave CH42 .... 66 F1
Byrom La WA3 .... 36 F2
Byrom St Liverpool L1,L3 .. 90 B4
Southport PR9 .... 4 F7
Byron Ave Liverpool L12 .. 54 A7
Prescot L35 .... 56 F3
Byron Cl Birkenhead CH43 . 77 F8
Formby L37 .... 9 F4
Huyton-w-R L36 .... 56 A1
3 Orrell WN5 .... 25 F7
St Helens WA10 .... 44 A5
Byron Ct Liverpool L25 .... 70 A3
Warrington WA2 .... 61 C2
Byron Rd Crosby L23 ..... 26 C4
Maghull L31 .... 20 D3
Byron St Bootle L20 ...... 38 A5
Liverpool L19 .... 81 C5
Byton Wlk L33 .... 30 A4
Byway The L23 .... 26 E5

C

'C' Ct WN4 .... 35 B2
Cabes Cl L14 .... 55 A6
Cabin La Maghull L31 .... 19 F4
Southport,Churchtown Moss
PR9 .... 2 F3
Southport,Halsall Moss L39 .. 8 C5
Cable Rd
Hoylake CH47 .... 63 B7
Prescot L35 .... 56 F4
Cable St Formby L37 ..... 10 A4
Liverpool L1 .... 90 A3
Southport PR8 .... 4 B7
Cables Ret Pk L34 ...... 56 D5
Cabot Cl WA5 .... 60 C1
Cabot Gn L25 .... 69 E5
Cadbury Cl L12 .... 40 B2
Caddick Rd L34 .... 41 B5
Cadnam Rd L25 .... 70 D5
Cadogan St L15,L7 .... 68 D8
Cadwell Rd L31 .... 20 B5
Caernarvon Cl CH49 ..... 65 A6
Caernarvon Ct CH63 ..... 78 F4
Caerwys Gr CH42 .... 66 E4
Cain's Brewery* L8 ..... 67 E6
Caird St L6 .... 53 A3
Cairn Ct WA9 .... 57 D8
Cairnmore Rd L18 .... 69 A2
Cairns St L8 .... 68 A6
Cairo St Liverpool L4 ..... 38 E1
St Helens WA10 .... 43 D1
Caister Cl WN8 .... 24 E8
Caithness Dr Crosby L23 .. 26 F3
Wallasey CH45 .... 51 C6
Caithness Gdns 4 CH43 . 65 F1
Caithness Rd L18 .... 69 B1
Calday Gr WA11 .... 45 A8
Calday Grange Cl CH48 .. 63 D1
Calday Grange Gram Sch
CH48 .... 63 D1
Caldbeck Ave WA2 ...... 61 D2
Caldbeck Cl WN4 .... 35 B4
Caldbeck Gr WA11 .... 33 C1
Caldbeck Rd CH62 .... 79 E2
Calder Ave
Birkenhead CH43 .... 66 A2
Ormskirk L39 .... 13 E4
Calder Cl
Kirkby L33 .... 30 A6
Widnes WA8 .... 73 F3
Calder Dr
Liverpool L18 .... 69 C4
Maghull L31 .... 20 F2
Rainhill L35 .... 57 C3
Calder Edge L18 .... 69 C4
Calder Grange L18 ...... 69 E3
Calder Park Ct L18 ...... 69 D4
Calder Rd Bebington CH63 78 D5
Liverpool L5 .... 52 F6
Calderfield Rd L18 ...... 69 D5
Calderhurst Dr WA10 .... 43 B6
Calders The L18 .... 69 C3
Calders View Ct L18 ..... 69 C3
Calderstones & Harthill
Botanic Gdns* L18 ..... 69 D4
Calderstones Ave L18 ... 69 C4
Calderstones Ct L18 ..... 69 C4
Calderstones Rd L18 .... 69 C4
Calderstones Sch L18 ... 69 C4
Calderwood Pk L27 ...... 70 D6
Caldicott Ave CH62 ...... 88 D7
Caldon Cl L21 .... 27 A1
Caldway Dr L27 .... 70 E6
Caldwell Ave WA5 .... 60 F2
Caldwell Cl L33 .... 29 F5
Caldwell Dr CH49 .... 65 B2
Caldwell St WA9 .... 44 D3
Caldy Chase Dr CH48 ... 75 D7
Caldy Ct 3 CH48 .... 63 B1
Caldy Gr WA11 .... 44 D5
Caldy Mews CH48 .... 75 D7
Caldy Rd
Liverpool L9 .... 39 A7
Wallasey CH45 .... 51 B5
West Kirby CH48 .... 75 D7
Caldy Wood CH48 .... 75 D7
Caldywood Dr L35 .... 56 E3
Caledonia St L7,L8 ...... 67 F8
Caledonian Cres L21 .... 27 A1
Calgarth Rd L36 .... 55 C5
California Rd L13 .... 53 D7
Callaghan Cl L5 .... 52 D5
Callander Rd L6 .... 53 D3
Callands Prim Sch WA5 . 60 E2
Callands Rd WA5 .... 60 D2
Callard Cl L27 .... 70 C6
Callestock Cl L11 .... 40 D6
Callington Cl L14 .... 55 A6
Callon Ave WA11 .... 44 E5
Callow Rd L15 .... 68 D7
Calmet Cl L5 .... 52 E6
Calne Cl CH61 .... 76 D7
Calstock Cl WA5 .... 74 E3
Calthorpe St L19 .... 81 B7
Calthorpe Way CH43 .... 65 D6
Calton Ave L15,L18 ...... 69 A5
Calvados Cl L17 .... 68 C1
Calveley Ave CH62 ...... 88 F4
Calveley Cl CH43 .... 65 E3
Calveley Rd L26 .... 83 A6
Calver Rd WA2 .... 61 A3
Calverhall Way WN4 .... 35 A3
Cam St L25 .... 69 F2
Camarthen Cres L8 ...... 67 D6
Camberley Cl PR8 .... 3 E5
Camberley Dr L25 .... 82 D8
Camberley Ho L25 .... 82 D8
Camberwell Park Rd
WA8 .... 73 D4
Camborne Ave L25 ...... 70 C1
Cambourne Ave WA11 ... 44 D7
Cambourne Rd WA5 ...... 59 F6
Cambria Street N 13 L6 .. 53 B3
Cambria Street S 14 L6 .. 53 B3
Cambrian Cl CH46 .... 64 B7
Cambrian Ct PR9 .... 4 D8
Cambrian Rd CH46 .... 64 C7
Cambrian Way L25 .... 70 B3
Cambridge Arc 5 PR8 .... 4 B7
Cambridge Ave
Crosby L23 .... 26 D5
Cambridge Ave *continued*
Litherland L21 .... 38 B8
Southport PR9 .... 1 F2
Cambridge Ct Liverpool L7 67 F8
Southport PR9 .... 1 F2
Cambridge Dr Crosby L23 26 C5
Liverpool L26 .... 82 F8
Cambridge Gdns PR9 ..... 1 F2
Cambridge Rd
Bebington CH62 .... 88 E8
Birkenhead CH42 .... 66 B2
Bootle L20 .... 38 D2
Crosby L23 .... 26 C5
Formby L37 .... 9 D1
Liverpool L9 .... 39 B8
Orrell WN5 .... 25 F8
Seaforth L21,L22 .... 37 E8
Skelmersdale WN8 .... 15 E1
Southport PR9 .... 1 E2
St Helens WA10 .... 43 E4
Wallasey CH45 .... 51 B7
Cambridge St
16 Liverpool,Edge Hill L7 ... 67 F8
Liverpool,Wavertree L15 ... 68 D8
Prescot L34 .... 56 D6
Cambridge Wlks 6 PR8 .. 4 B7
Camdale Cl L28 .... 55 B7
Camden Pl 1 CH41 ...... 66 E6
Camden St L3 .... 90 C4
Camelford Rd L11 .... 40 C5
Camelia Ct L17 .... 68 A2
Camellia Gdns WA9 ..... 59 B7
Camelot Cl WA12 .... 45 F4
Camelot Terr 8 L20 ..... 38 B4
Cameo Cl L6 .... 53 B4
Cameron Ct WA2 .... 61 A4
Cameron Rd CH46 .... 50 B3
Cameron St L7 .... 53 C2
Camm St WN2 .... 36 B8
Camp Rd Garswood WN4 .. 34 E4
Liverpool L25 .... 70 B1
Campania St L19 .... 81 C4
Campbell Cres Kirkby L33 29 D6
Warrington WA5 .... 74 F6
Campbell Dr L14 .... 54 E3
Campbell Sq L1 .... 90 B2
Campbell St Bootle L20 ... 38 B3
Liverpool L1 .... 90 B2
St Helens WA10 .... 43 E4
Campbeltown Rd CH41 ... 66 F4
Camperdown St CH41 ... 66 F6
Camphill Rd L25 .... 82 A8
Campion Cl WA11 .... 44 B7
Campion Gr WN4 .... 34 F4
Campion RC High Sch L5 52 E4
Campion Way L36 .... 70 F7
Campsey Ash WA8 .... 72 F4
Canal Bank Cotts L31 ... 20 C7
Canal Bank Pygons Hill
L31 .... 20 C7
Canal St Bootle L20 ...... 38 B2
Newton-le-W WA12 .... 45 F3
St Helens WA10 .... 43 F2
Canal View L31 .... 29 A3
Canal View Ct L21 ...... 27 A2
Canalside Gr L5 .... 52 C5
Canberra Ave
St Helens WA9 .... 57 E8
Warrington WA2 .... 61 D3
Canberra La L11 .... 40 C5
Canberra Sq WA2 .... 61 D2
Candia Twr L5 .... 52 E6
Candleston Cl WA5 ...... 60 E1
Canning Pl Liverpool L1 .. 90 A2
Liverpool L1 .... 90 A3
Canning Rd PR9 .... 5 A6
Canning St
Birkenhead CH41 .... 66 F7
2 Crosby L22 .... 26 D1
Liverpool L8 .... 67 F7
Canniswood Rd WA11 ... 45 A6
Cannock Gn L31 .... 20 B1
Cannon Hill CH43 .... 66 B6
Cannon Mount CH43 ..... 66 B6
Cannon St WA9 .... 58 C3
Canon Rd L6 .... 53 C7
Canon St WA7 .... 84 F3
Canon Wilson Cl WA11 .. 45 D6
Canova Cl L27 .... 70 F4
Canrow La L34 .... 41 E5
Cansfield Gr WN4 .... 35 A4
Cansfield High Specialist
Language Coll WN4 .... 35 A4
Cansfield St WA10 ...... 44 A4
Canter Cl L9 .... 39 D8
Canterbury Ave
Crosby L22 .... 26 D3
Golborne WA3 .... 36 D1
Canterbury Cl Aintree L10 28 E2
Formby L37 .... 9 F5
Prescot L34 .... 56 E7
Southport PR8 .... 3 F4
Canterbury Pk L18 ...... 81 C8
Canterbury Rd
Birkenhead CH42 .... 67 A1
Wallasey CH44 .... 51 C3
Widnes WA8 .... 84 C8
Canterbury St Liverpool L3 52 E3
Liverpool,Garston L19 ..... 81 D4
St Helens WA10 .... 43 E5
Canterbury Way
Litherland L30 .... 27 F4
1 Liverpool L3 .... 52 F3
Cantlow Fold PR8 .... 7 A4
Cantsfield St L7 .... 68 C7
Canvey Cl L15 .... 69 B7
Cape Rd L9 .... 39 C6
Capesthorne Cl WA8 .... 84 E8

Capesthorne Rd WA2 ...61 D2
Capilano Pk L39 ...21 C8
Capitol Trad Est L33 ...30 C2
Capper Gr L36 ...55 E3
Capricorn Cres L14 ...55 A5
Capricorn Way L20 ...38 B4
Capstick Cres L25 ...70 B6
Captain's La
Ashton-in-M WN4 ...35 C3
Bootle L30 ...38 E8
Captains Cl L30 ...38 D8
Captains Gn L30 ...38 D8
Caradoc Rd L21 ...38 A6
Caravan Pk The WA9 ...58 A8
Caraway Cl L23 ...27 B5
Caraway Gr WA10 ...43 D4
Carbis Cl L10 ...40 B6
Carden Cl L4 ...52 E7
Cardiff St WN8 ...15 D1
Cardigan Ave CH41 ...66 D6
Cardigan Cl
St Helens WA10 ...43 F2
Warrington WA5 ...60 D2
Cardigan Rd Southport PR8 .3 F1
Wallasey CH45 ...51 B7
Cardigan St L15 ...68 D8
Cardigan Way
Litherland L30 ...28 B4
Liverpool L6 ...53 B4
Cardinal Heenan RC High Sch
L14 ...54 D5
Cardus Cl CH46 ...64 B8
Cardwell Rd L19 ...81 D6
Cardwell St L7 ...68 B8
Carey Ave CH63 ...78 D6
Carey St WA8 ...73 B1
Carfax Rd L33 ...30 A4
Carfield WN8 ...24 E6
Cargill Gr CH42 ...79 B8
Carham Rd CH47 ...63 C6
Carisbrooke Cl CH48 ...75 C8
Carisbrooke Dr PR9 ...1 F1
Carisbrooke Pl L4 ...38 F1
Carisbrooke Rd L20,L4 ...38 E1
Carkington Rd L25 ...70 C1
Carl's Way L33 ...30 A6
Carland Cl L10 ...40 B6
Carlaw Rd CH42 ...66 A2
Carleen Cl L17 ...68 B2
Carleton House Prep Sch
L18 ...68 F3
Carlett Bvd CH62 ...88 F5
Carley Wlk L24 ...82 E2
Carlile Way L33 ...29 F6
Carlingford Cl L8 ...68 A7
Carlis Rd L32 ...40 F8
Carlisle Ave L30 ...27 F1
Carlisle Cl L4 ...53 D8
Carlisle Mews 16 CH43 ...66 C5
Carlisle Rd PR8 ...4 A2
Carlow Cl L24 ...83 D2
Carlow St WA10 ...43 D1
Carlton Ave WN8 ...25 A7
Carlton Cl
Ashton-in-M WN4 ...35 A5
Neston CH64 ...86 C2
Carlton La Hoylake CH47 ...63 C8
Liverpool L13 ...54 A4
Carlton Mt CH42 ...66 E3
Carlton Rd
Bebington CH63 ...79 B4
Birkenhead CH42 ...66 C4
Golborne WA3 ...36 D1
Southport PR8 ...7 C6
Wallasey CH45 ...51 B7
Carlton St Liverpool L3 ...52 B4
5 Prescot L34 ...56 D6
St Helens WA10 ...43 E3
Carlton Terr CH47 ...63 C8
Carlyon Way L26 ...82 E8
Carmarthen Cl WA5 ...60 D2
Carmel Cl Ormskirk L39 ...13 D2
7 Wallasey CH45 ...51 B8
Carmel Coll WA10 ...43 B1
Carmel Ct WA8 ...73 B4
Carmelite Cres WA10 ...43 A5
Carmichael Ave CH49 ...64 D2
Carnaby Cl L36 ...71 A8
Carnarvon Ct L9 ...39 A3
Carnarvon Rd Liverpool L9 39 A3
Southport PR8 ...3 F1
Carnarvon St WA9 ...57 D8
Carnatic Cl L18 ...68 F3
Carnatic Ct L18 ...68 E3
Carnatic Rd L17,L18 ...68 E3
Carnation Rd L9 ...39 B3
Carneghie Ct 1 PR8 ...3 F4
Carnegie Ave L23 ...26 D3
Carnegie Cres WA9 ...58 E8
Carnegie Dr WN4 ...35 A5
Carnegie Rd L13 ...53 E4
Carnforth Ave L32 ...29 F1
Carnforth Cl
7 Birkenhead CH41 ...66 C5
Liverpool L12 ...40 C1
Carnforth Rd L18 ...69 C2
Carno St L15 ...68 E8
Carnoustie Cl
Liverpool L12 ...54 F6
Southport PR8 ...3 F4
Wallasey CH46 ...49 B1
Carnoustie Gr WA11 ...45 A5
Carnsdale Rd CH46 ...64 F8
Carol Dr CH60 ...86 C8
Carole Cl WA9 ...58 E6
Carolina St L20 ...38 C3
Caroline Pl CH43 ...66 B5
Caronia St L19 ...81 C4
Carpathia St L19 ...81 C4
Carpenter's La CH48 ...63 B2
Carpenters Row L1 ...90 B2
Carr Bridge Rd CH49 ...65 C3
Carr Cl L11 ...40 B2
Carr Croft L21 ...27 B3
Carr Gate CH46 ...64 C7
Carr Hey CH46 ...64 B7
Carr Hey Cl CH49 ...65 C2
Carr House La
Birkenhead CH46 ...64 B8
Ince Blundell L38 ...18 E4
Carr La Hale L24,WA8 ...83 E4
Hoylake CH47 ...63 B6
Huyton-w-R L36 ...55 C1
Liverpool L11 ...40 A2
Maghull L31 ...19 F5
Prescot L34 ...56 B5
Southport PR8 ...7 F7
Wallasey CH46,CH47 ...49 A1
West Kirby CH48 ...63 E5
Carr La E L11 ...40 B3
Carr La Ind Est CH47 ...63 C6
Carr Meadow Hey L30 ...27 C3
Carr Mill Cres WN5 ...33 E4
Carr Mill Inf Sch WA11 ...44 B8
Carr Mill Jun Sch WA11 .33 C1
Carr Mill Rd
Billinge WA11,WN5 ...33 D3
St Helens WA11 ...44 C8
Carr Moss La
Haskayne L39 ...12 B8
Southport L39 ...8 D2
Carr Rd L20 ...38 D7
Carr Side La L29 ...19 A3
Carr St WA10 ...43 D5
Carr's Cres L37 ...9 E1
Carr's Cres W L37 ...9 D1
Carraway Rd L11 ...40 C6
Carrfield Ave L23 ...27 A3
Carriage Cl L24 ...83 D1
Carrick Ct L23 ...27 A3
Carrickmore Ave L18 ...69 A2
Carrington Rd CH45 ...51 C6
Carrington St CH41 ...66 A8
Carrock Rd CH62 ...79 E2
Carroll Cres L39 ...13 F7
Carrow Cl CH46 ...64 B7
Carrs Terr L35 ...56 D3
Carruthers St L3 ...52 C3
Carrville Way L12 ...41 A3
Carrwood Cl WA11 ...45 A6
Carrwood Pk PR8 ...4 B4
Carsdale Rd L18 ...69 A5
Carsgoe Rd CH47 ...63 C6
Carsington Rd L11 ...40 A2
Carstairs Rd L6 ...53 D4
Carsthorne Rd CH47 ...63 C6
Cartbridge La L26,L35 ...71 A2
Carter Ave WA11 ...32 A5
Carter St L8 ...67 F6
Carters The
Birkenhead CH49 ...64 C4
Litherland L30 ...28 A4
Carterton Rd CH47 ...63 C6
Cartier Cl WA5 ...60 C1
Cartmel Ave Maghull L31 ...20 E2
St Helens WA10 ...43 E7
Warrington WA2 ...61 C3
Cartmel Cl
11 Birkenhead CH41 ...66 C5
Huyton-w-R L36 ...55 D4
Southport PR8 ...4 F3
Warrington WA5 ...60 E2
Cartmel Dr
Birkenhead CH46 ...64 E7
Formby L37 ...10 B2
Liverpool L12 ...40 C1
Rainhill L35 ...57 A4
Cartmel Rd L36 ...55 C4
Cartmel Terr L11 ...40 C3
Cartmel Way L36 ...55 C4
Cartwright Cl WA11 ...31 F6
Cartwright Ct WA11 ...31 F7
Cartwrights Farm Rd
L24 ...82 A4
Carver St L3 ...52 F3
Caryl Gr L8 ...67 E4
Caryl St Liverpool L8 ...67 D5
Liverpool L8 ...67 D6
Liverpool L8 ...67 E4
Case Gr L35 ...56 E5
Case Rd WA11 ...45 D6
Cases St L1 ...90 B3
Cashel Rd CH44 ...51 B2
Caspian Pl L20 ...38 C3
Caspian Rd L4 ...39 D2
Cassia Cl L9 ...39 B4
Cassino Rd L36 ...55 E3
Cassio St L20 ...38 E2
Cassley Rd L24 ...83 A3
Cassville Rd L15,L18 ...69 A6
Castell Gr WA10 ...43 F3
Casterton St L7 ...68 C8
Castle Ave WA9 ...44 E3
Castle Cl CH46 ...50 A3
Castle Ct 4 CH48 ...63 B1
Castle Dr Formby L37 ...9 F1
Heswall CH60 ...85 F8
Castle Gn WA5 ...60 B2
Castle Hill 7 Liverpool L2 .90 A3
Newton-le-W WA12 ...46 E4
Castle Keep L12 ...54 B7
Castle La L40 ...14 E5
Castle Rd CH45 ...51 A6
Castle St Birkenhead CH41 .66 F6
Liverpool L2 ...90 A3
Liverpool,Woolton Hill L25 ..69 F2
Castle St *continued*
Southport PR9 ...4 B8
Widnes WA8 ...73 D1
Castle Wlk PR8 ...4 A6
Castlebridge Ct 5 CH42 .66 F1
Castlefield Cl L12 ...54 A7
Castlefield Rd L12 ...54 A8
Castlefields CH46 ...49 F4
Castleford Rise CH46 ...49 E3
Castleford St L15 ...69 A7
Castlegate Gr L12 ...54 B7
Castlegrange Cl CH46 ...49 E4
Castleheath Cl CH46 ...49 E3
Castlehey WN8 ...24 E6
Castlerigg Ct CH42 ...66 C1
Castlesite Rd L12 ...54 B7
Castleton Dr L30 ...28 B4
Castletown Cl L16 ...69 E8
Castleview Rd L12 ...54 B7
Castleway N CH46 ...50 A4
Castleway Prim Sch
CH46 ...50 A4
Castleway S CH46 ...50 A3
Castlewell L35 ...56 F4
Castlewood Rd L6 ...53 B5
Castor St L6 ...53 B5
Cat Tail La PR8 ...5 E1
Catchdale Moss La WA10 42 E5
Catford Cl WA8 ...72 C2
Catford Gn L24 ...82 F3
Catfoss Cl WA2 ...61 E1
Cath CE (Cathedral Church of
Christ) L1 ...90 C1
Cath RC (Metropolitan Cath
of Christ The King) L3 ..52 F1
Catharine St L8 ...67 F8
Catharine's La L39 ...13 F1
Cathcart St CH41 ...66 D7
Cathcart Street Prim Sch
CH41 ...66 D7
Cathedral Cl L1 ...90 C1
Cathedral Gate L1 ...90 C2
Cathedral Rd 2 L6 ...53 C6
Cathedral Wlk L3 ...52 F1
Catherine Ct L21 ...38 B6
Catherine St
Birkenhead CH41 ...66 D6
Bootle L21 ...38 B6
Catherine Way
Newton-le-W WA12 ...46 B2
St Helens WA11 ...44 F6
Catkin Rd L26 ...70 D2
Caton Cl PR9 ...1 F4
Catonfield Rd L18 ...69 D5
Cattan Gn L37 ...10 B3
Catterall Ave
St Helens WA9 ...58 D6
Warrington WA2 ...61 D2
Catterick Cl L26 ...82 F8
Catterick Fold PR8 ...4 F3
Caulfield Dr CH49 ...64 E3
Caunce Ave Golborne WA3 47 A7
Haydock WA11 ...45 B6
Newton-le-W WA12 ...46 C1
Causeway Cl CH62 ...79 B6
Causeway Ho CH46 ...49 E4
Causeway La L37 ...11 B1
Causeway The
Bebington CH62 ...79 B5
Liverpool L12 ...54 D4
Southport PR9 ...2 C5
Cavalier Dr L19 ...81 E5
Cavan Rd L11 ...53 E8
Cavell Cl L25 ...70 A1
Cavendish Ct
Liverpool L18 ...69 D3
Southport PR9 ...4 E8
5 Wallasey CH45 ...51 B8
Widnes WA8 ...72 F1
Cavendish Dr
Birkenhead CH42 ...66 D1
Liverpool L9 ...39 A3
Cavendish Gdns 8 L8 ...68 A5
Cavendish Rd
Birkenhead CH41 ...66 B7
Crosby L23 ...26 C3
Southport PR8 ...3 F3
3 Wallasey CH45 ...51 B8
Cavendish St
Birkenhead CH41 ...66 B8
Runcorn WA7 ...84 F2
Cavendish Wlk PR9 ...4 E8
Cavern Ct 6 L6 ...53 B3
Cawdor St Liverpool L8 ...68 A6
Runcorn WA7 ...84 F3
Cawfield Ave WA8 ...72 D1
Cawthorne Ave L32 ...40 E8
Cawthorne Cl L32 ...40 E8
Cawthorne Wlk L32 ...40 E8
Caxton Cl
Birkenhead CH43 ...65 C6
Widnes WA8 ...72 C3
Caxton Rd L35 ...57 E1
Cazneau St L3 ...52 D3
Cearns Cl CH43 ...66 A5
Cearns Rd CH43 ...66 A5
Cecil Dr WA10 ...43 A4
Cecil Rd Bebington CH62 ..79 B8
Birkenhead CH42 ...66 B2
Seaforth L21 ...37 F6
Wallasey CH44 ...51 B4
Cecil St Liverpool L15 ...68 D8
St Helens WA9 ...58 F7
Cedar Ave Bebington CH63 78 E4
Golborne WA3 ...47 F7
Widnes WA8 ...73 B2
Cedar Cl Liverpool L18 ...69 D3
Prescot L35 ...56 E4
Cedar Cres
Huyton-w-R L36 ...55 D1
Newton-le-W WA12 ...46 D2
Ormskirk L39 ...13 D4
Cedar Dr L37 ...9 C1
Cedar Gr Crosby L22 ...26 D2
Downall Green WN4 ...34 D5
Haydock WA11 ...45 E7
Liverpool L8 ...68 C6
Maghull L31 ...28 D6
Orrell WN5 ...25 F6
Skelmersdale WN8 ...15 E1
Cedar Rd Liverpool L9 ...39 B6
Prescot L35 ...56 D3
Warrington WA5 ...74 F6
Cedar St Birkenhead CH41 66 D5
Bootle L20 ...38 C4
Newton-le-W WA12 ...46 C2
Southport PR8 ...4 D4
St Helens WA10 ...43 D2
Cedar Terr L8 ...68 C6
Cedar Twrs L33 ...29 F3
Cedardale Pk WA8 ...73 E4
Cedardale Rd L9 ...39 A4
Cedars The
Birkenhead CH46 ...64 C7
Liverpool L12 ...40 F3
Cedarway CH60 ...86 B5
Cedarwood Cl CH49 ...64 B4
Cedarwood Ct L36 ...70 E8
Celandine Way WA9 ...59 B7
Celebration Dr L6 ...53 C5
Celendine Cl L15 ...68 E8
Celia St L20 ...38 D1
Celt St L6 ...53 C4
Celtic Rd CH47 ...48 E1
Celtic St 2 L8 ...68 A6
Cemeas Cl L3 ...52 C5
Cemetery Rd PR8 ...4 C4
Centenary Cl L4 ...53 C8
Central 12 Ret Pk PR9 ...4 C6
Central Ave
Bebington CH62 ...79 C1
Eccleston Park L34 ...57 A7
Liverpool L24 ...82 D3
Prescot L34 ...56 C5
Southport PR8 ...7 F8
Central Bldgs 2 L23 ...26 E4
Central Dr Haydock WA11 .45 B6
Liverpool L12 ...54 B5
Rainford WA11 ...31 F7
Central Liverpool Coll of F Ed
L1 ...90 C2
Central Par L24 ...82 E3
Central Park Ave CH44 ...51 C4
Central Park Ct CH44 ...51 B4
Central Rd
Bebington,New Ferry CH62 .79 B6
Bebington,Port Sunlight
CH62 ...79 C4
Central Sh Ctr L1 ...90 B3
Central Sq L31 ...20 D2
Central St WA10 ...44 A4
Central Sta L1 ...90 B3
Central Way Liverpool L24 .82 F2
Newton-le-W WA12 ...46 E2
Centre Way L36 ...55 E2
Centreville Rd L15,L18 ...69 A6
Centurion Cl CH47 ...48 E1
Centurion Dr CH47 ...48 E1
Century Bldgs L3 ...67 D5
Century Rd L23 ...26 D4
Ceres St L20 ...38 C1
Cestrian Dr CH61 ...77 A5
Chadlow Rd L32 ...40 F7
Chadwell Rd L33 ...29 F4
Chadwick Rd WA11 ...44 C7
Chadwick St
Birkenhead CH46 ...64 E8
Liverpool L3 ...52 B3
Chadwick Way L33 ...29 E6
Chaffinch Cl L12 ...40 F1
Chaffinch Glade L26 ...70 E1
Chain La WA11 ...44 E6
Chain Lane Sh Prec
WA11 ...44 D7
Chainhurst Cl L27 ...70 D5
Chalfont Ct PR8 ...4 A3
Chalfont Rd L18 ...69 D1
Chalfont Way L28 ...55 B7
Chalgrave Cl WA8 ...73 F3
Chalkwell Dr CH60 ...86 C7
Challis St CH41 ...50 E1
Challoner Cl L36 ...70 F8
Chalon Way E WA10 ...44 A3
Chalon Way Ind Est
WA10 ...44 A2
Chalon Way W WA10 ...44 A3
Chaloner Gr L19 ...80 F6
Chaloner St L1 ...90 B1
Chamberlain Dr L33 ...29 F5
Chamberlain St
Birkenhead CH41 ...66 F4
St Helens WA10 ...43 D3
Wallasey CH44 ...51 A2
Chambres Rd PR8 ...4 D5
Chambres Rd N PR8 ...4 D6
Chancel St L4 ...52 E7
Chancellor Ct L8 ...68 A8
Chancery La WA9 ...44 E3
Chandler Way WA3 ...47 E8
Chandlers Ct WA7 ...84 E1
Chandley Cl PR8 ...7 A5
Chandos St 9 L7 ...53 B1
Changford Gn L33 ...30 A3
Changford Rd L33 ...30 A3
Channel Rd L23 ...26 B3
Channel Reach L23 ...26 B3
Channel The CH45 ...50 E8
Channell Rd L6 ...53 C3
Chantrell Rd CH48 ...63 F2
Chantry Cl CH43 ...65 C6
Chantry Wlk
Ashton-in-M WN4 ...34 F5
Heswall CH60 ...86 A6
Chapel Alley L37 ...9 F3
Chapel Ave L9 ...39 A5
Chapel Ct Hoylake CH47 ..63 C7
St Helens WA10 ...43 D1
Chapel End Prim Sch
WN5 ...33 E4
Chapel Gdns L5 ...52 D5
Chapel Ho Maghull L31 ...20 D1
Seaforth L22 ...37 D8
Chapel La
Burtonwood WA5 ...59 F6
Formby L37 ...9 F3
Kirkby L31 ...29 A4
Litherland L30 ...27 F5
Litherland,Netherton L30 ..28 A5
St Helens,Eccleston WA10 ..43 B4
St Helens,Rainhill L35,WA9 .57 E2
Widnes WA8 ...72 C4
Chapel Mews L39 ...13 F4
Chapel Pl
Ashton-in-M WN4 ...35 B3
Liverpool L19 ...81 C6
Chapel Rd Hoylake CH47 ..63 C8
3 Liverpool,Cabbage Hall
L6 ...53 C6
Liverpool,Garston L19 ...81 C6
Warrington WA5 ...74 E3
Chapel St
Ashton-in-M WN4 ...35 B3
Haydock WA11 ...45 E6
Liverpool L3 ...90 A4
Newton-le-W WA12 ...46 B3
Ormskirk L39 ...13 F4
10 Prescot L34 ...56 D6
Southport PR8 ...4 B7
St Helens WA10 ...43 F5
Chapel Terr L20 ...38 B3
Chapel View WA11 ...32 F4
Chapel Yd L15 ...69 A7
Chapelhill Rd CH46 ...64 F8
Chapelhouse Wlk L37 ...10 A3
Chapman Cl Liverpool L8 ..67 E5
Widnes WA8 ...72 D4
Chapman Gr L34 ...56 E7
Chardstock Dr L25 ...70 C4
Charlecombe St CH42 ...66 D4
Charlecote St L8 ...67 F3
Charles Ave Southport PR8 .7 E6
Warrington WA5 ...74 F6
Charles Berrington Rd
L15 ...69 A6
Charles Best Gn L30 ...27 F4
Charles Rd CH47 ...63 B6
Charles St
2 Birkenhead CH41 ...66 D7
Golborne WA3 ...36 A1
St Helens WA10 ...44 A4
Charles Wlk L14 ...54 F3
Charlesbye Ave L39 ...14 B6
Charlesbye Cl L39 ...14 B6
Charleston Rd L8 ...67 F4
Charlesville CH43 ...66 B5
Charlesville Ct 4 CH43 ..66 B5
Charlesworth Cl L31 ...20 B5
Charley Wood Rd L33 ...30 C1
Charlock Cl L30 ...28 A4
Charlotte Rd CH44 ...51 D5
Charlotte Way 6 L1 ...90 B3
Charlotte's Mdw CH63 ...79 A4
Charlton Ct CH43 ...65 F6
Charlton Pl L13 ...54 A1
Charlton Rd L13 ...54 A1
Charlton Way W 2 WA10 43 F3
Charlwood Ave L36 ...55 E1
Charlwood Cl CH43 ...65 C6
Charmalue Ave L23 ...26 F4
Charmouth Cl
2 Liverpool L12 ...40 E3
Newton-le-W WA12 ...46 B4
Charnley's La PR9 ...2 E7
Charnock Ave WA12 ...45 F3
Charnock Cotts L11 ...40 A3
Charnock Rd L9 ...39 D3
Charnwood Cl L12 ...40 D3
Charnwood Rd L36 ...55 B3
Charnwood St WA9 ...44 E4
Charon Way WA5 ...60 B3
Charter Ho CH44 ...51 D4
Charterhouse Cl L25 ...70 B1
Charterhouse Dr L10 ...28 E2
Charterhouse Rd L25 ...70 B1
Chartmount Way L25 ...70 B4
Chartwell Gr L26 ...70 F1
Chartwell Rd PR8 ...7 B6
Chase Cl PR8 ...3 F4
Chase Heys PR9 ...2 A1
Chase The Bebington CH63 88 C5
Heswall CH60 ...86 A8
Huyton-w-R L36 ...70 F8
Chase Way L5 ...52 E4
Chaser Cl L9 ...39 C8
Chatburn Ave WA3 ...36 C1
Chater Cl L35 ...57 A5
Chatham Cl L21 ...37 F7
Chatham Ct L22 ...37 E8
Chatham Pl L7 ...53 B1
Chatham Rd CH42 ...67 A2
Chatham St L7 ...67 F8

Chatsworth Ave
Liverpool L9 .38 F5
Wallasey CH44 .51 C4
Chatsworth Cl WN4 .34 F4
Chatsworth Dr
Liverpool L7 .68 B8
Widnes WA8 .72 C3
Chatsworth Rd
Birkenhead CH42 .67 A2
Heswall CH61 .76 F5
Rainhill L35 .57 B4
Southport PR8 .7 B6
Chatterton Rd L14 .54 C4
Chaucer Dr L12 .40 F2
Chaucer Rd WA10 .43 D6
Chaucer St Bootle L20 .38 A4
Liverpool L3 .52 D3
Cheadle Ave L13 .53 F4
Cheapside Formby L37 .10 A2
Liverpool L2 .90 A4
Cheapside Alley 7 L2 .90 A4
Cheddar Cl L25 .69 F2
Cheddar Gr
Burtonwood WA5 .59 F7
Kirkby L32 .40 E7
Cheddon Way CH61 .76 E4
Chedworth Dr WA8 .72 C4
Chedworth Rd L14 .54 E4
Cheldon Rd L12 .40 C2
Chelford Ave WA3 .47 D8
Chelford Cl CH43 .65 C7
Chellowdene L23 .27 A6
Chelmarsh Ave WN4 .35 C3
Chelmsford Cl 8 L4 .52 D7
Chelsea Ct L12 .54 E8
Chelsea Lea L9 .38 F6
Chelsea Rd Bootle L21 .38 B6
Liverpool L9 .39 A6
Cheltenham Ave L17 .68 D6
Cheltenham Cl L10 .28 E1
Cheltenham Cres
Huyton-w-R L36 .55 D1
Wallasey CH46 .49 E3
Cheltenham Dr
Longshaw WN5 .25 D2
Newton-le-W WA12 .46 C5
Cheltenham Rd CH45 .50 E6
Cheltenham Way PR8 .4 F3
Chelwood Ave L14,L16 .54 E1
Chelwood Pk WA12 .35 B1
Chemical St WA12 .46 B3
Chemistry Rd L24 .82 C5
Chenotrie Gdns CH43 .65 D5
Chepstow Ave CH44 .51 C4
Chepstow Cl WA5 .60 E2
Chepstow St L4 .38 F1
Chequer Cl WN8 .24 F5
Chequer La WN8 .24 F6
Chequers Gdns L19 .68 F1
Cheriton Ave CH48 .63 D2
Cheriton Cl L26 .82 E8
Cheriton Pk PR8 .4 E3
Chermside Rd L17 .68 E1
Cherry Ave L4 .39 B1
Cherry Cl Liverpool L4 .39 B1
Newton-le-W WA12 .45 F4
Cherry Gdns L32 .40 F7
Cherry Gn L39 .13 B1
Cherry La L4 .53 D8
Cherry Rd PR8 .7 D2
Cherry Sq CH44 .51 B4
Cherry Tree Ave WA5 .74 F4
Cherry Tree Cl Hale L24 .83 E1
Haydock WA11 .45 A5
Prescot L35 .56 D3
Cherry Tree Cotts WA11 .33 A2
Cherry Tree Dr WA9 .45 A2
Cherry Tree La
Billinge WA11 .33 A2
Ormskirk L39 .13 B1
Cherry Tree Mews CH60 .86 A8
Cherry Tree Rd
Birkenhead CH46 .64 F8
Golborne WA3 .47 F8
Huyton-w-R L36 .70 E8
Cherry Vale L25 .70 B3
Cherry View L33 .30 A5
Cherrybank CH44 .51 B2
Cherrycroft WN8 .24 E6
Cherrydale Rd L18 .69 A4
Cherryfield Cres L32 .29 E2
Cherryfield Dr L32 .29 E2
Cherryfield Prim Sch
L32 .40 E7
Cherrysutton WA8 .72 B3
Cherwell Cl WA2 .61 D2
Cheryl Dr WA8 .73 D1
Cheshire Acre CH49 .65 A2
Cheshire Ave L10 .40 B7
Cheshire Cl WA12 .46 E3
Cheshire Gdns WA10 .43 E2
Cheshire Gr CH46 .64 E7
Cheshire Lines Path L39 .10 E6
Cheshire Way CH61 .76 F3
Chesnell Gr L33 .29 F5
Chesney Cl L8 .67 E6
Chesnut Gr
Birkenhead CH42 .66 D4
Bootle L20 .38 B4
Chesnut Rd L21 .37 F8
Chester Ave
Golborne WA3 .47 D8
Litherland L30 .27 F1
Southport PR9 .4 F8
Chester Cl L23 .27 B4
Chester Ct CH63 .78 F4
Chester Dr WN4 .35 D2
Chester High Rd CH64 .86 E4
Chester La WA9 .58 B4
Chester Rd
Heswall CH60,CH64 .86 C6
Hooton CH66 .89 A1
Huyton-w-R L36 .56 A4
Liverpool L6 .53 D5
Southport PR9 .4 F8
Chester Row WA12 .60 D8
Chester St
Birkenhead CH41 .66 F6
Liverpool L8 .90 C1
Prescot L34 .56 D6
Wallasey CH44 .51 A3
Widnes WA8 .73 B1
Chester Wlk L36 .56 A4
Chesterfield Cl PR8 .7 C4
Chesterfield Dr L33 .29 E5
Chesterfield High Sch
L23 .27 A4
Chesterfield Rd
Bebington CH62 .88 D4
Crosby L23 .27 A4
Southport PR8 .7 C5
Chesterfield St L8 .90 C1
Chesterton Dr WA2 .61 A5
Chesterton St L19 .81 C4
Chestnut Ave Crosby L23 .26 F6
Huyton-w-R L36 .70 D8
St Helens WA11 .44 F5
Warrington WA5 .74 F6
Widnes WA8 .73 B2
Chestnut Cl
Birkenhead CH49 .64 C2
Prescot L35 .56 E4
Chestnut Ct
3 Ormskirk L39 .13 F6
Widnes WA8 .72 D1
Chestnut Gr
Ashton-in-M WN4 .35 D4
Bebington CH62 .88 C8
Bootle L20 .38 B5
Golborne WA3 .47 F8
Liverpool L15 .69 A8
St Helens WA11 .44 D7
Chestnut Grange L39 .13 D3
Chestnut Ho 1 L20 .38 B4
Chestnut Lodge Spl Sch
WA8 .72 E1
Chestnut Rd L9 .39 C3
Chestnut St Liverpool L7 .52 F1
Southport PR8 .4 C5
Chestnut Way L37 .9 C1
Chestnut Wlk L31 .29 A4
Cheswood Cl L35 .56 E2
Cheswood Ct 4 CH49 .65 A2
Chetham Ct WA2 .61 A3
Chetwode Ave WN4 .35 B1
Chetwood Ave L23 .26 F5
Chetwood Dr WA8 .72 F4
Chetwynd Cl CH43 .65 F4
Chetwynd Rd CH43 .66 A5
Chetwynd St L17 .68 B3
Chevasse Wlk L25 .70 C3
Cheverton Cl CH49 .65 B3
Chevin Rd L9 .39 A5
Cheviot Ave
St Helens WA9 .44 F3
Warrington WA2 .61 A3
Cheviot Cl CH42 .66 D1
Cheviot Rd
Birkenhead CH42 .66 D1
Liverpool L7 .53 E2
Cheviot Way L33 .29 F6
Cheyne Cl L23 .26 A3
Cheyne Gdns L19 .80 F8
Cheyne Wlk WA9 .57 F6
Chichester Cl L15 .68 D8
Chidden Cl CH49 .64 C3
Chigwell Cl L12 .40 E3
Chilcott Rd L14 .54 C3
Childers St 1 L13 .54 A3
Childwall Abbey Rd L16 .69 E7
Childwall Ave
Birkenhead CH46,CH49 .64 D7
Liverpool L15 .68 D7
Childwall Bank Rd L16 .69 D7
Childwall CE Prim Sch
L16 .69 D5
Childwall Cl CH46 .64 D7
Childwall Cres L16 .69 D7
Childwall Five Ways L15 .69 C7
Childwall Gn CH49 .65 A2
Childwall Hts L25 .69 F7
Childwall La
Huyton-w-R L14 .55 A2
Liverpool L16,L25 .69 F6
Childwall Mount Rd L16 .69 D7
Childwall Par L14 .55 A2
Childwall Park Ave L16 .69 E6
Childwall Priory Rd L16 .69 D7
Childwall Rd L15 .69 B7
Childwall Sch L15 .69 C7
Childwall Valley Prim Sch
L25 .70 A7
Childwall Valley Rd L16,
L25,L27 .70 C6
Chilhem Cl 3 L8 .67 F4
Chilington Ave WA8 .84 D8
Chillerton Rd L12 .54 D8
Chillingham St 1 L8 .68 A3
Chiltern Cl
Ashton-in-M WN4 .35 C2
Kirkby L32 .29 C4
Liverpool L12 .40 F2
Chiltern Cres WA2 .61 A3
Chiltern Dr L32 .29 C4
Chiltern Pl WA2 .61 A3
Chiltern Rd
Birkenhead CH42 .66 C1
Southport PR8 .7 B6
St Helens WA9 .45 A3
Warrington WA2 .61 A3
Chilton Cl L31 .20 D1
Chilton Ct L31 .20 D1
Chilton Mews L31 .20 D1
Chilwell Cl WA8 .72 D4
Chimes Rd WN4 .34 F6
China Farm La CH48 .63 E3
Chindit Cl L37 .9 D2
Chippenham Ave CH49 .64 C3
Chipping Ave PR8 .7 A5
Chirk Way CH46 .64 F7
Chirkdale St L4 .38 E1
Chirton Cl WA11 .45 D7
Chisenhale St L3 .52 C4
Chisledon Cl WA11 .45 D7
Chislehurst Ave L25 .70 B6
Chislet Ct WA8 .72 E4
Chisnall Ave WA10 .43 C4
Chiswell St L7 .53 C2
Cholmley Dr WA12 .46 E2
Cholmondeley Rd CH48 .63 B2
Cholsey Cl CH49 .64 F4
Chorley Cl PR9 .2 F5
Chorley Rd L34 .56 B6
Chorley St WA10 .43 F4
Chorley Way CH63 .79 A1
Chorley's La WA8 .73 E3
Chorlton Cl L16 .69 F8
Chorlton Gr CH45 .50 D5
Chris Ward Cl 1 L7 .53 C1
Christ Church CE Prim Sch
Birkenhead CH41 .66 C5
Birkenhead,Moreton CH46 .64 E8
Bootle L20 .38 D4
Christ The King RC High Sch
& Sixth Form Ctr PR8 .4 B2
Christ The King RC Prim Sch
Bebington CH62 .88 E7
Liverpool L15 .69 C8
Christchurch Rd CH43 .66 B4
Christian Fellowship Sch
L7 .68 B8
Christian St L3 .52 E3
Christiana Hartley Maternity
Hospl PR8 .4 D5
Christie Cl CH66 .89 A2
Christie St WA8 .73 D1
Christleton Cl CH43 .65 D2
Christmas St L20 .38 D1
Christopher Cl
Liverpool L16 .69 D8
Rainhill L35 .57 B2
Christopher Dr CH62 .89 A5
Christopher St L4 .52 F8
Christopher Taylor Ho
L31 .28 D8
Christopher Way L16 .69 D8
Christophers Cl CH61 .77 A4
Christowe Wlk L11 .40 C5
Chudleigh Cl L26 .70 E1
Chudleigh Rd L13 .53 F3
Church Alley L1 .90 B3
Church Ave
Bickershaw WN2 .36 F8
Liverpool L9 .39 B7
Church Cl Formby L37 .10 A3
Southport PR9 .5 A8
Wallasey CH44 .51 D4
Church Close Ct L37 .10 A3
Church Cotts L25 .70 C5
Church Cres 9 CH44 .51 E2
Church Dr Bebington CH62 79 B6
Newton-le-W WA12 .46 C1
Orrell WN5 .25 D5
Church Drive Prim Sch
CH62 .79 B6
Church End L24 .83 D1
Church Farm Ct CH60 .85 F7
Church Fields L39 .13 E5
Church Gdns Bootle L20 .38 B3
Wallasey CH44 .51 D4
Church Gn Formby L37 .9 C2
Kirkby L32 .29 E3
Liverpool L16 .69 F7
Skelmersdale WN8 .15 F1
Church Gr L21 .37 F6
Church Hill CH44,CH45 .50 F5
Church Hill Rd L39 .13 D6
Church Ho 7 L39 .13 E6
Church La Aughton L39 .21 A7
Bebington,Bromborough
CH62 .79 D1
Bebington,Eastham CH62 .89 A4
Birkenhead CH49 .65 B2
Golborne WA3 .47 D7
Kirkby L34 .41 C4
Liverpool L17 .68 E1
Liverpool,Walton on the Hill
L4 .38 F2
Maghull L31 .20 A8
St Helens WA10 .43 A4
Thurstaston CH61 .76 B5
Wallasey CH44 .51 D4
Church Meadow La CH60 85 F7
Church Meadow Wlk
WA8 .84 B5
Church Mews
Birkenhead CH42 .67 A1
Liverpool L24 .82 B3
Church Mount 2 L7 .53 B1
Church Rd Banks PR9 .2 F6
Bebington CH63 .79 A4
Church Rd *continued*
Bickerstaffe L39 .22 E6
Birkenhead,Devonshire Pk
CH42 .66 D3
Birkenhead,Upton CH49 .65 A5
Bootle L20 .38 D6
1 Crosby L23 .26 E4
Formby L37 .10 A4
Hale L24 .83 E1
Haydock WA11 .45 E7
Huyton-w-R L36 .55 C3
Litherland L21 .38 C8
Litherland,Stanley Pk L21 .27 D1
Liverpool,Garston L19 .81 C5
Liverpool,Halewood L26 .70 F1
Liverpool,Stanley L13 .53 F3
Liverpool,Walton on the Hill
L4 .39 A2
Liverpool,Wavertree Green
L15,L18 .69 A6
Liverpool,Woolton Pk L25 .70 A3
Maghull L31 .28 D7
Rainford WA11 .32 A5
Seaforth L22 .37 E8
Skelmersdale WN8 .15 F1
Thornton Hough CH63 .87 B6
Wallasey CH44 .51 E2
West Kirby CH48 .63 B1
Church Rd N L15 .69 A7
Church Rd S L25 .70 A2
Church Rd W L4 .38 F2
Church Sq 11 WA10 .44 A3
Church St
Birkenhead CH41 .66 F6
Bootle L20 .38 A3
Golborne WA3 .36 B1
Liverpool L1 .90 B3
Newton-le-W WA12 .46 E4
Ormskirk L39 .13 E5
Orrell WN5 .25 E5
Prescot L34 .56 D6
Southport PR9 .4 C7
St Helens WA10 .44 A3
Up Holland WN8 .25 C7
Wallasey CH44 .51 D4
Church Terr
Ashton-in-M WN4 .35 B2
Birkenhead CH42 .66 D3
Church View Aughton L39 .21 A7
Bootle L20 .38 B3
Liverpool L12 .54 B7
Church View Ct 1 L39 .13 E5
Church Way Formby L37 .9 C2
Kirkby L32 .29 E3
Litherland L30 .27 D5
Church Wlk Bootle L20 .38 B3
St Helens WA10 .43 A4
Winwick WA2 .61 A6
Church Wlks 3 L39 .13 E5
Churchdown Cl L14 .54 F4
Churchdown Gr 3 L14 .54 E4
Churchdown Rd L14 .54 E4
Churchfield Rd L25 .70 C5
Churchfields Southport PR8 .3 F3
5 St Helens WA9 .58 C4
Widnes WA8 .73 B5
Churchgate PR9 .1 F1
Churchgate Mews PR9 .2 A1
Churchill Ave PR9 .1 F2
Churchill Gdns WA9 .57 C6
Churchill Gr CH44 .51 C5
Churchill Ho 6 L21 .37 F7
Churchill Ind Est L9 .39 C8
Churchill Way (Elevated Rd)
L1,L2,L3 .90 B4
Churchlands 13 CH44 .51 E2
Churchmeadow Cl CH44 .51 D4
Churchtown Ct PR9 .2 A2
Churchtown Prim Sch
PR9 .2 B2
Churchview Rd CH41 .66 B8
Churchway Rd L24 .83 A2
Churchwood Cl CH62 .79 D1
Churchwood Ct CH49 .65 B1
Churn Way CH49 .64 D4
Churnet St L4 .52 E8
Churston Rd L16 .69 E5
Churton Ave CH43 .65 F3
Churton Ct 5 L6 .53 A3
Ciaran Cl L12 .54 E8
Cicely St L7 .53 B1
Cinder La Bootle L20 .38 D7
Liverpool L18 .69 C5
Cinnamon Brow WN8 .25 C6
Cinnamon Brow CE Prim Sch
WA2 .61 F3
Cinnamon La WA2 .61 F2
Cinnamon La N WA2 .61 F3
Circular Dr
Bebington CH62 .79 B7
Birkenhead CH49 .64 D3
Heswall CH60 .76 F1
Circular Rd CH41 .66 D5
Circular Rd E L11 .53 F8
Circular Rd W L11 .53 F8
Cirencester Ave CH49 .64 C4
Cirrus Dr L39 .13 A1
Citrine Rd CH44 .51 D2
Citron Cl L9 .39 B4
City Gdns WA10 .43 F6
City Rd Liverpool L4 .38 F1
St Helens WA10 .43 F6
Civic Way Bebington CH63 .79 A5
Huyton-w-R L36 .55 E2
Clairville PR8 .3 F5
Clairville Cl L20 .38 C3
Clairville Ct 12 L20 .38 C3
Clairville Way L13 .53 E5
Clamley Ct L24 .83 A3
Clamley Gdns L24 .83 E2
Clandon Rd L18 .69 D1
Clanfield Ave WA8 .72 C3
Clanfield Rd L11 .40 B1
Clap Gate Cres WA8 .84 B5
Clapham Rd L4 .53 B7
Clare Cl WA9 .57 E7
Clare Cres CH44 .50 F4
Clare Mount Sch CH46 .50 A1
Clare Rd L20 .38 E2
Clare Villas L20 .38 D2
Clare Way CH45 .50 F5
Clare Wlk L10 .40 B7
Claremont Ave
Maghull L31 .28 B8
Widnes WA8 .73 C4
Claremont Cl L21 .37 F7
Claremont Dr
Ormskirk L39 .13 D3
Widnes WA8 .73 B4
Claremont Gdns PR8 .4 A4
Claremont Rd
Billinge WN5 .33 E5
Crosby L23 .26 E4
Liverpool L15 .68 E6
Seaforth L21 .37 F7
Southport PR8 .4 A4
West Kirby CH48 .63 B3
Claremont Terr 1 L23 .26 D5
Claremont Way CH63 .78 D8
Claremount Ct CH45 .50 F5
Claremount Dr CH63 .78 F4
Claremount Rd CH44,
CH45 .50 F6
Clarence Ave
Warrington WA5 .74 D6
Widnes WA8 .73 A4
Clarence Cl WA9 .44 C2
Clarence Ct WA12 .46 A4
Clarence High Sch L37 .9 F6
Clarence Rd
Birkenhead CH42 .66 C3
Southport PR8 .4 A4
Wallasey CH44 .51 D3
Clarence St
6 Ashton-in-M WN4 .34 F5
Golborne WA3 .36 A1
Liverpool L3 .90 C3
Newton-le-W WA12 .45 F4
Runcorn WA7 .84 F3
Clarendon Cl CH43 .66 C5
Clarendon Ct WA2 .60 F4
Clarendon Gr L31 .20 C5
Clarendon Rd
Liverpool,Cabbage Hill L6 .53 C6
Liverpool,Garston L19 .81 C6
3 Seaforth L21 .37 F6
Wallasey CH44 .51 D4
Claret Cl L17 .68 C1
Claribel St L8 .68 A6
Clarke Ave CH42 .66 E2
Clarke's Cres WA10 .43 B4
Classic Rd L13 .54 A4
Clatterbridge Hospl
CH63 .78 D1
Clatterbridge Rd
Bebington CH63 .78 E1
Thornton Hough CH63 .87 D8
Claude Rd L6 .53 C6
Claughton Cl 9 L7 .53 C1
Claughton Dr CH44 .51 B3
Claughton Firs CH43 .66 B4
Claughton Gn CH43 .66 B5
Claughton Pl CH41 .66 C6
Claughton Rd CH41 .66 D6
Claughton St WA10 .44 A3
Clavell Rd L19 .81 D8
Clay Brow Rd WN8 .24 E6
Clay Cross Rd L25 .69 F2
Clay La Burtonwood WA5 .59 E5
St Helens WA10 .42 E3
Clay St L3 .52 B4
Claydon Ct L26 .71 A1
Clayfield Cl L20 .38 D3
Clayford Cres L14 .54 C4
Clayford Pl L14 .54 B4
Clayford Rd L14 .54 C4
Clayford Way L14 .54 C4
Clayhill Light Ind Pk
CH64 .86 F2
Claypole Cl 8 L7 .68 C8
Clayton Ave WA3 .47 E8
Clayton Cl WA10 .43 E3
Clayton Cres Runcorn WA7 84 F1
Widnes WA8 .72 F1
Clayton La CH44 .51 A2
Clayton Mews WN8 .15 D1
Clayton Pl 22 CH41 .66 C5
Clayton Sq 2 L1 .90 B3
Clayton St
Birkenhead CH41 .66 C5
Skelmersdale WN8 .15 D1
Cleadon Cl 2 L32 .41 A7
Cleadon Rd L32 .41 A7
Cleadon Way WA8 .72 E4
Clearwater Cl L7 .53 B2
Cleary St L20 .38 B4
Cleaver Cotts L38 .18 A6
Clee Hill Rd CH42 .66 C1
Clegg St Liverpool L5 .52 E4
Skelmersdale WN8 .15 D1
Clematis Rd L27 .70 E6
Clement Gdns L3 .52 C4
Clementina Rd L23 .26 B4
Clemmey Dr L20 .38 E6
Clengers Brow PR9 .2 A3
Clent Ave L31 .20 C3

Clent Gdns L31 .20 C3
Clent Rd L31 .20 C3
Cleopas St L8 .67 F4
Cleve Way L37 .10 B2
Cleveland Bldgs L1 .90 B2
Cleveland Cl L32 .29 D4
Cleveland Dr
Ashton-in-M WN4 .35 C4
Golborne WA3 .36 D1
Cleveland Gdns WN4 .35 C4
Cleveland Rd WA2 .61 B3
Cleveland Sq L1 .90 B2
Cleveland St
Birkenhead CH41 .66 D8
St Helens WA9 .44 C1
Cleveley Pk L18 .69 D1
Cleveley Rd Hoylake CH47 .63 E8
Liverpool L18 .69 D1
Cleveleys Ave
Southport PR9 .2 A4
Widnes WA8 .73 D2
Cleveleys Rd PR9 .2 A3
Cleves The L31 .20 E3
Clieves Hills La L39 .12 E3
Clieves Rd L32 .29 F1
Clifden Ct L37 .9 F3
Cliff Dr CH44 .51 D5
Cliff Rd Southport PR9 .1 D1
Wallasey CH44 .51 A4
Cliff St L7 .53 C2
Cliff The CH45 .50 F8
Cliffe St 3 WA8 .73 C1
Clifford Holroyde Sch
L14 .54 D3
Clifford Rd Southport PR8 .4 A2
Wallasey CH44 .51 C3
Warrington WA5 .74 F4
Clifford St
Birkenhead CH41 .66 A8
Liverpool L3 .90 C4
Clifton Ave
Bebington CH62 .88 E3
Liverpool L26 .70 E1
Clifton Cres 11 CH41 .66 E6
Clifton Ct Birkenhead CH41 66 E5
Liverpool L19 .81 C8
Clifton Dr L10 .28 D2
Clifton Gr 2 Liverpool L5 .52 E4
Wallasey CH44 .51 D4
Clifton Rd
Ashton-in-M WN4 .34 F6
Billinge WN5 .33 D4
Birkenhead CH41 .66 D5
Formby L37 .10 A5
Liverpool L6 .53 D5
Southport PR8 .4 F6
Clifton Rd E L6 .53 D6
Clifton St Liverpool L19 .81 C6
St Helens WA10 .44 A4
Cliftonmill Mdw WA3 .46 F8
Cliftonville Rd L34 .56 E6
Clincton Cl WA8 .84 A8
Clincton View WA8 .84 A8
Clinning Rd PR8 .4 A2
Clint Rd L7 .53 C1
Clint Way 2 L7 .53 C1
Clinton Pl L12 .53 F7
Clinton Rd L12 .53 F7
Clipper View CH62 .79 B8
Clipsley Brook View
WA11 .44 F6
Clipsley Cres WA11 .45 B7
Clipsley La WA11 .45 C6
Clive Ave WA2 .61 C1
Clive Lo PR8 .3 F2
Clive Rd Birkenhead CH43 .66 C4
Southport PR8 .3 F2
Clock Face Colliery Ctry Pk*
WA9 .58 F3
Clock Face Rd WA8,WA9 .58 D3
Clocktower St WA10 .43 F3
Cloister Gn L37 .10 B2
Cloisters The Crosby L23 .26 D3
Formby L37 .9 F3
St Helens WA10 .43 B4
Clorain Cl L33 .30 A3
Clorain Rd L33 .30 A3
Close St WA9 .57 E7
Close The
Birkenhead,Egerton Pk
CH63 .66 D1
Birkenhead,Greasby CH49 .64 D2
Crosby L23 .26 D3
Huyton-w-R L28 .55 C7
Ince Blundell L38 .18 E3
Irby CH61 .76 D6
Liverpool L9 .38 F4
Newton-le-W WA12 .46 E1
St Helens,Blackbrook WA11 .44 F5
St Helens,Eccleston WA10 .43 A5
Closeburn Ave CH60 .85 E6
Cloudberry Cl L27 .70 E6
Clough Ave WA2 .61 B2
Clough Fold Prim Sch
WN8 .16 C2
Clough Gr WN4 .34 F5
Clough Rd L24 .82 E4
Clough The WN4 .34 D4
Clovelly Ave
St Helens WA9 .58 E6
Warrington WA5 .74 E7
Clovelly Ct CH49 .64 D3
Clovelly Dr
Skelmersdale WN8 .16 A8
Southport PR8 .7 E8
Clovelly Rd L4 .53 B6
Clover Ave L26 .70 D2
Clover Ct PR8 .4 C5
Clover Dr CH41 .50 E1
Clover Hey WA11 .44 B7
Cloverdale Dr WN4 .35 C2
Cloverdale Rd L25 .70 B7
Club St WA11 .33 A1
Clucas Gdns L39 .13 E6
Clwyd Gr L12 .54 B8
Clwyd St
2 Birkenhead CH41 .66 D6
2 Birkenhead CH41 .66 E6
Wallasey CH45 .51 B7
Clyde Rd L7 .53 E2
Clyde St
6 Birkenhead CH42 .66 F2
Liverpool L20 .52 C8
Clydesdale Rd
Hoylake CH47 .63 B8
Wallasey CH44 .51 D4
Coach House Ct L29 .27 F7
Coach Rd Bickerstaffe L39 .22 F2
Rainford L33,L39,WA11 .31 B5
Coachmans Dr L12 .40 E1
Coal Pit La L39 .23 D4
Coal St L1,L3 .90 C4
Coalbrookdale Rd CH64 .86 F2
Coalgate La L35 .56 C2
Coalport Wlk WA9 .57 C6
Coalville Rd WA11 .44 D6
Coastal Dr CH45 .50 E8
Coastal Rd
Southport,Birkdale PR8 .3 C3
Southport,Woodvale PR8 .7 A4
Coastguard La CH64 .86 B1
Coastline Mews PR9 .2 A4
Cob Moor Ave WN5 .25 D1
Cob Moor Rd WN5 .25 D1
Cobb Ave L21 .38 B6
Cobb's Brow Cotts L40 .15 F5
Cobb's Brow La L40,WN8 .16 B6
Cobb's Clough Rd L40 .15 F5
Cobbles The L26 .70 D2
Cobblestone Cnr L19 .81 A7
Cobbs Brow Prim Sch
WN8 .16 A3
Cobden Ave 2 CH42 .66 F3
Cobden Ct CH42 .66 F3
Cobden Pl
3 Birkenhead CH42 .66 F3
Liverpool L25 .69 F2
Cobden Rd PR9 .5 A6
Cobden St Liverpool L6 .52 F3
Liverpool,Woolton Hill L25 .69 F2
Newton-le-W WA12 .46 D4
Cobden View L25 .69 F2
Coberg St CH41 .66 D6
Cobham Ave L9 .38 F6
Cobham Rd CH46 .64 D7
Cobham Wlk L30 .27 E4
Coburg Dock (Marina)*
L3 .67 D6
Coburg Wharf L3 .67 C6
Cochrane St L5 .52 F5
Cock Glades L35 .56 D1
Cock Lane Ends WA8 .84 B4
Cockburn St L8 .67 F3
Cockerell Cl 3 L4 .52 F7
Cockerham Way L11 .40 C5
Cocklade La L24 .83 D1
Cockle Dick's La PR9 .1 E2
Cockshead Rd L25 .70 B5
Cockshead Way L25 .70 B6
Cockspur St L3 .90 A4
Cockspur St W L3 .90 A4
Coerton Rd L9 .39 B7
Cokers The CH42 .78 E8
Colbern Cl L31 .28 E8
Colby Cl L16 .69 E8
Colchester Rd PR8 .4 F3
Colden Cl L12 .54 E7
Coldstone Dr WN4 .34 D4
Coldstream Cl WA2 .61 E3
Cole Ave WA12 .46 C4
Cole Cres L39 .21 C8
Cole St CH43 .66 C6
Cole Street Prim Sch
CH43 .66 C6
Colebrooke Rd L17 .68 A3
Coleman Dr CH49 .64 C3
Colemere Dr CH61 .77 B6
Coleridge Ave WA10 .43 D4
Coleridge Dr CH62 .79 A7
Coleridge Gr WA8 .72 E1
Coleridge Rd WN5 .25 D1
Coleridge St Bootle L20 .38 A4
Liverpool L6 .53 B3
Coles Cres L23 .27 B6
Colesborne Rd L11 .40 B2
Coleshill Rd L11 .39 E3
Colette Rd L10 .40 B7
Coleus Cl L9 .39 B4
Colin Cl L36 .55 C2
Colin Dr L3 .52 C5
Colindale Rd L16 .69 E7
Colinmander Gdns L39 .13 C3
Colinton WN8 .24 E7
Colinton St L15 .68 E8
College Ave Crosby L23 .26 D2
Formby L37 .9 E4
College Cl
Birkenhead CH43 .65 B6
Formby L37 .9 D4
Southport PR8 .4 A3
Wallasey CH45 .50 E6
College Ct L12 .54 A5
College Dr CH63 .79 A7
College Fields L36 .55 E1
College Gn 2 L23 .26 D3
College La L1 .90 B3
College Path L37 .9 D5
College Rd Crosby L23 .26 D3
Up Holland WN8 .25 B8
College Rd N L23 .26 C5
College St WA10 .44 A5
College St N L6 .52 F3
College St S L6 .52 F3
College View Bootle L20 .38 C2
Huyton-w-R L36 .55 E2
Collier St WA7 .84 F3
Collin Rd CH43 .65 E8
Collingwood Rd
Bebington CH63 .79 B4
Newton-le-W WA12 .46 B3
Collins Cl L20 .38 A5
Collins Green La WA5 .45 E1
Collisdene Rd WN5 .25 E6
Colmoor Cl L33 .29 F6
Colmore Ave CH63 .79 A1
Colmore Rd L11 .39 E2
Colne Dr WA9 .58 D7
Colne Rd WA5 .59 F6
Colquitt St L1 .90 C2
Coltart Rd L8 .68 B6
Colton Rd L25 .70 A7
Colton Wlk L25 .69 F7
Columban Cl L30 .27 E3
Columbia Rd
Birkenhead CH43 .66 B4
Liverpool L4 .39 A2
Prescot L34 .56 E6
Columbine Cl WA8 .72 B4
Columbine Way WA9 .59 B7
Columbus Dr CH61 .76 E3
Columbus Quay L3 .67 E3
Columbus St 2 WN4 .34 F5
Columbus Way L21 .38 B7
Column Rd CH48 .63 D1
Colville Ct WA2 .61 A3
Colville Rd CH44 .51 A4
Colville St L15 .68 E8
Colwall Cl L33 .30 A2
Colwall Rd L33 .30 A2
Colwall Wlk L33 .30 A2
Colwell Cl L14 .55 A6
Colwell Rd L14 .55 A6
Colworth Rd L24 .82 B4
Colwyn Cl WA5 .60 E2
Colwyn Rd L13 .53 F2
Colwyn St CH41 .66 A8
Colyton Ave WA9 .58 D5
Combermere St
Liverpool L15 .68 D8
4 Liverpool,Toxteth L8 .67 F6
Comely Ave CH44 .51 D4
Comely Bank Rd CH44 .51 D4
Comer Gdns L31 .20 C3
Comfrey Gr L26 .70 E2
Commell Ct CH43 .66 B6
Commerce Way L8 .68 B7
Commercial Rd
Bebington CH62 .79 E3
Liverpool L20 .52 C7
Common Field Rd CH49 .65 B2
Common Rd WA12,WA5 .45 E3
Common St
Newton-le-W WA12 .45 E3
St Helens WA9 .57 D7
Commutation Row L3 .90 C4
Compass Ct CH45 .50 F8
Compton Cl WA11 .45 C7
Compton Rd Liverpool L6 .53 A4
Southport PR8 .4 B3
Wallasey CH41 .50 D1
Compton Way L26 .82 F6
Compton Wlk L20 .38 B4
Comus St L3 .52 D3
Concert St L1 .90 B3
Concorde Pl WA2 .61 D2
Concordia Ave CH49 .65 A5
Concourse Sh Ctr The
WN8 .16 B1
Concourse Way WA9 .45 A2
Condor Cl L19 .81 D6
Condron Rd N L21 .27 C1
Condron Rd S L21 .27 C1
Coney Cres L23 .27 B5
Coney La Huyton-w-R L36 .71 A8
Liverpool L36 .70 F7
Coney Wlk CH49 .64 D6
Congress Gdns WA9 .57 D7
Conifer Cl Kirkby L33 .29 E5
Liverpool L9 .39 B4
Conifer Ct L37 .10 A2
Conifer Gr WA5 .74 F7
Conifers The L31 .20 C3
Coningsby Dr CH45 .51 A4
Coningsby Gdns 13 WA3 .47 E8
Coningsby Rd L4 .53 A7
Coniston Ave
Ashton-in-M WN4 .35 B4
Bebington CH63 .88 C4
Birkenhead CH43 .65 C5
Orrell WN5 .25 F7
Prescot L34 .56 F6
Wallasey CH45 .50 E7
Warrington WA5 .74 D4
Coniston Cl Hooton CH66 .89 B2
Kirkby L33 .29 D4
Liverpool L9 .39 B7
Coniston Ct PR8 .7 C3
Coniston Dr WN2 .36 B8
Coniston Gr WA11 .44 A7
Coniston Ho L17 .68 D2
Coniston Rd Formby L37 .9 D2
Irby CH61 .76 D6
Maghull L31 .20 E2
Coniston St L5 .53 A5
Coniston Way WA11 .23 F2
Conleach Rd L24 .82 E3
Connaught Cl CH41 .66 A8
Connaught Dr WA12 .46 C2
Connaught Ho CH41 .66 F6
Connaught Rd L7 .53 B2
Connaught Way CH41 .66 A8
Connolly Ave L20 .38 E5
Conroy Way WA12 .60 C8
Conservation Ctr (Mus)
L1 .90 B4
Consett Rd WA9 .57 D6
Constance St Liverpool L3 .52 F2
St Helens WA10 .43 D2
Constantine Ave CH60 .77 A1
Convent Cl
Birkenhead CH42 .66 D4
Liverpool L19 .81 A7
Ormskirk L39 .13 E2
Conville Bvd CH63 .78 E8
Conway Ave WA5 .60 F2
Conway Cl
Bebington CH63 .78 D5
Kirkby L33 .29 D5
Warrington WA5 .74 F6
Conway Cres WN5 .33 E6
Conway Ct CH63 .78 F4
Conway Dr Billinge WN5 .33 F5
Birkenhead CH41 .66 D6
Newton-le-W WA12 .46 E3
Conway Ho L6 .53 C4
Conway Park Stn CH41 .66 E7
Conway Rd WN4 .35 E5
Conway St
Birkenhead CH41 .66 E6
Liverpool L5 .52 E5
Wallasey CH44 .51 B4
Conwy Dr L6 .53 B4
Conyers Ave PR8 .3 F3
Coogee Ave WA5 .74 E7
Cook Ave WA11 .45 F7
Cook Rd CH46 .50 B4
Cook St Birkenhead CH41 .66 D5
Liverpool L2 .90 A3
Prescot,Eccleston Lane Ends
L34 .56 D6
Prescot,Whiston L35 .56 F4
Cook's Ct L23 .26 D5
Cooke St WN4 .34 F6
Cookes Cl CH64 .86 E1
Cooks Rd L23 .26 D5
Cookson Rd L21 .38 A6
Cookson St L1 .90 C1
Coombe Rd CH61 .76 E7
Cooper Ave
Newton-le-W WA12 .45 F3
Warrington WA2 .61 B2
Cooper Ave N L18 .69 A2
Cooper Ave S L19 .69 A1
Cooper Cl L19 .81 A8
Cooper La WA11 .45 C6
Cooper St St Helens WA10 .43 F4
Widnes WA8 .73 B1
Cooper's La L33 .41 D7
Cooperage Cl L8 .67 E4
Coopers Row L22 .37 E8
Copeland Cl CH61 .76 E3
Copperas Hill L1,L3 .90 C3
Copperas St WA10 .43 F3
Copperfield Cl L8 .67 F5
Copperwood Dr L35 .56 F3
Coppice Cl CH43 .65 B6
Coppice Cres L36 .55 F4
Coppice Dr WN5 .25 D2
Coppice Gn WA5 .60 A1
Coppice Gr CH49 .64 C2
Coppice Grange CH46 .64 C7
Coppice La L35 .71 C7
Coppice Leys L37 .9 E3
Coppice The
Knowsley L34 .41 D3
Liverpool L6 .53 C6
Wallasey CH45 .51 A7
Coppins The WA2 .61 C2
Copple House Ct L10 .40 A7
Copple House La L10 .40 A7
Coppull Rd L31 .20 C4
Copse Gr CH61 .76 E7
Copse The Liverpool L18 .69 D5
Newton-le-W WA12 .46 B4
Copsmead CH46 .64 F8
Copthorne Rd L32 .29 B2
Copthorne Wlk L32 .29 B2
Copy Cl L30 .27 F5
Copy La L30,L9 .28 B3
Copy Way L30 .27 F5
Coral Ave Huyton-w-R L36 .55 D3
St Helens WA9 .57 F7
Coral Cl L32 .29 C2
Coral Dr L20 .38 C3
Coral Ridge CH43 .65 D6
Coral St L13 .54 A1
Coralin Way WN4 .34 F7
Corbet Cl L32 .29 C2
Corbet Wlk 4 L32 .29 C2
Corbridge Rd L16 .69 C7
Corbyn St CH44 .51 E1
Corfu St CH43 .66 C6
Corinth Twr L5 .52 E6
Corinthian Ave L13 .54 A4
Corinthian Com Prim Sch
L13 .54 B4
Corinthian St
5 Birkenhead CH42 .66 F2
Seaforth L21 .37 F7
Corinto St L8 .67 F6
Corkdale Rd L9 .39 B5
Cormorant Ct CH45 .50 E8
Cormorant Dr WA7 .84 E2
Corn Mill Cl WN4 .34 D4
Corn Mill Lo L31 .20 C2
Corn St L8 .67 E5
Cornbrook WN8 .24 E7
Corncroft Rd L34 .41 D3
Corndale Rd L18 .69 A4
Cornel Way L36 .70 F8
Cornelian Gr WN4 .34 F5
Cornelius Dr CH61 .76 F5
Corner Brook L28 .54 F7
Cornerhouse La WA8 .72 D3
Cornett Rd L9 .39 B7
Corney St L7 .68 C7
Cornfields Cl L19 .81 B6
Cornflower Way CH46 .50 A2
Cornforth Way WA8 .72 F3
Cornhill L1 .90 B2
Cornice Rd L13 .54 A4
Corniche Rd CH62 .79 B6
Cornwall Cl CH62 .79 B7
Cornwall Ct CH63 .78 F4
Cornwall Dr CH43 .66 A1
Cornwall Rd WA8 .73 B3
Cornwall St WA9 .44 E2
Cornwall Way PR8 .7 C2
Cornwallis St Liverpool L1 90 B1
Liverpool L1 .90 C2
Cornwood Cl L25 .70 B7
Corona Ave L31 .20 C5
Corona Rd
Bebington CH62 .79 C6
Crosby L22 .26 D1
Liverpool L13 .54 A4
Coronation Ave
Formby L37 .10 A2
Huyton-w-R L14 .54 E3
Wallasey CH45 .51 B7
Coronation Bldgs
Wallasey CH44 .51 B4
West Kirby CH48 .63 C4
Coronation Dr
Bebington CH62 .79 D3
Crosby L23 .26 D3
Haydock WA11 .46 A7
Huyton-w-R L14 .54 E3
Newton-le-W WA12 .46 E1
Prescot L35 .56 C3
Warrington WA5 .74 F4
Widnes WA8 .84 C8
Coronation Rd Crosby L23 26 D4
Hoylake CH47 .62 F6
Maghull L31 .20 D3
St Helens WA10 .43 C5
Coronation St WN4 .34 D6
Coronation Wlk
Billinge WN5 .33 D4
Southport PR8 .4 A7
Coroner's La WA8 .73 A4
Coronet Rd L11 .40 C3
Coronet Way WA8 .84 B8
Corporation Rd CH41 .66 C8
Corporation St
4 Southport PR8 .4 B7
St Helens WA10 .44 A3
Corpus Christi RC Prim Sch
WA11 .31 F7
Corrie Dr CH63 .78 F4
Corsewall St L7 .68 D8
Corsican Gdns L35 .57 C7
Cortsway CH49 .64 E5
Cortsway W CH49 .64 D5
Corwen Cl
Birkenhead,Moreton CH46 .64 F7
Birkenhead,Upton CH43 .65 B6
Warrington WA5 .60 E1
Corwen Cres L14 .54 F2
Corwen Dr L30 .28 B4
Corwen Rd Hoylake CH47 .63 C7
Liverpool L4 .53 C8
Cosgate Cl WN5 .25 E5
Cosgrove Cl L6 .53 D7
Cossack Ave WA2 .61 C1
Costain St L20 .52 C7
Cotham St 1 WA10 .44 A3
Coton Way L32 .29 C3
Cotsford Cl L36 .55 C4
Cotsford Pl L36 .55 C4
Cotsford Rd L36 .55 C4
Cotsford Way L36 .55 C4
Cotswold Ave WA3 .47 D6
Cotswold Cres L26 .82 E7
Cotswold Gr WA9 .45 A3
Cotswold Pl WA2 .61 B4
Cotswold Rd
Birkenhead CH42 .66 C1
Warrington WA2 .61 B3
Cotswold St L7 .53 B2
Cottage Cl Bebington CH63 88 C5
Kirkby L32 .40 E7
Ormskirk L39 .13 D4
Cottage Dr E CH60 .85 F5
Cottage Dr W CH60 .85 F5
Cottage La Heswall CH60 .85 F5
Ormskirk L39 .13 D5
Cottage Mews L39 .13 D5
Cottage Pl 9 WA9 .58 C4
Cottage St CH41 .66 D7
Cottenham St 8 L7 .53 B3
Cotterdale Cl
2 St Helens WA9 .58 C6
Warrington WA5 .74 F7
Cottesbrook Cl L11 .40 A3
Cottesbrook Pl L11 .40 A3
Cottesbrook Rd L11 .40 A3

Cottesmore Dr CH60 86 D8
Cottesmore Way WA3 36 B1
Cotton Dr L39 13 D6
Cotton St L3 52 B4
Cottonwood L17 68 A2
Cottrell Cl L19 81 C4
Cottys Brow PR9 1 F3
Coudray Rd PR9 1 E1
Coulport Cl L14 55 A4
Coulsdon Pl L8 68 A4
Coulthard Rd CH42 79 A8
Coulton Rd WA8 73 F3
Coultshead Ave WN5 33 E6
Council Ave WN4 35 B3
Council St L35 57 A5
Countess Pk L11 40 C2
Countisbury Dr L16 69 E6
County Dr WA10 43 E2
County Rd Kirkby L32 29 E2
Liverpool L4 38 F1
Ormskirk L39 13 E6
Court Ave L26 71 A1
Court Hey L31 20 E1
Court Hey Ave L14,L36 55 A2
Court Hey Dr L16 54 F1
Court Hey Rd L16 54 F1
Court Mews PR9 2 A1
Court Rd PR9 4 C8
Court The Bebington CH63 79 A4
Huyton-w-R L28 55 C7
Southport PR9 4 B8
Courtenay Ave L22 26 C2
Courtenay Rd Crosby L22 26 C2
Hoylake CH47 63 A6
Liverpool L25 70 A4
Courtfield L39 13 D7
Courtfields Cl L12 54 B5
Courtgreen L39 13 D7
Courthope Rd L4 39 B1
Courtland Rd L18 69 B5
Courtney Ave CH44 51 A3
Courtney Rd CH42 79 A8
Courtyard The WA12 46 E4
Courtyard Wks L33 30 C2
Covent Gdn L2 90 A3
Coventry Ave L30 27 F1
Coventry Rd L15 69 A6
Coventry St 8 CH41 66 D6
Coverdale Ave L35 57 D3
Coverdale Cl WA5 74 F7
Covertside CH48 63 D2
Cowan Dr L6 53 A4
Cowanway WA8 72 F5
Cowdrey Ave CH43 50 C1
Cowley Cl CH49 64 D5
Cowley Hill La WA10 43 E4
Cowley Language Coll WA10 43 E6
Cowley Rd L4 39 A1
Cowley St WA10 44 A5
Cowper Rd L13 54 B3
Cowper St Bootle L20 38 A5
St Helens WA9 44 C1
Cowper Way L36 56 A1
Coyford Dr PR9 2 A4
Coylton Ave L35 57 D2
Crab St WA10 43 F4
Crab Tree Cl L24 83 E2
Crabtree Cl Liverpool L27 70 E5
Newton-le-W WA12 46 E3
Cradley WA8 72 C2
Crag Gr WA11 33 B1
Craigburn Rd L13 53 E6
Craighurst Rd L25 70 A7
Craigleigh Gr CH62 88 F4
Craigmore Rd L18 69 A1
Craigs Rd L13 53 E6
Craigside Ave L12 54 A7
Craigwood Way L36 55 B3
Craine Cl L4 53 B8
Cramond Ave 1 L15,L18 69 A5
Cranberry Cl
St Helens WA10 43 F5
Liverpool L27 70 E6
Cranborne Ave CH47 48 E1
Cranborne Rd L15 68 D7
Cranbourne Ave
Birkenhead CH41 66 A7
Birkenhead,Saughall Massie CH46 64 D7
Cranbrook Ave WN4 35 A4
Crane Ave WA9 58 D6
Cranehurst Rd L4 39 B2
Cranes La L40 14 E7
Cranfield Rd L23 27 A5
Cranford Cl CH62 88 F4
Cranford Rd L19 81 B8
Cranford St CH44 51 C2
Cranham Ave WA3 47 E7
Crank Hill WA11 32 E4
Crank Rd
Billinge WA11,WN5 33 B8
Crank WA11 32 E2
Crank,King's Moss WA11 32 F7
St Helens WA11 43 C7
Crankwood Rd WN2,WN7 36 D5
Cranleigh Gdns L23 26 D4
Cranleigh Pl L25 70 A6
Cranleigh Rd L25 70 A6
Cranmer St Liverpool L5 52 C5
Liverpool L5 52 D6
Cranmore Ave L23 26 F2
Cranshaw Ave WA9 58 D3
Cranshaw La WA8 73 B6
Cranston Cl WA10 43 C5
Cranston Rd L33 30 C2
Crantock Cl
Liverpool,Croxteth L11 40 C4
Liverpool,Halewood L26 82 F8
Crantock Gr WA10 43 C7
Cranwell Cl L10 28 C2
Cranwell Rd
Birkenhead CH49 64 B3
Liverpool L25 70 A7
Cranwell Wlk L25 70 A7
Crask Wlk L33 29 F4
Craven Ave WA3 47 E7
Craven Cl CH41 66 D6
Craven Ct WA2 60 F4
Craven Lea L12 40 E4
Craven Rd Liverpool L12 54 C6
Rainhill L35 57 C3
Craven St
Birkenhead CH41 66 C6
Liverpool L3 90 C4
Cravenwood Rd L26 82 F7
Crawford Ave
Liverpool L18 68 F5
Maghull L31 20 B3
Widnes WA8 72 B1
Crawford Cl Liverpool L12 54 D7
St Helens WA9 58 D4
Crawford Dr L15 54 A1
Crawford Pk L18 68 F3
Crawford Rd WN8 24 D2
Crawford St WA9 58 E3
Crawford Village Prim Sch WN8 24 E3
Crawford Way L7 53 F1
Crawley Ave WA2 61 A3
Crawshaw Ct L36 55 B4
Crediton Ave PR9 2 B5
Crediton Cl L11 40 C5
Creek The CH45 50 E8
Cremona Cnr 3 L22 26 E1
Cremorne Hey L28 55 B7
Crescent Ave
Ashton-in-M WN4 35 A4
Formby L37 9 E1
Crescent Ct 6 L21 38 A6
Crescent Gn L39 13 B1
Crescent Rd Crosby L23 26 B5
Liverpool L9 39 B4
Seaforth L21 38 A6
Southport PR8 3 F3
Wallasey CH44 51 C4
Crescent The
Bebington CH63 78 E5
Birkenhead CH49 64 D3
Bootle L20 38 E6
Crosby,Thornton L23 27 A6
Crosby,Waterloo L22 26 E1
Heswall,Gayton CH60 86 B6
Heswall,Pensby CH61 76 F6
Huyton-w-R L36 56 B2
Liverpool L24 82 C4
Maghull L31 28 C6
Prescot L35 56 F4
Southport PR9 2 C3
West Kirby CH48 63 A2
Crescents The L35 57 A4
Cressida Ave CH63 78 E7
Cressingham Rd 2 CH45 51 B8
Cressington Ave CH42 66 D1
Cressington Espl L19 81 A6
Cressington Sta L19 81 A7
Cresson CH43 65 F5
Cresswell Cl Liverpool L26 71 A1
Warrington WA5 60 D2
Cresswell St 7 L6 53 A4
Crestor Rd L25 69 F3
Creswell St WA10 43 E3
Cretan Rd L15 68 D7
Crete Twr L5 52 E6
Crewe Gn CH49 65 A2
Cricket Path Formby L37 9 F5
Southport PR8 3 F3
Cricklade Cl L20 38 B4
Cringles Dr L35 71 A7
Crispin Rd L27 70 E5
Crispin St WA10 43 E3
Critchley Rd L24 83 A3
Critchley Way L33 29 F5
Crockett's Wlk WA10 43 B5
Crockleford Ave PR8 4 E3
Crocus Ave CH41 65 F7
Crocus Gdns WA9 59 A7
Crocus St L5 52 D7
Croft Ave Bebington CH62 79 D1
Golborne WA3 35 F2
Orrell WN5 25 D5
Croft Ave E CH62 79 D2
Croft Bsns Pk CH62 79 E2
Croft Cl CH43 65 E4
Croft Ct PR9 2 C4
Croft Dr Birkenhead CH46 64 F7
West Kirby CH48 75 C7
Croft Dr E CH48 75 E6
Croft Dr W CH48 75 C7
Croft Edge CH43 66 B3
Croft End WA9 44 F1
Croft Field L31 20 E1
Croft Gn CH62 79 D3
Croft Heys L39 13 B1
Croft La Bebington CH62 79 D1
Liverpool L9 39 D7
Croft St WA3 47 A8
Croft The
Birkenhead CH49 64 D2
Huyton-w-R L28 55 A8
Kirkby L32 40 F7
Liverpool L12 54 B7
Maghull L31 20 B5
Croft The *continued*
Orrell WN5 25 D3
Croft Way L23 27 B5
Crofters La L33 30 A5
Crofters The CH49 64 D4
Croftlands WN5 25 D4
Crofton Cres L13 54 B3
Crofton Rd
Birkenhead CH42 66 E3
Liverpool L13 54 B3
Runcorn WA7 84 E1
Croftson Ave L39 13 F7
Croftsway CH60 85 D8
Croftwood Gr L35 56 E2
Cromarty Rd Liverpool L13 53 F2
3 Wallasey CH44 50 F4
Cromdale Gr WA9 44 E2
Cromdale Way WA5 74 E6
Cromer Dr CH45 51 A5
Cromer Rd Hoylake CH47 63 A7
Liverpool L17 68 E1
Southport PR8 3 E2
Cromer Way L26 82 F6
Cromfield L39 13 C2
Cromford Rd L36 55 E5
Crompton Ct L18 69 D5
Crompton Dr
Liverpool L12 40 E3
Winwick WA2 61 A6
Crompton St L5 52 D5
Cromptons La L16,L18 69 D5
Cromwell Ave WA2 60 D3
Cromwell Cl
Newton-le-W WA12 46 A4
Ormskirk L39 13 C2
Cromwell Rd 6 L4 38 F2
Crondall Gr L15 69 B7
Cronton Ave Prescot L35 56 C1
Wallasey CH46 49 F3
Cronton CE Prim Sch WA8 72 C6
Cronton Farm Ct WA8 72 E4
Cronton La
Rainhill L35,WA8 57 B1
Widnes WA8 72 F5
Cronton Park Ave WA8 72 C6
Cronton Park Cl WA8 72 C6
Cronton Rd
Cronton L35,WA8 72 C5
Huyton-w-R L35,L36 71 B7
4 Liverpool L15 69 A5
Cronulla Dr WA5 74 E7
Crookall St WN4 35 C4
Crookhurst Ave WN5 33 D6
Croome Dr CH48 63 D2
Cropper St L1 90 C3
Cropper's La L39 14 A1
Croppers Hill WA10 43 E3
Croppers Hill Ct WA10 43 E3
Croppers Rd WA2 61 F3
Cropton Rd L37 9 F3
Crosby Cl CH49 64 F6
Crosby Gn L12 54 A7
Crosby Gr St Helens WA10 43 D1
Willaston CH64 88 B1
Crosby High Sch L23 26 E5
Crosby Rd PR8 4 A3
Crosby Rd N L22 26 E1
Crosby Rd S L21 37 F7
Crosender Rd L23 26 C3
Crosfield Cl 5 L7 53 C1
Crosfield Rd Liverpool L7 53 C1
Prescot L35 56 F4
Wallasey CH44 51 C3
Crosfield Wlk 4 L7 53 C1
Crosgrove Rd L4 39 C1
Crosland Rd L32 30 A1
Cross Barn La L38 18 E3
Cross Farm Prim Sch L27 70 F4
Cross Farm Rd WA9 44 C1
Cross Gn L37 10 A2
Cross Green Cl L37 10 A2
Cross Hey L21 27 B2
Cross Hey Ave CH43 65 D5
Cross Hillocks La L35, WA8 71 E3
Cross La Bebington CH63 78 F4
Newton-le-W WA12 46 B4
Orrell WN5 25 D3
Prescot L35 56 D4
Wallasey CH45 50 D4
Cross Meadow Ct WA9 44 C2
Cross Pit La WA11 31 F6
Cross St Bebington CH62 79 B5
Birkenhead CH41 66 F6
Crosby L22 26 D1
Golborne WA3 47 A7
Prescot L34 56 E7
Southport PR8 4 B6
5 St Helens WA10 44 A3
Widnes WA8 73 C1
Cross The Bebington CH62 79 D1
Ince Blundell L38 18 E4
Crossacre Rd L25 70 B7
Crossdale Rd
Bebington CH62 88 D5
Crosby L23 26 C3
Crossdale Way WA11 33 B1
Crossens Way PR9 2 C6
Crossfield Rd WN8 24 C8
Crossfield St WA9 44 B3
Crossford Rd L14 55 A5
Crossgates WA8 73 F3
Crosshall Brow L40 14 C4
Crosshall St L1,L2 90 B4
Crossings The WA12 46 C3
Crossledge Way L16 69 F7
Crossley Dr Heswall CH60 85 D8
Liverpool L15 69 B8
Crossley Rd WA10 43 D1
Crossvale Rd L36 55 E1
Crossway Birkenhead CH43 65 E8
Widnes WA8 84 D8
Crossway Cl WN4 35 E5
Crossway The CH63 87 C4
Crossways
Bebington CH62 79 D3
Liverpool L25 69 F6
Crosswood Cres L36 55 C3
Crosthwaite Ave CH62 88 F4
Croston Ave L35 57 B5
Croston Cl WA8 72 C3
Croston's Brow PR9 1 F3
Crouch St 10 Liverpool L5 53 A6
St Helens WA9 58 D8
Crow La WN8 16 F3
Crow La E WA12 46 C4
Crow La W WA12 46 A4
Crow Orch Prim Sch WN8 15 F2
Crow St L8 67 D6
Crow Wood La WA8 73 D2
Crow Wood Pl WA8 73 D3
Crow Wood Rd WA3 36 D1
Crowe Ave WA2 61 B2
Crowland Cl PR9 5 A6
Crowland St PR9 5 A6
Crowland Way L37 10 B2
Crowmarsh Cl CH49 64 F4
Crown Acres Rd L25 82 C8
Crown Ave WA8 84 B8
Crown Bldgs
3 Crosby L23 26 E4
Southport PR8 7 F8
Crown Cl L37 10 A2
Crown Fields Cl WA12 46 B5
Crown Gdns WA12 46 B4
Crown Park Dr WA12 46 B5
Crown Rd L12 54 C7
Crown St Liverpool L7 53 A1
Liverpool,Edge Hill L7,L8 68 A8
Newton-le-W WA12 46 A3
St Helens WA9 57 D7
Crownway L36 55 D4
Crowther St WA10 43 E3
Croxdale Rd L14 55 A6
Croxdale Rd W
Huyton-w-R L14 55 A7
Liverpool L14 54 F7
Croxteth Ave Bootle L21 38 B7
Rainford WA11 31 F7
Wallasey CH44 51 B4
Croxteth Cl L31 20 E3
Croxteth Com Comp Sch L11 40 C5
Croxteth Com Prim Sch L11 40 D4
Croxteth Ct 4 L8 68 B6
Croxteth Ctry Pk* L12 40 D2
Croxteth Dr L17 68 D5
Croxteth Gate L17 68 C5
Croxteth Gr L8 68 C6
Croxteth Hall* L12 40 D1
Croxteth Hall La L11,L12 40 C2
Croxteth La L28,L34 41 C1
Croxteth Rd Bootle L20 38 B5
Liverpool L8 68 B5
Croxteth View L32 40 F6
Croyde Cl PR9 2 B5
Croyde Pl WA9 58 C4
Croyde Rd L24 83 A3
Croydon Ave L18 68 F5
Croylands St L4 52 E8
Crucian Way L12 40 D3
Crump St L1 90 C1
Crutchley Ave CH41 66 B8
Cubbin Cres L5 52 D6
Cubert Rd L11 40 D4
Cuckoo Cl L25 70 A4
Cuckoo La L25 70 A5
Cuckoo Way L25 70 A4
Cuerden St L3 90 B4
Cuerdley Gn WA5 74 A2
Cuerdley Rd WA5 74 C3
Cullen Ave L20 38 D5
Cullen Cl CH63 88 C4
Cullen St L8 68 C7
Culme Rd L12 53 F7
Culzean Cl L12 40 E3
Cumber La L35 56 F3
Cumberland Ave
Birkenhead CH43 66 A2
Litherland L30 27 C3
Liverpool L17 68 D6
St Helens WA10 57 B8
Cumberland Cl L6 53 D7
Cumberland Cres WA11 45 A6
Cumberland Gate L30 28 A3
Cumberland Rd
Southport PR8 4 D5
Wallasey CH45 51 C7
Cumberland St L1 90 A4
Cumbria Way L12 40 C2
Cummings St L1 90 C2
Cummins Ave L37 9 E5
Cumpsty Rd L21 27 C1
Cunard Ave CH44 51 D5
Cunard Cl CH43 65 C6
Cunard Rd L21 38 B7
Cunliffe Ave WA12 46 B5
Cunliffe St L2 90 A4
Cunningham Cl
Warrington WA5 74 F5
West Kirby CH48 75 C6
Cunningham Dr
Bebington CH63 88 C7
Runcorn WA7 84 E1
Cunningham Rd
Liverpool L13 54 A2
Widnes WA8 84 D8
Cunscough La L31,L39 21 D3
Cuper Cres L36 55 D4
Curate Rd L6 53 C7
Curlender Cl CH41 50 E1
Curlender Way L24 83 E2
Curlew Ave CH49 64 D6
Curlew Cl CH49 64 D6
Curlew Ct CH46 49 C1
Curlew Gr L26 70 E1
Curlew Way CH46 49 C1
Curran Way L33 29 D5
Currans Rd WA2 61 B2
Curtana Cres L11 40 C3
Curtis Rd L4 39 C1
Curwell Cl CH63 79 B3
Curzon Ave
Birkenhead CH41 66 B7
1 Wallasey CH45 51 B7
Curzon Rd
Birkenhead CH42 66 B2
Crosby L22 26 E1
Hoylake CH47 63 A7
Southport PR8 4 E5
Curzon St 4 WA7 84 F1
Cusson Rd L33 30 B1
Custley Hey L28 55 B8
Custom House La L1 90 A3
Cut La Haskayne L39,L40 12 F6
Kirkby L33 41 F7
Cygnet Cl L39 13 C2
Cygnet Ct L33 30 A2
Cynthia Rd WA7 84 F1
Cypress Ave WA8 73 B2
Cypress Cl L13 29 A3
Cypress Croft CH63 79 B3
Cypress Gdns L35 57 C7
Cypress Rd
Huyton-w-R L36 70 D8
Southport PR8 4 F6
Cyprian's Way L30 27 E3
Cyprus Gr 5 L8 68 A4
Cyprus St L34 56 D6
Cyprus Terr 6 CH45 51 B7
Cyril Gr L17 68 E2

D

D'Arcy Cotts CH63 87 B6
Dacre St Birkenhead CH41 66 E6
Liverpool L20 38 B1
Dacre's Bridge La L35 71 D6
Dacy Rd L5 53 A6
Daffodil Cl WA8 73 E4
Daffodil Gdns WA9 59 A7
Daffodil Rd
Birkenhead CH41 65 F7
Liverpool L15 69 B7
Dagnall Ave WA5 60 F2
Dagnall Rd L32 29 D1
Dahlia Cl L9 39 B4
Dailton Rd WN8 25 A7
Dairy Farm Rd WA11 31 C7
Dairylands Cl L16 69 C6
Daisey Mews L21 38 B6
Daisy Ave WA12 46 C2
Daisy Bank Rd WA5 74 F4
Daisy Mount L31 28 E8
Daisy St L5 52 D7
Daisy Way PR8 4 C2
Dakin Wlk L33 29 F2
Dalby Cl WA11 44 C5
Dale Acre Dr L21,L30 27 C3
Dale Ave Bebington CH62 88 D8
Heswall CH60 76 F1
Dale Cl Maghull L31 20 C2
Widnes WA8 84 A8
Dale Cres WA9 58 D6
Dale Ct CH60 76 F1
Dale End Rd CH61 77 C4
Dale Gdns CH60 76 D1
Dale Hey Hooton CH66 88 E2
Wallasey CH44 51 B3
Dale La L33 30 B4
Dale Mews L25 70 B4
Dale Rd Bebington CH62 88 D6
Golborne WA3 47 A7
Dale St L19 81 C5
Dale St (Queensway) L1, L2 90 A4
Dale The WA5 74 F5
Dale View WA12 46 E4
Dale View Cl CH61 77 A5
Daleacre Com Prim Sch L21 27 C3
Dalebrook Cl L25 70 B7
Dalecrest WN5 25 D1
Dalegarth Ave L12 40 F1
Dalehead Pl WA11 33 B1
Dalehurst Cl CH44 51 D4
Dalemeadow Rd L14 54 D3
Dales Row L36 56 B2
Dales Wlk L37 10 A6
Daleside Ave WN4 35 A8
Daleside Cl CH61 76 F6
Daleside Rd L33 29 F3
Daleside Wlk L33 29 F3
Dalesway CH60 85 E8
Dalewood L12 40 E3
Dalewood Gdns L35 56 F2
Daley Pl L20 38 E7
Daley Rd L21 27 C1

Dallam Prim Sch WA5 60 F1
Dallas Gr 3 L9 39 A6
Dallington Ct 3 L13 54 B2
Dalmeny St L17 68 B3
Dalmorton Rd CH45 51 C8
Dalry Cres L32 40 F7
Dalry Wlk L32 40 F7
Dalrymple St L5 52 D5
Dalston Dr WA11 33 B1
Dalton Cl L12 40 C2
Dalton Gr WN4 35 A4
Dalton Rd CH45 51 C7
Dalton St Michael's CE Prim Sch WN8 16 D5
Daltry Cl L12 54 A7
Dam La Ashton-in-M WN4 35 F3
Winwick WA3 61 F7
Dam Wood Rd L24 82 E2
Damerham Mews L25 70 A7
Damfield La L31 28 D8
Damian Dr WA12 46 A5
Damson Rd L27 70 E6
Dan's Rd WA8 73 E2
Danbers WN8 24 F6
Danby Cl L5 52 F5
Danby Fold L35 57 B3
Dane Cl CH61 76 F6
Dane Ct L35 57 C3
Dane St L4 38 F1
Danefield Pl L19 81 D8
Danefield Rd
Birkenhead CH49 64 C2
Liverpool L19 81 D8
Danefield Terr L19 81 D7
Danehurst Rd Liverpool L9 39 B7
Wallasey CH45 50 F7
Danesbury Cl WN5 33 E4
Danescourt Rd
Birkenhead CH41 66 A8
Liverpool L12 54 C5
Danescroft WA8 72 B3
Daneswell Dr CH46 49 F1
Daneswell Rd L24 83 A2
Daneville Rd L4 39 D2
Daneway PR8 7 B6
Danger La CH46 49 F1
Daniel Cl L20 38 A6
Daniel Davies Dr L8 68 A7
Daniels La WN8 24 C7
Dannette Hey L28 55 C7
Dansie St L3 52 F1
Dante Cl L9 39 C8
Danube St L7,L8 68 C7
Dapple Heath Ave L31 29 A3
Darby Gr L19 81 B6
Darby Rd L19 81 A8
Darent Rd WA11 45 B7
Daresbury Ave PR8 7 A5
Daresbury Cl L32 29 C2
Daresbury Ct WA8 73 E3
Daresbury Expressway WA7 84 F2
Daresbury Rd
St Helens WA10 43 B5
Wallasey CH44 51 A4
Darfield WN8 24 F7
Dark Entry L34 41 E1
Dark La Maghull L31 20 E1
Ormskirk L40 14 C6
Darley Ave WA2 61 E3
Darley Cl WA8 72 B3
Darley Ct L12 54 C6
Darley Dr L12 54 C6
Darleydale Dr CH62 88 F5
Darlington Cl CH44 51 D4
Darlington St CH44 51 D4
Darmond Rd L33 30 A3
Darmond's Gn CH48 63 B3
Darmonds Green Ave L6 53 D7
Darnley St L8 67 E5
Darrel Dr L7 68 C7
Darrel St L7 68 C7
Darsefield Rd L16 69 E7
Dartington Rd L16 69 D8
Dartmouth Ave L10 28 C2
Dartmouth Dr
Litherland L30 27 C3
St Helens WA10 43 C6
Darvel Ave WN4 34 C4
Darwall Rd L19 81 D8
Darwen Gdns WA2 61 D1
Darwen St L5 52 B5
Darwick Dr L36 71 A8
Darwin Gr WA9 57 E7
Daryl Rd CH60 86 A8
Daulby St L3 52 F2
Dauntsey Brow L25 70 B7
Dauntsey Mews L25 70 B7
Davenham Ave CH43 65 F3
Davenham Cl CH43 65 F2
Davenham Rd L37 9 F3
Davenhill Pk L10 28 C2
Davenport Cl CH48 75 C6
Davenport Gr L33 29 E4
Davenport Rd CH60 85 E7
Daventree Rd CH45 51 B5
Daventry Rd L17 68 E2
David St L8 67 F4
Davids Wlk L25 70 C3
Davidson Rd L13 54 A3
Davies Ave WA12 46 C4
Davies St Bootle L20 38 D4
Liverpool L1,L2 90 A4
St Helens WA9 44 C4
Davis Rd CH46 50 B3
Davy Cl WA10 43 B5
Davy St L5 53 A6
Dawber Cl 4 L6 53 A4
Dawber St WN4 35 D4
Dawley Cl WN4 35 A3
Dawlish Cl L25 82 C8
Dawlish Dr PR9 2 A5
Dawlish Rd Irby CH61 76 C5
Wallasey CH44 51 A4
Dawlish Way WA3 35 F1
Dawn Cl WA9 57 E7
Dawn Wlk L10 40 B6
Dawpool CE Prim Sch CH61 76 B6
Dawpool Cotts CH48 76 A6
Dawpool Dr
Bebington CH62 88 C7
Birkenhead CH46 64 E8
Dawpool Farm CH61 76 B5
Dawson Ave
Birkenhead CH41 66 B8
Southport PR9 2 C5
St Helens WA9 58 D7
Dawson Gdns L31 20 C2
Dawson Rd L39 13 F7
Dawson St L1 90 B3
Dawson Way 12 L1 90 B3
Dawstone Rd CH60 86 A7
Dawstone Rise CH60 85 F7
Day St L13 54 A3
Daybrook WN8 24 F7
Dayfield WN8 25 B7
Days Mdw 1 CH49 64 C3
De Grouchy St CH48 63 B3
De La Salle RC High Sch L11 40 B2
De La Salle Sch WA10 43 B4
De Villiers Ave L23 26 E5
De-Haviland Way WN8 24 E8
Deacon Cl L22 37 D8
Deacon Ct Liverpool L25 70 B2
Seaforth L22 37 D8
Deacon Rd WA8 73 B1
Deacon Trad Est WA12 46 A2
Deakin St CH41 65 F8
Dealcroft L25 69 F2
Dean Ave CH45 50 E6
Dean Cl Billinge WN5 33 D3
Up Holland WN8 25 C7
Dean Cres WA2 61 B2
Dean Ct WA3 47 A7
Dean Dillistone Ct L1 90 C1
Dean Ho L22 37 D8
Dean Mdw WA12 46 C4
Dean Patey Ct L1 90 C1
Dean Rd WA3 47 A7
Dean St L22 37 D8
Dean Way WA9 58 B2
Dean Wood Ave WN5 25 E8
Deanacres L25 70 A2
Deane Rd L7 53 C2
Deans Ct L37 9 F5
Deans Way CH41 65 F8
Deansburn Rd L13 53 E6
Deanscales Rd L11 40 A2
Deansgate La L37 10 B5
Deansgate La N L37 10 A6
Deansway WA8 84 C8
Deanwood Cl L35 56 F2
Dearham Ave WA11 44 B7
Dearne Cl L12 54 E5
Dearnford Ave CH62 88 D6
Dearnford Cl CH62 88 D6
Dearnley Ave WA11 44 E5
Deauville Rd L9 39 C7
Debra Cl L31 29 B4
Dee Cl L33 29 F6
Dee Ct L25 70 C3
Dee Ho L25 70 C3
Dee La CH48 63 A2
Dee Park Cl CH60 86 B6
Dee Park Rd CH60 86 B5
Dee Rd L35 57 B3
Dee Side CH60 85 C8
Dee View Rd CH60 85 F8
Deeley Cl L7 53 C1
Deep Dale WA5 74 F6
Deepdale WA8 72 C3
Deepdale Ave
Billinge WA11 33 C1
Bootle L20 38 A5
Deepdale Cl CH43 65 C6
Deepdale Dr L35 57 D3
Deepdale Rd L25 70 A7
Deepfield Dr L36 70 F8
Deepfield Rd L15 68 F6
Deepwood Gr L35 56 E2
Deerbarn Dr L30 28 B4
Deerbolt Cl L32 29 C3
Deerbolt Cres L32 29 C3
Deerbolt Way L32 29 C3
Deeside Cl CH43 65 B6
Deeside Ct CH64 86 B1
Deighton Cl WN5 25 E6
Deirdre Ave WA8 73 A1
Delabole Rd L11 40 D5
Delafield Cl WA2 61 F3
Delagoa Rd L10 39 F6
Delamain Rd L13 53 E6
Delamere Ave
Bebington CH62 88 E4
Golborne WA3 47 E6
St Helens WA9 58 A3
Widnes WA8 72 C1
Delamere Cl
Bebington CH62 88 E4
Birkenhead CH43 65 B6
Liverpool L12 40 D3
Delamere Ct CH62 88 E4
Delamere Gr 3 CH44 51 E2
Delamere Rd
Skelmersdale WN8 15 F2
Southport PR8 7 B5
Delamere Way WN8 25 A7
Delamore Pl L4 38 E1
Delamore St L4 38 E1
Delavor Cl CH60 85 E8
Delavor Rd CH60 85 E8
Delaware Cres L32 29 C3
Delaware Rd L20 38 C4
Delf La Haskayne L39 12 A4
Liverpool,Hunt's Cross L24 82 B5
Liverpool,Walton on the Hill L4 39 A2
Delfby Cres L32 30 A1
Dell Cl CH63 88 B6
Dell Ct CH43 65 F1
Dell Gr CH42 79 B8
Dell La CH60 86 B7
Dell Prim Sch The CH42 67 B1
Dell St 2 L7 53 C2
Dell The Birkenhead CH42 67 B1
Liverpool L12 54 E8
Up Holland WN8 25 B7
Dellfield La L31 20 E1
Dellside Cl WN4 34 D5
Dellside Gr WA9 58 C8
Delph Cl L39 13 C1
Delph Common Rd L39 13 D1
Delph Ct L21 38 A8
Delph La Formby L37 9 C3
Ormskirk L39 13 C1
Prescot L35 56 F5
Warrington WA2 60 F4
Winwick WA2 61 E6
Delph Mdw Gdns WN5 33 D4
Delph Park Ave L39 13 B1
Delph Rd L23 26 D8
Delph Side Com Prim Sch WN8 24 C8
Delph Top L39 14 A6
Delphside Cl WN5 25 D5
Delphside Rd WN5 25 D5
Delphwood Dr WA9 44 B1
Delta Cres WA5 60 C2
Delta Dr L12 54 E8
Delta Rd Bootle L21 38 B7
St Helens WA9 44 F4
Delta Rd E CH42 67 B1
Delta Rd W CH42 67 B1
Deltic Way Kirkby L33 30 B1
Liverpool L30 39 A8
Delves Ave CH63 78 F3
Delyn Cl CH42 66 E1
Demesne St CH44 51 E3
Denbigh Ave Southport PR9 1 F3
St Helens WA9 58 C7
Denbigh Rd Liverpool L9 38 F3
Wallasey CH44 51 D3
Denbigh St L5 52 B5
Dencourt Rd L11 40 B1
Dene Ave WA12 45 F4
Denebank Rd L4 53 B7
Denecliff L28 55 B8
Denehurst Cl WA5 74 F4
Denes Way L28 55 A7
Deneshey Rd CH47 63 C8
Denford Rd L14 54 F5
Denham Cl 1 L12 41 A3
Denholme
Skelmersdale WN8 24 F7
Up Holland WN8 25 A7
Denise Ave WA5 74 E5
Denise Rd L10 40 B7
Denison Gr WA9 57 E7
Denman Dr L6 53 C4
Denman Gr 4 CH44 51 E2
Denman St 7 L7 53 B3
Denman Way L6 53 C4
Denmark Rd PR9 2 A2
Denmark St L22 26 D1
Dennett Cl L31 28 D7
Dennett Rd L35 56 C4
Denning Dr CH61 76 D7
Dennis Ave WA10 57 C7
Denny Cl CH49 64 F4
Densham Ave WA2 61 B2
Denshaw WN8 24 F7
Denston Cl CH43 65 B7
Denstone Ave L10 28 D3
Denstone Cl L25 82 B8
Dentdale Dr L5 52 E4
Denton Dr CH45 51 C6
Denton Gr L6 53 C5
Denton St Liverpool L8 67 F4
Widnes WA8 73 C1
Dentons Green La WA10 43 E5
Dentwood St L8 68 A4
Denver Rd L32 29 C1
Depot Rd L33 30 D4
Derby Bldgs L7 53 B1
Derby Cl WA12 46 B3
Derby Ct L37 9 E5
Derby Dr WA11 32 A5
Derby Gr L31 28 D6
Derby Hill Cres L39 14 A5
Derby Hill Rd L39 14 A5
Derby La L13 54 A4
Derby Rd
Birkenhead CH41,CH42 66 D4
Bootle L20 38 B2
Formby L37 9 E5
Golborne WA3 47 C8
Huyton-w-R L36 55 E2
Liverpool L20 52 C7
Skelmersdale WN8 23 C8
Southport PR9 4 C7
Wallasey CH45 51 A6
Derby Rd *continued*
Widnes,Barrow's Green WA8 73 D4
Widnes,Lunts Heath WA8 73 B4
Derby Row WA12 60 D8
Derby Sq Liverpool L1 90 A3
8 Prescot L34 56 E6
Derby St Huyton-w-R L36 56 A2
Liverpool,Garston L19 81 C4
Liverpool,Stanley L13 53 F3
Newton-le-W WA12 46 B3
Ormskirk L39 13 F5
Prescot L34 56 C6
Derby St W L39 13 E5
Derbyshire Hill Rd WA9 45 A2
Dereham Ave CH49 65 A7
Dereham Cres L10 39 F7
Derek Ave WA2 61 E1
Derna Rd L36 55 D3
Derrbourne Cl L25 69 F2
Derringstone Cl WA10 43 D1
Derrylea L9 39 D7
Derwent Ave Formby L37 9 D2
Golborne WA3 36 C1
Prescot L34 56 F6
Southport PR9 1 F1
Derwent Cl
Bebington CH63 78 D5
Kirkby L33 29 D4
Maghull L31 20 F2
Rainhill L35 57 B3
Derwent Dr Bootle L21 38 D8
Heswall CH61 76 F4
Hooton CH66 89 B2
Wallasey CH45 51 A6
Derwent Rd
Ashton-in-M WN4 35 E5
Bebington CH63 78 D5
Birkenhead CH43 66 B4
Crosby L23 26 F2
Hoylake CH47 63 E8
Orrell WN5 25 F8
St Helens WA11 44 B7
Widnes WA8 72 C1
Derwent Rd E L13 54 A4
Derwent Rd W L13 53 F4
Derwent Sq L13 54 A4
Desborough Cres L12 54 A7
Desford Ave WA11 44 D6
Desford Cl CH46 49 B1
Desford Rd L19 80 F8
Desilva St L36 56 A2
Desmond Cl CH43 65 C6
Desmond Gr L23 26 F3
Desoto Rd WA8 84 E5
Desoto Rd E WA8 84 F6
Desoto Rd W WA8 84 F6
Deva Cl L33 29 E7
Deva Rd CH48 63 A2
Deveraux Dr CH44 51 C3
Deveraux Rd CH44 51 C3
Deverell Gr L15 54 B1
Deverell Rd L15 54 B1
Deverill Rd CH42 66 E1
Devilla Cl L14 55 A5
Devisdale Gr CH43 65 C7
Devizes Dr CH61 76 D7
Devoke Ave WA11 33 A1
Devon Ave
Up Holland WN8 25 B6
Wallasey CH44,CH45 51 C5
Devon Cl L23 26 A3
Devon Dr CH61 76 E4
Devon Farm Way L37 10 B3
Devon Gdns
Birkenhead CH42 66 F1
Liverpool L16 69 E5
Devon Pl WA8 73 B3
Devon St Liverpool L3,L6 52 F2
St Helens WA10 43 D4
Devon Way
Huyton-w-R L36 56 A4
Liverpool L16 69 E6
Devondale Rd L18 69 A5
Devonfield Rd L9 38 F5
Devonport St L8 67 F5
Devonshire Cl
Birkenhead CH43 66 B5
Kirkby L33 29 E4
Devonshire Gdns WA12 46 C2
Devonshire Park Prim Sch CH42 66 C2
Devonshire Pl
Birkenhead CH43 66 A5
Liverpool L5 52 E6
Devonshire Rd
Birkenhead CH43 66 B5
Birkenhead,Upton CH49 64 E5
Crosby L22,L23 26 C3
Heswall CH61 76 E4
Liverpool L8 68 A5
Southport PR9 5 A8
St Helens WA10 43 D5
Wallasey CH44 51 B4
West Kirby CH48 63 C1
Devonshire Rd W L8 68 A5
Devonwall Gdns L8 68 B5
Dewberry Cl 3 CH42 66 D4
Dewberry Fields WN8 25 B7
Dewey Ave L9 39 B8
Dewlands Rd L21 37 F8
Dewsbury Rd L4 53 C7
Dexter St L8 67 E6
Dexter Way WN8 25 B6
Deycroft Ave L33 30 A4
Deycroft Wlk L33 30 A4
Deyes Ct L31 20 E1
Deyes End L31 20 E1
Deyes High Sch L31 20 D1
Deyes La Maghull L31 20 D1
Maghull,Moss Side L31 20 F1
Deysbrook La L12,L28 54 F8
Deysbrook Side L12 54 C6
Deysbrook Way L12 54 D8
Dial Rd CH42 66 D3
Dial St 5 L7 53 C2
Diamond Bsns Pk WA11 32 B4
Diamond St L3,L5 52 D4
Diana Rd L20 38 D7
Diana St L4 53 A8
Diane Rd WN4 35 E5
Dibb La L23 26 C7
Dibbins Gn CH63 88 B7
Dibbins Hey CH63 79 B2
Dibbinsdale Rd CH63 88 B7
Dibbinview Gr CH63 79 B2
Dicconson St WA10 44 A4
Dicconson Way L39 14 A5
Dicconson's La L39 12 D4
Dick's La L40 14 F4
Dickens Ave CH43 65 F1
Dickens Cl CH43 65 F1
Dickens Dr WN2 36 C8
Dickens Rd WA10 57 C8
Dickens St L8 67 F6
Dickenson St L1 90 B2
Dicket's Brow L40 14 F3
Dicket's La L40,WN8 15 A2
Dickinson Cl Formby L37 9 F2
Haydock WA11 45 A6
Dickinson Ct PR8 4 A2
Dickinson Rd L37 9 F2
Dickson St L3 52 B4
Didcot Cl L25 82 D8
Didsbury Cl L33 29 F2
Digg La CH46 49 D1
Digmoor Dr WN8 24 C7
Digmoor Rd Kirkby L32 40 F7
Skelmersdale WN8 24 D6
Dignum Mead L27 70 E5
Dilloway St WA10 43 E4
Dinas La L36 55 B4
Dinesen Rd L19 81 C7
Dingle Ave
Newton-le-W WA12 45 F2
Up Holland WN8 25 C8
Dingle Brow L8 68 A3
Dingle Cl L39 13 C1
Dingle Gr L8 68 A4
Dingle Grange 5 L8 68 A3
Dingle La L17,L8 68 A3
Dingle Mount L8 68 A3
Dingle Rd
Birkenhead CH42 66 C4
Liverpool L8 68 A3
Up Holland WN8 25 B7
Dingle Vale L17,L8 68 A3
Dingley Ave L9 38 F6
Dingwall Dr CH49 64 E3
Dinmore Rd CH44 51 B4
Dinnington Ct WA8 72 E3
Dinorwic Rd Liverpool L4 53 A6
Southport PR8 4 A2
Dinsdale Rd CH62 79 E2
District CE Prim Sch The WA12 46 A4
Ditchfield L37 10 A2
Ditchfield Pl WA8 84 B8
Ditchfield Rd
Warrington WA5 74 E3
Widnes WA8 84 B8
Ditton CE Prim Sch WA8 72 A1
Ditton La CH46 49 E3
Ditton Prim Sch WA8 72 E1
Ditton Rd WA8 84 D6
Dixon Ave WA12 46 C5
Dixon Cl WA11 46 A8
Dixon Rd L33 41 B8
Dobbs Dr L37 10 A4
Dobson St L6 53 A4
Dock Rd Liverpool L19 81 B5
Wallasey CH41,CH44 51 C1
Widnes WA8 84 F5
Dock Rd N CH62 79 C6
Dock Rd S CH62 79 D4
Doctor's La L37 10 E2
Dodd Ave
Birkenhead CH49 64 D3
St Helens WA10 43 C4
Dodd's La L31 20 D2
Doddridge Rd 6 L8 67 E5
Dodleston Cl CH43 65 D4
Dodman Rd L11 40 D5
Dodson Cl WN4 35 C3
Dodworth Ave PR8 4 E5
Doe Park Ctyd L25 82 B8
Doe's Meadow Rd CH63 88 B7
Dolly's La PR9 5 D8
Dolomite Ave L24 81 F6
Domar Cl L32 29 F1
Dombey St L8 67 F6
Domingo Dr L33 29 D5
Dominic Cl L16 69 E8
Dominic Rd L16 69 E8
Dominion St L6 53 C5
Domville L35 56 E2
Domville Dr CH49 65 A3
Domville Rd L13 54 A1
Donalds Way L17 68 E1
Donaldson St L5 53 A6
Doncaster Dr CH49 64 F6
Donegal Rd 1 L13 54 B2
Donne Ave CH63 79 A3

Donne Cl CH63 ....79 A3
Donnington Cl L36 ....70 D8
Donnington Lo PR8 ....3 F6
Donsby Rd L9 ....39 B6
Dooley Dr L30 ....28 B4
Doon Cl L4 ....52 E8
Dorbett Dr L23 ....26 F2
Dorchester Cl CH49 ....64 F4
Dorchester Dr L33 ....30 A5
Dorchester Pk CH43 ....65 D3
Dorchester Rd
Liverpool L25 ....70 B6
Up Holland WN8 ....25 A7
Dorchester Way WA5 ....59 F6
Doreen Ave CH46 ....64 D8
Dorgan Cl L35 ....57 C4
Doric Gn WN5 ....25 D3
Doric Rd L13 ....54 A4
Doric St
4 Birkenhead CH42 ....66 F2
Seaforth L21 ....37 F7
Dorien Rd L13 ....53 F2
Dorincourt CH43 ....66 A4
Dorking Gr L15 ....69 B6
Dorothy St Liverpool L7 ....53 B1
St Helens WA9 ....57 E8
Dorothy Wlk WN2 ....35 F8
Dorrit St L8 ....67 F6
Dorset Ave Liverpool L15 ....68 D7
Southport PR8 ....7 C2
Dorset Cl L20 ....38 D3
Dorset Dr CH61 ....76 E4
Dorset Gdns CH42 ....66 F1
Dorset Rd Huyton-w-R L36 56 A3
Liverpool L6 ....53 D5
St Helens WA10 ....43 D1
Wallasey CH45 ....51 A7
West Kirby CH48 ....63 C3
Douglas Arc 18 CH41 ....66 E6
Douglas Ave Billinge WN5 ....33 D3
St Helens WA9 ....59 B6
Up Holland WN8 ....25 B7
Douglas Cl Liverpool L13 ....53 F4
Widnes WA8 ....73 F3
Douglas Dr
Birkenhead CH46 ....64 D8
Maghull L31 ....20 F2
Ormskirk L39 ....13 D7
Orrell WN5 ....25 F7
Douglas Pl L20 ....38 B1
Douglas Rd Liverpool L4 ....53 B6
Southport PR9 ....2 C4
West Kirby CH48 ....63 D3
Douglas St
Birkenhead CH41 ....66 E6
St Helens WA10 ....43 D3
Douglas Way L33 ....29 F6
Doulton Cl CH43 ....65 B7
Doulton Pl L35 ....56 C2
Doulton St WA10 ....43 D3
Douro Pl L13 ....53 F2
Douro St L3,L5 ....52 E4
Dove Ct L25 ....70 B3
Dove Rd L9 ....38 F6
Dove St Golborne WA3 ....36 A2
Liverpool L8 ....68 B7
Dovecot Ave L14 ....54 F4
Dovecot Pl L14 ....54 F4
Dovecot Prim Sch L14 ....55 A3
Dovecote Dr WA11 ....45 C7
Dovecote Gn WA5 ....60 A1
Dovedale Ave
Bebington CH62 ....88 E5
Maghull L31 ....20 C2
Dovedale Cl
Birkenhead CH43 ....65 F2
Warrington WA2 ....61 E3
Dovedale Cres WN4 ....35 A8
Dovedale Ct WA8 ....72 B3
Dovedale Inf & Jun Schs L18 ....69 A5
Dovedale Rd
Ashton-in-M WN4 ....35 A8
Hoylake CH47 ....63 B8
Liverpool L18 ....69 A4
Wallasey CH45 ....51 A7
Dovepoint Rd CH47 ....48 E1
Dover Cl CH41 ....66 D7
Dover Gr L16 ....69 F8
Dover Rd Maghull L31 ....28 C6
Southport PR8 ....3 F2
Dover St L3 ....52 F1
Dovercliffe Rd L13 ....54 B3
Dovercroft L25 ....69 F2
Dovesmead Rd CH60 ....86 C7
Dovestone Cl L7 ....68 B8
Dovey St L8 ....68 A5
Doward St WA8 ....73 C2
Dowhills Dr L23 ....26 B5
Dowhills Pk L23 ....26 B6
Dowhills Rd L23 ....26 B5
Downall Green RC Prim Sch WN4 ....34 E6
Downall Green Rd WN4 ....34 E6
Downbrook Way WN4 ....35 D5
Downes Gn CH63 ....79 A1
Downham Cl L25 ....69 F5
Downham Ct CH60 ....86 A8
Downham Dr CH60 ....86 A8
Downham Gn L25 ....69 F5
Downham Rd CH42 ....66 E3
Downham Rd N CH61 ....77 A2
Downham Rd S CH60 ....77 A1
Downham Way L25 ....69 F5
Downham Wlk WN5 ....25 D1
Downholland Moss La L37 ....10 C4
Downholland-Haskayne CE Prim Sch L39 ....11 E3
Downing Cl CH43 ....66 B3
Downing Rd L20 ....38 E2
Downing St 3 L5 ....53 A5
Downland Way WA9 ....44 F2
Downlands Rd L27 ....70 F4
Downs Rd WA10 ....43 D2
Downs The L23 ....26 B3
Downside WA8 ....72 B3
Downside Cl L30 ....27 E4
Downside Dr L10 ....28 F1
Downway La WA9 ....45 A1
Dowsefield La L18,L25 ....69 E3
Dragon Cl L11 ....40 C4
Dragon Cres L35 ....56 F4
Dragon Dr L35 ....56 E3
Dragon La L35 ....56 E3
Dragon Wlk 1 L11 ....40 C4
Dragon Yd WA8 ....73 B4
Drake Cl Liverpool L10 ....40 A7
Ormskirk L39 ....13 C2
Prescot L35 ....56 E2
Warrington WA5 ....60 D1
Drake Cres L10 ....40 A7
Drake Gdns WA9 ....57 E6
Drake Pl L10 ....39 F7
Drake Rd Liverpool L10 ....40 A7
Neston CH64 ....86 E1
Wallasey CH46 ....50 B4
Drake St Bootle L20 ....38 B1
St Helens WA10 ....43 D4
Drake Way L10 ....40 A7
Drakefield Rd L11 ....39 E3
Draw Well Rd L33 ....30 D2
Draycott St L8 ....67 F3
Drayton Cl Irby CH61 ....76 D5
Runcorn WA7 ....84 F1
Drayton Cres WA11 ....44 D6
Drayton Rd
3 Liverpool L4 ....39 A2
Wallasey CH44 ....51 D3
Drennan Rd L19 ....81 E8
Drewell Rd L18 ....68 F3
Drewitt Cres PR9 ....2 D4
Driffield Rd L34 ....56 C6
Drinkwater Gdns 2 L3 ....52 E3
Drive The L12 ....54 B5
Driveway L35 ....56 F2
Droitwich Ave CH49 ....64 C4
Dromore Ave L18 ....69 A3
Dronfield Way L25 ....69 F7
Druid St WN4 ....35 C2
Druids Pk L18 ....69 E4
Druids Way CH49 ....65 A2
Druids' Cross Gdns L18 ....69 D4
Druids' Cross Rd L18 ....69 D4
Druidsville Rd L18 ....69 E4
Drum Cl L14 ....55 A5
Drummer's La WN4 ....34 E7
Drummond Ct WA8 ....73 B4
Drummond Rd Crosby L23 27 B5
Hoylake CH47 ....63 B6
Liverpool L4 ....39 C1
Drummoyne Ct L23 ....26 A5
Druridge Dr WA5 ....74 F4
Drury La L2 ....90 A3
Dryburgh Way 5 L4 ....52 E8
Dryden Ave WN4 ....34 F6
Dryden Cl
Birkenhead CH43 ....65 C7
Prescot L35 ....56 E3
Dryden Gr L36 ....55 F1
Dryden Pl WA2 ....61 C2
Dryden Rd L15,L7 ....53 E1
Dryden St Bootle L20 ....38 A5
Liverpool L5 ....52 D4
Dryebeck Gr WA9 ....58 D6
Dryfield Cl CH49 ....64 D4
Dublin St L3 ....52 B4
Ducie St L8 ....68 B6
Duck Pond La CH42 ....66 A2
Duckinfield St L3 ....52 F1
Duddingston Ave
Crosby L23 ....26 E2
2 Liverpool L15,L18 ....69 A5
Duddon Ave L31 ....20 F2
Duddon Cl CH43 ....65 F3
Dudley Cl CH43 ....66 B4
Dudley Cres CH65 ....89 B3
Dudley Gr L23 ....26 E2
Dudley Pl WA9 ....44 D3
Dudley Rd Liverpool L18 ....68 F5
Wallasey CH45 ....51 A8
Dudley St WN4 ....35 A5
Dudlow Ct L18 ....69 C5
Dudlow Dr L18 ....69 C5
Dudlow Gdns L18 ....69 C6
Dudlow Grange L18 ....69 C5
Dudlow La L18 ....69 C5
Dudlow Nook Rd L18 ....69 C6
Dugdale Cl L19 ....81 A7
Duke Ave PR8 ....4 C4
Duke Cl WA7 ....84 F2
Duke Of York Cotts CH62 79 A6
Duke St Ashton-in-M WN4 ....35 C3
Birkenhead CH41 ....66 C8
Formby L37 ....9 F2
Golborne WA3 ....36 A1
Liverpool L1 ....90 B2
Liverpool,Garston L19 ....81 C6
Newton-le-W WA12 ....46 B3
4 Prescot L34 ....56 D6
Seaforth L22 ....37 D8
Southport PR8 ....4 A5
St Helens WA10 ....43 F4
Duke St *continued*
Wallasey CH45 ....51 B8
Duke Street Gate CH41 ....66 C8
Duke Street La L1 ....90 B2
Duke's Wood La WN8 ....24 D3
Dukes Rd L5 ....52 E6
Dukes Terr L1 ....90 C2
Dukes Way L37 ....9 F2
Dulas Gn L32 ....30 A1
Dulas Rd Kirkby L32 ....30 A1
Liverpool L15 ....69 B6
Dulverton Rd L17 ....80 E8
Dumbarton St L4 ....38 F1
Dumbrees Gdns L12 ....54 E8
Dumbrees Rd L12 ....54 F8
Dumbreeze Gr L34 ....41 D4
Dumfries Way L33 ....29 D6
Dunacre Way L26 ....82 F7
Dunbabin Rd L15,L16 ....69 C6
Dunbar Cres PR8 ....7 F8
Dunbar Rd PR8 ....3 F1
Dunbar St L4 ....38 F2
Dunbeath Ave L35 ....57 D2
Dunbeath Cl L35 ....57 D1
Dunblane Cl WN4 ....34 C4
Duncan Ave WA12 ....46 C5
Duncan Cl WA10 ....43 F2
Duncan Dr CH49 ....64 D4
Duncan St
Birkenhead CH41 ....66 F6
Liverpool L1 ....90 C1
St Helens WA10 ....43 E3
Duncansby Cres WA5 ....74 E6
Duncansby Dr CH63 ....88 C4
Dunchurch Rd L14 ....54 F5
Duncombe Rd N L19 ....81 B7
Duncombe Rd S L19 ....81 B7
Duncote Cl
Birkenhead CH43 ....66 A4
Rainhill L35 ....57 A5
Dundale Rd L13 ....54 B3
Dundalk Rd WA8 ....84 E8
Dundas St L20 ....38 B1
Dundee Cl WA2 ....61 F4
Dundee Gr CH44 ....51 A3
Dundonald Rd L17 ....68 E1
Dundonald St CH41 ....66 A8
Dunedin Ct CH47 ....63 A6
Dunedin St WA9 ....57 E8
Dunes Dr L37 ....9 C4
Dunes Way L5 ....52 C6
Dunfold Cl L32 ....29 F1
Dungeon La Liverpool L24 .82 F1
Skelmersdale WN8 ....16 C7
Dunham Ave WA3 ....35 F1
Dunham Cl CH62 ....88 F3
Dunham Rd L15 ....54 B1
Dunkeld Cl 1 L6 ....53 A3
Dunkeld St 2 L6 ....53 A3
Dunkerron Cl L27 ....70 D7
Dunkirk Rd PR8 ....3 F2
Dunlin Ave WA12 ....46 C4
Dunlin Cl Liverpool L27 ....70 E4
Warrington WA2 ....61 E3
Dunlin Ct L25 ....70 A5
Dunlins Ct CH45 ....50 E8
Dunlop Ave PR8 ....7 C2
Dunlop Dr L31 ....29 B4
Dunlop Rd L24 ....82 C2
Dunluce St L4 ....38 E1
Dunmail Ave WA11 ....33 C1
Dunmore Rd L13 ....53 F3
Dunmow Way L25 ....82 C8
Dunnerdale Rd L11 ....40 A2
Dunnett St L20 ....38 B1
Dunning Cl CH49 ....64 E5
Dunnings Bridge Rd L30, L31 ....28 A3
Dunnock Cl Liverpool L25 .70 A5
Warrington WA2 ....61 E3
Dunraven Rd CH48 ....63 A2
Dunriding La WA10 ....43 D3
Dunscroft WA9 ....58 D7
Dunsdale Dr WN4 ....35 C3
Dunsdon Cl L18,L25 ....69 E4
Dunsdon Rd L25 ....69 E5
Dunsford WA8 ....72 B3
Dunsmore Cl WA11 ....45 C7
Dunsop Ave WA9 ....58 D4
Dunstall Cl CH46 ....49 E3
Dunstan La L7 ....68 C8
Dunstan St L15 ....68 E8
Dunster Gr Heswall CH60 .86 B7
St Helens WA9 ....58 D4
Dunster Rd PR8 ....7 E8
Durant's Cotts L31 ....28 E7
Durban Ave L23 ....26 E5
Durban Rd Liverpool L13 ....54 B3
Wallasey CH45 ....51 C6
Durban St WN2,WN7 ....36 E4
Durden St L7 ....68 C7
Durham Ave L30 ....28 A1
Durham Mews E L30 ....28 A1
Durham Mews W L30 ....28 A1
Durham Rd Seaforth L21 ....37 F7
Widnes WA8 ....73 B3
Durham St Liverpool L19 ....81 D4
Skelmersdale WN8 ....15 D2
Durham Way
Huyton-w-R L36 ....56 A3
Litherland L30 ....28 A1
Durley Dr CH43 ....65 E1
Durley Rd L9 ....39 B6
Durliston Cl WA8 ....72 C2
Durning Rd L7 ....53 C1
Durrant Rd 3 L11 ....53 E8
Durrell Way WA3 ....47 E8
Dursley L35 ....56 F2
Dursley Dr WN4 ....35 D4
Durston Rd L16 ....69 D8
Dutton Dr CH63 ....78 F2
Duxbury Cl Maghull L31 ....20 E3
Rainford WA11 ....32 A7
Duxford Ct WA2 ....61 E1
Dwerryhouse La L11,L12 ....40 B2
Dwerryhouse St L8 ....67 D6
Dyer St WA3 ....35 F1
Dyers La L39 ....13 E4
Dyke St L6 ....53 A4
Dykin Cl WA8 ....73 E3
Dykin Rd WA8 ....73 E3
Dymchurch Rd L24 ....82 B4
Dymoke Rd 2 L11 ....40 C3
Dymoke Wlk L11 ....40 C3
Dyson Hall L9 ....39 D5
Dyson Hall Dr L9 ....39 D5
Dyson St L4 ....38 F1

E

Eager La L31 ....20 B8
Eagle Cres WA11 ....32 A6
Eagle Dene L10 ....40 A6
Eagle Park Dr WA2 ....61 A1
Eaglehall Rd L9 ....39 F4
Eaglehurst Rd L25 ....70 B4
Eagles Ct L32 ....29 E2
Eaglesfield Cl 2 WA9 ....58 D7
Ealing Rd L9 ....39 B7
Eamont Ave PR9 ....2 B5
Eardisley Rd L15,L18 ....69 B6
Earhart Cl WN8 ....24 E8
Earl Rd L20 ....38 E4
Earl St Bebington CH62 ....79 B8
St Helens WA9 ....44 C4
Earl's Cl L23 ....26 D3
Earle Cl WA12 ....45 F3
Earle Cres CH64 ....86 D1
Earle Dr CH64 ....86 D1
Earle Rd L7 ....68 C8
Earle St 1 Liverpool L3 ....90 A4
Newton-le-W WA12 ....46 A3
Earlestown Sta WA12 ....46 B3
Earlsfield Rd L15 ....68 F6
Earlston Rd CH45 ....51 B6
Earlswood WN8 ....16 E1
Earlswood Cl 2 CH46 ....64 B8
Earlwood Gdns L35 ....56 E2
Earp St L19 ....81 C6
Easby Cl L37 ....10 A2
Easby Rd 5 L4 ....52 D7
Easby Wlk L4 ....52 D7
Easedale Dr PR8 ....7 B4
Easedale Wlk L33 ....29 D5
Easenhall Cl WA8 ....73 C5
Easington Rd WA9 ....57 D6
East Albert Rd L17 ....68 B4
East Ave WA3 ....36 C1
East Cl L34 ....57 A7
East Dam Wood Rd L24 ....83 A2
East Farm Mews CH48 ....75 F8
East Front L35 ....56 E1
East La L29 ....19 B2
East Lancashire Rd
Golborne WA11,WA12,WA3 .46 C7
Haydock WA11 ....45 C8
Knowsley L34 ....41 C6
Liverpool L11 ....40 C5
St Helens WA10,WA11 ....43 C7
East Leigh WN8 ....16 D1
East Mains L24 ....83 A3
East Mead L39 ....13 B2
East Meade L31 ....20 C2
East Millwood Rd L24 ....83 A4
East Mount WN5 ....25 F6
East Orchard La L9 ....39 E7
East Prescot Rd L13,L14 .54 D4
East Rd
Liverpool,Broad Green L14 .54 C2
Liverpool,Halewood L24,L26 83 A5
Maghull L31 ....20 F1
East Side WA9 ....44 C2
East St Ashton-in-M WN4 ....35 D4
Crosby L22 ....26 D1
Liverpool L3 ....90 A4
Prescot L34 ....56 E6
Southport PR9 ....4 D7
Wallasey CH41,CH44 ....51 E1
Widnes WA8 ....73 D1
East Way CH46 ....49 F1
Eastbank St PR8 ....4 B6
Eastbank Street Sq 9 PR8 ....4 B7
Eastbourne Mews L9 ....39 B7
Eastbourne Rd
Birkenhead CH41 ....66 C6
Crosby L22 ....26 B2
Liverpool L9 ....39 B7
Southport PR8 ....4 A3
Eastbury Cl WA8 ....73 C5
Eastcliffe Rd L13 ....54 B3
Eastcote Rd L19 ....81 C8
Eastcott Cl CH49 ....64 C3
Eastcroft Park Sch L33 ....29 F5
Eastcroft Rd CH44 ....51 C2
Eastdale Rd L15 ....68 F8
Easter Ct WA5 ....60 B2
Eastern Ave
Bebington CH62 ....79 D3
Liverpool L24 ....82 F3
Eastern Dr L19 ....81 A7
Eastfield Dr L17 ....68 C3
Eastfield Wlk L32 ....29 C1
Eastham Cl L16 ....54 F1
Eastham Cres WA9 ....58 C4
Eastham Ctry Pk★ CH62 .89 A8
Eastham Gn L24 ....82 E4
Eastham Mews CH62 ....89 A4
Eastham Rake CH62,CH64 88 D3
Eastham Rake Sta CH63 .88 D3
Eastham Village Rd CH62 ....89 A5
Eastlake Ave L5 ....52 F5
Eastleigh Dr CH61 ....76 D7
Eastman Rd L13 ....53 E7
Easton Rd Bebington CH62 79 B8
Huyton-w-R L36 ....55 A3
Eastpark Ct CH44 ....51 E3
Eastview Cl CH43 ....65 D4
Eastway Birkenhead CH49 .64 E4
Maghull L31 ....20 E1
Widnes WA8 ....72 D1
Eastway Prim Sch CH46 .49 F1
Eastwell Rd WN4 ....35 A3
Eastwood L17 ....68 A3
Eastwood Ave WA12 ....46 F3
Eastwood Rd WA5 ....59 F7
Eaton Ave Bootle L21 ....38 B7
Bootle,Orrell Pk L20 ....38 D5
Wallasey CH44 ....51 C4
Eaton Cl Huyton-w-R L36 ....55 D2
Liverpool L12 ....54 A7
Eaton Gdns L12 ....54 D4
Eaton Grange L12 ....54 C5
Eaton Pl L34 ....56 D6
Eaton Rd Birkenhead CH43 66 B5
Liverpool,Cressington Pk L19 ....81 A6
Liverpool,Sandfield Pk L12 .54 C5
Maghull L31 ....28 D6
St Helens WA10 ....43 D6
West Kirby CH48 ....63 B1
Eaton Rd N L12 ....54 A7
Eaton St Liverpool L3 ....52 C3
Prescot L34 ....56 D7
Wallasey CH44 ....51 B5
Eaves La WA9 ....58 C6
Eaves Prim Sch WA9 ....58 C6
Eavesdale WN8 ....24 E8
Ebenezer Howard Rd L21 ....27 C1
Ebenezer Rd L7 ....53 C3
Ebenezer St
Birkenhead CH42 ....67 A2
St Helens WA11 ....44 F6
Eberle St L2 ....90 A4
Ebony Cl CH46 ....64 B8
Ebony Way L33 ....29 E5
Ebor La L5 ....52 E4
Ebor Lo PR8 ....4 A5
Ebrington St L19 ....81 C7
Eccles Dr L25 ....70 B7
Eccles Gr WA9 ....58 E3
Eccles Rd L37 ....9 D1
Ecclesall Ave L21 ....38 D8
Ecclesfield Rd WA10 ....43 A6
Eccleshall Rd CH62 ....79 C6
Eccleshill Rd L13 ....54 A5
Eccleston Ave CH62 ....79 C1
Eccleston Cl CH43 ....65 F3
Eccleston Gdns
St Helens WA10 ....43 B1
St Helens,Portico WA10 ....57 A8
Eccleston Lane Ends Prim Sch L34 ....56 F7
Eccleston Mere Prim Sch WA10 ....43 A3
Eccleston Pk L35 ....57 A6
Eccleston Rd 1 L9 ....39 A6
Eccleston St Prescot L34 .56 D6
St Helens WA10 ....43 E3
Edale Cl CH62 ....88 E5
Edale Rd L18 ....69 B4
Edburton Ct WA3 ....47 A8
Eddisbury Rd
5 Wallasey CH44 ....51 C5
West Kirby CH48 ....63 A4
Eddisbury Way L12 ....54 A7
Eddleston St WN4 ....34 F6
Eden Ave Rainford WA11 ....31 E7
Southport PR9 ....1 F2
Eden Cl Kirkby L33 ....29 F6
Rainhill L35 ....57 B2
Eden Dr N L23 ....27 A3
Eden Dr S L23 ....27 A3
Eden St 6 L8 ....68 B7
Eden Vale L30 ....27 E4
Edendale WA8 ....72 B2
Edenfield Cl PR8 ....4 E3
Edenfield Cres L36 ....55 F4
Edenfield Rd L15 ....69 A6
Edenhall Dr L25 ....70 C2
Edenhurst WN8 ....24 E8
Edenhurst Ave
Huyton-w-R L16 ....70 A8
2 Wallasey CH44 ....51 C5
Edenhurst Cl L37 ....9 C2
Edenhurst Ct L36 ....55 B4
Edenhurst Dr L37 ....9 C2
Edenpark Rd CH42 ....66 C3
Edgar Ct Birkenhead CH41 66 D7
Litherland L21 ....27 B1
Edgar St L3 ....52 D3
Edgbaston Cl L36 ....55 C1
Edgbaston Way CH43 ....65 C8
Edge Gr L7 ....53 E2
Edge Green La WA3 ....35 F2
Edge Green Rd WN4 ....35 F4
Edge Green St WN4 ....35 D4
Edge Hall Rd WN5 ....25 E5
Edge Hill Coll of H Ed L39 ....14 A3
Edge Hill Sta L7 ....68 C8

Edge La Crosby L23 27 B5
Liverpool L13,L7 53 D2
Edge Lane Dr L13 54 B2
Edge Lane Ret Pk L13 53 F2
Edge St WA9 57 C6
Edgefield Cl CH43 65 D4
Edgefold Rd L32 29 F1
Edgehill Rd CH46 64 D8
Edgeley Gdns L9 38 F6
Edgemoor Cl
Birkenhead CH43 65 B7
Crosby L23 27 B5
Liverpool L12 54 D5
Edgemoor Dr Crosby L23 27 A5
Irby CH61 76 C7
Liverpool L10 40 A7
Edgemoor Rd L12 54 D5
Edgerley Pl WN4 35 A3
Edgerton Rd
Birkenhead CH43 66 A6
Golborne WA3 47 F8
Edgewood Dr CH62 88 D5
Edgewood Rd
Birkenhead CH49 64 F6
Hoylake CH47 48 D1
Edgeworth Cl WA9 58 E8
Edgeworth Rd WA3 35 F1
Edgeworth St WA9 58 E7
Edgley Dr L39 14 A5
Edgworth Rd L4 53 B6
Edinburgh Cl L30 39 A8
Edinburgh Dr
Birkenhead CH43 66 A1
Huyton-w-R L36 71 A8
Edinburgh Rd Formby L37 9 E1
Liverpool L7 53 A2
Wallasey CH45 51 B5
Widnes WA8 84 A8
Edinburgh Twr L5 52 E5
Edington St L15 68 E8
Edith Rd Bootle L20 38 D6
Liverpool L4 53 A6
Wallasey CH44 51 E3
Edith St Runcorn WA7 84 F3
St Helens WA9 58 F7
Edith Villas L20 38 E4
Edmondson St WA9 44 F3
Edmonton Cl L5 52 D6
Edmund St L3 90 A4
Edna Ave L10 40 A7
Edrich Ave CH43 65 C8
Edward Dr WN4 35 B4
Edward Jenner Ave L30 27 F3
Edward Rd Hoylake CH47 63 C6
Prescot L35 56 F5
Warrington WA5 74 D6
Edward St Haydock WA11 45 A6
Liverpool L3 90 C3
St Helens WA9 44 D1
Widnes WA8 73 D1
Edward's La L24 82 B6
Edwards Lane Ind Est
L24 82 B6
Edwards Way WA8 84 C8
Edwin St WA8 73 C1
Effingham St L20 38 B1
Egan Rd CH43 65 F8
Egbert Rd CH47 63 C8
Egdon Cl WA8 73 E2
Egerton WN8 24 D8
Egerton Ct 12 CH45 51 B8
Egerton Dr CH48 63 B2
Egerton Gdns CH42 66 E1
Egerton Gr CH45 51 B5
Egerton Park Cl CH42 66 E1
Egerton Rd
Bebington CH62 79 B7
Liverpool L15 68 D7
Prescot L34 56 C6
Egerton St
Abram Brow WN2 36 B7
Liverpool L8 67 F7
Runcorn WA7 84 F3
St Helens WA9 44 D1
Wallasey CH45 51 C8
Egerton Wharf CH41 66 E8
Eglington Ave L35 56 D2
Egremont Cl L27 71 A4
Egremont Lawn L27 71 A4
Egremont Prim Sch
CH44 51 D4
Egremont Prom CH44,
CH45 51 D5
Egypt St WA8 84 F7
Eight Acre La L37 10 B6
Eighth Ave L9 39 D7
Eilian Gr L14 54 D2
Elaine Cl Ashton-in-M WN4 35 D5
Widnes WA8 73 C1
Elaine Price Ct 2 WA7 84 F1
Elaine St L8 67 F6
Elbow La L37 9 F3
Elcombe Ave WA3 47 E7
Elder Gdns L19 81 B8
Elder Gr CH48 63 B2
Elderberry Cl 3 L11 40 C2
Elderdale Rd L4 53 B7
Elderflower Rd WA10 43 E5
Eldersfield Rd L11 40 B2
Elderswood Rd L35 57 C4
Elderwood Rd CH42 66 E3
Eldon Cl WA10 43 E2
Eldon Gdns WN4 35 A6
Eldon Gr L3 52 D4
Eldon Ho CH43 66 A4
Eldon Pl L3 52 D4
Eldon Rd Birkenhead CH42 66 F2
Wallasey CH44 51 B4
Eldon St Liverpool L3 52 C4
St Helens WA10 43 E2
Eldonian Way L3,L5 52 C4
Eldons Croft PR8 7 D5
Eldred Rd L16 69 C6
Eleanor Pk CH43 65 C8
Eleanor Rd
Birkenhead CH43 65 D8
Bootle L20 38 D6
Wallasey CH46 49 D1
Eleanor St L20 38 B1
Elephant La WA9 57 E7
Elfet St CH41 65 F8
Elgar Ave CH62 88 E5
Elgar Rd L14 54 F5
Elgin Ave WN4 34 D4
Elgin Ct L35 57 D2
Elgin Dr CH45 51 C6
Elgin Way CH41 66 E7
Elimu Study Sch L8 68 B7
Eliot Cl CH62 79 A7
Eliot St L20 38 B5
Eliza St WA9 58 F7
Elizabeth Ave PR8 7 E6
Elizabeth Rd Bootle L20 38 D6
Haydock WA11 45 E7
Huyton-w-R L36 71 A8
Liverpool L10 40 B6
Elizabeth St
Liverpool L3,L7 52 F2
St Helens,Clock Face WA9 58 E3
St Helens,Sutton WA9 58 E8
Elizabeth Terr WA8 72 D1
Elkan Cl WA8 73 E2
Elkan Rd WA8 73 E2
Elkstone Rd L11 40 B1
Ellaby Rd L35 57 C4
Ellamsbridge Rd WA9 58 E8
Ellel Gr L6 53 C5
Ellen Gdn WA9 58 E7
Ellen St WA9 58 E7
Ellen's Cl 5 L6 53 A2
Ellen's La CH62,CH63 79 B5
Elleray Dr L8 67 F4
Elleray Park Rd CH45 51 A7
Elleray Park Sch CH45 51 A7
Ellerbrook Way L39 13 E6
Ellergreen Rd L11 40 A2
Ellerman Rd L8,L17 67 F3
Ellerslie Ave L35 57 C5
Ellerslie Rd L13 53 E6
Ellerton Cl WA8 72 D3
Ellerton Way L12 40 E3
Ellesmere Dr L10 28 C3
Ellesmere Gr CH45 51 B7
Ellesmere Rd WN4 34 F4
Elliot St Liverpool L1 90 B3
St Helens WA10 43 D4
Elliott Ave WA3 36 B1
Ellis Ashton St L36 56 B1
Ellis Pl L8 67 F5
Ellis Rd WN5 33 D4
Ellis St WA8 84 F7
Ellison Dr WA10 43 C4
Ellison Gr L36 55 E2
Ellison St L13 53 F4
Ellison Twr L5 52 E5
Ellon Ave L35 57 D2
Elloway Rd L24 83 A3
Ellwood Cl L24 83 E2
Elm Ave Birkenhead CH49 64 D6
Crosby L23 26 F6
Downall Green WN4 34 D5
Golborne WA3 36 A1
Newton-le-W WA12 46 C2
Widnes WA8 73 B2
Elm Bank 7 L5 52 F7
Elm Cl Heswall CH61 77 A4
Liverpool L12 40 F3
Elm Ct Bebington CH63 78 D6
Crosby L23 26 C4
Skelmersdale WN8 15 E1
Elm Dr Billinge WN5 33 D5
Birkenhead CH49 64 C3
Formby L37 9 D1
Seaforth L21 37 F6
Elm Gdns Rainford WA11 31 F6
1 Seaforth L21 38 A6
Elm Gr Birkenhead CH42 66 D4
Hoylake CH47 63 C7
Liverpool L7 53 A1
Prescot L34 56 F7
Skelmersdale WN8 15 E1
Widnes WA8 73 B1
Elm Hall Dr L18 69 A5
Elm Ho Crosby L22 26 D1
Prescot L34 56 C6
Elm House Mews L25 70 B4
Elm Park Dr PR8 7 E5
Elm Park Rd CH45 51 A7
Elm Pl L39 13 E4
Elm Rd Abram Brow WN2 36 C7
Bebington CH63 78 F7
Birkenhead,Devonshire Pk
CH42 66 D3
Birkenhead,Prenton CH42 66 B2
Haydock WA11 45 E7
Heswall CH61 76 F6
Kirkby L32 29 D3
Liverpool L4 39 A2
Seaforth L21 37 F6
Southport PR8 4 B4
St Helens WA10,WA9 57 E8
Warrington,Cinnamon Brow
WA5 74 F4
Warrington,Winwick Quay
WA2 61 A4
Elm Rd N CH42 66 B2
Elm St Birkenhead CH41 66 D6
Huyton-w-R L36 56 A2
Elm Terr Hoylake CH47 63 C7
Liverpool L7 53 C2
Elm Tree Rd WA3 47 F8
Elm Vale L6 53 D3
Elmar Rd L17 68 E2
Elmbank Rd
Bebington CH62 79 B6
Liverpool L18 68 E5
Elmbank St CH44 51 C3
Elmcroft Cl L9 39 D6
Elmcroft La L38 18 A3
Elmdale Cl L37 9 D2
Elmdale Rd L9 39 A4
Elmdene Ct CH49 64 C2
Elmer's Green La WN8 16 C4
Elmers Gn WN8 16 D2
Elmers Green Prim Sch
WN8 16 D1
Elmers Wood Rd WN8 16 D2
Elmfield Cl WA9 57 E8
Elmfield Rd L9 39 A5
Elmham Cres L10 39 F7
Elmhurst Rd L25 70 B7
Elmore Cl L5 52 F5
Elmridge WN8 24 D8
Elmridge Ct WA3 47 F8
Elms House Rd L13 53 F2
Elms Rd L31 28 D6
Elms Sch The L28 55 B8
Elms The Golborne WA3 47 F7
Hoylake CH47 63 C7
Liverpool L8 68 A4
Maghull L31 20 D3
Runcorn WA7 84 F1
Southport,Birkdale PR8 3 F6
Southport,Blowick PR8 4 C5
Elmsbury St 1 WN4 34 F5
Elmsdale Rd L18 69 A5
Elmsett Cl WA5 74 E5
Elmsfield Cl L25 70 A5
Elmsfield Pk L39 21 A6
Elmsfield Rd L23 27 B6
Elmsley Ct L18 69 A3
Elmsley Rd L18 68 F4
Elmstead WN8 24 D8
Elmswood Ave L35 57 D1
Elmswood Ct L18 68 F3
Elmswood Gr L36 55 C3
Elmswood Rd
Birkenhead CH42 66 D4
Liverpool L17,L18 68 E2
Wallasey CH44 51 D4
Elmtree Cl L12 54 C7
Elmtree Gr CH43 65 E8
Elmure Ave CH63 78 D5
Elmway Cl L13 53 F2
Elmwood WN8 16 C3
Elmwood Ave
Ashton-in-M WN4 35 A2
Crosby L23 27 A5
Elmwood Dr CH61 76 F2
Elphin Gr L4 39 A1
Elric Wlk L33 29 F3
Elsbeck Gr WA9 58 D6
Elsie Rd L4 53 B6
Elsinore Ct L23 26 C3
Elsinore Hts L26 83 A7
Elsmere Ave L17 68 C3
Elson Rd L37 9 D1
Elstead Gr WN4 34 D4
Elstead Rd Kirkby L32 29 C1
Liverpool L9 39 E4
Elston Ave WA12 46 C5
Elstow St 6 L5 52 D7
Elstree Rd L6 53 D3
Elswick WN8 24 C8
Elswick Gn PR9 2 A5
Elswick Rd PR9 1 F4
Elswick St L8 67 F3
Elsworth Cl L37 17 C8
Eltham Ave L21 27 B1
Eltham Cl
Ashton-in-M WN4 35 D3
Birkenhead CH49 65 B2
Widnes WA8 73 E3
Eltham Gn CH49 65 B2
Eltham St L7 53 D2
Eltham Wlk WA8 73 E3
Elton Ave Crosby L23 26 C4
Litherland L30 27 E3
Elton Cl Bebington CH62 88 E3
Golborne WA3 47 E7
Elton Dr CH63 79 A3
Elton Head Rd L35,WA9 57 E6
Elton St L4 38 F2
Elvington Rd L38 18 A2
Elway Rd WN4 35 C4
Elwick Dr L11 40 C2
Elwood Cl L33 29 E6
Elworth Ave WA8 73 A5
Elworthy Ave L26 70 F1
Elwy St L8 68 A5
Elwyn Dr L26 83 A8
Elwyn Rd CH47 48 E1
Ely Ave CH46 64 C8
Ely Cl L30 27 F1
Ely Mews PR9 2 A2
Ember Cres 4 L6 52 F4
Embledon St L8 68 B7
Emerald Cl L30 28 B3
Emerald St L8 67 F3
Emerson Cl L38 18 A4
Emerson St L8 67 F7
Emery St L4 38 F1
Emily St L35 57 C7
Emlyn St WA9 44 D1
Emmanuel Rd PR9 1 F2
Emmaus CE & RC Prim Sch
L12 40 F3
Emmett St WA9 44 C1
Empire Rd L21 38 B6
Empress Cl L31 20 B1
Empress Rd Liverpool L7 53 B2
Liverpool,Cabbage Hall L6 53 C6
Wallasey CH44 51 C4
Emstrey Wlk 1 L32 29 C2
Endborne Rd L9 39 A6
Endbutt La L23 26 E3
Enderby Ave WA11 44 D6
Endfield Pk L19 81 B8
Endmoor Rd L36 55 D5
Endsleigh Rd Crosby L22 26 B2
Liverpool L13 53 E3
Enerby Cl CH43 65 C7
Enfield Ave L23 26 E4
Enfield Park Rd WA2 61 F4
Enfield Rd L13 54 B2
Enfield St WA10 43 E2
Enfield Terr CH43 66 B5
Enford Dr WA9 58 D7
Engine La L37 18 E8
English Martyrs RC Prim Sch
WA11 45 E7
English Martyrs RC Sch
L21 38 C8
Enid Pl WN2 35 F8
Enid St L8 67 F6
Ennerdale WN8 24 D8
Ennerdale Ave
Ashton-in-M WN4 35 B5
Bebington CH62 88 F4
Billinge WA11 33 B1
Maghull L31 20 E2
Warrington WA2 61 B3
Ennerdale Cl Formby L37 9 D3
Kirkby L33 29 D5
Ennerdale Ct CH45 50 F8
Ennerdale Dr Bootle L21 38 D8
Ormskirk L39 13 B2
Ennerdale Rd
Birkenhead CH43 65 E1
Formby L37 9 E3
Liverpool L9 39 D6
Wallasey CH45 50 F8
Ennerdale St 3 L3 52 D4
Ennis Cl L24 83 D2
Ennis Ct L11 40 B3
Ennis Rd L12 54 E6
Ennisdale Dr CH48 63 D2
Ennismore Rd Crosby L23 26 C5
Liverpool L13 53 F3
Ensor St L20 38 B1
Enstone WN8 16 D1
Enstone Ave L21 27 A1
Enstone Rd L25 82 B6
Ensworth Rd L18 69 B5
Enterprise Way L15 53 E1
Enterprise Workshops
Kirkby L33 30 B1
Southport PR9 5 A6
Epping Ave WA9 58 B3
Epping Cl L35 57 D2
Epping Ct CH60 77 A1
Epping Gr L15 69 B6
Epsom Cl L10 28 E1
Epsom Dr WN2 35 F7
Epsom Gr L33 30 A6
Epsom Rd CH46 49 F3
Epsom St WA9 44 F4
Epsom Way L5 52 D5
Epstein Ct 5 L6 53 B3
Epworth Cl
Birkenhead CH43 66 A6
Burtonwood WA5 59 F7
Epworth St L6,L7 52 F2
Eremon Cl L9 39 D8
Erfurt Ave CH63 79 A4
Eric Fountain Rd CH65 89 D3
Eric Gr CH44 51 A4
Eric Rd CH44 51 A4
Eric St WA8 73 C2
Erica Ct CH60 76 E1
Eridge St L8 68 A3
Erin Cl L8 67 E6
Erl St L9 39 A6
Ermine Cres L5 52 F5
Ernest Cookson Sch L12 54 A6
Errington Ct L17 80 F8
Errington St L5 52 C6
Errol St L17 68 B3
Erskine Cl WA11 44 E6
Erskine Ind Est 5 L6 52 F3
Erskine Rd CH44 51 C3
Erskine St L6 52 F2
Erskine St Ind Est 4 L7 53 A2
Erylmore Rd L18 69 A1
Escolme Dr CH49 64 E3
Escor Rd L25 70 A6
Escort Cl L25 82 C8
Eshe Rd L23 26 C4
Eshe Rd N L23 26 C4
Eshelby Cl L22 26 F1
Esher Cl Bebington CH62 79 B8
Birkenhead CH43 65 C7
Esher Rd Bebington CH62 79 B8
Liverpool L6 53 C3
Esk St L20 52 B8
Eskbank WN8 24 C8
Eskbrook WN8 16 C1
Eskburn Rd L13 53 E6
Eskdale WN8 24 B8
Eskdale Ave
Bebington CH62 88 E5
Ormskirk L39 13 C2
Eskdale Ave *continued*
St Helens WA11 44 B8
Wallasey CH46 49 C1
Warrington WA2 61 C3
Eskdale Cl L37 9 D2
Eskdale Dr Formby L37 9 D2
Maghull L31 20 E2
Eskdale Rd
Ashton-in-M WN4 35 B4
Liverpool L9 39 A6
Eslington St L19 81 A7
Esmond St L6 53 B5
Esonwood Rd L35 56 D3
Espin St 3 L4 38 F1
Esplanade
Birkenhead CH42 67 B2
Southport PR8 3 F7
Esplanade The
Birkenhead CH42 67 B1
4 Bootle L20 38 C3
Seaforth L22 37 D8
Esplen Ave L23 26 F5
Essex Rd Huyton-w-R L36 56 B4
Southport PR8 8 A8
West Kirby CH48 63 C3
Essex St L8 67 F5
Essex Way L20 38 D4
Esther St WA8 73 C1
Esthwaite Ave WA11 44 C8
Estuary Banks L24 81 F4
Estuary Banks Bsns Pk
L24 81 F4
Estuary Bvd L24 81 F4
Etal Cl 3 L11 40 B1
Ethel Rd CH44 51 D3
Ethelbert Rd CH47 63 C8
Etna St L13 53 F3
Eton Ct L18 69 D5
Eton Dr Aintree L10 28 D2
Heswall CH63 86 F6
Eton Hall Dr WA9 58 C7
Eton St L4 38 F1
Eton Way WN5 25 F8
Etruria St L19 81 C4
Etruscan Rd L13 54 A4
Ettington Dr PR8 7 A5
Ettington Rd L4 53 B7
Ettrick Cl L33 29 D6
Eurolink WA9 57 F4
Europa Bvd
Birkenhead CH41 66 E6
Warrington WA5 60 D3
Euston Gr CH43 66 C5
Euston St L4 38 F2
Evans Cl WA11 45 F7
Evans Rd Hoylake CH47 63 B7
Liverpool L24 82 C5
Evans St L34 56 D7
Evellynne Cl L32 29 D2
Evelyn Ave Prescot L34 56 E6
St Helens WA9 44 E3
Evelyn Com Prim Sch
L34 56 E7
Evelyn Rd CH44 51 C3
Evelyn St WA9 44 E3
Evenwood
Skelmersdale WN8 16 D1
5 St Helens WA9 58 C6
Evenwood Ct WN8 16 C1
Everard Rd PR8 4 D4
Everdon Wood L33 29 F3
Evered Ave L9 39 A4
Everest Rd
Birkenhead CH42 66 D2
Crosby L23 26 E4
Evergreen Cl
Birkenhead CH49 64 E6
Liverpool L27 70 E6
Evergreen Way WA9 59 A7
Evergreens The L37 9 D4
Everite Rd WA8 84 B7
Everleigh Cl CH43 65 B7
Eversleigh Dr CH63 79 A4
Eversley
Skelmersdale WN8 16 D1
Widnes WA8 72 B2
Eversley Pk CH43 66 B3
Eversley St Liverpool L8 68 A6
Liverpool L8 68 A7
Everton Brow L3,L5 52 E4
Everton Gr WA11 44 D5
Everton Rd Liverpool L6 52 F4
Southport PR8 4 A4
Everton St WN4 34 D5
Everton Valley L4,L5 52 E7
Everton View L20 38 B2
Every St L6 53 B4
Evesham Cl L25 69 F2
Evesham Rd Liverpool L4 39 D1
Wallasey CH45 50 F6
Evington WN8 16 D1
Ewanville L36 55 E1
Ewart Rd Huyton-w-R L16 70 A8
Seaforth L21 38 A7
St Helens WA11 44 B6
Ewden Cl L16 69 E7
Exchange Pas E 5 L2 90 A4
Exchange Pas W 4 L2 90 A4
Exchange Pl L35 57 C3
Exchange St 7 WA10 44 A3
Exchange St E L2 90 A4
Exchange St W 4 L2 90 A3
Exeley L35 56 E2
Exeter Cl L10 28 E1
Exeter Rd Bootle L20 38 C2

Exeter Rd *continued*
Wallasey CH44 .51 C5
Exeter St WA10 .43 D3
Exford Rd L12 .54 D8
Exmoor Cl Heswall CH61 .76 F5
Southport PR9 .2 B6
Exmouth Cl CH41 .66 D6
Exmouth Gdns [3] CH41 .66 D6
Exmouth St CH41 .66 D6
Exmouth Way
[1] Birkenhead CH41 .66 D6
Burtonwood WA5 .59 F6
Express Ind Est WA8 .84 A7
Extension View WA9 .58 D8

F

FACT (Mus) L1 .90 C2
Factory La WA8 .73 B3
Factory Row WA10 .43 E1
Fair View WN5 .33 D5
Fair View Ave WN5 .33 D5
Fair View Pl [3] L8 .68 A4
Fairacre Rd L19 .81 A8
Fairacres Rd CH63 .79 A4
Fairbairn Rd L22 .26 E1
Fairbank St L15 .68 E7
Fairbeech Ct CH43 .65 C7
Fairbeech Mews CH43 .65 C7
Fairbourne Cl WA5 .60 E3
Fairbrook Dr CH41 .50 E1
Fairbrother Cres WA2 .61 D2
Fairburn WN8 .16 B3
Fairburn Cl WA8 .73 E3
Fairburn Rd L13 .53 E6
Fairclough Cl L35 .57 B3
Fairclough Cres WA11 .45 A6
Fairclough La CH43 .66 B4
Fairclough Rd
Huyton-w-R L36 .55 C5
Rainhill L35 .57 B3
St Helens WA10 .43 C4
Fairclough St
Burtonwood WA5 .59 E6
Liverpool L1 .90 B3
Newton-le-W WA12 .46 B3
Fairfax Pl L11 .39 D2
Fairfax Rd
Birkenhead CH41 .66 E4
Liverpool L11 .39 E2
Fairfield L23 .26 E4
Fairfield Ave L14,L36 .55 A2
Fairfield Cl
Huyton-w-R L36 .55 A2
Ormskirk L39 .13 E7
Fairfield Cres
Birkenhead CH46 .64 D8
Huyton-w-R L36 .55 A2
Liverpool L6 .53 D4
Fairfield Dr Ormskirk L39 .13 E7
West Kirby CH48 .63 E3
Fairfield Gdns WA11 .32 E2
Fairfield High Sch WA8 .73 B3
Fairfield Hospl WA11 .32 E2
Fairfield Inf Sch WA8 .73 B2
Fairfield Jun Sch WA8 .73 B2
Fairfield Rd
Birkenhead CH42 .66 E2
Southport PR8 .7 C5
St Helens WA10 .43 D5
Widnes WA8 .73 B2
Fairfield St L7 .53 E3
Fairford Cres L14 .54 B4
Fairford Rd L14 .54 B4
Fairhaven Kirkby L33 .29 E5
Skelmersdale WN8 .16 C3
Fairhaven Cl CH42 .66 F2
Fairhaven Dr CH63 .88 C5
Fairhaven Rd Southport PR9 .2 B4
Widnes WA8 .73 C2
Fairholme L19 .80 F6
Fairholme Ave
Ashton-in-M WN4 .35 B4
Eccleston Park L34 .57 A6
Neston CH64 .86 D1
Fairholme Cl L12 .54 A8
Fairholme Mews L23 .26 E4
Fairholme Rd L23 .26 E4
Fairhurst Terr [10] L34 .56 E6
Fairlawn Cl CH63 .88 A6
Fairlawn Ct CH43 .65 F5
Fairlawne Cl L33 .29 E5
Fairlie WN8 .16 C3
Fairlie Cres L20 .38 D7
Fairlie Dr L35 .57 D2
Fairlie Prim Sch WN8 .16 C3
Fairmead Rd Liverpool L11 .39 E2
Wallasey CH46 .49 F1
Fairoak Cl CH43 .65 C7
Fairoak Mews CH43 .65 C7
Fairstead WN8 .16 C3
Fairthorn Wlk L33 .30 A3
Fairview Ave CH45 .51 B5
Fairview Cl
Ashton-in-M WN4 .35 B4
Birkenhead CH43 .66 B3
Fairview Rd CH43 .66 B3
Fairview Way CH61 .76 F3
Fairway Huyton-w-R L36 .56 A4
Southport PR8 .1 C2
St Helens WA10 .43 C5
Fairway Cres CH62 .79 D4
Fairway Ct CH47 .63 A6
Fairway N CH62 .79 D3
Fairway S CH62 .79 D3
Fairway The L12 .54 D4
Fairways Bebington CH42 .78 B8
Crosby L23 .26 D5
Fairways Cl L25 .82 B8
Fairways Ct L37 .9 C5
Fairways The
Garswood WN4 .34 D2
Liverpool L25 .82 D8
Skelmersdale WN8 .16 D3
West Kirby CH48 .75 D6
Falcon Cres L27 .70 F4
Falcon Hey L10 .40 A6
Falcon Rd CH41,CH43 .66 C4
Falcondale Rd WA2 .61 B6
Falconer St L20 .38 A6
Falconers Gn WA5 .60 B2
Falconhall Rd L9 .39 F4
Falkirk Ave WA8 .72 F3
Falkland WN8 .16 C3
Falkland Dr WN4 .34 C4
Falkland Rd Southport PR8 .4 D5
Wallasey CH44 .51 D4
Falkland St
Birkenhead CH41 .66 A8
Liverpool L3 .52 F2
Falklands App L11 .39 E2
Falkner Sq L8 .68 A8
Falkner St L1,L7,L8 .67 F8
Fallbrook Dr L12 .40 B1
Fallow Cl [6] WA9 .58 C4
Fallowfield L33 .29 E4
Fallowfield Rd L15 .69 A6
Fallows Way L35 .71 C8
Falmouth Dr WA5 .74 E3
Falmouth Rd L11 .40 D5
Falstaff St L20 .52 C8
Far Meadow La CH61 .76 D7
Far Moss Rd L23 .26 B6
Faraday Rd Knowsley L33 .41 B7
Liverpool L13 .53 E1
Faraday St L5 .53 A5
Farefield Ave WA3 .35 F2
Fareham Cl CH49 .64 D6
Fareham Rd L7 .53 D2
Faringdon Cl L25 .82 B6
Faringdon Rd WA2 .61 B6
Farley Ave CH62 .79 C1
Farley La WN8 .16 F3
Farlow Rd CH42 .66 F1
Farm Cl Birkenhead CH49 .64 C4
Southport PR9 .5 A8
St Helens WA9 .58 D3
Farm Meadow Rd WN5 .25 E5
Farm Rd WA9 .58 D3
Farm View L21 .27 B2
Farm Way WA12 .46 E1
Farmbrook Rd L25 .70 B7
Farmdale Cl L18 .69 B2
Farmdale Dr L31 .20 E1
Farmer Pl L20 .38 E7
Farmer's La WA5 .60 A6
Farmfield Dr CH43 .65 C7
Farmside CH46 .49 F3
Farmview Cl L27 .70 C7
Farnborough Gr L26 .70 F1
Farnborough Rd PR8 .7 F8
Farnborough Road Inf & Jun Schs PR8 .8 A8
Farndale WA8 .73 A5
Farndale Cl WA5 .74 F7
Farndale Gr WN4 .35 C2
Farndon Ave
St Helens WA9 .58 B4
Wallasey CH45 .50 E6
Farndon Dr CH48 .63 E3
Farndon Way CH43 .65 F4
Farnham Cl L32 .29 F1
Farnworth Ave CH46 .49 F4
Farnworth CE Prim Sch WA8 .73 A4
Farnworth Cl WA8 .73 B4
Farnworth Gr L33 .29 E5
Farnworth Rd WA5 .74 C4
Farnworth St Liverpool L6 .53 B3
St Helens WA9 .44 C4
Widnes WA8 .73 B4
Farr Hall Dr CH60 .85 E7
Farr Hall Rd CH60 .85 F8
Farrar St L13 .53 E7
Farrell Cl L31 .29 B4
Farrier Rd L33 .30 A2
Farrier Wlk WA9 .58 C4
Farriers Way
Birkenhead CH48 .64 B2
Bootle L30 .38 F8
Farringdon Cl WA9 .57 F6
Farrington Dr L39 .13 E6
Farthing Cl L25 .82 B7
Farthingstone Cl L35 .57 A6
Fatherside Dr L30 .27 C3
Faulkner Cl PR8 .7 C6
Faulkner Gdns PR8 .7 C6
Faversham Rd L11 .39 E3
Fawcett WN8 .16 B3
Fawcett Rd L31 .20 D3
Fawley Rd Liverpool L18 .69 C2
Rainhill L35 .57 E1
Fazakerley Cl L9 .39 A4
Fazakerley High Sch L10 .39 F7
Fazakerley Prim Sch L10 .39 F7
Fazakerley Rd
Liverpool L9 .39 A4
Prescot L35 .56 E4
Fazakerley St L3 .52 B2
Fazakerley Sta L9 .39 D7
Fearnhead Cross WA2 .61 F2
Fearnley Rd CH41 .66 D5
Fearnley Way WA12 .46 C1
Fearnside St L7 .68 C8
Feather La CH60 .85 F8
Feeny St WA9 .58 B2
Feilden Rd CH63 .79 A4
Felicity Gr CH46 .49 D1
Fell Gr WA11 .44 A8
Fell St Liverpool L7 .53 B2
Wallasey CH44 .51 E2
Fell View PR9 .2 D6
Felltor Cl L25 .69 F3
Fellwood Gr L35 .56 E3
Felmersham Gn L11 .39 F3
Felspar Rd L32 .40 F7
Felstead WN8 .16 B2
Felstead Ave L25 .70 C2
Felsted Dr L10 .28 E1
Felthorpe Cl CH49 .65 B7
Felton Cl CH46 .64 C8
Felton Ct L17 .68 C3
Felton Gr L13 .53 F3
Feltons WN8 .16 B2
Feltwell Rd L4 .53 B6
Feltwood Cl L12 .54 F7
Feltwood Rd L12 .54 F8
Feltwood Wlk L12 .54 F7
Fendale Ave CH46 .50 A1
Fender Ct CH49 .65 D1
Fender Hts CH46 .50 A1
Fender La CH43,CH46 .50 B1
Fender Prim Sch CH49 .65 C3
Fender View Rd CH46 .65 A8
Fender Way
Birkenhead CH43 .65 B7
Heswall CH61 .77 A4
Fenderside Rd CH43 .65 C8
Fenham Dr WA5 .74 F4
Fenney Ct WN8 .16 C1
Fenton Cl
Liverpool,Speke L24 .82 D3
Liverpool,Warbreck Pk L30 .39 B8
St Helens WA10 .43 F4
Widnes WA8 .72 C3
Fenton Gn L24 .82 D2
Fenwick St L2 .90 A3
Ferguson Ave CH49 .64 D3
Ferguson Dr WA2 .61 D1
Ferguson Rd
Litherland L21 .27 C1
Liverpool L11 .53 E8
Fern Ave WA12 .46 D2
Fern Bank Maghull L31 .20 E1
Rainford WA11 .31 E7
Fern Cl Liverpool L27 .70 E4
Skelmersdale WN8 .15 E1
Fern Gdns L34 .56 F7
Fern Gr Birkenhead CH43 .65 D4
Bootle L20 .38 C4
Liverpool L8 .68 C6
Fern Hey L23 .27 B5
Fern Lodge L8 .68 C6
Fernbank Ave L36 .55 D2
Fernbank Dr L30 .28 A4
Fernbank La CH49 .64 F7
Ferndale WN8 .16 C2
Ferndale Ave
Birkenhead CH48 .64 B1
Wallasey CH44 .51 C4
Ferndale Cl
Bold Heath WA8 .73 E7
Liverpool L9 .39 A7
Ferndale Rd Crosby L22 .26 E2
Hoylake CH47 .63 B8
Liverpool L15 .68 E6
Fernhill [9] CH45 .51 B8
Fernhill Ave L20 .38 E3
Fernhill Cl L20 .38 E3
Fernhill Dr L8 .68 A6
Fernhill Gdns L20 .38 E3
Fernhill Mews E L20 .38 E3
Fernhill Mews W L20 .38 E3
Fernhill Rd L20 .38 E4
Fernhill Sports Ctr L20 .38 D6
Fernhill Way L20 .38 E3
Fernhill Wlk WA9 .58 C3
Fernhurst Gate L39 .13 B1
Fernhurst Rd L32 .29 C1
Fernie Cres L8 .67 F5
Fernlea Ave WA9 .57 D7
Fernlea Gr WN4 .34 D5
Fernlea Mews CH43 .65 C8
Fernlea Rd CH60 .86 A8
Fernleigh Rd L13 .54 B3
Fernley Rd PR8 .4 A5
Ferns Cl CH60 .76 C1
Ferns Rd CH63 .78 D5
Fernwood Dr L26 .82 E8
Fernwood Rd L17 .68 E3
Ferny Brow Rd CH49 .65 B3
Ferny Knoll Rd WA11 .23 F4
Ferrer St WN4 .34 F6
Ferrey Rd L10 .40 A7
Ferries Cl CH62 .79 B8
Ferry Rd CH62 .89 A6
Ferry View Rd CH44 .51 E2
Ferryside CH44 .51 E2
Ferryside La PR9 .2 C5
Festival Ave WA2 .61 D2
Festival Cres WA2 .61 D2
Festival Ct L11 .40 B3
Festival Rd WA11 .32 A5
Ffrancon Dr CH63 .78 F7
Fiddler's Ferry Rd WA8 .73 D1
Fidler St WA10 .43 D1
Field Ave L21 .38 A8
Field Cl Bebington CH62 .79 C8
St Helens WA9 .58 D3
Field Hey La CH64 .88 B1
Field Ho L12 .54 A7
Field La Litherland L21 .38 A8
Liverpool L10 .40 B7
Field Rd St Helens WA9 .58 D3
Wallasey CH45 .51 B7
Field St Liverpool L3 .52 E3
Skelmersdale WN8 .15 D2
Field View L21 .27 A1
Field Way L35 .57 C5
Field Wlk Crosby L23 .27 B5
Ormskirk L39 .14 B5
Field's End L36 .70 E8
Fieldfare Cl L25 .70 A5
Fieldgate WA8 .84 B6
Fielding St L6 .53 A3
Fieldings The L31 .20 B4
Fieldlands PR8 .5 A2
Fieldsend Cl L27 .70 E4
Fieldside Rd CH42 .66 E2
Fieldton Rd L11 .40 B3
Fieldview WN8 .25 A7
Fieldview Dr WA2 .61 C1
Fieldway Bebington CH63 .78 D8
Heswall CH60 .77 C1
Hoylake CH47 .63 F7
Huyton-w-R L36 .70 F8
Liverpool L15 .69 C8
Maghull L31 .28 E7
Wallasey CH45 .51 A5
Widnes WA8 .73 E2
Fieldway Ct CH41 .66 C8
Fifth Ave Birkenhead CH43 .65 B7
Liverpool,Aintree L9 .39 D7
Liverpool,Fazakerley L9 .39 E7
Filbert Cl L33 .29 F6
Filby Gdns WA9 .57 E6
Filton Rd L14 .55 B6
Finborough Rd L4 .39 C1
Finch Ave WA11 .32 A5
Finch Cl Huyton-w-R L14 .55 A6
St Helens WA9 .58 D3
Finch Ct CH41 .66 D7
Finch Dene L14 .54 F6
Finch La Huyton-w-R L14 .55 A6
Liverpool,Halewood Village L26 .83 B7
Liverpool,Mill Yard L14 .54 F5
Finch Lea Dr L14 .55 A5
Finch Meadow Cl L9 .39 F4
Finch Pl L3 .52 F2
Finch Rd L14 .55 A6
Finch Way L14 .54 F5
Fincham Cl L14 .55 B5
Fincham Gn L14 .55 B5
Fincham Rd L14 .55 A5
Fincham Sq L14 .55 A5
Finchdean Cl [3] CH49 .64 C4
Finchley Dr WA11 .44 C7
Finchley Rd L4 .53 B7
Findlay Cl WA12 .46 C2
Findley Dr CH46 .49 F3
Findon WN8 .16 C2
Findon Rd L32 .40 F8
Fine Jane's Way PR9 .5 B8
Fingall Rd L15 .69 B6
Finger House La WA8 .58 D1
Fingland Rd L15 .68 E7
Finlan Rd WA8 .84 F7
Finlay Ave WA5 .74 E3
Finlay Ct L30 .27 F4
Finlay St L6 .53 C3
Finney Gr WA11 .45 E6
Finney The CH48 .75 D6
Finningley Ct WA2 .61 E1
Finsbury Pk WA8 .73 C5
Finstall Rd CH63 .79 A2
Finvoy Rd L13 .53 E7
Fiona Wlk L10 .40 B7
Fir Ave L26 .83 A8
Fir Cl L26 .83 A8
Fir Cotes L31 .20 E1
Fir Gr L9 .39 C8
Fir La L15 .69 A7
Fir Rd L22 .26 E2
Fir St Southport PR8 .4 F6
St Helens WA10 .57 D8
Widnes WA8 .73 C2
Fir Tree Ave WA3 .47 F8
Fir Tree Cl Crank WA11 .32 F7
Skelmersdale WN8 .24 D7
Fir Tree Dr N L12 .40 E4
Fir Tree Dr S L12 .40 E3
Fir Tree La
Burtonwood WA5 .60 A7
Haskayne L39 .12 F3
Ormskirk L39 .13 A2
Fir Tree Wlk WA3 .47 F8
Fir Way CH60 .86 B5
Firbeck WN8 .16 C1
Firbrook Ct CH43 .50 C1
Firdale Rd L9 .39 A4
Firdene Cres CH43 .65 E4
Fire Station Rd L35 .56 F5
Firethorne Rd L26 .70 D2
Firman Cl WA5 .60 B1
Firs Ave CH63 .78 F3
Firs Cl L37 .9 D5
Firs Cres L37 .9 D5
Firs La L39 .12 E3
Firs Link L37 .9 D4
Firscraig L28 .55 C7
Firshaw Rd CH47 .48 C1
First Ave Birkenhead CH43 .65 C6
Crosby L23 .26 D4
Liverpool,Aintree L9 .39 C7
Liverpool,Fazakerley L9 .39 E6
Rainhill L35 .57 B4
Firstone Gr L32 .40 E8
Firswood Rd L40,WN8 .15 C3
Firthland Way WA9 .44 F2
Firwood WN8 .16 D3
Firwood Gr WN4 .35 A2
Fisher Ave
Abram Brow WN2 .36 C7
Prescot L35 .56 D2
Warrington WA2 .61 B2
Fisher Dr Orrell WN5 .25 E7
Southport PR9 .4 F7
Fisher Pl L35 .56 D2
Fisher St Liverpool L8 .67 D6
St Helens WA9 .58 E8
Fishermans Cl L37 .9 E6
Fishers La CH61 .76 F4
Fishguard Cl [2] L6 .52 F4
Fishwicks Ind Est WA11 .45 F8
Fistral Cl L10 .40 B6
Fistral Dr WA10 .43 B6
Fitzclarence Way L6 .52 F4
Fitzgerald Rd L13 .54 A3
Fitzpatrick Ct L3 .52 C4
Fitzroy Way [14] L6 .53 A3
Five Ways CH64 .86 F3
Fiveways WA10 .43 A4
Fiveways Pk CH64 .86 F3
Flail Cl CH49 .64 C4
Flambards CH49 .65 B3
Flamstead WN8 .16 C1
Flander Cl WA8 .72 C2
Flatfield Way L31 .20 E1
Flatman's La L39 .11 E1
Flatt La CH43 .65 F3
Flawn Rd L11 .53 E8
Flaxfield Rd L37 .10 A3
Flaxhill CH46 .49 D1
Flaxman St [8] L7 .53 C2
Flaxton WN8 .16 C1
Flaybrick Cl CH43 .65 E8
Fleck La CH48 .63 D1
Fleet La WA9 .44 E2
Fleet St L1 .90 B3
Fleetcroft Rd CH49 .65 A2
Fleetwood Cl PR9 .1 F3
Fleetwood Cotts L30 .27 E4
Fleetwood Dr WA12 .46 B4
Fleetwood Gdns L33 .29 F5
Fleetwood Pl L25 .69 F2
Fleetwood Rd PR9 .1 E3
Fleetwood's La L30 .27 D4
Fleming Ct L3 .52 C4
Fleming Dr
Ashton-in-M WN4 .35 D4
Winwick WA2 .61 A6
Fleming Ho L17 .68 C3
Fleming Rd L24 .82 C6
Fleming Way CH46 .50 A2
Flemington Ave L4 .39 D1
Fletcher Ave
Birkenhead CH42 .66 E2
Prescot L34 .56 E7
Fletcher Cl CH49 .65 A3
Fletcher Dr L19 .81 A7
Flimby WN8 .16 D1
Flint Dr L12 .40 D1
Flint St L1 .90 B1
Flintshire Gdns WA10 .43 F2
Flora Mans L6 .53 C3
Flora St WN4 .35 B2
Floral Wood L17 .68 A2
Flordon WN8 .16 D2
Florence Ave CH60 .76 F1
Florence Cl L9 .38 F3
Florence Melly Com Prim Sch L4 .39 C1
Florence Nightingale Cl L30 .27 F4
Florence Rd CH44 .51 E3
Florence St
Birkenhead CH41 .66 D6
Liverpool L4 .52 F8
St Helens L35 .57 C7
Florentine Rd L13 .54 A4
Florey Ho L17 .68 C3
Florida Ct L19 .81 B8
Flowermead Cl CH47 .48 F1
Fluker's Brook La L34 .41 B2
Flyde Road Ind Est PR9 .2 B4
Foinavon Cl L9 .38 F7
Fold St WA3 .36 A1
Folds La WA11 .44 B7
Folds Rd WA11 .44 F5
Folds The CH63 .87 A6
Foley Cl L4 .52 E7
Foley St L4 .52 E7
Folkestone Rd PR8 .4 F3
Folly La CH44 .50 E5
Fontenoy St L3 .90 B4
Fonthill Cl L4 .52 D7
Fonthill Rd L4 .52 D8
Ford Ave L33 .29 E6
Ford Cl Birkenhead CH49 .65 B4
Bootle L20 .38 E7
Litherland L21 .27 B2
Ford Dr CH49 .65 B5
Ford La Birkenhead CH49 .65 B5
Litherland L21 .27 B3
Ford Rd Birkenhead CH49 .65 A5
Prescot L35 .56 F6
Ford St L3 .52 C3
Ford View L21 .27 B3
Ford Way CH49 .65 B4
Ford Way Mews CH49 .65 A4
Fordcombe Rd L25 .70 C4
Fordham Cl PR8 .4 E3
Fordham St L4 .52 E8
Fordhill View CH46 .65 A8
Fordland Cl WA3 .36 E1

Fordlea Rd L12 54 A8
Fordlea Way L12 54 B8
Forefield Inf Sch L23 27 A4
Forefield Jun Sch L23 27 A4
Forefield La L23 27 A4
Foreland Cl WA5 74 C7
Forest Cl Hoylake CH47 48 E1
Prescot L34 56 F7
Forest Ct CH43 65 F6
Forest Dr Huyton-w-R L36 55 C3
Skelmersdale WN8 16 C3
Forest Gn L12 54 B8
Forest Gr L34 56 F7
Forest Lawn L12 54 B8
Forest Mead WA10 43 A3
Forest Rd
Birkenhead CH43 66 A6
Heswall CH60 86 A8
Hoylake CH47 48 D1
Southport PR8 4 D6
St Helens WA9 58 A2
Forfar Rd L13 53 D6
Forge Cl Cronton WA8 72 C5
Westhead L40 14 E4
Forge Cotts 6 L17 68 C4
Forge Rd WA5 74 F5
Forge St L20 52 C8
Formby Bridge L37 9 E2
Formby Bsns Pk L37 10 B3
Formby By-Pass
Formby L37 10 B5
Hightown L37,L38 18 B8
Formby Cl WA5 74 F4
Formby Fields L37 10 A2
Formby Gdns L37 9 F4
Formby High Sch L37 9 E4
Formby La Formby L37 10 B2
Haskayne L39 12 F1
Formby Rd WA10 43 D1
Formby St L37 9 E2
Formby Sta L37 9 E2
Formosa Dr L10 39 F7
Formosa Rd L10 39 F6
Formosa Way L10 39 F7
Fornalls Green La CH47 63 E7
Forres Gr WN4 34 D4
Forrest St L1 90 B2
Forrester Ave L35 57 C7
Forresters Cl WN2 36 E8
Forshaw Ave WA10 57 C8
Forshaw's La WA5 59 E8
Forster St WA3 36 A1
Forsythia Cl L9 39 C3
Fort St CH45 51 C7
Forth St L20 52 C8
Forthlin Rd L18 69 C1
Forton Lo 3 L23 26 C4
Forwood Rd CH62 88 D8
Foscote Rd L33 30 A4
Foster Cl L35 57 A5
Foster Rd L37 9 D2
Foster St Liverpool L20 52 C7
Widnes WA8 73 B1
Fosters Cl PR9 5 B8
Fosters Gr WA11 44 F5
Fosters Green Rd WN8 16 D3
Fosters Rd WA11 44 F6
Foul La PR8,PR9 5 A5
Foundry La WA8 84 C5
Foundry St
Newton-le-W WA12 46 B3
St Helens WA10,WA9 44 A3
Fountain Ct L23 26 A5
Fountain Rd Knowsley L34 41 D3
4 Wallasey CH45 51 B7
Fountain St
Birkenhead CH42 66 D3
St Helens WA9 57 C6
Fountains Ave WA11 45 F7
Fountains Cl L4 52 F2
Fountains Ct 4 L4 52 D7
Fountains Rd L4 52 D7
Fountains The L39 13 E6
Fountains Way L37 10 B2
Four Acre Dr L21 27 B2
Four Acre La WA9 58 C4
Four Acre Lane Sh Ctr
WA9 58 B4
Four Lane Ends WA9 57 F7
Four Lanes End CH63 87 D5
Fouracres L31 28 B7
Fourth Ave
Birkenhead CH43 65 B6
Liverpool,Aintree L9 39 D7
Liverpool,Fazakerley L9 39 E7
Fourways Cl L27 70 D7
Fowell Rd CH45 51 B8
Fowler Cl 7 L7 53 C1
Fox Cover Rd CH60 86 D7
Fox Hey Rd CH44 50 F4
Fox Pl WA10 44 A4
Fox St Birkenhead CH41 66 C6
Liverpool L3,L5 52 E4
Fox's Bank La L35 71 F7
Foxcote WA8 72 B2
Foxcovers Rd CH63 79 A3
Foxdale Cl
Birkenhead CH43 66 A5
Southport PR8 4 E3
Foxdale Rd L15 68 F6
Foxdell Cl L13 54 A2
Foxes Ct 6 CH43 66 B5
Foxes The CH61 77 A6
Foxfield Cl WA2 61 E3
Foxfield Rd CH47 63 D8
Foxfield Sch CH46 64 D8
Foxfold WN8 16 D3
Foxglove Ave L26 70 E1
Foxglove Cl
2 Golborne WA3 47 D8
Liverpool L9 39 F4
Foxglove Rd CH41 65 F7
Foxhill Cl Formby L37 9 C3
Liverpool L8 68 A6
Foxhill La L26 70 F2
Foxhouse La L31 20 F1
Foxhunter Dr L9 39 C8
Foxleigh L26 70 E1
Foxley Heath WA8 84 E8
Foxshaw Cl L35 56 D1
Foxton Cl St Helens WA11 44 D5
Wallasey CH46 49 B1
Foxwood Liverpool L12 54 E8
St Helens L35 57 C7
Foxwood Cl Orrell WN5 25 E5
West Kirby CH48 63 E3
Foy St WN4 35 B3
Frailey Cl PR8 7 C4
Frampton Rd L4 39 D2
Frances Ct 2 L17 68 C4
Francine Cl L3 52 C5
Francis Ave
Birkenhead CH43 66 B6
Birkenhead,Moreton CH46 64 D8
Francis Cl Rainhill L35 57 C4
Widnes WA8 84 C8
Francis St WA9 58 F7
Francis Way L16 69 D8
Frank St 3 Liverpool L8 67 E5
Widnes WA8 73 C1
Frankby Ave CH44 51 A4
Frankby Cl CH49 64 B3
Frankby Gr CH49 64 F5
Frankby Rd
Birkenhead CH48,CH49 64 B3
Hoylake CH47 63 D8
Liverpool L4 53 C8
West Kirby CH48 63 E2
Frankby Stiles CH48 63 F2
Franklin Pl 8 L6 53 B5
Franklin Rd CH46 50 A4
Franton Wlk 2 L32 29 C2
Fraser Rd WA5 74 D6
Fraser St L3 90 C4
Frawley Ave WA12 46 C5
Freckleton Dr L33 30 A5
Freckleton Rd
Southport PR9 1 F4
St Helens WA10 43 C1
Freda Ave 4 WA9 58 C6
Frederick Banting Cl L30 27 F4
Frederick Gr L15 69 A8
Frederick Lunt Ave L34 41 D3
Frederick St
Ashton-in-M WN4 35 A5
Liverpool L1 90 A2
St Helens WA9 58 F8
Widnes WA8 73 B1
Frederick Terr WA8 84 A4
Freedom Cl L7 68 A8
Freehold St L7 53 E3
Freeland St L4 52 E7
Freeman St
Birkenhead CH41 66 E7
Liverpool L7 68 C8
Freemantle Ave WA9 57 F7
Freemasons' Row L3 52 D3
Freemont Rd L12 54 A7
Freeport Gr L9 39 B7
Freesia Ave L9 39 B4
Freme Cl L11 40 B3
French St St Helens WA10 43 D1
Widnes WA8 73 D1
Frenchfield St WA9 58 D3
Frensham Cl CH63 78 F2
Freshfield Cl L36 55 C3
Freshfield Ct L37 9 E4
Freshfield Prim Sch L37 10 A4
Freshfield Rd Formby L37 9 E4
Liverpool L15 68 F6
Freshfield Sta L37 9 E5
Freshford WA9 58 D6
Freshwater Cl WA5 74 D7
Friar St 1 Liverpool L5 53 A5
St Helens WA10 43 F6
Friars Ave WA5 74 E5
Friars Cl CH63 78 F5
Friars Wlk L37 10 B2
Friarsgate Cl L18 69 C5
Friary RC Prim & Inf Sch
L5 52 E4
Friends La WA5 74 D6
Frinsted Rd L11 40 A1
Frobisher Rd CH46 50 A4
Frodsham Dr WA11 44 D5
Frodsham St
Birkenhead CH41 66 E4
Liverpool L4 38 F1
Frogmore Rd L13 53 E3
Frome Cl CH61 76 D7
Frome Way L25 70 D1
Frontfield Ct WA9 44 C2
Frost Dr CH61 76 C6
Frost St L7 53 C2
Fry St WA9 44 F3
Fuchsia Wlk CH49 64 C2
Fulbeck WA8 72 C2
Fulbrook Cl CH63 78 F2
Fulbrook Rd CH63 78 F2
Fulford Cl L12 54 F6
Fulford Pk CH46 64 E8
Fullerton Gr L36 55 E4
Fulmar Cl Liverpool L27 70 E5
St Helens WA11 44 B6
Fulmar Gr L12 40 E3
Fulshaw Cl L27 70 D6
Fulton Ave CH48 63 E3
Fulton St L5 52 B6
Fulwood Ave PR8 4 D4
Fulwood Cl L17 68 D2
Fulwood Dr L17 68 C2
Fulwood Pk L17 68 D1
Fulwood Rd Golborne WA3 47 E7
Liverpool L17 68 C2
Fulwood Way L21 27 C4
Funchal Ave L37 9 D1
Furlong Cl
Ashton-in-M WN2 35 F7
Liverpool L9 39 D8
Furness Ave Formby L37 9 F3
Liverpool L12 40 C1
Ormskirk L39 13 E4
St Helens WA10 43 E7
Furness Cl Southport PR8 7 B3
Birkenhead CH49 64 E6
Furness St L4 52 E7
Furze Way CH46 49 E1
Fylde Rd PR9 2 B4

G

Gable Ct L11 39 E3
Gable Mews L37 10 A1
Gable St WA12 46 B3
Gable View L11 39 E3
Gables Cl WA2 61 F3
Gabriel Cl CH46 64 F8
Gainford Cl WA8 72 C3
Gainford Rd L14 55 A6
Gainsborough Ave L31 28 B8
Gainsborough Cl L12 54 E5
Gainsborough Ct WA8 72 B1
Gainsborough Rd
Birkenhead CH49 64 F6
Liverpool L15 68 E6
Southport PR8 3 E3
Wallasey CH45 50 E5
Gairloch Cl WA2 61 F4
Gaisgill Ct WA8 72 C1
Gala Cl 2 L14 54 E4
Galbraith Cl 3 L17 68 C2
Gale Ave WA5 60 F1
Gale Rd Kirkby L33 41 C8
Litherland L21 27 C1
Galemeade L11 40 B3
Galion Way WA8 72 F3
Gallagher Ind Est CH44 51 B2
Gallery The L37 9 F3
Galloway Dr WN8 25 B6
Galloway Rd L22 26 E2
Galloway St L7 68 D8
Galston Ave L35 57 D2
Galston Cl L33 29 D6
Galsworthy Ave L30 38 E7
Galsworthy Pl L30 38 E8
Galsworthy Wlk L30 38 E7
Galton St L3 52 B3
Galtres Ct CH63 78 E8
Galtres Pk CH63 78 E8
Gambier Terr L1 67 F7
Gamble Ave WA10 43 E6
Gamlin St CH41 66 A8
Gamston Wood L32 29 C1
Ganney's Meadow Rd
CH49 65 C2
Gannock St 6 L7 53 C2
Gantley Ave WN5 25 D3
Gantley Cres WN5 25 D3
Gantley Rd WN5 25 D4
Ganton Cl Southport PR8 4 E3
Widnes WA8 73 B4
Ganworth Cl L24 82 E2
Ganworth Rd L24 82 E3
Garden Cotts L12 54 D4
Garden Ct CH42 66 C1
Garden Hey Rd
Birkenhead CH46 64 C6
Hoylake CH47 48 C1
Garden La Liverpool L9 39 D7
Liverpool,Everton L5 52 F4
1 Wallasey CH46 49 E1
Garden Lodge Gr L27 70 D5
Garden St L25 70 A2
Garden View 14 L20 38 C3
Garden Wlk L34 56 D6
Gardeners View L33 30 A6
Gardeners Way L35 57 C5
Gardenia Gr L17 68 A2
Gardens Rd CH63 79 B5
Gardenside CH46 50 B4
Gardenside St L6 52 F3
Gardiner Ave WA11 45 C6
Gardiners Pl WN8 23 E8
Gardner Ave L20 38 E7
Gardner Rd Formby L37 10 B4
Liverpool L13 53 E5
Gardner's Dr L6 53 D4
Gardner's Row L3 52 D3
Gareth Ave WA11 44 B6
Garfield Terr CH49 65 A5
Garfourth Cl L19 81 D7
Garfourth Rd L19 81 D7
Garmoyle Cl L15 68 E7
Garmoyle Rd L15 68 E6
Garnet St Liverpool L13 53 F1
St Helens WA9 58 D7
Garnett Ave L4 52 E8
Garnett Gn L39 13 D4
Garnett Pl WN8 24 A7
Garnetts La
Tarbock Green L35 71 D1
Widnes WA8 84 A3
Garrick Ave CH46 64 C8
Garrick Par PR8 4 A6
Garrick Rd CH43 77 F8
Garrick St L7 68 C7
Garrigill Cl WA8 73 C5
Garrowby Dr L36 55 C3
Garsdale Ave L35 57 D2
Garsdale Cl 2 WA5 74 F7
Garsfield Rd 1 L4 53 E8
Garside Ave WA3 47 D7
Garstang Rd PR9 2 A5
Garston CE Prim Sch
L19 81 D6
Garston Ind Est L19 81 C4
Garston Old Rd L19 81 C7
Garston Sta L19 81 D6
Garston Way L19 81 D5
Garswood Ave WA11 32 A7
Garswood Cl Maghull L31 20 E3
Wallasey CH46 49 E4
Garswood Cres WN5 33 E4
Garswood Old Rd WA11,
WN4 33 E1
Garswood Prim Sch
WN4 34 C4
Garswood Rd Billinge WN5 33 F4
Garswood WA11,WN4 34 C3
Garswood St
Ashton-in-M WN4 35 B3
Liverpool L8 67 F3
St Helens WA10 44 A4
Garswood Sta WN4 34 D3
Garter Cl L11 40 C3
Garth Bvd CH63 78 E8
Garth Ct L22 26 E1
Garth Dr L18 69 C4
Garth Rd L32 41 A8
Garth The
Birkenhead CH43 65 F5
Huyton-w-R L36 55 E3
Garth Wlk 6 L32 41 A8
Garthdale Rd L18 69 B4
Garthowen Rd L7 53 D2
Garton Dr WA3 36 E1
Gartons La WA9 58 C3
Garway L25 70 C3
Garwood Cl
Warrington WA5 60 B1
Warrington WA5 60 C1
Gascoyne St L3 52 C3
Gaskell Ct WA9 44 F3
Gaskell Rake L30 27 D5
Gaskell St WA9 44 D2
Gaskell's Brow WN4 34 E5
Gaskill Rd L24 82 D4
Gatclif Rd L13 53 E7
Gateacre Brow L25 70 B4
Gateacre Com Comp Sch
L25 70 A5
Gateacre Ct L25 69 F7
Gateacre Park Dr L25 69 F6
Gateacre Rise L25 70 B4
Gateacre Vale Rd L25 70 B3
Gategill Gr WN5 25 D3
Gates La L29 19 C1
Gateside Cl L27 70 E5
Gathurst Ct WA8 84 D8
Gathurst Rd WN5 25 E8
Gatley Dr L31 28 E7
Gatley Wlk L24 82 F4
Gautby Rd CH41 50 E1
Gavin Rd WA8 84 B7
Gaw Hill La L39 13 B3
Gaw Hill View L39 13 B3
Gawsworth Cl
Birkenhead CH43 65 F3
St Helens WA10 43 B3
Gawsworth Rd WA3 35 F1
Gaybeech Cl CH43 65 B8
Gayhurst Ave WA2 61 F2
Gayhurst Cres L11 40 A2
Gaynor Ave WA11 45 F7
Gayton Ave
Bebington CH63 78 C8
Wallasey CH45 51 B8
Gayton Farm Rd CH60 86 A5
Gayton La CH60 86 B6
Gayton Mill Cl CH60 86 B7
Gayton Parkway CH60 86 C5
Gayton Prim Sch CH60 86 A6
Gayton Rd CH60 86 A6
Gaywood Ave L32 40 F8
Gaywood Cl
Birkenhead CH43 65 C7
5 Kirkby L32 40 F8
Gaywood Ct L23 26 B3
Gaywood Gn 4 L32 40 F8
Gelling St L8 67 F5
Gellings La L34 41 A5
Gellings Rd L34 41 A5
Gemini Bsns Pk WA5 60 E3
Gemini Cl L20 38 B4
Gemini Dr L14 54 F4
Geneva Cl L36 55 D4
Geneva Rd Liverpool L6 53 C3
Wallasey CH44 51 D2
Genista Cl L9 39 A3
Genoa Cl L25 70 B7
Gentwood Par L36 55 D4
Gentwood Rd L36 55 D3
George Dr PR8 7 E5
George Hale Ave L34 55 E6
George Harrison Cl 1
L6 53 B3
George Moore Ct L23 27 C6
George Rd CH47 63 C6
George St
Ashton-in-M WN4 35 C4
Birkenhead CH41 66 E7
George St *continued*
Liverpool L2 90 A4
Newton-le-W WA12 46 A4
St Helens WA10 44 A3
George Terr WN5 25 D5
George's Dock Gates L2,
L3 52 B1
George's La PR9 2 F8
George's Prec WA5 74 D6
Georges Dockway L3 52 B1
Georges Par L3 52 B1
Georges Pierhead L3 52 B1
Georgia Ave
Bebington CH62 79 E3
Kirkby L33 29 D6
Georgia St 9 L20 38 C3
Georgian Cl
Eccleston Park L35 57 A6
Liverpool L26 82 F6
Georgian Pl L37 9 E1
Geraint St L8 67 F6
Gerald Rd CH43 66 A4
Gerard Ave CH45 51 A7
Gerard Rd Wallasey CH45 50 F6
West Kirby CH48 63 B3
Gerard St
Ashton-in-M WN4 35 B3
Liverpool L3 90 C4
Gerards Ct WA11 44 C8
Gerards La WA9 58 D7
Germander Cl L26 70 E1
Gerneth Cl L24 82 C4
Gerneth Rd L24 82 B4
Gerosa Ave WA2 61 B8
Gerrard Pl WN8 23 F7
Gerrard Rd WN5 33 E5
Gerrard's La L26 70 F3
Gertrude Rd L4 53 B6
Gertrude St
Birkenhead CH41 66 F6
St Helens WA9 57 D7
Geves Gdns L22 26 E1
Ghyll Gr WA11 33 B1
Gibbon's Rd WN4 34 D3
Gibbons Ave WA10 43 C3
Gibraltar Row L3 52 B2
Gibson Cl CH61 76 F3
Gibson Rd L8 67 F6
Gibson Terr CH44 51 D5
Giddygate La L31 29 B7
Gidlow Rd L13 53 F3
Gidlow Rd S L13 53 F2
Gilbert Cl CH63 78 F2
Gilbert Rd L35 56 F5
Gilbert St L1 90 B2
Gilbrook Sch CH41 66 F6
Gildart St L3 52 F2
Gildarts Gdns L3 52 C4
Gilead St L7 53 B2
Gilescroft Ave L33 30 A4
Gill St L3 52 F2
Gillar's La WA10 42 E3
Gillars Green Dr WA10 43 A3
Gillbrook Sq 4 CH41 65 F8
Gilleney Gr L35 57 A5
Gillibrands Rd WN8 24 A7
Gillmoss Cl L11 40 C4
Gillmoss Ind Est L10,L11 40 B6
Gillmoss La L11 40 C5
Gills La CH61 77 B4
Gilman St 3 L4 53 A7
Gilmour (Southbank) Inf Sch
L19 81 B7
Gilmour Jun Sch L19 81 B7
Gilmour Mount CH43 66 B4
Gilpin Ave L31 20 E2
Gilroy Rd Liverpool L6 53 B3
West Kirby CH48 63 D3
Giltbrook Cl WA8 72 F3
Gilwell Ave CH46,CH49 64 E7
Gilwell Cl CH46 64 E7
Ginnel The CH62 79 B5
Gipsy Gr L18 69 E5
Gipsy La L16,L18 69 E5
Girton Ave
Ashton-in-M WN4 34 F4
Bootle L20 38 E2
Girtrell Cl CH49 64 D5
Girtrell Rd CH49 64 D5
Girvan Cres WN4 34 D4
Gisburn Ave WA3 35 F2
Givenchy Cl L16 69 E8
Givenchy Ct 1 L17 68 C2
Gladden Pl WN8 23 E8
Glade Rd L36 55 E4
Glade The CH47 48 D1
Gladeswood Rd L33 30 B1
Gladeville Rd L17 68 E3
Gladica Cl L36 56 B2
Gladstone Ave
Huyton-w-R L16 70 A8
2 Seaforth L21 37 F7
Gladstone Cl CH41 66 C6
Gladstone Hall Rd CH62 79 B4
Gladstone Rd
5 Birkenhead CH42 66 F3
Liverpool,Edge Hill L7 53 B1
Liverpool,Garston L19 81 C6
Liverpool,Walton L9 39 A3
Seaforth L21 37 F7
Southport PR9 4 F6
Wallasey CH44 51 D3
Gladstone St
1 Liverpool,Vauxhall L3 52 C3
Liverpool,Woolton Hill L25 69 F2

Gladstone St *continued*
St Helens WA10 43 D3
Gladstone Way WA12 46 B4
Gladsville Rd L27 70 F4
Glaisdale Cl WN4 35 C3
Glaisdale Dr PR8 4 F3
Glaisher St L5 53 A6
Glamis Cl CH43 65 D3
Glamis Dr PR9 2 B3
Glamis Gr WA9 58 C7
Glamis Rd L13 53 E6
Glamorgan Cl WA10 43 F2
Glan Aber Pk L12 54 E8
Glasier Rd CH46 49 C1
Glaslyn Way L9 39 A3
Glassonby Cres L11 40 A1
Glassonby Way 3 L11 40 A1
Glastonbury Cl L6 53 D7
Glasven Rd L33 29 F3
Gleadmere WA8 72 C2
Gleaston Cl CH62 79 D1
Gleave Cres L6 53 A4
Gleave Rd WA5 59 F6
Gleave St WA10 44 A5
Glebe Ave WN4 35 C2
Glebe Cl L31 20 B1
Glebe End L29 27 F7
Glebe Hey L27 70 E5
Glebe Hey Rd CH49 65 A3
Glebe La WA8 73 B5
Glebe Pl PR8 4 B7
Glebe Rd
Skelmersdale WN8 24 A8
Wallasey CH45 51 A6
Glebelands Rd CH46 64 E8
Glegg St L3 52 B4
Gleggside CH48 63 C2
Glegside Rd L33 30 A2
Glen Park Rd CH45 51 A7
Glen Rd L13 54 B2
Glen Ronald Dr CH49 64 D5
Glen The Bebington CH62 79 C3
Liverpool L18 69 C3
Glen Vine Cl L16 69 F8
Glenacres L25 70 A3
Glenalmond Rd CH44 51 D4
Glenathol Rd L18 69 C2
Glenavon Rd
Birkenhead CH43 66 A1
3 Liverpool L16 54 C1
Glenbank L22 26 C2
Glenbank Cl L9 39 A5
Glenburn Ave CH62 88 E4
Glenburn High Sch WN8 24 B8
Glenburn Rd
Skelmersdale WN8 16 A1
Wallasey CH44 51 D3
Skelmersdale WN8 15 F2
Glenby Ave L23 26 F2
Glencairn Rd L13 53 F3
Glencoe Rd CH45 51 C6
Glenconner Rd L16 54 E1
Glencourse Rd WA8 73 A5
Glencoyne Dr PR9 2 B5
Glencroft Cl L36 55 C5
Glendale Ave WN4 35 C4
Glendale Cl L8 67 F3
Glendale Gr
Bebington CH63 79 B2
Kirkby L33 30 A5
Glendale Rd WA11 44 A7
Glendale Way L37 9 F2
Glendevon Rd
Huyton-w-R L36 55 E1
Liverpool L16 54 D1
Glendower Ct 3 L23 26 B3
Glendower Rd L22 26 E1
Glendower St L20 38 C1
Glendyke Rd L18 69 C3
Gleneagles Cl
Golborne WA3 47 F7
Heswall CH61 76 F3
Kirkby L33 29 D6
Gleneagles Dr
Haydock WA11 45 A5
Southport PR8 7 C3
Widnes WA8 73 B5
Gleneagles Rd L14,L16 54 D1
Glenfield Cl
Birkenhead CH43 65 C8
Wallasey CH46 49 B1
Glenfield Rd L15 69 A6
Glengariff St L13 53 E7
Glenham Cl CH47 63 E8
Glenhead Rd L19 81 B8
Glenholm Rd L31 28 C7
Glenluce Rd L19 69 B1
Glenlyon Rd L15,L16 69 C8
Glenmarsh Cl
Bebington CH63 78 D5
Liverpool L12 54 C6
Glenmarsh Way L37 10 B3
Glenmaye Cl L12 40 E2
Glenmore Ave L18 69 A3
Glenmore Rd CH43 66 A4
Glenn Bldgs 2 L23 26 E5
Glenn Pl WA8 72 E1
Glenpark Dr PR9 2 B4
Glenrose Rd L25 70 A3
Glenrose Terr PR8 4 A5
Glenside L18 69 C2
Glentrees Cl CH49 64 D5
Glentrees Rd L12 54 B8
Glentworth Cl L31 28 D7
Glenville Cl L25 70 B4
Glenway L33 29 F6
Glenway Cl L12 40 F4
Glenwood Cl L35 56 F2
Glenwood Dr CH61 76 E7
Glenwyllin Rd L22 26 F1
Globe Rd L20 38 B4
Globe St L4 52 E7
Gloucester Ave WA3 47 B8
Gloucester Ct 18 L6 53 A3
Gloucester Pl L6 53 A3
Gloucester Rd Bootle L20 38 D4
Huyton-w-R L36 56 A3
Liverpool L6 53 D5
Southport PR8 3 F5
Wallasey CH45 50 E6
Widnes WA8 73 B3
Gloucester Rd N L6 53 D6
Gloucester St WA9 44 D2
Glover Pl L20 38 B4
Glover St Birkenhead CH42 66 C4
Newton-le-W WA12 46 C3
St Helens WA10 43 F3
Glover's Brow L32 29 C4
Glover's La L30 27 E4
Glovers Ct L32 29 C3
Glyn Rd CH44 51 B5
Glynn Ave CH62 88 E7
Glynn St L15 68 F8
Glynne Gr L16 70 A8
Glynne St L20 38 D6
Godetia Cl L9 39 F4
Godshill Cl WA5 74 D7
Golborne Dale Rd WA3, WA12 47 A5
Golborne Enterprise Pk WA3 36 A1
Golborne Jun & Inf Sch WA3 47 A8
Golborne Rd
Ashton-in-M WN4 35 E4
Golborne WA3 47 C8
Winwick WA2 61 A7
Golborne St WA12 46 E4
Golbourne High Sch WA3 36 C1
Golbourne St Thomas' CE Jun & Inf Sch WA3 36 B1
Gold Triangle Complex WA8 84 C5
Goldcliffe Cl WA5 60 D3
Goldcrest Cl L12 40 F4
Goldcrest Mews L26 70 E1
Golden Gr 3 L4 39 A1
Goldfinch Cl L26 70 E1
Goldfinch Farm Rd L24 82 C3
Goldie St L4 52 F7
Goldsmith Rd 1 CH43 65 F1
Goldsmith St Bootle L20 38 A4
Liverpool L6 53 B3
Goldsmith Way 2 CH43 65 F1
Goldsworth Fold L35 57 B3
Golf Links Rd CH42 78 B8
Golf Rd L37 9 E5
Gondover Ave L9 38 F6
Gonville Rd L20 38 D2
Gooch Dr WA12 46 D2
Good Shepherd Cl L11 40 B2
Goodacre Rd L9 39 B7
Goodaker's Mdw 2 CH49 65 A2
Goodakers Ct 10 CH49 65 A2
Goodall Pl L4 52 E8
Goodall St L4 38 E1
Goodban St WA9 58 E8
Goodison Ave L4 52 F8
Goodison Park (Everton Football Club) L4 52 F8
Goodison Pl L4 38 F1
Goodison Rd L4 38 F1
Goodlass Rd L24 82 A6
Goodleigh Pl WA9 58 C5
Goodwood Cl L36 55 D1
Goodwood Ct WA9 57 D6
Goodwood Dr CH46 49 F3
Goodwood St L5 52 D5
Goose Green The CH47 48 D1
Goostrey Cl CH63 79 B1
Gordale Cl Liverpool L8 68 A4
Warrington WA5 74 F7
Gordon Ave
Bebington CH62 88 E7
Birkenhead CH49 64 E3
Crosby L22 26 C2
Garswood WN4 34 E4
Haydock WA11 45 F7
Maghull L31 20 C3
Southport PR9 1 C1
Gordon Ct CH49 64 E3
Gordon Dr Huyton-w-R L14 54 E3
Liverpool L19 81 A7
Gordon Pl L18 69 A3
Gordon Rd Seaforth L21 37 F6
Wallasey CH45 51 C7
Gordon St
Birkenhead CH41 66 C6
Liverpool L15 68 E7
Southport PR9 4 C8
Gordonstoun Cres WN5 25 F7
Gore Dr L39 13 E3
Gore St L8 67 E6
Gore's La WA11 33 A5
Gores La Crank WA11 32 F6
Formby L37 9 F5
Gores Rd L33 30 C1
Gorleston Mews 10 L32 40 F8
Gorleston Way L32 29 F1
Gorse Ave L12 40 B1
Gorse Cres CH44 51 C2
Gorse Hey Ct L12,L13 54 A5
Gorse La CH48 63 E1
Gorse Rd CH47 63 D8
Gorse Way L37 9 C4
Gorsebank Rd L18 68 E5
Gorsebank St CH44 51 C3
Gorseburn Rd L13 53 E6
Gorsedale Pk CH44 51 D2
Gorsedale Rd
Liverpool L18 69 A4
Wallasey CH44 51 C2
Gorsefield Formby L37 10 A6
St Helens WA9 57 D7
Gorsefield Ave
Bebington CH62 88 D5
Crosby L23 27 A5
Gorsefield Cl CH62 88 D5
Gorsefield Rd CH42 66 C3
Gorsehill Rd
Heswall CH60 77 A1
Wallasey CH45 51 A8
Gorselands Ct L17 68 D2
Gorsewood Cl L25 70 C5
Gorsewood Gr L25 70 C5
Gorsewood Rd L25 70 B5
Gorsey Ave L30 27 C3
Gorsey Brow WN5 33 E5
Gorsey Brow Cl WN5 33 D5
Gorsey Cop Way L25 70 A6
Gorsey Croft L34 56 F7
Gorsey La Haskayne L39 11 B7
Hightown L38 18 B2
Litherland L21 27 C2
St Helens WA5,WA9 59 C5
Wallasey CH41,CH44 51 B2
Widnes WA8 73 E1
Gorsey Pl WN8 24 B7
Gorseyville Cres CH63 78 E5
Gorseyville Rd CH63 78 E5
Gorst St 11 L4 52 F7
Gort Rd L36 55 E3
Gorton Rd L13 54 B2
Goschen St
6 Liverpool,Everton L5 52 F7
Liverpool,Stanley L13 53 F3
Gosford St L8 67 F4
Gosforth Rd PR9 4 F8
Gosport Cl WA2 61 F1
Goswell St L15 68 E8
Gotham Rd CH63 79 B3
Gothic St CH42 66 F2
Gough Ave WA2 61 B2
Gough Rd L13 53 E7
Gourley Rd L13 54 B1
Gourley's La CH48 63 D1
Government Rd CH47 63 B7
Govett Rd WA9 57 D7
Gower St Bootle L20 38 B5
Liverpool L1,L3 90 A2
St Helens WA9 44 D1
Gowrie Gr L21 38 B7
Goyt Hey Ave WN5 33 E5
Graburn Rd L37 9 F4
Grace Ave L10 40 A7
Grace Cl CH45 51 B5
Grace Rd L9 39 A6
Grace St Liverpool L8 67 F4
St Helens WA9 58 C8
Gradwell St L1 90 B3
Graeme Bryson Ct L11 39 F1
Grafton Cres L8 67 E6
Grafton Dr
Birkenhead CH49 65 B4
Southport PR8 7 A5
Grafton Gr L8 67 E4
Grafton Rd CH45 51 B7
Grafton St
Birkenhead CH43 66 B5
Liverpool L8 67 E4
Liverpool L8 67 E5
Liverpool L8 67 E6
Liverpool,Dingle L8 67 F3
Newton-le-W WA12 46 B3
St Helens WA10 43 D3
Grafton Wlk CH48 63 C2
Graham Cl WA8 72 C1
Graham Dr L26 83 A8
Graham Rd
West Kirby CH48 63 A3
Widnes WA8 84 C8
Graham St WA9 44 C4
Graham's Rd L36 55 F2
Grain Ind Est L8 67 E4
Grainger Ave
Birkenhead CH43 65 F1
Bootle L20 38 E5
West Kirby CH48 63 B3
Graley Cl L26 82 F6
Grammar School La CH48 63 D1
Grampian Ave CH46 64 E8
Grampian Rd L7 53 E2
Grampian Way
Bebington CH62 88 E4
Birkenhead CH46 64 E8
Golborne WA3 36 D1
Granams Croft L30 27 D4
Granard Rd L15 69 A6
Granary Way L3 67 D6
Granborne Chase L32 29 B3
Granby Cl PR9 1 F3
Granby Cres CH63 79 A2
Granby St L8 68 A6
Grand National Ave L9 28 B1
Grandison Rd L4 39 C1
Grange Ave
Liverpool,Halewood L25 82 D7
Liverpool,Mill Yard L12 54 E5
Grange Ave *continued*
Southport PR9 4 E8
Wallasey CH45 51 B6
Grange Ave N L12 54 F5
Grange Cl WA3 47 C6
Grange Cotts CH63 78 A6
Grange Cres CH66 89 A1
Grange Cross Cl CH48 63 E1
Grange Cross Hey CH48 63 E1
Grange Cross La CH48 63 E1
Grange Ct CH43 66 A3
Grange Dr Heswall CH60 76 F2
St Helens WA10 57 B8
Thornton Hough CH63 87 A7
Widnes WA8 72 D1
Grange Farm Cres CH48 63 E3
Grange La Formby L37 9 E5
Liverpool L25 70 A5
Grange Mews L25 70 B4
Grange Mount
Birkenhead CH43 66 C5
Heswall CH60 76 F1
West Kirby CH48 63 D2
Grange Old Rd CH48 63 C2
Grange Park Rd WA10 57 C8
Grange Pk L31 28 F7
Grange Pl CH41 66 C6
Grange Prim Sch L30 27 E5
Grange Rd
Ashton-in-M WN4 34 F6
Birkenhead CH41 66 D6
12 Birkenhead CH41 66 E6
Haydock WA11,WA12 45 D5
Heswall CH60 76 F2
Hightown L38 17 E6
Litherland L30 28 B2
Southport PR9 4 E7
West Kirby CH48 63 B2
Grange Rd E 8 CH41 66 E6
Grange Rd W CH41,CH43 66 C6
Grange St L6 53 D5
Grange Terr L15 68 F7
Grange The Southport PR9 2 C3
Wallasey CH44 51 C4
Grange Vale CH42 67 A1
Grange Valley WA11 45 D6
Grange Valley Prim Sch WA11 45 D5
Grange View 15 CH43 66 C5
Grange Way L25 70 A5
Grange Weint L25 70 B4
Grange Wlk CH48 63 D1
Grangehurst Ct L25 70 B4
Grangemeadow Rd L25 70 A5
Grangeside L25 70 A5
Grangewood L16 54 F1
Granite Terr L36 56 A2
Granston Cl WA5 60 E2
Grant Ave L15 68 F6
Grant Cl Huyton-w-R L14 55 A3
St Helens WA10 43 E4
Warrington WA5 60 D1
Grant Ct 11 L20 38 C3
Grant Rd Huyton-w-R L14 55 A4
Wallasey CH46 50 C4
Grantham Cl
Heswall CH61 76 E4
Southport PR8 4 A1
Grantham Cres WA11 44 D5
Grantham Rd Kirkby L33 29 E5
Southport PR8 4 A1
Grantham St L6 53 B3
Grantham Way L30 28 B4
Grantley Rd L15 69 B6
Grantley St WN4 35 A5
Granton Cl L37 9 E3
Granton Rd L5 53 A6
Grantwood WN4 35 A5
Granville Ave L31 20 C2
Granville Cl Ormskirk L39 21 B8
Wallasey CH45 50 E6
Granville Ct Southport PR9 1 D1
3 Wallasey CH45 50 E6
Granville Pk L39 21 C8
Granville Pk W L39 21 B8
Granville Rd Liverpool L15 68 D7
Liverpool,Garston L19 81 C6
Southport PR8 3 D4
Granville St WA9 44 D3
Grappenhall Way CH43 65 C7
Grasmere Ave
Birkenhead CH43 65 C5
Orrell WN5 25 F8
Prescot L34 56 F6
St Helens WA11 44 B7
Up Holland WN8 25 B7
Warrington WA2 61 E3
Grasmere Cl Kirkby L33 29 D4
St Helens WA11 44 B7
Grasmere Ct
9 Birkenhead CH41 66 C5
St Helens WA11 44 B7
Grasmere Dr
Ashton-in-M WN4 35 B5
Bootle L21 38 E8
Wallasey CH45 51 A6
Grasmere Fold WA11 44 B7
Grasmere Gdns L23 26 F3
Grasmere Ho
Huyton-w-R L36 55 E2
Liverpool L17 68 D2
Grasmere Rd Formby L37 9 D3
Hightown L38 18 A4
Maghull L31 20 D2
Grasmere St L5 53 B5
Grasmere Terr WN2 36 B8
Grassendale Ct L19 81 A7
Grassendale Espl L19 80 F6
Grassendale La L19 81 A7
Grassendale Rd L19 81 A7
Grassington Cres L25 70 C2
Grassmoor Cl CH62 88 E8
Grasswood Rd CH49 65 C3
Grasville Rd CH42 66 E3
Gratrix Rd CH62 88 D8
Gratton Pl WN8 24 A8
Grave-Yard La L39 22 A6
Gravel Cl PR9 2 F5
Gravel La PR9 2 F5
Gray Ave WA11 45 D6
Gray Gr L36 70 F8
Gray St L20 38 A5
Graylands Pl L4 39 C1
Graylands Rd
Bebington CH62 79 C6
Liverpool L4 39 C2
Grayling Dr L12 40 D3
Grays Ave L35 56 F6
Grayson Mews CH41 66 F7
Grayson St L1 90 B2
Graysons Rd WA11 31 F8
Grayston Ave WA9 58 D6
Greasby Inf Sch CH49 64 C2
Greasby Jun Sch CH49 64 D1
Greasby Rd
Birkenhead CH49 64 E4
Wallasey CH44 51 A4
Great Ashfield WA8 72 D3
Great Charlotte St
Liverpool L1 90 B3
Liverpool L1 90 B4
Great Crosby RC Prim Sch L23 26 E4
Great Crosshall St L3 90 B4
Great Delph WA11 45 D7
Great George Pl L1 90 C1
Great George Sq L1 90 C1
Great George St L1 90 C1
Great George's Rd L22 37 E8
Great Hey L30 27 D5
Great Homer St L5 52 E5
Great Howard St L3,L5 52 B4
Great Meols Prim Sch CH47 48 E1
Great Mersey St L5 52 D6
Great Nelson St L3,L5 52 D4
Great Newton St L3 52 F1
Great Orford St L3 52 F1
Great Richmond St L3 52 E3
Great Sankey High Sch WA5 74 E7
Greaves St L8 67 F5
Grebe Ave WA10 57 B7
Grecian St L21 37 F8
Grecian Terr L5 52 F6
Gredington St L8 68 A4
Greek St Liverpool L3 90 C4
Runcorn WA7 84 F3
Green Bank CH63 78 A2
Green Croft L23 27 B5
Green End La WA9 58 C8
Green End Pk L12 54 A7
Green Gates L36 55 E6
Green Hey Dr L30 27 D3
Green Heys Dr L31 20 F1
Green Jones Brow WA5 59 F6
Green La Bebington CH63 79 A5
Birkenhead CH41 66 E4
Burtonwood WA5 59 E7
Crosby,Thornton L23 27 B6
Crosby,Waterloo L22 26 C2
Formby L37 9 F5
Litherland L21 27 B2
Liverpool L3 90 C3
Liverpool,Calderstones L16, L18 69 C5
Liverpool,Calderstones L18 69 B5
Liverpool,Stanley L13 53 F4
Maghull L31 20 A2
Maghull L31 20 C1
Ormskirk L39 13 E6
Orrell WN5 25 D3
Rainford WA11 32 A5
Seaforth L21 38 A7
Skelmersdale L40 16 A6
St Helens WA10 42 F5
Wallasey CH45 50 D6
Wallasey CH45,CH46 50 C5
Widnes WA8 72 E1
Winwick WA2 61 A7
Skelmersdale L40,WN8 15 F6
Green La N L16 69 D6
Green Lane Ave L39 13 E6
Green Lane Cl WA2 61 A7
Green Lane Sta CH41 66 F4
Green Lawn
Birkenhead CH42 66 F1
Huyton-w-R L36 56 A4
Green Lawn Gr CH42 66 F1
Green Leach Ave WA11 44 B7
Green Leach Ct WA11 44 B7
Green Leach La WA11 44 B7
Green Link L31 20 B2
Green Mdws WA3 47 E5
Green Mount CH49 65 A5
Green Oaks Way WA8 73 C1
Green Park Dr L31 20 B1
Green Park Prim Sch L31 20 B2
Green Pk L30 27 F5
Green Rd L34 56 C7
Green St L3,L5 52 C4
Green The Bebington CH62 79 D5
Crosby L23 26 D5
Hale L24 83 D1
Liverpool L13 54 C2

Green The *continued*
Prescot L34 56 F7
Thornton Hough CH63 87 C4
West Kirby CH48 75 D7
Green Way L36 55 B4
Green Way Cl L36 55 B4
Green Wlk PR8 7 D5
Green's La L31 12 C1
Greenacre L40 14 E4
Greenacre Cl L25 82 C8
Greenacre Rd L25 82 C8
Greenacres Cl CH43 65 C8
Greenacres Dr CH63 88 C7
Greenall Ave WA5 74 D4
Greenall Ct 15 L34 56 D6
Greenall St
Ashton-in-M WN4 35 B5
St Helens WA10 43 E4
Greenbank
Abram Brow WN2 36 B7
Ormskirk L39 13 C2
Seaforth L22 37 E8
Greenbank Ave
Maghull L31 20 C3
Orrell WN5 25 D3
3 Wallasey CH45 51 B7
Greenbank Cres WA10 43 F3
Greenbank Ct L17 68 E5
Greenbank Dr
Heswall CH61 77 A3
Liverpool L15,L17 68 E5
Liverpool,Gillmoss L10 40 B7
Southport PR8 3 E2
Greenbank High Sch PR8 3 E1
Greenbank La L17,L18 68 E5
Greenbank Prim Sch L18 68 F5
Greenbank Rd
Birkenhead CH42 66 C3
Liverpool L18 68 F5
West Kirby CH48 63 C4
Greenburn Ave WA11 33 C1
Greencroft Rd CH44 51 C3
Greendale Rd
Bebington CH62 79 B5
Liverpool L25 69 F4
Greene's Rd L35 56 D2
Greenfield Cl
Newton-le-W WA12 46 C4
Southport PR9 2 A3
Greenfield Dr L36 70 F8
Greenfield Gr L36 70 F8
Greenfield La
Heswall CH60 76 C2
Litherland L21 27 A1
Greenfield Rd
Liverpool L13 54 A3
Southport PR8 5 C1
St Helens WA10 43 E5
Greenfield View WN5 33 D4
Greenfield Way
Liverpool L18 69 C1
Wallasey CH44 51 B4
Greenfield Wlk L36 55 F1
Greenfields Ave CH62 88 C7
Greenfields Cres
Ashton-in-M WN4 35 B4
Bebington CH62 88 C7
Greenfinch Cl 1 L12 40 F3
Greenfinch Gr L26 70 E1
Greenford Cl WN5 25 D6
Greenford Rd PR8 7 C4
Greengables Cl 7 L8 68 A5
Greenham Ave L33 29 F6
Greenhaven WN5 25 B7
Greenhaven Cl L10 40 A7
Greenheath Way CH46 49 F3
Greenhey Pl WN8 23 F8
Greenheys Ct 5 L8 68 B6
Greenheys Gdns 7 L8 68 B6
Greenheys Rd Irby CH61 76 C5
Liverpool L8 68 B6
Wallasey CH44 51 B4
Greenhill Ave L18 69 C4
Greenhill Cl L18 69 B2
Greenhill Cres WN5 33 F5
Greenhill Pl L36 55 E1
Greenhill Rd Billinge WN5 33 F5
Liverpool,Grassendale L19 81 C8
Liverpool,Mossley Hill L18 69 B2
Greenholme Cl L11 40 A3
Greenhow Ave CH48 63 B3
Greenlake Rd L18 69 B2
Greenland St L1 90 B1
Greenlands L36 55 E1
Greenlea Cl
Bebington CH63 78 F6
Orrell WN5 25 D5
Greenleaf St L8 68 C7
Greenleas Cl CH45 50 D5
Greenleas Prim Sch
CH45 50 D6
Greenleas Rd CH45 50 D5
Greenleigh Rd L18 69 B2
Greenloon's Dr L37 9 C3
Greenloon's Wlk L37 9 C2
Greenock Mews WA8 72 E3
Greenock St L3 52 B3
Greenodd Ave L12 40 C1
Greenore Dr L24 83 D2
Greenough Ave L35 57 C5
Greenough St L25 69 F2
Greens Wlk L17 68 E3
Greensbridge La L26,L35 71 B2
Greenscres 4 L22 26 D1
Greenshank Cl WA12 46 C4
Greenside L6 52 F3
Greenside Ave
Aintree L10 28 E2

Greenside Ave *continued*
Liverpool L15 69 A7
Greenside Cl L33 30 A6
Greenslate Ct WN5 25 E3
Greenslate Rd WN5 25 E3
Greenville Cl CH63 78 F5
Greenville Dr L31 20 C1
Greenville Rd CH63 78 F5
Greenway
Ashton-in-M WN4 35 A4
Bebington CH62 79 D3
Birkenhead CH49 64 E5
Crosby L23 27 A5
Heswall CH61 76 E4
Neston CH64 86 B2
Warrington WA5 74 E7
Greenway Ave WN8 24 B8
Greenway Cl WN8 15 E2
Greenway Rd
Birkenhead CH42 66 D3
Liverpool L24 83 A3
Runcorn WA7 84 F1
Widnes WA8 73 B1
Greenway The L12 54 E4
Greenways WN5 25 E3
Greenways Sch L19 80 F7
Greenwell Rd WA11 45 C6
Greenwich Ave WA8 73 D4
Greenwich Ct L9 39 B8
Greenwich Rd L9 39 B7
Greenwood Cl
Ormskirk L39 13 C1
Prescot L34 56 E6
Greenwood Cres WA2 61 E2
Greenwood Ct 7 WA9 58 C4
Greenwood Dr WA12 46 D2
Greenwood Gdns PR8 4 A5
Greenwood La CH44 51 C5
Greenwood Rd
Birkenhead CH49 65 B3
Hoylake CH47 63 E8
Liverpool L18 69 B1
Greetby Hill L39,L40 14 A6
Greetby Pl WN8 24 A8
Greetham St L1 90 B2
Gregory Cl L16 69 E8
Gregory Way L16 69 E8
Gregson Ct CH45 51 C8
Gregson Rd Liverpool L14 54 C2
Prescot L35 56 D5
Widnes WA8 73 C1
Gregson St L6 52 F3
Gregson's Ave L37 9 E5
Grenfell Cl CH64 86 C1
Grenfell Pk CH64 86 C1
Grenfell Rd L13 53 E8
Grennan Ct 8 CH45 51 B8
Grennan The CH45 51 B8
Grenville Cres CH63 88 C7
Grenville Dr CH61 76 E3
Grenville Rd
4 Birkenhead CH42 66 F3
Neston CH64 86 F1
Grenville St S L1 90 C2
Grenville Way CH42 66 F3
Gresford Ave
Birkenhead CH43 66 A2
Liverpool L17 68 E6
West Kirby CH48 63 C3
Gresford Cl Prescot L35 56 F3
Warrington WA5 60 E1
Gresham St L7 53 E2
Gresley Cl 6 L7 53 C1
Gressingham Rd L18 69 C2
Gretton Rd L14 55 B5
Grey Rd Ashton-in-M WN4 35 A4
Liverpool L9 39 A4
Grey St L8 67 F6
Greyfriars WN4 34 F4
Greyfriars Rd PR8 7 B6
Greyhound Farm Rd L24 82 C4
Greystoke Cl CH49 64 F4
Greystokes L39 13 D2
Greystone Cres L14 54 E3
Greystone Pl L10 39 F7
Greystone Rd
Huyton-w-R L14 54 E2
Liverpool L10 39 F7
Warrington WA5 74 F4
Gribble Rd L10 40 A7
Grierson St L8 68 B7
Grieve Rd L10 40 A7
Griffin Ave CH46 64 E8
Griffin Cl Liverpool L11 40 C4
St Helens WA10 42 F4
Griffin Mews WA8 73 B3
Griffin St WA9 58 E7
Griffith's Rd L36 55 E2
Griffiths Cl CH49 64 C3
Griffiths Dr PR9 4 F8
Griffiths St L1 90 C2
Griffon Ho PR9 1 F2
Grimrod Pl WN8 24 A7
Grimshaw La L39 13 E7
Grimshaw Rd WN8 24 D8
Grimshaw St Bootle L20 38 B2
Golborne WA3 36 A1
St Helens WA9 58 C6
Grinfield St L7 53 A1
Grinshill Cl L8 68 A6
Grinstead Cl PR8 3 F1
Grinton Cres L36 55 D2
Grisedale Ave WA2 61 B3
Grisedale Cl L37 9 E3
Grisedale Rd CH62 88 F8
Grizedale WA8 72 B2
Grizedale Ave WA11 44 B8
Groarke Dr WA5 74 D5

Groes Rd L19 81 B7
Grogan Sq L20 38 D6
Gronow Pl L20 38 E6
Grosmont Rd L32 40 F8
Grosomont Rd 1 L32 41 A8
Grosvenor Ave Crosby L23 26 E2
3 Golborne WA3 47 D8
West Kirby CH48 63 B2
Grosvenor Cl
Litherland L30 27 F3
Southport PR8 3 E3
Grosvenor Ct
1 Birkenhead CH43 66 B5
Liverpool L18 68 E3
Prescot L34 56 D6
Grosvenor Dr CH45 51 B8
Grosvenor Gdns
Newton-le-W WA12 46 C2
Southport PR8 3 F3
Grosvenor Pl
Birkenhead CH43 66 A5
Southport PR8 3 F3
Grosvenor Rd
Birkenhead CH43 66 B5
Haydock WA11 45 B7
Hoylake CH47 63 B6
Liverpool L15 68 E7
Liverpool,Cressington Pk
L19 81 A6
7 Liverpool,Walton on the Hill
L4 38 F2
Maghull L31 28 D7
Prescot L34 56 D6
Southport PR8 3 E4
St Helens WA10 43 D2
Wallasey CH45 51 B8
Widnes WA8 73 B5
Grosvenor St Liverpool L3 52 D3
Wallasey CH44 51 B4
Grove Ave CH60 76 F1
Grove Ho L8 68 C6
Grove Mans CH45 50 E6
Grove Mead L31 20 F1
Grove Park Ave L12 54 B8
Grove Pk Liverpool L8 68 C6
Ormskirk L39 13 F7
Southport PR9 4 F8
Grove Pl Hoylake CH47 63 B7
Liverpool L4 52 E7
Grove Rd Birkenhead CH42 66 F2
Hoylake CH47 63 B7
Liverpool L6 53 D3
Up Holland WN8 25 C8
Wallasey CH45 50 F7
Grove Side L7 68 A8
Grove Sq CH62 79 A7
Grove St Ashton-in-M WN4 35 A4
Bebington CH62 79 B7
Bootle L20 38 A4
Liverpool,Edge Hill L7,L8 68 A8
Liverpool,Wavertree L15 68 F8
Runcorn WA7 84 F3
Southport PR8 4 A4
Grove St Inf Sch CH62 79 B7
Grove Terr Hoylake CH47 63 B7
Southport PR8 4 A5
Grove The Bebington CH63 79 A5
Birkenhead CH43 66 B3
Golborne WA3 36 D1
Huyton-w-R L28 55 C7
Liverpool L13 53 F5
Ormskirk L39 21 C7
St Helens WA10 43 C5
Wallasey CH44 51 C3
Warrington WA5 74 F4
Grove Way L7 68 A8
Grovedale Dr CH46 50 A1
Grovedale Rd L18 68 F5
Grovehurst Ave L14 54 F4
Groveland Ave
Hoylake CH47 63 B7
Wallasey CH45 50 D6
Groveland Rd CH45 50 D6
Grovelands L7 68 A8
Groves The
Birkenhead CH43 66 A5
Kirkby L32 40 E7
Groveside CH48 63 A2
Grovewood Prescot L35 56 F3
Southport PR8 3 E5
Grovewood Ct CH43 66 B3
Grovewood Gdns L35 56 E3
Grundy Cl Southport PR8 4 E5
Widnes WA8 72 F3
Grundy St Golborne WA3 47 A7
Liverpool L5 52 C6
Guardian Ct CH48 63 B1
Guelph St L7 53 A2
Guernsey Rd Liverpool L13 54 A4
Widnes WA8 73 E3
Guffitt's Rake CH47 48 E1
Guffitts Cl CH47 48 E1
Guild Hey L34 41 D4
Guildford Ave L30 27 F1
Guildford Rd PR8 8 A8
Guildford St CH44 51 D4
Guildhall Rd L9 39 A6
Guillemot Way L26 70 E1
Guilsted Rd L11 40 A2
Guinea Gap CH44 51 E3
Guion Rd L21 38 B7
Guion St L6 53 B4
Gullivers World Theme Pk*
WA5 60 E1
Gulls Way CH60 85 E7
Gunning Ave WA10 43 B5
Gunning Cl WA10 43 B5
Gurnall St 13 L4 52 F7

Gutticar Rd WA8 72 B1
Gwendoline Cl CH61 77 A5
Gwendoline St L8 67 F6
Gwenfron Rd 10 L6 53 B3
Gwent Cl L6 53 B5
Gwent St L8 68 A6
Gwladys St L4 38 F1
Gwladys Street Prim Sch
L4 39 A1
Gwydir St L8 68 A5
Gwydrin Rd L18 69 C5

H

Hackett Ave L20 38 D6
Hackins Hey L2 90 A4
Hackthorpe St L5 52 E7
Hadassah Gr L17 68 C4
Hadden Cl L35 57 A4
Haddock St L20 38 B1
Haddon Ave L9 38 F6
Haddon Dr Heswall CH61 76 F4
Widnes WA8 72 C3
Haddon Rd
Birkenhead CH42 67 A2
Golborne WA3 36 D2
Haddon St 5 WN4 34 F5
Haddon Wlk L12 40 E3
Hadfield Ave CH47 63 B7
Hadfield Cl WA8 73 E2
Hadfield Gr L25 70 C3
Hadleigh Cl WA5 74 E5
Hadleigh Rd L32 29 F1
Hadley Ave CH62 79 C1
Hadstock Ave L37 9 D1
Hadwens Bldgs L3 90 A4
Haggerston Rd L4 39 A2
Hague Bush Cl WA3 36 E1
Hahnemann Rd L4 38 E2
Haig Ave Birkenhead CH46 64 F8
Southport PR8 4 E5
Haig Rd WA8 73 A1
Haigh Cres L31 20 C4
Haigh Ct PR8 4 F6
Haigh Rd L22 26 E1
Haigh St L3,L6 52 F3
Haileybury Ave L10 28 D2
Haileybury Rd L25 82 B8
Hailsham Rd L19 80 F8
Halby Rd L9 39 B6
Halcombe Rd L12 54 D7
Halcyon Rd CH41 66 C4
Haldane Ave CH41 65 F7
Haldane Rd L4 39 A2
Hale Bank Rd WA8 83 F5
Hale Bank Terr WA8 84 A4
Hale CE Prim Sch L24 83 E1
Hale Ct WA8 84 A4
Hale Dr L24 82 E2
Hale Gate Rd Hale WA8 83 F3
Widnes WA8 84 A3
Hale Gr WN4 34 F5
Hale Rd
Liverpool,Kirkdale L4 38 E1
Liverpool,Speke L24 82 C3
Liverpool,Speke L24 82 E2
Wallasey CH45 51 C6
Widnes WA8 84 C7
Widnes,Ditton WA8 84 C8
Hale Road Ind Est WA8 84 B4
Hale St L2 90 A4
Hale View Rd L36 56 A2
Halebank CE Prim Sch
WA8 84 A5
Halefield St WA10 43 F4
Halewood 'Triangle' Ctry Pk
L26 82 E8
Halewood Ave WA3 35 F1
Halewood CE Prim Sch
L26 71 A1
Halewood Cl L25 70 B4
Halewood Comp Sch L26 82 E7
Halewood Dr
Liverpool L25 70 B2
Liverpool L25 70 C2
Halewood Lane Ends
L26 83 A8
Halewood Pl L25 70 C3
Halewood Rd L25 70 C3
Halewood Sta L26 82 F8
Halewood Way L25 70 C2
Haley Rd N WA5 59 E6
Haley Rd S WA5 59 E5
Half Crown St L5 52 C6
Halfpenny Cl L19 81 B7
Halidon Ct L20 38 A4
Halifax Cl WA2 61 D2
Halifax Cres L23 27 B6
Halifax Rd PR8 7 C5
Halkirk Rd L18 69 C1
Halkyn Ave L17 68 D6
Halkyn Dr L5 53 A5
Hall Ave WA8 72 A1
Hall Brow Cl L39 14 B4
Hall Dr Birkenhead CH49 64 C2
Kirkby L32 29 E3
Hall Farm CH62 89 A4
Hall Gn WN8 25 B7
Hall Green Cl WN8 25 B7
Hall La Bickerstaffe L39 22 E4
Burtonwood WA5 60 B8
Cronton L35 72 C8
Huyton-w-R L36 56 A2
Ince Blundell L38 18 F3
Kirkby L32 29 E2
Kirkby,Simonswood L33 30 A8
Liverpool,Kensington L7 53 A2

Hall La *continued*
Liverpool,Walton L9 39 B6
Maghull L31 28 D8
Maghull,Lydiate L31 20 B7
Orrell WN5 25 F4
Prescot L34,L35 56 D5
Skelmersdale L40 15 A6
St Helens WA9 59 A4
Hall Nook WA5 74 F3
Hall Rd WA11 45 E7
Hall Rd E L23 26 B6
Hall Rd W L23 26 A6
Hall Road Sta L23 26 A6
Hall St Ashton-in-M WN2 35 E7
Southport PR9 4 C7
St Helens WA9 58 E3
St Helens,Pocket Nook
WA10,WA9 44 B4
Hall Terr WA5 74 E7
Hall Wood Ave WA11 34 F1
Hall's Cotts WA10 43 D6
Hallam Wlk 3 L7 53 C1
Hallbridge Gdns WN8 25 B8
Hallcroft WN8 16 C2
Hallfields Rd WA2 61 D1
Hallmoor Cl L39 13 E2
Hallows Ave WA2 61 D1
Hallsands Rd L32 40 E8
Hallside Cl L19 81 A8
Halltine Cl L23 26 A6
Hallville Rd L18 69 B5
Halsall Bldgs 6 PR9 4 C8
Halsall Cl L23 26 E5
Halsall Ct L39 13 D6
Halsall Gn CH63 79 B1
Halsall La Formby L37 9 F3
Haskayne L39 12 D6
Ormskirk L39 13 D6
Halsall Rd Bootle L20 38 C5
Southport PR8 8 A8
Halsall St L34 56 D7
Halsall's Cotts WA8 83 E5
Halsbury Rd Liverpool L6 53 C3
Wallasey CH45 51 B6
Halsey Ave L12 53 F7
Halsey Cres L12 53 F7
Halsnead Ave L35 56 C1
Halsnead Cl L13 54 A1
Halsnead Com Prim Sch
L35 56 D2
Halstead Rd Liverpool L9 38 F6
Wallasey CH44 51 C3
Halstead Wlk 5 L32 29 C1
Halton Chase L40 14 E4
Halton Cres CH49 64 B3
Halton Hey L35 56 D1
Halton Rd Maghull L31 20 D3
9 Wallasey CH45 51 A6
Warrington WA5 74 F6
Halton St WA11 45 E6
Halton View Rd WA8 73 C1
Halton Wlk L25 70 C6
Halton Wood L32 29 B3
Halville Rd CH44 51 C3
Halyard Ho CH60 76 C2
Hamble Dr 2 WA5 74 F3
Hambledon Dr CH49 64 D4
Hambleton Cl
Liverpool L11 40 B4
Widnes WA8 72 C3
Hamblett Cres WA11 44 B6
Hamblett Sch WA10 43 D6
Hamer Ho CH45 50 E5
Hamer St WA10 43 F4
Hamil Cl CH47 48 E1
Hamilton Cl CH64 86 B2
Hamilton Ct L23 26 B4
Hamilton La CH41 66 E7
Hamilton Rd
Garswood WN4 34 D4
Liverpool L5 52 F5
St Helens WA10 43 C6
Wallasey CH45 51 A8
Hamilton Sq CH41 66 F7
Hamilton Square Sta
CH41 66 F7
Hamilton St CH41 66 F6
Hamlet Ct L17 68 C3
Hamlet Rd CH45 50 F6
Hamlin Rd L19 81 D6
Hammersley Ave WA9 58 C3
Hammersley St WA9 58 C3
Hammill Ave WA10 43 E6
Hammill St WA10 43 D5
Hammond Rd L33 30 C3
Hammond St WA9 44 D2
Hamnett Rd L34 56 E7
Hampden Gr CH42 66 E4
Hampden Rd CH42 66 E4
Hampden St L4 38 F2
Hampshire Ave L30 27 C3
Hampshire Gdns WA10 43 F2
Hampson Cl WN4 35 B2
Hampson St L6 53 C5
Hampstead Rd
Liverpool L6 53 C4
Wallasey CH44 51 C3
Hampton Chase CH43 65 D3
Hampton Cl WA8 73 E3
Hampton Court Rd L12 54 D5
Hampton Dr WA8 72 C5
Hampton Pl WA11 44 B6
Hampton Rd Formby L37 9 E1
Southport PR8 4 C5
Hampton St L8 67 F7

Hanbury Rd L4 53 D8
Handel Ct L8 68 B6
Handel Rd L27 70 C6
Handfield Pl 5 L5 53 A5
Handfield Rd L22 26 E1
Handfield St L5 53 A5
Handford Ave CH62 88 F5
Handley Ct L19 80 F8
Handley St WA7 84 F3
Hands St L21 38 B6
Handsworth Wlk PR8 4 F3
Hanford Ave L9 38 F6
Hankey Dr L20 38 E5
Hankey St WA7 84 F2
Hankin St L5 52 D5
Hankinson St L13 54 A1
Hanley Cl WA8 72 C1
Hanley Rd WA8 72 C1
Hanlon Ave L20 38 D6
Hanmer Rd L32 29 B2
Hannah Cl CH61 76 E3
Hannan Rd L6 53 C3
Hanns Hall Rd CH64 87 D1
Hanover Cl CH43 65 F6
Hanover St L1 90 B3
Hans Rd 9 L4 39 A1
Hansard Ct WA9 57 D7
Hansby Cl WN8 24 E8
Hanson Pk CH43 65 E5
Hanson Rd L9 39 C5
Hanstock Cl WN5 25 E5
Hants La L39 13 E6
Hanwell St L6 53 B6
Hanworth Cl L12 40 E3
Hapsford Rd L21 38 B6
Hapton St L5 52 E6
Harbern Cl L12 54 D6
Harbord Rd L22 26 C1
Harbord St L7 53 B1
Harbord Terr L22 26 C1
Harborne Dr CH63 78 F2
Harbury Ave PR8 7 A4
Harcourt Ave CH44 51 E3
Harcourt St
Birkenhead CH41 66 C7
Liverpool L4 52 D7
Hard La WA10 43 E6
Hardacre St L39 13 F6
Hardie Ave CH46 49 C1
Hardie Cl WA9 58 A3
Hardie Rd L36 56 A3
Harding Ave
Bebington CH63 79 A4
Warrington WA2 61 E1
Harding Cl L5 53 A5
Hardinge Rd L19 81 D8
Hardknott Rd CH62 88 E8
Hardman St L1 90 C2
Hardshaw Ctr WA10 44 A3
Hardshaw St
St Helens WA10 44 A3
St Helens WA10 44 A4
Hardwick Rd WN4 35 A5
Hardy St Liverpool L1 90 B1
Liverpool L1 90 C2
Liverpool,Garston L19 81 D4
Hare Croft L28 54 F8
Harebell Cl L37 9 F1
Harebell St L5 52 D7
Harefield Gn L24 82 D3
Harefield Rd L24 82 D3
Hares La PR8 5 D1
Haresfinch Rd WA10, WA11 44 B6
Haresfinch View WA11 44 B6
Harewell Rd L11 40 A1
Harewood Ave PR8 7 C6
Harewood Cl L36 55 E3
Harewood Rd CH45 51 A7
Harewood St 3 L6 53 A4
Harford Cl WA5 74 F4
Hargate Rd L33 29 F2
Hargate Wlk 3 L33 29 F2
Hargrave Ave CH43 65 E3
Hargrave Cl CH43 65 E3
Hargrave La
Bebington CH64 88 A4
Thornton Hough CH63,CH64 87 F5
Hargreaves Ct WA8 73 D1
Hargreaves Rd L17 68 C3
Hargreaves St
Southport PR8 4 C6
St Helens WA9 44 E3
Harington Cl L37 9 D3
Harington Gn L37 9 D3
Harington Rd L37 9 D4
Harke St L7 68 B8
Harker St L3 52 E3
Harland Dr WN4 35 C3
Harland Gn L24 82 F3
Harland Rd CH42 66 D4
Harlech Cl WA5 60 E2
Harlech Ct CH63 78 F4
Harlech Rd L23 26 C3
Harlech St
Ashton-in-M WN4 34 F5
Liverpool L4 38 F1
Wallasey CH44 51 E2
Harleston Rd L33 30 A3
Harleston Wlk L33 30 A3
Harley Ave CH63 78 C8
Harley St 2 L9 39 A6
Harlian Ave CH46 64 D7
Harlow Cl WA9 57 F7
Harlow St L8 67 F4
Harlyn Cl L26 82 E6
Harlyn Gdns WA5 74 D3
Harmony Way L13 54 A1
Harold Ave WN4 35 A5
Harold Magnay Sch L25 69 F4
Harold Rd WA11 45 F7
Haroldene Gr L34 55 F5
Harp's Croft L30 27 C3
Harper Rd L9 39 A4
Harper St 3 L6,L7 53 A2
Harptree Cl L35 56 E3
Harradon Rd L9 39 B7
Harridge La L39 12 F8
Harrier Dr Liverpool L26 70 E1
Skelmersdale WN8 24 E8
Harrier Rd WA2 61 F2
Harringay Ave L18 68 F5
Harrington Ave CH47 63 C7
Harrington Rd Crosby L23 26 D4
Litherland L21 27 D1
Liverpool L3 67 E4
Harrington St L2 90 A3
Harris Cl CH63 79 A2
Harris Dr L20,L30 38 D7
Harris Gdns WA9 44 B1
Harris St St Helens WA10 43 E4
Widnes WA8 73 C1
Harrismith Rd L10 39 F6
Harrison Dr Bootle L20 38 E3
Haydock WA11 45 A6
Rainford WA11 31 F8
Wallasey CH45 50 E7
Harrison Hey L36 55 E1
Harrison Sq WA5 60 F1
Harrison St WA8 84 B6
Harrison Way Liverpool L3 67 E4
Newton-le-W WA12 46 C4
Harrock Wood Cl CH61 76 E6
Harrocks Cl L30 27 D5
Harrod Dr PR8 3 E3
Harrogate Cl
Bebington CH62 88 D4
Warrington WA5 60 A1
Harrogate Dr L5 52 F5
Harrogate Rd
Bebington CH62 88 D4
Bebington,Dacre Hill CH42 79 A8
Harrogate Way PR9 2 C6
Harrogate Wlk CH42 79 A8
Harrops Croft L30 27 E4
Harrow Cl Litherland L30 27 F2
Orrell WN5 25 F8
Wallasey CH44 50 F5
Harrow Dr L10 28 D2
Harrow Gr CH62 88 E8
Harrow Rd Liverpool L4 53 B6
Wallasey CH44 50 F5
Harrowby Cl L8 68 A7
Harrowby Rd
Birkenhead CH42 66 D4
Seaforth L21 37 F7
Wallasey CH44 51 E4
Harrowby Rd S CH42 66 C4
Harrowby St 4 L8 68 A7
Harsnips WN8 16 C2
Harswell Cl WN5 25 E5
Hart St Liverpool L3 90 C4
Southport PR8 4 E6
Hart's La WN8 24 F8
Hartdale Rd Crosby L23 27 B6
Liverpool L18 69 A4
Hartford Cl CH43 65 F3
Harthill Ave L18 69 B4
Harthill Mews CH43 50 C1
Harthill Rd L18 69 C4
Hartington Ave CH41 66 B7
Hartington Rd
Liverpool L8 68 C6
Liverpool,Garston L19 81 D6
Liverpool,Sandfield Pk L12 54 C6
St Helens WA10 43 D5
Wallasey CH44 51 B4
Hartington Terr L19 81 B6
Hartismere Rd CH44 51 D3
Hartland WN8 16 C2
Hartland Ave PR9 2 B5
Hartland Cl WA8 73 A5
Hartland Gdns WA9 57 D6
Hartland Rd L11 39 E2
Hartley Ave L9 39 B5
Hartley Cl 4 L4 52 F7
Hartley Cres PR8 3 F2
Hartley Ct L14 54 D2
Hartley Gr Kirkby L33 29 F5
St Helens WA10 57 C8
Hartley Quay L3 90 A2
Hartley Rd PR8 3 F2
Hartnup St
Liverpool,Anfield L5 53 A6
Liverpool,Everton L5 52 F6
Harton Cl WA8 72 E3
Hartopp Rd L25 70 A6
Hartopp Wlk L25 70 A7
Hartsbourne Ave L25 70 A6
Hartsbourne Cl L25 69 F7
Hartsbourne Wlk L25 70 A7
Hartshead WN8 16 C2
Hartswell Cl WA3 36 A2
Hartwell St L21 38 B6
Hartwood Cl 5 L32 41 A7
Hartwood Rd Kirkby L32 40 F7
Southport PR9 4 D7
Hartwood Sq L32 40 F7
Harty Rd WA11 45 A5
Harvard Cl WA2 61 A3
Harvard Gr L34 56 E7
Harvest La CH46 49 D1
Harvest Way 10 WA9 58 C4
Harvester Way
Birkenhead CH49 64 C4
Litherland L30 28 A4
Harvey Ave
Birkenhead CH49 64 D3
Newton-le-W WA12 45 F3
Harvey Ct Golborne WA3 36 A1
Warrington WA2 61 B3
Harvey La WA3 35 F1
Harvey Rd Wallasey CH46 50 A2
Wallasey,Liscard CH45 51 A6
Harvington Dr PR8 7 B5
Harwich Gr L16 69 F8
Harwood Rd L19 81 D6
Haselbeech Cl L11 39 F3
Haselbeech Cres L11 39 F3
Haseldine St WN4 34 F6
Hasfield Rd L11 40 B2
Haslam Dr L39 13 D7
Haslemere L35 56 F3
Haslemere Dr WA5 74 D4
Haslemere Ind Est WN4 35 A8
Haslemere Rd L25 70 B6
Haslemere Way L25 70 B6
Haslingden Cl L13 54 B2
Haslington Gr L26 83 A6
Hassal Rd CH42 79 A8
Hastie Cl L27 70 E5
Hastings Ave WA2 61 B4
Hastings Dr L36 71 A8
Hastings Rd Crosby L22 26 B2
Southport PR8 3 E1
Haswell Dr L28 55 B8
Hatchmere Cl CH43 65 F3
Hatfield Cl
2 Liverpool L12 41 A3
St Helens WA9 57 F7
Hatfield Gdns L36 55 F1
Hatfield Rd Bootle L20 38 E3
Southport PR8 7 C6
Hathaway L31 28 B7
Hathaway Cl L25 70 A6
Hathaway Rd L25 70 A6
Hatherley Ave L22,L23 26 E2
Hatherley Cl 3 L8 68 A7
Hatherley St Liverpool L8 68 A7
Wallasey CH44 51 E2
Hathersage Rd L36 55 F5
Hatherton Gr L26 83 A6
Hatton Ave CH62 88 E3
Hatton Cl CH60 76 D1
Hatton Garden Ind Est L3 90 B4
Hatton Gdn L1,L2,L3 90 B4
Hatton Hill Prim Sch L21 27 B2
Hatton Hill Rd L21 27 A1
Hattons La L16 69 C6
Hauxwell Gr WA11 44 B6
Havannah La WA9 45 B3
Havelock Cl WA10 43 F3
Haven Brow L39 21 C8
Haven Rd L10 39 F8
Haven Wlk L31 20 C4
Havergal St 3 WA7 84 F1
Haverstock Rd L6 53 D3
Haverton Wlk L12 40 E3
Haverty Prec WA12 46 B1
Hawarde Cl WA12 46 A4
Hawarden Ave
Birkenhead CH43 66 C6
Liverpool L17 68 E6
Wallasey CH44 51 C4
Hawarden Ct CH63 78 F4
Hawarden Gr L21 38 A6
Hawdon Ct 9 L7 68 C8
Hawes Ave WA11 44 C8
Hawes Cres WN4 35 B5
Hawesside St PR9 4 C7
Haweswater Ave WA11 45 A6
Haweswater Cl L33 29 D5
Haweswater Gr L31 20 F2
Hawgreen Rd L32 29 B1
Hawick Cl L33 29 D6
Hawke Gn L36 71 A7
Hawke St L3 90 C3
Hawker Dr WN8 24 E8
Hawkesworth St 8 L4 53 A6
Hawkhurst Cl 1 L8 67 F4
Hawkins Rd CH64 86 F1
Hawkins St L6 53 C3
Hawks Way CH60 85 E8
Hawksclough WN8 16 D2
Hawkshead Ave L12 40 C1
Hawkshead Cl L31 20 E2
Hawkshead Dr L21 38 D8
Hawkshead Rd
Bebington CH62 79 E1
Burtonwood WA5 59 E6
Hawkshead St PR8,PR9 4 D7
Hawksmoor Cl L10 40 A7
Hawksmoor Rd L10 40 A7
Hawksmore Cl CH49 64 D6
Hawkstone St L8 68 A5
Hawksworth Cl L37 10 A6
Hawksworth Dr L37 10 A6
Hawley's Cl WA5 60 F1
Hawley's La WA2,WA5 61 A1
Haworth Dr L20 38 D7
Hawthorn Ave
Downall Green WN4 34 D5
Newton-le-W WA12 46 D3
Orrell WN5 25 F6
1 Widnes WA8 73 B2
Hawthorn Cl WN5 33 D5
Hawthorn Cotts CH60 85 F8
Hawthorn Cres WN8 15 E1
Hawthorn Dr
Heswall CH61 76 F2
Hawthorn Dr continued
St Helens WA10 43 B4
West Kirby CH48 63 E2
Hawthorn Gr 5 L7 53 B1
Hawthorn Rd
Huyton-w-R L36 55 C2
Neston CH64 86 C1
Prescot L34 56 E6
Hawthorne Ave
Liverpool L26 82 F6
Warrington WA5 74 F6
Hawthorne Cl WA11 45 A5
Hawthorne Cres L37 10 A2
Hawthorne Dr CH64 88 B1
Hawthorne Gr
Southport PR9 4 F7
Wallasey CH44 51 E2
Hawthorne La CH62 88 D8
Hawthorne Rd
Birkenhead CH42 66 D3
Bootle L20,L21,L70 38 D5
St Helens WA9 58 D6
Hawthorns Gr L12 54 B6
Haxted Gdns L19 81 D6
Haydn Rd L14 54 F6
Haydock High Sch WA11 45 C6
Haydock La
Ashton-in-M WA11 34 E1
Haydock WA11 45 C7
Haydock La Ind Est WA11 45 E8
Haydock Lane Ind Est WA11 34 E1
Haydock Park Gdns WA12 35 B1
Haydock Park Race Course WA12 35 D1
Haydock Park Rd L10 28 E3
Haydock Rd CH45 51 C7
Haydock St
Ashton-in-M WN4 35 B2
Newton-le-W WA12 46 A3
St Helens WA10 44 A3
Hayes Ave L35 56 E5
Hayes Dr L31 29 B3
Hayes St WA10 57 C8
Hayfield Cl L26 71 A1
Hayfield Rd L39 13 E7
Hayfield Sch CH49 65 A6
Hayfield St 14 L4 52 F7
Hayfield Way 8 WA9 58 C4
Hayles Cl L25 70 A6
Hayles Gn L25 70 A6
Hayles Gr L25 70 A6
Haylock Cl L8 67 F4
Hayman's Cl L12 54 A7
Hayman's Gn L12 54 A7
Hayman's Gr L12 54 A7
Haymans Gn L31 20 E1
Haymarket Lodge PR9 1 D1
Hayscastle Cl WA5 60 E1
Haywood Cl WA3 36 E1
Haywood Gdns WA10 43 D2
Hazel Ave Kirkby L32 29 C3
Prescot L35 56 E4
Hazel Ct 12 Liverpool L8 68 A4
Ormskirk L39 13 E5
Hazel Gr Bebington CH63 78 E4
Crosby L23 26 F3
Golborne WA3 47 B8
Irby CH61 76 D7
Liverpool L9 39 B6
Southport PR8 4 E7
St Helens WA10 43 C3
Hazel La WN8 16 B4
Hazel Mews L31 29 B3
Hazel Rd Birkenhead CH41 66 D5
Hoylake CH47 63 B7
Huyton-w-R L36 55 F5
Hazelbank Gdns L37 9 E5
Hazeldale Rd L9 39 A4
Hazeldene Ave
Heswall CH61 77 B6
Wallasey CH45 51 A5
Hazeldene Way CH61 77 B7
Hazelfield Ct 2 WA9 58 C4
Hazelhurst Rd L4 53 B7
Hazelmere Ho L17 68 D2
Hazelslack Rd L11 40 A2
Hazelwood
Birkenhead CH49 64 D5
Southport PR8 3 F1
Hazelwood Cl
St Helens WA9 58 B3
Widnes WA8 84 A8
Hazelwood Gr L26 70 D2
Hazlehurst Cl L37 9 C2
Hazlehurst Gr WN4 35 C4
Hazleton Rd L14 54 C3
Head St L8 67 E6
Headbolt La Kirkby L33 29 F4
Southport L39 8 A4
Headbourne Cl L25 69 F7
Headbourne Ct L25 69 F7
Headingley Cl
Huyton-w-R L36 70 C8
St Helens WA9 58 C6
Headingly Ave WN8 15 D1
Headington Rd CH49 64 D5
Headland Cl
Golborne WA3 47 E6
West Kirby CH48 75 B8
Headley Cl WA10 43 F3
Headworth Gdns WA9 57 D6
Heald St WA12 45 F3
Heales Fold PR9 2 D5
Healy Cl L27 71 A4
Heanor Dr PR8 4 F3
Hearne Rd WA10 43 D4
Heartwood Cl L9 39 A7
Heath Cl Liverpool L25 69 F5
Prescot L34 56 F7
West Kirby CH48 75 B8
Heath Dale CH63 78 F3
Heath Dr Birkenhead CH49 65 A6
Heswall CH60 76 F1
Heath Hey L25 69 F5
Heath La Golborne WA3 47 F2
Willaston CH64 88 C1
Heath Rd
Ashton-in-M WN4 35 C2
Bebington CH63 78 F5
Huyton-w-R L36 55 B5
Liverpool L19,L18 81 D8
Warrington WA5 74 F5
Widnes WA8 72 D2
Heath St Ashton-in-M WN4 35 C2
Golborne WA3 47 A8
St Helens WA9 57 D7
Heath View L21 27 B3
Heathbank Ave Irby CH61 76 D7
Wallasey CH44 51 A3
Heathbank Rd CH42 66 D3
Heathcliff Ho L4 39 B1
Heathcote Cl 1 L7 68 C8
Heathcote Gdns CH63 78 F5
Heathcote Rd L4 38 F2
Heather Bank CH63 78 D6
Heather Brae
Huyton-w-R L34 56 A5
Newton-le-W WA12 46 A4
Heather Brow CH43 65 F7
Heather Cl Formby L37 10 B5
Kirkby L33 29 E4
Liverpool L4 52 F8
Southport PR8 7 D2
Heather Ct L4 52 F8
Heather Dene CH62 79 D2
Heather Gr WN4 35 E4
Heather Rd
Bebington CH63 78 D4
Heswall CH60 77 A1
Heather Way L23 27 C6
Heatherdale Cl CH42 66 C4
Heatherdale Rd L18 69 A4
Heatherdene Rd CH48 63 B3
Heatherlea Cl WN8 25 C7
Heatherleigh
St Helens WA9 57 D6
West Kirby CH48 75 D6
Heatherleigh Cl L9 39 A7
Heathers Croft L30 27 E3
Heatherways L37 10 A6
Heathey La PR8 8 F8
Heathfield Ave WA9 57 E8
Heathfield Cl Bootle L21 38 C6
Formby L37 10 A6
Heathfield Dr L33 29 E4
Heathfield Ho CH61 77 A6
Heathfield Pk WA8 72 D3
Heathfield Rd
Bebington CH63 78 F4
Birkenhead CH43 66 C4
Crosby L22 26 C2
Liverpool L15,L18 69 B6
Maghull L31 28 F7
Southport PR8 7 F6
Heathfield St L1 90 C3
Heathgate WN8 16 C2
Heathgate Ave L24 83 A2
Heathland Rd WA9 58 C4
Heathlands The CH46 49 E3
Heathmoor Ave WA3 47 D6
Heathmoor Rd CH46 49 D1
Heathside CH60 76 D1
Heathview Cl WA8 84 A5
Heathview Rd WA8 84 A5
Heathwaite Cres L11 40 A1
Heathway CH60 86 B7
Heathwood L12 54 B5
Heathy La L39 11 B8
Heatley Cl CH43 65 C7
Heaton Cl Liverpool L24 82 F3
Up Holland WN8 25 A7
Hebburn Way L12 41 A3
Hebden Par 3 L11 40 C3
Hebden Rd L11 40 B3
Hebdon Cl WN4 35 A5
Hedgebank Cl L9 39 D8
Hedgecote L32 40 E7
Hedgecroft L23 27 C6
Hedgefield Rd L25 70 B6
Hedgerows The WA11 45 F7
Hedges Cres L13 53 E7
Hedingham Cl L26 71 A1
Helen Bank Dr WA11 31 F7
Helen St Ashton-in-M WN4 35 A4
Golborne WA3 35 F1
Helena Rd WA9 58 F7
Helena St
Birkenhead CH41 66 E5
Liverpool,Walton L9 38 F3
11 Liverpool,Wavertree L7 53 B1
Helford Cl L35 57 A6
Helford Rd L11 40 D5
Heliers Rd L13 54 B2
Hell Nook WA3 35 F1
Helmdon Cl 2 L11 40 A1
Helmingham Gr CH41 66 E4
Helmsdale WN8 16 C2
Helmsley Rd L26 82 F7
Helsby Ave CH62 88 F3
Helsby Rd L9 39 B7
Helsby St Liverpool L7 53 A1
St Helens WA9 44 E1
Helston Ave Liverpool L26 70 F1

Helston Ave *continued*
St Helens WA11 44 D7
Helston Cl Southport PR9 2 B5
Warrington WA5 74 E5
Helston Gn L36 56 B3
Helston Rd L11 40 D5
Helton Cl CH43 65 E3
Hemans St L20 38 A4
Hemer Terr L20 38 A5
Hemingford St CH41 66 D6
Hemlock Cl L12 40 D3
Hemmingsway L35 57 A3
Hempstead Cl WA9 57 F7
Henderson Cl
Birkenhead CH49 64 E6
Warrington WA5 74 D6
Henderson Dr WA11 32 A8
Henderson Rd
Huyton-w-R L36 56 A3
2 Widnes WA8 73 A1
Widnes,Lower House WA8 84 F8
Hendon Rd L6 53 D4
Hendon Wlk CH49 64 C3
Hengest Cl L33 29 E6
Henglers Cl 7 L6 53 A3
Henley Ave L21 38 A8
Henley Cl CH63 79 A2
Henley Ct Southport PR9 1 E1
St Helens WA10 43 D1
Henley Dr PR9 1 F1
Henley Rd L18 69 B5
Henllan Gdns WA9 58 F7
Henlow Ave L32 40 F8
Hennawood Cl 5 L6 53 B5
Henrietta Gr L34 55 F5
Henry Edward St L3 52 D3
Henry Hickman Cl L30 27 F4
Henry St Birkenhead CH41 66 E6
Liverpool L1 90 B2
Liverpool,Stanley L13 53 F2
St Helens WA10 43 F4
4 Widnes WA8 73 C1
Henthorne Rd CH62 79 B8
Henthorne St CH43 66 C5
Hepworth Cl WN3 35 F2
Herald Ave L24 81 F6
Herald Cl L11 40 C3
Herald St L19 81 C6
Heralds Cl WA8 84 C8
Heralds Gn WA5 60 A2
Herbarth Cl L9 38 F3
Herbert St
Burtonwood WA5 59 E6
St Helens WA9 58 F7
Herbert Taylor Cl L6 53 C5
Herberts La CH60 85 F8
Herculaneum Ct L8 67 F3
Herculaneum Rd L8 67 E4
Herdman Cl L25 70 B5
Hereford Ave
Birkenhead CH49 64 E6
Golborne WA3 47 B8
Hereford Cl
Ashton-in-M WN4 35 C2
St Helens WA10 43 F2
Hereford Dr L30 27 F1
Hereford Gr WN8 25 B6
Hereford Rd Liverpool L15 69 A6
Seaforth L21 37 F7
Southport PR9 4 F7
Heriot St L5 52 D6
Heriot Wlk L5 52 D6
Herm Rd L5 52 C5
Hermes Cl L30 38 E8
Hermes Rd L11 40 C6
Hermitage Gr L20 38 D6
Hermitage Green La
WA2,WA12 61 A8
Hermitage The CH60 85 F7
Hero St L20 38 D2
Heron Ct L26 70 E1
Heron Gr WA11 32 B5
Heron Rd CH47,CH48 64 A6
Herondale Rd L18 69 A5
Heronhall Rd L9 39 F4
Heronpark Way CH63 79 B2
Herons Ct L31 20 B4
Herrick St L13 53 F3
Herschell St L5 53 A6
Hertford Dr CH45 51 C6
Hertford Rd L20 38 C2
Hertford St WA9 44 D2
Hesketh Ave CH42 66 D1
Hesketh Cl WA5 74 F4
Hesketh Ct WA11 32 A4
Hesketh Dr Heswall CH60 77 A1
Maghull L31 20 F1
Southport PR9 1 F1
Hesketh Grange Cotts
CH63 87 A7
Hesketh Links Ct PR9 1 E2
Hesketh Lo L37 9 E3
Hesketh Meadow La
WA3 47 F8
Hesketh Rd Hale L24 83 E2
Southport PR9 1 D2
Hesketh St 5 L17 68 C4
Heskin Cl Kirkby L32 40 E7
Maghull L31 20 D4
Rainhill L35 57 B3
Heskin Hall Ct L39 13 D8
Heskin La L39 13 D8
Heskin Rd L32 40 E7
Heskin Wlk L32 40 E7
Hessle Dr CH60 85 F7
Hester Cl L38 17 F4
Heswall Ave
Bebington CH63 78 C8
Heswall Ave *continued*
St Helens WA9 58 B4
Heswall Mount CH61 77 A5
Heswall Prep Sch CH60 76 F2
Heswall Prim Sch CH60 77 A1
Heswall Rd L9 39 B7
Heswall Sta CH60 86 D8
Hetherlow Twrs L4 39 A3
Hever Dr L26 71 A1
Heversham WN8 16 C2
Heward Ave 1 WA9 58 C6
Hewitson Ave L13 53 F6
Hewitson Rd L13 53 F6
Hewitt Ave WA10 43 D4
Hewitt Bsns Pk WN5 25 E4
Hewitt's La L33,L34 41 E7
Hewitts Pl 8 L2 90 A4
Hexagon The 1 L20 38 C3
Hexham Cl Litherland L30 28 A1
St Helens WA9 57 D6
Hey Green Rd L15 68 E8
Hey Lock Cl WA12 60 C8
Hey Pk L36 55 F2
Hey Rd L36 55 F2
Hey Wood Cl WA12 60 C8
Heyburn Rd L13 53 E6
Heydale Rd L18 69 A4
Heydean Rd L18 69 C1
Heydean Wlk L18 69 C1
Heydon Cl L37 9 D1
Heyes Ave Haydock WA11 45 D5
Rainford WA11 32 A6
Heyes Dr CH45 50 C4
Heyes Gr WA11 32 A6
Heyes Mount L35 57 C2
Heyes Rd Orrell WN5 25 E6
Widnes WA8 84 C8
Heyes St L5 53 A5
Heyes The L25 70 B2
Heyescroft L39 22 D6
Heygarth Dr CH49 64 D4
Heygarth Prim Sch CH62 88 E5
Heygarth Rd CH62 88 E5
Heygreen Com Prim Sch
L15 68 E8
Heys Ave CH62 88 D8
Heys The Bebington CH62 88 F5
Southport PR8 3 D4
Heyscroft Rd L25 70 B2
Heysham Lawn L27 71 A4
Heysham Rd
Litherland L30,L9 28 A2
Liverpool L27 71 A3
Southport PR9 4 F7
Heysmoor Hts 6 L8 68 B6
Heysome Cl WA11 32 E4
Heythrop Dr CH60 86 D8
Heyville Rd CH63 78 E5
Heywood Ave WA3 36 B1
Heywood Bvd CH61 77 A6
Heywood Cl Formby L37 9 E3
Heswall CH61 77 A6
Heywood Ct L15 54 C1
Heywood Gdns
Golborne WA3 36 B1
Prescot L35 56 E2
Heywood Rd L15 69 C8
Heyworth St L5 52 F5
Hickmans Rd CH41,CH44 51 B1
Hickory Gr L31 29 A2
Hicks Rd Crosby L22 26 E1
Seaforth L21 38 A7
Hickson Ave L31 20 C3
High Bank Cl CH43 65 D5
High Beeches L16 54 F1
High Beeches Cres WN4 35 A6
High Carrs L36 55 B8
High Clere Cres L36 55 E5
High La Bickerstaffe L39 22 C8
Ormskirk L39,L40 14 A8
High Moss L39 13 E3
High Mount CH60 85 F8
High Park Pl PR9 5 A8
High Park Rd PR9 5 A8
High Park St L8 68 A5
High St Bebington CH62 79 E1
Golborne WA3 47 A8
Hale L24 83 D1
Liverpool L2 90 A4
Liverpool,Wavertree L15 68 F8
Liverpool,Woolton L25 70 A2
Newton-le-W WA12 46 D4
Prescot L34 56 D6
Runcorn WA7 84 F2
Skelmersdale WN8 15 E1
Highacre Rd CH45 51 A7
Higham Ave
St Helens WA10 42 F3
Warrington WA5 60 F1
Higham Sq 4 L5 52 E4
Highbank Dr L19 81 E6
Highbanks L31 20 C3
Highcroft Ave CH63 79 A5
Highcroft Gn CH63 79 A5
Highcroft The CH63 78 F5
Higher Ashton WA8 72 F3
Higher Bebington Jun Sch
CH63 78 D6
Higher Bebington Rd
CH63 78 E5
Higher End Pk L30 27 E5
Higher La Liverpool L9 39 D6
Rainford WA11 32 C5
Skelmersdale WN8 16 C7
Up Holland WN8 25 E7
Higher Moss La L37 11 A2
Higher Parr St WA9 44 C3
Higher Rd
Liverpool L26,WA8 83 C5
Liverpool,Speke L25,L26 82 E7
Higher Side Com Comp Sch
L35 56 F3
Higher View WN8 25 C6
Highfield L33 29 F5
Highfield Ave WA3 46 F8
Highfield Cl CH44 51 A4
Highfield Cres
Birkenhead CH42 66 F1
Widnes WA8 73 A2
Highfield Ct CH42 66 F1
Highfield Dr
Birkenhead CH49 64 D4
Crank WA11 32 E4
Highfield Gr
Birkenhead CH42 66 F1
Crosby L23 26 F5
Highfield La
Golborne WA3 47 C5
Winwick WA2 61 C7
Highfield Pk L31 20 F1
Highfield Rd
Birkenhead CH42 66 F1
Litherland L21 38 A8
Liverpool,Stonycroft L13 54 A4
Liverpool,Walton L9 38 F4
Ormskirk L39 13 E7
Southport PR9 2 B3
Widnes WA8 73 A2
Highfield S CH42 79 A8
Highfield Sch
Birkenhead CH43 65 F6
Liverpool L26 83 A7
Highfield St
Liverpool L2,L3 90 A4
St Helens WA9 58 D8
Highfield View L13 54 A4
Highfields Heswall CH60 76 F1
Prescot L34 56 C6
Highgate Cl CH60 76 F2
Highgate Ct 13 L7 53 B1
Highgate Rd Maghull L31 20 D3
Up Holland WN8 25 B7
Highgate St L7 53 A1
Highgreen Rd CH42 66 C3
Highgrove Pk L19 81 A8
Highlands Rd WA7 84 F1
Highmarsh Cres WA12 46 B4
Highmeadow WN8 25 A6
Highoaks Rd L25 70 B1
Highpark Rd CH42 66 C3
Highsted Gr L33 29 F5
Hightor Rd L25 69 F3
Hightown Sta L38 18 A4
Highville Rd L16 69 D6
Highwood Ct L33 29 F4
Highwoods Cl WN4 35 B5
Higson Ct L8 68 A3
Hilary Ave Golborne WA3 36 D1
Huyton-w-R L14 54 F2
Hilary Cl Liverpool L4 53 C8
Prescot L34 56 E7
Warrington WA5 74 D6
Widnes WA8 73 E3
Hilary Dr CH49 65 A6
Hilary Mans CH44 51 A4
Hilary Rd L4 53 C8
Hilberry Ave L13 53 E5
Hilbre Ave Heswall CH60 85 E6
Wallasey CH44 51 A4
Hilbre Cl PR9 1 F1
Hilbre Ct CH48 63 A1
Hilbre Dr PR9 1 F1
Hilbre High Sch CH48 63 D3
Hilbre Island Nature
Reserve★ CH47 62 B4
Hilbre Point CH47 62 F5
Hilbre Rd CH48 63 B1
Hilbre St Birkenhead CH41 66 D8
Liverpool L3 90 C3
Hilbre View CH48 63 C2
Hilcrest Rd L4 39 D1
Hilda Rd L12 54 E5
Hildebrand Cl L4 53 C8
Hildebrand Rd L4 53 C8
Hilden Rd WA2 61 E1
Hill Crest L20 38 E2
Hill Gr CH46 64 E7
Hill Rd CH43 65 E6
Hill Ridge CH43 65 D5
Hill Rise View L39 13 A1
Hill School Rd WA10 57 A8
Hill St Crosby L23 26 F3
Liverpool L8 67 D6
Liverpool L8 67 E6
7 Prescot L34 56 D6
Southport PR9 4 B7
St Helens WA10 44 A5
Hill Top La CH60 86 B8
Hill Top Rd WA11 32 B2
Hill View WA8 72 F5
Hill View Dr CH49 65 A6
Hillam Rd CH45 50 D6
Hillary Cres L31 20 D1
Hillary Dr L23 27 A4
Hillary Rd CH62 88 E5
Hillary Wlk L23 27 A4
Hillbark Rd CH48,CH49 64 B1
Hillbeck Cres WN4 34 D4
Hillbrae Ave WA11 33 A1
Hillburn Dr CH41 50 E1
Hillcrest Maghull L31 20 F1
Skelmersdale WN8 24 B8
Hillcrest Ave L36 56 A2
Hillcrest Dr CH49 64 C3
Hillcrest Par L36 56 A2
Hillcrest Rd Crosby L23 27 A4
Ormskirk L39 13 E6
Hillcroft Rd Liverpool L25 69 F4
Wallasey CH44 51 C2
Hilldean WN8 25 C8
Hillerton Cl L12 40 B2
Hillfield Dr CH61 76 F3
Hillfoot Ave L25 82 C7
Hillfoot Cl CH43 65 C8
Hillfoot Gn L25 82 A7
Hillfoot Rd L25 82 A8
Hillhead Rd L20 38 E2
Hillingden Ave L26 82 F7
Hillingdon Ave CH61 76 F2
Hillingdon Rd L15 69 B6
Hillock La WN8 16 D7
Hills Moss Rd WA9 58 F7
Hills Pl L15 69 A7
Hillside Ave
Ashton-in-M WN4 34 F8
Huyton-w-R L36 55 D6
Newton-le-W WA12 45 F2
Ormskirk L39 13 D3
St Helens WA10 43 E6
Hillside Cl Billinge WN5 33 D5
Birkenhead CH41 66 E4
Bootle L20 38 E2
Hillside Com Prim Sch
WN8 24 D8
Hillside Cres L36 55 D6
Hillside Ct
Birkenhead CH41 66 E4
Liverpool L25 70 B3
Hillside Ct Flats L25 70 B2
Hillside Dr L25 70 B3
Hillside Gr WA5 74 F4
Hillside High Sch L20 38 E3
Hillside Prim Sch CH43 65 D5
Hillside Rd
Birkenhead CH43 65 D8
Birkenhead,Tranmere CH41 66 E4
Heswall CH60 86 A7
Huyton-w-R L36 55 E5
Liverpool L18 69 B5
Southport PR8 3 E1
Wallasey CH44 50 F4
West Kirby CH48 63 D2
Hillside St L6 52 F3
Hillside Sta PR8 3 E1
Hillside View CH43 66 A3
Hillsview Rd PR8 7 C4
Hilltop Rd L16 69 D7
Hilltop Wlk L39 13 C3
Hillview L17 68 E2
Hillview Ave CH48 63 B3
Hillview Ct CH43 65 C8
Hillview Gdns L25 69 F3
Hillview Mans CH48 63 B3
Hillview Rd CH61 76 C7
Hillwood Cl CH63 79 A1
Hilton Cl CH41 66 D6
Hilton Ct L30 27 D4
Hilton Gr CH48 63 A3
Hilton St WN4 35 C3
Hinchley Gn L31 20 B1
Hinckley Rd WA11 44 C6
Hind St CH41 66 E5
Hindburn Ave L31 20 F2
Hinderton Dr
Heswall CH60 85 F6
West Kirby CH48 63 E1
Hinderton La CH64 87 A1
Hinderton Rd
Birkenhead CH41 66 E5
Neston CH64 87 B1
Hindle Ave WA5 60 F1
Hindley Beech 1 L31 20 C2
Hindley Wlk L24 82 D2
Hindlip St 4 L8 68 A3
Hinson St 6 CH41 66 E6
Hinton St Bootle L21 38 B6
Liverpool L6 53 C3
Historic Warship Mus★
CH44 51 D1
HM Customs & Exise National
Mus★ L3 90 A2
Hobart Dr L33 29 E6
Hobart St WA9 57 E8
Hoblyn Rd CH43 65 E8
Hockenhall Alley L2 90 A4
Hockenhull Cl CH63 79 A2
Hodder Ave L31 20 F2
Hodder Cl WA11 44 B7
Hodder Rd L5 52 F6
Hodder St L5 52 F6
Hodge St PR8 4 B7
Hodgkinson Ave WA5 60 F1
Hodnet Dr WN4 35 C3
Hodson Pl L6 53 A4
Hodson St PR8 4 C6
Hogarth Dr CH43 65 D3
Hogarth St 3 L21 38 A6
Hogarth Wlk L4 52 D8
Hoggs Hill La L37 9 F1
Hoghton Cl WA9 58 F8
Hoghton Gr PR9 4 C8
Hoghton Pl 3 PR9 4 B7
Hoghton Rd Hale L24 83 E2
St Helens WA9 58 F7
Hoghton St PR9 4 C7
Holbeck St L4 53 C7
Holborn Ct WA8 72 F3
Holborn Dr L39 13 C3
Holborn Hill
Birkenhead CH41 66 E4
Ormskirk L39 13 C4
Holborn Sq CH41 66 E4
Holborn St L7 53 A2
Holbrook Cl
St Helens WA9 58 C6
Warrington WA5 74 E5
Holcombe Ave WA3 47 C8
Holcombe Cl CH49 64 D4
Holden Gr L22 26 C2
Holden Rd Crosby L22 26 C2
Prescot L35 56 C4
Holden Rd E L22 26 C2
Holden St L8 68 A8
Holden Terr L22 26 C2
Holdsworth St L7 53 B2
Holford Way WA12 46 F3
Holgate L23,L29 27 B7
Holgate Dr WN5 25 E6
Holgate Pk L23 27 B7
Holin Ct CH43 66 A7
Holkham Cl WA8 72 F1
Holkham Gdns WA9 57 D6
Holland Bsns Pk L40 15 C4
Holland Ct Litherland L30 27 D4
Skelmersdale WN8 24 D2
Holland Gr CH60 76 F1
Holland Moor Prim Sch
WN8 24 E7
Holland Moss WN8 24 A5
Holland Pl 4 L7 53 B1
Holland Rd
Liverpool,Halewood L26 82 E6
Liverpool,Speke L24 82 E2
Wallasey CH45 51 C7
Holland St L7 53 D3
Holland Way L26 82 E6
Holland's La WN8 15 A1
Holley Ct L35 57 C3
Holliers Cl L31 20 E1
Hollies Rd L26 82 F8
Hollies The Liverpool L25 69 E3
Southport PR8 3 F6
Hollin Hey Cl WN5 33 D3
Hollingbourne Pl L11 40 A3
Hollingbourne Rd L11 40 A3
Hollinghurst Rd L33 29 F5
Hollingwood Cl WN4 35 A3
Hollingworth Cl L9 39 B3
Hollinhey Cl L30 28 A5
Hollins Cl Garswood WN4 34 D4
Liverpool L15 69 A8
Hollins Dr WA2 61 A6
Hollins La WA2 60 E6
Hollins Park Hospl WA2 60 F6
Hollins Way WA8 84 B5
Hollocombe Rd L12 40 B2
Hollow Croft L28 41 B1
Holloway WA7 84 F1
Holly Ave Bebington CH63 78 F3
Newton-le-W WA12 46 D3
Holly Bank Ct L18 69 C5
Holly Bank Gr WA9 44 C4
Holly Cl Hale L24 83 D2
Skelmersdale WN8 15 E1
St Helens WA10 43 B4
Westhead L40 14 E4
Holly Cres WA11 32 A5
Holly Ct L20 38 B5
Holly Farm Ct WA8 72 E4
Holly Farm Rd L19 81 D6
Holly Fold La L39,WA11 23 E3
Holly Gr Birkenhead CH42 66 E4
Huyton-w-R L36 55 B2
Seaforth L21 37 F6
Holly Hey L35 56 D1
Holly La Ormskirk L39 13 B4
Skelmersdale L39,WA11 23 E4
Holly Lodge Girls Coll
L13 53 F5
Holly Lodge Girls' Coll
L13 54 A6
Holly Mount Liverpool L12 54 A6
St Helens WA10 43 D2
Holly Pl CH46 64 F7
Holly Rd Golborne WA3 47 C8
Haydock WA11 45 A6
Liverpool L7 53 D2
Warrington WA5 74 E5
Holly St L20 38 C4
Holly Terr WA5 74 F5
Hollybank Ct
5 Birkenhead CH41 66 D5
Widnes WA8 72 F1
Hollybank Rd
Birkenhead CH41 66 D5
Liverpool L18 68 E5
Hollybrook Rd PR8 4 A5
Hollybush Sq WA3 36 E1
Hollycourt L5 53 A6
Hollydale Rd L18 69 A5
Hollyfield Rd L9 38 F5
Hollyhurst Cl L8 68 A5
Hollymead Cl L25 70 B4
Hollyrood L34 56 A5
Hollytree Rd L25 70 B3
Hollywood Rd L17 68 E3
Holm Cotts CH43 65 F2
Holm Hey Rd CH43 65 F1
Holm Hill CH48 63 C1
Holm La CH43 65 F2
Holm View Cl CH43 66 A3
Holman Rd L19 81 D6
Holmdale Ave PR9 2 C4
Holme Cl L34 57 A7
Holme Rd WA10 43 C3
Holme St L5 52 C6
Holmefield Ave L19 69 A1

114 Kin – Lea

Kingsway *continued*
Newton-le-W WA12 46 C2
Prescot L34,L35 56 E5
Southport PR8 4 A7
St Helens WA11 44 A8
Wallasey CH45 51 A6
Widnes WA8 73 A1
Kingsway (Tunnel) L3, CH44 52 B3
Kingsway Ct 4 L3 52 D4
Kingsway Ind Pk L3,L5 52 D4
Kingsway Par L36 55 C4
Kingsway Prim Sch CH44 51 D2
Kingswell Cl L7 68 B8
Kingswood Ave
Crosby L22 26 F2
Liverpool L9 39 B7
Kingswood Bvd CH63 78 E8
Kingswood Ct L33 29 F4
Kingswood Dr L23 26 D3
Kingswood Pk PR8 3 F5
Kingswood Rd
4 Wallasey CH44 51 C5
Warrington WA5 60 A2
Kington Rd CH48 63 A3
Kinley Gdns L20 38 E5
Kinloch Cl L26 83 A7
Kinloch Way L39 13 D6
Kinloss Rd CH49 64 C3
Kinmel Cl
Birkenhead CH41 66 D7
Liverpool L4 53 D8
Kinmel St Liverpool L8 68 A5
St Helens WA9 58 C8
Kinnaird Rd CH45 51 A6
Kinnaird St L8 68 A3
Kinnerton Cl CH46 64 B8
Kinnock Pk WA5 59 E6
Kinross Ave WN4 34 C4
Kinross Cl WA2 61 F4
Kinross Rd Liverpool L10 39 F7
Seaforth L22 37 E8
Wallasey CH45 50 D6
Kinsman Ho L19 80 F7
Kintbury St WN2 35 F7
Kintore Cl CH63 88 C4
Kintore Dr WA5 74 D6
Kintore Rd L19 81 B7
Kipling Ave
2 Birkenhead CH42 66 F1
Huyton-w-R L36 71 A8
Warrington WA2 61 C1
Kipling Cres WA8 84 F8
Kipling Gr WA9 58 A3
Kipling St L20 38 A5
Kirby Cl CH48 63 C1
Kirby Mount CH48 75 C8
Kirby Park Mans 2 CH48 63 B1
Kirby Pk CH48 63 C1
Kirby Rd L20 38 D6
Kirby's Cotts L31 21 B3
Kirk Rd L20 38 C6
Kirk St L5 52 E6
Kirk Stone Rd W L21 27 B2
Kirkacre Ave WA12 60 C8
Kirkbride Cl L27 71 A4
Kirkbride Lawn L27 71 A4
Kirkbride Wlk L27 71 A4
Kirkburn Cl 13 L8 67 F4
Kirkby Bank Rd L33 30 C2
Kirkby CE Prim Sch L32 29 E2
Kirkby Row L32 29 D3
Kirkby Row Cotts L32 29 C3
Kirkby Sta L32 29 C3
Kirkcaldy Ave WA5 74 D6
Kirkdale Gdns WN8 25 A7
Kirkdale Rd L5 52 E6
Kirkdale St Lawrence CE Prim Sch L4 52 D8
Kirkdale Sta L20 38 D1
Kirkdale Vale L4,L5 52 E7
Kirket Cl CH63 79 A4
Kirket La CH63 79 A4
Kirkfield Gr CH42 67 A1
Kirkham Ave WA3 47 E6
Kirkham Rd Southport PR9 2 A4
Widnes WA8 73 C2
Kirkham St WN2 36 B8
Kirklake Bank L37 9 C2
Kirklake Rd L37 9 D2
Kirkland Ave CH42 66 D2
Kirkland Cl L9 38 F7
Kirkland Rd CH45 51 C8
Kirkland St WA10 43 F4
Kirklands The CH48 63 C2
Kirklees Rd PR8 3 F1
Kirkmaiden Rd L19 81 B8
Kirkman Fold L35 57 B3
Kirkmore Rd L18 69 A2
Kirkmount CH49 65 A5
Kirkside Cl L12 40 D3
Kirkstall Dr L37 10 B2
Kirkstall Rd PR8 3 F2
Kirkstead Way WA3 47 A8
Kirkstead Wlk L31 29 B3
Kirkstone Ave
St Helens WA11 44 C8
Warrington WA2 61 C2
Kirkstone Rd N L21 27 C1
Kirkstone Rd S L21,L30, L20 38 D8
Kirkway Bebington CH63 78 D7
Birkenhead,Greasby CH49 64 E4
Birkenhead,Upton CH49 64 F5
Wallasey CH45 51 B7
Kitchen St L1 90 B1
Kitchener Dr L9 38 F6
Kitchener St WA10 43 E4
Kitling La L34 41 B5
Kitling Rd L34 41 C5
Kiverley Cl L18 69 E3
Kiveton Dr WN4 35 C2
Knap The CH60 86 A6
Knaresborough Rd CH44 50 F4
Knight Rd WA5 59 F6
Knight St L1 90 C2
Knighton Rd L4 39 D1
Knights Grange WA9 44 C4
Knightsbridge Cl WA8 73 D4
Knightsbridge Ct CH43 65 D3
Knightsbridge Wlk L33 29 D6
Knightsway L22 26 F2
Knob Hall Gdns PR9 1 F3
Knob Hall La PR9 1 F3
Knoclaid Rd L13 53 E7
Knoll The CH43 66 A3
Knolle Park Mews L25 69 F3
Knotty Ash Prim Sch L12 54 D4
Knotty Mews L25 70 C3
Knowl Hey Rd L26 83 A6
Knowle Ave PR8 7 C6
Knowle Cl L12 40 C2
Knowles House Ave WA10 42 F3
Knowles St
Birkenhead CH41 66 C7
Widnes WA8 73 C2
Knowsley Ave WA3 36 B1
Knowsley Bsns Pk L34 41 B6
Knowsley Cl CH42 67 A1
Knowsley Com Coll L32 29 D2
Knowsley Comm Coll L36 55 D3
Knowsley Ct CH42 67 A1
Knowsley Expressway
Liverpool L35,WA8 83 F8
Tarbock Green L35 71 D4
Knowsley Hey Sch L36 55 F2
Knowsley Hts L36 55 E5
Knowsley Ind Pk
Kirkby L33 30 C2
Knowsley L33 41 B7
Knowsley La
Huyton-w-R L34,L36 55 D6
Knowsley L34 41 C4
Knowsley Park La L34 56 C7
Knowsley Rd
Birkenhead CH42 67 A1
Bootle L20 38 B5
Liverpool L19 81 A6
Ormskirk L39 13 F5
Rainhill L35 57 D2
Southport PR9 1 C1
St Helens WA10 43 D3
Wallasey CH45 51 A6
Knowsley Saf Pk* L34 42 C2
Knowsley St 1 L4 38 F2
Knowsley View WA11 31 E8
Knowsley Village Sch L34 41 C3
Knox Cl CH62 79 B6
Knox St CH41 66 F6
Knutsford Cl WA10 43 B2
Knutsford Gn CH46 49 E1
Knutsford Rd CH46 49 E1
Knutsford Wlk L31 20 D4
Kramar Wlk 1 L33 29 F2
Kremlin Dr L13 54 A5
Kylemore Ave L18 69 A2
Kylemore Cl CH61 76 E3
Kylemore Ct L26 82 E7
Kylemore Dr CH61 76 F3
Kylemore Rd CH43 66 A4
Kylemore Way
Heswall CH61 76 E3
Liverpool L26 82 E7
Kynance Rd L11 40 D5

L

Laburnum Ave
Huyton-w-R L36 70 E8
St Helens WA11 44 D7
Laburnum Cres L32 29 D3
Laburnum Ct 14 L8 68 A4
Laburnum Dr WN8 15 D1
Laburnum Gr Irby CH61 76 D6
Liverpool L15 69 A8
Maghull L31 20 F1
Southport PR8 4 F7
Laburnum La WA5,WA8 74 C5
Laburnum Pl L20 38 D3
Laburnum Rd
Birkenhead CH43 66 C4
Golborne WA3 47 F7
Liverpool L7 53 D3
Wallasey CH45 51 B7
Laburnum St WN4 35 B2
Lace St L3 90 B4
Lacey Rd L34 56 E5
Lacey St WA10 57 D8
Lad La L3 52 B2
Laddock Cl L4 53 C7
Lady Alice's Dr L40 14 E8
Lady Chapel Cl L1 90 C1
Lady Green Ct L38 18 E3
Lady Green La L38 18 D4
Lady Lever Art Gall The* CH62 79 B6
Lady's Wlk L40 14 C6
Ladybarn Ave WA3 46 F7
Ladybower Cl L7 68 B8
Ladyewood Rd CH44 51 C3
Ladyfield CH43 65 C7
Ladyfields L12 54 B5
Ladymount RC Prim Sch CH61 76 F3
Ladypool L24 83 C2
Ladysmith Ave WN4 35 C3
Ladysmith Rd L10 39 F6
Ladywood Rd WA5 60 D1
Laffak Rd WA11 44 D7
Lafford La WN8 25 C8
Lagan Ho CH46 49 E4
Laggan St L7 53 B2
Lagrange Arc 8 WA10 44 A3
Laird Cl CH41 65 F8
Laird St CH41 66 A8
Lairds Pl L3 52 D4
Laithwaite Cl WA9 58 B3
Lake Pl CH47 63 B7
Lake Rd Hoylake CH47 63 B7
Liverpool L15 69 A7
Lake St 5 L4 53 A7
Lake View L35 71 E8
Lakeland Ave WN4 35 C4
Lakeland Cl L1 90 B2
Lakemoor Cl WA9 58 D7
Lakenheath Rd L26 82 E6
Lakes Dr WN5 25 E6
Lakes Rd L9 39 D7
Lakeside Ave WN5 25 E3
Lakeside Cl WA8 84 A8
Lakeside Ct
Rainford WA11 32 A6
Wallasey CH45 51 C8
Lakeside Gdns WA11 32 A6
Lakeside Lawn L27 71 A3
Lakeside View L22 37 D8
Lakeview Ct PR9 4 B8
Laleston Cl WA8 84 E8
Lambert St L3 90 C4
Lambert Way L3 90 C4
Lambeth Ct CH47 63 A7
Lambeth Rd L4,L5 52 D7
Lambeth Wlk L4 52 D7
Lambourn Ave WA8 72 C5
Lambourne WN8 16 B4
Lambourne Gr WA9 45 A4
Lambourne Rd L4 39 D1
Lambrigg Row 18 L4 52 F7
Lambshear La L31 20 C4
Lambton Rd L17 68 B3
Lamerton Cl WA5 74 D4
Lammermoor Rd L18 69 A2
Lampeter Cl WA5 60 E2
Lampeter Rd L6 53 C6
Lamport Cl WA8 73 E3
Lamport St 2 L8 67 E5
Lanark Cl WA10 43 F2
Lanark Gdns WA8 72 E3
Lancashire Gdns WA10 43 F2
Lancaster Ave Crosby L23 26 D3
Golborne WA3 47 C8
Liverpool L17 68 D6
Prescot L35 56 D3
Wallasey CH45 51 C5
Widnes WA8 72 A2
Lancaster Cl
Bebington CH62 79 B6
Liverpool L5 52 D6
Maghull L31 20 F1
Newton-le-W WA12 45 F4
Southport PR8 3 E4
Warrington WA2 61 F2
Lancaster Cres WN8 15 E1
Lancaster Dr PR9 2 F5
Lancaster Gate PR9 2 F5
Lancaster Gdns PR8 3 E4
Lancaster Ho PR8 3 E4
Lancaster Rd Formby L37 9 E1
Huyton-w-R L36 56 A4
Southport PR8 3 E4
Widnes WA8 73 B3
Lancaster St Liverpool L5 52 D6
Liverpool,Walton L9 38 F3
Lancaster Wlk
Huyton-w-R L36 56 A4
Liverpool L5 52 D6
Lance Cl L5 52 F5
Lance Gr L15 69 A7
Lance La L15 69 A7
Lancefield Rd L9 38 F5
Lancelyn Ct CH63 79 A3
Lancelyn Terr CH63 78 F4
Lancing Ave WA2 61 A4
Lancing Cl L25 70 D1
Lancing Dr L10 28 D2
Lancing Rd L25 70 D1
Lancing Way L25 70 D1
Lancots La WA9 58 D8
Land End L31 21 C1
Land Gate La WN4 35 B8
Land La PR9 2 D4
Lander Rd L21 38 C6
Lander Road Prim Sch L21 38 C6
Landford Ave L9 39 E4
Landford Pl L9 39 E4
Landgate Ind Est WN4 35 A8
Landican La CH43,CH49, CH63 77 E7
Landican Rd CH49,CH61 77 B7
Landmark The L5 52 E5
Landor Cl Golborne WA3 47 E8
Liverpool L3 52 C5
Landseer Rd L5 52 F5
Lane Ends WA8 83 D5
Lane Head Ave WA3 47 F8
Lanfranc Cl L16 69 E8
Lanfranc Way L16 69 E8
Lang La CH48 63 B3
Lang Lane S CH48 63 C2
Langbar L35 56 E2
Langdale Ave Formby L37 9 D2
Golborne WA3 36 C1
Heswall CH61 76 F4
Langdale Cl Formby L37 9 D2
Kirkby L32 29 F1
Warrington WA2 61 E2
Widnes WA8 84 C8
Langdale Cres WN2 36 B8
Langdale Dr L31 20 E2
Langdale Gdns PR8 3 F1
Langdale Gr WA11 44 B7
Langdale Rd
Bebington CH63 78 F4
Liverpool L15 68 E6
Wallasey CH45 51 A7
Langdale St L20 38 D3
Langdowne Way L36 55 E2
Langfield WA3 47 E7
Langfield Gr CH62 88 D5
Langford L24 83 C2
Langford Rd L19 80 F8
Langham Ave L17 68 C3
Langham Ct L4 52 F8
Langham St L4 52 F8
Langham St Ind Est L4 52 F8
Langholm Rd WN4 34 C4
Langholme Hts L11 39 F4
Langland Cl Liverpool L4 53 D8
Warrington WA5 60 E2
Langley Ave WA12 46 C1
Langley Cl Bebington CH63 79 A2
Golborne WA3 36 C1
Hightown L38 17 F2
Liverpool L12 40 F3
Langley Rd CH63 79 A2
Langley St L8 67 E6
Langrove St L5 52 E5
Langsdale St Liverpool L3 52 E3
Liverpool L3,L6 52 F3
Langshaw Lea L27 70 F4
Langstone Ave CH49 64 C3
Langton Cl
Newton-le-W WA12 46 A4
Widnes WA8 72 B3
Langton Rd Kirkby L33 29 F5
Liverpool L15 68 D7
Langtree WN8 16 B3
Langtree St WA9 44 C3
Langtry Cl L4 52 D8
Langtry Rd L4 52 D8
Lansbury Ave WA9 44 E3
Lansbury Rd L36 56 A2
Lansdown L12 54 A6
Lansdowne Cl CH41 66 A8
Lansdowne Ct 6 CH43 65 F8
Lansdowne Ho CH41 66 F6
Lansdowne Pl
5 Birkenhead CH43 65 F8
Liverpool L5 52 F6
Lansdowne Rd
Birkenhead CH41,CH43 65 F8
Southport PR8 4 E6
Wallasey CH45 50 F7
Lanville Rd L19 69 B1
Lanyork Rd L3 52 B3
Lapford Cres L33 30 A4
Lapford Wlk L33 30 A4
Lapwing Cl Liverpool L12 40 F1
Newton-le-W WA12 46 C3
Lapwing Ct L26 70 E1
Lapworth Cl 3 CH46 64 B8
Lapworth St L5 52 D6
Larch Ave
Newton-le-W WA12 46 C2
Warrington WA5 74 E5
Widnes WA8 73 B2
Larch Cl Billinge WN5 33 D5
Golborne WA3 47 F6
Liverpool L19 80 F7
Skelmersdale WN8 15 E1
Larch Ct 13 L8 68 A4
Larch Gr Birkenhead CH43 65 E8
Liverpool L15 54 A1
Larch Lea 2 L6 53 B5
Larch Rd Birkenhead CH41 66 D5
Haydock WA11 45 E7
Huyton-w-R L36 55 D2
Larch St PR8 4 E6
Larch Twrs L33 29 F3
Larch Way L37 9 D4
Larchdale Gr L9 39 B4
Larchfield Rd L23 27 B5
Larchwood Ave L31 28 C7
Larchwood Cl
Heswall CH61 76 F3
Liverpool L25 70 B5
Larchwood Dr CH63 78 F7
Larcombe Ave CH49 64 F5
Lark La L17 68 C4
Lark Way L17 68 C3
Larkfield Cl L17 68 C2
Larkfield Ct PR9 2 A3
Larkfield Gr L17 68 C2
Larkfield La PR9 2 A3
Larkfield Prim Sch PR9 2 A3
Larkfield Rd L17 68 C2
Larkfield View L15 68 E8
Larkhill WN8 16 B4
Larkhill Ave CH49 65 A7
Larkhill Cl L13 53 E7
Larkhill Gr L13 17 F3
Larkhill La Formby L37 9 C4
Liverpool L13 53 E7
Larkhill Pl L13 53 F7
Larkhill View L13 53 F7
Larkhill Way CH49 65 A7
Larkin Cl CH62 79 A7
Larkspur Cl 3 PR8 4 D6
Larksway CH60 86 B8
Larton Farm Cl CH48 63 E3
Larton Rd CH48 63 E3
Lartonwood CH48 63 E3
Lascelles Rd L19 81 D7
Lascelles St WA9 44 C3
Latchford Rd CH60 86 B6
Late Moffatt Rd W L9 39 B7
Latham Ave
Newton-le-W WA12 46 C4
Ormskirk L39 14 A5
Latham Ho WA12 46 B4
Latham St L5 52 D6
Latham Way CH63 79 B2
Lathbury La L17 68 E5
Lathom Ave
2 Seaforth L21 37 F6
Wallasey CH44 51 B4
Lathom Cl 1 L21 37 F6
Lathom Dr Maghull L31 20 E3
Rainford WA11 31 F7
Lathom High Sch WN8 15 F3
Lathom La L40 14 C7
Lathom Rd
Bickerstaffe L39 22 F8
Bootle L20 38 C5
Huyton-w-R L36 55 E2
Southport PR9 1 C1
Lathum Cl L35 56 E5
Latimer Cl 2 WN5 25 F7
Latimer St L5 52 D5
Latrigg Rd L17 68 E2
Lauder Cl L33 29 D6
Launceston Dr WA5 74 E3
Laund The CH45 50 F5
Laurel Ave Bebington CH63 78 E4
Heswall CH60 76 F1
Newton-le-W WA12 46 D3
Laurel Bank WA8 73 A3
Laurel Ct WA11 44 B7
Laurel Dr
Skelmersdale WN8 15 E2
St Helens WA10 42 F4
Willaston CH64 88 B1
Laurel Gr
Ashton-in-M WN4 35 B4
Crosby L22 26 D2
Golborne WA3 47 D8
Huyton-w-R L36 70 E8
Liverpool L8 68 C6
Southport PR8 4 E7
Laurel Rd
Birkenhead CH42 66 D4
Liverpool L7 53 D2
Prescot L34 56 E6
St Helens,Blackbrook WA11 44 F5
St Helens,West Pk WA10 43 D2
Laurelbanks CH60 76 E1
Laurelhurst Ave CH61 77 A4
Laurels The CH46 49 E3
Lauren Cl L36 56 B2
Laurence Deacon Ct 1 CH41 66 D7
Lauriston Rd L4 39 C1
Laurus Cl L27 70 F5
Lavan Cl L6 53 A3
Lavan St 3 L6 53 A3
Lavender Cres 7 L34 56 E6
Lavender Gdns
Crosby L23 27 B5
St Helens WA9 59 A7
Lavender Way L9 39 B4
Lavender Wlk WN4 34 D5
Lavrock Bank L8 67 E4
Lawford Dr CH60 86 C8
Lawler Gr L34 56 E7
Lawler St L21 38 B6
Lawns Ave Bebington CH63 88 B6
Orrell WN5 25 C5
Lawns The
Birkenhead CH43 65 D7
Southport PR9 1 F2
Lawnside Cl CH42 66 F1
Lawrence Cl L19 81 A7
Lawrence Com Prim Sch L15 68 D7
Lawrence Ct WN2 36 B8
Lawrence Gr L15 68 E7
Lawrence Rd
Liverpool L15 68 E7
St Helens WA10 43 C6
Lawrenson St WA10 43 E3
Lawson St PR9 5 A7
Lawson Wlk L12 40 D3
Lawswood L37 9 E5
Lawton Ave L20 38 E5
Lawton Rd Crosby L22,L23 26 D2
Huyton-w-R L36 55 C1
Rainhill L35 57 D2
Lawton St L1 90 C3
Laxey St L8 67 E6
Laxton Rd L25 82 C7
Layford Cl L36 55 D6
Layford Rd L36 55 D5
Layton Ave CH43 65 F1
Layton Cl L25 70 C2
Layton Rd L25 70 C2
Lazenby Cres WN4 34 F3
Lea Cl CH43 65 E4
Lea Cres L39 13 F7
Lea Cross Gr WA8 72 C3
Lea Ct L39 13 E7
Lea Green Bsns Pk WA9 57 F4
Lea Green Ind Est WA9 58 A3

Lea Green Rd WA9 58 A4
Lea Green Sta WA9 58 B5
Lea Rd CH44 51 D5
Leach Croft L28 55 A7
Leach La WA9 58 D5
Leach St 4 WA10 43 F4
Leach Way CH61 76 C6
Leacroft WN4 34 F6
Leadenhall Cl L5 52 F6
Leafield Cl CH61 76 F6
Leafield Rd L25 82 B6
Leagate L10 39 F8
Leamington Ave
Newton-le-W WA12 46 C1
Southport PR8 7 D5
Leamington Com Prim Sch
L11 39 D2
Leamington Rd
Liverpool L11 39 D2
Southport PR8 7 D5
Leander Rd CH45 51 A5
Leas Pk CH47 63 A4
Leas The Heswall CH61 77 B6
Wallasey CH45 50 E7
Leasowe Ave CH45 50 E6
Leasowe Gdns CH46 49 E4
Leasowe Prim Sch CH46 50 B4
Leasowe Rd Liverpool L9 39 B7
Wallasey CH45,CH46 50 C5
Leasowe Sta CH46 50 A2
Leasoweside CH46 50 A4
Leather La L2 90 A4
Leather's La L26 82 F7
Leatherbarrows La
Kirkby L31 29 A6
Maghull L31 28 F7
Leathwood L31 28 E8
Leaway CH49 64 D4
Leawood Gr CH46 64 F8
Leckwith Rd L30 28 B2
Leda Gr 3 L17 68 C4
Ledburn WN8 16 B3
Ledbury Cl
Birkenhead CH43 65 E2
Liverpool L12 40 F4
St Helens WA10 43 B3
Ledger Rd WA11 45 A5
Ledmore Gr WN4 34 D3
Ledsham Cl CH43 65 E4
Ledsham Rd L32 29 C2
Ledsham Wlk L32 29 C2
Ledson Gr L39 21 B7
Ledson Pk L33 29 F6
Ledsons Gr L31 29 A3
Lee Cl L35 57 D1
Lee Ct WA2 61 C2
Lee Hall Rd L25 70 C5
Lee La WN2 36 B8
Lee Park Ave L25 70 C5
Lee Rd CH47 63 C7
Lee St WA9 58 E8
Lee Vale Rd L25 70 C4
Leece St L1 90 C2
Leecourt Cl L12 54 D5
Leeds St L3 52 C3
Leeming Cl L19 81 C5
Lees Ave CH42 66 F2
Lees La Liverpool L12 54 D7
Skelmersdale WN8 16 E7
Lees Rd L33 30 B2
Leeside Ave L32 29 F1
Leeside Cl L32 29 F1
Leeswood 6 Crosby L22 26 E1
Skelmersdale WN8 16 B3
Leeswood Rd CH49 65 A4
Leeward Dr L24 82 A4
Legh Rd Bebington CH62 79 B7
Haydock WA11 45 B6
Legh St Ashton-in-M WN4 35 B2
Golborne WA3 47 A8
Newton-le-W WA12 46 A3
Legh Vale Prim Sch
WA11 45 B6
Legion La CH62 79 D1
Legion Rd WA10 57 D8
Leicester Ave L22 26 D2
Leicester Rd L20 38 D4
Leicester St Southport PR9 4 B8
St Helens WA9 57 D8
Leigh Ave WA8 73 A1
Leigh Bridge Way L5 52 C5
Leigh Green Cl 4 WA8 84 C8
Leigh Pl L1 90 B3
Leigh Rd CH48 63 B3
Leigh St L1 90 B3
Leighs Hey Cres L32 29 F2
Leighton Ave
Hoylake CH47 63 E8
Maghull L31 20 D2
Leighton Chase CH64 86 D1
Leighton Rd
Birkenhead CH41 66 E4
Neston CH64 86 D2
Leighton St L4 38 E1
Leinster Gdns WA7 84 F3
Leinster Rd L13 54 B3
Leinster St WA7 84 F3
Leison St L4 52 D7
Leiston Cl CH61 76 E7
Lemon Cl L7 53 C1
Lemon Gr L8 68 C6
Lemon St L5 52 D6
Lemon Tree Wlk WA10 43 D1
Lendel Cl L37 9 E3
Lenfield Dr WA11 44 F6
Lenham Way L24 82 B4
Lennox Ave CH45 51 B7
Lennox La CH43 50 C1
Lenthall St L4 38 F2
Lenton Ave L37 9 D4
Lenton Rd L25 70 C5
Leo Cl L14 54 F4
Leominster Rd CH44 51 B4
Leon Cl WA5 74 D7
Leonard Cheshire Dr L30 27 F3
Leonard St WA9 58 F7
Leonards Cl L36 55 D6
Leonora St 18 L8 68 A4
Leopold Gr WA9 58 C5
Leopold Rd Crosby L22 26 C2
Liverpool L7 53 B2
Leopold St CH44 51 E3
Lesley Rd PR8 4 E7
Leslie Ave CH49 64 D3
Leslie Rd WA10 57 C8
Lesseps Rd L8 68 C7
Lessingham Rd WA8 72 F3
Lester Cl L4 52 E7
Lester Dr Irby CH61 76 C7
St Helens WA10 43 A5
Lester Gr L36 55 F4
Lestock St L8 90 C1
Leta St Liverpool L4 38 F1
Liverpool L4 39 A1
Letchworth St L6 53 C5
Lethbridge Cl L5 52 D6
Lethbridge Rd PR8 4 D5
Letitia St L8 67 F5
Leven St L4 52 E8
Levens Hey CH46 64 D8
Levens Way 1 WA8 84 C8
Lever Ave 11 CH44 51 E2
Lever Cswy CH63 78 B7
Lever St WA9 58 D3
Lever Terr CH42 66 E3
Leveret Rd L24 83 A3
Leverhulme Ct CH63 79 A4
Leveson Rd L13 54 B1
Lewis Ave WA5 60 F2
Lewis Ct PR9 4 D8
Lewis Gr WA8 72 D1
Lewis St WA10 43 E3
Lewisham Rd
Bebington CH62 79 C6
Liverpool L11 40 A1
Lexham Rd L14 54 C3
Lexington Way L33 29 D6
Lexton Dr PR9 2 B3
Ley Cl WA9 58 C4
Leybourne Ave PR8 7 F7
Leybourne Cl L25 70 A6
Leybourne Gn L25 70 A6
Leybourne Gr L25 70 A5
Leybourne Rd L25 70 A6
Leyburn Cl L32 40 E7
Leyburn Rd CH45 50 F6
Leyfield Cl L12 54 D6
Leyfield Ct L12 54 D6
Leyfield Rd L12 54 D6
Leyfield Wlk L12 54 D6
Leyland Cl PR9 2 E5
Leyland Gr WA11 45 B6
Leyland Green Rd WN4 34 C5
Leyland Rd Rainford WA11 31 F6
Southport PR9 1 C1
Leyland St 8 L34 56 D6
Leyland Way L39 13 F5
Liberton Ct 11 L5 53 A6
Liberty St L15 68 E7
Libra Cl L14 55 A5
Library St 3 WA10 44 A3
Lichfield Ave Crosby L22 26 D3
Golborne WA3 47 D8
Lichfield Cl L30 28 A1
Lichfield Gr WN4 35 C2
Lichfield Rd
Liverpool,Halewood L26 82 E6
Liverpool,Wavertree Green L15 69 A6
Lichfield St CH45 51 C7
Lickers La L35 56 E2
Liddell Ave L31 29 B4
Liddell Ct CH45 50 D5
Liddell Rd L12 53 F7
Lidderdale Rd L15 68 E6
Lidgate Cl L33 29 F5
Lifeboat Rd L37 9 B1
Liffey St L8 68 B7
Lifton Rd L33 30 A2
Lightbody St L5 52 C5
Lightburn St 5 WA7 84 F1
Lightfoot Cl CH60 86 B7
Lightfoot La CH60 86 B7
Lighthorne Dr PR8 7 A4
Lighthouse Rd CH47 63 B6
Lightshaw La WA3 36 B4
Lightwood Dr 3 L7 68 C8
Lightwood St 5 L7 68 C8
Lilac Ave
Downall Green WN4 34 D5
Southport PR8 7 D2
Widnes WA8 73 B2
Lilac Gr Billinge WN5 33 D4
Huyton-w-R L36 70 D8
Skelmersdale WN8 15 E1
St Helens WA11 44 F5
Lilac Rd WA3 36 A1
Lilford Ave L9 38 F6
Lilford Dr WA5 74 F6
Lilley Ct L7 53 D3
Lilley Rd L7 53 D2
Lillian Rd L4 53 B6
Lillie Cl CH43 65 C8
Lilly Gn L4 39 B1
Lilly Gr L4 39 B1
Lilly Vale L7 53 D3
Lillyfield CH60 85 F6
Lily Ave WA12 46 D2
Lily La WN2 35 F7
Lily Pl WN4 35 C2
Lily Rd L21 38 B6
Lily St WN4 35 E5
Limbo La CH49 76 D8
Lime Ave Bebington CH63 78 D4
3 Widnes WA8 73 B2
Lime Cl Abram Brow WN2 36 C7
Liverpool L13 54 A4
Lime Ct WN8 15 E1
Lime Gr Bootle L21 38 A6
Golborne WA3 47 E6
Liverpool L8 68 C6
Rainford WA11 31 F6
Skelmersdale WN8 15 E1
Lime St Liverpool L1 90 B4
Southport PR8 4 E6
Lime Street Sta L3,L1 90 C4
Lime Tree Cl L9 39 B4
Lime Tree Gr CH60 86 C8
Lime Tree Way L37 9 C2
Lime Vale Rd WN5 33 C3
Limedale Rd L18 69 B5
Limefield Dr WN8 24 E7
Limehurst Gr CH62 88 D6
Limekiln Ct L5 52 D4
Limekiln La
Burtonwood WA5 59 E3
1 Liverpool L3 52 D3
Liverpool L3,L5 52 D4
Wallasey CH41,CH44 51 A2
Limes The
Birkenhead CH49 64 F5
Golborne WA3 47 D6
Limont Rd PR8 7 D5
Linacre La Bootle L20 38 D5
Maghull L37 19 B7
Widnes WA8 72 E5
Linacre Prim Sch L20 38 C5
Linacre Rd L20,L21 38 B6
Linaker Dr L39 12 B8
Linaker Prim Sch PR8 4 B5
Linaker St PR8 4 B5
Linbeck Gr WA3 36 E1
Linbridge Rd L14 54 F6
Lincoln Ave WA3 36 D1
Lincoln Cl Huyton-w-R L36 56 B3
Liverpool L6 53 B4
Lincoln Cres WA11 44 B6
Lincoln Dr Aintree L10 28 D3
Ashton-in-M WN4 35 D2
Wallasey CH45 51 C6
Lincoln Gn L31 28 B8
Lincoln Rd Southport PR8 4 A1
St Helens WA10 43 D2
Lincoln Sq WA8 73 B2
Lincoln St
Birkenhead CH41 51 A1
Liverpool L19 81 D4
Lincoln Way
Huyton-w-R L36 56 B3
Rainhill L35 57 D1
Lincombe Rd L36 55 C4
Lind St L4 38 F1
Lindale Cl CH46 50 A1
Lindale Dr 11 WA9 58 C4
Lindale Rd L7 53 E3
Lindby Cl L32 41 A8
Lindby Rd L32 41 A8
Linden Ave
Ashton-in-M WN4 34 F5
Crosby L23 26 C4
Litherland L30 27 F2
Orrell WN5 25 E6
Linden Ct 1 Crosby L23 26 B3
Orrell WN5 25 E6
Widnes WA8 72 F4
Linden Dr
Birkenhead CH43 65 E1
Huyton-w-R L36 70 E8
Linden Gr Billinge WN5 33 C3
Orrell WN5 25 E6
Wallasey CH45 51 B7
Linden Rd L27 70 E5
Linden Way
St Helens WA10 43 B4
Widnes WA8 72 F4
Linden Wlk WN5 25 E6
Lindens WN8 16 B4
Lindens The
3 Birkenhead CH43 66 C5
Maghull L31 28 C7
Lindenwood 6 L32 40 F8
Lindeth Ave CH44 51 B3
Lindfield Cl 4 L8 67 F4
Lindholme WN8 16 C3
Lindisfarne Dr L12 41 A3
Lindley Ave WN5 25 C5
Lindley Cl 6 L7 68 C8
Lindley St L7 68 C8
Lindrick Cl L35 57 A4
Lindsay Rd L4 53 D8
Lindsay St WA9 58 E3
Lindwall Cl CH46 50 C1
Linear Pk CH46 49 C1
Linear View WA12 46 C1
Lineside Cl L25 70 B5
Linford Gr WA11 44 C5
Ling St L7 53 B2
Lingdale Ave CH43 65 F6
Lingdale Ct
Birkenhead CH43 65 F7
Hoylake CH48 62 F3
Lingdale Rd
Birkenhead CH41,CH43 65 F7
West Kirby CH48 63 A3
Lingdale Rd N CH41 65 F7
Lingdales L37 10 B5
Lingfield Cl
Huyton-w-R L36 55 D1
Litherland L30 28 A1
Lingfield Gr L14 54 D2
Lingfield Rd Liverpool L14 54 D2
Runcorn WA7 84 E1
Lingford Cl L27 70 F4
Lingham Cl CH46 49 D2
Lingham La
Wallasey CH46 49 C3
Wallasey,Moreton CH46 49 D1
Lingham Prim Sch CH46 49 D1
Lingholme Rd WA10 43 E4
Lingley Green Ave WA5 74 D8
Lingley Rd WA5 74 D6
Lingmell Ave WA11 33 C1
Lingmell Rd L11,L12 54 B8
Lingtree Rd L32 29 B3
Lingwell Ave WA8 72 D2
Lingwood Rd WA5 74 F6
Linhope Way L17 68 C3
Link Ave Crosby L23 27 A5
St Helens WA11 44 E5
Link Rd L36 56 B1
Linkfield Cl L27 70 D6
Links Ave PR9 1 F3
Links Cl Bebington CH63 88 B6
Wallasey CH45 50 F7
Links Hey Rd CH48 75 E6
Links Rd L32 30 A1
Links The CH43 65 F5
Links View
Birkenhead CH43 65 E5
Wallasey CH45 50 F8
Linkside CH63 78 D7
Linkside Ave WA2 61 B6
Linkside Ct L23 26 A5
Linkside Rd L25 70 C1
Linkstor Rd L25 69 F3
Linksway CH45 50 F7
Linkway WA10 43 B6
Linkway Ave WA8 35 E5
Linkway E WA10,WA9 44 B2
Linkway W WA10 44 A2
Linner Rd L24 82 D3
Linnet Cl Liverpool L17 68 C5
Newton-le-W WA12 46 C3
Warrington WA2 61 D3
Linnet Ho L8 68 B5
Linnet La L17 68 C4
Linnet Way L33 29 E7
Linnets Way CH60 85 E8
Linslade Cl L33 29 F4
Linslade Cres L33 29 F4
Linton Ave WA3 35 F2
Linton St 1 L4 38 F1
Linum Gdns WA9 59 B7
Linville Ave L23 26 B4
Linwood Gr L35 56 E2
Linwood Rd CH42 66 E3
Lionel St WA9 58 F7
Lions Cl 2 CH43 65 F6
Lipton Cl L20 38 C2
Lisburn La L13 53 E7
Lisburn Rd L17 68 E2
Liscard Cres CH44,CH45 51 B4
Liscard Gr CH44,CH45 51 A4
Liscard Ho CH44 51 B4
Liscard Prim Sch CH44,
CH45 51 C5
Liscard Rd Liverpool L15 68 D7
Wallasey CH44 51 C4
Liscard Village CH45 51 B5
Liscard Way CH44 51 B4
Lisieux RC Inf Sch L11 39 F2
Lisleholme Cl L12 54 C6
Lisleholme Cres L12 54 C6
Lisleholme Rd L12 54 C6
Lismore Ct L23 26 C4
Lismore Pk PR8 3 E4
Lismore Rd L18 69 A2
Lister Cres L7 53 C2
Lister Dr L13,L6 53 E4
Lister Drive Inf Sch L13 53 E4
Lister Jun Sch L13 53 E4
Lister Rd L7 53 C2
Liston St L4 38 F2
Litcham Cl CH49 65 A7
Litchborough Gr L35 57 A6
Litherland Ave CH46 49 D1
Litherland Cres WA11 44 C7
Litherland High Sch L21 27 D2
Litherland Moss Prim Sch
L21 27 D1
Litherland Pk L21 38 B8
Litherland Rd Bootle L20 38 C4
Bootle L20 38 C5
Lithou Cl L5 52 D5
Little Acre L31 28 E8
Little Barn Hey L30 27 D5
Little Bongs L12 54 D4
Little Brewery La L37 9 F6
Little Brook La L32 40 D8
Little Canning St 1 L8 67 F7
Little Catharine St L8 67 F7
Little Croft L35 56 D3
Little Crosby Rd L23 26 E6
Little Ct L3 52 C4
Little Delph WA11 45 C7
Little Digmoor Prim Sch
WN8 24 B6
Little Hardman St 2 L1 90 C2
Little Heath Rd L24 82 E3
Little Hey La L37 10 B4
Little Heyes St L5 53 A6
Little Howard St L3 52 B4
Little Huskisson St L8 67 F7
Little La Neston CH64 86 C1
Southport PR9 2 B1
Little Moss Hey L28 55 C7
Little Parkfield Rd L17 68 B4
Little St WA9 44 E1
Little St Bride St 12 L7,L8 67 F8
Little Storeton La CH63 78 A6
Little Woolton St L69 53 A1
Littlecote Cl 16 WA9 58 C4
Littledale Rd
Liverpool L14 54 D3
Wallasey CH44 51 D3
Warrington WA5 74 F7
Littlemore Cl CH49 64 D5
Littler Rd WA11 45 A5
Littlestone Cl WA8 73 A4
Littleton Cl CH43 65 E4
Littlewood Cl L35 56 E2
Littondale Ave L35 57 D2
Liver Ind Est L9 39 C4
Liver St L1 90 A2
Livermore Ct L8 68 C6
Liverpool Ave PR8 7 D5
Liverpool Coll L18 68 F4
Liverpool Com Coll L3 90 C3
Liverpool Com Coll
(Bankside) L13 53 F5
Liverpool Com Coll (Old
Swan Ctr) L13 54 A3
Liverpool Com Coll
(Riversdale Ctr) L19 80 E7
Liverpool Com Coll The Arts
Ctr L8 67 F8
Liverpool Comm Coll L3 52 C3
Liverpool Hope Univ Coll
Liverpool L3 52 F3
Liverpool,Childwall L16 69 D6
Liverpool Inst (Blackburne
House) L8 67 F8
Liverpool Inst for the
Performing Arts L1 90 C2
Liverpool John Lennon
Airport L24 82 C2
Liverpool Mus & Planetarium
L3 90 B4
Liverpool Old Rd L37 7 C1
Liverpool Pl WA8 72 C1
Liverpool Rd
Ashton-in-M WN4 35 A3
Bickerstaffe L39 22 C5
Crosby L22,L23 26 E3
Formby L37 10 A1
Garswood WA11,WN4 34 D2
Haydock WA11 45 B8
Hightown L37 18 A8
Huyton-w-R L36 55 D4
Maghull L31 20 D4
Neston CH64 86 F1
Neston CH64 86 F3
Ormskirk L39 13 B2
Royal Oak L39 21 F4
Skelmersdale WN8 23 C8
Southport PR8 4 A3
Southport,Birkdale Hills PR8 7 E6
St Helens WA10 43 F3
Warrington WA5,WA8 74 E6
Widnes WA8 72 C1
Liverpool Rd N L31 20 C2
Liverpool Rd S
Maghull L31 20 C1
Maghull L31 28 C7
Liverpool Row WA12 60 D8
Liverpool St WA10 43 F3
Liverpool Womens Hospl
L8 68 A8
Liversidge Rd CH42 66 D4
Livesley's La
Great Altcar L37 10 F2
Haskayne L37 11 A2
Livingston Ave L17 68 C4
Livingston Ct L17 68 C3
Livingston Dr L17 68 C3
Livingston Dr N L17 68 C3
Livingston Dr S L17 68 C3
Livingstone Gdns CH41 66 C7
Livingstone Rd CH46 50 B4
Livingstone St
2 Ashton-in-M WN4 35 A5
Birkenhead CH41 66 C7
Llanrwst Cl L8 67 E5
Lloyd Ave CH41 66 B7
Lloyd Cl L6 52 F4
Lloyd Cres WA12 45 F3
Lloyd Dr CH49 64 D3
Lloyd Rd L34 56 E7
Lloyd St WA11 44 F6
Lobelia Ave L9 39 B4
Lochinvar St L9 38 F3
Lochmore Rd L18 69 B1
Lochryan Rd L19 81 B8
Lock Rd CH62 89 A8
Lock St WA9 44 C5
Locke St L19 81 C4
Locker Ave WA2 61 B2
Locker La WN4 35 F4
Locker Pk CH49 64 C4
Lockerbie Cl WA2 61 E4
Lockerby Rd L7 53 D2
Lockett Bsns Pk WN4 35 C5
Lockett Rd
Ashton-in-M WN4 35 C6
Widnes WA8 73 B3
Lockfields View L3,L5 52 C5
Lockington Cl 23 L8 68 A4

Lockton Rd L34 .41 B5
Loddon Cl CH49 .65 B7
Lodge La Bebington CH62 .79 B6
Haydock WA11,WA12,WN4 .46 B8
Liverpool L8 .68 B7
Rainford L39,WA11 .23 D1
Widnes WA8 .72 B4
Lodge Rd Orrell WN5 .25 E4
Widnes WA8 .84 B8
Lodwick St L20 .38 B1
Lofthouse Gate WA8 .72 F4
Logan Rd CH41 .51 B1
Logfield Dr L19 .81 D4
Lognor Rd L32 .29 C2
Lognor Wlk L32 .29 C2
Logwood Rd L36 .71 A8
Lombard Rd CH46 .49 F2
Lombardy Ave CH49 .64 B2
Lomond Gr CH46 .64 F8
Lomond Rd L7 .53 E2
London Fields WN5 .33 E5
London La PR8 .8 D8
London Rd Liverpool L3 .52 F2
Liverpool L3 .90 C4
London Row WA12 .60 D8
London Sq 2 PR8 .4 B7
London St PR8,PR9 .4 B7
Londonderry Rd L13 .53 E7
Long Acres Rd CH64 .86 E2
Long Ave L9 .39 B6
Long Hey L35 .56 D2
Long Hey Rd CH48 .75 E7
Long Heys or Back La WN8 .16 F5
Long La Bickerstaffe L39 .22 B7
Crosby L23,L29 .27 A8
Formby L37 .9 E4
Liverpool L9 .39 E4
Liverpool,Garston L19 .81 C7
Liverpool,Hartley's Village L9 .39 C5
Liverpool,Wavertree L15 .68 F8
Maghull L29 .19 B1
Ormskirk L39 .21 F8
Skelmersdale WN8 .24 E3
Warrington WA2 .61 B1
Long Lane Com Prim Sch WA2 .61 B2
Long Mdw Heswall CH60 .85 F6
St Helens WA10 .43 B4
Long Meanygate PR9 .5 F8
Long Moss L30 .27 C2
Longacre PR9 .1 F3
Longacre Cl CH45 .50 D5
Longacres CH46 .64 D5
Longborough Rd L34 .41 C2
Longcliffe Dr PR8 .7 C4
Longcroft Ave L19 .81 E7
Longcroft Sq L19 .81 E7
Longdale La L29 .27 D8
Longden Rd WN4 .35 A3
Longdown Rd L10 .40 B6
Longfellow Dr CH62 .79 A7
Longfellow St Bootle L20 .38 A5
Liverpool L8 .68 C7
Longfield L37 .10 B5
Longfield Ave L23 .26 E6
Longfield Cl CH49 .64 D4
Longfield Pk WA9 .58 D4
Longfield Rd Bootle L21 .38 B6
Warrington WA2 .61 C1
Longfield Wlk L23 .26 E6
Longfold L31 .20 E1
Longford Rd PR8 .4 A2
Longford St L8 .68 A3
Longhey WN8 .16 C4
Longland Rd CH45 .51 B6
Longmead Ave WN4 .35 C4
Longmeadow Rd L34 .41 D4
Longmoor Cl L10 .39 E7
Longmoor Com Prim Sch L9 .39 B6
Longmoor Gr L9 .39 B6
Longmoor La L10,L9 .39 D7
Longreach Rd L14 .54 F3
Longridge Ave
Birkenhead CH49 .64 E6
St Helens WA11 .44 D5
Longridge Wlk 10 L4 .52 E8
Longshaw Ave WN5 .25 E1
Longshaw Cl WN5 .25 E1
Longshaw Comm
Billinge WN5 .33 E8
Longshaw WN5 .25 E1
Longshaw Old Rd WN5 .25 E1
Longshaw St WA5 .60 F1
Longstone Wlk L7 .68 B8
Longton Ave WA3 .47 C7
Longton Ct PR8 .7 C5
Longton Dr L37 .10 A6
Longton La L35 .57 B4
Longton Lane Com Prim Sch L35 .57 B5
Longview Ave Rainhill L35 57 A4
Wallasey CH45 .51 B5
Longview Com Sch L36 .55 E6
Longview Cres L36 .55 F3
Longview Dr L36 .56 A3
Longview La L36 .55 F4
Longview Rd
Huyton-w-R L36 .55 F3
Rainhill L35 .57 A4
Longville St L8 .67 E5
Longwood Cl WA11 .32 C1
Longworth Way L25 .70 A3
Lonie Gr WA10 .57 C8
Lonsboro Rd CH44 .51 C3
Lonsdale Ave
Ormskirk L39 .13 F7
St Helens WA10 .57 B7
Wallasey CH45 .51 A6
Lonsdale Cl Litherland L21 27 B2
Warrington WA5 .74 F8
3 Widnes WA8 .84 C8
Lonsdale Mews L21 .27 B2
Lonsdale Rd Formby L37 .9 F3
Litherland L21 .27 B2
Liverpool L26 .82 E6
Southport PR8 .4 D4
Lonsdale Villas CH45 .51 A6
Looe Cl WA8 .72 E2
Looe Rd L11 .40 D5
Looms The CH64 .86 B2
Loomsway CH61 .76 D6
Loraine St L5 .52 F5
Lord Nelson St L1,L3 .90 C4
Lord Sefton Way L37 .10 E2
Lord St Ashton-in-M WN4 .35 D4
Birkenhead CH41 .66 E7
Liverpool L2 .90 A3
Liverpool,Garston L19 .81 D4
Newton-le-W WA12 .46 A3
Runcorn WA7 .84 F3
Southport PR8,PR9 .4 B7
St Helens WA10 .44 A5
Lord St W PR8 .4 A6
Lordens Cl L14 .55 A5
Lordens Rd L14 .55 A5
Lords Ave CH43 .65 C8
Lords Fold WA11 .31 E7
Loreburn Rd L15 .69 B6
Lorenzo Dr L11 .53 F8
Loretto Dr CH49 .65 A6
Loretto Rd CH44 .50 F4
Lorn Ct 17 CH41 .66 E6
Lorn St CH41 .66 E6
Lorne Ct CH43 .66 B4
Lorne Rd Birkenhead CH43 66 A5
Crosby L22 .26 D1
Lorne St L7 .53 E3
Lorton Ave WA11 .44 A8
Lorton St L8 .68 B7
Lostock Cl WN5 .33 E5
Lothair Rd L4 .53 A7
Lothian St L8 .68 A5
Lotus Gdns WA9 .59 A7
Loudon Gr L8 .68 A6
Lough Gn CH63 .79 A2
Loughlin Dr L33 .30 A5
Loughrigg Ave WA11 .33 B1
Louis Braille Cl L30 .27 F4
Louis Pasteur Ave L30 .27 F4
Lourdes Hospl L18 .68 F5
Love La Liverpool L3 .52 B4
Wallasey CH44 .51 B3
Lovel Rd L24 .82 D3
Lovel Terr WA8 .84 B5
Lovel Way L24 .82 D3
Lovelace Rd L19 .81 B7
Lovett Dr L35 .56 E5
Low Bank Rd WN4 .34 F4
Low Hill L6 .53 A3
Low Wood Gr CH61 .77 C4
Low Wood St L6 .53 A2
Lowcroft WN8 .16 C3
Lowden Ave L21 .27 B1
Lowe St Golborne WA3 .47 A8
St Helens WA10 .43 F4
Lowe St S WA10 .43 F3
Lowe's La WN8 .15 F8
Lowell St L4 .38 F1
Lower Alt Rd L38 .17 F4
Lower Appleton Rd WA8 .73 B1
Lower Bank View L20 .38 B1
Lower Breck Rd L6 .53 C5
Lower Carr La L37 .19 B7
Lower Castle St L2 .90 A3
Lower Cl L26 .83 A8
Lower Farm Rd L25 .70 A7
Lower Flaybrick Rd CH43 65 E8
Lower Gill St L3 .52 F2
Lower Gn CH49 .65 A3
Lower Hey L23 .27 B5
Lower House La
Liverpool L11 .40 A3
Widnes WA8 .84 F8
Lower La L10,L9 .39 F6
Lower Lee Sch L25 .69 E4
Lower Mersey View L20 .38 B1
Lower Prom Southport PR8 .4 A7
Southport PR9 .4 B8
Lower Rd Bebington CH62 .79 B6
Liverpool L26,WA8 .83 C7
Lower Sandfield L25 .70 B4
Lower Thingwall La CH61 .77 C5
Lowerson Cres L11 .53 E8
Lowerson Rd L11 .53 E8
Lowes Gn L37 .10 B3
Loweswater Cl WA2 .61 B3
Loweswater Cres WA11 .45 A6
Loweswater Way L33 .29 D4
Lowfield Ind Est WA9 .57 F5
Lowfield La WA9 .57 F5
Lowfield Rd L14 .54 C3
Lowfields Ave CH62 .88 E3
Lowfields Cl CH62 .88 E3
Lowlands Rd WA7 .84 F2
Lowndes Rd L6 .53 D6
Lowry Bank CH44 .51 E3
Lowry Cl L33 .29 E6
Lowther Ave Aintree L10 .28 D2
Maghull L31 .20 F2
Lowther Cres WA10 .57 B8
Lowther Dr L35 .57 C3
Lowther St L8 .68 A7
Lowton Gdns WA3 .47 B5
Lowton Rd WA3 .36 C1
Lowton West Prim Sch WA3 .47 D8
Lowwood Gr CH41 .66 D5
Lowwood Rd CH41 .66 D5
Loxdale Cl 24 L8 .68 A4
Loxley Rd PR8 .4 D4
Loxwood Cl L25 .70 B7
Loyola Hey L35 .72 E8
Lucan Rd L17 .68 E2
Lucania St L19 .81 C4
Lucerne Rd CH44 .51 D2
Lucerne St L17 .68 C3
Lucius Cl L9 .38 F7
Lucknow St 4 L17 .68 C4
Ludlow WN8 .16 C4
Ludlow Ct 1 CH48 .63 B1
Ludlow Dr Ormskirk L39 .13 D7
West Kirby CH48 .63 B1
Ludlow Gr CH62 .79 D1
Ludlow St L4 .38 F1
Ludwig Rd 7 L4 .53 B6
Lugard Rd L17 .68 E2
Lugsmore La WA10 .43 D1
Luke St Ashton-in-M WN4 .35 D5
Liverpool L8 .67 F6
Wallasey CH44 .51 E2
Lulworth WN8 .16 C4
Lulworth Ave L22 .26 C1
Lulworth Lo PR8 .3 F5
Lulworth Rd Liverpool L25 70 C5
Southport PR8 .3 F5
Lumber La WA5 .59 F8
Lumby Ave L36 .55 E3
Lumina CH62 .79 E1
Lumley Rd CH44 .51 D3
Lumley St L19 .81 B7
Lumley Wlk L24 .83 E1
Lunar Dr L30 .27 F4
Lunar Rd L9 .39 B6
Lune Ave L31 .20 E2
Lune St L23 .26 E4
Lune Way WA8 .72 C1
Lunehurst 12 WA3 .47 E8
Lunesdale Ave 3 L9 .39 B7
Lunsford Rd L14 .54 F4
Lunt Ave Litherland L30 .28 A2
Prescot L35 .56 E3
Lunt La L29 .27 D8
Lunt Rd Bootle L20 .38 C5
Lunt L29 .27 D8
Maghull L29 .19 C1
Lunt's Heath Rd WA8 .73 B5
Lunts Heath Prim Sch WA8 .73 B5
Luntswood Gr WA12 .46 A4
Lupin Dr WA11 .45 F6
Lupton Dr L23 .27 A4
Luscombe Cl L26 .83 A8
Lusitania Rd L4 .39 B2
Luther Gr WA9 .45 B2
Luton Gr L4 .52 F8
Luton St L5 .52 C6
Lutyens Cl 2 L4 .52 F7
Luxmore Rd L4 .39 A1
Lycett Rd Liverpool L4 .53 C7
Wallasey CH44 .50 E5
Lyceum Pl Liverpool L1 .90 B3
15 Liverpool L1 .90 B3
Lyceum St 16 L1 .90 B3
Lydbrook Cl 6 CH42 .66 F3
Lydbury Cl WA5 .60 D2
Lydbury Cres L32 .40 F8
Lydford Rd L12 .54 B8
Lydia Ann St L1 .90 B2
Lydia Wlk L10 .40 B7
Lydiate La
Crosby L23,L29,L30 .27 C6
Liverpool L25,L26 .70 D2
Willaston CH64 .87 E1
Lydiate Pk L23 .27 B6
Lydiate Prim Sch L31 .20 C4
Lydiate Rd L20 .38 C5
Lydiate Station Rd L31 .19 E5
Lydiate The CH60 .85 F7
Lydieth Lea L27 .70 E6
Lydney Rd L36 .55 B4
Lydstep Ct WA5 .60 E2
Lyelake Cl L32 .29 F1
Lyelake La L40 .14 F2
Lyelake Rd L32 .29 F1
Lyle St L5 .52 D5
Lyme Cl L36 .56 A6
Lyme Com Prim Sch WA12 .45 F4
Lyme Cross Rd L36 .55 F6
Lyme Gr L36 .55 F5
Lyme St Haydock WA11 .45 E6
Newton-le-W WA12 .45 F4
Lymecroft L25 .69 F2
Lymington Gr L30 .27 F3
Lymington Rd CH44 .50 F4
Lymm Rd CH43 .65 C7
Lynas Gdns L19 .81 B8
Lynas St CH41 .66 D8
Lynbridge Cl WN5 .25 E5
Lyncot Rd L9 .39 B8
Lyncroft Rd CH44 .51 C2
Lyndale WN8 .16 B4
Lyndale Ave
Bebington CH62 .88 E4
Warrington WA2 .61 F2
Lyndale Sch The CH62 .88 F5
Lyndene Rd L25 .70 A7
Lyndhurst Maghull L31 .20 D1
Skelmersdale WN8 .16 B4
Lyndhurst Ave
Heswall CH61 .77 A3
Liverpool L18 .69 A3
Lyndhurst Cl CH61 .77 A5
Lyndhurst Rd Crosby L23 .27 A4
Hoylake CH47 .48 E1
Irby CH61 .76 C6
Liverpool L18 .68 F3
Southport PR8 .4 B2
Wallasey CH45 .50 F6
Lyndhurst Way L36 .55 E2
Lyndon Dr L18 .69 B4
Lyndor Cl L25 .70 B1
Lyndor Rd L25 .70 B1
Lyneham L35 .56 F2
Lynholme Rd L4 .53 B7
Lynmouth Rd L17 .80 E8
Lynn Cl WA10 .43 C4
Lynnbank CH43 .66 B4
Lynnbank Rd L18 .69 D5
Lynscott Pl L16 .69 D8
Lynsted Rd L14 .54 F3
Lynton Cl Heswall CH60 .86 B6
Liverpool L19 .81 B8
Warrington WA5 .74 E4
Lynton Cres WA8 .72 E2
Lynton Ct Crosby L23 .26 B4
Hoylake CH47 .63 A6
Lynton Dr Bebington CH63 79 A3
Southport PR8 .3 E1
Lynton Gn L25 .69 F4
Lynton Gr WA9 .58 C5
Lynton Rd Huyton-w-R L36 .56 B3
Southport PR8 .3 E1
Wallasey CH45 .50 E6
Lynton Way WA10 .43 B6
Lynwood Ave
Golborne WA3 .47 E6
Ormskirk L39 .13 C3
Wallasey CH44 .51 A3
Lynwood Cl WN8 .24 D7
Lynwood Dr CH61 .76 E6
Lynwood End L39 .13 C3
Lynwood Gdns L9 .38 F5
Lynwood Rd L9 .39 A5
Lynxway The L12 .54 D4
Lyon Cl WA10 .43 F3
Lyon Rd L4 .53 B6
Lyon St Ashton-in-M WN4 .34 F7
Liverpool L19 .81 D4
St Helens WA10 .43 F3
Lyons Cl CH46 .49 E1
Lyons Pl L25 .82 D8
Lyons Rd Southport PR8 .4 A5
Wallasey CH46 .49 E1
Warrington WA5 .74 F4
Lyra Rd L22 .26 D1
Lyster Rd L20 .38 A3
Lytham Cl L10 .28 F1
Lytham Ct L32 .29 C3
Lytham Rd
Ashton-in-M WN4 .34 F5
Southport PR9 .2 A4
Widnes WA8 .73 C2
Lytham Way L12 .54 E6
Lytles Cl L37 .10 A2
Lyttelton Rd L17 .68 E2
Lytton Ave CH42 .66 F1
Lytton Gr L21 .38 A6
Lytton St L6 .52 F3

M

Mab La L12,L14 .54 F7
Mab Lane JMI Sch L12 .54 F7
Macalpine Cl CH49 .65 A6
Macbeth St L20 .38 C1
Macdermott Rd WA8 .84 F5
Macdona Dr CH48 .75 B8
Macdonald Ave WA11 .44 E5
Macdonald Dr CH49 .64 D3
Macdonald Rd CH46 .64 C8
Macdonald St L15 .68 E8
Mace Rd L11 .40 C3
MacFarren St 2 L13 .54 A3
Mack Gr L30 .27 D2
Mackenzie Rd CH46 .50 B3
Macket's La L25 .82 C7
Mackets Cl L25 .70 C1
Mackets Prim Sch L25 .70 D1
MacQueen St 2 L13 .54 A2
Maddock Rd CH44 .51 D5
Maddock St CH41 .66 C8
Maddocks St 1 L13 .54 A2
Maddrell St L3 .52 B4
Madeira Dr L25 .70 B7
Madelaine St L8 .68 A6
Madeley Cl CH48 .63 B1
Madeley Dr CH48 .63 B1
Madeley St L6 .53 C3
Madeline McKenna Ct WA8 .72 C3
Madison Sq L1 .90 C2
Madryn Ave L33 .30 A2
Madryn St L8 .68 A5
Maelor Cl CH63 .88 C6
Mafeking Cl 1 L15 .68 F8
Mafeking Pl WN4 .35 C3
Magazine Ave CH45 .51 B7
Magazine Brow CH45 .51 C7
Magazine La
Bebington CH62 .79 E4
Wallasey CH45 .51 C7
Magazine Rd CH62 .79 D3
Magazine Wlk CH62 .79 D3
Magazines Prom CH45 .51 C7
Magdala St L7,L8 .68 C7
Magdalen Dr WN4 .34 F4
Magdalene Sq L30 .27 F4
Maggots Nook Rd WA11 .24 A1
Maghull Com Prim Sch L31 .28 C7
Maghull High Sch L31 .28 C8
Maghull La L31 .21 B1
Maghull Smallholdings Est L31 .20 F3
Maghull Sta L31 .28 E7
Magnolia Cl Liverpool L26 70 D2
St Helens WA11 .44 F5
Magnolia Wlk CH49 .64 C2
Magnum St L5 .52 F5
Magnus Cl L13 .53 F5
Maguire Ave L20 .38 E4
Maharishi School of the Age of Enlightenment L40 .16 A5
Mahon Ave L20 .38 D6
Mahon Ct 7 L8 .67 F7
Maiden Cl WN8 .15 C2
Maiden La L13 .53 D7
Maidford Rd L14 .54 F4
Maidstone Cl L25 .82 C7
Maidstone Dr L14 .54 F5
Main Ave WA10 .57 C7
Main Cl WA11 .45 A6
Main Dr L35 .56 E1
Main La WA3 .47 F3
Main Rd CH62,CH63 .79 B4
Main St WN5 .33 E5
Mains Ave WN2 .35 F7
Mainside Rd L32 .29 F1
Maintree Cres L24 .83 A4
Mainwaring Rd
Bebington CH62 .88 D8
Wallasey CH44 .51 D3
Mairscough La L39 .12 B1
Maitland Cl L8 .68 B7
Maitland Rd CH45 .51 C8
Maitland St 4 L8 .68 B7
Majestic Mews WN5 .25 D5
Major St L5 .52 D6
Makepeace Wlk 2 L8 .67 F6
Makerfield Dr WA12 .46 A5
Makin St L4 .38 F2
Malcolm Ave WA2 .61 D1
Malcolm Cres CH63 .88 C6
Malcolm Gr L20 .38 D1
Malcolm Pl L15 .53 F1
Malden Rd L6 .53 C3
Maldon Cl L26 .82 F6
Maldwyn Rd CH44 .51 B5
Maley Cl L8 .68 A4
Malham Cl PR8 .4 E3
Malhamdale Ave L35 .57 D2
Malika Pl WN4 .34 E6
Malin Cl L24 .83 D2
Mall The L5 .53 A5
Mallaby St CH41 .66 A8
Mallard Cl Liverpool L12 .40 F3
Liverpool,Halewood L26 .70 E1
Ormskirk L39 .13 C2
Warrington WA2 .61 D3
Mallard Gdns WA9 .57 E6
Mallard Ho L31 .20 B4
Mallard Way
St Helens WA11 .44 B6
Wallasey CH46 .49 C1
Mallards The PR9 .2 C3
Mallee Ave PR9 .2 A3
Mallee Cres PR9 .2 A3
Malleson Rd L13 .53 E7
Mallins Cl L8 .68 A4
Mallory Ave L31 .20 B4
Mallory Gr WA11 .44 D6
Mallory Rd CH42 .66 D2
Mallow Rd L6 .53 C3
Mallow Way L36 .70 F8
Mallowdale Cl CH62 .88 F5
Malmesbury Cl 2 CH49 .64 C4
Malmesbury Rd L11 .39 E2
Malpas Ave CH43 .66 A2
Malpas Dr CH63 .78 E7
Malpas Gr CH45 .51 A6
Malpas Rd Liverpool L11 .40 D5
Wallasey CH45 .51 A6
Malt House Ct WA10 .43 C6
Malt St L7 .68 B8
Malta Cl L36 .55 D3
Malta St L8 .67 F5
Malta Wlk 5 L8 .67 F5
Maltkiln La L39 .21 E8
Malton Ave WA3 .47 E7
Malton Cl WA8 .72 C5
Malton Rd L25 .70 C2
Malvern Ave L14 .54 F2
Malvern Cl
Ashton-in-M WN4 .35 B4
Kirkby L32 .29 C4
Malvern Cres L14 .54 F2
Malvern Gr Aintree L10 .28 C2
Birkenhead CH42 .66 D2
Malvern Prim Sch L14 .54 F2
Malvern Rd Bootle L20 .38 C5
Haydock WA9 .45 A4
Liverpool L6 .53 C3
Wallasey CH45 .50 D5
Malverns The CH43 .66 A3
Malwood St L8 .67 F4
Manchester Rd
Prescot L34 .56 C5
Southport PR9 .4 C7
Manchester Row WA12 .60 D8
Mandela Ct L8 .68 B5
Mandela Ho L15 .68 E7

Mandeville Rd PR8 ....7 B5
Mandeville St L4 ....38 F2
Manesty's La L1 ....90 B3
Manfield WN8 ....16 A3
Manfred St 1 L6 ....53 A2
Manica Cres L10 ....39 F6
Manion Ave L31 ....20 B5
Manion Cl L31 ....20 B5
Manley Ave WA3 ....35 F2
Manley Cl CH43 ....65 F3
Manley Pl WA9 ....57 E7
Manley Rd Crosby L22 ....26 D2
Huyton-w-R L36 ....71 A8
Mann Island L3 ....52 B1
Mann St L8 ....67 E6
Mannering Ct 11 L17 ....68 C4
Mannering Rd L17 ....68 C4
Manners La CH60 ....85 E6
Manning Rd PR8 ....4 E6
Manning St WA10 ....43 F3
Manningham Rd L4,L6 ...53 C6
Mannington Cl CH47 ....63 E8
Manor Ave Crosby L23 ...26 D5
Golborne WA3 ....47 C8
Newton-le-W WA12 ....45 F4
Rainhill L35 ....57 C2
Manor Cl Bootle L20 .....38 E2
Garswood WN4 ....34 C3
Manor Cres L25 ....70 B1
Manor Ct Birkenhead CH49 64 C3
Golborne WA3 ....47 C8
Irby CH61 ....76 D6
7 Liverpool L17 ....68 C4
West Kirby CH48 ....63 A3
Manor Dr
Birkenhead CH49 ....65 A6
Crosby L23 ....26 D5
Litherland L30 ....28 B3
Manor Farm Rd L36 .....55 F1
Manor Gr Kirkby L32 .....29 B2
Skelmersdale WN8 ....15 F1
Manor High Sch L23 ....26 C6
Manor Hill CH43 ....66 A6
Manor Ho Bebington CH62 88 D8
Liverpool L17 ....68 B3
Manor House Cl
Billinge WA11 ....33 B1
Maghull L31 ....20 C1
Manor House Dr WN8 ...24 E3
Manor La Birkenhead CH42 67 A2
Wallasey CH44,CH45 .....51 C5
Manor Lo L37 ....9 E4
Manor Mans 3 CH44 ...51 C5
Manor Mews CH44 ....51 C5
Manor Pl Bebington CH62 .79 D5
Widnes WA8 ....72 B1
Manor Prim Sch CH43 ...65 C7
Manor Rd Bebington CH62 .88 E6
Crosby L23 ....26 C5
Haydock WA11 ....45 F7
Hoylake CH47 ....63 C7
Irby CH61 ....76 D6
Liverpool L25 ....70 B1
Southport PR9 ....2 A2
Thornton Hough CH63 ....87 A7
Wallasey CH44,CH45 .....51 C5
Widnes WA8 ....72 B1
Manor Rd Sta CH47 .....63 C7
Manor St Golborne WA3 ..36 B1
St Helens WA9 ....44 C2
Manor The WA11 ....32 C4
Manor View L12 ....40 F1
Manor Way L25 ....70 B1
Manorbier Cres L9 ......39 A3
Manorside Cl CH49 ......64 F6
Manorwood Dr L35 ......56 F2
Mansart Cl WN4 ....35 D3
Manse Gdns WA12 ....46 D4
Mansell Cl WA8 ....73 C5
Mansell Dr L26 ....82 E6
Mansell Rd L6 ....53 B3
Mansfield St
Golborne WA3 ....35 F1
Liverpool L3 ....52 E3
Mansion Dr L11 ....40 B4
Manston Rd WA5 ....74 F3
Manton Rd L6 ....53 C3
Manvers Rd L16 ....54 E1
Manville Rd CH45 ....51 B7
Manville St WA9 ....44 C1
Manx Jane's La PR9 .....2 A4
Maple Ave Golborne WA3 .47 F7
Haydock WA11 ....45 B7
Newton-le-W WA12 ....46 D2
5 Widnes WA8 ....73 B1
Maple Cl Billinge WN5 ....33 D5
Bootle L21 ....38 A6
Formby L37 ....9 C1
Liverpool L12 ....40 D3
Prescot L35 ....56 E3
Maple Cres
Huyton-w-R L36 ....55 D2
Warrington WA5 ....74 F3
Maple Dr WN2 ....36 B7
Maple Gr Bebington CH62 .88 C8
Liverpool L8 ....68 C6
Prescot L35 ....56 E5
St Helens WA10 ....43 C3
Maple Rd WA2 ....61 B6
Maple St Ashton-in-M WN4 35 A6
Birkenhead CH41 ....66 D5
Southport PR8 ....4 E6
Maple Tree Gr CH60 .....77 C1
Maple Twrs L33 ....29 F3
Mapledale Rd L18 ....69 B5
Maples Ct CH43 ....66 A3
Mapleton Cl CH43 ....65 E1
Maplewood 9 Kirkby L32 .40 F8
Maplewood *continued*
Skelmersdale WN8 ....16 A4
Southport PR9 ....1 F2
Maplewood Cl
Liverpool L27 ....70 E5
Widnes WA8 ....84 A7
Maplewood Gr CH43 ....65 E8
Maranatha Bglws CH60 ..77 A1
Marathon Cl L6 ....52 F4
Marble Cl L20 ....38 C2
Marble Pl PR8 ....4 B7
Marbury Rd L32 ....29 C2
Marc Ave L31 ....29 B4
March Rd L6 ....53 D5
Marcham Way 2 L11 ....40 B1
Marchant Cl L30 ....39 B8
Marchbank Rd WN8 .....15 D1
Marchfield Rd L9 ....38 F5
Marchwood Way L25 .....70 A7
Marcien Way WA8 ....72 F3
Marcot Rd L6 ....53 D4
Marcross Cl WA5 ....60 E1
Marcus St CH41 ....66 D7
Marcus Street Workshops
CH41 ....66 D7
Mardale Ave
St Helens WA11 ....44 B8
Warrington WA2 ....61 C3
Mardale Cl Liverpool L27 ..71 A3
Southport PR8 ....7 B4
Mardale Lawn L27 ....71 A3
Mardale Rd L36 ....55 C5
Mardale Wlk
Huyton-w-R L36 ....55 C5
Liverpool L27 ....71 A3
Mareth Cl L18 ....69 A2
Marford Rd L12 ....54 B7
Marfords Ave CH63 ......88 C7
Margaret Ave Bootle L20 .38 C6
St Helens WA9 ....58 C8
Margaret Beavan Sch
L12 ....54 A7
Margaret Ct WA10 ....43 D1
Margaret Rd Crosby L23 ..26 A5
Liverpool L4 ....38 E2
Margaret St Liverpool L6 ..53 A4
St Helens WA9 ....58 E3
Margery Rd WA10 ....43 C1
Maria Rd L9 ....38 F3
Marian Ave WA12 ....45 F3
Marian Cl L35 ....57 C2
Marian Cl The L30 ....27 E4
Marian Dr
Birkenhead CH46 ....64 E8
Rainhill L35 ....57 B2
Marian Rd WA11 ....45 E7
Marian Sq L30 ....27 F3
Marian Way The L30 .....27 E3
Marians Dr L39 ....13 E7
Maricourt RC High Sch
Maghull L31 ....28 D8
Maghull L31 ....28 E8
Marie Curie Ave L30 .....27 F3
Marigold Way WA9 ....59 A7
Marina Ave Litherland L21 .38 B8
St Helens WA9 ....58 C7
Marina Cres
Huyton-w-R L36 ....55 D1
Litherland L30 ....28 A1
Marina Ct CH47 ....63 A2
Marina Dr WA2 ....61 C1
Marina Rd L37 ....9 F1
Marine Cres L22 ....37 D8
Marine Dr Heswall CH60 ..85 D6
Southport,Birkdale PR8 ....3 E7
Southport,Marshside PR8,
PR9 ....1 D4
Marine Gate Mans PR9 ...4 B8
Marine Par PR8 ....4 A8
Marine Park Mans CH45 .37 B1
Marine Pk CH48 ....63 B3
Marine Prom CH45 ....37 B1
Marine Rd CH47 ....63 A7
Marine Terr Seaforth L22 .37 D8
Wallasey CH45 ....51 C7
Mariners Rd Crosby L23 ..26 B3
Wallasey CH45 ....51 C7
Mariners Way 3 L20 .....38 C3
Mariners Wharf L3 ....67 D6
Marion Gr L18 ....69 B2
Marion Pl WN2 ....35 F8
Marion Rd L20 ....38 D6
Marion St CH41 ....66 E6
Maritime Cl WA12 ....46 C5
Maritime Ct
Birkenhead CH49 ....65 B1
Litherland L30 ....27 F5
12 Liverpool L6 ....53 B3
Liverpool,Sandfield Park
L12 ....54 A8
Southport PR9 ....4 B8
Maritime Ent Pk L20 ....38 B4
Maritime Grange 15
CH44 ....51 E2
Maritime Lo L5 ....52 F6
Maritime Pk 19 CH41 ....66 C5
Maritime Pl L3 ....52 E3
Maritime View CH42 .....66 D3
Maritime Way L1 ....90 B2
Marius Cl L4 ....52 F8
Mark Rake CH62 ....79 D1
Mark Rd L38 ....17 F4
Mark St L5 ....52 E7
Market App WN4 ....35 B3
Market Cross 5 L39 .....13 E5
Market Pl
Birkenhead CH41 ....66 F6
Prescot L34 ....56 D6
Market Sq 9 L1 ....90 B3
Market St
Birkenhead CH41 ....66 E6
Hoylake CH47 ....63 B7
Newton-le-W WA12 ....46 A3
Southport PR8 ....4 B7
10 St Helens WA10 .....44 A3
Market Way
8 Liverpool L1 ....90 B3
6 Ormskirk L39 ....13 E5
Markfield Cres
Liverpool L25 ....70 C1
St Helens WA11 ....44 C5
Markfield Rd L20 ....38 C5
Markham Dr PR8 ....4 E2
Markham Gr CH43 ....65 F8
Marksway CH61 ....77 A4
Marl Gr WN5 ....25 D4
Marl Rd Kirkby L33 ....30 C3
Litherland L30 ....28 B3
Marland WN8 ....16 A4
Marlborough WN8 ....16 A4
Marlborough Ave
Litherland L30 ....28 A2
Maghull L31 ....20 D3
Marlborough Cres WA8 ..73 A5
Marlborough Gdns 5 PR9 4 C8
Marlborough Gr CH43 ...66 C4
Marlborough Pl 5 L3 ...52 C3
Marlborough Rd
Crosby L23 ....26 D3
Liverpool L13 ....53 E6
Prescot L34 ....56 E7
Seaforth L22 ....37 E8
Southport PR9 ....4 C7
Wallasey CH45 ....51 C7
Marlborough St 4 L3 ...52 C3
Marlbrook Rd L25 ....70 B6
Marldon Ave L23 ....26 E2
Marldon Rd L11,L12 ......54 B8
Marled Hey L28 ....55 A8
Marlew Day Hospl WA9 .57 C5
Marley Cl L35 ....57 E1
Marlfield La CH61 ....77 A4
Marlfield Rd L12 ....54 B6
Marline Ave CH63 ....88 C6
Marling Pk WA8 ....72 B1
Marlowe Cl Liverpool L19 .81 C5
Widnes WA8 ....72 F1
Marlowe Dr L12 ....54 A6
Marlowe Rd CH44 ....51 A4
Marlsford St L6 ....53 C3
Marlston Ave CH61 ......76 F6
Marlwood Ave CH45 ......50 E5
Marmaduke St L7 ....53 B1
Marmion Ave L20 ....38 E7
Marmion Cl WA3 ....36 E1
Marmion Rd Hoylake CH47 63 B7
Liverpool L17 ....68 C4
Marmonde St L4 ....52 E8
Marnock Cl WN2 ....36 F8
Marnwood Rd L32 ....29 D1
Marnwood Wlk 6 L32 ...29 C1
Marple Cl CH43 ....65 E3
Marquis St
Bebington CH62 ....79 B7
Birkenhead CH41 ....66 E4
Liverpool L3 ....90 C4
Marram Cl CH46 ....50 A1
Marron Ave WA2 ....61 B2
Marryat Cl WA2 ....61 A6
Marsden Ave WA10 ......43 D4
Marsden Cl CH44 ....51 D5
Marsden Ct
12 Wallasey CH45 ....51 B7
Widnes WA8 ....72 E4
Marsden Rd Liverpool L26 .82 F6
Southport PR9 ....4 E7
Marsden St 12 L6 ....53 A3
Marsden Way 13 L6 .....53 A3
Marsh Ave L20 ....38 E6
Marsh Brows L37 ....9 E2
Marsh Hall Pad WA8 .....73 B4
Marsh La Bebington CH63 .78 C7
Bootle L20 ....38 C4
Hightown L37,L38 ....18 E6
Warrington WA5 ....74 C2
Marsh St Liverpool L20 ...38 D1
St Helens WA9 ....44 C3
Marshall Ave
St Helens WA9 ....58 C8
Warrington WA5 ....60 F2
Marshall Cl L33 ....29 F5
Marshall Pl L3 ....52 C4
Marshall St CH41 ....66 C8
Marshall's Cl L31 ....20 C4
Marshalls Cross Rd WA9 .58 B7
Marshallsay L37 ....10 A2
Marsham Cl CH49 ....65 A7
Marsham Rd L25 ....70 C5
Marshfield Cl L36 ....55 F3
Marshfield Ct CH46 ......49 E3
Marshfield Rd L11 ....40 B1
Marshgate WA8 ....84 B6
Marshgate Rd L12 ....40 C2
Marshlands Rd 1 CH45 ..50 E6
Marshside Cl L8 ....67 F5
Marshside Nature Reserve★
PR9 ....1 E5
Marshside Prim Sch PR9 .2 A5
Marshside Rd PR9 ....1 F4
Marshway Dr WA12 ......46 B5
Marsland Gr WA9 ....58 E8
Marston Cl
Bebington CH62 ....88 E3
Birkenhead CH43 ....65 F3
Marston Cres L38 ....18 A2
Marten Ave CH63 ....88 C7
Martensen St L7 ....53 B1
Martin Ave
Newton-le-W WA12 ....46 C5
St Helens WA10 ....43 F6
Warrington WA2 ....61 E1
Martin Cl Irby CH61 .....76 C6
Liverpool L18 ....69 A1
Rainhill L35 ....57 A4
Martin Gr L35 ....56 E5
Martin Rd L18 ....69 A1
Martin's La CH44 ....51 C4
Martindale Rd
Bebington CH62 ....79 E1
Billinge WA11 ....33 C2
Liverpool L18 ....69 D5
Martine Cl L31 ....29 B4
Martinhall Rd L9 ....39 F4
Martins La WN8 ....24 D7
Martland Ave Aintree L10 .28 E2
Golborne WA3 ....47 E7
Martland Rd L25 ....70 C4
Martlesham Cres CH49 ..64 B3
Martlett Rd L12 ....54 D5
Martock L35 ....56 F2
Marton Cl L24 ....82 D3
Marton Gn L24 ....82 D2
Marton Rd L36 ....55 E6
Marvin St L6 ....53 A3
Marwood Twr L5 ....52 E6
Mary Ave PR8 ....7 E6
Mary Rd L20 ....38 D6
Mary St WA9 ....58 E3
Mary Stockton Ct 5 L21 .38 A6
Marybone L3 ....52 D3
Maryfield L23 ....26 E3
Maryfield Cl WA3 ....47 A7
Maryland Ho 8 L20 .....38 C3
Maryland La CH46 ....49 D1
Maryland St L1 ....90 C2
Marylebone Ave WA9 ....57 F6
Maryport Cl L5 ....52 F6
Maryton Grange L18 .....69 D2
Maryville Rd L34 ....56 E6
Marywell Cl WA9 ....58 D7
Masefield Ave WA8 ......84 F8
Masefield Cl CH62 ....79 A7
Masefield Cres L30 ......38 D8
Masefield Dr WA2 ....61 A5
Masefield Gr Liverpool L16 69 F8
St Helens WA10 ....43 D5
Masefield Pl L30 ....38 E8
Masefield Rd L23 ....27 C6
Maskell Rd L13 ....53 F3
Mason Ave WA8 ....73 B4
Mason Cl WN4 ....35 D4
Mason St Abram WN2 ....36 B8
Crosby L22 ....26 D1
Liverpool L7 ....53 A1
Liverpool,Woolton L25 ....70 A2
Wallasey CH45 ....51 B8
Massam Cl WA11 ....32 A6
Massam's La L37 ....9 F6
Massey Ave WA5 ....60 F2
Massey Pk CH45 ....51 A5
Massey St
Birkenhead CH41 ....66 D8
St Helens WA9 ....58 C8
Masters Way L19 ....81 D4
Matchwood Cl L19 ....81 D5
Matchworks The L19 ....81 E5
Mather Ave Golborne WA3 47 E6
Liverpool L18,L19 ....69 C2
St Helens WA9 ....44 E3
Mather Ct 3 CH43 ......66 B5
Mather Rd CH43 ....66 B5
Mathew St L2 ....90 A3
Mathieson Rd WA8 ......84 E5
Matlock Ave
7 Liverpool L9 ....39 A6
Southport PR8 ....4 B4
Matlock Cl Southport PR8 ..4 B4
Warrington WA5 ....60 A1
Matlock Cres PR8 ....4 B4
Matlock Rd PR8 ....4 B4
Matthew Arnold Prim Sch
L8 ....68 A3
Matthew Cl 16 CH44 ....51 E2
Matthew St CH44 ....51 E2
Maud Roberts Ct L21 ....38 A8
Maud St L8 ....68 A6
Maunders Ct L23 ....27 A5
Maureen Wlk L10 ....40 B7
Mauretania Rd L4 ....39 A2
Maurice Jones Ct CH46 ..49 E1
Mavis Dr CH49 ....65 A3
Mawdsley Cl L37 ....10 B3
Mawdsley Terr L39 ......13 F7
Max Rd L14 ....54 F6
Maxton Rd L6 ....53 C3
Maxwell Cl CH49 ....65 A6
Maxwell Pl L13 ....53 F6
Maxwell Rd L13 ....53 F6
Maxwell St WA10 ....43 E3
May Ave Abram Brow WN2 .36 C7
Wallasey CH44 ....51 D2
May Cl L21 ....38 B6
May Pl Liverpool L3 ......90 C3
Liverpool,Broad Green L13 .54 A2
May Rd CH60 ....86 A8
May St Bootle L20 ....38 C5
Golborne WA3 ....36 B2
Liverpool L3 ....90 C3
Maybank Cl PR9 ....2 A1
Maybank Gr L17 ....68 F1
Maybank Rd CH42 ....66 D4
Maybury Way L17 ....68 C2
Mayer Ave CH63 ....78 F4
Mayew Rd CH61 ....76 F6
Mayfair Ave Crosby L23 ..26 E5
Huyton-w-R L14 ....54 F3
Mayfair Cl Hightown L38 ..17 F2
1 Liverpool L6 ....53 B4
Warrington WA5 ....74 D7
Mayfair Gr WA8 ....72 D1
Mayfayre Ave L31 ....20 B5
Mayfield L4 ....52 E8
Mayfield Ave Formby L37 ..9 C1
St Helens WA9 ....57 E8
Widnes WA8 ....72 B1
Mayfield Cl L12 ....54 C6
Mayfield Ct Formby L37 ...9 F5
Widnes WA8 ....73 A2
Mayfield Dr CH62 ....89 B6
Mayfield Gdns
Liverpool L19 ....81 A7
Neston CH64 ....86 E1
Mayfield Rd
Bebington CH63 ....79 A3
Liverpool L19 ....81 A7
Up Holland WN8 ....25 B7
Wallasey CH45 ....50 F5
Mayfield St WN4 ....35 A3
Mayfields Ho CH62 ......79 B7
Mayfields N CH62 ....79 B7
Mayfields S CH62 ....79 B7
Mayflower Ave L24 ......82 A6
Mayflower Ind Est L37 ..10 A1
Mayford Cl L25 ....70 B6
Mayhall Ct L31 ....20 D2
Maypole Ct L30 ....27 D5
Maypole Ind Est WN2 ...36 C7
Mayrick Cl WA12 ....46 A3
Maytree Cl L27 ....70 C6
Maytree Wlk WN8 ....16 B4
Mayville Rd L18 ....69 B5
Mazzini Cl L5 ....52 E4
Mc Clellan Pl WA8 ......73 B1
McBride St L19 ....81 C6
McCormack Ave WA9 ....44 E3
McCulloch St WA9 ....44 C3
McFarlane Ave WA10 ....43 C4
McGill Ct 9 CH41 ....66 D7
McGough Cl WA9 ....58 A3
McGregor St L5 ....52 F5
McKee Ave WA2 ....61 B2
McKeown Cl 2 L5 ....52 D5
Mckinley Way WA8 ....72 F3
McMinnis Ave WA9 ....45 B2
McVinnie Rd L35 ....56 F6
Mead Ave L21 ....38 C8
Meade Cl L35 ....57 D1
Meade Rd L13 ....53 E6
Meadfoot Rd CH46 ....49 D1
Meadow Ave Southport PR8 4 C4
St Helens WA9 ....58 D3
Meadow Bank
Maghull L31 ....20 B2
3 Ormskirk L39 ....13 F5
Meadow Bank Sch L10 ..39 F8
Meadow Brook Cl L10 ...40 B7
Meadow Brow PR9 ....2 D5
Meadow Cl
Newton-le-W WA12 ....45 F3
Skelmersdale WN8 ....24 D7
Westhead L40 ....14 E4
Widnes WA8 ....72 D3
Meadow Clough WN8 ....16 B4
Meadow Cres CH49 ......65 B2
Meadow Ct L11 ....40 B4
Meadow Dr
Huyton-w-R L36 ....70 F8
Ormskirk L39 ....13 C2
Meadow Hey L20 ....38 A6
Meadow Hey Cl L25 .....70 B3
Meadow La
Birkenhead CH42 ....66 F2
Liverpool L11,L12 ....54 B8
Maghull L31 ....20 F1
Southport PR8 ....7 D3
St Helens WA9 ....44 F2
Willaston CH64 ....87 F1
Meadow Oak Dr L25 .....70 A4
Meadow Pk 2 CH42 .....66 F2
Meadow Rd CH48 ....63 F3
Meadow St CH45 ....51 A8
Meadow The CH49 ....65 B3
Meadow View
Litherland L21 ....27 B3
Southport PR8 ....4 D4
Meadow Way L12 ....40 B1
Meadow Wlk CH61 ....76 E3
Meadowbank Cl L12 .....54 E5
Meadowbridge Cl L40 ...14 E4
Meadowbrook Rd CH46 .64 D7
Meadowcroft
Ashton-in-M WN4 ....34 F6
Formby L37 ....9 F2
Heswall CH60 ....77 C1
Skelmersdale WN8 ....16 B4
St Helens WA9 ....58 C6
Meadowcroft Pk L12 ....54 D4
Meadowcroft Rd CH47 ...48 E1
Meadowfield WN8 ....25 A7
Meadowfield Cl
3 Birkenhead CH42 ......66 F2
Liverpool L9 ....39 A7
Meadows The
Maghull L31 ....20 D1
Rainhill L35 ....57 C3
Meadowside CH46 ....50 B4
Meadowside Ave WN4 ...35 A8
Meadowside Dr L33 .....29 F6
Meadowside Rd CH62 ...88 D8

Mona St Birkenhead CH41 .65 F7
Bootle L20 .38 D6
St Helens WA10 .43 D3
Monaghan Cl L9 .39 A7
Monash Rd L11 .53 F8
Monastery La WA9 .58 E7
Monastery Rd
4 Liverpool L6 .53 C6
St Helens WA9 .58 E7
Mond Rd Liverpool L10 .40 A7
5 Widnes WA8 .73 A1
Monfa Rd Bootle L20 .38 C6
Bootle L20 .38 D6
Monica Dr WA8 .73 A5
Monica Rd L25 .70 B1
Monica Terr WN4 .35 B2
Monk Rd CH44,CH45 .51 B4
Monk St Birkenhead CH41 .66 F6
Liverpool L5 .52 F6
Monk's Way CH48 .63 C2
Monkfield Way L19 .81 D4
Monks Carr La L37,L38 .19 A6
Monks Cl L37 .10 A1
Monks Dr L37 .10 A1
Monks Ferry CH41 .66 F6
Monks Way
Bebington CH63 .78 F4
Liverpool L25 .70 B2
Monksdown Prim Sch L11 .40 A1
Monksdown Rd L11 .40 A1
Monksferry Wlk L19 .80 F7
Monkswell Dr L15 .69 A8
Monkswell St L8 .68 A3
Monkswood Cl WA5 .60 E2
Monmouth Cres WN4 .35 D2
Monmouth Dr L10 .28 F1
Monmouth Gr WA9 .44 D2
Monmouth Rd CH44 .50 F4
Monro Cl L8 .67 F4
Monro St L8 .67 F4
Mons Sq 5 L20 .38 C3
Montagu Mews L37 .9 E5
Montagu Rd L37 .9 E5
Montague Rd L13 .54 A2
Montclair Dr L18 .69 B6
Monterey Rd L13 .54 B2
Montfort Dr L19 .81 A7
Montgomery Ave PR9 .5 B6
Montgomery Cl L35 .56 D2
Montgomery Hill
Birkenhead CH48 .64 A1
Irby CH48 .76 A8
Montgomery Ho 8 L21 .37 F7
Montgomery Rd
Huyton-w-R L36 .55 E4
Liverpool L9 .39 A7
Widnes WA8 .84 D8
Montgomery Way 3 L6 .53 B4
Montpelier Dr 8 L8 .67 F4
Montpellier Cres CH45 .51 A8
Montreal Rd L27 .70 E5
Montreal St WN7 .36 E4
Montrey Cres WN4 .34 C3
Montrose Ave CH44 .51 E1
Montrose Cl WA2 .61 F4
Montrose Ct Hoylake CH47 63 B6
Liverpool L12 .54 F7
Montrose Dr PR9 .1 F1
Montrose Pl L26 .82 F6
Montrose Rd L13 .53 E6
Montrose Way L13 .53 F2
Montrovia Cres L10 .39 F6
Monville Rd L9 .39 C7
Moor Cl Crosby L23 .26 F5
Southport PR8 .7 D2
Moor Coppice L23 .26 F5
Moor Ct L10 .40 A7
Moor Dr Crosby L23 .26 F4
Skelmersdale WN8 .24 D7
Moor Ho 4 L23 .26 E5
Moor La Crosby L23 .26 F5
Heswall CH60 .85 F8
Ince Blundell L38,L23 .18 E2
Liverpool L10 .40 A7
Liverpool L32 .40 B8
Liverpool,Walton L4 .39 A2
Maghull L29 .19 D1
Southport PR8 .7 C2
Widnes WA8 .84 F7
Moor La S WA8 .84 F7
Moor Pl L3 .90 C4
Moor Rd WN5 .25 E6
Moor St Liverpool L2 .90 A3
Ormskirk L39 .13 F5
Moorbridge Cl L30 .28 A5
Moorcroft Rd
Huyton-w-R L36 .55 E5
Liverpool L18 .69 D1
Wallasey CH45 .50 D5
Moore Ave
Birkenhead CH42 .66 E2
St Helens WA9 .45 B3
Moore Cl WA8 .73 D2
Moore Dr WA11 .45 F6
Moore St L20 .38 B5
Moore's Ho 11 L4 .38 F2
Mooreway L35 .57 E1
Moorfield L33 .29 F5
Moorfield Ctr The L33 .29 F6
Moorfield Dr CH64 .86 C1
Moorfield Prim Sch WA8 .73 D3
Moorfield Rd Crosby L23 .27 A5
St Helens WA10 .43 D5
Widnes WA8 .73 D3
Moorfields L2 .90 A4
Moorfields Ave CH43 .65 D4
Moorfields Sta L2 .90 A4
Moorfoot Rd WA9 .44 F3
Moorfoot Way L33 .29 D6
Moorgate L39 .13 E4
Moorgate Ave L23 .26 F4
Moorgate La 8 L32 .41 A8
Moorgate Rd L32 .41 A7
Moorgate St 8 L7 .53 B1
Moorhey Rd L31 .28 D6
Moorhouses L38 .17 F3
Moorings Cl CH64 .86 B1
Moorings The
6 Birkenhead CH41 .66 D5
Heswall CH60 .85 C8
Maghull L31 .20 B4
West Kirby CH48 .63 A2
Moorland Ave L23 .26 E5
Moorland Cl CH60 .86 A7
Moorland Pk CH60 .86 A7
Moorland Rd
Ashton-in-M WN4 .35 E5
Birkenhead CH42 .66 E3
Maghull L31 .28 D6
Moorlands Rd L23 .27 B6
Moorside Cl L23 .26 F4
Moorside Com Prim Sch WN8 .24 E7
Moorside Ct WA8 .84 F7
Moorside Rd L23 .26 F4
Moorway CH60 .86 B8
Moorwood Cres WA9 .58 C4
Moray Cl WA10 .43 E5
Morcott La L24 .83 D2
Morden Ave WN4 .35 B3
Morden St L6 .53 C3
Morecambe St L6 .53 C5
Morecroft Rd CH42 .67 A1
Morella Rd L4 .53 C8
Morello Cl WA10 .43 F5
Morello Dr CH63 .79 B2
Moret Cl L23 .27 A5
Moreton Ave 1 WA9 .58 C4
Moreton Cl WA3 .35 F1
Moreton Gr CH45 .50 E6
Moreton Rd CH49 .64 F6
Moreton Sta CH46 .49 E2
Morgan Ave WA2 .61 C2
Morgan Mews L30 .27 D3
Morgan St WA9 .44 D3
Morland Ave CH62 .88 D6
Morley Ave CH41 .66 B8
Morley Rd Southport PR9 .4 E8
Wallasey CH41,CH44 .51 A3
Morley St Liverpool L4 .52 E7
St Helens WA10 .43 F5
Morley Way 1 WA10 .43 F4
Morningside L23 .26 F3
Morningside Pl L11 .39 F1
Morningside Rd L11 .53 F8
Morningside View L11 .53 F8
Morningside Way L11 .53 F8
Mornington Ave L23 .26 E2
Mornington Rd
Southport PR9 .4 C7
Wallasey CH45 .51 B6
Mornington St L8 .67 E5
Morpeth Cl CH46 .64 B8
Morpeth Rd CH47 .63 A5
Morpeth St L8 .67 F7
Morpeth Wharf CH41 .66 F8
Morris Cl WA11 .45 A5
Morris Ct CH43 .65 F5
Morris Rd WN8 .25 A7
Morris St WA9 .44 E1
Morrissey Cl WA10 .43 D4
Morston Ave L32 .40 E8
Morston Cres L32 .40 E8
Morston Wlk L32 .40 E8
Mortimer St CH41 .66 F6
Mortlake Cl WA8 .72 C3
Morton St L8 .67 F5
Morvah Cl 2 L12 .40 C2
Morval Cres L4 .38 E2
Morven Cl WA2 .61 E3
Morven Gr PR8 .4 E7
Moscow Dr Liverpool L13 .53 F5
Liverpool L13 .54 A5
Mosedale Ave WA11 .33 B1
Mosedale Rd
Bebington CH62 .79 E2
Liverpool L9 .39 A5
Moseley Ave CH44,CH45 .51 A4
Moseley Rd CH63 .79 A1
Moses St L8 .67 F4
Mosley St PR8 .4 B4
Moss Ave WN5 .25 D3
Moss Bank L39 .13 D2
Moss Bank Ct L39 .13 D2
Moss Bank Pk L21 .38 A8
Moss Bank Rd WA11 .33 B2
Moss Brow WA11 .31 E7
Moss Cotts L40 .15 A3
Moss Delph La L39 .13 C1
Moss End Way L33 .30 D3
Moss Gate Gr L14 .55 A3
Moss Gate Rd L14 .55 A3
Moss Gdns PR8 .4 C2
Moss Gn L37 .10 B4
Moss Gr Birkenhead CH42 .66 C2
Liverpool L8 .68 C4
Moss Green Way WA9 .45 A1
Moss La Bickerstaffe L39 .22 F2
Birkenhead CH42 .66 B2
Crank WA11 .32 E5
Formby L37,L39 .10 E5
Golborne WA3 .47 B5
Hightown L38,L23 .18 C2
Kirkby L33 .29 F7
Kirkby,Northwood L33 .30 B3
Moss La *continued*
Litherland L21 .27 D1
Liverpool L9,L20 .38 F6
Maghull L31 .20 E2
Maghull,Lydiate L31 .20 D5
Skelmersdale WN8 .23 F6
Southport PR9 .5 B8
St Helens WA11 .43 B7
St Helens,Moss Nook WA9 .45 A1
Moss Lane View WN8 .23 F6
Moss Nook L39 .13 C2
Moss Nook La Kirkby L31 .29 B7
Rainford WA11 .31 E6
Rainford WA11 .31 F5
Moss Pits Cl L10 .39 F7
Moss Pits La
Liverpool,Fazakerley L10 .39 E7
Liverpool,Wavertree Green L15 .69 B7
Moss Rd Orrell WN5 .25 D3
Southport PR8 .4 C2
Moss Side Formby L37 .10 B4
Huyton-w-R L14 .55 A3
Moss St Liverpool L3,L6,L7 .52 F2
Liverpool,Garston L19 .81 C6
Prescot L34 .56 D7
Moss View Litherland L21 .38 C8
Maghull L31 .20 F1
Ormskirk L39 .13 E4
Moss Way L11 .40 C4
Mossborough Hall La WA11 .31 C2
Mossborough Rd WA11 .31 E4
Mossbrow Rd L36 .55 E4
Mosscraig L28 .55 C7
Mosscroft Cl L36 .56 A4
Mosscroft Prim Sch L36 .56 A3
Mossdale Dr L35 .57 D3
Mossdale Rd
Ashton-in-M WN4 .35 A8
Kirkby L33 .29 F5
Mossdene Rd CH44 .50 F4
Mossfield Rd L9 .38 F6
Mossgiel Ave PR8 .7 B5
Mosshill Cl L31 .20 C3
Mosslake 19 L8 .67 F8
Mosslands WA10 .43 A4
Mosslands Dr CH44,CH45 .50 E4
Mosslands Sch The CH45 .50 E4
Mosslawn Rd L32 .30 A1
Mosslea Pk L18 .68 F4
Mossley Ave
Bebington CH62 .88 D8
Liverpool L18 .68 F5
Mossley Ct L18 .69 A3
Mossley Hill Dr L17 .68 E4
Mossley Hill Hospl L18 .68 E3
Mossley Hill Rd L18,L19 .68 F2
Mossley Hill Sta L18 .69 A3
Mossley Rd CH42 .66 E3
Mosspits Jun & Inf Schs L15 .69 B6
Mossville Cl L18 .69 A2
Mossville Rd L18 .69 B2
Mossy Bank Rd CH44 .51 D4
Mostyn Ave Aintree L10 .28 C2
Heswall CH60 .85 C8
Liverpool L19 .81 D8
West Kirby CH48 .63 B1
Mostyn Cl L4 .52 E7
Mostyn Gdns CH64 .86 B1
Mostyn House Sch CH64 .86 C1
Mostyn Sq CH64 .86 B1
Mostyn St CH44 .51 B2
Mother Teresa RC Prim Sch L5 .52 D4
Motherwell Cl WA8 .72 E3
Motherwell Cres PR8 .4 F3
Mottershead Rd WA8 .73 A1
Mottram Cl L33 .29 F2
Moughland La WA7 .84 F1
Mould St L5 .52 D5
Mounsey Rd CH42 .66 D5
Mount Ave
Bebington CH63 .78 D7
Bootle L20 .38 D7
Heswall CH60 .85 F8
Mount Carmel Sch L39 .13 D2
Mount Cl L32 .29 C4
Mount Cres Kirkby L32 .29 C4
Orrell WN5 .25 F6
Mount Ct Heswall CH60 .85 F8
6 Wallasey CH45 .51 A8
Mount Dr CH63 .78 D7
Mount Gr CH41 .66 C5
Mount Grove Pl 5 CH41 .66 C5
Mount Haven Cl CH49 .65 A5
Mount House Cl L37 .10 B5
Mount House Rd L37 .10 B5
Mount Mews CH60 .85 F8
Mount Olive CH43 .66 A3
Mount Park Ct L25 .70 A3
Mount Pk Bebington CH63 .78 D7
Liverpool L25 .70 A3
Mount Pleasant
Birkenhead CH43 .66 B3
Crosby L22 .26 D1
Liverpool L1,L3,L7 .90 C3
Liverpool L3,L7 .52 F1
Widnes WA8 .73 B2
Mount Pleasant Ave WA9 .45 B3
Mount Pleasant Flats 6 L22 .26 D1
Mount Pleasant Rd CH45 51 B7
Mount Prim Sch CH45 .51 A8
Mount Rd Bebington CH63 78 D5
Mount Rd *continued*
Birkenhead,Egerton Pk CH42 .66 D1
Birkenhead,Upton CH49 .65 A5
Kirkby L32 .29 B3
Wallasey CH45 .51 A7
West Kirby CH48 .63 C1
Mount St Crosby L22 .26 D1
Liverpool L1 .90 C2
Liverpool,Woolton L25 .70 A2
Southport PR9 .4 D7
Widnes WA8 .73 B1
Mount The Heswall CH60 .85 F8
Skelmersdale WN8 .24 B8
Wallasey CH44 .51 C4
Mount Vernon L7 .53 A1
Mount Vernon Gn 9 L7 .53 A2
Mount Vernon Rd L7 .53 A1
Mount Vernon St 6 L7 .53 A2
Mount Vernon View 7 L7 .53 A2
Mount Wood Rd CH42 .78 C8
Mountfield Ct WN5 .25 F7
Mountview Cl 5 L8 .68 A5
Mountway CH63 .78 D7
Mountwood WN8 .16 A4
Mountwood Lo PR8 .7 C5
Mowbray Ave WA11 .44 C5
Mowbray Ct 1 L20 .38 C1
Mowbray Gr Liverpool L13 .54 A1
Liverpool L13 .54 A1
Mowcroft La WA5 .74 B3
Moxon St WA10 .43 D2
Moxon Way WN4 .35 D4
Moyles Cl WA8 .72 D2
Mozart Cl L8 .68 B6
Much Woolton RC Prim Sch L25 .70 B2
Muirfield Cl L12 .54 E6
Muirfield Dr PR8 .7 C4
Muirfield Rd L36 .55 C1
Muirhead Ave L13 .53 F7
Muirhead Ave E L11,L12 .40 B1
Mulberry Ave
Golborne WA3 .47 F7
St Helens WA10 .43 C3
Mulberry Cl L33 .29 F6
Mulberry Gr CH44 .51 D3
Mulberry Pl L7 .67 F8
Mulberry Rd CH42 .66 F2
Mulberry St L7 .67 F8
Mulcrow Cl WA9 .44 D4
Mulgrave St L8 .68 A7
Mullberry St L7 .52 F1
Mullen Cl WA5 .60 F1
Mulliner St L7 .68 C7
Mullins Ave WA12 .46 C5
Mullion Cl Liverpool L26 .82 E8
Southport PR9 .2 B5
Mullion Rd L11 .40 C5
Mullion Wlk L11 .40 C5
Mullrea Cl L27 .70 C6
Mullwood Cl L12 .40 F3
Mulveton Rd CH63 .78 F3
Mumfords Gr CH47 .48 E1
Mumfords La CH47 .48 E1
Muncaster Cl CH62 .79 D1
Muncaster Dr WA11 .32 B6
Munro Ave WN5 .25 E6
Munster Rd L13 .54 B3
Murat Gr L22 .26 D1
Murat St L22 .26 D1
Murcote Rd L14 .54 F5
Muriel Cl WA5 .74 D6
Muriel St L4 .53 A8
Murphy Gr WA9 .44 E4
Murray Gr CH48 .63 A3
Murrayfield Dr CH46 .49 F4
Murrayfield Hospl CH61 .77 D5
Murrayfield Rd L25 .70 B6
Murrayfield Wlk L25 .70 B6
Mus of Liverpool Life★ L3 .67 B8
Musker Ct L23 .26 F3
Musker Dr L30 .27 C3
Musker Gdns L23 .26 F3
Musker St L23 .26 F3
Muspratt Rd L21 .38 A6
Muttocks Rake L30 .27 D5
Myddleton La WA2 .61 C6
Myers Ave L35 .57 A5
Myers Ct L23 .26 F2
Myers Rd E L23 .26 E3
Myers Rd W L23 .26 D3
Myerscough Ave L20 .38 E5
Mynsule Rd CH63 .78 F3
Myrtle Ave
Ashton-in-M WN4 .34 F6
Haydock WA11 .45 B7
Newton-le-W WA12 .46 C2
Myrtle Gr Billinge WN5 .33 D4
Crosby L22 .26 D2
Southport PR9 .4 E7
Wallasey CH44 .51 E3
Widnes WA8 .84 D8
Myrtle Par L7 .67 F8
Myrtle St L7,L8 .68 A8
Mystic Mews 9 L39 .13 E5

N

N Brooke Way CH49 .65 A3
Naburn Dr WN5 .25 E5
Naburn Gr CH46 .64 E7
Nairn Ave WN8 .16 B5
Nairn Cl CH63 .88 D4
Nansen Gr 4 L4 .39 A1
Nant Park Ct CH45 .51 C8
Nantwich Cl CH49 .65 A2
Napier Cl WA10 .43 E3
Napier Dr CH46 .64 F8
Napier Rd CH62 .79 B8
Napier St Bootle L20 .38 B1
St Helens WA10 .43 E3
Napier Terr PR8 .4 A5
Naples Rd CH44 .51 D3
Napps Cl L25 .69 F7
Napps Way Heswall CH61 .77 A2
Liverpool L25 .69 F8
Napps Wlk L25 .69 F7
Nares Cl WA5 .60 C1
Narrow Croft Rd L39 .13 B1
Narrow La L39 .13 B1
Narrow Lane (Clieves Hills) L39 .12 E6
Narrow Moss La L39,L40 .13 E8
Naseby Cl CH43 .65 C4
Naseby St L4 .38 F2
Natal Rd L9 .39 B6
Nathan Dr WA11 .45 E6
Nathan Gr L33 .29 F4
National Wildflower Ctr The★ L16 .54 F1
Naughton Lea WA8 .72 D3
Navigation Cl L30 .28 A4
Navigation Wharf L3 .67 D5
Naylor Ave WA3 .47 B8
Naylor Rd
Birkenhead CH43 .65 E8
Widnes WA8 .73 D1
Naylor St L3 .52 D3
Naylor's Rd Liverpool L25 .70 D5
Liverpool L27 .70 D7
Naylorsfield Dr L27 .70 C6
Nazeby Ave L23 .27 A3
Neale Dr CH49 .64 E3
Neasham Cl L26 .82 F8
Nedens Gr L31 .20 C3
Nedens La L31 .20 C3
Needham Cres CH43 .65 D4
Needham Rd L7 .53 C2
Needham Way WN8 .16 B5
Needwood Dr CH63 .78 F3
Neil St WA8 .73 C2
Neills Rd WA5 .59 B6
Neilson Rd L17 .68 C3
Neilson St L17 .68 B3
Nell's La L39 .20 F5
Nelson Ave L35 .56 E2
Nelson Ct
Birkenhead CH42 .67 A1
Southport PR8 .3 F4
Nelson Dr CH61 .76 E3
Nelson Ho CH42 .67 A1
Nelson Pl L35 .56 E2
Nelson Rd
Birkenhead CH42 .67 A1
Bootle L21 .38 B7
Liverpool L7 .53 B1
Nelson St Bootle L20 .38 B2
Liverpool L1 .90 B1
Liverpool L1 .90 C2
Liverpool,Wavertree L15 .68 E8
Newton-le-W WA12 .46 A3
Southport PR8 .4 A6
Wallasey CH45 .51 C7
Nelson's Croft CH63 .79 A3
Nelville Rd L9 .39 C7
Neptune Ent Ctr CH41 .66 D8
Neptune St CH41 .66 D8
Ness Gr L32 .29 C2
Neston Ave WA9 .58 B4
Neston Gdns CH41 .66 B8
Neston High Sch CH64 .86 F1
Neston Rd CH63,CH64 .86 F5
Neston Road Cotts CH63 87 A6
Neston St L4 .38 F1
Neston St Mary's CE Prim Sch CH64 .86 F1
Netherby St L8 .67 F4
Netherfield WA8 .84 E8
Netherfield Cl CH43 .65 C4
Netherfield Rd N L5 .52 E6
Netherfield Rd S L5,L6 .52 F4
Netherley Rd
Tarbock Green L35,L27 .71 C3
Widnes WA8 .72 A2
Netherton Gn L30 .27 F5
Netherton Grange L30 .28 B3
Netherton Ind Est L30 .38 F8
Netherton La L30 .27 E5
Netherton Moss Prim Sch L30 .27 E3
Netherton Park Prim Sch L30 .27 F1
Netherton Park Rd L21 .38 D8
Netherton Rd
Birkenhead CH46 .64 E8
Bootle L20 .38 D6
Liverpool L18,L19 .69 A1
Netherton Way L20,L21, L30 .38 E8
Netherwood Rd L11 .39 E2
Netley St L4 .52 E8
Nettle Hill CH48 .63 B3
Nettlestead Rd L11 .40 A1
Neva Ave CH46 .64 D8
Neverstitch Cl WN8 .15 F2
Neverstitch Rd WN8 .15 D2
Nevill St PR8 .4 B7
Neville Ave St Helens WA9 45 B2
Warrington WA2 .61 D1

Neville Cl CH43 65 C4
Neville Rd Bebington CH62 88 E8
Crosby L22 26 E1
Wallasey CH44 51 A4
Neville St WA12 46 A3
Nevin St 10 L6 53 A3
Nevison St 12 L7 53 B1
Nevitte Cl L28 55 A8
New Acres Cl CH43 65 C8
New Bank Pl WA8 72 B1
New Bank Rd WA8 72 B1
New Barn Ave WN4 35 C3
New Barnet WA8 72 F4
New Bartram Ct 9 L17 68 C4
New Bird St L1 90 B1
New Brighton Prim Sch CH45 51 C8
New Brighton Sta CH45 51 A8
New Chester Rd
Bebington CH42,CH62 79 C5
Bebington,Eastham CH62 88 E7
Birkenhead CH41,CH42 66 F4
Hooton CH62,CH66 89 A2
New Cotts L12 54 E8
New Court Way L39 13 F5
New Cross St Prescot L34 56 D7
1 St Helens WA10 43 F3
6 St Helens WA10 43 F4
New Cswy L37,L38 18 B8
New Cut Cl PR8 8 A8
New Cut La Knowsley L34 42 A8
Rainford L33,WA11 31 B1
Shirdley Hill L39,PR8 8 D6
New Ferry By-Pass CH62 79 B7
New Ferry Rd CH62 79 B8
New Fold WN5 25 C4
New Fort Way L20 38 A6
New Foul La PR8 5 A4
New Glade Hill WA11 44 E6
New Grey Rock Cl 4 L6 53 B4
New Hall L10 39 F8
New Hall Dr PR8 5 C1
New Hall La L11 39 E1
New Hayes Dr L18 69 D1
New Hedley Gr L5 52 C5
New Henderson St L8 67 E5
New Hey L12 54 B5
New Hey Rd CH49 65 C3
New Heyes CH64 86 E1
New Heys Comp Sch L19 69 D1
New Hutte La L26 82 F6
New Hutte Prim Sch L26 82 E6
New Islington L3 90 C4
New La Haskayne L39 11 E3
Ormskirk L39 13 E2
Southport PR9 2 E3
New Market Rd L21 38 B7
New Meadow La L37 18 F8
New Mersey Ret Pk L24 81 F5
New Mill Stile L25 70 A3
New Park Prim Sch L6 53 B3
New Quay L3 52 B2
New Rd Formby L37 10 A5
Liverpool L13 53 E5
Prescot L34 56 E7
New Red Rock View L6 53 B4
New Road Ct L13 53 E5
New School La CH66 89 B1
New St Ashton-in-M WN4 35 C4
Haskayne L39 12 B8
St Helens WA9 58 C7
Wallasey CH44 51 E2
New Tower Ct CH45 51 C8
New Way L39 22 C2
New Way Bsns Ctr CH44 51 D2
Newark Cl
Birkenhead CH43 65 C4
Huyton-w-R L36 55 D6
Litherland L30 28 B5
Newark St L4 38 F1
Newbold Cres CH48 63 E3
Newbold Gr L12 40 F2
Newborough Ave
Crosby L23 27 A4
9 Liverpool L18 68 F5
Newborough Cl WA5 60 E2
Newborough Sch L25 69 F3
Newbridge Cl
Birkenhead CH49 65 B3
Garswood WN4 34 D3
Warrington WA5 60 D2
Newburn CH43 66 B5
Newburn Cl WN8 16 B5
Newburn St 7 L4 39 A2
Newburns La CH43 66 B3
Newbury Cl
Huyton-w-R L36 55 D1
Widnes WA8 73 A3
Newbury Rd WN8 16 B5
Newbury Way
Liverpool L12 54 E5
Wallasey CH46 49 F3
Newby Ave L35 57 A4
Newby Cl PR8 7 B3
Newby Ct L37 9 F3
Newby Dr Huyton-w-R L36 55 C3
Skelmersdale WN8 16 B5
Newby Gr L12 40 C2
Newby Pl WA11 44 A8
Newby St L4 52 F8
Newcastle Rd L15 69 A6
Newchurch Cl L27 70 F4
Newcombe St L6 53 B5
Newcroft Rd L25 69 F4
Newdales Cl CH43 65 C8
Newdown Rd L11 40 D5
Newdown Wlk L11 40 D5
Newell Rd CH44,CH45 51 B5
Newenham Cres L14 54 E3
Newfield Cl L23 27 C6
Newfield Sch L23 27 B5
Newfields WA10 43 D4
Newgate Rd WN8 24 F7
Newhall La CH47 63 B6
Newhall St L1 90 C1
Newhaven Rd
Wallasey CH45 51 C7
Warrington WA2 61 B4
Newholme Cl L12 40 E3
Newhope Rd CH41 66 C7
Newhouse Rd L15 68 D7
Newick Rd L32 29 C1
Newington L1 90 C3
Newland Cl WA8 72 C3
Newland Ct L17 68 C3
Newland Dr CH44,CH45 51 A4
Newlands Dr WA3 47 D8
Newlands Rd
Bebington CH63 79 B4
St Helens WA11 44 C7
Newling St CH41 66 C7
Newlyn Ave Litherland L21 27 B1
Maghull L31 20 E1
Newlyn Cl CH47 48 E2
Newlyn Dr
Ashton-in-M WN4 35 B1
Skelmersdale WN8 24 D7
Newlyn Gdns WA5 74 D3
Newlyn Gr WA11 44 D7
Newlyn Rd Hoylake CH47 48 E2
Liverpool L11 40 D5
Newlyn Wlk L11 40 D5
Newman St L4 52 D7
Newmarket Gdns WA9 57 C6
Newmorn Ct L17 68 C2
Newport Ave CH45 50 D7
Newport Cl CH43 65 C4
Newport Ct L5 52 C5
News La WA11 23 F2
Newsham Cl WA8 72 B4
Newsham Dr L6 53 D5
Newsham Rd L36 71 A8
Newsham St L5 52 D5
Newstead Ave L23 26 B3
Newstead Dr WN8 16 B5
Newstead Rd Hale WA8 83 F6
Liverpool L8 68 C7
Newstet Rd L33 30 C2
Newton Bank Sch WA12 46 E4
Newton Cl L12 54 B8
Newton Comm Hospl WA12 46 B2
Newton Cross La CH48 63 E2
Newton Ct L13 53 E1
Newton Dr
Skelmersdale WN8 16 B5
West Kirby CH48 63 E2
Newton Gr WA2 61 F3
Newton La WA12 46 E6
Newton Park Dr WA12 46 F3
Newton Park Rd CH48 63 E2
Newton Rd
Billinge WN5,WA9,WN4 33 F6
Golborne WA12,WA3 47 D5
Hoylake CH47 63 C7
Liverpool L13 53 E3
St Helens WA9 45 A3
Wallasey CH44 51 A4
Warrington WA2,WA12 60 F8
Winwick WA2 61 A5
Newton St
Birkenhead CH41 66 C7
Southport PR9 5 A7
Newton Way
Birkenhead CH49 64 F5
Liverpool L3 52 F1
Newton Wlk 4 L20 38 B4
Newton-le-Willows Com High Sch WA12 46 D5
Newton-le-Willows Prim Sch WA12 46 D3
Newton-le-Willows Sta WA12 46 E3
Newtown Gdns L32 29 E2
Newway L14 55 A5
Nicander Rd L18 68 F5
Nicholas Rd Crosby L23 26 B3
Widnes WA8 84 C8
Nicholas St 3 L3 52 D3
Nicholl Rd WA10 43 A5
Nicholls Dr CH61 76 F4
Nicholson St WA9 44 E4
Nickleby Cl L8 67 F5
Nickleford Hall Dr WA8 72 F6
Nicol Mere Dr WN4 35 A5
Nicol Mere Sch WN4 35 A5
Nicol Rd WN4 35 B5
Nicola Ct CH45 51 C6
Nidderdale Ave L35 57 D3
Nigel Rd CH60 86 C8
Nightingale Cl Kirkby L32 29 B3
Liverpool L27 70 F5
Nightingale Rd L12 40 F3
Nimrod St L4 38 F1
Nine Tree Prim Sch L28 41 A1
Ninth Ave L9 39 D7
Nipe La WN8 24 B5
Nithsdale Rd L15 68 E6
Nixon St L4 38 F2
Nixon's La PR8 7 E7
Nixons La WN8 24 D7
Noctorum Ave CH43 65 C4
Noctorum Dell CH43 65 D4
Noctorum La CH43 65 E5
Noctorum Rd CH43 65 E5
Noctorum Way CH43 65 D3
Noel Gate L39 13 B1
Noel St L8 68 C7
Nolan St PR8 4 C5
Nook La Golborne WA3 47 B8
St Helens WA9 44 F1
Nook Rise L15 69 B8
Nook The Birkenhead CH43 66 B5
Birkenhead,Frankby CH48 64 B2
Liverpool L25 70 C3
St Helens WA10 43 B6
Noon Ct WA12 46 B1
Noonan Cl L9 38 F4
Norbeck Ave L14 54 F2
Norbreck Ave L14 54 F2
Norburn Cres L37 9 F2
Norbury Ave
Bebington CH63 78 E5
Billinge WN5 33 D6
8 Liverpool L18 68 F5
Norbury Cl
Bebington CH63 78 F5
Kirkby L32 29 D2
Southport PR9 2 C5
Norbury Fold L35 57 E1
Norbury Rd L32 29 D2
Norbury Wlk L32 29 D2
Norcliffe Rd L35 57 B4
Norcote Lo L37 9 E4
Norcott Dr WA5 59 F6
Norfield L39 13 F5
Norfolk Cl
Birkenhead CH43 65 C4
Bootle L20 38 D4
Norfolk Dr
Warrington WA5 74 E6
West Kirby CH48 63 C1
Norfolk Gr PR8 3 F1
Norfolk Pl Bootle L21 38 A7
Widnes WA8 84 C8
Norfolk Rd Longshaw WN5 25 E1
Maghull L31 28 C7
Southport PR8 3 F1
St Helens WA10 43 D1
Norfolk St L1 90 B1
Norgate St 16 L4 52 F7
Norland St WA8 73 D1
Norland's La
Cronton L35,WA8 72 F7
Rainhill L35 72 E8
Norlands Ct CH42 66 E1
Norley Ave CH62 88 E3
Norley Dr WA10 43 B3
Norley Pl L26 82 E6
Norma Rd L22 26 E1
Norman Ave
Haydock WA11 46 A7
Newton-le-W WA12 46 E3
Norman Pannell Sch The L27 70 E5
Norman Rd Bootle L20 38 C7
Crosby L23 26 D3
Wallasey CH44 51 E2
Norman Salisbury Ct 1 WA10 44 A4
Norman St
Birkenhead CH41 65 F8
Liverpool L3 52 F2
Normandale Rd L4 39 D1
Normandy Rd L36 55 D3
Normanhurst L39 14 A4
Normans Rd WA9 58 F7
Normanston Cl CH43 66 B4
Normanston Rd CH43 66 B4
Normanton Ave L17 68 C3
Normington Cl L31 20 C4
Norris Cl CH43 65 C4
Norris Green Cres L11 39 F1
Norris Green Rd L12 54 B6
Norris Green Way 6 L11 40 A1
Norris House Dr L39 21 C8
Norris Rd L34 56 C6
Norris Way L37 10 B3
Norseman Cl L12 54 B8
North Atlantic Cl L36 55 E4
North Ave Aintree L10 28 E2
Golborne WN7 36 F4
Liverpool L24 82 A6
North Barcombe Rd L16 69 D7
North Breeze Hill 8 L4, L9 38 F2
North Cantril Ave L12 54 F8
North Cheshire Trad Est CH43 77 E8
North Cl CH62 79 C2
North Dingle Liverpool L4 52 D8
Liverpool L4 52 E7
North Dr Heswall CH60 86 A7
Liverpool,Sandfield Pk L12 54 B6
Liverpool,Victoria Pk L15 69 A8
Wallasey CH45 50 F8
North Dunes L38 17 F4
North End La
Hightown L38 18 A6
Liverpool L26 70 E3
North Florida Rd WA11 45 D8
North Front L35 56 E1
North Gr L18 69 C1
North Hill St L8 68 A6
North John St
Liverpool L2 90 A3
St Helens WA10 43 F3
North Leach Dr PR8 7 A5
North Linkside Rd L25 70 C1
North Manor Way L25 70 C2
North Meade L31 20 C2
North Mersey Bsns Ctr L33 30 D4
North Moor La L39 12 F8
North Moss La L37 10 D7
North Mossley Hill Rd L17,L18 68 F3
North Mount Rd L32 29 C4
North Par Hoylake CH47 63 B7
Kirkby L32 29 E2
Liverpool L24 82 E3
Neston CH64 86 B2
North Park Brook Rd WA5 60 E1
North Park Rd L32 29 C4
North Parkside Wlk L12 54 A8
North Perimeter Rd L33 30 D4
North Rd Bebington CH65 89 E3
Birkenhead CH42 66 D3
Liverpool,Broad Green L13, L14 54 C2
Liverpool,Cressington Pk L19 81 A6
Liverpool,Halewood L26 82 E5
Southport PR9 2 C4
St Helens WA10 43 F5
West Kirby CH48 63 A2
North St Ashton-in-M WN4 35 D5
Haydock WA11 45 E6
Liverpool L1,L2,L3 90 B4
Newton-le-W WA12 45 F4
Southport PR9 4 C8
North Sudley Rd L17 68 E2
North View
Huyton-w-R L36 56 A2
Liverpool L7 53 A1
Warrington WA5 74 E7
North William St 5 CH44 51 E2
North Wirral Coastal Pk* CH46 49 E4
Northam Cl PR9 2 A5
Northbrook Cl L8 68 A7
Northbrook Rd CH44 51 D3
Northbrook St L8 68 A7
Northcote Cl 1 L5,L6 52 F4
Northcote Prim Sch L9 39 A3
Northcote Rd Liverpool L9 38 F3
Wallasey CH45 50 D5
Northdale Rd L15 68 F8
Northern La WA8 72 A3
Northern Perimeter Rd L30 28 B5
Northern Rd L24 82 E4
Northern Rd The L23 26 F4
Northfield WN8 16 B4
Northfield Cl Kirkby L33 30 A4
St Helens WA9 58 D3
Northfield Ct WN3 36 C1
Northfield Rd L20 38 E6
Northgate Rd L13 54 A5
Northmead Rd L19 81 E7
Northolt Ct WA2 61 E1
Northop Rd 8 CH45 51 A6
Northpark Ct CH44 51 E3
Northridge Rd CH61 77 A5
Northumberland Gr L8 67 D5
Northumberland St L8 67 E5
Northumberland Terr L5 52 E6
Northumberland Way L30 27 C3
Northway Heswall CH60 77 D1
Liverpool L15 54 B1
Maghull L31,L39 20 E4
Ormskirk L39 13 A1
Skelmersdale WN8 16 B2
Warrington WA2 61 B2
Widnes WA8 72 D1
Northway Prim Sch
Liverpool L15 54 B1
Maghull L31 20 E3
Northways CH62 79 D3
Northwich Cl L23 27 B6
Northwood Ave WA12 46 F3
Northwood Rd
Birkenhead CH43 65 F1
Huyton-w-R L36 55 F4
Norton Ave WA5 74 E5
Norton Dr CH61 76 C7
Norton Gr Maghull L31 28 D6
St Helens WA9 57 D7
Norton Rd CH48 63 A3
Norton St Bootle L20 38 B5
Liverpool L3 90 C4
Norton Terr L20 38 B5
Norville Rd L14 54 C2
Norwich Ave
Ashton-in-M WN4 35 D3
Golborne WA3 47 D8
Norwich Dr CH49 65 A7
Norwich Rd L15 69 A6
Norwich Way L32 29 E2
Norwood Ave
Ashton-in-M WN4 34 F6
Golborne WA3 47 F7
Litherland L21 27 B1
Southport PR9 4 E7
Norwood Cres PR9 4 E7
Norwood Ct CH49 64 D3
Norwood Gdns PR9 4 F7
Norwood Gr
2 Liverpool L6 53 B4
Rainford WA11 32 A6
Norwood Prim Sch PR9 4 E7
Norwood Rd
Birkenhead CH49 64 D4
Southport PR8,PR9 4 F6
Wallasey CH44 51 B2
Norwyn Rd L11 39 E2
Nostell Rd WN4 35 A5
Notre Dame RC Coll L5 52 F7
Nottingham Cl L35 57 C5
Nottingham Rd L36 55 C1
Nowshera Ave CH61 76 F5
Nuffield Cl CH49 64 F4
Nugent House Sch WN5 33 D4
Nun Cl CH43 66 B3
Nunn St WA9 44 D3
Nunsford Cl L21 27 D2
Nunthorpe Rd L34 41 B5
Nurse Rd CH61 77 B6
Nurseries The L37 10 A2
Nursery Ave L39 14 A6
Nursery Cl
Birkenhead CH43 66 C3
Liverpool L25 82 C8
Widnes WA8 73 D3
Nursery Dr L37 9 F2
Nursery La L19 81 C7
Nursery Rd Maghull L31 20 C4
St Helens WA9 57 D7
Nut St WA9 57 D7
Nutgrove Ave WA9 57 D7
Nutgrove Hall Dr WA9 57 D6
Nutgrove Methodist Prim Sch WA9 57 D7
Nutgrove Rd WA9 57 D7
Nuthall Rd PR8 4 F3
Nuttall St L7 53 C1
Nyland Rd L36 55 E5

O

O'Brien Gr WA9 44 E4
O'Connell Cl WA11 45 C6
O'Connell Rd L3 52 D4
O'Connor Gr L33 29 E6
O'Keeffe Rd WA9 44 C4
O'Neill St L20 38 B4
O'Reilly Ct L3 52 C4
O'Sullivan Cres WA11 44 E5
Oak Ave Abram Brow WN2 36 C7
Birkenhead CH49 64 D6
Golborne WA3 47 B8
Haydock WA11 45 E7
Liverpool L9 39 B6
Newton-le-W WA12 46 D3
Ormskirk L39 13 D4
Oak Bank CH41 66 C5
Oak Cl Birkenhead CH46 64 D7
Liverpool L12 40 F1
Prescot L35 56 E3
Oak Cres WN8 15 D1
Oak Ct 15 L8 68 A4
Oak Gn L39 13 F5
Oak Hall Bldg 10 L5 53 B5
Oak La L12 40 C2
Oak La N L11,L12 40 D2
Oak Leigh L13 53 E5
Oak Meadows Ct L35 57 E1
Oak Rd Bebington CH63 78 F7
Hooton CH66 88 E1
Huyton-w-R L36 70 D8
Prescot L35 56 E3
Warrington WA5 74 F3
Oak St Bootle L20 38 C4
Southport PR8 4 E6
St Helens WA9 58 E8
Oak Terr L7 53 C2
Oak Tree Ct WN8 16 D3
Oak Vale L13 54 B2
Oak View L24 83 A3
Oakbank Rd L18 68 E5
Oakbank St CH44 51 C3
Oakbourne Cl 5 L17 68 C2
Oakdale Ave CH44 51 D2
Oakdale Cl L32 29 C1
Oakdale Dr CH49 64 C2
Oakdale Rd Crosby L22 26 D2
Liverpool L18 69 A5
Wallasey CH41,CH44 51 D2
Oakdene Cl CH62 88 D5
Oakdene Ct L35 57 D2
Oakdene Prim Sch L35 57 D2
Oakdene Rd
Birkenhead CH42 66 C3
Liverpool L4 53 B7
Oakenden Cl WN4 35 A6
Oakenholt Rd
Birkenhead CH46 64 E8
2 Wallasey CH46 49 E1
Oakes St L3 52 F2
Oakfield L4 53 B6
Oakfield Ave
Golborne WA3 35 F1
Liverpool L25 70 A4
Oakfield Cl WA9 57 D7
Oakfield Com Prim Sch WA8 84 B8
Oakfield Dr Formby L37 9 D4
Huyton-w-R L36 70 F8
Widnes WA8 84 A8
Oakfield Gr L36 70 F8
Oakfield Rd
Bebington CH62 88 C8
Hightown L38 17 F2
Liverpool L4 53 A6
Oakfields L39 14 A5
Oakgate Cl L11 40 B3
Oakham Ct PR9 4 C8
Oakham Dr Aintree L10 28 F1
Wallasey CH46 49 B1
Oakham St L8 67 E6
Oakhill Cl Liverpool L12 40 D3
Maghull L31 20 D2
Oakhill Cottage La L31 20 D4

Oakhill Dr L31 20 D4
Oakhill Pk L13 54 B2
Oakhill Rd Liverpool L13 54 B3
Maghull L31 20 D3
Oakhurst Cl L25 70 B5
Oakland Cl L21 38 C6
Oakland Ct CH43 66 A5
Oakland Dr CH49 65 A6
Oakland Rd L19 80 F8
Oakland Vale CH45 51 C8
Oaklands L35 57 C3
Oaklands Ave L23 26 E5
Oaklands Ct WA9 58 C4
Oaklands Dr
Bebington CH63 79 A6
Heswall CH61 77 A1
Oaklands Rd WA3 47 F7
Oaklands Terr CH61 77 A2
Oaklea Rd CH61 76 F6
Oakleaf Mews CH43 65 D5
Oaklee Gr L33 30 A4
Oakleigh WN8 24 D2
Oakleigh Gr CH63 78 F6
Oakley Ave WN5 33 E6
Oakley Cl L12 40 E3
Oakmere Cl Liverpool L9 39 A7
Wallasey CH46 49 E4
Oakmere Dr
Birkenhead CH49 64 C4
Warrington WA5 74 F3
Oakridge Cl CH62 79 C2
Oakridge Rd CH62 79 C2
Oaks Cl WA9 58 D3
Oaks La CH61 77 A4
Oaks The Bebington CH62 88 C8
Liverpool L12 40 F3
Southport PR8 3 F6
St Helens WA9 58 D4
Oaksmeade Cl L12 40 F2
Oakston Ave L35 57 D2
Oaksway CH60 86 C6
Oakthorn Gr WA11 45 C6
Oaktree Pl CH42 66 F3
Oaktree Rd WA10 43 A5
Oakwood WN8 16 D3
Oakwood Ave
Ashton-in-M WN4 35 A2
Southport PR8 7 D6
Oakwood Cl L25 70 B5
Oakwood Dr
Birkenhead CH43 65 E8
Huyton-w-R L36 55 F1
Southport PR8 7 E5
Oakwood Pk CH62 88 D5
Oakwood Rd L26 82 F7
Oakworth Cl L33 29 E4
Oakworth Dr
Bebington CH62 79 C7
Huyton-w-R L36 71 A7
Oarside Dr CH45 51 A6
Oatfield La L21 27 B2
Oatlands Rd L32 29 C2
Oatlands The CH48 63 C1
Oban Dr Garswood WN4 34 C4
Heswall CH60 86 A8
Oban Rd L4 53 B6
Oberon St L20 38 C1
Observatory Rd CH43 65 E8
Ocean Pk CH44 51 D1
Ocean Rd L21 38 B7
Ocean View [7] CH45 51 A8
Oceanic Rd L13 53 F2
Octavia Ct L36 55 F1
Octavia Hill Rd L21 27 C1
Odsey St L7 53 C2
Odyssey Ctr CH41 66 C8
Off Botanic Rd PR9 2 A1
Ogden Cl L11 54 A8
Ogle Cl L35 56 E5
Oglet La L24 82 D1
Oil St L3 52 B4
Okehampton Rd L16 69 D8
Okell Dr L26 70 D1
Old Acre L38 17 F3
Old Alder La WA2,WA5 60 D5
Old Barn Rd
[6] Liverpool L4 53 B6
Wallasey CH44 51 A3
Old Bidston Rd CH41 66 B8
Old Boston WA11 46 A7
Old Boston Trad Est
WA11 46 B8
Old Boundary Way L39 13 F6
Old Chester Rd
Bebington CH42,CH63 78 F8
Birkenhead CH41,CH42 66 F2
Old Church Cl L9 39 B7
Old Church Yd [1] L2 90 A3
Old Clatterbridge Rd
CH63 78 F2
Old Colliery Rd L35 56 D3
Old Colliery Yd WN4 34 C3
Old Court House Rd
CH62 79 D5
Old Distillery Rd L24 82 C5
Old Dover Rd L36 70 C8
Old Eccleston La WA10 43 C3
Old Engine La WN8 15 C2
Old Farm Rd Crosby L23 26 F4
Kirkby L32 40 F6
Old Gorsey La CH41,CH44 51 C1
Old Greasby Rd CH49 64 F5
Old Hall L35 71 E8
Old Hall Bsns Pk PR9 5 A5
Old Hall Cl L31 28 D7
Old Hall Dr WN4 35 A2
Old Hall Gdns WA11 32 A7
Old Hall La L32 29 D2
Old Hall Rd
Bebington CH62 79 F1
Maghull L31 28 D7
Old Hall St L2,L3 90 A4
Old Haymarket L1 90 B4
Old Hey Wlk WA12 46 C1
Old Higher Rd WA8 83 D5
Old Hutte La L26 83 A6
Old Kennel Cl L12,L14 54 F8
Old La Formby L37 9 F6
Haskayne L39 11 E3
Heswall CH60 86 D8
Maghull L31 20 E4
Prescot L34,L35 56 F6
Rainford WA11 31 F7
Rainhill L35 57 B3
Old Leeds St L3 52 B2
Old Links Cl PR9 5 B8
Old Lodge Cl L12 54 B8
Old Maryland La CH46 49 E1
Old Mdw L34 41 C4
Old Meadow Rd CH61 76 E4
Old Mill Ave WA9 58 D5
Old Mill Cl Heswall CH60 86 B7
Liverpool L15 69 A8
Old Mill Hill L39 13 D3
Old Mill La Formby L37 9 F4
Knowsley L34 41 E4
Liverpool L15 69 A8
Old Mill Lane Cotts L34 41 E4
Old Moss La L39 11 C5
Old Nook La WA11 44 E6
Old Orch L35 56 E1
Old Park La PR9 5 A8
Old Post Office Pl [1] L1 90 B3
Old Prescot Cl L31 21 C2
Old Pump La CH49 64 C3
Old Quarry The L25 70 A2
Old Racecourse Rd L31 28 B8
Old Rd WN4 35 A4
Old Rectory Gn
Aughton L39 21 A7
Sefton L29 27 F7
Old Riding L14 54 F5
Old Roan Sta L30 28 B3
Old Ropery [6] L2 90 A3
Old Rough La L33 29 F2
Old School House La
WA2 61 A7
Old School Pl WN4 35 A3
Old School Way CH41 65 E7
Old Thomas La L14 54 D1
Old Town Cl WN8 23 D8
Old Town Ct L37 9 E4
Old Town La L37 9 E4
Old Town Way WN8 23 D8
Old Upton La WA8 72 E4
Old Wargrave Rd WA12 46 C3
Old Whint Rd WA11 45 A6
Old Wood Rd CH61 76 F3
Oldbridge Rd L24 82 F3
Oldershaw Sch The CH45 51 A5
Oldfield L35 56 F4
Oldfield Cl CH60 76 E2
Oldfield Cotts CH60 76 C2
Oldfield Dr CH60 76 D2
Oldfield Gdns CH60 76 D1
Oldfield La CH48 64 A5
Oldfield Rd Heswall CH60 76 D1
Liverpool L19 81 A8
Wallasey CH45 50 F6
Oldfield St WA10 43 F5
Oldfield Way CH60 76 E1
Oldgate WA8 84 C7
Oldham Pl L1 90 C3
Oldham St L1 90 C2
Oleander Dr WA10 43 C4
Olga Rd WA9 58 C7
Olinda St CH62 79 B7
Olive Cl L31 29 A2
Olive Cres CH41 66 E4
Olive Gr Huyton-w-R L36 55 D2
Litherland L30 28 A1
Liverpool L15 54 A1
Skelmersdale WN8 15 E1
Southport PR8 4 E7
Olive La L15 69 A8
Olive Mount CH41 66 E4
Olive Mount Hts L15 69 A8
Olive Mount Rd L15 69 A8
Olive Mount Wlk L15 69 B8
Olive Rd L22 37 E8
Olive Vale L15 68 F8
Olivedale Rd L18 68 F5
Oliver La CH41 66 E6
Oliver Lyme Rd L34 56 E6
Oliver Lymm Ho [6] L34 56 E6
Oliver Rd WA10 57 C8
Oliver St CH41 66 D6
Oliver St E CH41 66 E6
Olivetree Rd L15 54 B1
Olivia Cl CH43 65 C4
Olivia Mews CH43 65 C4
Olivia St L20 38 D1
Olivia Way L36 56 B2
Ollerton Cl CH43 65 C4
Ollerton Pk WA5 59 E7
Ollery Gn L30 28 B4
Olney St L4 38 F2
Olton St L15 68 E8
Olympia St L6 53 A3
Olympic Way L30 39 B8
Omega Blvd WA5 59 D1
Onslow Cres PR8 4 A2
Onslow Rd
Bebington CH62 79 B8
Liverpool L6 53 C3
[10] Wallasey CH45 51 B8
Ontario Cl L27 70 E5
Opal Cl Litherland L21 38 C8
Liverpool L6 53 B4
Openfields Cl L26 70 E2
Oppenheim Ave WA10 57 C8
Oran Way L36 55 D3
Orange Gr Liverpool L8 68 C6
Warrington WA2 61 E2
Orange Tree Cl L28 55 B8
Orb Cl L11 40 C3
Orb Wlk [3] L11 40 C4
Orchard Ave L14,L16 54 D1
Orchard Cl
Eccleston Park L34 57 A7
Prescot L35 56 E1
St Helens WA11 44 D7
Orchard Ct
Birkenhead CH41 66 F3
Maghull L31 28 C8
Orchard Dale L23 26 F4
Orchard Dene L35 57 C3
Orchard Gdns L35 71 E8
Orchard Grange CH46 64 C7
Orchard Hey
Litherland L30 28 B4
Maghull L31 28 E8
St Helens WA10 43 A3
Orchard La PR8 7 D4
Orchard Lo [1] L39 13 F6
Orchard Rd CH46 49 E1
Orchard St WN4 35 C3
Orchard The
Huyton-w-R L36 55 E2
Liverpool L17 68 F1
Ormskirk L39 13 D5
Wallasey CH45 51 A7
Orchard View L39 13 D1
Orchard Way
Bebington CH63 78 D6
Widnes WA8 72 A3
Orchards The Orrell WN5 25 E5
Southport PR8 7 D4
Orchid Cl WN8 25 B6
Orchid Gr L17 67 F3
Orchid Way WA9 59 B7
Orford Cl L24 83 E2
Orford Gn WA2 61 D1
Orford St L15 68 F8
Oriel Cl Aintree L10 28 D3
[2] Liverpool L2 90 A3
Oriel Cres L20 38 C1
Oriel Ct CH42 66 B1
Oriel Dr L10 28 D3
Oriel Lodge L20 38 C2
Oriel Rd Ashton-in-M WN4 34 F4
Birkenhead CH42 66 E3
Bootle L20 38 C2
Liverpool L20 38 C1
Oriel St L3 52 C3
Orient Dr L25 70 B3
Origen Rd L16 54 D1
Oriole Cl WA10 57 B7
Orion Blvd WA5 59 E1
Orith Ave WA10 42 F3
Orkney Cl St Helens WA11 44 D7
Widnes WA8 73 E3
Orlando Cl CH43 65 C4
Orlando St L20 38 C1
Orleans Rd L13 54 A3
Ormande St WA9 44 B1
Orme Ho L39 14 A5
Ormerod Ct CH63 79 A5
Ormesby Gdns WA9 57 E6
Ormesby Gr CH63 88 B6
Ormiston Rd CH45 51 B7
Ormond Ave L40 14 E4
Ormond Cl WA8 72 C2
Ormond Mews CH43 65 C4
Ormond St Liverpool L3 90 A4
Wallasey CH45 51 B5
Ormond Way CH43 65 C4
Ormonde Ave L31 28 C7
Ormonde Cres L33 30 A2
Ormonde Dr L31 28 C8
Orms Way L37 9 E3
Ormsby St L15 68 E7
Ormside Gr [7] WA9 58 D7
Ormskirk & District General
Hospl L39 14 A4
Ormskirk Bsns Pk [2] L39 13 F6
Ormskirk CE Prim Sch
L39 14 A6
Ormskirk Coll L39 13 E5
Ormskirk Lathom Park CE
Prim Sch L40 15 A8
Ormskirk Old Rd L39 22 F7
Ormskirk Rd
Aintree L10,L30,L9 28 B2
Bickerstaffe L39 22 E7
Knowsley L34 41 D4
Rainford WA11 23 D1
Rainford WA11 31 E7
Skelmersdale WN8 15 C1
Skelmersdale,Tanhouse
WN8 24 D7
Up Holland WN8 25 A7
Ormskirk Sch L39 14 B5
Ormskirk St WA10 44 A3
Ormskirk Sta L39 13 F5
Orphan Dr Liverpool L6,L3 53 D4
Liverpool L7 53 D3
Orphan St L7 68 A8
Orrell Gdns WN5 25 F6
Orrell Hey L20 38 D7
Orrell Hill La L38 18 C4
Orrell Holgate Prim Sch
WN5 25 E5
Orrell La L20,L9 38 F7
Orrell Mount L20 38 C7
Orrell Newfold Com Prim Sch
WN5 25 D4
Orrell Park Sta L9 39 A6
Orrell Prim Sch L20 38 D5
Orrell Rd Bootle L20,L21 38 C7
Orrell WN5 25 E7
Wallasey CH45 51 C7
Orrell St WA9 44 C3
Orrell Sta WN5 25 E4
Orrell Water Pk★ WN5 25 E4
Orret's Meadow Rd CH49 65 B3
Orrets Meadow Sch
CH46 64 F8
Orry St L5 52 D5
Orrysdale Rd CH48 63 A3
Orsett Rd L32 40 F8
Orston Cres CH63 79 B2
Ortega Cl CH62 79 C7
Orthes St L3 52 F1
Orton Rd L16 69 C8
Orton Way WN4 34 F3
Orville St WA9 58 F7
Orwell Cl Formby L37 9 D1
St Helens WA9 58 A3
Orwell Rd L4 52 D8
Osbert Rd L23 26 B4
Osborne Ave
Wallasey CH45 51 B7
Warrington WA2 61 D1
Osborne Ct
Bebington CH62 79 B6
St Helens WA10 57 C8
Osborne Gr
Huyton-w-R L34 56 A5
Wallasey CH45 51 B6
Osborne Ho L15 69 A8
Osborne Rd
Ashton-in-M WN4 35 A4
Birkenhead CH43 66 B5
Formby L37 9 E1
Golborne WA3 47 E7
Litherland L21 27 C1
Liverpool L13 53 E6
Southport PR8 7 B6
St Helens WA10 43 A5
Wallasey CH45 51 C7
Osborne Vale [8] CH45 51 B7
Osborne Wood L17 68 D1
Osbourne Cl CH62 88 E7
Osmaston Rd CH42 66 A1
Osprey Cl Liverpool L27 70 F5
Warrington WA2 61 E3
Ossett Cl CH43 65 C4
Osterley Gdns L9 38 F6
Oteley Ave CH62 88 D8
Othello Cl L20 38 C1
Otterburn Cl CH46 64 B8
Otterspool Dr L17 80 D8
Otterspool Rd L17 68 D1
Otterton Rd L11 40 C5
Ottery Cl PR9 2 A5
Ottley St L6 53 C3
Otway St L19 81 C4
Oulton Cl Birkenhead CH43 65 E2
Maghull L31 20 B4
Oulton Gdns WA9 57 E6
Oulton La L36 70 D8
Oulton Rd L16 69 D6
Oulton Way CH43 65 E3
Oundle Dr L10 28 C3
Oundle Pl L25 82 B7
Oundle Rd CH46 49 E1
Our Lady & St Edward's RC
Prim Sch CH41 66 B8
Our Lady & St Philomena's
RC Prim Sch L9 39 F4
Our Lady & St Swithin's RC
Prim Sch L11 40 C5
Our Lady Immaculate Prim
Sch L5 52 E6
Our Lady Of Compassion RC
Prim Sch L37 10 A3
Our Lady of Good Help RC
Prim Sch L15 69 A8
Our Lady of Lourdes RC Prim
Sch PR8 4 A1
Our Lady of Lourdes RC Sch
CH46 50 B4
Our Lady of Mount Carmel
RC Prim Sch L8 67 F5
Our Lady of Perpetual
Succour RC Prim Sch
WA8 84 A8
Our Lady of Pity RC Prim Sch
CH49 64 D2
Our Lady of Reconciliation
RC Prim Sch L3 52 C4
Our Lady of the Assumption
RC Prim Sch L25 70 B6
Our Lady of Walsingham RC
Jun Sch L30 27 F2
Our Lady of Walsingham RC
Prim Sch L30 27 F2
Our Lady Queen of Peace RC
High Sch WN8 15 F4
Our Lady Queen of Peace RC
Prim Sch L21 27 B2
Our Lady Star of the Sea RC
Prim Sch L21 38 A6
Our Lady's Bishop Eton RC
Prim Sch L18 69 C5
Our Lady's RC High Sch
L6 53 A4
Our Lady's RC Prim Sch
L34 56 D7
Out La L25 70 B3
Outer Forum L11 39 E2
Outlet La L31,L39 21 F1
Outlook The L38 17 F4
Oval Sports Ctr The
CH63 78 F7
Oval The CH45 50 F6
Overbrook La L34 41 C5
Overbury St L7 68 B8
Overchurch Inf Sch CH49 64 F6
Overchurch Jun Sch
CH49 64 F6
Overchurch Rd CH46,
CH49 64 E6
Overdale Ave CH61 77 D5
Overdale Prim Sch L33 29 F4
Overdale Rd CH64 88 A1
Overdene Wlk L32 29 F1
Overgreen Gr CH46 49 D1
Overstrand CH48 63 A2
Overton Ave L21 27 B1
Overton Cl
Birkenhead CH43 65 F3
Kirkby L32 29 D1
Overton Rd CH44 51 B4
Overton St L7 53 B1
Overton Way CH43 65 F3
Ovington Dr PR8 4 E3
Ovolo Rd L13 54 A4
Owen Ave L39 13 F6
Owen Cl WA10 43 D1
Owen Dr L24 82 B3
Owen Rd Knowsley L33 41 C7
Liverpool L4 52 D8
Rainhill L35 57 C2
Owen St WA10 43 D1
Owen's La L39 11 E2
Owlsfield WA12 46 E3
Ox La L35 71 C6
Oxborough Cl WA8 72 F4
Oxbow Rd L12 54 E8
Oxendale Cl L8 68 B7
Oxenham Rd WA2 61 A3
Oxenholme Cres L11 40 A1
Oxford Ave Bootle L20 38 E3
Litherland L21 38 B8
Oxford Cl L17 68 C2
Oxford Ct Crosby L22 26 C2
[6] Southport PR8 3 F4
Oxford Dr Crosby L22 26 C2
Heswall CH63 86 F6
Liverpool L26 83 A8
Oxford Gdns PR8 3 E4
Oxford Ho L20 38 E3
Oxford Rd Bootle L20 38 D3
Crosby L22 26 C1
Huyton-w-R L36 56 A3
Liverpool L9 39 B8
Orrell WN5 25 F8
Skelmersdale WN8 15 E1
Southport PR8 3 E4
Wallasey CH44 51 C4
Oxford St Liverpool L7 52 F1
Newton-le-W WA12 46 B3
[2] St Helens WA10 43 F4
St Helens WA10 43 F5
Oxford St E L7 53 A1
Oxhouse Rd WN5 25 D4
Oxley Ave CH46 50 B3
Oxley St WA9 58 D7
Oxton Cl
Liverpool,Aigburth L17 68 C2
Liverpool,Kirkby L32 40 B8
Widnes WA8 72 C4
Oxton Ct CH43 66 B4
Oxton Rd Birkenhead CH41 66 C5
Wallasey CH44 51 B3
Oxton St L4 52 F8
Oxton St Saviour's CE Prim
Sch CH43 66 A3

P

Pacific Rd
Birkenhead CH41 66 F7
Bootle L20 38 B4
Packenham Rd L13 53 F6
Padbury St L8 68 A5
Paddington L7 53 A1
Paddock Cl L23 26 B6
Paddock Dr CH64 86 D2
Paddock Gr WA9 58 D3
Paddock Hey L27 70 D6
Paddock Rd WN8 24 C5
Paddock The
Ashton-in-M WN4 34 F6
Birkenhead,Saughall Massie
CH46 64 C7
Birkenhead,Upton CH49 65 B5
Formby L37 10 A5
Heswall CH60 86 C8
Kirkby L32 40 D7
Liverpool L25 70 B4
Ormskirk L39 13 C3
Prescot L34 56 F7
Southport PR8 7 C4
Padeswood Cl WA9 58 C6
Padgate Com High Sch
WA2 61 F2
Padstow Cl Liverpool L26 70 E1
Southport PR9 2 A5
Warrington WA5 74 E3
Padstow Dr WA10 43 B6
Padstow Rd
Birkenhead CH49 64 C2
Liverpool L16 69 D8

Per – Pri 123

Perth St L6 .53 A3
Peter Mahon Way L20 .38 B4
Peter Price's La CH63 .78 E4
Peter Rd Liverpool L4 .38 E1
  Liverpool L4 .38 F2
Peter St Ashton-in-M WN4 .35 C3
  Golborne WA3 .47 A8
  Liverpool L1 .90 B4
  St Helens WA10 .43 F4
  8 Wallasey CH44 .51 E2
Peter's La L1 .90 B3
Peterborough Dr L30 .27 F4
Peterborough Rd L15 .69 A6
Peterhouse Sch PR9 .2 B3
Peterhouse Wlk WN4 .34 F4
Peterlee Cl WA9 .57 F7
Peterlee Way L30 .28 A1
Petersfield Cl L30 .28 A1
Peterstone Cl WA5 .60 D2
Peterwood CH42 .67 A1
Petham Ct WA8 .72 E4
Petherick Rd L11 .40 C5
Petton St L5 .52 F6
Petunia Cl Huyton-w-R L14 .55 A4
  St Helens WA9 .59 A7
Petworth Ave WA2 .61 B3
Petworth Cl L24 .82 B4
Petworth Rd PR8 .7 B6
Peveril St L9 .38 F3
Pex Hill Ct WA8 .72 E5
Pharmacy Rd L24 .82 C5
Pheasant Field L24 .83 C2
Pheasant Gr L26 .70 E1
Philbeach Rd L11,L4 .39 D2
Philharmonic Ct 5 L8 .67 F8
Philip Dr PR8 .7 F6
Philip Gr WA9 .58 C7
Philip Leverhulme Lodge CH62 .79 B6
Philip Rd WA8 .84 B8
Philips Dr WA5 .74 E6
Phillimore Rd L6 .53 C3
Phillip Gr L12 .54 F5
Phillip's Cl L37 .9 F2
Phillip's La L37 .9 F2
Phillips Cl L23 .27 B6
Phillips St L3 .52 C3
Phillips Way CH60 .85 E8
Phipps' La WA5 .59 E7
Phoenix Ave WA5 .60 F2
Phoenix Dr L14 .55 B5
Phoenix Prim Sch L7 .53 E2
Physics Rd L24 .82 C5
Phythian Cl L6 .53 B3
Phythian Cres WA5 .74 F4
Phythian St Liverpool L6 .53 A3
  St Helens WA11 .44 F6
Picadilly WN5 .33 E5
Pickerill Rd CH49 .64 D3
Pickering Rake L30 .27 D5
Pickering Rd CH45 .51 B8
Pickering St L6 .53 A5
Pickering's Pasture (Nature Reserve)★ WA8 .84 B3
Pickerings Rd WA8 .84 B5
Pickmere Dr
  Bebington CH62 .88 F3
  Bebington CH62 .88 F4
Pickop St 6 L3 .52 C3
Pickwick St L8 .67 F6
Pickworth Way L31 .29 B3
Picow Farm Rd WA7 .84 E1
Picow St 1 WA7 .84 F1
Picton Cl Bebington CH62 .88 E3
  Birkenhead CH43 .65 F4
Picton Cres L15 .68 E8
Picton Gr L15 .68 D8
Picton Rd Crosby L22 .26 D1
  Liverpool L15 .68 E8
Piele Rd WA11 .45 E8
Piercefield Ct L37 .10 A5
Piercefield Rd L37 .9 F5
Pierpoint St WA3 .47 A7
Pighue La Liverpool L13 .54 A1
  Liverpool L13,L7 .53 F1
Pigot St WA10 .43 E3
Pigotts Rake L30 .27 D5
Pike House Rd WA10 .43 A5
Pike Pl WA10 .43 B4
Pikelaw Pl WN8 .24 C5
Pikes Bridge Fold WA10 .43 A4
Pikes Hey Rd CH48 .75 F7
Pilch Bank Rd L14 .54 E4
Pilch La L14,L36 .54 F3
Pilch La E L36 .55 A2
Pilgrim Cl WA2 .61 A6
Pilgrim St
  Birkenhead CH41 .66 F6
  Liverpool L1 .90 C2
Pilkington Rd PR8 .4 D5
Pilkington St WA11 .31 F6
Pilling Cl PR9 .1 F5
Pilling La L31 .20 A5
Pilling Pl WN8 .24 C5
Pilot Gr L15 .68 D8
Pimblett Rd WA11 .45 E7
Pimblett St WA3 .47 A7
Pimbley Gr E L31 .28 C6
Pimbley Gr W L31 .28 C6
Pimbo La
  Skelmersdale WN8 .24 F3
  Up Holland WN8 .25 A4
Pimbo Rd
  Crank WA11,WN8 .32 E7
  Skelmersdale WN8 .24 C5
Pimhill Cl L8 .68 A6
Pimlico Rd WA7 .84 E2
Pincroft Way 3 L4 .52 D7
Pine Ave Bebington CH63 .78 F3
  Newton-le-W WA12 .46 D2
  Ormskirk L39 .13 F7
  St Helens WA10 .43 F6
  4 Widnes WA8 .73 B2
Pine Cl Haydock WA11 .45 C6
  Huyton-w-R L36 .55 D4
  Kirkby L32 .29 C3
  Prescot L35 .56 E3
  Skelmersdale WN8 .15 F1
Pine Crest L39 .13 B2
Pine Ct Birkenhead CH41 .66 D6
  11 Liverpool L8 .68 A4
Pine Dale WA11 .31 E7
Pine Dr L39 .13 F6
Pine Gr Bootle L20 .38 D4
  Crosby L22 .26 D2
  Golborne WA3 .47 C8
  Ormskirk L39 .13 F7
  Southport PR9 .4 D7
Pine Lodge L4 .53 B8
Pine Mews L1 .90 C1
Pine Rd CH60 .86 C8
Pine Tree Ave CH43 .65 C4
Pine Tree Rd L36 .70 D8
Pine View Dr CH61 .77 A3
Pine Walks
  Bebington CH42 .78 B8
  Birkenhead CH42 .66 B1
Pine Way CH60 .76 E2
Pinedale Cl CH43 .65 D4
Pinehey CH64 .86 D1
Pinehurst Ave Crosby L22 .26 C2
  Liverpool L4 .53 C7
Pinehurst Rd L4 .53 C7
Pinehurst Road Prim Sch L4 .53 C7
Pinemore Rd L18 .69 A2
Pineridge Cl CH62 .79 C2
Pines The Bebington CH63 .79 B3
  Liverpool L12 .40 F4
  Southport PR8 .3 F6
Pinetop Cl L6 .53 C4
Pinetree Cl
  Birkenhead CH46 .64 F8
  Litherland L30 .27 F3
Pinetree Ct CH45 .50 F5
Pinetree Dr CH48 .63 D1
Pinetree Gr CH46 .64 F8
Pinewood
  Ashton-in-M WN4 .35 A2
  Skelmersdale WN8 .16 D3
Pinewood Ave Formby L37 .9 D1
  Liverpool L12 .40 D3
Pinewood Cl
  Abram Brow WN2 .36 C7
  Formby L37 .9 D2
  Liverpool L27 .70 E6
  Southport PR8 .5 C1
Pinewood Cres WN5 .25 E6
Pinewood Dr CH60 .86 B8
Pinewood Gdns L33 .29 E5
Pinewood Rd WA5 .59 F7
Pinfold CH47 .63 A4
Pinfold Cl Litherland L30 .27 E5
  Southport PR8 .7 B3
Pinfold Cres L32 .41 A8
Pinfold Ct 3 L23 .26 D5
Pinfold Dr WA10 .43 A3
Pinfold La Knowsley L34 .41 C3
  Southport PR8 .7 B3
  West Kirby CH48 .63 A4
Pinfold Pl WN8 .24 D4
Pinfold Rd L25 .82 C7
Pingot Rd WN5 .33 E5
Pingwood La L33 .30 A5
Pinnington Pl L36 .55 E2
Pinnington Rd L35 .56 E3
Pintail Cl WA11 .44 B6
Piper's Cl CH60 .85 D8
Piper's End CH60 .85 D8
Piper's La CH60 .76 C1
Pipers The WA3 .47 F8
Pipistrelle Rise CH43 .65 E4
Pipit Ave WA12 .46 C3
Pipit Cl L26 .70 E2
Pirrie Rd L9 .39 D3
Pit Hey Pl WN8 .24 C5
Pit La WA8 .73 A4
Pit Pl L25 .70 A2
Pitch Cl CH49 .64 D4
Pitsmead Rd L32 .29 E1
Pitt St Liverpool L1 .90 B2
  Southport PR9 .4 F6
  St Helens WA9 .44 C3
  St Helens WA9 .44 C4
Pitts House La PR9 .5 B8
Pitville Ave L18 .69 A3
Pitville Cl L18 .69 A2
Pitville Gr L18 .69 A3
Pitville Rd L18 .69 A3
Pitville Terr WA8 .84 C7
Plane Cl L9 .39 C3
Plane Tree Gr WA11 .46 A7
Plane Tree Rd CH63 .78 E5
Planetree Rd L12 .54 F8
Plantation Bsns Pk CH62 79 F2
Plantation Prim Sch L26 .82 F8
Plantation Rd CH62 .79 F2
Planters The
  Birkenhead CH49 .64 C4
  Litherland L30 .28 A4
Platt Gr CH42 .79 A8
Platts St WA11 .45 A6
Plattsville Rd L18 .69 A5
Playfield Rd L12 .54 F7
Playfield Wlk L12 .54 F7
Pleasance Way WA12 .46 D4
Pleasant Hill St L8 .67 D6
Pleasant St Bootle L20 .38 B2
  Liverpool L3 .90 C3
  Wallasey CH45 .51 B7
Pleasant Street Prim Sch L3 .90 C3
Pleasant View L20 .38 B2
Pleasington Cl CH43 .65 E4
Pleasington Dr CH43 .65 E4
Plemont Rd L13 .54 A5
Plessington RC High Sch Tech Coll CH63 .79 A7
Plex La L39 .12 C5
Plex Moss La
  Haskayne L39 .11 D8
  Southport PR8,L39,L37 .7 E1
Plimsoll St 6 L7 .53 B1
Plough La L40 .15 A4
Plover Cl WA12 .46 C3
Plover Way WA3 .47 E8
Pluckington Rd L36 .56 B3
Plum Tree Cl
  Eccleston Park L35 .57 A6
  Huyton-w-R L28 .55 B8
Plumbers Way L36 .55 F2
Plumer St
  Birkenhead CH41 .66 A8
  Liverpool L15 .68 E8
Plumley Gdns WA8 .72 A1
Plumpton La L39 .8 E2
Plumpton St L6 .52 F4
Plymyard Ave CH62 .88 D5
Plymyard Cl CH62 .88 D5
Pocket Nook St WA9 .44 C4
Pocklington Ct WA2 .61 F1
Podium Rd L13 .54 A4
Poets Cnr CH62 .79 B5
Poets Gn L35 .56 F3
Poleacre Dr WA8 .72 D2
Poll Hill Rd CH60 .76 F1
Pollard Rd L15 .54 A1
Pollitt Cres WA9 .58 C3
Pollitt Sq CH62 .79 C8
Polperro Cl WA5 .74 E3
Pomfret St L8 .68 A6
Pomona St L3 .90 C3
Pond Cl L6 .53 C4
Pond Green Way WA9 .44 F1
Pond View Cl CH60 .86 C8
Pond Wlk WA9 .45 A1
Ponsonby Rd CH45 .50 E5
Ponsonby St L8 .68 A6
Pontville Residential Sch L39 .13 D3
Pool Bank CH62 .79 B6
Pool End WA9 .44 F2
Pool Hey L28 .55 B8
Pool Hey La PR8,PR9 .5 B3
Pool La Bebington CH62 .79 D5
  Birkenhead,Woodchurch CH49 .65 A2
Pool St Birkenhead CH41 .66 D7
  Southport PR9 .2 D5
Poolbank Rd CH62 .79 B7
Poole Ave WA2 .61 B2
Poole Cres WA2 .61 B2
Poole Rd CH44 .51 D5
Poolside Wlk PR9 .2 C4
Poolwood Rd CH49 .65 B3
Pope St L20 .38 B5
Poplar Ave
  Birkenhead CH49 .64 F5
  Crosby L23 .26 F5
  Downall Green WN4 .34 D5
  Newton-le-W WA12 .46 D3
  St Helens WA10 .43 A4
  Warrington WA5 .74 E3
Poplar Bank
  Huyton-w-R L36 .55 E2
  Southport PR9 .1 D1
Poplar Ct 7 L8 .68 A4
Poplar Dr Bebington CH63 .79 A4
  Kirkby L32 .29 D3
  Liverpool L5 .53 A5
  Skelmersdale WN8 .15 F1
Poplar Farm Cl CH46 .64 C6
Poplar Gr Haydock WA11 .45 C6
  Prescot L35 .56 E5
  Seaforth L21 .37 F6
  St Helens WA10 .43 C3
Poplar Rd
  Birkenhead CH43 .66 B4
  Haydock WA11 .45 C6
  Liverpool L25 .70 A3
Poplar St Golborne WA3 .36 B1
  Southport PR8 .4 E6
Poplar Terr 9 CH45 .51 B7
Poplar Way L4 .52 D8
Poplars Ave
  Warrington WA2 .61 A4
  Warrington WA2 .61 C3
Poplars Pl WA2 .61 D2
Poplars The WA3 .36 B1
Poppleford Cl L25 .70 D5
Poppy Cl Southport PR8 .4 B2
  Wallasey CH46 .50 A2
Poppy La L39 .14 B1
Porchester Rd L11 .39 F1
Porchfield Cl L11 .40 B3
Porlock Ave Liverpool L16 .69 E5
  St Helens WA9 .58 C5
Porlock Cl Heswall CH60 .86 B6
  Warrington WA5 .74 E4
Port Cswy CH62 .79 D4
Port of Liverpool Euro Rail Terminal L21 .37 E7
Port Sunlight Her Ctr★ CH62 .79 B5
Port Sunlight Sta CH62 .79 B5
Portal Mews CH61 .76 F3
Portal Rd CH61 .76 F3
Portal Way L10,L11 .40 C6
Portbury Cl CH62 .79 C6
Portbury Way CH62 .79 C6
Portbury Wlk CH62 .79 C6
Portelet Rd L13 .53 F4
Porter Ave WA12 .46 C5
Porter Cl L35 .57 E1
Porter St L3 .52 B4
Portgate Cl L12 .40 C2
Porthcawl Cl WA8 .72 C3
Portia Ave CH63 .78 E7
Portia Gdns CH63 .78 E7
Portia St 2 L20 .38 C1
Portico Ave L35 .57 A6
Portico Ct L35 .57 A6
Portico La L35 .57 A6
Portland Ave L22 .26 C2
Portland Cl WN2 .36 A8
Portland Gdns L3 .52 C4
Portland Pl L5 .52 E4
Portland Prim Sch CH41 .66 A8
Portland St
  Birkenhead CH41 .66 A8
  Liverpool L5 .52 C4
  Newton-le-W WA12 .45 F4
  Runcorn WA7 .84 F3
  Southport PR8 .4 B5
  Wallasey CH45 .37 A1
Portland Way WA9 .44 F1
Portlemouth Rd L11 .40 C5
Portloe Ave L26 .70 F1
Portman Rd L15 .68 D7
Porto Hey Rd CH61 .76 D5
Porton Rd L32 .29 C1
Portreath Way WA10 .43 B6
Portree Ave CH63 .88 D5
Portree Cl L9 .39 A5
Portrush St L13 .53 E6
Portway L25 .82 C7
Portwood Cl L7 .68 B8
Post Office Ave 1 PR9 .4 B7
Potter Pl WN8 .24 D5
Potters La Hale WA8 .83 F5
  Liverpool L18 .69 C5
Pottery Cl L35 .56 C3
Pottery Fields 1 L34 .56 E6
Pottery La L35,L36 .56 C3
Poulevara Ho L13 .54 B2
Poulsom Dr L30 .27 D3
Poulter Rd L9 .39 B7
Poulton Bridge Rd CH41, CH44 .51 A3
Poulton Cl L26 .82 E6
Poulton Ct PR9 .4 F7
Poulton Dr
  7 Ashton-in-M WN4 .34 F5
  Widnes WA8 .84 D8
Poulton Green Cl CH63 .78 F1
Poulton Hall Rd
  Bebington CH63 .88 A7
  Wallasey CH44 .51 A3
Poulton Lancelyn Prim Sch CH63 .79 A2
Poulton Prim Sch CH44 .51 B3
Poulton Rd
  Bebington CH63 .79 A2
  Southport PR9 .4 F7
  Wallasey CH44 .51 C3
Poulton Royd Dr CH63 .78 F2
Poulton Vale CH44 .51 A2
Poverty La L31 .28 F8
Povey Rd WA2 .61 D1
Powderworks La L31 .21 C3
Powell Dr WN5 .33 D3
Powell St WA9 .58 E7
Power Rd Bebington CH62 .79 F1
  Bebington,Rock Ferry CH42 79 A8
Powis St L8 .68 A5
Pownall Sq 10 L3 .90 A4
Pownall St L1 .90 B2
Poynter St WA9 .57 E7
Pratt Rd L34 .56 C6
Precinct CH63 .79 A3
Precinct The CH62 .79 D1
Precincts The 4 L23 .26 E4
Preece Cl WA8 .72 D4
Preesall Cl PR9 .1 F4
Preesall Way L11 .40 C5
Premier St Liverpool L5 .52 F5
  2 Liverpool L5 .53 A5
Prentice Rd CH42 .66 E1
Prenton Ave WA9 .58 C4
Prenton Dell Ave CH43 .78 A8
Prenton Dell Rd CH43 .77 F8
Prenton Farm Rd CH43 .78 A8
Prenton Gn L24 .82 E3
Prenton Hall Rd CH43 .65 F1
Prenton High Sch for Girls CH42 .66 D1
Prenton Jun Sch CH43 .66 A1
Prenton La CH42 .66 B1
Prenton Park (Tranmere Rovers FC) CH42 .66 C2
Prenton Park Rd CH42 .66 C2
Prenton Prep Sch CH43 .66 B3
Prenton Rd E CH42 .66 D3
Prenton Rd W CH42 .66 C2
Prenton Village Rd
  Bebington CH43 .78 A8
  Birkenhead CH43 .65 F1
Prenton Way CH43 .65 D1
Prentonwood Ct CH42 .66 C1
Prescot Ctr 14 L34 .56 D6
Prescot Dr L6 .53 E3
Prescot Gn L39 .13 D3
Prescot Mus★ L34 .56 D6
Prescot Prim Sch L34 .56 E6
Prescot Rd Kirkby L31,L32 .29 C6
  Liverpool L6,L7,L13 .53 E3
  Ormskirk L31,L39 .21 D6
  St Helens WA10 .43 D2
  Tarbock Green WA8 .71 F5
  Widnes WA8 .72 D2
Prescot Sch L34 .56 C7
Prescot St Liverpool L3,L7 .52 F2
  Wallasey CH45 .51 A8
Prescot Sta L35 .56 E5
Prescott Ave WA3 .35 F2
Prescott Rd WN8 .24 F4
Prescott St WA3 .36 A1
Preseland Rd L23 .26 E3
Pressfield Sch PR9 .2 A3
Prestbury Ave
  Birkenhead CH43 .65 E2
  Southport PR8 .7 B5
Prestbury Cl
  Birkenhead CH43 .65 E2
  Widnes WA8 .84 E8
Prestbury Dr WA10 .43 B3
Prestbury Rd L11 .39 F4
Preston Ave L34 .56 C5
Preston Gr L6 .53 C5
Preston New Rd PR9 .2 B4
Preston Rd PR9 .4 E8
Preston St Liverpool L1 .90 B4
  St Helens WA9 .58 A2
Preston Way L23 .27 A4
Prestwick Cl WA8 .72 F3
Prestwick Dr L23 .26 C6
Prestwood Cres L14 .54 F4
Prestwood Pl WN8 .24 F4
Prestwood Rd L14 .54 F4
Pretoria Rd
  Ashton-in-M WN4 .35 B4
  Liverpool L9 .39 B6
Price Gr WA9 .45 A2
Price St Birkenhead CH41 .66 D7
  Liverpool L1 .90 B2
Price Street Bsns Ctr CH41 .66 C8
Price's La CH43 .66 B4
Pride Cl WA12 .46 E2
Priesthouse Cl L37 .10 A3
Priesthouse La L37 .10 A3
Primary Ave L30 .28 B4
Primrose Cl Formby L37 .10 B5
  Southport PR9 .2 C6
  Warrington WA2 .61 D2
  Widnes WA8 .72 E1
Primrose Ct 13 CH45 .51 B8
Primrose Dr L36 .55 E5
Primrose Gr
  Haydock WA11 .45 E7
  6 Wallasey CH44 .51 E2
Primrose Hill
  Bebington CH62 .79 B6
  Liverpool L3 .90 B4
Primrose Rd
  Birkenhead CH41 .65 F7
  Liverpool L18 .69 C5
Primrose St L4,L5 .52 D7
Primrose View WN4 .35 C2
Primula Dr Golborne WA3 .47 D8
  Liverpool L9 .39 B4
Prince Albert Mews L1 .90 C1
Prince Alfred Rd L15 .69 A6
Prince Andrew's Gr WA10 .43 C6
Prince Charles Gdns PR8 .3 F4
Prince Edward St CH41 .66 C7
Prince Edwin St L5 .52 E4
Prince St
  Ashton-in-M WN4 .35 A5
  Seaforth L22 .37 E8
Prince William St L8 .67 E6
Princes Ave
  Bebington CH62 .88 E6
  Crosby L23 .26 D4
  Liverpool L8 .68 A6
  West Kirby CH48 .63 B2
Princes Bvd CH63 .78 E8
Princes Ct L8 .68 B6
Princes Gate E 1 L8 .68 B6
Princes Gate Ho 3 L8 .68 B6
Princes Gate W 2 L8 .68 B6
Princes Gdns L3 .52 C3
Princes Par L3 .52 B2
Princes Park Man L8 .68 B5
Princes Pl WA8 .72 E1
Princes Rd Liverpool L8 .68 A6
  St Helens WA10 .43 C1
Princes Sch L8 .68 A7
Princes St Bootle L20 .38 B1
  Liverpool L2 .90 A4
  Newton-le-W WA12 .46 B3
  Southport PR8 .4 A6
Princes Way WA11 .44 A8
Princess Ave
  Ashton-in-M WN4 .35 C3
  Haydock WA11 .46 A7
  St Helens WA10 .43 E6
  Warrington WA5 .74 E7
Princess Dr
  Huyton-w-R L14,L36,L12 .55 A5
  Liverpool L14 .54 F7
Princess Pavement 14 CH41 .66 E6
Princess Rd
  Ashton-in-M WN4 .35 C3
  11 Wallasey CH45 .51 B7

RENAISSANCE SPEKE
WAY
P82

Reedale Rd L18 69 A4
Reeds Ave E CH46 50 A3
Reeds Ave W CH46 49 F3
Reeds Brow WA11 32 B8
Reeds La CH46 49 F3
Reeds Rd L36 55 E4
Reeds The L39 13 D6
Reedville CH43 66 B5
Reedville Gr CH46 49 F2
Reedville Rd CH63 78 F5
Reeves Ave L20 38 E5
Reeves St WA9 44 E3
Regal Cres WA8 84 B8
Regal Ct PR8 7 D5
Regal Dr WA10 43 C5
Regal Rd L11 40 C3
Regal Wlk L4 52 F7
Regency Gdns PR8 3 E4
Regent Ave
Ashton-in-M WN4 34 F5
Haydock WA11 45 B7
Huyton-w-R L14 54 E2
Litherland L30 27 F3
Regent Cl PR8 3 F4
Regent Ct 2 PR9 4 C8
Regent Mews PR8 3 F4
Regent Pk L36 55 E5
Regent Rd Bootle L20,L5 38 B1
Crosby L23 26 D4
Liverpool L20,L5 52 B6
Southport PR8 3 F4
Wallasey CH45 50 D6
Widnes WA8 73 B1
Regent St Liverpool L3 52 B4
Newton-le-W WA12 46 A3
Regents Cl CH61 77 B6
Regents Rd WA10 43 C1
Regents Way CH63 78 D8
Regina Ave L22 26 C2
Regina Rd L9 39 A6
Reginald Rd WA9 58 E6
Reginald Rd Ind Pk WA9 58 E6
Reigate Cl L25 70 C3
Renacres La L39 8 F6
Rendal Cl L5 53 A5
Rendcombe Gn L11 39 F3
Rendel Cl WA12 46 D2
Rendel St CH41 66 D7
Rendelsham Cl CH49 64 E5
Renfrew Ave
Bebington CH62 88 E5
St Helens WA11 44 E7
Renfrew St L7 53 A2
Renfrey Cl L39 13 E8
Rennell Rd L14 54 C3
Rennie Ave WA10 43 C4
Renown Way L24 82 A6
Renshaw St L1 90 C3
Renville Rd L14 54 C2
Renwick Ave L35 57 A4
Renwick Rd L9 39 B5
Renwick Sq WN4 34 F3
Repton Gr L10 28 C2
Repton Rd L16 69 D8
Reservoir Rd
Birkenhead CH42 66 B1
Liverpool L25 69 F3
Reservoir Rd N CH42 66 B1
Reservoir St Liverpool L6 53 A4
St Helens L35 57 C7
Rest Hill Rd CH63 78 C5
Retford Rd L33 30 A2
Retford Wlk 5 L33 29 F2
Reva Rd L14 54 F3
Revesby Cl WA8 72 D2
Rex Cohen Ct L17 68 E5
Rexmore Rd L18 69 A2
Rexmore Way L15 68 E7
Reynolds Ave WA9 45 B2
Reynolds Cl L6 53 A4
Reynolds Way L25 70 A3
Rhiwlas St L8 68 A5
Rhodesia Rd L9 39 C6
Rhodesway CH60 86 B7
Rhona Cl CH63 88 C4
Rhona Dr WA5 74 E6
Rhosesmor Cl L32 40 F6
Rhosesmor Rd L32 40 F6
Rhuddlan Cl L13 53 F2
Rhyl St Liverpool L8 67 F5
Widnes WA8 84 F7
Rialto Cl 11 L8 67 F7
Ribble Ave Maghull L31 20 E2
Rainhill L35 57 C3
Southport PR9 2 C4
Ribble Cl WA8 73 F3
Ribble Cres WN5 33 C3
Ribble Ho L25 70 C3
Ribble Rd L25 70 C3
Ribble St CH41 50 F1
Ribbledale Rd L18 69 A4
Ribbler's La Kirkby L32 40 E7
Kirkby L34 40 F6
Ribblesdale Ave 2 L9 39 B7
Ribblesdale Cl CH62 88 F5
Ribchester Way L35 71 A7
Rice Hey Rd CH44 51 C4
Rice La Liverpool L9 39 A4
Wallasey CH44 51 D4
Rice Lane Jun Sch L9 39 A5
Rice Lane Sta L9 39 A5
Rice St L1 90 C2
Rich View CH43 66 B3
Richard Allen Way 5 L6 52 F4
Richard Chubb Dr CH44, CH45 51 D6
Richard Evans Com Prim Sch
Haydock WA11 45 A6
Richard Evans Com Prim Sch *continued*
St Helens WA11 44 F6
Richard Gr L12 54 F5
Richard Hesketh Dr L32 29 C2
Richard Kelly Cl L4 53 D8
Richard Kelly Dr L4 39 D2
Richard Kelly Pl L4 53 D8
Richard Martin Rd L21 27 C1
Richard Rd L23 26 A5
Richards Gr WA9 44 E4
Richardson Rd CH63 78 E8
Richardson St L7 68 C7
Richland Rd L13 53 F5
Richmond Ave
Haydock WA11 45 B7
Litherland L21 38 A8
Richmond Cl
Bebington CH63 79 A6
Hightown L38 17 F2
St Helens WA10 42 F4
Richmond Cres L30 27 F3
Richmond Ct Bootle L21 38 B7
5 Crosby L23 26 E5
Richmond Gdns WA12 46 C2
Richmond Gr L31 20 E3
Richmond Pk L6 53 C5
Richmond Rd
Ashton-in-M WN4 34 F5
Bebington CH63 78 F6
Crosby L23 26 E5
Southport PR8 3 F2
Richmond Row L3 52 E3
Richmond St Liverpool L1 90 B3
Wallasey CH45 37 B1
Widnes WA8 73 C1
Richmond Terr L6 53 B5
Richmond Way
Heswall CH61 76 F2
Heswall,Thingwall CH61 77 A6
Huyton-w-R L35 71 A7
Rickaby Cl CH63 88 C8
Rickman St L4 52 D7
Rickman Way L36 70 F8
Riddock Rd L21 38 B6
Ridge Cl PR9 2 C5
Ridge The CH60 76 D2
Ridgeborne Cl WA5 60 D2
Ridgefield Rd CH61 76 F5
Ridgemere Rd CH61 76 F5
Ridgetor Rd L25 70 A3
Ridgeview Rd CH43 65 D5
Ridgeway WA3 47 E7
Ridgeway Dr L31 20 E3
Ridgeway High Sch
CH43 65 D4
Ridgeway The
Bebington CH63 78 D8
Cronton WA8 72 C6
Heswall CH60 86 B7
Hoylake CH47 63 E7
Liverpool L25 70 A3
Ridgewell Ave 4 WA3 47 D8
Ridgewood Dr
Heswall CH61 76 F5
St Helens WA9 58 D6
Ridgewood Way L9 39 A7
Ridgmont Ave L11 39 F2
Riding Cl WA9 58 C4
Riding Fold L26 70 D2
Riding Hill Rd L34 41 D2
Riding Hill Wlk L34 41 D2
Riding La
Ashton-in-M WN4 35 F5
Haskayne L39 11 E4
Riding St Liverpool L3 52 F2
Southport PR8 4 B6
Ridings Hey CH43 65 D4
Ridings The
Birkenhead CH43 65 D5
Southport PR9 2 A3
Ridley Gr CH48 63 A3
Ridley La L31 20 D1
Ridley Rd L6 53 C3
Ridley St CH43 66 C5
Ridsdale 2 WA8 84 C8
Ridsdale Lawn L27 71 A3
Riesling Dr L33 29 E5
Rigby Dr CH49 64 D2
Rigby Rd L31 20 B3
Rigby St Ashton-in-M WN4 35 A3
Golborne WA3 47 A8
Liverpool L3 90 A4
St Helens WA10 43 F4
Riley Ave L20 38 D5
Rimington Ave WA3 36 C1
Rimmer Ave L16 55 A1
Rimmer Cl L21 38 B7
Rimmer Gn PR8 5 D1
Rimmer Gr WA9 44 E3
Rimmer St L3 90 C4
Rimmer's Ave Formby L37 9 E6
Southport PR8 4 B6
Rimmerbrook Rd L25 70 B7
Rimmers Ct CH41 65 F7
Rimmington Rd L17 68 E2
Rimrose Bsns Pk L20 38 A4
Rimrose Rd L20 38 A4
Rimrose Valley Country Pk*
L23 27 A3
Rimrose Valley Rd L23 27 B4
Ringcroft Rd L13 54 B2
Ringley Ave WA3 35 F1
Ringo Starr Dr 4 L6 53 B3
Ringsfield Rd L24 83 A2
Ringway CH64 86 E1
Ringway Rd L25 70 C4
Ringways CH62 79 D3
Ringwood CH43 66 A3
Ringwood Ave L14 54 F2
Ringwood Ct CH43 66 A3
Rio Ct L34 56 D7
Ripley Ave L21 27 B1
Ripley Cl L31 20 E1
Ripon Ave WA3 47 D8
Ripon Cl Huyton-w-R L36 56 B3
Litherland L30 27 F1
Newton-le-W WA12 46 C5
Southport PR8 4 F3
Ripon Dr WN4 35 D2
Ripon Rd CH45 50 F6
Ripon St Birkenhead CH41 66 E4
Liverpool L4 38 F1
Risbury Cl L11 39 F2
Rishton Cl 10 L5 53 A5
Rishton St 8 L5 53 A5
Ritchie Ave L9 39 C6
Ritherup La L35 57 C4
Ritson St L8 68 B6
Rivacre Rd CH62,CH65, CH66 89 C2
River Avon St
3 Liverpool L8 68 B7
1 Liverpool L8 68 C7
River Cl L37 10 B1
River Gr CH62 79 B8
River St CH41 66 D6
River View
Bebington CH62 79 C8
Crosby L22 26 C2
Riverbank Cl CH60 85 F6
Riverbank Rd
Heswall CH60 85 E6
Liverpool L19 81 A7
Rivermeade PR8 4 D4
Riverpark Gdns L8 67 E6
Rivers St WN5 25 E6
Riversdale Cl L33 29 F4
Riversdale Ct
Liverpool L19 80 F8
West Kirby CH47 63 A3
Riversdale Mews
Liverpool L19 80 F8
West Kirby CH48 63 A2
Riversdale Rd
Liverpool L19 80 F7
3 Seaforth L21 37 F7
Wallasey CH44 51 D4
West Kirby CH48 63 A2
Riverside Bebington CH62 79 B5
Hightown L38 17 F4
Liverpool L12 40 E1
West Kirby CH48 75 B8
Riverside Cl L20 38 A5
Riverside Dr L17 68 B2
Riverside Gr WA9 58 D7
Riverside Prim Sch CH44 51 E3
Riverside Trad Est WA5 74 D1
Riverside View L17 68 C1
Riverslea Rd L23 26 B2
Riverview Hts L19 80 F7
Riverview Rd CH44 51 E3
Riverview Wlk 9 L8 67 F4
Riverwood Rd CH62 79 F1
Riviera Dr
Birkenhead CH42 66 D1
Liverpool L11 40 C4
Rivington Ave
Birkenhead CH43 65 E4
Golborne WA3 36 C1
St Helens WA10 43 F6
Rivington Cl PR8 4 A3
Rivington Dr
Bickershaw WN2 36 F8
Up Holland WN8 25 C7
Rivington Prim Sch
WA10 43 E5
Rivington Rd
St Helens WA10 43 D4
Wallasey CH44 51 D3
Rivington St WA10 43 D3
RL Hughes Prim Sch
WN4 35 A3
Road N L6 53 D6
Roadside Ct WA3 47 C8
Roadwater Cl L25 70 B7
Rob La WA12 46 E5
Robarts Rd L4 53 B6
Robbin's Bridge L31 20 E5
Robeck Rd L13 54 B1
Robert Dr CH49 64 E3
Robert Gr L12 54 E5
Robert St
4 Birkenhead CH41 66 D7
Widnes WA8 73 B1
Roberts Ave WA11 45 A5
Roberts Dr L20 38 E7
Roberts Prim Sch L20 38 E7
Roberts St L3 52 B3
Robertson St L8 67 E5
Robin Way CH49 65 B2
Robin's La WA11 33 A8
Robina Rd WA9 58 D8
Robins La WA9 58 D8
Robins Lane Comm Prim Sch
WA9 58 C8
Robinson Mews CH41 66 F6
Robinson Pl WA9 44 D3
Robinson Rd L21 27 C1
Robsart St L5 52 E5
Robson Pl WN2 36 B8
Robson St
Liverpool,Everton L5 52 F6
Liverpool,Old Swan L13 54 A1
Robson Way 3 WA3 47 F8
Roby Cl L35 57 C4
Roby Mount Ave L36 55 D2
Roby Park Prim Sch L36 55 A3
Roby Rd Huyton-w-R L36 55 C2
Huyton-w-R,Bowring Park L14,L36 54 F1
Roby St Bootle L20 38 C4
Liverpool L15 68 E7
St Helens WA10 43 D1
Roby Sta L36 55 C2
Roby Well Way WN5 33 D5
Rocastle Cl 17 L6 53 A3
Rochester Ave L30 27 F1
Rochester Cl WA3 47 A8
Rochester Gdns WA10 43 D1
Rochester Rd CH42 67 A1
Rock Ave CH60 76 F1
Rock Bank CH49 65 A5
Rock Cl CH42 66 F2
Rock Ferry By-Pass
CH42 67 A2
Rock Ferry High Sch
CH42 78 F8
Rock Ferry Prim Sch
CH42 66 F2
Rock Ferry Sta CH42 66 F2
Rock Gr L13 54 A3
Rock La Aintree L31 28 F5
Widnes WA8 72 F4
Rock La E CH42 67 A2
Rock La W CH42 66 F1
Rock Mount Cl L25 69 F3
Rock Mount Pk L25 69 F3
Rock Park Rd CH42 67 B1
Rock Ret Pk CH41 66 F5
Rock St Golborne WA3 36 A2
Liverpool L13 54 A3
St Helens WA10 57 C8
Rock View Kirkby L31 29 A4
Liverpool L5 52 E6
Rockbank Rd L13 53 F5
Rockbourne Ave L25 69 F5
Rockbourne Gn L25 69 F5
Rockbourne Way L25 69 F5
Rockfield Cl WA8 72 D2
Rockfield Gdns 2 L31 20 C2
Rockfield Rd L4 53 A7
Rockford Ave L32 40 E7
Rockford Cl L32 40 E7
Rockford Wlk L32 40 E7
Rockhill Rd L25 70 B2
Rockhouse St L6 53 C5
Rockingham Ct L33 29 F4
Rockland Rd Crosby L22 26 E2
Wallasey CH45 50 F7
Rocklands Ave CH63 79 A7
Rocklands La CH63 87 C8
Rockley St 8 L4 52 E8
Rockmount Rd L17 68 F1
Rockpoint Ave CH45 51 C7
Rockside Rd L18 69 A1
Rockville Rd L13,L14 54 C1
Rockville St CH42 66 F2
Rockwell Cl L12 54 D8
Rockwell Rd L12 54 E8
Rocky Bank Rd CH42 66 D3
Rocky La Heswall CH60 85 F8
Liverpool,Anfield L6 53 C5
Liverpool,Childwall L15,L16 69 D8
Rocky La S CH60 86 A8
Roderick Rd 1 L4 39 A2
Roderick St 3 L3 52 E3
Rodick St L25 69 F2
Rodmell Rd L9 39 B6
Rodney St
Birkenhead CH41 66 E5
Liverpool L1 90 C2
St Helens WA10 43 E4
Roe Alley L1 90 B3
Roe La PR9 4 E8
Roe St L1 90 B4
Roe-Park Mews PR9 4 D8
Roeburn Way WA5 74 D3
Roedean Cl Liverpool L25 82 B8
Maghull L31 20 D2
Roehampton Dr L23 26 C6
Roemarsh Cl L11 40 B2
Roften Ind Est CH66 88 D1
Rogers Ave L20 38 E5
Rogerson's Gn L26 70 E2
Rokeby Ave WA3 36 D1
Rokeby Cl L3 52 E3
Rokeby St L3 52 E3
Rokeden WA12 46 D4
Roker Ave CH44 51 A3
Rokesmith Ave L7 68 C8
Roklis Ct CH49 65 A4
Roland Ave
Bebington CH63 78 E6
Runcorn WA7 84 F1
St Helens WA11 44 C7
Roleton Cl L30 28 B4
Rolleston Dr
Bebington CH63 79 A4
Wallasey CH45 50 F6
Rolling Mill La WA9 58 F8
Rollo St L4 52 E7
Roman Cl WA12 46 C2
Roman Rd
Ashton-in-M WN4 35 A5
Bebington CH43,CH63 78 A8
Hoylake CH47 48 D1
Rome Cl L36 55 D3
Romer Rd L6 53 C3
Romford Way L26 82 F6
Romiley Dr WN8 15 F2
Romilly St L6 53 B3
Romley St L4 38 F1
Romney Cl WA8 73 E2
Romsey Ave L37 10 B2
Romulus St L7 53 D2
Ronald Cl L22 26 F1
Ronald Rd L22 26 F1
Ronald Ross Ave L30 27 F3
Ronald St L13 53 F3
Ronaldshay WA8 73 E2
Ronaldsway
Birkenhead CH49 64 F6
Crosby L23 27 A6
Heswall CH60 85 F6
Liverpool L10 40 A7
Liverpool,Halewood Village L26 83 A8
Ronan Cl L20 38 A4
Ronan Rd WA8 84 E5
Rone Cl CH46 64 D8
Rookery Ave WN4 35 B2
Rookery Dr Liverpool L19 80 F8
Rainford WA11 32 A5
Rookery La WA11 32 B5
Rookery Rd PR9 1 F1
Rookery The WA12 46 D4
Rookley Cl L27 70 F4
Rooks Way CH60 85 E8
Rooley The L36 55 D1
Roosevelt Dr L9 39 B8
Roper St Liverpool L8 67 F5
St Helens WA9 44 C4
Ropers Bridge Cl L35 56 D2
Ropewalks Sq 4 L1 90 C2
Rosalind Ave CH63 78 E7
Rosalind Way L20 38 D1
Rosclare Dr CH45 50 F6
Roscoe Ave WA12 46 E3
Roscoe Cl L35 71 A7
Roscoe Inf Sch L13 53 E7
Roscoe Jun Sch L13 53 E7
Roscoe La L1 90 C2
Roscoe Pl L1 90 C2
Roscoe St Liverpool L1 90 C2
St Helens WA10 43 D3
Roscommon St L5 52 E4
Roscote Cl CH60 85 F7
Roscote The CH60 85 F7
Rose Ave
Abram Brow WN2 36 B7
Bootle L20 38 C7
Haydock WA11 45 E6
St Helens WA9 58 C7
Rose Bank Rd L16 69 D7
Rose Brae L18 69 B4
Rose Brow L25 70 A4
Rose Cres
Skelmersdale WN8 15 E1
Southport PR8 7 C2
Widnes WA8 84 F7
Rose Ct L15 68 E7
Rose Dr WA11 32 A5
Rose Hill Liverpool L3 52 D3
Southport PR8,PR9 4 D6
Rose Hill View WN4 34 F7
Rose La L18 69 A3
Rose Lea Cl WA8 73 A4
Rose Mount
Birkenhead CH43 66 B4
Crosby L22 26 C1
Rose Mount Dr CH45 51 A6
Rose Pl Birkenhead CH42 66 D4
Liverpool L3 52 D3
Liverpool L3 52 E3
Ormskirk L39 13 D2
Rainford WA11 32 A5
Rose St Liverpool L1 90 B4
Liverpool,Woolton Hill L25 69 F2
Widnes WA8 84 F7
Rose Terr L18 69 A4
Rose Vale L5 52 E5
Rose View Ave WA8 73 A2
Rose Villas L15 69 A7
Roseacre CH48 63 A3
Roseate Ct CH45 50 E8
Rosebank Rd L36 55 C5
Rosebank Way L36 55 C5
Rosebay Cl L37 10 A3
Roseberry Rd WN4 35 A5
Rosebery Ave Crosby L22 26 C2
Wallasey CH44 51 C4
Rosebery Gr CH42 66 B2
Rosebery Rd WA10 43 D5
Rosebery St Liverpool L8 68 A7
Southport PR9 5 A6
Rosebourne Cl L17 68 C2
Rosebrae Ct CH60 77 A1
Rosecroft CH62 88 C6
Rosecroft Cl L39 13 E6
Rosecroft Ct CH47 63 A6
Rosedale Ave Crosby L23 26 F4
Golborne WA3 47 C7
Rosedale Cl L9 39 B4
Rosedale Rd
Birkenhead CH42 66 E3
Liverpool L18 69 B5
Rosefield Ave CH63 78 E7
Rosefield Rd L25 70 C1
Rosegarth Gn L14 54 B4
Roseheath Dr L26 83 A6
Roseheath Prim Sch L26 82 F7
Rosehill Ave WA9 59 B5
Rosehill Bsns Pk 1 PR9 4 D6
Rosehill Ct L25 70 A4
Rosehill Dr L39 13 C2
Rosehill Mans L39 13 C2
Roseland Cl L31 20 B4
Roselands Ct CH42 66 E1

126 Ros – St E

Roselea Dr PR9 .....2 C4
Rosemary Cl
Birkenhead CH43 .....65 E8
Liverpool L7 .....68 A8
Rosemary Ct L37 .....9 F3
Rosemary Dr WA12 .....46 F3
Rosemary La Formby L37 ...9 F3
Haskayne L39 .....12 B4
Rosemead Ave CH61 .....77 A4
Rosemont Rd L17 .....68 F2
Rosemoor Dr L23 .....27 A5
Rosemount Cl CH43 .....66 A3
Rosemount Cotts WA2 ...61 B8
Rosemount Pk CH43 .....66 A3
Roseside Dr L27 .....70 F6
Rosewarne Cl L17 .....68 B2
Rosewell Ct L28 .....55 B6
Rosewood Cl
Abram Brow WN2 .....36 B7
Huyton-w-R L28 .....55 B7
Liverpool L27 .....70 E5
Rosewood Dr CH46 .....64 B8
Rosewood Gdns 1 L11 ...40 B1
Roseworth Ave L9 .....39 A7
Rosina Cl WN4 .....34 F6
Roskell Rd L25 .....82 C7
Roslin Ct CH43 .....66 B4
Roslin Rd Birkenhead CH43 66 B4
Irby CH61 .....76 D6
Roslyn St CH42 .....66 F3
Ross Ave CH46 .....50 C4
Ross Cl Billinge WN5 .....33 E6
Knowsley L34 .....41 D3
Ross St WA8 .....73 B1
Ross Tower Ct CH45 .....51 C8
Rossall Ave L10 .....28 D3
Rossall Cl L24 .....83 E2
Rossall Rd Liverpool L13 ..54 B2
Wallasey CH46 .....49 F1
Widnes WA8 .....73 D2
Rossendale Cl CH43 .....65 D4
Rossett Ave L17 .....68 E6
Rossett Cl WA5 .....60 E2
Rossett Rd L23 .....26 C3
Rossett St L6 .....53 C5
Rossini St L21 .....38 A6
Rosslyn Ave L31 .....28 B8
Rosslyn Cres CH46 .....64 E8
Rosslyn Dr CH46 .....64 E8
Rosslyn Pk 1 CH46 .....64 E7
Rosslyn St L17 .....68 B3
Rossmore Gdns L4 .....53 C8
Rostherne Ave
Golborne WA3 .....47 D8
Wallasey CH44 .....51 A3
Rostherne Cres WA8 .....72 D2
Rosthwaite Gr WA11 .....33 B1
Rosthwaite Rd L12 .....54 C6
Rostron Cres L37 .....9 E1
Rothay Dr WA5 .....74 D3
Rothbury Cl CH46 .....64 C8
Rothbury Ct WA9 .....58 B2
Rothbury Rd L14 .....54 F6
Rotherham Cl L36 .....55 F4
Rotherwood CH43 .....65 D5
Rotherwood Cl CH63 .....78 D6
Rothesay Ct CH63 .....78 F4
Rothesay Dr
Bebington CH62 .....88 E4
Crosby L23 .....26 F3
Rothesay Gdns 3 CH43 ...65 F1
Rothley Ave PR8 .....7 A4
Rothsay Cl WA11 .....44 E6
Rothwell Cl L39 .....13 D5
Rothwell Dr Ormskirk L39 .13 B2
Southport PR8 .....7 A4
Rothwell Rd WA3 .....36 C1
Rothwell St 5 L6 .....53 A4
Rothwells La L23 .....27 B7
Rotten Row PR8 .....3 F6
Rotunda St L5 .....52 D5
Roughdale Ave Kirkby L32 40 F7
St Helens WA9 .....58 B4
Roughdale Cl L32 .....40 F7
Roughsedge Ho L28 .....55 B8
Roughwood Dr L33 .....29 F3
Round Hey L28 .....55 A8
Round Meade The L31 ...20 C2
Roundabout The WA8 ...72 D6
Roundway The L38 .....17 F3
Roundwood Dr WA9 .....44 B1
Routledge St WA8 .....73 B1
Row The CH47 .....63 B7
Rowan Ave Golborne WA3 .47 F7
Liverpool L12 .....40 F1
Rowan Cl
St Helens,Blackbrook WA11 .44 F5
St Helens,Laffak WA11 ...44 D7
Warrington WA5 .....74 F6
Rowan Ct Bebington CH63 .78 D6
Birkenhead CH49 .....64 C2
Liverpool L17 .....68 E2
Rowan Dr L32 .....29 D3
Rowan Gr Bebington CH63 .78 E4
Huyton-w-R L36 .....70 D8
Rowan La WN8 .....16 B4
Rowan Park Sch L21 .....27 D2
Rowan Tree Cl CH49 .....64 B3
Rowans The L39 .....21 A7
Rowena Cl L23 .....26 F4
Rowsley Gr L9 .....39 B7
Rowson Ct 6 CH45 .....51 B8
Rowson St Prescot L34 ...56 D7
Wallasey CH45 .....51 B7
Rowthorn Cl WA8 .....84 E8
Rowton Cl CH43 .....65 F3
Roxborough Cl WA5 .....60 A6
Roxborough Wlk L25 .....70 C3
Roxburgh Ave
Birkenhead CH42 .....66 D2
Liverpool L17 .....68 C3
Roxburgh St L20,L4 .....38 E1
Royal Ave WA8 .....72 A1
Royal Birkdale Golf Links
PR8 .....3 D3
Royal Cl L37 .....10 A1
Royal Cres L37 .....10 A1
Royal Croft L12 .....54 B4
Royal Gr WA10 .....43 D1
Royal Infmy L3 .....52 F2
Royal Liver Building L3 ..52 B1
Royal Liverpool Children's
Hospl The L7 .....67 F8
Royal Liverpool Univ Hospl
L3,L7 .....52 F2
Royal Mail St L3 .....90 C3
Royal Pl WA8 .....84 B8
Royal Quay L3 .....90 A2
Royal School for the Blind
L15 .....69 A7
Royal St L4 .....52 E7
Royal Standard Way 8
CH42 .....66 F3
Royal Terr PR8 .....4 A7
Royal The CH47 .....62 F6
Royden Ave CH44 .....51 D5
Royden Cres WN5 .....33 E5
Royden Pk* CH48 .....64 A1
Royden Rd Billinge WN5 ..33 E5
Birkenhead CH49 .....64 E6
Royden Way L3 .....67 E3
Royhsay Cl L5 .....52 F4
Roysten Gdns WA9 .....44 D2
Royston Ave CH44 .....51 D4
Royston Cl 2 WA3 .....47 E8
Royston St L7 .....53 B1
Royton Rd L22 .....26 F2
Rubbing Stone CH48 .....75 D6
Ruby Cl L21 .....38 C8
Ruby St L8 .....68 A3
Rudd Ave WA9 .....45 B2
Rudd St CH47 .....63 B7
Ruddington Rd PR8 .....4 E2
Rudgate L35 .....56 E2
Rudgrave Cl CH43 .....65 D4
Rudgrave Mews CH44 ...51 D5
Rudgrave Pl CH44 .....51 D5
Rudgrave Sq CH44 .....51 D5
Rudley Wlk L24 .....82 F2
Rudloe Ct WA2 .....61 F1
Rudston Jun & Inf Schs
L16 .....69 D8
Rudston Rd L16 .....69 D7
Rudyard Cl L14 .....54 C3
Rudyard Rd L14 .....54 D3
Ruff La L39,L40 .....14 B4
Rufford Ave L31 .....20 E3
Rufford Cl Liverpool L10 ..39 F8
Prescot L35 .....56 F5
Widnes WA8 .....72 C2
Rufford Dr PR9 .....2 F5
Rufford Rd Bootle L20 ...38 C5
Liverpool L6 .....53 D3
Rainford WA11 .....31 F8
Southport PR9 .....2 C4
Wallasey CH44 .....51 C3
Rufford St 4 WN4 .....34 F5
Rufford Wlk WA11 .....44 F6
Ruffwood Sch L33 .....29 F3
Rugby Dr Aintree L10 .....28 F1
Orrell WN5 .....25 F8
Rugby Rd Liverpool L9 ...39 B8
Wallasey CH44 .....50 F4
Ruislip Cl L25 .....70 C2
Ruislip Ct WA2 .....61 F1
Rullerton Rd CH44,CH45 .51 A4
Rumford Pl L2,L3 .....90 A4
Rumford St L2 .....90 A3
Rumney Pl L4 .....52 E8
Rumney Rd L4 .....52 E8
Rumney Rd W L4 .....52 D8
Runcorn Docks Rd WA7 ..84 E2
Runcorn Sta WA7 .....84 F2
Rundle Rd L17 .....68 E1
Rundle St CH41 .....66 A8
Runic St L13 .....53 F2
Runnell The CH64 .....86 D4
Runnell's La L23 .....27 C5
Runnymede L36 .....55 D4
Runnymede Cl L25 .....70 A4
Runnymede Ct 2 WA8 ...73 C1
Runnymede Dr WA11 .....45 A6
Runnymede Gdns 5
WA8 .....73 C1
Runnymede Wlk WA8 .....73 C2
Runton Rd L25 .....70 C5
Rupert Dr L6 .....53 A3
Rupert Rd L36 .....55 D3
Ruscar Cl L26 .....70 E2
Ruscolm Cl WA5 .....74 D7
Ruscombe Rd L14 .....55 A5
Rushden Rd L32 .....30 A1
Rushey Hey Rd L32 .....29 F1
Rushgreen Cl CH43 .....65 C7
Rushlake Dr L27 .....70 D5
Rushmere Rd L11 .....39 F2
Rushmoor Ave WN4 .....35 E4
Rusholme Cl L26 .....83 A6
Rushton Ave WA12 .....46 B4
Rushton Cl WA8 .....72 F3
Rushton Pl L25 .....70 A2
Rushton's Wlk L30 .....27 D4
Rushy Park WA11 .....44 C6
Rushy View WA12 .....46 A4
Ruskin Ave
Birkenhead CH42 .....66 F1
Newton-le-W WA12 .....46 C4
Wallasey CH44 .....51 A3
Warrington WA2 .....61 C2
Ruskin Cl L20 .....38 C3
Ruskin Dr WA10 .....43 D5
Ruskin St L4 .....38 E1
Ruskin Way
Birkenhead CH43 .....65 E3
Huyton-w-R L36 .....55 D1
Rusland Ave CH61 .....76 F4
Rusland Rd L32 .....40 F8
Russel Ct WA8 .....73 B4
Russell Ave PR9 .....5 A7
Russell Ct PR9 .....2 B4
Russell Pl L3 .....90 C3
Russell Rd
Birkenhead CH42 .....67 A2
Huyton-w-R L36 .....56 B2
Liverpool L18 .....68 F5
Liverpool,Garston L19 ...81 C6
Runcorn WA7 .....84 E1
Southport PR9 .....5 A6
Wallasey CH44 .....50 E5
Russell St
Birkenhead CH41 .....66 E7
Liverpool L3 .....90 C3
Russet Cl
Liverpool,Netherley L27 ...70 E5
St Helens WA10 .....43 F5
Russian Ave L13 .....53 F5
Russian Dr L13 .....53 F5
Ruth Evans Ct L35 .....57 A4
Rutherford Cl L13 .....53 E1
Rutherford Rd
Liverpool L18 .....69 B6
Maghull L31 .....28 E7
St Helens WA10 .....43 C6
Rutherglen Ave L23 .....26 F2
Ruthin Cl WA5 .....60 E3
Ruthven Ct L21 .....38 A7
Ruthven Rd Litherland L21 38 A7
Liverpool L13 .....54 B1
Rutland Ave
Golborne WA3 .....47 D7
Liverpool L17 .....68 D6
Liverpool,Rutland Village
L26 .....83 A8
Rutland Cl 4 L5 .....53 A5
Rutland Cres L39 .....13 E7
Rutland Dr WN4 .....35 C4
Rutland Ho Crosby L23 ...26 B3
Liverpool L17 .....68 D5
Rutland Rd PR8 .....4 D5
Rutland St Bootle L20 ...38 D4
Runcorn WA7 .....84 F2
St Helens WA10 .....43 F5
Rutland Way L36 .....56 B3
Rutter Ave WA5 .....60 F2
Rutter St L8 .....67 E5
Ryburn Rd L39 .....13 E4
Rycot Rd L24 .....82 C4
Rycroft Rd Hoylake CH47 ..63 E8
Liverpool L10 .....39 E7
Wallasey CH44 .....51 C2
Rydal Ave
Birkenhead CH43 .....65 C5
Crosby L23 .....26 F2
Formby L37 .....9 D3
Orrell WN5 .....25 F7
Prescot L34 .....56 F6
Rydal Bank
Bebington CH63 .....79 A7
Wallasey CH44 .....51 C4
Rydal Cl Aintree L10 .....28 F2
Ashton-in-M WN4 .....35 C4
Heswall CH61 .....76 F4
Kirkby L33 .....29 D4
Rydal Gr WA11 .....44 A7
Rydal Pl WN2 .....36 B8
Rydal Rd L36 .....55 E1
Rydal St Liverpool L5 .....53 A5
Newton-le-W WA12 .....46 C3
Rydal Way WA8 .....72 C1
Rydecroft L25 .....69 F2
Ryder Cl Ormskirk L39 ...13 C2
Rainhill L35 .....57 A4
Ryder Cres Ormskirk L39 ..13 C1
Southport PR8 .....7 E7
Ryder Rd WA8 .....73 B4
Rydinge The L37 .....10 A6
Rye Cl WA9 .....58 D4
Rye Gr L12 .....54 E6
Rye Hey Rd L32 .....29 F2
Rye Moss La L37 .....19 B8
Ryecote L32 .....40 E7
Ryecroft L21 .....27 B3
Ryecroft Ave WA3 .....36 E1
Ryecroft Rd CH60 .....86 C7
Ryedale Cl L8 .....68 B7
Ryefield La L21 .....27 B3
Ryegate Rd L19 .....81 B8
Ryeground La L37 .....10 A5
Ryland Pk CH61 .....77 A5
Rylands Hey CH49 .....64 D4
Ryleys Gdns L2 .....90 A4
Rymer Gr 2 L4 .....39 A1
Rymers Gn L37 .....9 E4

S

Sables Ct 3 CH45 .....51 A8
Sackville Rd WA10 .....43 C6
Sacred Heart RC High Sch
L23 .....26 E3
Sacred Heart RC High Sch
(Lower) L23 .....26 E3
Sacred Heart RC Prim Sch
Kirkby L33 .....29 F2
Liverpool L7 .....53 A2
Wallasey CH46 .....49 F1
Saddle Cl L9 .....39 D8
Sadler St WA8 .....73 C1
Sadler's La WA11 .....42 E7
Saffron Cl WA3 .....47 E8
Saffron Gdns WA9 .....44 D2
Saffron Mews L23 .....27 B6
Sagar Fold L39 .....21 D8
SS Peter & Paul RC High Sch
WA8 .....72 F2
SS Peter & Paul's RC Prim
Sch L33 .....29 F6
St Aelred's RC Tech Coll
WA12 .....46 D4
St Agnes RC Prim Sch
L36 .....55 F1
St Agnes Rd
Huyton-w-R L36 .....55 F2
Liverpool L4 .....52 D8
St Aidan's CE Prim Sch
WN5 .....33 E5
St Aidan's Cl WN5 .....33 E6
St Aidan's Ct CH43 .....65 F6
St Aidan's RC Prim Sch
L36 .....55 F3
St Aidan's Terr 1 CH43 ..65 F6
St Aidan's Way L30 .....27 E3
St Aidans CE Comm Sch
WA9 .....58 E3
St Aiden's Gr L36 .....55 C7
St Alban Rd WA5 .....74 E5
St Alban's RC Prim Sch
CH44 .....51 B4
St Alban's Rd
Birkenhead CH43 .....66 A6
Bootle L20 .....38 C3
Wallasey CH44 .....51 B4
St Alban's Sq L20 .....38 C2
St Albans L6 .....53 B5
St Albans Cl WA11 .....46 A7
St Albans Ct L5 .....52 C5
St Albert's RC Prim Sch
L28 .....55 A8
St Alexander Cl 3 L20 ..38 D1
St Aloysius RC Prim Sch
L36 .....55 C4
St Ambrose Barlow RC High
Sch L30 .....28 A5
St Ambrose Croft L30 ...27 E4
St Ambrose Gr L4 .....53 B6
St Ambrose RC Prim Sch
L24 .....83 A2
St Ambrose Rd WA8 .....73 C1
St Ambrose Way 6 L5 ...52 F4
St Andrew Gdns L3 .....90 C4
St Andrew Rd L4 .....53 B6
St Andrew St L3 .....52 F1
St Andrew's CE Prim Sch
Bebington CH63 .....78 F6
Warrington WA2 .....61 C3
St Andrew's Dr L23 .....26 C6
St Andrew's Dr L36 .....55 C7
St Andrew's Gr L30 .....27 C3
St Andrew's Pl PR8 .....4 B6
St Andrew's RC Prim Sch
L26 .....82 D7
St Andrew's Rd
Birkenhead CH43 .....66 B6
Crosby L23 .....26 B6
St Andrew's View L33 ...29 E5
St Andrews Ave L12 .....54 E6
St Andrews Ct L22 .....37 E8
St Andrews Gr WA11 .....44 B6
St Andrews Maghull CE Prim
Sch L31 .....20 D1
St Andrews Pl L17 .....68 C3
St Andrews Rd
Bebington CH63 .....79 A4
Bootle L20 .....38 C6
St Andrews Villas L36 ...55 B3
St Ann Pl L35 .....57 C4
St Ann's CE Prim Sch
L35 .....57 C3
St Anne St
Birkenhead CH41 .....66 C8
5 Birkenhead CH41 .....66 D7
Liverpool L3 .....52 E3
St Anne Terr CH41 .....66 C7
St Anne's (Stanley) JMI Sch
L13 .....54 A3
St Anne's Cl
6 Birkenhead CH41 .....66 D7
Formby L37 .....9 F6
St Anne's Cotts L14 .....54 C3
St Anne's Path L37 .....9 F6
St Anne's Pl CH41 .....66 C8
St Anne's RC Prim Sch
Bebington CH42 .....78 F8
Huyton-w-R L36 .....55 D1
Liverpool L7 .....68 B8
Ormskirk L39 .....13 E4
St Helens WA9 .....58 D7
St Anne's Rd Formby L37 ..9 F6
Huyton-w-R L36 .....55 F1
Liverpool L17 .....68 F1
Ormskirk L39 .....13 D4
Widnes WA8 .....73 B2
St Annes Ct Liverpool L3 ..52 E3
Liverpool,Aigburth L17 ...68 E1
St Annes Gdns L17 .....68 F1
St Annes Gr L17 .....68 F1
St Annes Rd PR9 .....1 F4
St Annes Way CH41 .....66 D7
St Anns Rd WA10 .....43 C3
St Anselm's Coll CH43 ...66 A6
St Anthony of Padua RC Prim
Sch L18 .....68 F4
St Anthony Pl WA2 .....61 B6
St Anthony's Cl L36 .....55 C7
St Anthony's Gr L30 .....27 D3
St Anthony's Rd L23 .....26 B4
St Anthony's Sh Ctr 5
L5 .....52 D5
St Asaph Dr WA5 .....60 E3
St Asaph Gr L30 .....27 F1
St Augustine of Canterbury
RC High Sch WA11 .....44 E5
St Augustine St 1 L5 ...52 D5
St Augustine's Way L30 ..27 E4
St Austel Cl WA5 .....74 E3
St Austell Cl CH46 .....49 B1
St Austells Rd L4 .....38 E2
St Austin's RC Prim Sch
Liverpool L19 .....81 A7
St Helens WA9 .....57 D7
St Bartholomew's RC Prim
Sch L35 .....57 E1
St Basil's RC Prim Sch
WA8 .....72 A2
St Bede's RC High Sch
L39 .....13 D4
St Bede's RC Inf Sch
WA8 .....73 A1
St Bede's RC Jun Sch
WA8 .....73 A1
St Bedes Cl L39 .....13 D3
St Benet's RC Prim Sch
L30 .....27 F4
St Benet's Way L30 .....27 E3
St Bernard's Cl
Litherland L30 .....27 D3
7 Liverpool L8 .....68 B7
St Bernard's Dr L30 .....27 D3
St Brendan's Cl L36 .....55 C7
St Bride St 10 L8 .....67 F8
St Bride's Rd CH44 .....51 D5
St Brides Cl WA5 .....74 E3
St Bridget's CE Prim Sch
CH48 .....63 B1
St Bridget's Gr L30 .....27 D3
St Bridget's La CH48 .....63 B1
St Bridget's RC Prim Sch
WA2 .....61 E3
St Bridgets Cl WA2 .....61 F3
St Brigid's Cres L5 .....52 C5
St Brigid's RC Prim Sch
L28 .....55 A7
St Catherine's Hospl
CH42 .....66 D3
St Catherine's RC Prim Sch
WA3 .....47 E7
St Catherine's Rd L20 ...38 C3
St Catherines Cl L36 .....55 E1
St Catherines Gdns CH42 66 D4
St Cecilia's RC Inf Sch
L13 .....53 E5
St Cecilia's RC Jun Sch
L13 .....53 E5
St Chad's Dr L32 .....29 E2
St Chad's Par L32 .....29 E2
St Charles RC Prim Sch
L17 .....68 C2
St Christopher's Ave L30 27 D4
St Christopher's Dr L36 .55 C7
St Christopher's RC Prim Sch
L24 .....82 D4
St Clair Dr PR9 .....2 A1
St Clares RC Prim Sch
L15 .....68 E6
St Cleopas' CE Jun Mix Inf
Sch L8 .....67 F4
St Columba's Cl CH44 ...51 D5
St Columba's RC Prim Sch
L36 .....55 E5
St Cuthbert's Cl
3 Liverpool L12 .....40 E3
Southport PR9 .....2 A2
St Cuthbert's RC Com High
Sch WA9 .....44 F1
St Cuthbert's RC Prim Sch
L13 .....53 F3
St Cuthbert's Rd PR9 .....2 A2
St Cyrils Cl L27 .....70 C6
St Damian's Croft L30 ...27 E3
St David Rd
Bebington CH62 .....89 A6
Birkenhead CH43 .....66 A6
St David's Rd 5 L4 .....53 B6
St Davids Cl L35 .....57 C4
St Davids Dr WA5 .....60 E2
St Davids Gr L30 .....27 D2
St Davids La CH43 .....65 D5
St Davids Rd L14 .....55 B5
St Domingo Gr L5 .....53 A6
St Domingo Rd L5 .....52 E6
St Domingo Vale L5 .....53 A6
St Dominic's RC Jun & Inf
Sch L14 .....55 B6
St Dunstan's Gr L30 .....27 D3
St Edmond's Rd L20 .....38 C2
St Edmund Arrowsmith RC
High Sch
Ashton-in-M WN4 .....35 B2
Prescot L35 .....56 F5
St Edmund of Canterbury RC
High Sch L14 .....55 B6
St Edmund's & St Thomas' RC
Prim Sch L22 .....26 D1
St Edmund's RC Prim Sch
WN8 .....15 F1
St Edmunds Rd CH63 .....78 F5

St Edward's Coll L12 54 B5
St Edwards Cl CH41 66 B8
St Edwards Mews CH41 66 B8
St Elizabeth's RC Jun Sch L21 38 C6
St Elmo Rd CH44 51 D5
St Finbar's RC Prim Sch L8 68 A3
St Francis de Sales RC Inf Sch L4 38 E2
St Francis de Sales RC Mix Jun Sch L4 38 E1
St Francis of Assisi RC Prim Sch, Garston L19 81 C6
St Francis Xavier's Coll L25 69 F4
St Gabriel's Ave L36 56 A2
St Gabriel's CE Prim Sch L36 56 A2
St George of England High Sch L20 38 D6
St George's Ave WA10 43 C5
St George's Ct WA8 84 D8
St George's Hill L5 52 E6
St George's Mount CH45 51 B8
St George's Pk CH45 51 B8
St George's Pl
Liverpool L1 90 B4
Southport PR9 4 B7
St George's Prim Sch CH45 50 F5
St George's Prim Sch (annexe) CH45 50 F6
St George's RC Prim Sch L31 28 D7
St George's Rd Formby L37 9 E4
Hightown L38 17 F5
Huyton-w-R L36 55 E5
Wallasey CH45 50 E6
St George's Way
11 Liverpool L1 90 B3
Thornton Hough CH63 87 A7
St Georges Ave CH42 66 D2
St Georges Ct L31 28 D8
St Georges Gr
Birkenhead CH46 64 D8
Litherland L30 27 D2
St Georges Rd WA10 43 D2
St Gerard's Cl L5 52 D6
St Gerard's RC Prim Sch L5 52 D6
St Gregory's Croft L30 27 E4
St Gregory's RC Prim Sch
Liverpool L27 70 E5
Maghull L31 20 C4
St Helen's Cl CH43 66 B6
St Helens Central Sta WA10 44 B3
St Helens Coll WA10 43 F3
St Helens Coll (Tech Campus) WA9 44 B4
St Helens Coll Newton Campus WA12 46 B4
St Helens Hospl WA9 44 C1
St Helens Junction Sta WA9 58 F7
St Helens Linkway L35, WA9 57 F4
St Helens PACE WA9 45 A3
St Helens Rd
Ormskirk L39 14 A2
Prescot L34,WA10 56 E7
Rainford WA11 32 B1
St Helens Ret Pk WA9 44 B3
St Helens RLFC WA10 43 C3
St Hilary Brow CH44 50 F4
St Hilary Dr CH45 50 F5
St Hilda St 9 L4 52 E8
St Hilda's CE High Sch L17 68 D5
St Hildas Ct L17 68 D6
St Hugh's Cl CH43 66 B6
St Hugh's RC Prim Sch L7 68 D7
St Ives Ct CH43 66 A7
St Ives Gr L13 53 F3
St Ives Rd CH43 66 A6
St Ives Way L26 70 F1
St James CE Prim Sch WA11 45 E6
St James Cl
Birkenhead CH49 64 D4
Ormskirk L40 14 C3
St James Cres WN2 36 F8
St James Ct 4 CH45 51 B8
St James Dr L20 38 B4
St James Mews L20 38 B4
St James Mount L35 57 C2
St James Pl Liverpool L8 67 E6
Southport PR8 4 B5
St James RC Sch WN8 16 B4
St James Rd
Birkenhead CH41,CH43 65 F8
Liverpool L1 90 C1
Rainhill L35 57 C2
Wallasey CH45 51 B8
St James St Liverpool L1 90 B1
Southport PR8 4 B6
St James Way L30 27 D4
St James' Cl L12 54 A6
St James' RC Prim Sch
Bootle L20 38 B4
Orrell WN5 25 D4
St James' Rd
Huyton-w-R L36 55 E1
Orrell WN5 25 D4
Prescot L34 56 E6
St Jerome's RC Prim Sch L37 9 C3
St Jerome's Way L30 27 E4
St Joan of Arc RC Prim Sch L20 38 A5
St John Almond RC High Sch L19 81 D6
St John Bosco High Sch L11 40 B3
St John Bosco RC Prim Sch L31 20 B2
St John Fisher RC Prim Sch
Knowsley L34 41 D4
Widnes WA8 73 D1
St John Southworth's RC Prim Sch WN4 35 D4
St John St
Birkenhead CH41 66 D6
Newton-le-W WA12 46 A3
St Helens WA10 43 D1
St John Stone RC Prim Sch PR8 7 D2
St John Vianney RC Prim Sch WA9 57 E6
St John's Ave L9 39 A5
St John's CE Prim Sch
Crosby L22 26 D1
Southport PR9 2 C5
Southport,Ainsdale PR8 7 D4
St John's Cl CH47 63 D8
St John's Ct L22 26 D1
St John's Ctr & Mkt L1 90 B3
St John's La L1 90 B4
St John's Pavement 6 CH41 66 D6
St John's Pl L22 26 D1
St John's RC Inf Sch CH63 78 F7
St John's RC Jun Sch CH63 78 F7
St John's RC Prim Sch
Liverpool L4 52 E7
Skelmersdale WN8 16 C1
St John's Rd
Bebington CH62 89 A5
Crosby L22 26 D1
Huyton-w-R L36 55 F1
Liverpool L20 38 C1
Southport PR8 3 F1
Wallasey CH45 50 E5
St John's Sq
Birkenhead CH41 66 D6
10 Liverpool L1 90 B3
St John's St WN2 36 B8
St John's Terr L20 38 B1
St John's Way 5 L1 90 B3
St Johns Ct PR8 7 D4
St Joseph's Cl L36 55 C7
St Joseph's Cl WA5 74 E5
St Joseph's RC Prim Sch
Birkenhead CH49 65 A5
Huyton-w-R L36 55 F3
Wallasey CH44 51 D2
Warrington WA5 74 E5
St Joseph's The Worker RC Prim Sch L32 29 E1
St Josephs Cl WA9 44 C1
St Josephs Cres L3 52 E3
St Jude's Cl L36 55 C7
St Julie's RC High Sch L25 70 A1
St Julie's RC Prim Sch WA10 43 A4
St Kilda's Rd CH46 64 D7
St Laurence Cl 10 CH41 66 D7
St Laurence Dr 11 CH41 66 D7
St Laurence Gr L32 40 F8
St Laurence's RC Prim Sch
Birkenhead CH41 66 D7
Kirkby L32 29 F1
St Lawrence Cl 1 L8 68 A4
St Leo's RC Prim Sch L35 56 E2
St Leonard's Cl L30 27 D4
St Lucia Rd CH44 51 D5
St Luke's Ave WA3 47 D8
St Luke's Bldg 2 PR8 4 D6
St Luke's CE Prim Sch
Formby L37 9 D1
Golborne WA3 47 E7
St Luke's Church Rd L37, L38 17 C8
St Luke's Cres WA8 73 B4
St Luke's Ct L4 39 A2
St Luke's Dr Formby L37 9 C2
Orrell WN5 25 E4
St Luke's Gr Litherland L30 27 D4
Southport PR9 4 E7
St Luke's Halsall CE Prim Sch L23 26 D5
St Luke's Pl 3 L1 90 C2
St Luke's RC Prim Sch
Prescot L35 56 F4
Skelmersdale WN8 24 E6
St Luke's Rd Crosby L23 26 E4
Southport PR9 4 D7
St Helens WA10 43 D4
St Luke's Way L36 55 C7
St Lukes Cl L14 54 F6
St Lukes Ho WN4 35 D4
St Malachy's RC Prim Sch L8 67 E5
St Margaret Mary's RC Inf Sch L14 54 F3
St Margaret Mary's RC Jun Sch L14 54 F3
St Margaret of Antioch CE Prim Sch L8 67 F7
St Margaret's Anfield CE Prim Sch L6 53 C5
St Margaret's Ave WA2 61 D1
St Margaret's CE Prim Sch WA2 61 C1
St Margaret's Gr L30 27 C3
St Margaret's Rd CH47 63 A6
St Margarets CE High Sch L17 68 E1
St Margarets CE Prim Sch WA2 61 C2
St Marie's RC Prim Sch L33 30 A3
St Mark's Gate WA10 43 F5
St Mark's Gr L30 27 C4
St Mark's RC Prim Sch
Liverpool L26 83 A8
Skelmersdale WN8 24 E8
St Mark's Rd L36 55 F1
St Mark's St WA11 45 A6
St Marks Ct 2 CH43 66 B5
St Martin's Mews 1 L5 52 E4
St Martins Gr L32 40 F7
St Mary's & St Paul's CE Prim Sch L35 56 D4
St Mary's & St Thomas' CE Prim Sch WA10 43 F4
St Mary's Arc 12 WA10 44 A3
St Mary's Ave
Billinge WN5 33 C4
4 Liverpool L4 39 A2
Wallasey CH44 51 B4
St Mary's CE Prim Sch
Bebington CH62 89 A5
Bootle L20 38 B3
St Mary's CE Prim Sch, West Derby L12 54 B7
St Mary's Cl 1 L20 38 B3
St Mary's Cl Hale L24 83 E2
Liverpool L13 53 F1
St Mary's Coll Prep Sch L23 26 E4
St Mary's Ct CH49 65 A4
St Mary's Gate CH41 66 F6
St Mary's Gdns PR8 7 F7
St Mary's Gr
5 Liverpool L4 39 A2
Litherland L30 27 C2
St Mary's La L4 39 A2
St Mary's Mkt WA10 44 A3
St Mary's Pl 6 L4 39 A2
St Mary's RC Coll CH45 50 E6
St Mary's RC Inf Sch WA12 46 C4
St Mary's RC Jun Sch WA12 46 B3
St Mary's RC Prim Sch
Billinge WN5 33 D4
Crosby L23 26 D8
St Mary's Rd Crosby L22 26 F1
Huyton-w-R L36 55 F2
Liverpool L19 81 B7
Warrington WA5 74 F5
St Mary's St
Liverpool,Woolton L25 70 A2
Wallasey CH44 51 B4
St Marys Ct L25 70 A2
St Mathew's Cl L36 55 F3
St Mathew's RC Prim Sch WN8 24 D7
St Mathews Cl L4 39 D2
St Matthew's RC Prim Sch L4 53 E8
St Matthews Ave L21 38 D8
St Matthews CE Prim Sch WA9 57 D7
St Matthews Gr WA10 57 C8
St Mawes Cl WA8 72 E2
St Mawes Way WA10 43 B6
St Mawgan Ct WA2 61 F2
St Michael & All Angels RC Prim Sch CH49 65 D2
St Michael Rd L39 20 F7
St Michael's Church Rd L17 68 C2
St Michael's Cl
Liverpool L17 68 C2
Southport PR9 1 F3
Widnes WA8 84 C7
St Michael's Gr
Litherland L30 27 C3
Liverpool L6 53 B4
St Michael's in the Hamlet Com Prim Sch L17 68 B3
St Michael's RC Prim Sch
Liverpool L6 53 B4
Widnes WA8 84 C7
St Michael's Rd
Crosby L23 26 C6
Liverpool L17 68 B3
Widnes WA8 84 C7
St Michael's Road Ind Est WA8 84 C7
St Michael's Sta L17 68 B2
St Michaels Ct L36 55 E3
St Michaels Gr CH46 64 D8
St Michaels Pk L39 21 A7
St Michaels Rd WA9 58 A3
St Monica's Dr L30 27 D4
St Monica's RC Prim Sch L20 38 E5
St Nicholas CE Prim Sch L23 26 B3
St Nicholas Gr 1 WA9 58 D7
St Nicholas Pl L3 52 B1
St Nicholas RC Inf Sch L3 52 F1
St Nicholas Rd L35 56 D1
St Nicholas' Dr L30 27 D4
St Nicholas' Rd CH45 50 D5
St Oswald's Ave CH43 50 C1
St Oswald's Bidston CE Prim Sch CH43 50 C1
St Oswald's CE Prim Sch L30 27 F3
St Oswald's La L30 27 F3
St Oswald's Mews CH43 50 C1
St Oswald's RC Inf & Jun Sch L13 54 A2
St Oswald's RC Prim Sch WN4 35 B3
St Oswald's St L13 54 A2
St Oswalds Cl WA2 61 B6
St Oswalds Ct L30 27 F3
St Oswalds Rd WN4 35 A2
St Paschal Baylon Blvd L16 70 A8
St Paschal Baylon's RC Prim Sch L16 69 F8
St Patrick's Cl L33 29 E5
St Patrick's Dr L30 27 D4
St Patrick's RC Prim Sch
Liverpool L8 67 F6
Southport PR9 2 A2
St Paul of the Cross RC Prim Sch WA5 59 E6
St Paul St WA10 43 E3
St Paul's & St Timothy's RC Inf Sch L12 54 C6
St Paul's Ave 10 CH44 51 E2
St Paul's Cl CH42 66 E2
St Paul's Ct L35 56 D4
St Paul's Pas PR8 4 A6
St Paul's Pl L20 38 D2
St Paul's RC Jun Sch L12 54 C6
St Paul's RC Prim Sch CH43 65 C7
St Paul's Rd
Birkenhead CH42 66 F3
Wallasey CH44 51 E2
St Paul's Sq Liverpool L3 90 A4
Southport PR8 4 A6
St Paul's St PR8 4 A6
St Paul's Villas 1 CH42 66 F2
St Pauls Cl L33 29 D5
St Pauls Mans 4 PR8 4 A6
St Peter & St Paul RC Prim Sch
St Helens WA11 44 B7
Wallasey CH45 51 B8
St Peter's Ave L37 9 D4
St Peter's CE Prim Sch
Formby L37 10 A5
Heswall CH60 85 F8
Newton-le-W WA12 46 E4
St Peter's Cl Formby L37 9 D4
Heswall CH60 85 F7
St Peter's Ct CH42 67 A1
St Peter's Mews CH42 67 B1
St Peter's RC High Sch WN5 25 F7
St Peter's RC Prim Sch CH43 65 C4
St Peter's Rd
Birkenhead CH42 67 A1
Liverpool L9 39 C6
Southport PR8 4 A3
St Peter's Row L31 28 D6
St Peter's Way CH43 65 C4
St Peters Cl L33 29 D5
St Peters Ct L17 68 B4
St Philip (Westbrook) CE Prim Sch WA5 60 C1
St Philip's Ave L21 38 C7
St Philip's CE Prim Sch
Bootle L21 38 C8
Southport PR8 4 C5
St Raymond's RC Prim Sch L30 27 E4
St Richards Cl 2 L20 38 D1
St Richards RC Prim Sch WN8 15 D1
St Robert Bellarmine RC Prim Sch L20 38 D7
St Sebastian's RC Prim Sch L7 53 D2
St Seiriol Gr CH43 66 A6
St Silas CE Prim Sch L8 68 A5
St Stephen Rd WA5 74 F5
St Stephen's Ave WA2 61 B3
St Stephen's Ct L25 70 B4
St Stephen's Gr L30 27 D3
St Stephen's RC Prim Sch WA2 61 B2
St Stephen's Rd
Birkenhead CH42 66 B1
Hightown L38 17 F4
St Stephens Cl
Heswall CH60 86 C6
Liverpool L25 70 C5
St Stephens Ct CH42 66 B1
St Stephens Pl 4 L3 52 D3
St Teresa's RC Inf Sch PR8 4 A4
St Teresa's RC Jun & Inf Schs L11 39 F2
St Teresa's RC Prim Sch WA10 43 D4
St Teresa's Rd WA10 43 D4
St Theresa's RC Prim Sch WA9 58 C3
St Thomas Becket RC High Sch L36 56 A3
St Thomas CE Prim Sch
Ashton-in-M WN4 35 C3
Maghull L31 20 D4
St Thomas Ct WA8 72 E1
St Thomas of Canterbury RC Prim Sch WA10 43 D6
St Thomas the Martyr CE Prim Sch WN8 25 B7
St Thomas's Ct WN8 25 C7
St Thomas's Dr L30 27 D3
St Vincent de Paul RC Prim Sch L1 90 B2
St Vincent Rd
Birkenhead CH43 66 A6
Wallasey CH44 51 D5
Warrington WA5 74 F5
St Vincent St L3 90 C4
St Vincent Way L3 90 C4
St Vincent's Cl L12 54 E6
St Vincent's RC Prim Sch WA5 74 F3
St Vincent's Sch L14 54 E6
St Vincent's Way PR8 4 A4
St Werburgh's RC Prim Sch CH42 66 D5
St Werburgh's Sq 13 CH41 66 E6
St Wilfrid's RC High Sch L21 38 C7
St William of York RC Prim Sch L23 27 B5
St William Rd L23 27 B5
St William Way L23 27 B5
St Winefride's RC Inf Sch L20 38 C2
St Winefride's RC Jun Sch L20 38 C3
St Winifred Rd
Rainhill L35 57 B5
Wallasey CH45 51 B7
Saker St 17 L4 52 F7
Salacre Cl CH49 65 A4
Salacre Cres CH49 65 A4
Salacre La CH49 65 A4
Salacre Terr CH49 65 A5
Salcombe Dr
Liverpool L25 82 B7
Southport PR9 2 A5
Salem View CH43 66 B3
Salerno Dr L36 55 D3
Saleswood Ave WA10 43 A3
Salford Ct PR8 7 C5
Salford Rd PR8 7 C5
Saline Cl L14 55 A6
Salisbury Ave
Litherland L30 28 A1
West Kirby CH48 63 A2
Salisbury Ct CH42 66 E1
Salisbury Dr CH62 79 B7
Salisbury Ho 2 L20 38 B4
Salisbury Pk L16 69 D5
Salisbury Rd
1 Ashton-in-M WN4 35 A5
Bootle L20 38 B5
Haydock WA11 45 E8
Liverpool,Anfield L5 53 A6
Liverpool,Cressington Pk L19 81 A6
Liverpool,Wavertree L15 68 D8
Wallasey CH45 51 A8
Salisbury St
Birkenhead CH41 66 D5
Golborne WA3 47 A8
Liverpool L3 52 F3
3 Prescot L34 56 D6
Southport PR9 5 A6
Salisbury Terr L15 68 F8
Salkeld Ave WN4 34 F3
Sallowfields WN5 25 D5
Sally's La PR9 2 A2
Salop St L4 52 F8
Saltash Cl L26 82 E8
Saltburn Rd CH45 50 D5
Saltergate Rd 20 L8 68 A4
Salthouse Quay L3 90 A2
Saltney St L3 52 B4
Saltpit La L31 20 E1
Salvia Way L33 29 D5
Salvin Cl WN4 35 D3
Salwick Cl PR9 1 F5
Samaria Ave CH62 79 C7
Samaria Ho CH41 66 F6
Sambourn Fold PR8 7 A5
Samphire Gdns WA9 59 B7
Samuel St WA9 57 D7
Samwoods Ho WN4 35 A5
Sanbec Gdns WA8 72 D5
Sandalwood Cl
Liverpool L6 53 B5
Warrington WA2 61 D2
Sandalwood Dr CH43 65 D4
Sandalwood Gdns WA9 58 C7
Sandbeck St L8 67 F3
Sandbourne CH46 65 A8
Sandbrook Ct CH46 64 E8
Sandbrook Gdns WN5 25 D5
Sandbrook La CH46 64 F8
Sandbrook Prim Sch CH46 65 A8
Sandbrook Rd
Liverpool L25 70 A7
Orrell WN5 25 C5
Southport PR8 7 D4
Sandbrook Way PR8 7 C3
Sandcliffe Rd CH45 50 E7
Sandeman Rd L4 53 D8
Sanderling Rd Kirkby L33 30 A3
Newton-le-W WA12 46 C4

Sanderson Cl WA5 74 D6
Sandfield L36 55 D2
Sandfield Ave CH47 48 D1
Sandfield Cl
Bebington CH63 78 D6
3 Golborne WA3 47 E8
Liverpool L12 54 C5
Sandfield Cotts L39 13 D2
Sandfield Cres WA10 43 F3
Sandfield Park Sch L12 54 B5
Sandfield Pk
Heswall CH60 85 D8
Ormskirk L39 13 D2
Sandfield Pk E L12 54 C6
Sandfield Pl L20 38 B4
Sandfield Rd
Bebington CH63 78 D6
Birkenhead CH49 65 B2
Bootle L20 38 D3
Liverpool L25 70 B4
St Helens WA10 43 A5
Wallasey CH45 51 B7
Sandfield Terr 10 CH45 51 B7
Sandfield Wlk L13 54 B4
Sandford Dr L31 20 D2
Sandford Rd WN5 25 C5
Sandford St CH41 66 E7
Sandforth Cl L12 54 A6
Sandforth Ct L12 54 A5
Sandforth Rd L12 54 B6
Sandgate Cl L24 82 B4
Sandham Gr CH60 86 D7
Sandham Rd L24 83 A4
Sandhead St L7 68 D8
Sandhey Rd CH47 63 C8
Sandheys CH64 86 C1
Sandheys Ave L22 26 C1
Sandheys Cl L4 52 E7
Sandheys Dr PR9 1 F1
Sandheys Gr L22 26 C2
Sandheys Rd 13 CH45 51 B7
Sandheys Terr L22 26 C1
Sandhills L38 17 F3
Sandhills Bsns Pk L5 52 C6
Sandhills Ind Ctr L5 52 C6
Sandhills La L20 52 C7
Sandhills Sta L20 52 C7
Sandhills The CH46 49 E3
Sandhills View CH45 50 D5
Sandhurst 2 L23 26 C4
Sandhurst Cl Formby L37 9 C1
Seaforth L21 37 F7
Sandhurst Dr L10 28 E2
Sandhurst Rd
Liverpool L26 83 A6
Rainhill L35 57 B4
Sandhurst St L17 68 B3
Sandhurst Way L31 20 B5
Sandicroft Rd L12 40 F2
Sandilands Gr L38 17 F3
Sandino St L8 67 E6
Sandiway Bebington CH63 88 C6
Hoylake CH47 48 D1
Huyton-w-R L36 55 F1
Prescot L35 56 D2
Sandiway Ave WA8 72 A1
Sandiway Ct PR9 4 E8
Sandiways L31 20 E1
Sandiways Ave L30 28 A2
Sandiways Rd CH45 50 E6
Sandlea Ho CH48 63 A2
Sandlea Pk CH48 63 A2
Sandlewood Gr L33 29 F4
Sandling Dr WA3 36 A2
Sandon Cl L35 57 B4
Sandon Gr WA11 32 A6
Sandon Lodge 8 L21 38 A6
Sandon Pl WA8 73 D1
Sandon Prom CH44 51 E4
Sandon Rd Southport PR8 3 F1
Wallasey CH44 51 E4
Sandon St Crosby L22 26 D1
15 Liverpool L8 67 F8
Sandon Way L5 52 B6
Sandon Way Ind Est L5 52 B6
Sandown Ct
4 Liverpool L15 68 F8
1 Southport PR9 4 C8
Sandown La L15 68 F8
Sandown Park Rd L10 28 E3
Sandown Rd Liverpool L15 53 F1
Seaforth L21 37 F7
Sandpiper Cl
Birkenhead CH49 64 D6
Newton-le-W WA12 46 C4
Sandpiper Gr L26 70 E1
Sandpipers CH47 63 B7
Sandra Dr WA12 46 E3
Sandridge Rd
Heswall CH61 76 F5
Wallasey CH45 51 B7
Sandringham Ave
Hoylake CH47 63 C7
2 Seaforth L22 37 E8
Sandringham Cl
Bebington CH62 79 A7
Hoylake CH47 63 C7
Kirkby L33 29 E5
Sandringham Ct
Golborne WA3 47 E7
Southport PR9 4 B8
Sandringham Dr
Liverpool L17 68 B4
St Helens WA9 58 C7
Wallasey CH45 51 A8
Sandringham Mews
CH47 63 C7
Sandringham Rd
Formby L37 9 E1
Liverpool L13 53 E6
Maghull L31 28 C8
Seaforth L22 37 E8
Southport PR8 3 E3
Southport,Ainsdale PR8 7 C5
Widnes WA8 73 A4
Sandrock Cl CH45 51 B7
Sandrock Rd CH45 51 B7
Sands Rd L18 68 F4
Sandstone Cl L35 57 C1
Sandstone Dr Rainhill L35 57 A5
West Kirby CH48 63 E2
Sandstone Mews WA8 72 E4
Sandstone Rd E L13 54 A4
Sandstone Rd W L13 53 F4
Sandstone Wlk CH60 86 A7
Sandwash Cl WA11 32 B4
Sandway Cres L11 40 A2
Sandy Brow La
Golborne WA3 47 E2
Kirkby L33 41 E8
Sandy Gn L9 39 C6
Sandy Gr L13 53 F6
Sandy Ho 5 L21 37 F7
Sandy Knowe L15 69 A8
Sandy La Cronton WA8 72 D5
Golborne WA3 46 F8
Heswall CH60 77 A1
Hightown L38 18 A3
Irby CH61 76 C7
Kirkby L31 29 A6
Liverpool,Hartley's Village
L9 39 C6
Liverpool,Tuebrook L13 53 F6
Maghull,Holt Green L39 21 B6
Maghull,Lydiate L31 20 C5
Ormskirk L40 14 D7
Orrell WN5 25 D4
Seaforth L21 38 A7
Skelmersdale WN8 15 D1
St Helens WA11 43 F8
Wallasey CH45 50 E6
Warrington WA8 74 B6
Warrington,Longford WA2 61 C2
West Kirby CH48 63 B1
Sandy La Ctr WN8 15 D1
Sandy La N CH61 76 C8
Sandy Lane W WA2 61 B3
Sandy Rd Seaforth L21 37 F7
Seaforth L21 38 A7
Sandy Way CH43 66 A5
Sandymount Dr
Bebington CH63 78 F4
Wallasey CH45 51 A7
Sandyville Gr 2 L4 53 E8
Sandyville Rd L4 53 E8
Sanfield Cl L39 13 E6
Sangness Dr PR8 4 E3
Sankey For Penketh Sta
WA5 74 F6
Sankey Rd Maghull L31 28 D7
St Helens WA11 44 F5
Sankey St Golborne WA3 47 A8
Liverpool L1 90 C2
Newton-le-W WA12 46 A3
St Helens WA9 44 D2
Sankey Valley Ind Est
WA12 46 A2
Sankey Valley Pk★
WA11 44 E7
Santon Ave L13 53 E5
Santon Dr WA3 47 E8
Sanvino Ave PR8 7 D5
Sapphire Dr L33 29 E5
Sapphire St L13 53 F1
Sarah's Croft L30 27 E3
Sark Rd L13 53 F4
Sarsfield Ave 1 WA3 47 D8
Sartfield Cl L16 69 E8
Sarum Rd L25 70 B7
Satinwood Cl WN4 34 F2
Satinwood Cres L31 29 A2
Saughall Massie La CH49 64 F5
Saughall Massie Rd
Birkenhead CH46,CH49 64 D6
West Kirby CH48 63 E4
Saughall Rd CH46 64 C6
Saunby St L19 81 C4
Saunders Ave L35 56 D4
Saunders St PR9 1 C1
Saundersfoot Cl WA5 60 E2
Saunderton Cl WA11 45 C7
Savia High Sch L30 38 E8
Saville Rd Liverpool L13 54 B2
Maghull L31 20 C3
Savon Hook L37 10 B1
Savoylands Cl 6 L17 68 C2
Sawdon Ave PR8 4 E3
Sawley Ave WA3 36 D1
Sawpit La L36 55 F2
Sawyer Dr WN4 35 D3
Saxby Rd L14 55 A6
Saxenholme PR8 3 F5
Saxon Cl L6 53 B5
Saxon Ct WA10 43 E4
Saxon Lodge PR8 3 F5
Saxon Rd Crosby L23 26 D3
Hoylake CH47 63 C8
Southport PR8 3 F5
Wallasey CH46 49 F1
Saxon Terr 4 WA8 73 B1
Saxon Way L33 29 E6
Saxonia Rd L4 39 B2
Saxony Rd L7 53 A2
Sayce St WA8 73 B1
Scafell Ave WA2 61 C3
Scafell Cl CH62 88 D3
Scafell Lawn L27 71 A3
Scafell Rd WA11 44 A7
Scafell Wlk L27 71 A4
Scaffold La L38 18 D4
Scape La L23 26 E5
Scargreen Ave L11 39 F3
Scarisbrick Ave
Bootle L21 38 B7
Southport PR8 4 A7
Scarisbrick Cl L31 20 E3
Scarisbrick Cres L11 39 D3
Scarisbrick Ct PR8 4 C6
Scarisbrick Dr L11 39 D2
Scarisbrick New Rd PR8 4 D5
Scarisbrick Pl L11 39 D2
Scarisbrick Rd
Liverpool L11 39 D2
Rainford WA11 31 F7
Scarisbrick St
Ormskirk L39 13 E6
Southport PR9 4 B7
Scarsdale Rd L11 39 F1
Scarth Hill La
Ormskirk L39 14 A2
Ormskirk L40 14 B2
Scarth Pk WN8 24 C7
Sceptre Cl WA12 46 A3
Sceptre Rd L11 40 C3
Sceptre Wlk L11 40 C3
Scholar St L7 68 C7
Scholes La WA10,WA9 57 C7
Scholes Pk WA10 57 B7
Schomberg St L6 53 B3
School Ave L37 9 F3
School Brow WN5 33 E5
School La Liverpool L27 70 C7
Ormskirk L39 13 C1
Southport PR8 4 B2
Wallasey CH46 49 F1
School Dr WN5 33 E5
School Hill CH60 85 F7
School House Cotts
CH47 63 C7
School House Gn L39 13 F5
School La Aintree L10 28 E1
Bebington,Higher Bebington
CH63 78 D5
Bebington,New Ferry CH62 79 B7
Bold Heath WA8 73 E7
Bootle L21 38 A7
Formby L37 9 F3
Garswood WN4 34 C3
Haskayne L39 11 F4
Hooton CH66 88 F1
Hoylake CH47 63 B7
Hoylake,Meols CH47 48 D1
Huyton-w-R L36 56 A2
Irby CH61 76 B6
Kirkby L31 29 A5
Knowsley L34 41 B5
Litherland L21 38 B8
Liverpool L1 90 B3
Liverpool,Hunt's Cross L25 82 B8
Maghull L31 21 A1
Neston CH64 87 B2
Neston,Parkgate CH64 86 B1
Skelmersdale WN8 15 E1
St Helens L35 57 F1
Up Holland WN5,WN8 25 C7
Wallasey CH44 50 E5
Wallasey,Bidston CH43 50 C1
Westhead L40 14 E3
School Rd Hightown L38 17 F4
Warrington WA2 61 C1
School St
Ashton-in-M WN4 35 D5
Golborne WA3 47 A8
Newton-le-W WA12 46 B3
St Helens WA11 44 F6
School Terr WA3 47 A8
School Way Liverpool L24 82 B4
Widnes WA8 73 D3
Schoolfield Cl CH49 65 B2
Schoolfield Rd CH49 65 B2
Science Rd L24 82 C4
Scone Cl L11 40 C3
Score La L16 69 D8
Score The St Helens WA9 58 A7
St Helens WA9 58 C8
Scorecross WA9 58 B8
Scoresby Rd CH46 50 B3
Scorpio Cl L14 55 A5
Scorton St L6 53 C5
Scotchbarn La L34,L35 56 F6
Scoter Rd L33 29 F2
Scotia Ave CH62 79 C7
Scotia Rd L13 54 A4
Scotia Wlk 1 WA3 47 F8
Scotland Rd L3,L5 52 D4
Scott Ave Huyton-w-R L36 71 A8
Prescot L35 56 F3
Widnes WA8 84 F8
Scott Cl Liverpool L4 52 F7
Maghull L31 20 D1
Scott Dr L39 13 F7
Scott Rd WA3 36 D2
Scott St Bootle L20 38 B5
Southport PR9 5 A7
Wallasey CH45 51 B5
Scott Wlk WA12 46 C1
Scotts Ave WA9 58 A3
Scotts Pl CH41 65 F7
Scotts Quays CH44 51 F1
Scythes The
Birkenhead CH49 64 D4
Scythes The *continued*
Litherland L30 28 B4
Scythia Cl CH62 79 C7
Sea Ct CH45 50 F7
Sea Rd CH45 50 F7
Sea View Rd L20 38 B4
Seabank Ave CH44 51 C5
Seabank Cott CH47 48 E2
Seabank Ct CH48 63 A1
Seabank Rd Heswall CH60 85 E6
Southport PR9 4 B8
Wallasey CH44,CH45 51 C6
Seacombe Aquarium★
CH44 51 F2
Seacombe Prom CH44 51 E3
Seacombe Twr L5 52 E6
Seacombe View CH44 51 E2
Seacroft Cl L14 55 A6
Seacroft Cres PR9 2 B5
Seacroft Rd L14 55 A6
Seafield L37 10 A2
Seafield Ave Crosby L23 26 F4
Heswall CH60 85 E6
Seafield Dr CH45 51 A7
Seafield Rd
Bebington CH62 79 B8
6 Bootle L20 38 B4
Liverpool L9 38 F5
Southport PR8 7 C6
Seaford Pl WA2 61 A4
Seafore Cl L31 20 B4
Seaforth & Litherland Sta
L21 38 A7
Seaforth Dr CH46 64 E7
Seaforth Rd L21 38 A6
Seaforth Vale N L21 38 A6
Seaforth Vale W L21 38 A6
Seagram Cl L9 39 C8
Sealand Ave L37 9 E2
Sealand Cl L37 9 D2
Sealy Cl CH63 79 A1
Seaman Rd L15 68 E7
Seaport St L8 68 B6
Seascale Ave WA10 57 B8
Seath Ave WA9 44 E4
Seathwaite Cl L23 26 B3
Seathwaite Cres L33 29 D4
Seaton Cl L12 41 A3
Seaton Gr WA9 57 D6
Seaton Pl WN8 15 E3
Seaton Rd
Birkenhead CH42 66 C4
1 Wallasey CH45 51 A6
Seaton Way PR9 2 A5
Seaview CH47 63 B7
Seaview Ave
Bebington CH62 89 B6
Irby CH61 76 D6
Wallasey CH45 51 B5
Seaview La CH61 76 D6
Seaview Rd CH44,CH45 51 A5
Seaview Terr L22 26 C1
Seawood Gr CH46 64 D7
Second Ave
Birkenhead CH43 65 C6
Crosby L23 26 D4
Liverpool,Aintree L9 39 D7
Liverpool,Fazakerley L9 39 E6
Rainhill L35 57 B4
Sedbergh Ave L10 28 C3
Sedbergh Rd CH44 50 F5
Sedburgh Gr L36 55 C3
Sedburn Rd L32 41 A7
Seddon Cl WA10 42 F3
Seddon Pl WN8 15 E3
Seddon Rd Liverpool L19 81 C6
St Helens WA10 57 B8
Seddon St Liverpool L1 90 B2
St Helens WA10 43 F7
Seddons Ct 1 L34 56 D6
Sedgefield Rd CH46 65 A8
Sedgemoor Rd L11 39 F3
Sedgewick Cres WA5 59 E6
Sedgley Wlk L36 55 F5
Sedley St L6 53 B5
Sedum Gr L33 29 D5
Seeds La L9 39 C8
Seel Rd L36 56 A2
Seel St L1 90 B2
Seeley Ave CH41 66 A7
Sefton Ave Bootle L21 38 B7
Orrell WN5 25 D5
Widnes WA8 73 A3
Sefton Cl Kirkby L32 29 C3
Orrell WN5 25 D5
Sefton Dr Aintree L10 28 E2
Crosby L23 27 A7
Kirkby L32 29 C3
Liverpool L8 68 C5
Maghull L31 28 B8
Sefton Fold Dr WN5 33 D5
Sefton Fold Gdns WN5 33 D5
Sefton Gdns L39 21 D7
Sefton Gr L17 68 C4
Sefton Ho L9 39 B7
Sefton La L31 28 B8
Sefton Lane Ind Est L31 28 A8
Sefton Mill Ct L29 27 F7
Sefton Mill La L29 27 F7
Sefton Moss La L30 27 D2
Sefton Moss Villas L21 38 B8
Sefton Park Palm Ho★
L17 68 D4
Sefton Park Rd L8 68 B5
Sefton Rd
Ashton-in-M WN4 34 F6
Bebington CH62 79 A8
Birkenhead CH42 67 A1
Sefton Rd *continued*
Bootle L20 38 D5
Formby L37 9 E2
Litherland L21 38 B8
Liverpool L9 39 A4
Liverpool,Fazakerley L9 39 E7
Orrell WN5 25 D5
Wallasey CH45 51 B7
Sefton St Litherland L21 38 B7
Liverpool L3,L8 67 D5
Newton-le-W WA12 45 F3
Southport PR8 4 C5
Sefton View Crosby L23 27 A4
Litherland L21 38 B8
Orrell WN5 25 D5
Sefton Villas L20 38 E4
Segar's La PR8,L39 8 B4
Seiont Ho 3 L8 67 F5
Selborne L35 56 F2
Selborne Cl 1 L8 68 A7
Selborne St L8 68 A7
Selbourne Cl CH49 65 C3
Selby Cl WA10 43 D2
Selby Dr L37 10 B2
Selby Gr L36 56 B3
Selby Pl WN8 15 D2
Selby Rd L9 39 A6
Selby St CH45 51 B5
Seldon St L7 53 B2
Selina Rd L4 38 F2
Selkirk Ave
Bebington CH62 88 E4
Garswood WN4 34 D4
Selkirk Dr WA10 43 B5
Selkirk Rd L13 53 F2
Sellar St L4 52 E7
Selsdon Rd L22 26 C2
Selsey Cl L7 68 B8
Selside Lawn L27 71 A4
Selside Wlk L27 70 F4
Selston Cl CH63 79 A2
Selworthy Gn L16 69 D6
Selworthy Rd
Southport PR8 3 D3
Southport PR8 3 E3
Selwyn Cl
Newton-le-W WA12 46 B5
Widnes WA8 73 E3
Selwyn St L4 38 E1
Senate Bsns Pk L30 38 F8
Senator Rd WA9 57 D7
Sennen Rd L32 40 F8
Sentinel Way L30 39 A8
Sephton Dr L39 13 F7
September Rd L6 53 D6
Serenade Rd L33 29 F6
Sergrim Rd L36 55 D3
Serin Cl WA12 46 C3
Serpentine N The L23 26 A5
Serpentine Rd CH44 51 C4
Serpentine S The L23 26 B4
Serpentine The
Crosby L23 26 A4
Liverpool L19 81 A8
Ormskirk L39 21 D8
Servia Rd L21 38 B7
Servite Cl L22 26 C2
Servite Ct L25 70 C1
Servite Ho L17 68 B4
Sessions Rd L4 52 E7
Seth Powell Way L36 55 D5
Settrington Rd L11 39 F1
Seven Acre Rd L23 27 B5
Seven Acres La CH61 77 A5
Sevenoaks Ave PR8 7 B5
Sevenoaks Cl L5 52 E5
Seventh Ave L9 39 D7
Severn Cl Billinge WN5 33 D3
St Helens WA9 58 C6
Warrington WA2 61 E2
Widnes WA8 73 F3
Severn Rd
Ashton-in-M WN4 35 E5
Kirkby L33 29 F6
Rainhill L35 57 B3
Severn St
Birkenhead CH41 51 A1
Liverpool L5 52 F6
Severs St L6 53 B4
Sewell St L34 56 D6
Sexton Ave WA9 45 B2
Sexton Way L14 54 E2
Seymour Ct
Birkenhead CH42 66 E4
Liverpool L14 54 D1
Seymour Dr L31 20 E3
Seymour Pl W 14 CH45 51 B8
Seymour Rd Bootle L21 38 B7
Liverpool L14 54 D2
Seymour St
Birkenhead CH42 66 E4
Bootle L20 38 B2
Liverpool L3 90 C4
Wallasey CH45 51 B8
Seymour Terr L3 90 C4
Shacklady Rd L33 30 A4
Shackleton Rd CH46 50 B4
Shadwell Cl L5 52 B5
Shadwell St L5 52 B5
Shaftesbury Ave
Southport PR8 8 A8
Warrington WA5 74 E2
Shaftesbury Gr PR8 4 A1
Shaftesbury Rd
Crosby L23 26 D4
Southport PR8 4 A1
Shaftesbury St L8 67 E6
Shaftesbury Terr L13 54 A3

Southport & Formby District General Hospl PR8 .4 E4
Southport Botanic Gdns* PR9 .2 B2
Southport Coll PR9 .4 C7
Southport General Infmy PR8 .4 D5
Southport Holiday Village PR8 .6 F6
Southport New Rd PR9 .2 F5
Southport Old Rd L37 .10 B7
Southport Pleasureland* PR8 .3 F7
Southport Rd Bootle L20 .38 E4
Crosby L23 .27 A7
Formby L37 .10 A5
Haskayne L39 .12 A6
Maghull L31,L39 .20 B5
Ormskirk L39,L40 .13 D8
Southport PR8 .5 B2
Southport St WA9 .45 A3
Southport Sta PR8 .4 B4
Southport Zoo* PR8 .3 F7
Southridge Rd CH61 .77 A5
Southward Rd WA11 .46 A7
Southwark Gr L30 .27 F1
Southway
Skelmersdale WN8 .16 B1
Widnes WA8 .84 D8
Southwell Cl WA3 .47 C8
Southwell Pl 4 L8 .67 E5
Southwell St L8 .67 E5
Southwick Rd CH42 .66 E3
Southwold Cres WA5 .74 E5
Southwood Cl 9 L32 .41 A8
Southwood Rd L17 .68 B3
Southworth La WA2,WA3 .61 E7
Southworth Rd WA12 .46 F4
Sovereign Hey 11 L11 .40 C3
Sovereign Rd L11 .40 C3
Sovereign Way
Liverpool L11 .40 C3
Wallasey CH41 .51 D1
Spa Fold L40 .15 A4
Spa La L40,WN8 .15 C4
Sparks La CH61 .77 B6
Sparling St L1 .90 B1
Sparrow Hall Cl L9 .39 F4
Sparrow Hall Rd L9 .39 F4
Sparrowhawk Cl L26 .70 E1
Spawell Cl WA3 .47 E8
Speakman Ave WA12 .46 C5
Speakman Rd WA10 .43 D5
Speakman St WA7 .84 F3
Speedwell Cl
11 Golborne WA3 .47 E8
Heswall CH60 .86 C8
Speedwell Dr CH60 .86 C8
Speedwell Rd CH41 .65 F7
Speke Bvd Liverpool L24 .82 C4
Liverpool L24,WA8 .82 D4
Speke Church Rd L24 .82 B3
Speke Com Sch L24 .82 E3
Speke Hall* L24 .81 F2
Speke Hall Ave L24 .82 B3
Speke Hall Rd L25 .82 B6
Speke Rd
Liverpool,Garston L19 .81 D5
Liverpool,Speke L19,L24 .81 E5
Liverpool,Walton L25 .82 C8
Widnes WA8 .84 C6
Speke Town La L24 .82 C4
Spekeland Rd L7 .68 C8
Spellow La L4 .52 F8
Spence Ave L20 .38 D5
Spencer Ave CH46 .50 A1
Spencer Cl L36 .70 F8
Spencer Gdns WA9 .58 D8
Spencer Pl L20 .38 D7
Spencer St L6 .52 F4
Spencer's La
Aintree L10,L31 .28 F3
Orrell WN5 .25 D7
Southport L39 .8 B3
Spencers La WN8 .24 B7
Spenser Ave CH42 .66 F1
Spenser Cl WA8 .72 F1
Spenser Rd CH64 .86 E1
Spenser St L20 .38 B4
Spice St L9 .39 B5
Spicer Gr L32 .29 E2
Spindle Cl 3 L6 .52 F4
Spindle Hillock WN4 .34 D4
Spindrift Ct CH48 .63 A1
Spindus Rd L24 .82 B3
Spinnakers The L19 .80 F7
Spinney Ave WA8 .72 A1
Spinney Cl Kirkby L33 .41 C8
Ormskirk L39 .13 D3
St Helens WA9 .58 C4
Spinney Cres L23 .26 B6
Spinney Gn WA10 .43 A2
Spinney Rd L33 .41 D8
Spinney The
Bebington CH63 .79 B3
Formby L37 .10 A5
Heswall CH60 .86 C5
Huyton-w-R L28 .55 A7
Neston CH64 .86 F2
Prescot L34 .56 C7
West Kirby CH48 .63 E2
Spinney View L33 .41 D8
Spinney Way L36 .55 C3
Spinney Way The WA11 .31 F6
Spion Kop WN4 .35 A3
Spires Gdns WA2 .61 A7
Spires The WA10 .43 A4
Spital Heyes CH63 .79 B3
Spital Rd CH62,CH63 .79 C3
Spital Sta CH63 .79 B3
Spitfire Rd L24 .81 F6
Spofforth Rd L15,L7 .68 D8
Spooner Ave L21 .38 C8
Sprainger St L3 .52 B4
Sprakeling Pl L20 .38 E7
Spray St WA10 .43 E4
Spreyton Cl L12 .40 C2
Sprig Cl L9 .39 D8
Spring Bank Rd 1 L4 .53 B5
Spring Cl Kirkby L33 .30 A5
Southport PR8 .4 A5
Spring Field WA11 .23 E2
Spring Gdns L31 .28 E8
Spring Gr L12 .54 C6
Spring Rd WN5 .25 F8
Spring St CH41 .66 F3
Spring Vale CH45 .50 E7
Springbourne Rd L17 .68 B2
Springbrook Cl WA10 .43 A4
Springcroft CH64 .86 C1
Springdale Cl L12 .54 D7
Springfield L3 .52 E3
Springfield Ave
Golborne WA3 .46 F8
Litherland L21 .38 C8
West Kirby CH48 .63 F2
Springfield Cl
Birkenhead CH49 .65 C2
Formby L37 .9 C2
St Helens WA10 .57 C8
Springfield Cotts 2 L23 .26 D5
Springfield La WA10 .43 A4
Springfield Pk WA11 .45 C7
Springfield Rd
Maghull L39 .20 F6
St Helens WA10 .57 C8
Widnes WA8 .84 A8
Springfield Sch L32 .40 E7
Springfield Sq L4 .52 F8
Springfield Way L12 .54 E8
Springhill Ave CH62 .88 D6
Springmeadow Rd L25 .70 A5
Springmount WA3 .47 E7
Springpool WA9 .58 D7
Springs Cl L20 .38 D4
Springside Cl L14 .55 C6
Springvale WA11 .32 A8
Springville Rd L9 .39 C7
Springwell Ct L20 .38 D6
Springwell Rd Bootle L20 .38 D6
Bootle L20 .38 D7
Springwood Ave L19,L25 .81 E7
Springwood Gr L32 .40 F7
Springwood Heath Prim Sch L19 .81 D8
Springwood Way CH62 .79 A8
Spruce Cl
4 Birkenhead CH42 .66 D4
Golborne WA3 .47 F7
Spruce Gr L28 .55 B7
Spruce Way L37 .9 C3
Sprucewood Cl 3 L6 .53 B5
Spur Cl L11 .40 C3
Spur The L23 .26 D3
Spurgeon Cl L5 .52 F5
Spurling Rd WA5 .59 F6
Spurrier's La L31 .29 D8
Spurstow Cl CH43 .65 F3
Spymers Croft L37 .10 A6
Squibb Dr CH46 .50 A2
Squires Ave 3 WA8 .73 A1
Squires Cl WA11 .45 B6
Squires St L7 .68 A8
Squirrel Gn L37 .9 C5
Stable Cl CH49 .64 D4
Stable Yd L12 .40 D1
Stables Bsns Ctr The L13 53 E7
Stables Ct WA9 .44 C2
Stackfield The CH48 .63 F3
Stadium Mews L20 .38 E4
Stadium Rd CH62 .79 E2
Stadt Moers Ctry Pk* L35 .56 C2
Stafford Cl L36 .56 A4
Stafford Moreton Way L31 .20 D1
Stafford Rd Southport PR8 .4 A1
St Helens WA10 .43 D1
Stafford St Liverpool L3 .90 C4
Skelmersdale WN8 .15 D1
Staffordshire Cl L5 .52 E6
Stag Rd L24 .81 E6
Stainburn Ave L11 .39 F3
Stainer Cl Liverpool L14 .54 F5
Newton-le-W WA12 .46 B5
Stainton Cl Liverpool L26 .82 E8
St Helens WA11 .44 B8
Stairhaven Rd L19 .69 B1
Stakes The CH46 .49 E3
Stalbridge Ave L18 .68 F5
Staley Ave L23 .26 F3
Staley St L20 .38 D6
Stalisfield Ave L11 .40 A1
Stalisfield Gr L11 .40 A2
Stalisfield Pl L11 .40 A2
Stalmine Rd L9 .39 A4
Stamford Rd
Skelmersdale WN8 .15 D2
Southport PR8 .4 B2
Stamford St L7 .53 C2
Stamfordham Dr L19 .81 D7
Stamfordham Gr L19 .81 D7
Stamfordham Pl L19 .81 D7
Stanbury Ave CH63 .79 A6
Stand Farm Rd L12 .40 F3
Stand Park Ave L30 .27 F2
Stand Park Cl L30 .27 F2
Stand Park Rd L16 .69 D6
Stand Parkway L30 .27 E3
Standale Rd L15 .68 F8
Standard Rd L11 .40 C4
Standen Cl WA10 .43 E4
Standhouse La L39 .13 C2
Standish Ave WN5 .33 E5
Standish Ct WA8 .84 D8
Standish Dr WA11 .32 A7
Standish St Liverpool L3 .90 B4
St Helens WA10,WA9 .44 B4
Standring Garden WA10 .57 B8
Stanfield (Merchant Taylors' Prep Sch for Girls) L23 .26 E3
Stanfield Ave L5 .52 F5
Stanfield Dr CH63 .78 F3
Stanford Ave 2 CH45 .51 B7
Stanford Cres L25 .82 D8
Stangate L31 .20 B2
Stanhope Dr
Bebington CH62 .79 D1
Huyton-w-R L36 .55 C3
Stanhope St Liverpool L8 .67 E6
St Helens WA10 .43 F5
Stanier Way L7 .53 C1
Staniforth Pl L16 .54 D1
Stanlawe Rd L37 .9 E6
Stanley Ave
Bebington CH63 .78 C8
Rainford WA11 .31 F7
Southport PR8 .3 F3
Wallasey CH45 .50 D6
Warrington WA5 .74 D7
Stanley Bank Rd WA11 .45 A7
Stanley Bglws L34 .41 C3
Stanley Cl Liverpool L4 .52 D7
Wallasey CH44 .51 E2
Widnes WA8 .73 C2
Stanley Cres L34 .56 C6
Stanley Ct CH42 .66 F3
Stanley Gdns L9 .38 F5
Stanley High Sch PR9 .1 F4
Stanley Ho L20 .38 B4
Stanley La CH62 .88 F4
Stanley Park Ave N L4 .39 B2
Stanley Park Ave S L4 .53 B8
Stanley Pk L21 .27 B1
Stanley Rd
Bebington CH62 .79 A8
Bootle L20 .38 C3
Formby L37 .9 E6
Hoylake CH47 .62 F6
Huyton-w-R L36 .55 E3
Liverpool L5 .52 D5
Maghull L31 .28 C6
Seaforth L22 .37 E8
Up Holland WN8 .25 B7
Wallasey CH41 .50 F1
Stanley Sch CH61 .77 A6
Stanley St Liverpool L1,L2 .90 A3
Liverpool,Fairfield L7 .53 E3
Liverpool,Garston L19 .81 C4
Newton-le-W WA12 .46 A3
Ormskirk L39 .13 F5
Southport PR9 .4 B8
Wallasey CH44 .51 E2
Stanley Terr Liverpool L18 .69 A3
7 Wallasey CH45 .51 B7
Stanley Villas 6 WA7 .84 F1
Stanley Way WN8 .15 E3
Stanlowe View L19 .80 F6
Stanmore Pk CH49 .64 B3
Stanmore Rd L15 .69 B6
Stannanought Rd WN8 .16 E2
Stanner Cl WA5 .60 D2
Stanney Cl CH62 .88 E3
Stannyfield Cl L23 .27 B6
Stannyfield Dr L23 .27 B6
Stansfield Ave L31 .20 F1
Stanstead Ave 1 WA5 .74 F3
Stanton Ave L21 .27 A1
Stanton Cl Haydock WA11 .45 C6
Litherland L30 .27 D5
Stanton Cres L32 .29 C2
Stanton Rd
Bebington CH63 .78 F3
6 Liverpool L18 .68 F5
Stanton Rd Prim Sch CH63 .79 A3
Stanwood Cl WA10 .42 F3
Stanwood Gdns L35 .56 E3
Stapehill Cl L13 .54 B2
Stapeley Gdns L26 .83 A6
Staplands Rd L14 .54 D2
Stapleford Rd L25 .70 C6
Staplehurst Cl L12 .40 E3
Stapleton Ave
Birkenhead CH49 .64 D4
Liverpool L24 .82 D3
Rainhill L35 .57 C4
Stapleton Cl Liverpool L25 70 B7
Rainhill L35 .57 C4
Stapleton Rd Formby L37 .9 D1
Rainhill L35 .57 C5
Stapleton Way WA8 .84 B5
Stapley Cl WA7 .84 F1
Star Inn Cotts WA11 .32 A5
Star St L8 .67 E6
Starling Gr L12 .40 F1
Startham Ave WN5 .33 D3
Starworth Dr CH62 .79 C7
Statham Ave WA2 .61 C2
Statham Rd
Birkenhead CH43 .65 C8
Statham Rd *continued*
Skelmersdale WN8 .15 E3
Statham Way L39 .13 E4
Station App Hoylake CH47 63 E8
Ormskirk L39 .13 F5
Wallasey CH46 .49 E2
Station Ave WN5 .25 D5
Station Mews
Garswood WN4 .34 D3
Kirkby L32 .29 C3
Station Rd Banks PR9 .2 F5
Birkenhead CH41 .50 F1
Garswood WN4 .34 C3
Haskayne L39 .11 E7
Haydock WA11 .45 C6
Heswall CH60 .85 F6
Heswall,Barston CH61 .77 E5
Hoylake CH47 .63 B6
Huyton-w-R L36 .55 C2
Kirkby L31 .29 B3
Liverpool L25 .70 B5
Maghull L31 .28 E8
Maghull,Lydiate L31 .20 A6
Ormskirk L39 .13 F6
Prescot L34 .56 D5
Rainhill L35 .57 C3
Runcorn WA7 .84 F2
Southport PR8 .7 C5
St Helens WA9 .58 E7
Thurstaston CH61 .75 F4
Wallasey CH44 .51 A4
Warrington WA5 .74 F6
Warrington,Penketh WA5 .74 E3
Station St L35 .57 C3
Statton Rd L13 .54 B1
Staveley Rd Liverpool L19 .81 B8
Skelmersdale WN8 .15 E3
Southport PR8 .7 D4
Stavert Cl L11 .40 B3
Staverton Pk L32 .29 C1
Stavordale Rd CH46 .65 A8
Steble St L8 .67 F5
Steel Ave CH45 .51 C6
Steel Ct L5 .52 C6
Steeple The CH48 .75 D6
Steeple View L33 .29 E5
Steeplechase Cl L9 .39 C8
Steers Croft L28 .55 A8
Stein Ave WA3 .47 E8
Steinberg Ct L3 .52 C4
Steley Way L34 .56 D5
Stella Prec L21 .38 A6
Stephen Way L35 .57 B5
Stephens La L2 .90 A4
Stephenson Ct 11 L7 .53 C1
Stephenson Ho L7 .68 A8
Stephenson Rd
4 Liverpool L13 .54 A2
Newton-le-W WA12 .46 D2
Stephenson St WN2 .36 B8
Stephenson Way
Formby L37 .10 C3
Liverpool L13,L15 .53 E1
Stepney Gr 1 L4 .39 A1
Sterling Way L5 .52 D6
Sterrix Ave L30 .27 C2
Sterrix Gn L21 .27 C2
Sterrix La L21,L30 .27 C2
Steve Biko Cl 2 L8 .68 B7
Stevenage Cl WA9 .57 F7
Stevens Rd CH60 .86 C7
Stevens St WA9 .57 D8
Stevenson Cres WA10 .43 D4
Stevenson Dr CH63 .78 F3
Stevenson St L15 .68 F8
Steward Ct L35 .56 F5
Steward's Ave WA8 .84 F8
Stewart Ave L20 .38 E4
Stewart Cl CH61 .76 F3
Stewerton Cl WA3 .35 F2
Stile Hey L23 .27 B5
Stiles Rd L33 .29 F6
Stiles The L39 .13 E5
Stillington Rd L8 .68 A4
Stirling Ave L23 .26 E3
Stirling Cres WA9 .58 C6
Stirling Ct PR9 .2 A2
Stirling Dr WN4 .34 D4
Stirling La L25 .82 D8
Stirling Rd L24 .82 B3
Stirling St CH44 .51 B2
Stockbridge La L36 .55 C5
Stockbridge Pl 6 L5 .53 A5
Stockbridge St L5 .53 A5
Stockdale Cl 2 L3 .52 C3
Stockdale Dr WA5 .74 E7
Stockley Cres L39 .22 E6
Stockmoor Rd L11 .39 F3
Stockpit Rd L33 .30 D2
Stocks Ave WA9 .44 E3
Stocks La WA5 .74 D5
Stockswell Rd WA8 .71 F4
Stockton Cres L33 .29 E6
Stockton Gr WA9 .57 D6
Stockton Wood Rd L24 .82 C3
Stockville Rd L18 .69 E4
Stockwell Farm Ct WA8 .72 E4
Stoddart Rd 2 L4 .39 A2
Stoke Cl CH62 .88 E3
Stoke St CH41 .66 C8
Stoker Way L9 .39 A5
Stokesay CH43 .65 D6
Stokesley Ave L32 .29 C2
Stone Cross La N WA3 .47 C7
Stone Cross La S WA3 .47 C6
Stone Cross Pk WA3 .47 B7
Stone Hall La WN8 .16 F4
Stone Hay L35 .56 D1
Stone Pit Cl WA3 .36 F1
Stone Pit La WA3 .47 F2
Stone Sq L20 .38 E6
Stone St Liverpool L3 .52 B4
6 Prescot L34 .56 D6
Stonebarn Dr L31 .20 C3
Stonebridge La L10,L11 .40 B6
Stoneby Dr CH45 .51 A7
Stonechat Cl
10 Golborne WA3 .47 E8
Liverpool L27 .70 E4
Stonecrop L18 .69 E5
Stonecross Cl L35 .57 C1
Stonecross Dr L35 .57 D1
Stonedale Cres L11 .40 B4
Stonefield Rd L14 .55 A4
Stonegate Dr L8 .67 F4
Stonehaven Cl L16 .69 F8
Stonehey Dr CH48 .75 C8
Stonehey Rd L32 .40 E8
Stonehey Wlk L32 .40 E8
Stonehill Ave
Bebington CH63 .79 A6
4 Liverpool L4 .53 B6
Stonehill St L4 .53 B6
Stonehouse Mews L18 .69 D3
Stonehouse Rd CH44 .50 E5
Stoneleigh Cl PR8 .7 C4
Stoneleigh Gr CH42 .78 F8
Stonemasons Ct L25 .70 A3
Stoneridge Ct CH43 .65 C8
Stoneville Rd L13 .54 A4
Stoneway Ct CH60 .85 F8
Stoney Hey Rd CH45 .51 A7
Stoney La L35 .57 A3
Stoney La Ind Est L35 .57 A4
Stoney View L35 .57 B3
Stoneycroft L13 .54 B4
Stoneycroft Cl L13 .54 A5
Stoneycroft Cres L13 .54 A5
Stoneyhurst Ave L10 .28 C3
Stonham Cl CH49 .64 E5
Stonyfield L30 .27 E5
Stonyhurst Cl WA11 .44 B7
Stonyhurst Rd L25 .70 B1
Stopford St 11 L8 .67 F4
Stopgate La Kirkby L33 .30 C7
Liverpool L11,L9 .39 D3
Store St L20 .38 D1
Storeton Cl CH43 .66 B3
Storeton La CH61 .77 C4
Storeton Rd CH42,CH43 .66 B2
Stormont Rd L19 .81 B6
Storrington Ave L11 .40 B3
Storrington Heys L11 .40 B3
Storrsdale Rd L18 .69 B3
Stour Ave L35 .57 C3
Stourcliffe Rd CH44 .51 A4
Stourport Cl 1 CH49 .64 C4
Stourton Rd Kirkby L32 .40 F8
Southport PR8 .7 C4
Stourton St CH44 .51 C2
Stourvale Rd L26 .82 F7
Stowe Ave L10 .28 E2
Stowe Cl L25 .82 B7
Stowell St L7 .67 F8
Stowford Cl L12 .40 C2
Strada Way L3 .52 F3
Strafford Dr L20 .38 E4
Straight Up La PR9 .5 D8
Strand Ave WN4 .35 B4
Strand Ho 7 L20 .38 C3
Strand Rd Bootle L20 .38 B3
Bootle L20 .38 C4
Hoylake CH47 .63 B7
Strand Sh Ctr L20 .38 C3
Strand St L1,L3 .90 A3
Strand The
Ashton-in-M WN4 .35 B4
Liverpool L2,L3 .90 A3
Strand View L20 .38 A3
Strange Rd WN4 .34 D3
Stratford Cl PR8 .7 A6
Stratford Rd L19 .80 F8
Strathallan Cl CH60 .76 E2
Strathcona Rd
Liverpool L15 .68 E8
Wallasey CH45 .51 C6
Strathcona St L15 .68 E7
Strathearn Rd CH60 .85 F7
Strathlorne Cl 7 CH42 .66 F3
Strathmore Ave WN4 .35 A5
Strathmore Dr L23 .26 E3
Strathmore Gr WA9 .58 C6
Strathmore Rd L6 .53 C4
Stratton Cl Liverpool L18 .69 E3
Wallasey CH44 .51 C5
Stratton Pk WA8 .72 F5
Stratton Rd L32 .29 C1
Stratton Wlk 4 L32 .29 C1
Strauss Cl L8 .68 B6
Strawberry Rd L11 .39 E2
Streatham Ave L18 .68 F5
Streatham House Sch L23 .26 D4
Street Hey La CH64 .88 B1
Stretford Cl L33 .29 E5
Stretton Ave Billinge WN5 .33 E5
Golborne WA3 .47 E7
St Helens WA9 .44 F3
Wallasey CH44 .51 A4
Stretton Cl
Bebington CH62 .88 E3
Birkenhead CH43 .65 E3
Liverpool L12 .41 A3
Stretton Dr PR9 .4 F8
Stretton Way L36 .71 C8
Strickland St WA10,WA9 .44 B4

Wharf St CH62 .79 C5
Wharfdale Cl 1 WA5 .74 F7
Wharfedale Ave CH42 .66 B2
Wharfedale Dr
Bebington CH62 .88 F5
Rainhill L35 .57 D3
Wharfedale Rd CH45 .50 F6
Wharfedale St L19 .81 E5
Wharmby Rd WA11 .45 E6
Wharncliffe Rd L13 .54 A3
Wharton Cl CH49 .64 D6
Wharton St WA9 .44 B1
Wheat Hill Rd L27,L36 .70 E8
Wheatacre WN8 .23 E8
Wheatcroft Rd L18 .69 D2
Wheatear Cl L27 .70 E4
Wheatfield Cl
Birkenhead CH46 .64 F7
Litherland L30 .28 B3
Wheatfield Rd WA8 .72 C5
Wheatfield View L21 .27 B2
Wheathills Ind Est L27 .70 E6
Wheatland Bsns Pk
CH44 .51 D2
Wheatland Cl WA9 .58 C4
Wheatland La CH44 .51 D2
Wheatland Rd CH60 .86 C7
Wheatlands Cl L27 .70 D7
Wheatley Ave Bootle L20 .38 E5
Newton-le-W WA12 .46 C5
Wheatsheaf Ave WA9 .58 D6
Wheatsheaf Wlk 4 L39 .13 E5
Wheeler Dr L31 .29 B4
Whelan Gdns WA9 .57 E6
Whernside WA8 .72 C3
Whetstone Ct 4 CH41 .66 D5
Whetstone La CH41,CH42 66 D5
Whickham Cl WA8 .72 F3
Whimbrel Ave WA12 .46 C3
Whimbrel Pk L26 .70 E1
Whinberry Dr L32 .29 D1
Whinbury Ct 15 WA9 .58 C4
Whinchat Ave WA12 .46 C4
Whinchat Cl WA3 .47 E7
Whincraig L28 .55 C7
Whinfell Rd L15 .54 C5
Whinfield Rd Crosby L23 .27 B6
Liverpool L9 .38 F6
Whinhowe Rd L11 .40 B2
Whinmoor Cl CH43 .65 D6
Whinmoor Rd
Liverpool L10 .40 A7
Liverpool,Sandfield Pk L12 .54 C5
Whinney Gr E L31 .28 C6
Whinney Gr W L31 .28 C6
Whiston Hospl L35 .56 F4
Whiston La L36 .56 B4
Whiston Sta L35 .56 E3
Whiston Willis Com Prim Sch
L35 .56 E3
Whitburn WN8 .15 D1
Whitburn Cl WN4 .34 D4
Whitburn Rd L33 .30 A4
Whitby Ave Southport PR9 .2 D6
Wallasey CH45 .50 E5
Warrington WA2 .61 D2
Whitby St L6 .53 D6
Whitcroft Rd L6 .53 D3
White House Cl WA11 .45 B6
White Lodge Ave L36 .55 D3
White Lodge Cl CH62 .88 D5
White Lodge Dr WN4 .35 D4
White Meadow Dr L23 .27 A6
White Moss Rd WN8 .23 C7
White Moss Rd S WN8 .23 D7
White Oak Lo L19 .80 F7
White Rock St L6 .53 B4
White St L1 .90 B2
White Thorn Sch L11 .39 F3
Whitebeam Cl L33 .29 F6
Whitebeam Dr L12 .40 D3
Whitebeam Gdns WA9 .57 C6
Whitebeam Wlk CH49 .64 B2
Whitechapel L1 .90 B3
Whitecroft Ave WA3 .36 E1
Whiteside Cl CH49 .65 A4
Whitefield Ave
Liverpool L4 .52 E8
Newton-le-W WA12 .46 E2
Whitefield Cl
Birkenhead CH49 .65 B3
Golborne WA3 .47 A8
Hightown L38 .17 F2
Whitefield Dr L32 .29 C1
Whitefield La L35 .71 A6
Whitefield Prim Sch L6 .53 A4
Whitefield Rd Liverpool L6 53 B5
Liverpool,Hartley's Village
L9 .39 A5
St Helens WA10 .43 D5
Whitefield Way 2 L6 .53 A4
Whitefriars WA10 .43 A4
Whitegate Cl L34 .41 D4
Whitegates Cl CH64 .87 E1
Whitegates Cres CH64 .87 E1
Whitehall Cl L4 .38 E1
Whitehart Cl L4 .39 B1
Whitehaven Cl PR8 .7 B3
Whiteheath Way CH46 .49 F3
Whitehedge Rd L19 .81 B7
Whitehey WN8 .23 E8
Whitehey Rd WN8 .23 E8
Whitehouse Ave L37 .10 A3
Whitehouse La
Formby L37 .10 A3
Heswall CH60,CH63 .77 D1
Whitehouse Rd L13 .54 B2
Whitelands Mdw CH49 .64 E5
Whiteledge Rd WN8 .24 B6
Whiteleys La L40 .14 D2
Whitely Gr L33 .30 A6
Whiterails Dr L39 .13 D6
Whiterails Mews L39 .13 D6
Whiteside Ave WA11 .44 E5
Whiteside Cl L5 .52 D5
Whiteside Rd WA11 .45 B6
Whitestock WN8 .23 E8
Whitestone Cl L34 .41 C2
Whitethorn Ave WA5 .74 F5
Whitethorn Dr L28 .55 B8
Whitewell Dr CH49 .64 F7
Whitewood Cl WN4 .35 A6
Whitewood Pk L9 .39 D6
Whitfield Ct 1 CH42 .66 D4
Whitfield Gr WA11 .45 A6
Whitfield La CH60 .77 A1
Whitfield St CH42 .66 D4
Whitford Rd CH42 .66 D4
Whitham Ave L23 .26 F3
Whithhaven Rd L5 .52 F6
Whithorn St L7 .68 D8
Whitland Rd L6 .53 D3
Whitledge Gn WN4 .35 A5
Whitledge Rd WN4 .35 A5
Whitley Cl WA7 .84 F1
Whitley Cres WN2 .36 B7
Whitley Dr 1 CH44,CH45 .51 C5
Whitley St L3 .52 B4
Whitlow Ave WA3 .35 F1
Whitman St L15 .68 E7
Whitmoor Cl L35 .57 E1
Whitney Pl L25 .70 C2
Whitney Rd L25 .70 C2
Whitstable Pk WA8 .72 E4
Whitstone Cl L18 .69 E2
Whitstone Dr WN8 .24 D7
Whittaker Ave WA2 .61 D2
Whittaker Cl L13 .53 F1
Whittaker St WA9 .44 D1
Whittier St L8 .68 C7
Whittle Ave
Haydock WA11 .45 A5
Warrington WA5 .60 A1
Whittle Cl L5 .52 E6
Whittle Dr L39 .13 E7
Whittle Hall La WA5 .74 F6
Whittle St Liverpool L5 .52 E6
St Helens WA10 .43 D1
Whittlewood Ct L33 .29 F4
Whitwell Cl WA5 .74 D7
Wicket Cl L11 .40 D5
Wickham Cl CH44 .51 E2
Wicks Cres L37 .9 C4
Wicks Gdns L37 .9 D3
Wicks Gn L37 .9 C3
Wicks Green Cl L37 .9 C3
Wicks La L37 .9 D3
Widdale Ave L35 .57 D3
Widdale Cl WA5 .74 F7
Widgeons Covert CH63 .86 F5
Widmore Rd L25 .70 C4
Widnes & Runcom Sixth
Form Coll WA8 .72 E5
Widnes Rd
Warrington WA5 .74 C3
Widnes WA5,WA8 .73 F2
Widnes Sta WA8 .73 A3
Wiend The
Bebington CH63 .79 A5
Birkenhead CH42 .66 D1
Wigan Rd
Ashton-in-M WN4 .35 A5
Billinge WN5 .33 F7
Golborne WA3 .36 B3
Ormskirk L39 .14 A5
Skelmersdale WN8 .23 F8
Westhead L40 .14 E4
Wight Moss Way PR8 .4 D3
Wightman Ave WA12 .46 C5
Wightman St L6 .53 B3
Wignall Cl L32 .40 E7
Wignalls Mdw L38 .17 F3
Wigston Cl PR8 .7 B4
Wilberforce Rd L4 .39 B2
Wilbraham Pl 4 L5 .52 D5
Wilbraham St Liverpool L5 52 D5
St Helens WA9 .58 E3
Wilbur St WA9 .58 E7
Wilburn St L4 .38 F1
Wilcock Cl L5 .52 D5
Wilcock Rd WA11 .46 B8
Wilcote Cl WA8 .73 C4
Wilcove WN8 .15 F1
Wild Arum Cl 8 WA3 .47 E8
Wild Pl L20 .38 E7
Wildbrook Dr CH41 .50 D1
Wildcherry Gdns L35 .57 C7
Wilde St L3 .90 C4
Wilfer Cl 4 L7 .68 C8
Wilfred Owen Dr CH41 .65 E7
Wilkes Ave CH46 .50 B3
Wilkie St L15 .68 E7
Wilkin St L4 .52 E7
Wilkinson St 18 CH41 .66 C5
Willan St CH43 .66 B4
Willard Ave WN5 .25 D3
Willard St L20 .38 D6
Willaston Dr L26 .83 A6
Willaston Rd Liverpool L4 .39 B1
Thornton Hough CH63,CH64 87 D4
Wallasey CH46 .49 D1
Willedstan Ave L23 .26 E3
William Beamont Com High
Sch WA2 .61 B1
William Brown St L3 .90 B4
William Ct CH64 .86 F2
William Gladstone CE Sch
The L21 .38 A7
William Harvey Cl L30 .27 F3
William Henry St
Bootle L20 .38 B2
Liverpool L3,L6 .52 E3
William Jessop Way L3 .52 B2
William Morris Ave L20 .38 E5
William Moult St L5 .52 D5
William Penn Cl WA5 .74 E5
William Rd WA11 .44 F6
William Roberts Ave L32 29 C2
William St
Birkenhead CH41 .66 E6
2 St Helens WA10 .44 A4
Wallasey CH44 .51 E2
Widnes WA8 .73 C1
William Wall Rd L21 .27 B2
Williams Ave Bootle L20 .38 E5
Newton-le-W WA12 .46 C5
Williams St L34 .56 D6
Williamson Art Gal & Mus★
CH43 .66 B5
Williamson Ct L25 .70 C1
Williamson Sq 13 L1 .90 B3
Williamson St Liverpool L1 90 B3
St Helens WA9 .44 C4
Williamson Student Village
L7 .53 A1
Williamson Tunnels Heritage
Ctr★ L7 .53 A1
Willingdon Rd L16 .54 E1
Willington Ave CH62 .88 E3
Willink Rd WA11 .44 C7
Willis Cl L35 .56 D2
Willis La L35 .56 D2
Williton Rd L16 .69 E5
Willmer Rd
Birkenhead CH42 .66 D5
Liverpool L4 .53 B7
Willoughby Cl WA5 .60 C1
Willoughby Dr WA10 .57 B8
Willoughby Rd Crosby L22 26 E1
Huyton-w-R L14 .54 F2
Wallasey CH44 .51 A4
Willow Ave
Huyton-w-R L36 .70 E8
Kirkby L32 .29 C3
Newton-le-W WA12 .46 E4
Prescot L35 .56 E3
2 Widnes WA8 .73 B2
Willow Bank Est WA12 .46 F4
Willow Cl L14 .54 E2
Willow Ct Bebington CH63 .78 D6
17 Liverpool L8 .68 A4
St Helens WA9 .58 D4
11 Wallasey CH45 .51 B8
Willow Dr WN8 .15 E1
Willow Gn Liverpool L25 .69 F4
2 Ormskirk L39 .13 F5
Willow Gr
Ashton-in-M WN4 .35 E5
Birkenhead CH46 .64 D7
Formby L37 .9 F4
Golborne WA3 .36 A1
Liverpool L15 .69 A8
Prescot L35 .56 E5
Southport PR9 .4 E7
Willow Hey Maghull L31 .28 E7
Skelmersdale WN8 .15 F1
Willow Ho 7 L21 .38 A6
Willow La CH63,CH64 .87 D3
Willow Lea CH43 .66 A4
Willow Moss Cl CH46 .50 A2
Willow Pk CH49 .64 C4
Willow Rd Haydock WA11 .45 E7
Liverpool L15 .68 E8
Newton-le-W WA12 .46 E4
St Helens WA10 .43 C3
Willow Tree Ave WA9 .58 D4
Willow Tree Prim Sch
WA9 .58 D4
Willow Way Crosby L23 .26 E5
Liverpool L11 .40 D6
Willow Wlk WN8 .16 B4
Willowbank Cl L36 .55 C5
Willowbank Holiday Home &
Touring Pk PR8 .7 B2
Willowbank Rd
Bebington CH62 .79 B6
Birkenhead CH42 .66 D3
Willowbrow Rd CH63,
CH64 .87 D3
Willowcroft Rd CH44 .51 C2
Willowdale WA12 .46 E3
Willowdale Rd
Liverpool L18 .68 F5
Liverpool,Hartley's Village
L9 .39 A4
Willowdene Ct L11 .40 D5
Willowfield Gr WN4 .35 A2
Willowherb Cl L26 .70 D2
Willowhey PR9 .1 F4
Willowmeade L11 .40 B3
Willows The Southport PR8 .3 F6
3 St Helens WA9 .58 C4
Wallasey CH45 .50 E7
Warrington WA5 .74 F5
Wills Ave L31 .20 C2
Willsford Ave L31 .29 B3
Wilmcote Gr PR8 .7 B4
Wilmere La WA8 .73 A6
Wilmot Ave WA5 .74 F6
Wilmot Dr WA3 .46 F7
Wilne Rd 3 CH45 .51 A6
Wilsden Rd WA8 .72 B1
Wilsford Cl WA3 .36 B1
Wilsham Rd WN5 .25 E5
Wilshaw Terr CH63 .87 B6
Wilson Ave CH44 .51 E4
Wilson Cl St Helens WA10 .43 F3
Widnes WA8 .73 D1
Wilson Gr L19 .81 C6
Wilson Rd Huyton-w-R L36 56 A1
Prescot L35 .56 D4
Wallasey CH44 .51 E4
Wilsons La L21 .38 B8
Wilstan Ave CH63 .78 D5
Wilton Gr 6 L13 .54 A2
Wilton Grange CH47 .63 A4
Wilton Rd
Birkenhead CH42 .67 A1
Huyton-w-R L36 .55 D1
Wilton St
Ashton-in-M WN4 .35 A6
Liverpool L3 .90 C4
Wallasey CH44 .51 B4
Wiltons Dr L34 .41 D3
Wiltshire Dr L30 .27 D3
Wiltshire Gdns WA10 .43 F2
Wimbledon St
Liverpool L15 .68 E7
Wallasey CH44,CH45 .51 B5
Wimborne Cl L14 .55 B6
Wimborne Pl L14 .55 B5
Wimborne Rd L14 .55 B5
Wimborne Way CH61 .76 D7
Wimbourne Ave CH61 .77 A5
Wimbrick Cl
Birkenhead CH46 .64 F8
Ormskirk L39 .13 D4
Wimbrick Cres L39 .13 D3
Wimbrick Ct CH46 .64 F8
Wimbrick Hey CH46 .65 A8
Wimpole St L7 .53 B2
Winchester Ave
Aintree L10 .28 D3
Ashton-in-M WN4 .35 A3
1 Crosby L22 .26 D3
Winchester Cl
Liverpool L25 .82 B7
4 Orrell WN5 .25 F7
Winchester Dr CH44,CH45 51 A5
Winchester Pl WA8 .84 C8
Winchester Rd
Ashton-in-M WA11 .34 E1
Liverpool L6 .53 C6
Longshaw WN5 .25 D2
Winchfield Rd L15 .68 F6
Windbourne Rd L17 .68 C2
Windermere Ave
St Helens WA11 .44 B8
Warrington WA2 .61 D3
Widnes WA8 .73 B4
Windermere Cres PR8 .7 C3
Windermere Ct 8 CH41 .66 C5
Windermere Dr
Kirkby L33 .29 D4
Liverpool L12 .40 C1
Maghull L31 .20 E2
Rainford WA11 .23 F2
Windermere Ho L17 .68 D2
Windermere Pl WA11 .44 A8
Windermere Rd
Abram WN2 .36 B8
Birkenhead CH43 .65 C5
Haydock WA11 .45 B6
Hightown L38 .18 A4
Orrell WN5 .25 F8
Windermere St
Liverpool L5 .53 B5
Widnes WA8 .73 B4
Windermere Terr L8 .68 B5
Windfield Cl L33 .30 A6
Windfield Gn L19 .81 D3
Windfield Rd L19 .81 D4
Windgate WN8 .15 F1
Windle Ash L31 .20 C2
Windle Ave L23 .27 A3
Windle City WA10 .43 F6
Windle Ct CH64 .86 E2
Windle Gr WA10 .43 C6
Windle Hall Dr WA10 .43 E7
Windle Smithies WA10 .43 C7
Windle St WA10 .43 F5
Windle Vale WA10 .43 E5
Windlebrook Cres WA10 .43 B6
Windlehurst Ave WA10 .43 E6
Windlehurst Com Prim Sch
WA10 .43 E6
Windleshaw Rd WA10 .43 E5
Windmill Ave Crosby L23 .26 F5
Ormskirk L39 .13 F5
Windmill Cl L33 .29 E5
Windmill Gdns
Birkenhead CH43 .65 C8
St Helens WA9 .44 D4
Windmill Hts WN8 .25 A8
Windmill La WA5 .74 E5
Windmill Rd WN8 .24 F7
Window La L19 .81 C4
Windrows WN8 .15 F1
Windsor Ave
Litherland L21 .38 A8
Newton-le-W WA12 .46 D2
Windsor Cl
Bebington CH62 .79 A7
Birkenhead CH49 .64 D3
Litherland L30 .27 F5
Windsor Com Prim Sch
L8 .67 F6
Windsor Ct 5 Liverpool L8 67 F6
Southport PR8 .3 E4
Windsor Day Hospl L8 .67 F7
Windsor Dr WA11 .46 A7
Windsor Mews CH62 .79 A7
Windsor Park Rd L10 .28 E3
Windsor Rd
Ashton-in-M WN4 .35 C1
Billinge WN5 .33 F5
Bootle L20 .38 E5
Crosby L23 .26 D5
Formby L37 .9 F1
Golborne WA3 .47 C8
Huyton-w-R L36 .55 B3
Liverpool,Tuebrook L13 .53 D6
5 Liverpool,Warbreck Pk
L9 .39 A6
Maghull L31 .28 C8
Prescot L35 .56 F4
Southport PR9 .4 D7
St Helens WA10 .43 D4
Up Holland WN8 .25 A8
Widnes WA8 .73 A4
Windsor St Liverpool L8 .67 F6
Wallasey CH45 .37 B1
Windsor View L8 .68 B7
Windus St WA10 .43 E3
Windy Arbor Brow L35 .71 C8
Windy Arbor Cl L35 .56 D1
Windy Arbor Rd L35 .56 D1
Windy Bank CH62 .79 B6
Windy Bank Ave WA3 .47 E8
Windy Harbour Rd PR8 .7 E7
Wineva Gdns L23 .26 F3
Winford St CH44 .51 D3
Winfrith Cl CH63 .78 F2
Winfrith Dr CH63 .78 F2
Winfrith Rd L25 .70 C4
Wingate Ave WA9 .57 D6
Wingate Cl CH43 .65 E4
Wingate Rd
Bebington CH62 .88 E5
Kirkby L33 .29 F3
Liverpool L17 .68 E2
Wingate Twrs L36 .55 D4
Wingate Wlk L33 .30 A3
Wingfield Cl L29 .27 D8
Wingrave Way L11 .40 B1
Winhill L25 .70 A4
Winhill Lodge L25 .70 A4
Winifred La L39 .21 B8
Winifred Rd L10 .40 B7
Winifred St L7 .53 B1
Winkle St 1 L8 .67 F5
Winmoss Dr L33 .30 A5
Winnard St WA3 .36 B2
Winnington Rd CH47 .63 A4
Winnipeg Dr L27 .70 E5
Winsford Cl WA11 .45 F7
Winsford Dr WA5 .59 E7
Winsford Rd L13 .53 F6
Winsham Cl L32 .40 F8
Winsham Rd L32 .40 F8
Winskill Rd L11 .40 A1
Winslade Ct L4 .39 B2
Winslade Rd L4 .39 B2
Winslow St L4 .52 F8
Winsor St CH41 .66 C5
Winstanley Coll WN5 .25 F3
Winstanley Ho
Bebington CH62 .79 B7
1 Crosby L22 .26 E1
Winstanley Ind Est WA2 .61 B1
Winstanley Rd
Ashton-in-M WN2 .35 F8
Bebington CH62 .79 B7
Crosby L22 .26 E2
Garswood WN4,WN5 .34 B6
Orrell WN5 .25 F3
Skelmersdale WN8 .23 F8
Winster Dr L27 .71 A3
Winsters The WN8 .15 F1
Winston Ave
Newton-le-W WA12 .46 C3
St Helens WA9 .45 B2
Winston Cres PR8 .4 E2
Winston Dr CH43 .65 C5
Winston Gr CH46 .64 E8
Winstone Rd L14 .55 A4
Winter Gr WA9 .45 B3
Winter St 9 L6 .53 A3
Winterburn Cres L12 .54 D7
Winterhey Ave CH44 .51 B3
Winterlea Dr L26 .83 A6
Winthrop Pk CH43 .65 E5
Winton Cl CH45 .51 A8
Winton Rd WA3 .47 E6
Winwick CE Prim Sch
WA2 .61 A6
Winwick La WA3 .47 E3
Winwick Link Rd WA2,
WA12 .61 C6
Winwick Park Ave WA2 .61 A6
Winwick Rd
Newton-le-W WA12 .46 F1
Warrington WA2 .61 A2
Winwick View WA5 .45 D1
Winwood Hall L25 .70 A1
Wirral Bsns Pk The CH49 64 F3
Wirral Cl CH63 .78 F3
Wirral Country Pk★
CH48 .75 D5
Wirral Ctry Pk★ CH61 .76 B2
Wirral Ed Ctr CH62 .88 D8
Wirral Gdns CH63 .78 F3
Wirral Gram Sch for Boys
CH63 .78 F4
Wirral Gram Sch for Girls
CH63 .78 F5
Wirral L Pk CH62 .79 E3

Addresses

Name and Address	Telephone	Page	Grid reference

Name and Address	Telephone	Page	Grid reference

Addresses

Name and Address	Telephone	Page	Grid reference

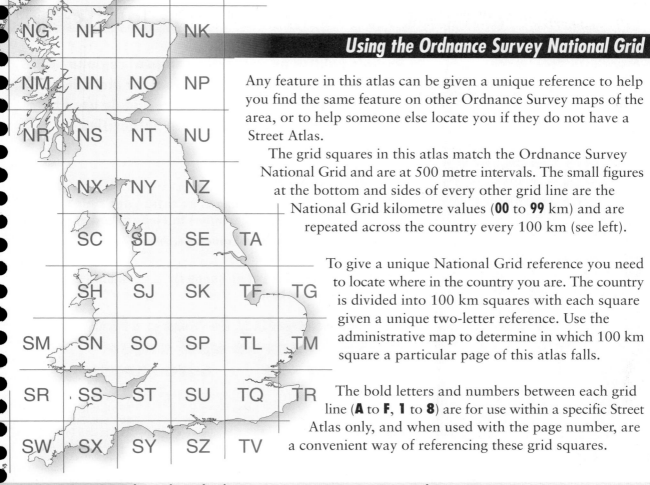

Any feature in this atlas can be given a unique reference to help you find the same feature on other Ordnance Survey maps of the area, or to help someone else locate you if they do not have a Street Atlas.

The grid squares in this atlas match the Ordnance Survey National Grid and are at 500 metre intervals. The small figures at the bottom and sides of every other grid line are the National Grid kilometre values (**00** to **99** km) and are repeated across the country every 100 km (see left).

To give a unique National Grid reference you need to locate where in the country you are. The country is divided into 100 km squares with each square given a unique two-letter reference. Use the administrative map to determine in which 100 km square a particular page of this atlas falls.

The bold letters and numbers between each grid line (**A** to **F**, **1** to **8**) are for use within a specific Street Atlas only, and when used with the page number, are a convenient way of referencing these grid squares.

Example   The railway bridge over DARLEY GREEN RD in grid square B1

Step 1: Identify the two-letter reference, in this example the page is in **SP**

Step 2: Identify the 1 km square in which the railway bridge falls. Use the figures in the southwest corner of this square: Eastings **17**, Northings **74**. This gives a unique reference: **SP 17 74**, accurate to 1 km.

Step 3: To give a more precise reference accurate to 100 m you need to estimate how many tenths along and how many tenths up this 1 km square the feature is (to help with this the 1 km square is divided into four 500 m squares). This makes the bridge about **8** tenths along and about **1** tenth up from the southwest corner.

This gives a unique reference: **SP 178 741**, accurate to 100 m.

Eastings (read from left to right along the bottom) come before Northings (read from bottom to top). If you have trouble remembering say to yourself "Along the hall, THEN up the stairs"!

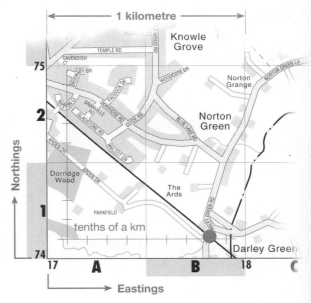

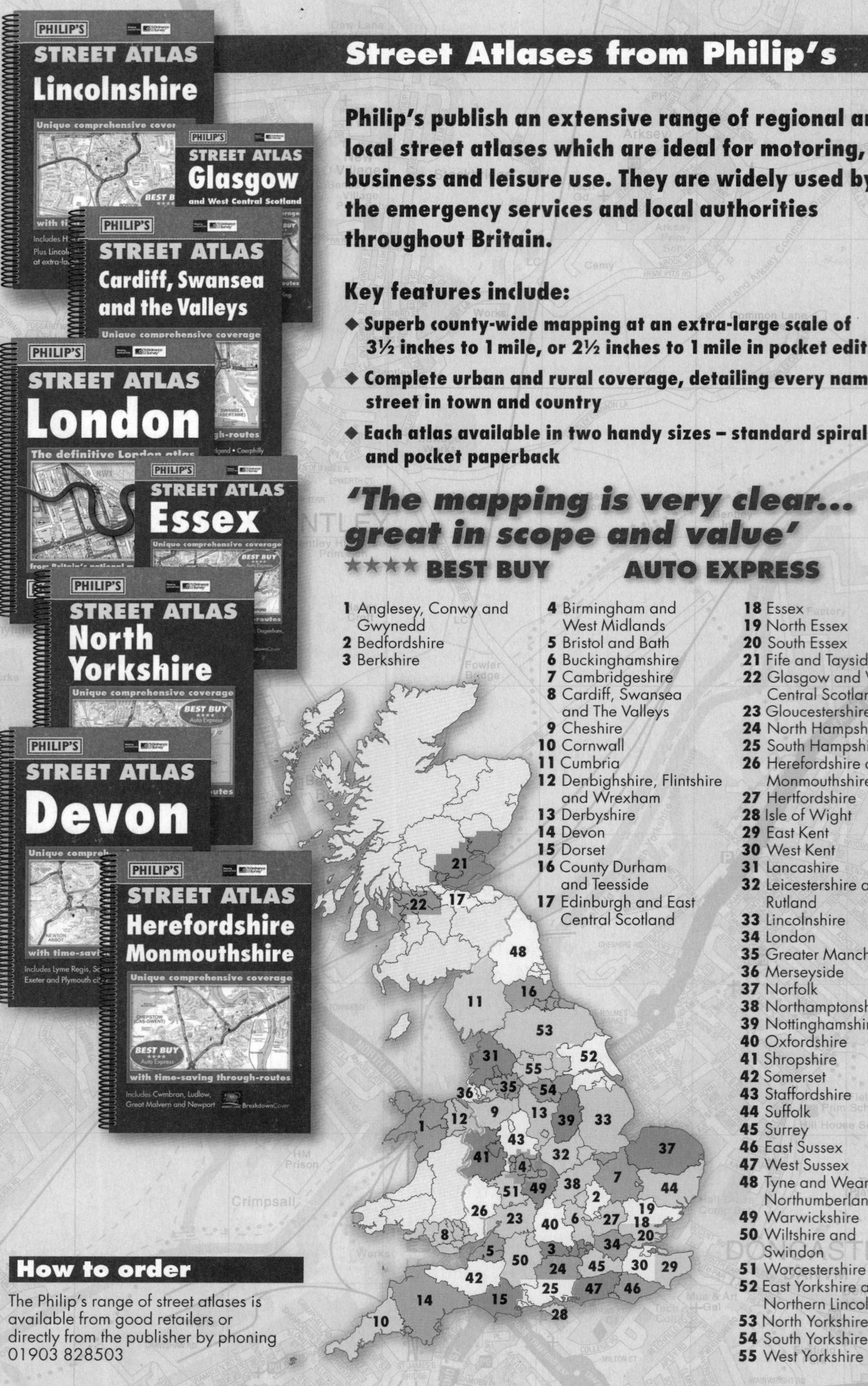

Street Atlases from Philip's

Philip's publish an extensive range of regional and local street atlases which are ideal for motoring, business and leisure use. They are widely used by the emergency services and local authorities throughout Britain.

Key features include:

◆ Superb county-wide mapping at an extra-large scale of 3½ inches to 1 mile, or 2½ inches to 1 mile in pocket editions

◆ Complete urban and rural coverage, detailing every named street in town and country

◆ Each atlas available in two handy sizes – standard spiral and pocket paperback

'The mapping is very clear... great in scope and value'

★★★★ BEST BUY   AUTO EXPRESS

<table>
<tr><td>1</td><td>Anglesey, Conwy and Gwynedd</td><td>4</td><td>Birmingham and West Midlands</td><td>18</td><td>Essex</td></tr>
<tr><td></td><td></td><td>5</td><td>Bristol and Bath</td><td>19</td><td>North Essex</td></tr>
<tr><td>2</td><td>Bedfordshire</td><td>6</td><td>Buckinghamshire</td><td>20</td><td>South Essex</td></tr>
<tr><td>3</td><td>Berkshire</td><td>7</td><td>Cambridgeshire</td><td>21</td><td>Fife and Tayside</td></tr>
<tr><td></td><td></td><td>8</td><td>Cardiff, Swansea and The Valleys</td><td>22</td><td>Glasgow and West Central Scotland</td></tr>
<tr><td></td><td></td><td>9</td><td>Cheshire</td><td>23</td><td>Gloucestershire</td></tr>
<tr><td></td><td></td><td>10</td><td>Cornwall</td><td>24</td><td>North Hampshire</td></tr>
<tr><td></td><td></td><td>11</td><td>Cumbria</td><td>25</td><td>South Hampshire</td></tr>
<tr><td></td><td></td><td>12</td><td>Denbighshire, Flintshire and Wrexham</td><td>26</td><td>Herefordshire and Monmouthshire</td></tr>
<tr><td></td><td></td><td>13</td><td>Derbyshire</td><td>27</td><td>Hertfordshire</td></tr>
<tr><td></td><td></td><td>14</td><td>Devon</td><td>28</td><td>Isle of Wight</td></tr>
<tr><td></td><td></td><td>15</td><td>Dorset</td><td>29</td><td>East Kent</td></tr>
<tr><td></td><td></td><td>16</td><td>County Durham and Teesside</td><td>30</td><td>West Kent</td></tr>
<tr><td></td><td></td><td>17</td><td>Edinburgh and East Central Scotland</td><td>31</td><td>Lancashire</td></tr>
<tr><td></td><td></td><td></td><td></td><td>32</td><td>Leicestershire and Rutland</td></tr>
<tr><td></td><td></td><td></td><td></td><td>33</td><td>Lincolnshire</td></tr>
<tr><td></td><td></td><td></td><td></td><td>34</td><td>London</td></tr>
<tr><td></td><td></td><td></td><td></td><td>35</td><td>Greater Manchester</td></tr>
<tr><td></td><td></td><td></td><td></td><td>36</td><td>Merseyside</td></tr>
<tr><td></td><td></td><td></td><td></td><td>37</td><td>Norfolk</td></tr>
<tr><td></td><td></td><td></td><td></td><td>38</td><td>Northamptonshire</td></tr>
<tr><td></td><td></td><td></td><td></td><td>39</td><td>Nottinghamshire</td></tr>
<tr><td></td><td></td><td></td><td></td><td>40</td><td>Oxfordshire</td></tr>
<tr><td></td><td></td><td></td><td></td><td>41</td><td>Shropshire</td></tr>
<tr><td></td><td></td><td></td><td></td><td>42</td><td>Somerset</td></tr>
<tr><td></td><td></td><td></td><td></td><td>43</td><td>Staffordshire</td></tr>
<tr><td></td><td></td><td></td><td></td><td>44</td><td>Suffolk</td></tr>
<tr><td></td><td></td><td></td><td></td><td>45</td><td>Surrey</td></tr>
<tr><td></td><td></td><td></td><td></td><td>46</td><td>East Sussex</td></tr>
<tr><td></td><td></td><td></td><td></td><td>47</td><td>West Sussex</td></tr>
<tr><td></td><td></td><td></td><td></td><td>48</td><td>Tyne and Wear and Northumberland</td></tr>
<tr><td></td><td></td><td></td><td></td><td>49</td><td>Warwickshire</td></tr>
<tr><td></td><td></td><td></td><td></td><td>50</td><td>Wiltshire and Swindon</td></tr>
<tr><td></td><td></td><td></td><td></td><td>51</td><td>Worcestershire</td></tr>
<tr><td></td><td></td><td></td><td></td><td>52</td><td>East Yorkshire and Northern Lincolnshire</td></tr>
<tr><td></td><td></td><td></td><td></td><td>53</td><td>North Yorkshire</td></tr>
<tr><td></td><td></td><td></td><td></td><td>54</td><td>South Yorkshire</td></tr>
<tr><td></td><td></td><td></td><td></td><td>55</td><td>West Yorkshire</td></tr>
</table>

How to order

The Philip's range of street atlases is available from good retailers or directly from the publisher by phoning 01903 828503